Multi-Party and Multi-Contract Arbitration in the Construction Industry

Multi-Party and Multi-Contract Arbitration in the Construction Industry

Dimitar Kondev

Ph.D., LL.M., Mag. Jur., MCIArb, MIR

WILEY Blackwell

This edition first published 2017

Registered Office
John Wiley & Sons Ltd, The Atrium, Southern Gate, Chichester, West Sussex, PO19 8SQ, United Kingdom.

Editorial Offices
9600 Garsington Road, Oxford, OX4 2DQ, United Kingdom.
The Atrium, Southern Gate, Chichester, West Sussex, PO19 8SQ, United Kingdom.

For details of our global editorial offices, for customer services and for information about how to apply for permission to reuse the copyright material in this book please see our web site at www.wiley.com/wiley-blackwell.

Library of Congress Cataloging-in-Publication data applied for

ISBN: 9781119251729

A catalogue record for this book is available from the British Library.

Wiley also publishes its books in a variety of electronic formats. Some content that appears in print may not be available in electronic books.

Cover design by Wiley
Cover image: Omar Jabri / EyeEm/Gettyimages

Set in 10/12.5pt Minion by SPi Global, Pondicherry, India

10 9 8 7 6 5 4 3 2 1

Contents

About the Author

Dimitar Kondev, Ph.D., LL.M., Mag. Jur., MCIArb, MIR, is an international lawyer specializing in construction law and dispute resolution.

Dimitar has dealt with international construction agreements based on the FIDIC Conditions of Contract and bespoke contracts for over a decade. He is currently working for White & Case LLP Paris on a research project in construction law. Before joining White & Case he worked as a senior associate and practising attorney-at-law at DGKV, one of the largest law firms in Bulgaria, where he provided legal advice on all aspects and stages concerning the realization of large-scale construction projects. Dimitar has also worked as of counsel at the family-owned law firm Law House Kondevi, Bourgas, Bulgaria.

Besides his professional background as an attorney, Dimitar has dealt with international construction law on an academic level. He obtained his LL.M. degree in international business law from the Vrije Universiteit Amsterdam. Dimitar's doctoral dissertation at Aarhus University in Denmark, which forms the basis of this book, focuses on construction law and dispute resolution.

Dimitar has written several articles for international peer-reviewed construction law journals such as the *International Construction Law Review* and *Construction Law International*. He has been teaching international construction law at Aarhus University since 2015. Dimitar is registered as a dispute adjudicator under the Bulgarian list of FIDIC adjudicators (BACEA National List).

Contact details: d_kondev@mail.bg.

Foreword

I am delighted to have been invited to write a foreword to this book. A proper discussion of multi-party and multi-contract arbitration issues in the construction sector is long overdue.

Disputes are inherent in the construction industry. Large construction projects invariably involve a multitude of contracting parties, who are generally bound by a series of bilateral contracts. Controversies arising under one of these contracts often have repercussions on parties not directly bound by that contract. For example, an employer's claim against the main contractor based on alleged defects in the subcontractor's work will often trigger a recourse claim by the main contractor against the subcontractor.

Parties to international commercial contracts, including construction contracts, regularly resort to arbitration as a main dispute resolution method because of the advantages that arbitration offers over litigation. Arbitration proceedings typically take place only between the (typically two) parties to the contract. Third parties, who are non-signatories to that contract, may not participate in the same proceedings. As a result, related disputes on similar points of law and fact, such as the one mentioned above, often have to be resolved in parallel arbitrations. This takes time, incurs costs and may result in inconsistent findings.

Multi-party arbitration is not a new topic. It has been the focal point of discussion and debate for several decades. Numerous articles and a number of other contributions have been written on the topic. In this context, it may seem surprising that very few of these contributions focus on the construction industry, where multi-party disputes occur on a regular basis. The present book is the first book on the market that provides for an in-depth analysis of the legal issues associated with multi-party and multi-contract arbitration in the construction industry.

Having the background of a practising lawyer and a scholar, the author has approached this intrinsically difficult subject and its attendant problems from both a theoretical and a practical perspective. In Chapters 1 and 2, the book opens with an introduction to the problem of multi-party arbitration. In Chapter 3, the author steps into the shoes of each major participant in construction projects with the purpose of identifying their potential interests in participating in this type of arbitration. Chapter 4 contains an in-depth analysis of the approaches to multi-party arbitration under arbitration rules commonly encountered in construction disputes. In this analysis, the author draws upon numerous articles and commentaries. In Chapter 5, different legislative approaches to the problem are described and evaluated. In Chapter 6, the book then focuses on the contractual solutions to multi-party arbitration in a wide range of popular international and domestic standard forms together with case law pertaining to them. The author critically analyses the contractual solutions available so far. The purpose is to inform users of the forms of potential pitfalls and complexities that may result from the application of these solutions. The guidelines for drafting multi-party arbitration clauses suggested by the author in Chapter 7 are of particular interest for practitioners. This chapter contains a practitioner-oriented discussion of how to create a proper multi-party arbitration clause. Last, but not least, the author has proposed an intriguing redraft of the arbitration clause in the FIDIC Red Book, which contracting parties willing to engage in multi-party arbitration may want to adopt.

The book is the first comprehensive work on the topic. It is well thought out, clearly structured and written in a straightforward style. It offers an up-to-date and comprehensive coverage of existing materials and case law, tacked with the author's original ideas as to how the current regulation of multi-party arbitration may be improved. In view of the importance of the issues it addresses, this book will be a precious reference work for practitioners and scholars alike.

Professor Torsten Iversen LL.D., Ph.D., LL.M. (Frankfurt a.M., Germany)
The University of Aarhus, Denmark

Preface

The topic of multi-party arbitration is not new. The perennial problems pertaining to multi-party arbitrations have been the subject of extensive debate and scholarly writings for more than two decades. Several books and numerous articles have been written on this subject.

There are several reasons why I decided to choose to write a book related to a subject that has received such extensive comment in recent years. First, most of the existing contributions focus on multi-party arbitration from a general perspective. Because of their broad scope they fail to consider in sufficient detail and precision the problems arising in the construction sector. Even though the construction sector does not have monopoly over multi-party disputes, the frequency of such disputes there is greater than in other commercial sectors. Moreover, multi-party construction disputes commonly arise under two or more contracts at the same time. For example, a main contract dispute concerning defects in the subcontractor's work may trigger a related subcontract dispute whereunder the main contractor will pursue his recourse claim against the subcontractor. The consistent resolution of these two disputes may require the conduct of a single arbitration with the participation of all three parties, which will bear the characteristics of both multi-party and multi-contract arbitration. This book aims at covering exactly this type of arbitration. Multi-party arbitrations based on multiple contracts often give rise to a number of challenges that are even more intricate than those arising in a mere multi-party arbitration.

Secondly, construction contracts and disputes have their own specifics, which distinguish them from other commercial sectors and deserve a separate analysis. For example, construction agreements commonly require the fulfilment of certain procedural requirements in order for a 'claim' to crystalize into a 'dispute'. Moreover, complex multi-tier dispute resolution provisions demanding dispute adjudication and other legal mechanisms as preconditions to arbitration are commonplace in the construction sector. All these procedural requirements can have a significant impact on the conduct of multi-party arbitral proceedings and are therefore discussed thoroughly in this book. In scholarly writings this is a subject that is commonly left in the dark.

Finally yet importantly, even though many scholarly writings have the potential to contribute to arbitration theory, they are of limited use to those practising in the field. These contributions confine themselves to identifying the problems pertaining to multi-party arbitration but they do not give any practical suggestions on how these problems can be solved. This book also aspires to contribute on a theoretical level but it has a clear practical approach to the problems discussed. It provides detailed guidelines for drafting multi-party arbitration clauses and contains some other practical suggestions as to how the current legal regulation of multi-party disputes can be improved in order to accommodate better the increased demand for efficient resolution of these disputes.

Therefore, I hope that this book will be useful to both scholars and practitioners.

I have endeavoured to state the law as it stood on 1 November 2016.

Dimitar Kondev

Acknowledgements

Throughout my work on this book I enjoyed the assistance of many individuals whom I would like to thank.

First, I would like to thank Professor Torsten Iversen from Aarhus University who acted as a main supervisor of my doctoral dissertation, a modified version of which formed the basis of the present book.

I would also like to thank the following individuals who contributed to this project with their ideas and suggestions: Christopher Seppälä (White & Case, Paris), His Honour Humphrey Lloyd (Atkin Chambers, London), Professor John Uff (Keating Chambers, London), John Marrin (Keating Chambers, London), Paul Buckingham (Keating Chambers, London), Anthony Lavers (White & Case, London), Professor David Mosey (King's College London), Professor Renato Nazzini (King's College London), Professor Ingeborg Schwenzer (University of Basel, Switzerland), Philipp Habegger (LALIVE, Zurich), Professor Sébastien Besson (Python & Peter, Geneva), Tobias Zuberbühler (Lustenberger, Zurich), Paolo Marzolini (Patocchini & Marzolini, Geneva), Dr Dorothee Schramm (Sidley, Geneva), Dr Herman Verbist (Everest, Ghent), Ian Heaphy (Turner & Townsend).

The views expressed in this book are, however, those of the author and do not necessarily reflect the views and opinions of the abovementioned persons.

I am also indebted to the following organizations and other entities for the permissions granted to me to quote and reproduce some material from the various standard forms examined in this book: ACA, AIA, CECA, ConsensusDocs, ENAA, FIDIC, IChemE, JCT, and NEC (Thomas Telford Ltd.). Similarly, I would also like to thank all the arbitral institutions mentioned in the book for granting me permissions to quote certain clauses from their arbitration rules.

Special thanks to Stephan Kyutchukov from DGKV, Sofia, who was the first who introduced me to the FIDIC Conditions of Contract many years ago.

On the personal side, I would like to say special thanks to those who supported me and encouraged me throughout my work on this book. They know how they are. Thank you for your endless support, understanding and patience.

List of Abbreviations

AAA	American Arbitration Association
ACA	Association of Consulting Architects
AIA	American Institute of Architects
CECA	Civil Engineering Contractors Association
CEPANI	Belgian Centre for Arbitration and Mediation
CIAR	Construction Industry Arbitration Rules
CIArb	Chartered Institute of Arbitrators
CIETAC	China International Economic and Trade Arbitration Commission
CIMAR	Construction Industry Model Arbitration Rules
DIA	Danish Institute of Arbitration
DIS	Deutsche Institution für Schiedsgerichtsbarkeit e.V. (German Institution of Arbitration)
ENAA	Engineering Advancement Association of Japan
FAA	Federal Arbitration Act (USA)
FCEC	Federation of Civil Engineering Contractors
FIDIC	Fédération Internationale des Ingénieurs Conseils (International Federation of Consulting Engineers)
FOSFA	Federation of Oils, Seeds and Fats Associations
GAFTA	Grain and Feed Trade Association
HKIAC	Hong Kong International Arbitration Centre
IBA	International Bar Association
ICC	International Chamber of Commerce, France
ICDR	International Centre for Dispute Resolution
ICE	Institution of Civil Engineers
IChemE	Institution of Chemical Engineers
JCAA	Japan Commercial Arbitration Association
JCT	Joint Contracts Tribunal
LCIA	London Court of International Arbitration
NEC	New Engineering Contract
RUAA	Revised Uniform Arbitration Act (USA)
SCC	Arbitration Institute of the Stockholm Chamber of Commerce
SIAC	Singapore International Arbitration Centre
UNCITRAL	United Nations Commission on International Trade Law
VBA	Voldgiftsnævnet for bygge- og anlægsvirksomhed (Danish Arbitration Board for Building and Construction)
VIAC	Vienna International Arbitral Centre

Chapter 1
Introduction

The present book deals with multi-party and multi-contract international arbitration in the construction sector. This chapter provides an introduction to the topic. The introduction starts with a brief overview of arbitration, its advantages over litigation and its general inability to deal sufficiently well with multi-party and multi-contract disputes arising in the construction sector (Section 1.1). Then, the scope of this book and its limitations are described, with a brief overview of the existing literature in the field (Section 1.2). The introduction also contains a concise description of the legal sources utilized in this book (Section 1.3). Finally, the structure of the book is outlined (Section 1.4) and its contribution and goals are stated (Section 1.5).

1.1 General background and research problem

Arbitration is the preferred method for resolution of disputes under international commercial transactions, including in the construction sector[1]. The perceived advantages of arbitration over litigation include the possibility to choose a neutral forum, to have a neutral tribunal in the constitution of which the parties may participate, the flexibility of the arbitral proceedings due to the lack of formal rigid rules of evidence, and the confidentiality of the arbitration process. Contracting parties also prefer arbitration because of the nature of the arbitral awards, which are binding and not subject to court review on the merits. This, in principle, makes arbitration faster than court proceedings. The direct recognition and enforceability of arbitral awards under the New York Convention on the Recognition and Enforcement of Foreign Arbitral Awards (the '**New York Convention**')[2] is pointed out as a further and probably the most significant advantage of arbitration.

[1] Gary Born (2009) *International Commercial Arbitration*, Kluwer Law International, The Hague, pp. 67–70, See also Julian Lew, Loukas Mistelis and Stefan Kröll (2003) *Comparative International Commercial Arbitration*, Kluwer Law International, The Hague, pp. 1–8, Alan Redfern and Martin Hunter with Nigel Blackaby and Constantine Partasides (2004) *Law and Practice of International Commercial Arbitration*, 4th edn, Sweet & Maxwell, London, pp. 22–27.

[2] Convention on the Recognition and Enforcement of Foreign Arbitral Awards, 10 June 1958, available at http://www.uncitral.org/pdf/english/texts/arbitration/NY-conv/XXII_1_e.pdf (accessed 25 July 2016).

Multi-Party and Multi-Contract Arbitration in the Construction Industry, First Edition.
Dimitar Kondev.

The growing international interdependency of commerce and the globalization of today's business world have led to complex contractual relations, which very often involve more than two parties bound by a multitude of contracts[3]. The relationships between the contracting parties are often intricate and frequently involve multilateral and divergent interests. As a result, there is a permanent trend for the number of multi-party actions in international commercial arbitration to increase, which is evident from recent statistical reports[4]. The increasing number of multi-party disputes has led to a higher demand for dispute resolution mechanisms capable of handling such disputes, such as joinder or intervention of third parties into pending proceedings and consolidation of parallel arbitrations.

Despite the predominant position of arbitration over litigation, today it is still argued that arbitration is not well equipped to handle a certain category of disputes arising under international business transactions, including in the construction sector[5]. From the perspective of the construction industry, this category comprises multi-party construction disputes and especially those arising under multiple contracts. As His Honour Humphrey Lloyd has pointed out:

> Given the complexity of construction work and the prevalence of contractual disputes in certain sections of the industry, it is not clear why multi-party arbitrations are so thin on the

[3]Nathalie Voser (2009) 'Multi-party Disputes and Joinder of Third Parties', in Albert Jan van den Berg (ed.) *50 Years of the New York Convention, ICCA International Arbitration Conference, ICCA Congress Series No. 14*, Kluwer Law International, Alphen aan den Rijn, p. 343.

[4]In 1998, approximately one-fifth of the cases administered by the ICC International Court of Arbitration involved more than two parties, whereas in 2007 the percentage of multi-party cases reached 31.1%. See Anne Marie Whitesell (2009) 'Multiparty Arbitration: The ICC International Court of Arbitration Perspective', in the Permanent Court of Arbitration (ed.) *Multiple Party Actions in International Arbitration*, Oxford University Press, New York, NY, p. 203. For a more recent statistical analysis about the ICC cases, see '2014 ICC Dispute Resolution Statistics', in *1 ICC Dispute Resolution Bulletin*, no. 1 (2015), p. 8, where it has been stated that one-third of the total number of filings in 2014 comprised multi-party cases. Similar information has been disclosed in an earlier ICC report: see '2012 Statistical Report', in *24 ICC International Court of Arbitration Bulletin*, no. 1 (2013), p. 10. A statistical analysis of all the disputes brought before the Swiss Federal Supreme Court revealed that the percentage of multi-party arbitration disputes grew from 25% in the early 1990s to 40% in 2005. See Felix Dasser, 'International Arbitration and Setting Aside Proceedings in Switzerland: A Statistical Analysis', in *25 ASA Bulletin*, no. 3 (2007), pp. 462–463. In 2002, more than 50% of the London Court of International Arbitration cases were multi-party proceedings. See Martin Platte, 'When Should an Arbitrator Join Cases?' in *18 International Arbitration* no. 1 (2002), pp. 71–75. See also Ruth Stackpool-Moore (2014) 'Joinder and Consolidation – Examining Best Practice in the Swiss, HKIAC and ICC Rules', in Nathalie Voser (ed.) *10 Years of the Swiss Rules of International Arbitration*, ASA Special Series No. 44, JurisNet LLC, New York, NY, p. 16, where the author has stated that more than one third of the new cases filed under the 2013 arbitration rules of the Hong Kong International Arbitration Centre involve multiple parties or multiple contracts.

[5]Nathalie Voser (2009) 'Multi-party Disputes and Joinder of Third Parties', in Albert Jan van den Berg (ed.) *50 Years of the New York Convention, ICCA International Arbitration Conference, ICCA Congress Series No. 14*, Kluwer Law International, Alphen aan den Rijn, p. 343. See also Kristina Maria Siig, 'Multi-party Arbitration in International Trade: Problems and Solutions', in *1 International Journal of Liability and Scientific Enquiry*, no. 1/2 (2007), p. 72, Richard Garnett, Henry Gabriel and Jeff Waincymer (2002) *A Practical Guide to International Commercial Arbitration*, Oceana Publications, New York, NY; Alan Redfern and Martin Hunter with Nigel Blackaby and Constantine Partasides (2004) *Law and Practice of International Commercial Arbitration*, 4th edn, Sweet & Maxwell, London, p. 200, and Clive Hardy, 'Multi-Party Arbitration: Exceptional Problems Need Exceptional Solutions', in *66 Arbitration: The Journal of the Chartered Institute of Arbitrators*, no. 1 (2000), p. 15.

ground, whereas the courts are full of actions involving many parties bound by contracts incorporating arbitration clauses[6].

This observation was made in 1991 but it still concerns a question of interest, which remains unsettled. Unlike judges in national courts, who usually have the power to review multi-party disputes by way of ordering consolidation of parallel proceedings or joinder of third parties in existing litigation on the basis of statutory provisions contained in civil procedure codes, arbitral institutions and tribunals do not have similar powers, mainly because of the consensual nature upon which their jurisdiction is based.

The attempts of the international arbitration community to provide for solutions for satisfactory resolution of multi-party disputes have resulted in the revision of the major sets of arbitration rules in recent years and also in the introduction of multi-party arbitration provisions in the national arbitration laws of some states. The present book examines the legal regulation in these rules and laws to identify whether this regulation provides for workable solutions that contracting parties in the construction industry may readily utilize. As it will be seen, a workable solution, in the author's opinion, is a solution that provides for a self-contained mechanism of resolution of multi-party and multi-contract disputes – a solution that can be put into operation upon the request of a contracting party without the need to obtain the explicit *ad hoc* consent of the other parties. Such *ad hoc* consent can hardly be obtained once the parties have entered into the contentious stage of their contractual relations. At the same time, a workable solution should necessarily result in an arbitral award that is capable of being recognized and enforced internationally without any difficulties.

In addition to the legal regime contained in the arbitration rules and laws, the author analyses the contractual regulation of multi-party arbitration in order to ascertain whether a workable solution can be found in parties' contracts. At a contractual level, however, relatively few international standard forms have dealt with this type of arbitration. The FIDIC Conditions of Contracts[7] and the NEC3[8], which are probably the most popular and widely used international standard forms, do not contain standard provisions dealing with multi-party arbitrations. Furthermore, *ad hoc* multi-party arbitration clauses are rarely met. Therefore, there is still a gap related to the lack of multi-party arbitration provisions in the contracts that the parties conclude. The present book aims, *inter alia*, to address this gap. It will analyse the available contractual provisions on multi-party arbitration, which are mostly contained in domestic standard forms, and provide some suggestions as to how this gap can be overcome.

On the basis of the analysis of the current regulation of multi-party disputes, as contained in the parties' contracts and the applicable arbitration rules and laws, the book provides some practical suggestions as to how the current regulation can be improved in order to meet the increasing demands of the business community for workable multi-party arbitration solutions.

---

[6] Humphrey Lloyd (1991) 'A National Experience', in P. Bellet, P. Bernardini, G. Bernini *et al.* (eds) *Multi-Party Arbitration: Views from International Arbitration Specialists*, Publication No. 480/1, ICC Publishing SA, Paris, p. 63.

[7] FIDIC is the French acronym of the International Federation of Consulting Engineers (www.fidic.org, accessed 25 July 2016) and the FIDIC Conditions of Contracts are a suite of contracts drafted by FIDIC. For further details about these contracts, please see Subsection 3.2.1 of this book.

[8] The original version of the NEC3 suite of contracts was launched in 2005, and it was drafted by the Institution of Civil Engineers in London. These standard forms were amended in 2006 and in 2013. For more details about NEC3, please see www.neccontract.com (accessed 25 July 2016) and Subsection 3.2.2 of this book.

1.2 Scope of the book, limitations and literature review

1.2.1 Scope of the book

As the title of the book suggests, it deals with arbitration of construction disputes that involve multiple parties and arise under two or more contracts[9]. More particularly, the book deals with those construction disputes that are multi-party and multi-contract at the same time, for example related disputes involving an employer, a main contractor and a subcontractor arising under a main contract and a subcontract.

The focus of this book is on construction arbitration for several reasons. These reasons have been described in more detail in Section 3.1 but will be briefly reiterated here. First, even though the construction industry does not have a monopoly over multi-party and multi-contract disputes and the problems pertaining thereto, the frequency of such disputes in the construction sector is generally greater than in other commercial sectors[10]. This is due to the multitude of parties and contracts involved in large construction projects. Therefore, construction disputes are very illustrative of the type of issues arising in multi-party and multi-contract arbitrations. Furthermore, construction projects have their own specifics, which deserve a separate analysis. Due to the long-term nature of many construction projects, there is a necessity for a prompt resolution of construction disputes while works are still under way. This has led to the emergence of multi-tier dispute resolution clauses in construction agreements, which add a further level of complexity to multi-party arbitration problems. In addition, there is a proliferation of standard form agreements in the construction industry. Some of these contracts, mostly domestic forms, contain multi-party arbitration provisions and have from time to time been subject to arbitral proceedings or litigated before local courts. Therefore, the provisions contained in these contracts, together with the case law pertaining to them, represent fruitful ground for specific sector-oriented research in construction arbitration.

1.2.2 Limitations

The present book deals with construction disputes that are both multi-party and multi-contract. Therefore, multi-party arbitral proceedings arising under a single contract (e.g. a consortium agreement) or those arising under several agreements executed between the same two parties (e.g. multiple main contracts between an employer and the same main contractor executed in relation to different construction projects) are outside the scope of this book. Furthermore, it is not the intention of this book to explore the notion of extension of an arbitration agreement to non-signatories, which has been subject to an extensive

[9]Strictly speaking, the use of the word *multiple* in respect of contracts may be understood as denoting *more* than two contracts. However, in international commercial arbitration it is commonly accepted that arbitrations arising under *two or more* contracts can be classified as multi-contract arbitrations. Therefore, for the purposes of this book, the existence of two contracts will be sufficient to categorize the disputes arising thereunder as multi-contract disputes or certain arbitration based on these disputes as multi-contract arbitration.

[10]John Marrin (2009) 'Multiparty Arbitration in the Construction Industry', in the Permanent Court of Arbitration (ed.) *Multiple Party Actions in International Arbitration*, Oxford University Press, New York, NY, pp. 398–399.

debate in recent years[11]. This notion has been invoked with regard to situations that are principally different from those discussed here. Unlike multi-contract arbitrations, which in most cases imply the existence of two or more arbitration agreements contained in several contracts, the notion of extension of the arbitration agreement to non-signatories presupposes the existence of one arbitration agreement only, which is *extended* to a third party or non-signatory on the basis of some of the theories employed to justify this notion[12].

Another limitation stems from the type of arbitration discussed here. The focus of the book is on international commercial arbitration. Some states have adopted a dual approach to commercial arbitration – they distinguish between domestic and international commercial arbitration in their statutes. This book mostly considers arbitration laws governing international commercial arbitration. However, on some occasions domestic arbitration statutes have also been considered because of their peculiar approach to multi-party arbitration. Other types of arbitration, which are not mentioned above, such as multi-party investor-state arbitration, mass claims and class-wide arbitration, are also outside the scope of the book. Contractual adjudication and other dispute resolution techniques, such as expert determination, are also not within the main focus of the book. However, the book occasionally touches upon the topic of construction adjudication[13]. This is necessary because of the direct relevance of adjudication to the conduct of multi-party arbitrations in some cases.

This book deals with multi-party arbitration in the strict sense of the term: arbitration where each of the multiple parties participates as a formal party in a proceeding that may result in a single arbitral award binding all parties. Therefore, related legal institutes, such as concurrent hearing of disputes and *name borrowing*, which are mainly known in common law countries, are also outside the scope of the book.

1.2.3 Literature review

Multi-party arbitration is not a new topic. Some of the first publications in the field are from the early 1980s[14]. Since then multi-party arbitration has been discussed extensively

---

[11] See, for example, Bernard Hanotiau (2005) *Complex Arbitrations: Multiparty, Multicontract, Multi-issue and Class Actions*, Kluwer Law International, The Hague. See also Pierre Mayer (2009) 'Extension of the Arbitration Clause to Non-signatories under French Law', in the Permanent Court of Arbitration (ed.) *Multiple Party Actions in International Arbitration*, Oxford University Press, New York, NY, pp. 189–199, and William Park (2009) 'Non-signatories and International Contracts: An Arbitrator's Dilemma', in the Permanent Court of Arbitration (ed.) *Multiple Party Actions in International Arbitration*, Oxford University Press, New York, NY, pp. 3–31.

[12] These theories include, *inter alia*, consent on the basis of conduct, the *group of companies doctrine*, the doctrine of *piercing the corporate veil*, representation and agency, assignment, etc.

[13] See, for example, Section 6.5 and Subsection 7.3.3.3 of this book.

[14] The International Council for Commercial Arbitration (ICCA) dealt with the topic of multi-party arbitration at the Warsaw Conference of 1980, a full report of which was published (see Polish Chamber of Foreign Trade (1982) *International Arbitration in Multi-Party Disputes, Materials of an International Symposium Warsaw June 29th – July 2nd 1980*, Wydawnictwo Prawnicze, Warsaw). See also Cornelis Voskuil and John Wade (eds) (1985) *Hague–Zagreb Essays 5 on the Law of International Trade, Reservation of Title, Multiparty Arbitration*, Martinus Nijhoff, The Hague.

in the legal literature in the form of several books[15] and numerous articles. Most of these legal sources have been quoted throughout this book on several occasions. The contributions in the field mostly focus on multi-party arbitration from a general perspective. Because of their broad scope, they fail to consider in sufficient detail and precision the problems arising in the construction sector. These contributions discuss issues such as the advantage of having multi-party arbitration in general, the general obstacles that such arbitration may cause and the extension of arbitration agreements to non-signatories.

The present book aims at addressing an existing gap in the legal literature. As far as the author is aware, there is no book written with a specific focus on multi-party and multi-contract arbitration problems arising in the international construction industry. The only contributions in the field are in the form of few articles. The author has found two of these articles especially stimulating. The first article was written by His Honour Humphrey Lloyd in 1991[16]. It is an excellent thought-provoking article. It briefly considers the interests of the different parties in the construction industry and poses a list of matters that should be considered by those drafting multi-party arbitration clauses. However, some of the content of this article is outdated because of some new developments in the field. The second article was published by John Marrin in 2009[17]. It is a very useful article, which provides a concise overview of the regulation of multi-party arbitration in the construction sector but does not go into detail about each of the reviewed levels of regulation due to the natural volume constraints stemming from the form of the contribution. Both articles recognize that further work is necessary in the field, especially with a view to the lack of contractual solutions to multi-party arbitration[18].

1.3 Sources used

Unlike research in domestic fields of law, where the available sources are more or less limited to those existing in the specific country, research in international commercial arbitration requires the use of a unique blend of legal sources, which are mutually intertwined[19]. The diversity of legal sources available in commercial arbitration is one of its specific features. Some of these sources are national (e.g. arbitration laws, case law)

[15] See, for example, Bernard Hanotiau (2005) *Complex Arbitrations: Multiparty, Multicontract, Multi-Issue and Class Actions*, Kluwer Law International, The Hague, and the Permanent Court of Arbitration (ed.) (2009) *Multiple Party Actions in International Arbitration*, Oxford University Press, New York, NY.

[16] Humphrey Lloyd (1991) 'A National Experience', in P. Bellet, P. Bernardini, G. Bernini *et al.* (eds) *Multi-Party Arbitration: Views from International Arbitration Specialists*, Publication No. 480/1, ICC Publishing SA, Paris, pp. 61–79.

[17] John Marrin (2009) 'Multiparty Arbitration in the Construction Industry', in the Permanent Court of Arbitration (ed.) *Multiple Party Actions in International Arbitration*, Oxford University Press, New York, NY, pp. 395–425.

[18] Ibid., p. 412. See also Humphrey Lloyd (1991) 'A National Experience', in P. Bellet, P. Bernardini, G. Bernini *et al.* (eds) *Multi-Party Arbitration: Views from International Arbitration Specialists*, Publication No. 480/1, ICC Publishing SA, Paris, pp. 63, 74.

[19] S. Strong (2009) *Research and Practice in International Commercial Arbitration. Sources and Strategies*, Oxford University Press, New York, NY, pp. 1–2 (para. 1.01), 12 (paras 2.11–2.12).

and others are international in their nature (e.g. international conventions). Furthermore, we can also speak of 'anational' or transnational sources, such as standard form contracts and arbitration rules[20]. Standard form agreements may be applied in different jurisdictions. Moreover, they can be subject to different governing laws. This is a consequence of the widely recognized principle of freedom of contract. Arbitration rules are published by arbitral institutions and other non-state bodies. They are detached from the peculiarities of any national legal system and may be applied to disputes irrespective of the governing law of the underlying contracts and the seat of arbitration. Some of the legal sources in international commercial arbitration are created by states (e.g. arbitration laws, case law) whereas others are drafted by private parties or institutions (e.g. arbitration agreements, arbitral awards, arbitration rules, or guidelines).

Regulation of multi-party arbitration can be found in three main types of legal sources. These sources can also serve as legal bases for the conduct of multi-party arbitrations[21]. These include the arbitration agreements contained in the parties' contracts, the arbitration rules referred to in these agreements, and the arbitration laws of the seat of arbitration (*lex arbitri*). All of these primary legal sources have been examined because they have direct relevance to the conduct of multi-party arbitrations.

As regards the first legal source, the arbitration agreements, the focus of the book is on both standard and *ad hoc* clauses contained in international construction agreements. Even though domestic construction agreements are in principle outside the scope of this book, some standard clauses in domestic forms addressing multi-party arbitration have also been examined. They can serve as a useful source of inspiration for the finding of contractual solutions on an international level. Most of these domestic forms originate from England or the United States.

As regards arbitration rules, the focus is on the rules published by the most prominent arbitral institutions not only in Europe but also worldwide[22]. The main criterion for the selection of these rules is their frequent application to construction disputes. Sometimes arbitration rules drafted for use in specific commercial sectors are published by entities, mostly private organizations, which are not arbitral institutions[23]. Some of these rules are also considered in this book to the extent they contain regulation of multi-party and multi-contract disputes in the construction sector.

The choice of a certain seat of arbitration will generally trigger the application of the arbitration law of that state (*lex arbitri*). Most states do not regulate multi-party arbitration in their legislation. Therefore, the rationale for the choice of the reviewed arbitration laws differ from the one adopted with regard to the arbitration rules. The emphasis is not

---

[20] Ibid.

[21] Kristina Maria Siig, 'Multi-party Arbitration in International Trade: Problems and Solutions', in *1 International Journal of Liability and Scientific Enquiry*, no. 1/2 (2007), pp. 77–78.

[22] These include the ICC International Court of Arbitration with the International Chamber of Commerce in Paris, France, the LCIA in London, the Swiss Chambers' Arbitration Institution, the International Centre for Dispute Resolution, the Arbitration Institute of the Stockholm Chamber of Commerce, some other nascent arbitral institutions in Asia and so forth.

[23] Examples of this type of rules are the ICE Arbitration Procedure, published by the Institution of Civil Engineers, and the Construction Industry Model Arbitration Rules (CIMAR) drafted by the Society of Construction Arbitrators.

on the arbitration laws of the states that are the most preferred seats of arbitration but on the laws of the states that have addressed multi-party arbitration in their statutes. The UNCITRAL Model Law on International Commercial Arbitration (the '**UNCITRAL Model Law**')[24] has also been taken into account. Even though this law is not binding in itself, it has been incorporated as arbitration law governing international commercial arbitration in many states.

National arbitration laws are of relevance not only because of the multi-party arbitration solutions they may contain. These laws will also come into play at the post-award stage if a setting aside of the award is requested or if the prevailing party tries to enforce the award. If the recognition or enforcement of the award is sought in third countries, certain international instruments, such as the New York Convention, may also apply. Therefore, the provisions of these instruments are also taken into consideration.

Apart from the legal sources described above, certain other sources have been used. Case law on multi-party arbitration has been examined, particularly in England and the United States, which are major contributors not only of domestic standard forms containing multi-party arbitration clauses but also of court decisions interpreting these clauses. The case law represents a persuasive source of authority because it sheds some light on various issues, such as the authority of courts to order consolidation in cases where parties' contracts are silent on the matter and the application of multi-party arbitration clauses contained in parties' contracts. Even though this case law may not be considered as a formal source of law outside the country where it has its origin, a judge or an arbitrator who is faced with a new controversial issue or is not certain as to how to approach a certain problem or to deal with a certain argument may want to consider this foreign case law if it deals with the same issue, problem or argument[25]. Moreover, case law from countries, which are considered as leaders in international commercial arbitration due to their longstanding expertise in the field, such as England, can be considered as a highly persuasive source of authority regardless of the place where arbitration takes place[26]. The same holds true about arbitral awards issued by arbitral tribunals acting under the auspices of reputable arbitral institutions. Even though arbitral awards are in principle not publicly available, certain arbitral institutions, such as, for example, the ICC International Court of Arbitration and the Swiss Chambers' Arbitration Institution, publish excerpts of some arbitral awards in their bulletins. Furthermore, certain awards or other information concerning the conduct of the proceedings have come within the public domain in other ways, for example, in the stage of enforcement of an award or in cases of statutory court-ordered consolidation of arbitrations.

Besides the abovementioned relevance of case law and arbitral awards, these two sources may be useful in other ways. In many cases, case law and arbitral awards deal

---

[24] UNCITRAL Model Law on International Commercial Arbitration, 1985, as amended in 2006, http://www.uncitral.org/pdf/english/texts/arbitration/ml-arb/07-86998_Ebook.pdf (accessed 25 July 2016).

[25] See Jan Smits (2006) 'Comparative Law and its Influence on National Legal Systems', in Mathias Reimann and Reinhard Zimmermann (eds) *The Oxford Handbook of Comparative Law*, Oxford University Press, Oxford, pp. 520, 525, 531–532.

[26] S. Strong (2009) *Research and Practice in International Commercial Arbitration. Sources and Strategies*, Oxford University Press, New York, NY, pp. 27–28 (paras 2.52–2.53), 85 (para 5.23).

with the question of how certain legal rules should be applied, for example how a certain multi-party arbitration clause should be construed and applied in practice, whether the preconditions for the application of this clause have been fulfilled and so forth. These sources are therefore particularly useful for those drafting multi-party arbitration clauses. They show the draftsman the pitfalls that he should try to avoid and may give him some ideas as to how to approach a certain matter.

Secondary legal sources have been used extensively in this book. These include treatises and articles on multi-party and multi-contract arbitration. Some soft law instruments have also been considered[27]. Even though these instruments are not binding, they can be indicative, for instance, of how an arbitrator may approach a request for multi-party arbitration or how a multi-party arbitration clause can be drafted. Statistical information provided by arbitral institutions has also been used on certain occasions.

1.4 Structure of the book

The book aims at dealing with multi-party arbitration from the perspective of the construction industry and it addresses some substantive and procedural legal problems in relation to this type of arbitration. In order to enable a better understanding of the problems described in the book, the latter begins with two introductory chapters. First, Chapter 2 provides a concise introduction to the topic of multi-party arbitration in general. The chapter deals with some terminology clarifications, explains how multi-party arbitration takes place in practice, and reveals the advantages and obstacles to the conduct of multi-party arbitrations. Chapter 3 focuses on the divergent economic interests pursued by the different stakeholders in construction projects on the basis of the different contractual models used in these projects. Chapter 4 scrutinizes the available solutions to multi-party arbitration problems in the arbitration rules most often applied in construction disputes. Chapter 5 deals with the approaches to multi-party arbitration problems available in the arbitration laws or case law of some states. Chapter 6 focuses on some contractual multi-party arbitration clauses. More particularly, this chapter investigates the approach of some of the most popular international standard form construction agreements to multi-party arbitration. In addition, the chapter discusses some popular domestic standard forms available in England, the United States and Denmark, which specifically address the matter. Chapter 7 reveals the author's ideas of how the current legal framework of multi-party arbitration can be improved in order to accommodate in a better way the type of construction disputes examined in the book. The final Chapter 8 summarizes the main observations and proposals made throughout the book.

---

[27] Some of the soft law instruments considered comprise the IBA Guidelines for Drafting International Arbitration Clauses, published by the International Bar Association, and Practice Guideline 15: Guidelines for Arbitrators on how to approach issues relating to Multi-Party Arbitrations, published by the Chartered Institute of Arbitrators (CIArb).

1.5 Aims and contribution of the book

The aims of the book are manifold. First, it aims to increase the awareness of the different stakeholders in the construction industry of the need for multi-party and multi-contract arbitration in the construction sector. As described in Chapter 3, there are often occasions where it can be beneficial for the parties to resolve their disputes in a multi-party context. Contracting parties in the construction industry should be aware of the solutions currently available and should ascertain whether these solutions respond to their needs. Secondly, the book aims to show these parties how to address the problem of multi-party arbitration in their contracts. Thirdly, the book aims to inform readers of the attempts undertaken by legislators, arbitral institutions and drafters of standard form agreements to handle multi-party arbitrations.

The book aims to be the first published monograph focusing on multi-party and multi-contract arbitration in the international construction sector. The present book also addresses the gap concerning the lack of contractual self-contained multi-party arbitration clauses by providing some guidelines for drafting of such clauses. Thus, the author's ideas in the book will not only contribute to the theoretical knowledge in the field of multi-party arbitration but will also be of practical value for scholars, practitioners and contracting parties. Furthermore, the book may provide incentives for draftsmen of standard form agreements to implement standardized solutions on multi-party arbitration issues in the near future.

The book may also be particularly useful for arbitrators who have to conduct multi-party arbitrations in the construction sector. These arbitrators will often face jurisdictional objections to the conduct of multi-party proceedings raised by a party not willing to participate in these proceedings. The content of the book can be useful for arbitrators when they have to take a decision on these jurisdictional objections. Furthermore, the book contains a detailed analysis on the interpretation of multi-party arbitration clauses contained in both standard form and some *ad hoc* contracts, and thus could facilitate arbitrators when dealing with contracts containing identical or similar clauses.

Likewise, the book might also be beneficial to judges when they are dealing with motions for setting aside, non-recognition or non-enforcement of arbitral awards rendered in a multi-polar setting, as the book contains an analysis of all grounds upon the occurrence of which such motions may be granted.

Finally, the book also proposes certain changes to the regulation of multi-party arbitration on the level of institutional arbitration rules. This book may therefore also serve arbitral institutions in their attempts to accommodate multi-party disputes arising under multiple contracts in a better way.

Chapter 2

Multi-Party Arbitration in General

This chapter provides a concise general introduction to the topic of multi-party arbitration. Its purpose is to enable a better understanding of the specific features of multi-party arbitration issues in the construction industry. The chapter briefly deals with the definition of *multi-party arbitration*, its relation with *multi-contract arbitration* and the *group-of-contracts doctrine* (Section 2.1). The chapter continues with an explanation of the legal techniques through which multi-party arbitration may take place in practice (Section 2.2). Finally, the advantages of multi-party arbitration (Section 2.3) and the obstacles to the conduct of such type of arbitration (Section 2.4) are discussed.

2.1 Terminology notes

2.1.1 Definition of multi-party arbitration

Several definitions of multi-party arbitration have been proposed in the legal doctrine. Pursuant to the most popular one, multi-party arbitration is '*an arbitration which deals with a dispute involving more than two parties*'[1]. Two types of multilateral disputes can be distinguished within this definition. First, a dispute involving more than two parties can look like a pure bipolar dispute involving two parties. A bipolar multi-party dispute would be a dispute where 'the parties can normally be divided into two camps: a Claimant camp and a Respondent Camp'[2], where the interests of the parties within each camp are coinciding or substantially the same. The second situation concerns multi-polar disputes where the parties cannot be divided into two camps because of their divergent interests. The International Court of Arbitration with the International Chamber of Commerce in Paris ('**ICC**') perceives a multilateral dispute as one falling within the second category. Thus, multi-party arbitration is defined by the ICC as an 'arbitration involving a confrontation

[1] Olivier Caprasse, 'The Setting up of the Arbitral Tribunal in Multi-Party Arbitration', in *International Business Law Journal*, no. 2 (2006), p. 197.

[2] Yves Derains and Eric Schwartz (2005) *A Guide to the ICC Rules of Arbitration*, 2nd edn, Kluwer Law International, The Hague, pp. 70–71.

Multi-Party and Multi-Contract Arbitration in the Construction Industry, First Edition.
Dimitar Kondev.

between more than two parties with opposing interests'[3], thereby implying that cases where the parties within each camp have identical interests (such as those in the first situation described above) will *de facto* constitute a normal bilateral arbitration[4]. Indeed, most of the complexities in today's international commercial arbitration are rooted exactly in this second type of multi-party arbitration.

Numerous situations may arise in the international business sector that can give rise to multi-party arbitrations[5]. To enumerate all such situations would be neither possible nor necessary for the purposes of this book. Multi-party disputes frequently occur in the construction sector as well. As mentioned in Section 1.2, the focus of this book is on multi-party construction disputes arising under two or more contracts concluded by different parties, for example, a dispute arising under a subcontract related to a dispute arising under a main contract. These disputes can give rise to the second type of multi-party arbitration, as defined by the ICC, since the different parties involved in the related disputes, for example the employer, the main contractor and the subcontractor, pursue their own economic interests, which are rarely identical.

2.1.2 Multi-party and multi-contract arbitration: divergent or similar concepts?

In addition to *multi-party arbitration*, the term *multi-contract arbitration* is also mentioned in the legal literature with regard to complex arbitrations. Both terms have often been used interchangeably in case law and legal doctrinal writings to designate the same thing, which has caused considerable confusion[6]. Indeed, these terms could sometimes be overlapping. However, it is very important to draw a clear distinction between them in order to avoid any misunderstanding.

2.1.2.1 Divergent concepts

The terms have two different variables, which result in different conceptual meanings. In its essence, multi-party arbitration is an arbitration that involves multiple parties with opposing interests. On the other hand, multi-contract arbitration is an arbitration based on two or more contracts. These terms have different ambits. Multi-party arbitration

[3] ICC Commission on International Arbitration, 'Final Report on Multi-party Arbitrations', in 6 *ICC International Court Arbitration Bulletin*, no. 1 (1995), pp. 26–50.

[4] Christopher Stippl, 'International Multi-party Arbitration: The Role of Party Autonomy', in 7 *The American Review of International Arbitration*, no. 1 (1996), pp. 48–49.

[5] Traditionally, multi-party disputes involve construction and major industrial projects (with related subcontracts), guarantees, defective products, commodities transactions, supply chains, or, more generally, back-to-back purchases / sales. In more recent times, other types of disputes have been mentioned, such as shareholders' and joint-venture arbitration, multi-party merger and acquisitions, trust arbitration, insurance and reinsurance disputes, maritime arbitration disputes and sports-related disputes. See Nathalie Voser (2009) 'Multi-party Disputes and Joinder of Third Parties', in Albert Jan van den Berg (ed.) *50 Years of the New York Convention, ICCA International Arbitration Conference, ICCA Congress Series No. 14*, Kluwer Law International, Alphen aan den Rijn, p. 343.

[6] Fernando Mantilla-Serrano (2010) 'Multiple Parties and Multiple Contracts: Divergent or Compatible Issues?', in Bernard Hanotiau and Eric Schwartz (eds) Multiparty Arbitration, Dossiers VII, ICC Institute of World Business Law, ICC Publication No. 701E, ICC Publishing SA, Paris, pp. 11–33. See also Bernard Hanotiau (2010) 'Introduction', in Bernard Hanotiau and Eric Schwartz (eds) *Multiparty Arbitration*, Dossiers VII, ICC Institute of World Business Law, ICC Publication No. 701E, ICC Publishing SA, Paris, pp. 7–8.

does not always result in multi-contract arbitration and vice versa. For example, multi-party arbitration is also possible in single-contract situations. This will be the case, for example, when an employer concludes a construction agreement containing an arbitration clause with a consortium of multiple contractors. The different members of the consortium are considered as separate legal entities and therefore the contract will involve more than two parties. Multi-party disputes thereunder could be either disputes between the employer and the members of the consortium or among the members of the consortium themselves. A contract between a single buyer and many sellers on the other side (e.g. a contract where the buyer purchases all the shares of a company from numerous sellers) will also fall within the group of single-contract situations.

This type of multi-party arbitration raises less intricate problems than disputes arising under multiple contracts. For example, if all the multiple parties are bound by a single contract containing a standard arbitration clause, which does not explicitly address multi-party arbitration, it can be assumed that all the parties should have anticipated that they might be involved in multi-party arbitration with the participation of the other parties bound by the same contract. On that basis it can be argued that all the parties have consented to multi-party arbitration. Such a conclusion, however, can hardly be made in cases of multi-contract disputes arising under two or more arbitration agreements binding non-identical parties.

It is also important to note that multi-contract arbitration does not necessarily presuppose the involvement of multiple parties. For example, disputes under multiple bilateral contracts executed between the same parties could give rise to multi-contract arbitration if the arbitral proceedings dealing with the disputes under the different contracts are consolidated in a single arbitration. This will be a pure bipolar multi-contract dispute, which does not bear the characteristics of multi-party arbitration.

2.1.2.2 Overlapping concepts

Arbitral proceedings may bear the characteristics of both multi-party and multi-contract arbitrations in a diversity of practical scenarios. These proceedings may concern both horizontal and vertical contractual relations. In the case of horizontal contractual relations, one party signs two or more separate contracts with different parties[7]. In the construction sector, this is the case where an employer signs separate agreements with different parties, for example with a designer and a main contractor or with several main contractors for the completion of different sections of the construction works. Vertical contractual relations comprise situations where each party signs two related contracts with two different parties[8]. For example, an employer concludes a contract with a main contractor, and the latter signs a separate contract with a subcontractor. The subcontractor, on his part, may have contracted with a sub-subcontractor or a supplier and so forth. Chain contracts of this kind can be found in other commercial sectors as well, for

---

[7] Bernard Hanotiau, 'Multiparty – Multicontract Arbitration: A General Presentation with Special Emphasis on Energy Disputes', in *The Lebanese Review of Arbitration*, no. 27 (2003), p. 9.

[8] Ibid.

instance in commodities trade where goods pass through different parties before reaching the end purchaser[9].

As mentioned in Section 1.2, this book focuses on related construction disputes arising under several agreements binding non-identical parties. These disputes can involve both the horizontal and vertical contractual relations discussed above. What is common in both types of contractual relations is that the parties under the executed multiple agreements are not identical but there may be a common legal and / or factual link in the disputes arising under these contracts, which may require their resolution in a single multi-party arbitration with the involvement of all parties with legal standing. For example, in the case of horizontal contractual relations, there might be defects in the construction works caused by multiple main contractors hired by the employer. Similarly, in the case of vertical contractual relations, there may be a subcontract dispute concerning a delay in the delivery of drawings for which the employer was ultimately responsible. If these disputes are to be reviewed in a single arbitration, this arbitration will bear the characteristics of both multi-party and multi-contract arbitrations. Therefore, in these cases the concepts of these two types of arbitration overlap. For the sake of brevity, only the term *multi-party arbitration* will be used throughout this book. However, the reader should bear in mind that whenever a reference has been made to multi-party arbitration, this reference also implies arbitration based on multiple contracts[10].

2.1.3 Group of contracts doctrine

Legal doctrinal writings dealing with complex arbitrations often refer to the so-called *group-of-contracts doctrine*. The doctrine concerns multiple related contracts not linked to the same arbitration agreement – multiple contracts each of which contains a separate arbitration agreement[11]. In principle, these contracts could be entered into either by the same or by different parties. In the latter case, the notion behind the *group-of-contracts doctrine* is very closely interwoven with the type of construction disputes examined in this book.

Pursuant to the *group-of-contracts doctrine*, disputes arising under multiple contracts can in certain cases be subject to a single unified jurisdiction if the undertakings of the different parties are *indivisible*[12]. Multi-party arbitration based on this doctrine

---

[9] For example, this is the case with regard to raw materials heavily traded on specialized commodity exchanges, where traders are usually bound to standard arbitration clauses under the rules of the respective commodity exchange. Examples of such commodity exchanges are the Grain and Feed Trade Association and the Sugar Association of London.

[10] For a detailed analysis of multi-contract arbitration from a general perspective, see Philippe Leboulanger, 'Multi-Contract Arbitration', in 13 *Journal of International Arbitration*, no. 4 (1996), pp. 43–99.

[11] Fernando Mantilla-Serrano (2010) 'Multiple Parties and Multiple Contracts: Divergent or Compatible Issues?', in Bernard Hanotiau and Eric Schwartz (eds) *Multiparty Arbitration*, Dossiers VII, ICC Institute of World Business Law, ICC Publication No. 701E, ICC Publishing SA, Paris, p. 13.

[12] Philippe Leboulanger, 'Multi-Contract Arbitration', in 13 *Journal of International Arbitration* no. 4 (1996), pp. 46–47.

requires the existence of an economic link between the different contracts. As Philippe Leboulanger has pointed out:

> Contractual relations usually involve long-term economic operations comprising a large number of distinct, but interrelated, contracts. In many cases, the different kinds of agreements seem to give rise to an indivisible transaction, an economical and operational unit 'hidden' behind a multi-contract façade, that actually amounts to one fundamental relationship[13].

Furthermore, F. X. Train has stated that two or more contracts are linked to each other when they are united in a relationship of economic or functional dependence[14]. A group of contracts that coexist to reach a common goal, such as a main contract and a subcontract, belongs to this category of linked contracts. Arguably, such a link can be found in international construction projects where the multiple contracts underlying the project are somehow related to its completion. These contracts contribute to the implementation of one and the same economic transaction, which, allegedly, creates a basis for the application of the *group-of-contracts doctrine*. However, under this doctrine the existence of an economic tie between several contracts is not the only precondition to the conduct of multi-party arbitration. Other important elements are the consent of the parties to resolve their disputes in a multi-party context and the compatibility of the arbitration agreements under the different contracts.

In order to avoid any terminological confusion, the author will not refer to the *group-of-contracts doctrine* as such in the present book. However, the theoretical observations underlying the doctrine, including in respect of the parties' consent and the compatibility of the arbitration agreements, will be duly explored in the following chapters. Thus, the notion of consent to multi-party arbitration in the construction industry will be systematically discussed in Chapters 4, 5, 6 and 7, and the issue of compatibility will be dealt with in Section 7.4.

2.2 Legal techniques introducing multi-party arbitration

Multi-party arbitration may be initiated in the following four ways: (i) by filing a single request for arbitration against multiple parties, (ii) joinder of a third party in a pending arbitration, (iii) intervention of a third party in a pending arbitration and (iv) consolidation of parallel arbitrations. Each of these legal techniques will be examined briefly below in order to facilitate the reader's apprehension of how multi-party arbitration may take place in practice. The issue pertinent to all these techniques is how to justify the participation in a single arbitration of parties that do not have a direct contractual relation and have arguably never agreed to arbitrate between themselves.

---

[13] Ibid.

[14] Francois-Xavier Train (2003) *Les Contrats liés devant l'arbitre du commerce international*, Bibliothèque de Droit Privé, LGDJ, Paris, quoted by Bernard Hanotiau (2005) *Complex Arbitrations: Multiparty, Multicontract, Multi-issue and Class Actions*, Kluwer Law International, The Hague, pp. 101–102 (§ 219).

Provisions introducing these legal techniques can be found in the parties' contracts, the arbitration rules chosen by the parties as applicable to their disputes or in the arbitration laws of some states. The particular procedural and other requirements concerning the application of these legal techniques will be discussed in the subsequent chapters.

2.2.1 Single request for arbitration

The first way to commence multi-party arbitration is by means of filing a single request for arbitration against multiple parties. This would be the case, for example, when an employer files a single request for arbitration against both a designer and a main contractor with whom the employer has contracted separately. Unlike the other legal techniques for multi-party arbitration, which presuppose the existence of one or more pending arbitrations, the single request for arbitration gives the start of the arbitration. This legal technique is explicitly addressed in some of the most popular institutional arbitration rules[15].

2.2.2 Joinder

The term *joinder* is often defined as the introduction of a new party in a pending arbitration upon the initiative of one of the disputants[16]. The third party could be either a signatory to the same arbitration agreement or a non-signatory. There are two classic examples of joinder. Under the first one, a claimant who has started proceedings against a respondent tries to join a third party in the pending case as an additional respondent. For instance, an employer has started an arbitration against one of the two main contractors working on the same construction project, and at a later stage decides to bring the second main contractor as an additional respondent in the same arbitration. In the second example, the respondent tries to join a third party in a pending arbitration. For instance, a main contractor may require the joinder of a subcontractor in his arbitration with the employer where the main contractor is a respondent. Joinder provisions can be found in most modern sets of institutional arbitration rules and in some national arbitration laws.

2.2.3 Intervention

Intervention is the acceding of a third party in a pending arbitration upon its own motion with the purpose of filing a claim against one or all of the parties to the pending arbitration. For example, a design professional may want to intervene in an arbitration

[15] See, for example, Article 9 of the ICC Rules of Arbitration and Article 10 of the CEPANI Rules.

[16] Martin Platte (2008) 'Multi-Party Arbitration: Legal Issues Arising Out of Joinder and Consolidation', in E. Gaillard and D. Di Pietro (eds) *Enforcement of Arbitration Agreements and International Arbitral Awards: The New York Convention in Practice*, Cameron May, London, pp. 481–499.

between an employer and a main contractor in order to introduce his claim against one of these disputants. The main difference from the joinder is that in the latter case the participation of the third party is requested by one of the parties to the pending arbitration. Arbitration rules rarely deal with the question of intervention[17]. Furthermore, very few states have addressed intervention in their arbitration laws[18].

The abovementioned observations concern the so-called *main intervention* – the intervention of a third party that introduces its own claim against one of the parties to the arbitration. Other forms of intervention are sometimes referred to in the legal literature. These may include the notion of *side intervention* and *amicus curie*. Side intervention (in German known as *einfacher Nebenintervenient*) generally designates the intervention of a third party that does not have a separate claim against one of the disputants. Such a party is not considered as a formal party to the proceedings, and it intervenes in the latter in order to assist one of the formal parties. For example, a subcontractor may intervene in proceedings between an employer and a main contractor in order to help the main contractor in better substantiating his claim against the employer. It is argued that the outcome of the proceedings will be binding on the intervening party[19].

The present book only deals with main intervention. Side intervention is a peculiar legal mechanism, which is primarily known in a few countries belonging to the Germanic legal system, such as Germany, Austria and Switzerland. Therefore, this mechanism is covered under the arbitration rules adopted by arbitral institutions in these countries[20]. While *amicus curiae* are typical for investment arbitration, they are rarely met in international commercial arbitrations[21].

2.2.4 Consolidation

In the legal literature, different connotations have been attributed to the term *consolidation*, which has caused much confusion. For example, the joinder of a third party in a pending arbitration is sometimes referred to as consolidation of disputes. In this book, consolidation is used as a term that denotes the act of uniting several pending arbitrations into a

---

[17] For example, the ICC Rules of Arbitration and the UNCITRAL Rules do not address intervention at all. An example of arbitration rules that envisage the possibility for intervention is the Swiss Rules of the Swiss Chambers' Arbitration Institution ('**Swiss Rules**'). See Article 4 (2) of the Swiss Rules.

[18] This is the case in Belgium and the Netherlands.

[19] See Nathalie Voser (2009) 'Multi-party Disputes and Joinder of Third Parties', in Albert Jan van den Berg (ed.) *50 Years of the New York Convention, ICCA International Arbitration Conference, ICCA Congress Series No. 14*, Kluwer Law International, Alphen aan den Rijn, p. 381. The author further explains that this form of participation in the proceedings is possible not only by way of intervention by the third party on its own notion but also upon the request of one of the formal parties to the proceedings.

[20] See, for example, Article 4(2) of the Swiss Rules and Article 14 of the Vienna Rules.

[21] Nikolaus Pitkowitz (2015) 'Chapter II: The Arbitrator and the Arbitration Procedure, Multi-Party Arbitrations – Joinder and Consolidation under the Vienna Rules 2013', in Christian Klausegger, Peter Klein, Florian Kremslehner *et al.* (eds) *Austrian Yearbook on International Arbitration*, Volume 2015, Manz'sche Verlags- und Universitätsbuchhandlung, Vienna, pp. 308–309.

single arbitration conducted before a single arbitral tribunal. In ICC arbitrations, the term *consolidation* is used in the same way[22].

Theoretically, consolidation of pending proceedings is possible with regard to two or more disputes arising under one and the same bipartite agreement and also with regard to disputes based on several agreements executed between the same two parties. However, these cases are not examined in the book. The focus hereof is on consolidation of disputes arising under separate agreements concluded between different parties. For example, there are two separate arbitrations. The first one is between an employer and a main contractor, and the second one – between the main contractor and a subcontractor, and the main contractor files a request for the merging of the two arbitrations. This legal mechanism finds regulation in most modern institutional arbitration rules. In some states, consolidation can also be ordered on the basis of provisions contained in national arbitration laws or on the basis of case law. The latter policy is addressed in Chapter 5.

2.3 *Advantages of multi-party arbitration*

2.3.1 Avoids risk of inconsistent findings

One of the main advantages of multi-party arbitration is that it avoids the risk of having inconsistent or conflicting arbitral awards in cases that face the same or similar points of law and / or fact[23]. This increases the efficiency of the dispute resolution process as a whole. This advantage can be easily seen in cases concerning recourse claims. A respondent in a pending arbitration might want to file a recourse claim against a third party that is not participating in the arbitration. In principle, the respondent will not be able to pursue this claim in the same arbitration if the third party does not have direct contractual relations with the claimant. Therefore, the respondent will have to introduce his claim against the third party in a separate arbitration, which will be conducted without the participation of the claimant in the first arbitration. However, the new arbitral tribunal dealing with this second arbitration will not be bound by the findings of the first tribunal as regards the facts of the case and the scope of liability of the respondent. As a result, the recourse claim may be dismissed in the second arbitration despite the fact that the claimant's identical claim against the respondent was successful in the first arbitration.

---

[22] See Jason Fry, Simon Greenberg and Francesca Mazza (2012) *The Secretariat's Guide to ICC Arbitration*, ICC Publication No. 729, ICC Publishing SA, Paris, pp. 111 (§ 3-347).

[23] Sigvard Jarvin (1991) 'Issues Related to Consolidation', in P. Bellet, P. Bernardini, G. Bernini *et al.* (eds) *Multi-Party Arbitration: Views from International Arbitration Specialists*, Publication No. 480/1, ICC Publishing SA, Paris, p. 200. See also Alan Redfern and Martin Hunter with Nigel Blackaby and Constantine Partasides (2004) *Law and Practice of International Commercial Arbitration*, 4th edn, Sweet & Maxwell, London, p. 200 (&3-73), Martin Platte (2008) 'Multi-Party Arbitration: Legal Issues Arising Out of Joinder and Consolidation', in E. Gaillard and D. di Pietro (eds) *Enforcement of Arbitration Agreements and International Arbitral Awards: The New York Convention in Practice*, Cameron May, London, p. 497, and Andreas Austmann, 'Commercial Multi-party Arbitration: A Case-By-Case Approach', in *1 The American Review of International Arbitration*, no. 3 (1990), pp. 347–348.

In the construction sector, such a situation can be observed in a scenario where the employer files a request for arbitration against a main contractor due to defects in the completed construction works, and the main contractor is of the opinion that these defects have been caused by a subcontractor. If the employer is awarded compensation, the main contractor would certainly like to pass on his liability towards the employer to the subcontractor who ultimately caused the defects. In principle, he would have to do that in a separate arbitration (provided, of course, that the subcontract also contains an arbitration agreement) because the subcontractor and the employer are not privy to each other. However, the second arbitral tribunal dealing with the main contractor's recourse claim against the subcontractor is not bound by the findings of the first tribunal. Therefore, the second tribunal may even reach the conclusion that there are no defects in the construction works. As a result, the main contractor will have to pay to the employer under the first arbitral award and will not be in a position to pass on the paid indemnification to the subcontractor under the second arbitral award. Apparently, this is an undesirable situation, which the main contractor would like to avoid. This risk will not occur if both claims – the employer's claim against the main contractor and the latter's recourse claim against the subcontractor – are to be reviewed in a single arbitration with the participation of all three parties.

However, the advantages resulting from such a single arbitration, including the avoidance of the risk of having inconsistent or conflicting awards, should always be considered in the light of the economic interests pursued by the different participants in construction projects. Multi-party proceedings can be advantageous for some parties but disadvantageous for other parties. This question will be further discussed in Chapter 3. It suffices to mention here that there might be parties that would actually benefit from the existence of inconsistencies in the separate awards. In the abovementioned scenario, for example, it will be the subcontractor who would benefit from an arbitral award that is inconsistent with a preceding award confirming the existence of defects in his works.

2.3.2 Less time and fewer costs

From an overall perspective, the conduct of a single arbitration instead of separate parallel proceedings dealing with identical or similar points of law and/or fact saves costs and time. As stated by Martin Platte: 'One of the main advantages joinder and consolidation provide is that they reduce the administrative and legal effort and thereby reduce cost, increase speed and – from a general point of view – make proceedings more efficient'[24].

This is especially true with regard to parties pursuing recourse claims against third parties – non-participants in the initiated arbitration. In the scenario discussed in Subsection 2.3.1, the main contractor will most likely invest less money and time in a single arbitration with the participation of all three parties than in two separate arbitrations against the employer and the subcontractor. However, this advantage

---

[24] Martin Platte (2008) 'Multi-Party Arbitration: Legal Issues Arising Out of Joinder and Consolidation', in E. Gaillard and D. di Pietro (eds) *Enforcement of Arbitration Agreements and International Arbitral Awards: The New York Convention in Practice*, Cameron May, London, p. 496.

should not be overestimated. The time and cost factor will ultimately depend on the circumstances of the specific case. Some authors argue, with some justification, that multi-party arbitration might sometimes increase the number of arbitrators in the panel, thus inflating the costs of the proceedings as well as the time needed to deliberate and arrive at the final disposition of the case[25]. Furthermore, joint hearings and presentation of evidence by multiple parties can also increase the time and costs involved in the proceedings[26]. Finally, the time and cost factor does not equally affect all parties. The party subject to more than one set of proceedings (e.g. the main contractor in the discussed scenario) will benefit from this factor but other parties involved in small parts of the dispute (e.g. the subcontractor) will most likely have to invest additional time and money because multi-party arbitration will trigger more costs and require more time than a bipolar arbitration[27].

2.3.3 Fewer factual errors

It is also often argued that multi-party arbitration decreases the risk of factual errors in arbitral awards. The arbitrators have to take into account the submissions and pleas made by multiple parties. This facilitates the understanding of the tribunal of the mutual rights and obligations under the related bilateral contracts. They are able to acquire a more complete and detailed picture of all the facts of the case because of the participation of all the parties in the dispute which may decrease the risk of factual errors[28].

---

[25] Andreas Austmann, 'Commercial Multi-party Arbitration: A Case-By-Case Approach', in *1 The American Review of International Arbitration*, no. 3 (1990), p. 349. See also Fritz Nicklisch, 'Multi-party Arbitration and Dispute Resolution in Major Industrial Projects', in *11 Journal of International Arbitration*, no. 4 (1994), pp. 64–68.

[26] See Fritz Nicklisch, 'Multi-party Arbitration and Dispute Resolution in Major Industrial Projects', in *11 Journal of International Arbitration*, no. 4 (1994), pp. 64–65. The author cited a report commenting on a real arbitration case. The case was commenced with a contractor's claim against the employer, who joined the architect and the technical consultant in the proceedings as third-party defendants. The author stated that 'the articulation of indemnity claims against the architect and the technical consultant involved substantial problems and a very considerable delay in the proceedings. Immediately after finalization of the terms of reference, it became apparent that, due to the various submission schedules, the first hearing addressing procedural issues ... could take place, at the earliest two years after the claimant's request for arbitration.'

[27] Andreas Austmann, 'Commercial Multi-party Arbitration: A Case-By-Case Approach', in *1 The American Review of International Arbitration*, no. 3 (1990), p. 349. See also Emmanuel Gaillard, 'The Consolidation of Arbitral Proceedings and Court Proceedings', in *14 ICC International Court of Arbitration Bulletin, Complex Arbitrations – Special Supplement* (2003), p. 37.

[28] Irene Ten Cate 'Multi-party and Multi-contract Arbitrations: Procedural Mechanisms and Interpretation of Arbitration Agreements under U.S. Law', in *15 The American Review of International Arbitration*, no. 1 (2004), pp. 137–138. See also Ruth Stackpool-Moore (2014) 'Joinder and Consolidation – Examining Best Practice in the Swiss, HKIAC and ICC Rules', in Nathalie Voser (ed.) *10 Years of the Swiss Rules of International Arbitration*, ASA Special Series No. 44, JurisNet LLC, New York, NY, pp. 17–18.

2.4 *Obstacles to multi-party arbitration*

2.4.1 Consensual nature of arbitration

The main obstacle to the conduct of multi-party arbitration is the consensual nature of arbitration[29]. Unlike state courts, which derive their jurisdiction from the state and the state legislation, the jurisdiction of arbitral tribunals is based on the agreement of the parties. Furthermore, arbitral tribunals do not have the wide-ranging powers of state judges to consolidate parallel proceedings or order joinder of third parties into existing proceedings.

The main principle in arbitration is that arbitral proceedings may only be held among parties that have agreed to submit their disputes to arbitration[30]. Therefore, the question of whether or not multi-party arbitration should be admitted should start from the interpretation of the intent of the parties as expressed in the relevant arbitration clause[31]. Construction projects are often characterized by a multitude of bilateral contracts: a main contract, a subcontract, a sub-subcontract, a supply agreement, a consultancy or professional services agreement with a project manager or a designer, and so forth. Even though these contracts are interlinked in the sense that they all pertain to the completion of the construction project, they remain distinct agreements with distinct scopes of works and responsibilities concluded by parties that are not identical. In the author's opinion, the presence of separate arbitration clauses contained in two or more of these contracts, which are silent on the question of multi-party arbitration, constitutes a strong presumption that each contracting party expects to resolve its dispute in a bipolar setting with its counterparty only[32]. Even if the separate arbitration clauses are identical or substantially similar, it cannot be assumed on the basis of this similarity *per se* that

---

[29] Kristina Maria Siig, 'Multi-party Arbitration in International Trade: Problems and Solutions', in *1 International Journal of Liability and Scientific Enquiry*, no. 1/2 (2007), p. 73: '[The] Achilles heel of arbitration is its core feature; that arbitration as a means of dispute resolution presupposes consensus between parties.'

[30] As stated in the *ad hoc* award of 17 November 1994 in *Banque Arabe et Internationale d'Investissement et. al.* v. *Inter-Arab Investment Guarantee Corporation*, in *XIII Yearbook Commercial Arbitration*, 1998, pp. 644–654: 'Contrary to litigation in front of state courts where any interested party can join or be adjoined to protect its interests, in arbitration only those who are parties to the arbitration agreement expressed in writing could appear in the arbitral proceedings either as claimants or defendants.'

[31] Bernard Hanotiau, 'Problems Raised by Complex Arbitrations Involving Multiple Contracts-Parties-Issues, An Analysis', in 18 *Journal of International Arbitration*, no. 3 (2001), p. 302. See also Kristina Maria Siig, 'Multi-party Arbitration in International Trade: Problems and Solutions', in *1 International Journal of Liability and Scientific Enquiry*, no. 1/2 (2007), p. 78.

[32] See also Gary Born (2014) *International Commercial Arbitration, Volume II: International Arbitral Procedures*, 2nd edn 2014, Kluwer Law International, Alphen aan den Rijn, p. 2075, where the author has stated: 'Further, there is a substantial argument that, by not agreeing affirmatively to permit consolidation (or joinder / intervention), the parties have agreed on arbitral procedures that exclude or are inconsistent with such measures; this is consistent with notions of privity of contract and confidentiality concerns.' See also Keechang Kim and Jason Mitchenson, 'Voluntary Third-Party Intervention in International Arbitration for Construction Disputes: A Contextual Approach to Jurisdictional Issues', in *30 Journal of International Arbitration*, no. 4 (2013), p. 413, where the authors have stated: 'Where an agreement is silent on third-party intervention, the presumption will be against multiparty proceedings.'

the parties have tacitly consented to multi-party arbitration. A similar view has been expressed by Fritz Nicklisch who has stated that 'The mere inclusion of a standard ICC arbitration clause in a number of contracts jointly serving the realisation of a large-scale project is not normally a conclusive indication of consent to multi-party arbitration'[33]. When commenting on the relation between a main contract and a subcontract, the same author was even more explicit:

> [In] terms of both substantive and procedural law, arbitration must take place *inter partes*, i.e. in a linear way between the individual contracts and not in proceedings involving three or more parties. In this instance, there is not the slightest indication of implied consent to multi-party arbitration. Indeed, the strict separation of contractual relationships by the parties themselves would appear to indicate precisely the opposite[34].

Therefore, an arbitration clause contained in a bilateral contract can, in principle, be invoked only by the parties bound by that contract. Thus, from a contractual standpoint a subcontractor is not bound by an arbitration clause contained in a main contract, and a main contractor is not bound by an arbitration clause contained in a contract concluded between an employer and a design professional[35]. Similarly, an employer is not bound by an arbitration clause contained in a subcontract, and an architect or an engineer hired by the employer is not bound by an arbitration clause contained in a main contract. As a result, multi-party arbitral proceedings may only be conducted if all the parties under the different bilateral contracts have agreed to resolve their disputes in a multi-party context. Otherwise, multi-party proceedings will infringe the parties' consent for the resolution of their contractual disputes in a bipolar context, and, most notably, the mechanism for appointment of arbitrators stipulated in their contracts, especially if the parties have agreed on a three-member arbitral tribunal where each party has the right to appoint an arbitrator. As will be seen in Chapter 5, the conduct of multi-party proceedings without parties' authorization on the basis of statutory provisions or case law may raise similar concerns.

---

[33] Fritz Nicklisch, 'Multi-Party Arbitration and Dispute Resolution in Major Industrial Projects', in *11 Journal of International Arbitration*, Issue 4 (1994), pp. 60–61, 71.

[34] Ibid. A similar statement has been made by Stavros Brekoulakis, see Stavros Brekoulakis (2010) *Third Parties in International Commercial Arbitration*, Oxford University Press, Oxford, pp. 100–101 (§ 3.16). According to the author: 'It would seem, however, that when there are several arbitration clauses in several contracts any attempt to ascertain consent to multiparty proceedings or third-party claims will be problematic. Unless clear evidence exists that the several parties wanted to allow for multiparty proceedings despite the fact that they signed different arbitration clauses, the presumption should be against multiparty proceedings and third-party claims.' See also Karim Youssef (2009) *Consent in Context: Fulfilling the Promise of International Arbitration. Multi-Party, Multi-Contract and Non-Contract Arbitration*, West Thomson, Eagan, MN, pp. 142–143, and Andrea Marco Steingruber (2012) *Consent in International Arbitration*, Oxford University Press, Oxford, para. 9.70. For an opposite opinion, see Jean-Francois Poudret and Sébastien Besson (2007) *Comparative Law of International Arbitration*, 2nd edn, Sweet & Maxwell, London / Schulthess, pp. 198–199, 898.

[35] Stavros Brekoulakis (2010) *Third Parties in International Commercial Arbitration*, Oxford University Press, Oxford, pp. 84–87 (§ 2.273, § 2.279 and § 2.284–§ 2.287), 186 (§ 6.42), 276 (§ 12.25).

In the United Kingdom, the consensual nature of arbitration is further underpinned with the doctrine of 'privity of contract'[36]. According to this doctrine 'no person can sue or be sued on a contract unless a party to it'[37]. Thus, only parties to a contract can enjoy the benefits and liabilities envisaged thereunder. Hence, a party's right and obligation to arbitrate its dispute under a contract applies only in respect of its contractual counterparty and cannot be extended to third parties outside the contract because these situations fall short of privity.

2.4.2 Arbitration as a two-party setup

Originally, arbitration was predominantly dealing with the resolution of bipolar disputes. Therefore, arbitration had a two-party setup. This did not suit the complexity of multi-polar arbitration disputes in cases where parties pursued their own specific interests, which were different from and sometimes contrary to the interests of the other parties[38]. This perception of arbitration as a mechanism for resolution of bipolar disputes has not been completely eradicated yet. This, for example, can be seen from the UNCITRAL Model Law, which does not even contemplate the existence of more than two parties. The traditional two-party set up can also be discerned in some institutional arbitration rules which do not contain provisions addressing multi-party arbitrations[39].

Not all arbitration rules addressing multi-party arbitrations take into account all the complexities of multi-party disputes. A brief comparison between the 1998 and the 2012 version of the Rules of Arbitration of the ICC ('**ICC Rules**') may exemplify this statement. The 1998 ICC Rules did not explicitly provide for the opportunity that in multi-party arbitration any party may make a claim against any other party. The silence of the rules on this matter was sometimes interpreted conservatively, i.e. in a way excluding the filing of claims between parties on the same side[40]. This issue has now been dealt with under the 2012 ICC Rules that acknowledge that possibility[41]. Another example is the consolidation provision in the 1998 ICC Rules (Article 4(6)), which could be applied only in cases of parallel arbitrations between the same parties. While

---

[36] For the application of the doctrine of privity of contract in construction law, see John Adriaanse (2010) *Construction Contract Law. The Essentials*, 3rd edn, Palgrave Macmillan, Basingstoke, pp. 6, 81–82, 103–104, 246, 310. See also Douglas Wood, Paul Chynoweth, Julie Adshead and Jim Mason (2010) *Law and the Built Environment*, Wiley Blackwell, Chichester, p. 77.

[37] Douglas Wood, Paul Chynoweth, Julie Adshead and Jim Mason (2010) *Law and the Built Environment*, Wiley Blackwell, Chichester, p. 77.

[38] Nathalie Voser (2009) 'Multi-party Disputes and Joinder of Third Parties', in Albert Jan van den Berg (ed.) *50 Years of the New York Convention, ICCA International Arbitration Conference, ICCA Congress Series No. 14*, Kluwer Law International, Alphen aan den Rijn, p. 351.

[39] For example, the DIS Arbitration Rules adopted by the German Institution of Arbitration (Deutsche Institution für Schiedsgerichtsbarkeit e.V.) do not contain any provisions dealing with consolidation, joinder or intervention.

[40] See Jason Fry, Simon Greenberg and Francesca Mazza (2012) *The Secretariat's Guide to ICC Arbitration*, ICC Publication No. 729, ICC Publishing SA, Paris, p. 105 (§ 3-325).

[41] Article 8(1) of the ICC Rules.

the 2012 ICC Rules have remained conservative, they have significantly broadened the scope of the consolidation provision[42].

In recent years, we are witnessing overhauls of the most popular sets of arbitration rules with the purpose of adapting them to multi-polar disputes. These revisions have introduced specific provisions dealing with the different legal techniques through which multi-party arbitration may take place[43]. Therefore, the traditional two-party setup of arbitral proceedings as an obstacle to multi-party arbitration is gradually fading away.

2.4.3 Arbitration as a confidential process

One of the main advantages of arbitration is its confidential nature. Arbitration awards are usually not published, and the proceedings are capable of being organized in a way ensuring that the underlying contract and any business secrets of the parties are not disclosed to third parties. Taking that into consideration, it is doubtful whether third parties should be allowed to participate in arbitral proceedings pending between two other parties. The weight of the confidentiality factor will ultimately depend on the specific facts of the case. For example, in a construction dispute between an employer and a main contractor where the joinder of a subcontractor is sought, the disclosure of certain elements of the main contract to the subcontractor, such as the agreed contract price, is often considered a sensitive issue, which the parties will try to avoid. Furthermore, it is sometimes considered as highly unusual for the employer to be cognizant of all the details of the subcontracts concluded by the main contractor[44].

However, the confidentiality issue should not be overrated. Indeed, it is a main principle in international commercial arbitration that hearings are held in camera[45]. However, many arbitration rules do not contain provisions expanding the confidentiality to the arbitral proceedings as a whole, including in respect of the submissions of the parties, their deliberations and so forth. There are, however, some exceptions. These comprise the confidentiality provision in the LCIA Rules adopted by the London Court of International Commercial Arbitration ('**LCIA Rules**')[46] and the provision in the Arbitration Rules of the Hong Kong International Arbitration Centre ('**HKIAC Rules**')[47]. Applicable national

[42] See Article 10 of the 2012 ICC Rules. The provision allows consolidation subject to parties' consent even in cases where the parties under the different arbitrations are not identical. This provision will be discussed further in Section 4.1 of this book.

[43] See, for example, Articles 7–10 of the ICC Rules under the title *Multiple Parties, Multiple Contracts and Consolidation*. See also Article 4 and Article 8 of the Swiss Rules, etc.

[44] See Fritz Nicklisch, 'Multi-party Arbitration and Dispute Resolution in Major Industrial Projects', in *11 Journal of International Arbitration*, no. 4 (1994), p. 69.

[45] See Article 26(3) of the ICC Rules, Article 28(3) of the UNCITRAL Rules, etc.

[46] Article 30 of the LCIA Rules spreads the confidentiality element to all documents and other materials created or submitted in relation to the proceedings.

[47] Article 42 of the HKIAC Rules stipulates that no party may publish, disclose or communicate any information relating to the arbitration and the award made in that arbitration. The deliberations of the arbitral tribunal are also confidential.

laws rarely contain confidentiality provisions[48]. Until recently, it was considered that there was a duty of confidentiality concerning international commercial arbitrations in France but this position changed in 2011[49]. Nowadays, the duty of confidentiality applies only to domestic arbitrations in France but not to international commercial arbitrations[50]. Moreover, it is true that arbitration awards are usually not published but in certain cases their content may enter the public domain, especially when it comes to the recognition and enforcement of these awards.

In addition, the confidentiality concerns stemming from the participation of third parties in arbitration between two other parties are not so acute when it comes to the type of construction disputes examined in this book. The parties who are likely to have an interest in consolidation of, or joining in, existing disputes are usually parties to whom the contractual relationship between the original parties is probably already known[51]. This is especially discernible in subcontracts, which are commonly drafted back-to-back to the respective main contracts. These subcontracts often contain provisions obliging the main contractor to disclose the main contract content or a certain part of it to the subcontractor. For example, the FIDIC Subcontract stipulates that the main contractor should make the main contract, except for certain confidential information, such as the contract price, available to the subcontractor for inspection[52]. Furthermore, the subcontractor is deemed to have acquired full knowledge of the relevant provisions of the main contract[53]. Other international standard forms contain similar provisions[54]. Thus, the subcontractor is usually cognizant of the content of the main contract, which diminishes the significance of the confidentiality factor. Similarly, an engineer or an architect who has to prepare the drawings for the contemplated construction works is usually aware of the main contract or material parts of it whereunder the relevant specifications have been stated. Even if there is a confidentiality agreement between some of the parties, it may be possible to conduct the multi-party proceedings in such a way that the obligations of the parties under this agreement are not breached.

---

[48] Under English law, there is an implied term of confidentiality in the arbitral proceedings. The position is spelt out in *Dolling-Baker v. Merrett* [1991] 2 All ER 890, and in *Hassneh Insurance Co. of Israel v. Mew* [1993] 2 Lloyd's Law Reports 243.

[49] A new Decree No. 2011-48 of 13 January 2011, which entered into force on 1 May 2011, introduced a major textual overhaul of French Arbitration Law.

[50] While Article 1464 of the French Code of Civil Procedure provides that domestic arbitral proceedings are confidential, unless the parties agree otherwise, the same confidentiality provision is not included in the list of provisions contained in Article 1506 that apply to international commercial arbitration.

[51] Kristina Maria Siig, 'Multi-party Arbitration in International Trade: Problems and Solutions', in *1 International Journal of Liability and Scientific Enquiry*, no. 1/2 (2007), p. 76.

[52] See sub-clause 2.1 [Subcontractor's Knowledge of Main Contract] of the FIDIC Subcontract. Pursuant to the clause, the main contractor should provide to the subcontractor a copy of the Appendix to Tender of the main contract together with the Particular Conditions of the main contract.

[53] Ibid.

[54] See, for example, Article 2.2 [Flow Down of the Main Contract] of the ICC Model Subcontract, published by the ICC in France. Pursuant to this clause, the subcontractor expressly confirms that he is bound to follow and give effect to the provisions of the main contract as if he were the main contractor to the extent the subcontract works are concerned. In order to allow the subcontractor to fulfil his obligations under this clause, the main contractor will have to disclose the content of the main contract to the subcontractor.

For example, anecdotal evidence suggests that multi-party arbitrations with the participation of employers, main contractors and subcontractors have been organized in a way ensuring that the subcontractors do not acquire knowledge of the contract price under the main contracts.

The weight of the confidentiality factor in the context of multi-party proceedings would very much depend on the availability of a confidentiality agreement concluded among the parties, the content of the relevant contracts and the relevant provisions under the applicable arbitration rules and arbitration law. In principle, however, the confidentiality element is a hurdle that can be easily overcome in the context of multi-party arbitrations in the construction sector.

2.4.4 Setting aside proceedings and non-recognition and / or non-enforcement of arbitral awards

The legislative framework governing recognition and enforcement of arbitral awards differs depending on the country where the award is rendered. If the recognition and enforcement of an award is sought in the same country as the one where the award is rendered, the principal position is that the local arbitration law applies. If, however, recognition and enforcement is sought in countries other than the one where the award is rendered, the provisions of the New York Convention come into play, provided, of course, that the relevant state where enforcement is sought is a signatory to the convention[55]. So far there are 156 state parties that have acceded to the convention. The high number of signatories illustrates the significance of the convention in the international arbitration world.

Recognition and enforcement of awards resulting from multi-party arbitral proceedings can give rise to serious concerns. First, the New York Convention presupposes the existence of an arbitration agreement in writing between the parties. Pursuant to Article II (2): 'The term "agreement in writing" shall include an arbitral clause in a contract or an arbitration agreement, signed by the parties or contained in an exchange of letters or telegrams.' This formal requirement was considered outdated and therefore UNCITRAL adopted a Recommendation in 2006[56] that encouraged states that had ratified the convention to apply Article II (2) 'recognizing that the circumstances described therein are not exhaustive.' However, this recommendation does not have any binding character. Because of the abovementioned formal requirement, some arbitral institutions and tribunals are still reluctant to deal with multi-party disputes arising under multiple contracts in cases where there is no arbitration agreement binding all the parties at

[55] However, in certain cases, the New York Convention will also apply with regard to awards rendered in the country where enforcement is sought (Article I(1) of the convention). These are awards that are treated as non-domestic awards under the law of that country.

[56] Recommendation Regarding the Interpretation of Article II, Paragraph 2, and Article VII, Paragraph 1, of the Convention on the Recognition and Enforcement of Foreign Arbitral Awards, done in New York, 10 June 1958 (2006), http://www.uncitral.org/uncitral/en/uncitral_texts/arbitration/2006recommendation.html (accessed 25 July 2016).

stake. However, the general tendency is that courts and arbitrators are inclined to give a flexible interpretation of this requirement and it would be unlikely that they would base their decision concerning multi-party arbitration solely on this factor[57].

Article V of the New York Convention contains an explicit list of grounds upon the existence of which recognition and enforcement of an arbitral award may be refused. For convenience, the relevant part of Article V has been reproduced below:

> 1. Recognition and enforcement of the award may be refused, at the request of the party against whom it is invoked, only if that party furnishes to the competent authority where recognition and enforcement is sought, proof that:
>   (a) ...the said [arbitration] agreement is not valid under the law to which the parties have subjected it or, failing any indication thereon, under the country where the award is made; or
>   (b) The party against whom the award is invoked was not given proper notice of the appointment of the arbitrator or of the arbitration proceedings or was otherwise unable to present his case; or
>   (c) The award deals with a difference not contemplated by or not falling within the terms of submission to arbitration, or it contains decisions on matters beyond the scope of the submission to arbitration...; or
>   (d) The composition of the arbitral authority or the arbitral procedure was not in accordance with the agreement of the parties, or, failing such agreement, was not in accordance with the law of the country where the arbitration took place; or...
> 2. Recognition and enforcement of an arbitral award may also be refused if the competent authority where recognition and enforcement is sought finds that:...
>   (b) The recognition or enforcement of the award would be contrary to the public policy of that country.

In most cases the grounds for setting aside an award under the domestic legislation of the country where the award is rendered are analogous to those under the New York Convention[58]. All these grounds may be considered as *stumbling blocks* when it comes to the recognition and enforcement of multi-party arbitral awards[59]. A specific aspect of multi-party arbitration based on multiple contracts is that the award often deals not only with one but with several arbitration agreements. If a party has not consented to resolve its contractual dispute in an arbitration with the participation of third parties not bound by the same contract, then this party may have valid arguments to resist the recognition and enforcement of a multi-party arbitral award rendered against it[60].

---

[57] See Bernard Hanotiau (2005) *Complex Arbitrations: Multiparty, Multicontract, Multi-issue and Class Actions*, Kluwer Law International, The Hague, pp. 9–10 (§ 17).

[58] See for example Article 34(2) of the UNCITRAL Model Law.

[59] Nathalie Voser (2009) 'Multi-party Disputes and Joinder of Third Parties', in Albert Jan van den Berg (ed.) *50 Years of the New York Convention, ICCA International Arbitration Conference, ICCA Congress Series No. 14*, Kluwer Law International, Alphen aan den Rijn, p. 352.

[60] Martin Platte (2008) 'Multi-Party Arbitration: Legal Issues Arising Out of Joinder and Consolidation', in E. Gaillard and D. di Pietro (eds) *Enforcement of Arbitration Agreements and International Arbitral Awards: The New York Convention in Practice*, Cameron May, London, pp. 483–490.

This can best be illustrated with an example from the construction industry. If a subcontractor is brought into an arbitration between an employer and a main contractor despite the subcontractor's objection, the subcontractor may have several arguments to resist the enforcement of the arbitration award. First, he may claim that the recognition and enforcement of the award should be refused on the ground of Article V (1) (a) because there was no arbitration agreement binding all three parties. Secondly, the subcontractor may also invoke Article V (1) (b) if he was joined in the proceedings after the constitution of the tribunal by asserting that he was not given proper notice of the appointment of the arbitrators because he did not participate in the process. The subcontractor may also lean on Article V (1) (c) and claim that the award contains decisions on matters that are beyond the scope of the bilateral arbitration clauses contained both in his agreement with the main contractor and in the agreement between the employer and the main contractor. The fourth and probably the most obvious argument would be that enforcement should be refused on the ground of Article V (1) (d) as the arbitral tribunal was constituted and the arbitral proceedings were conducted not in accordance with the subcontractor's agreement expressed in his arbitration clause with the main contractor. This will be the case, for example, if the subcontractor has agreed on a three-member tribunal with the right to appoint one of the arbitrators but he is deprived of this right because of his joinder in the arbitration between the employer and the main contractor where the arbitral tribunal has already been appointed. Furthermore, it has been argued by some authors that depriving a certain party of the right to appoint an arbitrator, whilst allowing other parties to make such an appointment, will result in unequal treatment of the parties which might run counter to the public policy of the country where the award is made and / or enforcement is sought[61]. In this case, Article V (2) (b) could also be invoked as a ground for refusal of the enforcement of the award as the composition of the arbitral tribunal is tainted by irregularities[62].

There are instances where some of the abovementioned grounds have been invoked by parties not satisfied with a multi-party arbitration award as a means of last resort in the country where the enforcement of the award is sought. Case law with regard to that matter differs. Examples of court decisions refusing enforcement of an award, albeit not in the construction sector, are the *Javor v. Francoeur* case[63], the *Sarhank Group v. Oracle*

[61] Ibid., pp. 491–494. See also Julian Lew, Harris Bor, Gregory Fullelove and Joanne Greenaway (eds) (2013) *Arbitration in England with Chapters on Scotland and Ireland*, Kluwer Law International, Alphen aan den Rijn, pp. 479–480 (para. 22.78), and Subsection 6.2.3.4 of this book.

[62] Klaus Peter Berger (1993) *International Economic Arbitration*, Kluwer Law and Taxation Publishers, The Hague, p. 315.

[63] *Javor v. Francoeur* 2003 BCSC 350, http://www.newyorkconvention1958.org/index.php?lvl=notice_display&id=957# (accessed 25 July 2016). In this case, the Supreme Court of British Columbia refused the enforcement of an arbitral award for payment of arbitration costs where the award was rendered against an individual who was not a signatory to the arbitration agreement.

Corporation case[64], and the most recent *Astro v. Lippo case*[65]. On the other hand, the US Court of Appeals for the Fourth Circuit in *International Paper Co.* v. *Schwabedissen Maschinen & Anlagen Gmbh* confirmed the enforcement of an award which involved a party that did not sign the arbitration agreement[66]. Reference should also be made to the *Pertamina* case where the US Court of Appeals for the Fifth Circuit confirmed a district court's decision concerning the enforcement of an arbitral award in a case where the arbitral tribunal decided to consolidate disputes arising under two closely related agreements[67].

For the above reasons, the risk of refusal of enforcement and / or setting aside of the award is a serious one, which should be carefully examined in each particular case and weighed against the advantages that multi-party arbitration can provide.

---

[64] *Sarhank Group v. Oracle Corporation* 404 F.3d 657 (2nd Cir. 2005), http://www.newyorkconvention1958.org/index.php?lvl=notice_display&id=746 (accessed 25 July 2016). The United States Court of Appeals for the Second Circuit refused the enforcement of an award against Oracle Corporation – the parent company of the signatory of the arbitration agreement. The court stated that 'an American non-signatory cannot be bound to arbitrate in the absence of a full showing of facts supporting an articulable theory based on American contract law or American agency law.'

[65] *PT First Media TBK v. Astro Nusantara International BV & Others* [2013] SGCA 57 in *1 Singapore Law Reports* (2014), pp. 372–452, https://leeshih.files.wordpress.com/2013/11/judgment-ca150151.pdf (accessed 1 August 2016). In this case, the Singapore Court of Appeal set aside an award rendered in Singapore on the ground that the arbitral tribunal allowed the joinder of third parties to a pending arbitration. The joined parties were part of the claimant's group of companies but were non-signatories to the arbitration agreement giving rise to the arbitration. This case is discussed in more detail in the context of the Arbitration Rules of the Singapore International Arbitration Centre (see Subsection 4.11.2 hereof).

[66] *International Paper Co.* v. *Schwabedissen Maschinen & Anlagen Gmbh* 206 F.3d 411 (4th Cir. 2000), http://caselaw.findlaw.com/us-4th-circuit/1451869.html (accessed 25 July 2016). The court confirmed that a party could be deprived of the right to assert that the lack of its signature precluded the enforcement of the arbitration clause against it in cases where such party had consistently argued that other provisions of the same contract should be enforced to its benefit.

[67] *Karaha Bodas Co. v. Perusahaan Pertambangan Minyak Dan Gas Bumi Negara*, et al, 364 F.3d 274 (5th Cir. 2004), Decision of 23 March 2004, reported in *23 ASA Bulletin* no. 2 (2005), pp. 360–378. The decision is also available at http://caselaw.findlaw.com/us-5th-circuit/1207034.html (accessed 25 July 2016). The disputes involved three parties KBC, Pertamina and PLN and two agreements (the first one between KBC and Pertamina and the second one among KBC, Pertamina and PLN). The contracts concerned the production of electricity from geothermal sources in Indonesia. They contained identical arbitration clauses referring to arbitration in Geneva subject to the UNCITRAL Arbitration Rules. The clauses were, however, silent on multi-party arbitration. Pertamina challenged the enforcement of the award on the ground that the tribunal had improperly consolidated the disputes under the separate agreements. The court decided that the contracts were so closely connected that the joint resolution of the disputes is justified. Moreover, one of the contracts was contractually stipulated to form an integral part of the other contract. Pertamina's attempts to resist the enforcement of the award in Hong Kong also failed as a result of similar reasoning adopted by the Hong Kong court (High Court of the Hong Kong Special Administrative Region, Court of First Instance, Decision of 27 March 2003, *Karaha Bodas Co. v. Perusahaan Pertambangan Minyak Dan Gas Bumi Negara*, in *21 ASA Bulletin* no. 3 (2003), pp. 667–684.)

2.4.5 Practical difficulties

The conduct of multi-party arbitration can often cause practical difficulties related to matters such as scheduling of meetings, conduct of hearings, collection of evidence to which all parties involved should have the right to react and appointment of experts and the participation of parties in considering their reports[68]. However, this disadvantage of multi-party arbitration should not be overestimated. It could only serve as an ancillary argument in a determination of whether multi-party arbitration should be allowed or not.

[68] See Fritz Nicklisch, 'Multi-party Arbitration and Dispute Resolution in Major Industrial Projects', in *11 Journal of International Arbitration*, no. 4 (1994), pp. 64–65, 68. See also Peter Binder (2013) *Analytical Commentary to the UNCITRAL Arbitration Rules*, Sweet & Maxwell, London, p. 121 (§ 10-004), and Julian Lew, Harris Bor, Gregory Fullelove and Joanne Greenaway (eds) (2013) *Arbitration in England with chapters on Scotland and Ireland*, Kluwer Law International, Alphen aan den Rijn, pp. 470–471 (para. 22.49).

Chapter 3
The Need for Multi-Party Arbitration in the Construction Sector

This chapter analyses the extent to which the different participants in construction projects are interested in multi-party arbitration. A complete apprehension of parties' positions on multi-party arbitration requires a prior understanding of the specifics of construction disputes (Section 3.1), the main types of international standard form construction agreements (Section 3.2) and the different contractual models used under these agreements (Section 3.3). Therefore, these three topics are dealt with before focusing on the parties' interests in multi-party arbitration (Section 3.4).

3.1 Specifics of construction disputes and construction arbitration

International construction disputes have their own specifics, which differentiate them from disputes in other commercial sectors and impinge on the way in which arbitral proceedings are conducted. These specifics are discussed below.

First, contracts concerning large-scale construction projects are usually long-term contracts. Construction works under these contracts can easily spread out over a period of time of several years. This requires dispute resolution mechanisms that provide for a fast resolution of disputes while construction works are still under way. In addition, construction disputes usually involve a high degree of technical complexity and demanding fact intensive investigations, which requires a timely and efficient system of claim management throughout the lifetime of the contract[1]. For these reasons, most international standard forms provide for a complex multi-tier system for resolution of disputes. A construction claim will often have to pass through several stages before it crystallizes into a dispute that can be brought before arbitration. These stages usually include a notice to an independent third party, such as an engineer, a fair determination by the third party, a review of the claim by a dispute adjudication board or a dispute review board, a notice of dissatisfaction against the decision of the board and, finally, an attempt to reach an amicable settlement. As mentioned in Subsection 2.1.3, the conduct of

[1] Jane Jenkins (2013) *International Construction Arbitration Law*, 2nd revised edn, Kluwer Law International, Alphen aan den Rijn, p. 1.

Multi-Party and Multi-Contract Arbitration in the Construction Industry, First Edition.
Dimitar Kondev.

multi-party proceedings based on multiple contracts requires, *inter alia*, the availability of two key elements – the parties' consent and the compatibility of the arbitration agreements in the different contracts. In terms of construction arbitration, however, the compatibility assessment should encompass not only the arbitration agreements but also the dispute resolution provisions as a whole, including in respect of the pre-arbitral phases of dispute resolution. As will be seen later on, the availability of different preconditions to arbitration under the different contracts or the non-fulfilment of some of these preconditions can be a serious obstruction to the conduct of multi-party arbitration[2]. This peculiarity of construction multi-party arbitration often gives rise to situations that are even more intricate than those observed in other commercial sectors.

Another inherent feature of construction projects is that they involve a multitude of parties with divergent interests. Therefore, the frequency of multi-party disputes in the construction industry is greater than in other commercial sectors. A large construction project will almost invariably involve multiple parties coming from different jurisdictions with different legal perceptions. These parties include an employer, a designer, a third-party certifier (often referred to as an engineer), a main contractor, subcontractors, a project manager, suppliers, lending banks, issuers of performance bonds, and so forth. The contractual relations deriving under a complex construction project are regulated under multiplicity of bilateral contracts. Thus, the employer will have direct contractual relations with a main contractor. The latter will then often subcontract parts of the work to several subcontractors under the terms of separate subcontracts. The subcontractors will have direct relations with sub-subcontractors and / or suppliers, etc. The designing phase of the construction project will be completed by an architect or an engineer on the basis of a separate contract, which, depending on the structure of the project, can be executed either with the employer or with the main contractor. Bipolar disputes arising under some of the abovementioned agreements will inevitably have repercussions on a number of parties different from the ones directly bound by the contract. As noted in Subsection 2.3.1, the typical example of such a bipolar controversy will be a claim for defects filed by an employer against a main contractor which concerns defects in the construction works performed by a subcontractor. If such a claim is resolved in a bipolar arbitration between the employer and the main contractor its outcome will have an impact on the relations between the main contractor and the subcontractor. If the main contractor is found non-liable, there will be no need for the latter to invoke the responsibility of the subcontractor. On the other hand, an unsuccessful outcome for the main contractor in the main contract arbitration would almost certainly result in a separate claim pursued by the latter against the subcontractor.

Another feature that differentiates construction disputes from disputes in other commercial sectors is the impact of sector-specific legislation, which addresses particular practices relevant to the construction industry, including in respect of dispute resolution[3]. An example of such a specific legislation can be found in England. Under the

---

[2] See ICC Case No. 5333 and ICC Case No. 5898 discussed in Subsection 6.2.2.

[3] Jane Jenkins (2013) *International Construction Arbitration Law*, 2nd revised edn, Kluwer Law International, Alphen aan den Rijn, p. 4.

provisions of the Housing Grants, Construction and Regeneration Act 1996 ('**HGCRA**')[4], dispute adjudication of construction claims under certain types of contracts and projects is mandatory[5]. Apparently, in these cases parties have to allow their disputes to be adjudicated whatever the contract may have said. Another example is the 2011 Arbitration Ordinance in Hong Kong (discussed in Section 5.6). It contains a specific consolidation provision applicable to construction projects where the work assigned under the main contract is subcontracted to subcontractors[6]. All these statutory provisions may influence the possibility for the conduct of multi-party arbitration in a significant way.

In addition, there is a proliferation of both domestic and international standard form construction agreements. Even bespoke construction contracts are often based on model clauses derived from these standard forms. The use of these contracts provides a fruitful ground for research for two main reasons. First, disputes arising under these contracts have either been litigated or arbitrated from time to time. Court decisions or arbitral awards on construction disputes can provide useful guidance on the dispute resolution provisions available in these contracts. Secondly, the solutions proposed in this book are capable of being applied to construction projects regulated under international standard forms because these solutions have taken into account the specific wording and structure of these forms.

All of the above features demonstrate that multi-party arbitration issues in international construction projects have their own standing, which deserves a separate analysis and a particular treatment.

3.2 *Introduction to international standard form construction agreements*

3.2.1 FIDIC Conditions of Contract

The FIDIC Conditions of Contract are probably the most popular and widely used international standard forms. The FIDIC suite of contracts is published by the International Federation of Consulting Engineers ('**FIDIC**')[7].

FIDIC published its first edition of a standard form in 1957. This was the Conditions of Contract (International) for Works of Civil Engineering Construction ('**Old Red Book**'). It was subsequently updated and amended over four editions. The fourth edition was published in 1987 and has been reprinted twice, in 1988 and in 1992, with editorial amendments. The editions of the Old Red Book up to the fourth edition are closely

---

[4] The Housing Grants, Construction and Regeneration Act 1996, http://www.legislation.gov.uk/ukpga/1996/53/contents (accessed 25 July 2016).

[5] Section 108 HGCRA.

[6] Section 101 of the Hong Kong Arbitration Ordinance (Cap. 609).

[7] The FIDIC acronym stands for the French version of the name – Fédération Internationale des Ingénieurs Conseils (www.fidic.org, accessed 25 July 2016). FIDIC currently has 94 member associations and associates coming from all over the world. It has its domicile in Geneva, Switzerland and it represents the consulting engineering industry globally.

based on a UK standard form construction agreement, and, more particularly, on the ICE Conditions of Contract[8]. In 1963, the Conditions of Contract for Electrical and Mechanical Works ('**Old Yellow Book**') was issued, and the third edition of this book was released in 1987. In 1994, FIDIC also published the first edition of the Conditions of Subcontract ('**Old FIDIC Subcontract**'), which was drafted primarily for use with the Old Red Book. In 1995, the Orange Book for design-build and turnkey contracts ('**Orange Book**') was also issued.

All of the above contracts concern the carrying out of works or the supply of plant and/or equipment. In addition to them, FIDIC published a series of client consulting agreements. The first one was the Client/Consultant Model Services Agreement ('**Old White Book**'), the second edition of which was published in 1991. The other consulting contracts include the Joint Venture (Consortium) Agreement[9] and the Sub-Consultancy Agreement[10].

In 1999, FIDIC issued an entirely new suite of contracts following a major overhaul of all the standard forms issued until then. The purpose and layout of the standard forms was changed in a material way. The most current standard forms, which are used nowadays for building and engineering works, comprise both the 1999 suite of contracts and some other standard forms released later on. The complete list of these contracts is as follows:

- Conditions of Contract for Construction for Building and Engineering Works Designed by the Employer, 1st edn, 1999 ('**FIDIC Red Book**'), which replaced the Old Red Book and is to be used for construction projects where the employer is responsible for the design stage of the project;
- Conditions of Contract for Construction for Building and Engineering Works Designed by the Employer, Multilateral Development Bank Harmonized Edition 2006 ('**FIDIC Pink Book**'), which is based on the FIDIC Red Book and is to be used as part of the standard bidding documents by the Multilateral Development Bank only;
- Conditions of Contract for Plant and Design-Build for Electrical and Mechanical Plant, and for Building and Engineering Works Designed by the Contractor, 1st edn, 1999 ('**FIDIC Yellow Book**'), which is based on the Old Yellow Book and the Orange Book and is intended to replace both. The Yellow Book is to be used for projects where the contractor takes responsibility for the design;
- Conditions for Contract for EPC/Turnkey Projects, 1st edn, 1999 ('**FIDIC Silver Book**') – an entirely new FIDIC contract, which foresees a higher degree of risk borne by the contractor, including for the design;

[8] See John Uff (2013) *Construction Law*, 11th edn, Sweet & Maxwell, London, Thomson Reuters, p. 403. See also Christopher Seppälä, 'The Development of Case Law in Construction Disputes Relating to FIDIC Contracts', in *26 International Construction Law Review*, part 1 (2009), p. 107.

[9] This is a contract to be entered into by consultants when forming a joint venture or a consortium for a certain project.

[10] This contract is to be used when a firm of consulting engineers hires another consulting firm to act as a subconsultant of the first firm.

- Short Form of Contract, 1st edn, 1999 ('**FIDIC Green Book**'), which is also a new FIDIC contract, used with regard to less complex construction projects with relatively small capital value;
- Conditions for Subcontract for Construction for Building and Engineering Works Designed by the Employer, 1st edn, 2011 ('**FIDIC Subcontract**'), which replaces the Old FIDIC Subcontract and is intended to be used in conjunction with the FIDIC Red Book;
- Conditions of Contract for Design, Build and Operate Projects, 1st edn 2008 ('**FIDIC Gold Book**'), which are suitable for *green field* projects only;
- Form of Contract for Dredging and Reclamation Works, 1st ed. 2006 ('**FIDIC Blue-Green Book**').

Some of the above agreements are currently under revision. The second editions of the FIDIC Red Book, the FIDIC Yellow Book and the FIDIC Silver Book are likely to be published in 2017. The FIDIC Subcontract will also be updated with a view to it being used in conjunction with the second edition of the FIDIC Red Book. FIDIC is also working on separate subcontracts to be used in conjunction with the second editions of the FIDIC Yellow Book and the FIDIC Silver Book.

In addition to the abovementioned agreements, FIDIC has issued two recent consultancy agreements. The first one is the Client/Consultant Model Services Agreement, 4th edn, 2006 ('**FIDIC White Book**'). It is a revised edition of the Old White Book. The FIDIC White Book is recommended for general use for the purposes of pre-investment and feasibility studies, designs and administration of construction and project management, both for employer-led design teams and for contractor-led design teams, where proposals for such services are invited on an international basis. The most recent consultancy book is the Model Representative Agreement, 1st edn, 2013 ('**Purple Book**'). This is intended for consultants who wish to enter into a contract with a representative for the provision of representative services. The Purple Book, together with the White Book and the earlier published Joint Venture (Consortium) Agreement and the Sub-Consultancy Agreement form the entire FIDIC collection of agreements for consulting services. This collection is also undergoing an extensive revision. New editions of the White Book, the Joint Venture (Consortium) Agreement and the Sub-Consultancy Agreement are expected to be released in 2017.

In addition, FIDIC is working on some new contracts that have not been released yet. These include a Contract for Tunnelling and Underground Works and a new design-build-operate contract, which will be known as the Bronze Book[11].

[11] Unlike the Gold Book, which is suitable for *green-field* projects only, the Bronze Book is going to be used for *brown-field* scenarios.

3.2.2 NEC contracts

The New Engineering Contracts ('**NEC**') are a suite of contracts published in London by the Institution of Civil Engineers. The first NEC contract was released in 1993. The second edition, known as NEC2, was launched in 1995, and the third edition NEC3 was released in June 2005. NEC3 was later amended in 2006 and subsequently in 2013. Wherever reference is made to NEC in this book, such reference shall be to the NEC3 family.

Specific features of NEC are that these contracts use simplified wording, avoiding legal jargon. They focus on strong project management principles by way of encouraging closer collaboration between contracting parties and avoiding disputes at an early stage through an early warning system[12]. Although NEC3 is primarily used in the United Kingdom, it has been stated that there are no real barriers for its use abroad[13]. Internationally, NEC has been used in more than 16 countries predominantly with common law background, such as South Africa, India, New Zealand, Hong Kong, Canada and Australia[14]. Occasionally, NEC3 has also been used in some civil law countries, such as the Netherlands, Norway, Denmark, Italy and Germany[15].

Currently, the NEC3 family of contracts comprises the following documents:

- Engineering and Construction Contract ('**ECC**')[16], which is used for the appointment of a contractor for engineering and construction works, including any level of design responsibility;
- Engineering and Construction Subcontract ('**ECS**') to be used in conjunction with the ECC;
- Professional Services Contract ('**PSC**') to be used for the appointment of a supplier to provide professional services;
- Term Service Contract to be used for the appointment of a supplier for a period of time to manage and provide services;
- Supply Contract to be used for local and international procurement of high-value goods and related services, including design;

---

[12] Nicholas Gould (2007) *NEC3: Construction Contract of the Future?* A paper presented to the Society of Construction Law international conference in Singapore, February 2007, Paper No. D84 (September), published by the UK Society of Construction Law (www.scl.org.uk, accessed 25 July 2016), pp. 1–2, 28.

[13] Humphrey Lloyd, 'Some Thoughts on NEC3', in *25 International Construction Law Review*, no. 4 (2008), pp. 468–469.

[14] See http://www.neccontract.com/international/index.asp (accessed 25 July 2016). See also Nicholas Gould (2007) *NEC3: Construction Contract of the Future?* A paper presented to the Society of Construction Law international conference in Singapore, February 2007, Paper No. D84 (September), published by the UK Society of Construction Law, pp. 1, 29.

[15] This information has been disclosed during a NEC3-accredited on-line course *International Application of NEC3 and Comparison to FIDIC* completed by the author in 2015.

[16] Under the ECC there are six different options reflecting the chosen contract strategy. These are: Option A (priced contract with activity schedule), Option B (priced contract with bill of quantities), Option C (target contract with activity schedule), Option D (target contract with bill of quantities), Option E (cost reimbursable contract), and Option F (management contract).

- Framework Contract to be used for the appointment of one or more suppliers to carry out construction work or to provide design or advisory services; and
- Adjudicator's Contract to be used for the appointment of an adjudicator to decide disputes under the NEC family of contracts.

For projects with less complexity, short versions of the contracts listed under the first five items are available. The NEC family is shown in Figure 1[17].

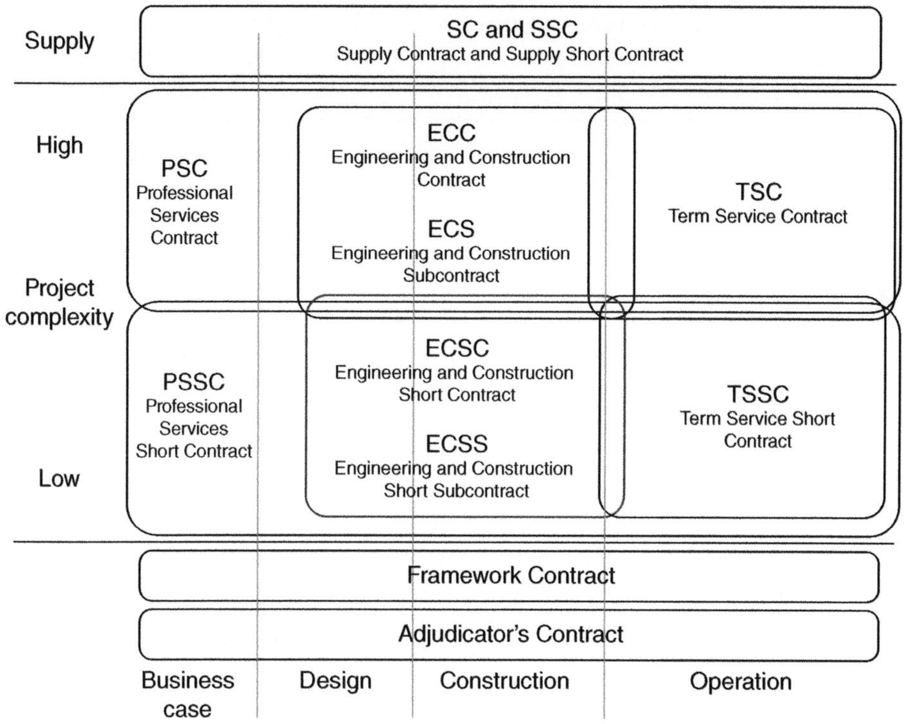

Figure 1 The NEC family.

3.2.3 ICC contracts

These contracts are published by the ICC in Paris and are the result of the work of the ICC Commission on Commercial Law and Practice[18]. Three standard forms have been published so far and these are briefly mentioned below.

The ICC Model Contract for the Turnkey Supply of an Industrial Plant ('**ICC Turnkey Supply Contract**')[19] was published in 2003. It regulates the relations between a supplier

---

[17] The diagram is available at http://www.neccontract.com/about/index.asp (accessed 25 July 2016). It is reproduced with permission granted by the copyright holders of NEC3.

[18] They should be distinguished from the ICC Infrastructure Conditions of Contract published by the Association of Consultancy and Engineering in the United Kingdom.

[19] ICC Model Contract for the Turnkey Supply of an Industrial Plant, ICC Publication No. 653, 2003 edn, ICC Publishing SA, Paris.

and a purchaser of equipment. The supplier's main obligation is to supply the equipment and assist the purchaser during erection and startup.

The ICC Model Turnkey Contract for Major Projects ('**ICC Turnkey Contract**')[20] was released in 2007 and is to be used with regard to international turnkey projects. The ICC Turnkey Contract aims at introducing equilibrium of the rights and obligations between the contracting parties and a balanced risk allocation[21]. The contract may be used both in civil law and common law countries. Design obligations under this contract principally lie with the contractor[22].

The third and most recent contract is the ICC Model Back-To-Back Subcontract to Turnkey Contracts for Major Projects ('**ICC Subcontract**')[23] issued in 2011. The contract contains the same features as the ICC Turnkey Contract but it regulates the relations between a main contractor and a subcontractor. As hinted by its full name, the ICC Subcontract contains back-to-back provisions to the ICC Turnkey Contract.

3.2.4 ENAA model forms

These standard form contracts are drafted by the Engineering Advancement Association of Japan ('**ENAA**') which is a non-profit organization established in Japan in 1978[24]. ENAA is supported by various national and local government agencies, research organizations and universities.

In 1986, the ENAA published the ENAA Model Form-International Contract for Process Plant Construction ('**ENAA Process Plant Model**'). The second edition of this contract was issued in 1992, and the third in March 2010. This is a turnkey lump-sum basis contract used for international projects related to the construction of process plants. With some modifications, it has also been used as part of the World Bank's standard bidding documents[25].

In 1996, the ENAA also published the Model Form-International Contract for Power Plant Construction, the second edition of which was issued in 2012. This is also a turnkey lump-sum basis contract used for the construction of power plants. Another contract belonging to the ENAA suite is the Model Form – International Contract for Engineering, Procurement and Supply for Plant Construction. Its first edition was published in 2007 and the current second edition is from 2013.

---

[20] ICC Model Turnkey Contract for Major Projects, ICC Publication No. 659, 2007 edn, ICC Publishing SA, Paris.

[21] Hefried Wöss, 'The ICC Model Turnkey Contract for Major Projects', in *3 Construction Law International*, no. 2 (2008), p. 11, http://www.woessetpartners.com/backoffice/manager/pdf/32.pdf (accessed 25 July 2016).

[22] Article 32.1 of the ICC Turnkey Contract.

[23] ICC Model Back-to-Back Subcontract to Turnkey Contracts for Major Projects, ICC Publication No. 706E, 2011 edn, ICC Publishing SA, Paris.

[24] For more details about ENAA and the standard forms published by it, see http://www.enaa.or.jp/EN/about/index.html (accessed 25 July 2016).

[25] See http://www.enaa.or.jp/EN/activities/model.html (accessed 25 July 2016).

3.2.5 IChemE contracts

The IChemE Contracts are a suite of contracts published by the British Institution of Chemical Engineers ('**IChemE**')[26]. There are two contract suites published by IChemE: forms for use in the United Kingdom and forms for international use. While there are several editions of the domestic contracts, the international suite is still in its first edition,which was published in 2007. This suite is closely modelled on the domestic standard forms but in order to make it suitable for international use the specific references to UK law have been removed. The international suite includes the following documents:

- International Form of Contract Lump Sum Contracts – The International Red Book;
- International Form of Contract Reimbursable Contracts – The International Green Book;
- International Form of Contract Target Cost Contracts – The International Burgundy Book;
- International Form of Contract Subcontracts – The International Yellow Book.

The titles of the contracts are illustrative of their intended purposes. So far the use of the international IChemE contracts remains limited to common law countries, such as Malaysia, Australia and Singapore.

In addition, two more contracts from the IChemE suite can be mentioned here. These are the Professional Services Contract – Short Form Agreement, which was issued in 2015, and the Professional Services Contract – Long Form Agreement, which is to be issued in 2017. It has been stated by the IChemE that both contracts are suitable for domestic and international use. These contracts can be used for any kind of consultancy services, such as design, feasibility and other studies, to be performed by a consultant hired by the employer.

3.2.6 PPC International and SPC International[27]

The Project Partnering Contract, also known as PPC2000, was published in 2000 by the UK Association of Consultant Architects ('**ACA**'). PPC2000 was amended in 2003, 2008 and most recently in 2013. It aims to foster a collaborative approach in construction projects and is described as the first standard form project partnering contract, which tries to bring all the major stakeholders in a construction project in a single document. Initially, the PPC was drafted for use in the United Kingdom. However, in 2007 an international version of the contract, known as PPC International, was published for use outside the United Kingdom. It has been stated that the PPC International has been used

[26] For more details about the IChemE and the standard forms published by it, see www.icheme.org (accessed 25 July 2016).

[27] Information about these contracts is available at http://www.ppc2000.co.uk/(accessed 25 July 2016).

successfully in West Africa and the Middle East and is under detailed consideration in countries, such as Australia, Singapore and Japan[28].

The Standard Form of Specialist Contract, SPC2000, allows the contractor to contract with specialist subcontractors on terms that are consistent with the PPC2000. The SPC2000 was amended in 2004 and 2008. The international version of this contract, SPC International, was published in 2004.

3.3 Contractual structures in construction projects

The structure of the particular construction project determines the type of claims that may arise under that project. The structure also has a direct impact on the parties' interests in the conduct of multi-party arbitration. Therefore, the main contractual models in the construction sector are discussed below.

3.3.1 'Build-only' projects

The *build-only* model represents the conventional type of construction contracting. Under this contractual scheme, the employer hires a design team, consisting of an engineer and / or an architect, which elaborates the design for the project. There is usually a tender for the construction works after the design or part of it is completed. The contractor who is awarded the tender should complete the works on the basis of the elaborated design and the employer's specifications. This is the model followed under the FIDIC Red Book and the FIDIC Pink Book, although a contractor working under these books may also carry out some part of the design[29]. The ECC can also be used as a *build-only* contract by choosing the appropriate option.

Under this model, the employer has direct contractual relations with both the design team and the main contractor. Typically, the employer does not have direct contractual links with other participants in the construction project, such as subcontractors and suppliers. However, certain schemes have evolved in the construction practice with the purpose of enabling the employer to hold subcontractors and suppliers liable for their contractual breaches. This is the purpose of the so-called collateral warranties, which usually represent separate contracts concluded between the employer and the subcontractor, respectively the supplier. They allow the employer not only to hold these parties liable for their breaches but also to 'step into the contractor's shoes' under these agreements in cases of their impending termination by the subcontractor, or respectively the supplier[30].

The '*build-only*' contractual scheme can be illustrated as in Figure 2.

---

[28] Katie Saunders and David Mosey, 'PPC2000: Association of Consultant Architects Standard Form of Project Partnering Contract', in *2 Lean Construction Journal*, no. 2 (2005), p. 65, also available at http://www.leanconstruction.org/media/docs/lcj/LCJ_05_004.pdf (accessed 25 July 2016).

[29] Sub-clause 1.8 [*Care and Supply of Documents*] of the FIDIC Red Book and the FIDIC Pink Book envisages that the specifications and drawings will be in the custody and care of the employer. The opportunity for contractor's design of parts of the works is addressed under sub-clause 4.1 [Contractor's General Obligations] of the FIDIC Red Book and the FIDIC Pink Book.

[30] Jane Jenkins (2013) *International Construction Arbitration Law*, 2nd revised edn, Kluwer Law International, Alphen aan den Rijn, p. 16.

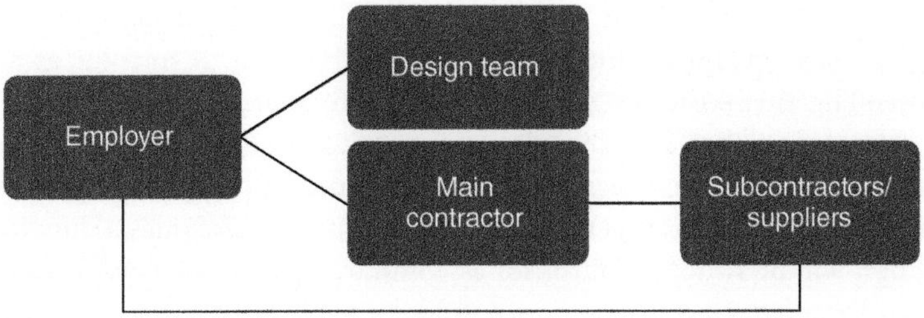

Figure 2 Build-only contractual scheme.

The advantage of this model from the employer's perspective is that the employer has a greater degree of supervision over the design prepared by the design team. However, a certain drawback is that the employer is usually responsible for the co-ordination between the design phase and the construction phase of the project. The contractor may not be held liable for flaws in the design. As a result, the employer is often faced with the problem of fragmented liability. In case of defects in the construction works, the employer has to ascertain whether these defects can be attributed to the design prepared by the design team or to the workmanship of the contractor. Such ascertainment is not a straightforward task, and it will frequently give rise to difficulties. The contractor will often argue that it was the design which caused the defects in order to excuse his poor workmanship. The design team will probably counterargue that the defects occurred during the contractor's completion of the construction works and / or because the design was not strictly followed by the contractor.

3.3.2 'Design-build' or 'turnkey' projects

Under *design-build* projects, sometimes also called *turnkey*[31] or EPC projects[32], the contractor takes responsibility for both the design and the completion of the construction works. *Design-build* contracting is increasingly the norm in international projects[33]. There is a single contractual relation between the employer and the contractor. The contractor concludes separate contracts with the design team and also with subcontractors and suppliers. The contractor is liable not only for the acts of his subcontractors but also for the work of the design team and for any defective products delivered by his suppliers.

The scope of the contractor's design liability will very much depend on the governing law and the content of the specific construction agreement. Within common law jurisdictions there are two types of design liability. The first concerns liability for the design at a professional duty of care level (or reasonable skill and care)[34]. In this case, the contractor is only responsible for the process leading to the result to be achieved but not

[31] The term *turnkey* means that the contractor is obliged to deliver to the employer a facility 'at the turn of a key' – i.e. a facility which is built and duly commissioned.

[32] '*EPC*' stands for '*engineer-procure-construct*' and indicates the range of services that should be undertaken by the contractor.

[33] William Godwin (2013) *International Construction Contracts. A Handbook*, Wiley Blackwell, Chichester, p. 33.

[34] Lukas Klee (2015) *International Construction Contract Law*, Wiley Blackwell, Chichester, pp. 47–48.

for the result itself[35]. The contractor's design liability can be invoked only if he has been negligent. The second liability is stricter than the first. It introduces a fitness-for-purpose obligation – the design has to be fit for the purposes specified in the contract. The contractor will be liable if the design is not fit for purpose, even if he has acted with reasonable skill and care. When it comes to *design-build* projects, the general rule under common law jurisdictions seems to be that a contractor assumes a duty to ensure that the design will be fit for its purposes as communicated to that contractor[36]. However, standard form agreements sometimes differ in their approach to design responsibility The FIDIC Conditions of Contract introduce a fitness-for-purpose obligation[37]. NEC3, however, contains a provision that the contractor's liability does not spread beyond the reasonable skill and care[38]. It is therefore recommendable that this matter should be explicitly addressed in *design-build* contracts.

Of the international standard forms discussed in Section 3.2 above, the FIDIC Yellow Book and the FIDIC Silver Book are *design-build* contracts. The ICC Turnkey Contract, the ENAA Process Plant Model and the IChemE International Red Book also follow the *design-build* model. The ECC can also be used for this type of contracting[39].

The employer normally does not have any contractual relations with the design team, the subcontractors and the suppliers. However, such relations may arise if these participants provide collateral warranties in favour of the employer. The *design-build* model is presented in Figure 3.

From the employer's perspective, the obvious advantage of this model is that it presupposes a single point of responsibility in the face of the contractor with regard to both design and construction works. In addition, the turnkey model of construction allows the project to progress on a 'fast-track' timetable with design, construction and procurement progressing in parallel[40]. Therefore, the successful completion of such projects will

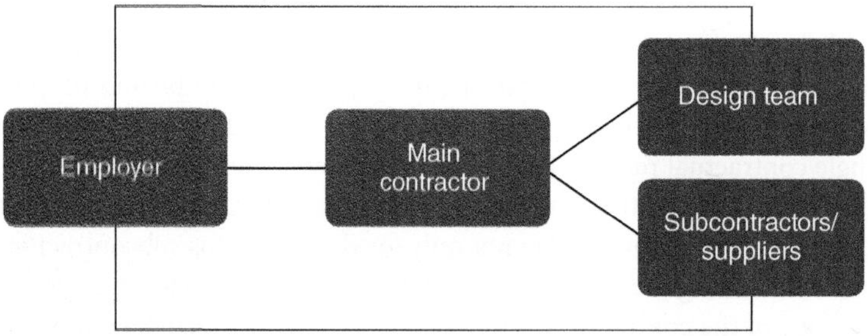

Figure 3 Design-build model.

[35] Ibid.

[36] Jeremy Glover and Simon Hughes (2006) *Understanding the FIDIC Red Book: A Clause-by-Clause Commentary*, 2nd edn, Sweet & Maxwell, London, pp. 72–73.

[37] See, for example, sub-clause 4.1 of the FIDIC Yellow Book and the FIDIC Silver Book.

[38] See Option X15 of the ECC.

[39] See Clause 21 of the ECC.

[40] Jane Jenkins (2013) *International Construction Arbitration Law*, 2nd revised edn, Kluwer Law International, Alphen aan den Rijn, p. 18.

require a high degree of management skills on behalf of the main contractor. He would have to manage in an efficient way not only the interface between the design and construction phases of the project but also the contractual interfaces among its sub-contractors and suppliers[41].

A disadvantage of the turnkey model for the employer is that the latter necessarily relinquishes his control over detailed design matters[42]. Under *design-build* projects, the employer sets out his design criteria in the employer's requirements or specifications, which form part of the contractual documentation. However, these requirements or specifications mostly concern the conceptual level of the design and do not deal with the detailed drawings of the project, which are to be procured by the contractor at a later date. The contractor has the freedom to elaborate the final design to the extent to which it is in compliance with the criteria set by the employer. Therefore, the employer's requests for design alterations during the performance of the contract can be considered as variations, which may trigger delays in completion and additional costs borne by the employer.

3.3.3 Construction management

In the construction management model, the employer concludes several bilateral contracts with different contractors and each contractor undertakes to complete a certain part of the works. The design is developed on the basis of a contract executed between the design team and the employer. The latter also appoints a project manager, also sometimes called a construction manager, who is not directly involved in the construction works and mainly has the task of coordinating the different activities concerning the project[43]. Under the FIDIC Conditions of Contract, the construction management model may occur in situations where the employer concludes separate FIDIC Red Book based contracts for different sections of the works with several contractors and also separate contracts based on the FIDIC White Book with the design team and the construction manager.

The construction management model can be illustrated as in Figure 4.

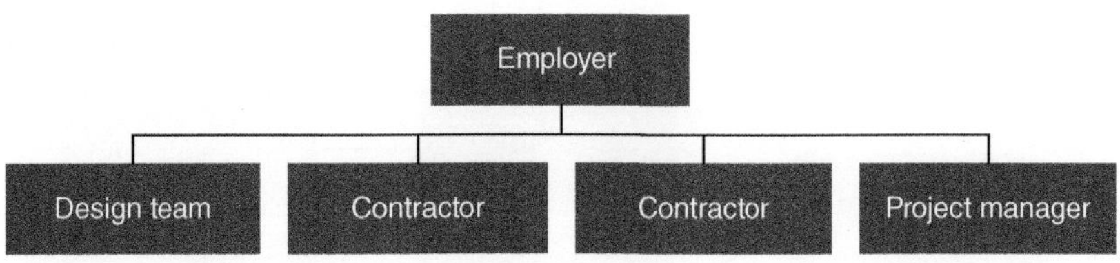

Figure 4 The construction management model.

[41] Jane Jenkins and James Stebbing (2006) *International Construction Arbitration Law*, Kluwer Law International, Alphen aan den Rijn, p. 23.
[42] John Uff (2013) *Construction Law*, 11th edn, Sweet & Maxwell, London, Thomson Reuters, p. 308.
[43] Jane Jenkins (2013) *International Construction Arbitration Law*, 2nd revised edn, Kluwer Law International, Alphen aan den Rijn, pp. 19–20.

The advantage of this model for the employer is that the latter has the possibility to exercise closer supervision over each stage of the project. Moreover, he is in direct contractual relations with all the parties, and therefore may pursue direct claims against each defaulting party. However, this advantage is a double-edged sword because the employer can be drawn as a respondent by multiple parties. The main drawback of the construction management model is that the employer is responsible for the interfaces between each separate bilateral contract, including between the design and construction phases of the project. As a result, the employer will face the same risk of fragmented liability as is borne by the employer under *build-only* contracts. However, this risk is even higher in the construction management model because it is spread over a greater number of participants and interfaces. A further disadvantage is the significant managerial burden on the employer who is responsible for the interfaces between all project activities[44].

3.3.4 Management contracting

Management contracting is a hybrid form of construction contracting, which has some of the features of both the construction management model and the traditional models of contract[45]. Under this scheme, the employer concludes a contract with the design team and another one with a management contractor. The management contractor assigns the construction works to subcontractors under the terms of separate agreements. The management contractor's role in the physical completion of the works is very limited. His role is mostly to co-ordinate the works of the subcontractors without necessarily being responsible for their acts and omissions. Direct contractual relations could be created between the employer and the subcontractors by means of collateral warranties. The model of management contracting can be illustrated as in Figure 5.

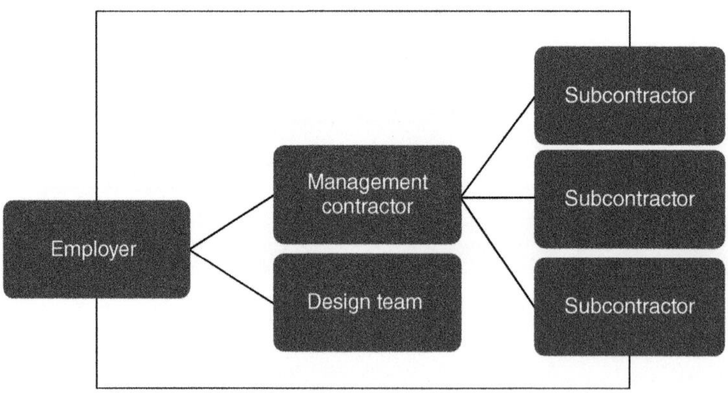

Figure 5 Management contracting model.

[44] Ibid.

[45] Ibid., pp. 20–21.

The main advantage for the employer is that it has a single contact point in the face of the management contractor. Furthermore, management contracting allows the appointment of the management contractor at a very early phase before the design is completed. The disadvantage is that the management contractor is usually not responsible for the defaults of the subcontractors to the employer, unless he has breached his coordination obligations under his agreement with the employer[46].

3.3.5 'Design-build-operate' ('DBO') model

This is also a hybrid model, which combines into one contract the *design-build* model with a long-term operation commitment. Therefore, the structure of this project looks similar to the *design-build* model. The contractor may undertake the operation by himself or may assign it to an operator. However, in the latter case the contractor will remain responsible to the employer during the operation period.

Design-build-operate contracting typically involves the private sector designing some piece of infrastructure, financing its construction and then operating and maintaining it during the operation period which could be as long as 20 or 30 years[47]. The rationale behind this period is that the employer, usually a state or a state agency, does not have the funds to finance the project and therefore grants to the contractor the right to operate it during the operation period at a profit and then hand it back to the employer. However, the contractor's obligation to finance the construction is not an indispensable element under DBO projects[48]. There may therefore be DBO projects where the responsibility for the financing rests with the employer.

The main advantage of DBO models for the employer is that there is a single contractor who is responsible for the design, build and operation phases of the project. During the operation period, the contractor will have to maintain the facility and remedy any and all defects. However, the employer will be deprived of the right to operate the facility during the term of the operation period because of the operation license granted in favour of the contractor.

The DBO model is represented in the FIDIC Gold Book. This book is suitable for *green field* projects only – projects to be constructed on undeveloped land – and not in respect of *brown field* projects – those dealing with refurbishment of existing facilities. The FIDIC Gold Book presupposes that the contractor who would assume design-build-operate obligations will be a joint venture or a consortium and the operation period is set to 20 years. The contractor does not have responsibility for the financing of the project. FIDIC is currently working on a new DBO contract, the Bronze Book, which will be suitable for *brown field* projects.

---

[46] Ibid., p. 21.

[47] William Godwin (2013) *International Construction Contracts. A Handbook*, Wiley Blackwell, Chichester, pp. 18–21.

[48] For that reason, DBO projects are sometimes further subdivided into two categories. The first one is the typical DBO project where the contractor does not have the obligation to finance the project, and the second one is the so-called 'design-build-finance-operate' or DBFO project where the contractor undertakes the responsibility for the financing.

3.3.6 Partnering and alliancing

Partnering and alliancing are alternative methods, which have largely grown out of dissatisfaction with traditional construction methods and the adversarial culture that they tend to promote[49]. Partnering and alliancing put a strong focus on the collaborative approach in construction. They aim to promote a non-adversarial approach in construction projects and early resolution of potential problems through co-operation between the parties. Partnering is a relatively broad concept, which can encompass various categories. The partnering arrangement, which may be either bilateral or multilateral, is often based on a non-binding document or arrangement but may also comprise a contract that is intended to have enforceable legal consequences[50]. Furthermore, the partnering arrangement may relate to a single project or to several projects[51]. Alliancing is generally understood to represent a more formal and binding arrangement with financial incentives based on profit and risk sharing[52]. In alliancing, there is often a single document which binds all the major participants in the project, such as the employer, the main contractor(s), the design team, any subcontractors and so forth. The purpose of this contractual commitment is that the allied participants work together as a single integrated team to generate mutual benefit, which is aligned with the actual project objectives[53].

The PPC International and SPC International follow the partnering and alliancing approach. NEC3 can also be used as a partnering and alliancing contract by choosing the relevant secondary option provided thereunder[54].

3.4 *Parties' interests in multi-party arbitration*

In the present section, the author tries to step into the shoes of each major participant in construction projects and explore its interest in participating in multi-party arbitration.

3.4.1 Employer

The employer is the party commissioning the construction works. In different standard forms, the employer may be referred to as the *owner*, *promoter*, *client* and so forth. The FIDIC Conditions of Contract use the term *employer*. The same term is also used in this book. The most common employer's claims against the main contractor are claims for delay damages for late completion, claims concerning defective works and claims for

[49] Jane Jenkins (2013) *International Construction Arbitration Law*, 2nd revised edn, Kluwer Law International, Alphen aan den Rijn, p. 20.

[50] John Uff (2013) *Construction Law*, 11th edn, Sweet & Maxwell, London, p. 365.

[51] Ibid.

[52] Ibid.

[53] Lukas Klee (2015) *International Construction Contract Law*, Wiley Blackwell, Chichester, pp. 61–62.

[54] See Option X12 (Partnering) of the ECC.

damages for performance failures. As regards claims for defective works, the employer may seek different forms of relief depending on the content of the contract and the law governing it. These forms typically include the reimbursement of the costs for the repair, if the remedial works have been undertaken by the employer or a third party appointed by the latter, a reduction of the contract price and / or specific performance in some jurisdictions.

3.4.1.1 Employer's position in 'design-build' and DBO contracting

It is often argued that the employer is not interested in multi-party arbitration as he will usually hold the main contractor responsible for any defects in the constructions works, regardless of whether such defects are caused by a faulty design provided by the engineer or the architect, the poor workmanship of the main contractor or his subcontractors or poor materials delivered by the main contractor's or the subcontractors' suppliers[55]. The employer's position will be similar when it comes to claims pursued by the main contractor against him. As John Marrin has pointed out:

> If [the employer] is to defend claims, he would prefer to defend claims from a single source, namely the main contractor. The employer may fear that a multiparty arbitration procedure will be open to abuse by a recalcitrant party, given that it increases the opportunity for procedural objections. Furthermore, should he need to advance claims, he may well hope to be able to hold the main contractor fully liable, leaving him to pursue claims against the other parties involved[56].

Therefore, the employer will prefer to arbitrate his dispute with the main contractor only and is not interested in the participation of other parties hired by the main contractor such as engineers, architects, subcontractors and / or suppliers, in the arbitral proceedings. Moreover, bringing these other parties into the arbitration will delay the dispute resolution process for the employer and increase the employer's costs. It is namely for this reason that the employer usually refrains from agreeing a multi-party arbitration clause in his contract with the main contractor. As a principal, the employer often imposes the content of this contract on the contractor, and a draft of it is usually included in the tender package preceding its execution.

---

[55] Humphrey Lloyd (1991) 'A National Experience', in P. Bellet, P. Bernardini, G. Bernini *et al.* (eds) *Multi-Party Arbitration: Views from International Arbitration Specialists*, Publication No. 480/1, ICC Publishing SA, Paris, pp. 69–72. See also Bernard Hanotiau (2005) *Complex Arbitrations: Multiparty, Multicontract, Multi-issue and Class Actions*, Kluwer Law International, The Hague, pp. 103–104 (§ 226), Christopher Stippl, 'International Multi-Party Arbitration: The Role of Party Autonomy', in *7 The American Review of International Arbitration*, no. 1 (1996), p. 53, and Piero Bernardini (1991) 'Examination of the Issues Involved in Drafting Arbitral Clauses', in P. Bellet, P. Bernardini, G. Bernini *et al.* (eds) *Multi-Party Arbitration: Views from International Arbitration Specialists*, Publication No. 480/1, ICC Publishing SA, Paris, pp. 100–101.

[56] John Marrin (2009) 'Multiparty Arbitration in the Construction Industry', in the Permanent Court of Arbitration (ed.) *Multiple Party Actions in International Arbitration*, Oxford University Press, New York, NY, pp. 398–399.

All of the abovementioned arguments are indeed true but, as will be seen below, they do not cover the whole range of contractual models in the construction industry. The employer's unwillingness to be involved in multi-party arbitration is understandable if the construction project is based on *design-build* or DBO contracting. In the employer's eyes, it does not matter whether the delay in completion or the poor workmanship, which resulted in defects and / or performance failures, is attributable to the main contractor, a subcontractor or the design team, as the main contractor is vicariously liable for the work undertaken by these parties. However, there are two important exceptions to this conventional position. The first is related to the provision of collateral warranties in construction projects, and the second to the figure of nominated subcontractors. Both exceptions are discussed below.

As mentioned in Subsection 3.3.1, collateral warranties are provided in favour of the employer by parties with which the employer usually does not have contractual links. The purpose of the warranties is to create a direct contractual relation between the employer and the respective architect, engineer, subcontractor or supplier, as the case may be, and to enable the employer to pursue direct claims against these parties, if needed. There may be instances in which the employer may wish to pursue a claim for reimbursement of costs for rectification of defects against both the main contractor and the subcontractor who actually caused the defects. This could be the case, for example, if the main contractor is facing financial difficulties impeaching his ability to pay the reimbursement sought. In such a case, the employer may well decide to increase his chances of recovery by way of filing a single request for arbitration against both the main contractor and the subcontractor.

Nominated subcontractors are often used in construction projects. The purpose of such a nomination by the employer is to ensure that certain specialist parts of the works are carried out by a specific subcontractor with relevant competence and experience and at the same time to retain employer's closer control over that part of the works. Even though the nomination of these subcontractors is made by the employer, they are typically hired by the main contractor. Nominated subcontractors are often imposed on the main contractor, which usually results in certain limitations in the liability of the main contractor for the nominated subcontractors' works[57]. For example, under the FIDIC Red Book the contractor is not obliged to employ a nominated subcontractor against whom he has raised reasonable objections, unless the employer agrees to indemnify the contractor against the consequences of such an employment[58]. As a result, the employer may not be able to hold the main contractor fully liable for the defaults of the nominated subcontractor[59]. This problem occurred in several reported cases in the United Kingdom,

---

[57] Humphrey Lloyd (1991) 'A National Experience', in P. Bellet, P. Bernardini, G. Bernini *et al.* (eds) *Multi-Party Arbitration: Views from International Arbitration Specialists*, Publication No. 480/1, ICC Publishing SA, Paris, p. 64. See also John Adriaanse (2010) *Construction Contract Law. The Essentials*, 3rd edn, Palgrave Macmillan, Basingstoke, pp. 252–256.

[58] See clause 5 [*Nominated Subcontractors*] of the FIDIC Red Book.

[59] Humphrey Lloyd (1991) 'A National Experience', in P. Bellet, P. Bernardini, G. Bernini *et al.* (eds) *Multi-Party Arbitration: Views from International Arbitration Specialists*, Publication No. 480/1, ICC Publishing SA, Paris, p. 64.

such as *Gloucestershire County Council v. Richardson*[60] and *Metropolitan Hospital Board v. Bickerton*[61]. This unsatisfactory solution has often forced employers to enter into direct contractual relations with nominated subcontractors in order to ensure recovery in case of the subcontractor's contractual breaches. In such a scenario, the employer might be willing to resolve his dispute in a multi-party context. This can be best illustrated with an example. There are defects in the construction works, and the employer decides to file a request for arbitration against the main contractor. However, in the course of the proceedings the main contractor states that he is not responsible for the defects that, in the main contractor's words, have been caused by a nominated subcontractor against whose appointment the main contractor had reasonable objections. The main contractor further presents documents substantiating his argument. Then, faced with the risk that the main contractor will not be held liable for the nominated subcontractor's work, the employer decides to join the nominated subcontractor in the proceedings in order to make sure that he will get the relief sought. The position will be similar in respect of suppliers nominated by the employer.

Collateral warranties and nominated subcontractors are not only met in *design-build* and DBO contracting but also in the other contractual models discussed in Section 3.3. Therefore, the above observations will be valid to those models as well.

3.4.1.2 Employer's position in 'build only' contracting

In the conventional *build only* construction project, the position of the employer is similar to the one under *design-build* contracting as far as the employer's claims pertain to defects in the construction works caused by subcontractors or suppliers. The employer is not interested in multi-party arbitration, except in cases of claims concerning collateral warranties or nominated subcontractors or suppliers.

However, the situation will be completely different if the defects are due, entirely or partially, to a faulty design provided by the architect or the engineer appointed by the employer under the terms of a consultancy or professional services agreement. As mentioned in Subsection 3.3.1, it will often be difficult for the employer to determine whether the design has caused or at least contributed to these defects. In these cases, for example, the issue of whether the plans and drawings in the agreement with the designer were followed by the main contractor will be directly relevant for both the agreement with the designer and the main contract[62]. The employer might therefore want to pursue his

---

[60] *Gloucestershire County Council v. Richardson* [1969] 1. A.C. 480. The main contractor discovered that the pre-cast concrete columns provided by a nominated supplier suffered from defects. The construction agreement did not allow the contractor to object to the employment of the nominated supplier. The court decided that the main contractor was not responsible for the quality and the fitness of the components put into the columns.

[61] *North West Metropolitan Hospital Board v. T A Bickerton & Son Ltd.* [1970] 1 W.L.R. 607. The case dealt with the consequences of a nominated subcontractor's repudiation and the question which party (i.e. the employer or the main contractor) should bear the costs for completion of the subcontractor's works. It was decided that the employer should bear these costs.

[62] Stavros Brekoulakis (2010) *Third Parties in International Commercial Arbitration*, Oxford University Press, Oxford, pp. 84–85 (§ 2.278).

claims against both the designer and the main contractor if he is not sure whom to blame for the deviations in the construction works[63]. For the same considerations, the employer may want to join the engineer or the architect in an arbitration initiated by the main contractor if the latter claims extension of time and additional costs for late delivery of the design for the project. In all these cases, the conduct of multi-party arbitration involving all three parties will save time and costs for the employer and eliminate the risk of inconsistent findings.

The above statements concerning the employer's position will also be valid with regard to other types of construction models where the designer is appointed by the employer. This will normally be the case in management contracting and construction management projects and sometimes also in partnering and alliancing projects.

3.4.1.3 *Employer's position in construction management projects*

Multi-party arbitration will often be beneficial to the employer in construction management projects. These projects presuppose the existence of numerous bilateral contracts concluded between the employer on one side and the contractors and the design team on the other side. If, for instance, several contractors have contributed to the late completion of the project, the employer will prefer to pursue his claims for delay damages against all the delinquent parties in a single arbitration. From the employer's perspective, this will avoid duplication of time and costs, as well as the risk of awards that are inconsistent as to who caused the delay and to what extent.

The employer will also be interested in multi-party arbitration if the arbitration is initiated by one of the contractors and the claim is linked to the default of some of the other contractors or the designer. For instance, one of the contractors may claim extension of time and/or additional payment because of the employer's failure to ensure timely access to the site. If the late access is attributable to another contractor appointed by the employer who, for example, was still working on the site on the contemplated access date, the employer may want to join the defaulting contractor in the pending arbitration.

3.4.1.4 *Employer's position in management contracting*

In management contracting, the employer has a stronger incentive to ask for collateral warranties from subcontractors because the management contractor mainly exercises management functions and is only responsible for the faults of the subcontractors to the

---

[63] A similar example was mentioned by John Marrin. See John Marrin (2009) 'Multiparty Arbitration in the Construction Industry', in the Permanent Court of Arbitration (ed.) *Multiple Party Actions in International Arbitration*, Oxford University Press, New York, NY, pp. 397–398. A highway authority has procured the construction of a new road bridge whose structure was designed by a consulting engineer and built by an engineering contractor. Both the engineer and the contractor were appointed by the authority under two separate contracts. The bridge failed but the cause remained uncertain. The contractor blamed the engineer's design whereas the engineer blamed the contractor's materials. The highway authority took the position that the damage must be the responsibility of one or other or both of the engineer and the contractor. In this case, John Marrin has concluded: 'there is, from the highway authority's point of view, an overwhelming case for being in position to pursue both the engineer and the contractor in the same arbitration.'

extent these faults are caused by his mismanagement. These collateral warranties would allow direct employer's redress against the defaulting subcontractor.

A management contracting project can be delayed for different reasons such as poor management on behalf of the management contractor, protracted work by a subcontractor or both. In cases of uncertainty about the exact cause of delay, the employer might want to pursue his claims for delay damages in single arbitration against both the management contractor and the respective subcontractor, provided that the latter has given a collateral warranty. Such an arbitration will probably be faster and cheaper than two separate arbitrations. It will also obviate the risk of inconsistencies stemming from the running of separate arbitrations against these two parties.

In other cases, however, the employer will have no interest in multi-party arbitration. For instance, a subcontractor files a claim for extension of time and additional payment against the management contractor claiming that he has been disrupted in his work by another subcontractor. The management contractor in this case may try to join the employer in the proceedings, if the employer has somehow contributed to this disruption, in order to pass on to him any liability towards the subcontractor. Apparently, the employer will try to avoid this scenario.

3.4.2 Contractor

The most common contractor's claims against the employer are claims for extension of time and / or additional payment. As regards subcontractors, the contractor will typically have claims that are identical to the employer's claims against the main contractor, such as claims for delay damages or claims concerning defective work.

It is mainly the contractor who is interested in the conduct of multi-party arbitration. As mentioned in Subsection 2.3.1, a single arbitration involving multiple parties will be beneficial for the party having a recourse claim against a third party. In the construction industry, the main contractor will have a recourse claim against a subcontractor in cases where the employer claims against the main contractor for defective work carried out by that same subcontractor. Arbitration involving all three parties will ensure that there will be no inconsistent findings that would trap the contractor in the middle without being able to obtain recovery from the party that indeed caused the defects, namely the subcontractor. Furthermore, from the contractor's perspective, single arbitration would usually be faster and less costly than two separate arbitrations.

The contractor will have the same standing in turnkey and DBO contracting if a designer's default has affected the main contractor's ability to perform the main contract. Poor design prepared by the architect or the engineer may result in defects in the construction works completed by the main contractor or his subcontractors. In addition, late delivery of the design to the main contractor may have a negative impact on the latter's work programme and delay the time for completion. If the employer starts arbitration against the main contractor concerning these defects or the delay in completion, the main contractor will try to bring the engineer or the architect in the same arbitration in order to bind him with the arbitral award and avoid the 'man-in-the-middle' problem resulting from inconsistent awards.

The contractor may also be interested in multi-party arbitration in case of claims pursued by parties hired by the contractor further down the contractual chain, for example subcontractors and suppliers. This is visible in cases where these parties claim against the main contractor for a main contract breach for which the employer is ultimately responsible. For example, the employer has given late access to the site to the main contractor, which has also triggered a main contractor's default in giving timely access to the site to the respective subcontractor. The main contractor would prefer to resolve the resulting disputes under both the main contract and the subcontract in a single arbitration in order to avoid the risk of irreconcilable findings stemming from the conduct of separate arbitrations (e.g. a subcontract arbitration granting additional payment and extension of time to the subcontractor and a main contract arbitration rejecting the main contractor's claim against the employer or granting only extension of time without additional payment to the main contractor).

However, the position of the main contractor is not always so straightforward. There are cases in which he may want to avoid the prospect of multi-party arbitration. As His Honour Humphrey Lloyd has pointed out:

> There will be instances in which the contractor will not wish to have such a single tribunal, for example where a sub-contractor's claim paints him in a bad light and might prejudice his position vis-à-vis the employer as where the employer claims that the work was done badly and the fault lies in the contractor not having given the proper instructions to the sub-contractor who actually carried out the work[64].

In addition, multi-party arbitration might sometimes result in disclosing certain information contained in one bilateral agreement to the party that is a non-signatory to that agreement. For example, as mentioned in Subsection 2.4.3, the disclosure of the main contract price to the subcontractor may be a sensitive issue, especially for the main contractor. Furthermore, sometimes the contractor has the benefit of a contractual limit of liability, which may be put at risk if third parties advance contribution claims against him in multi-party proceedings[65].

3.4.3 Subcontractor

The subcontractor's claims against the main contractor are often identical with the main contractor's claims against the employer – claims for extension of time and/or additional payment. Apparently the subcontractor's claims will have a different nature if directed against sub-subcontractors and suppliers further down the chain. Thereunder, the subcontractor may have claims concerning defective works completed by a sub-subcontractor

---

[64] Humphrey Lloyd (1991) 'A National Experience', in P. Bellet, P. Bernardini, G. Bernini *et al.* (eds) *Multi-Party Arbitration: Views from International Arbitration Specialists*, Publication No. 480/1, ICC Publishing SA, Paris, pp. 64–65.

[65] John Marrin (2009) 'Multiparty Arbitration in the Construction Industry', in the Permanent Court of Arbitration (ed.) *Multiple Party Actions in International Arbitration*, Oxford University Press, New York, NY, p. 399.

or defective products delivered by a supplier, or claims for delay damages against a sub-subcontractor. A peculiarity of the subcontractor's position is that he may be allowed to make direct claims against the employer in some jurisdictions, especially if these claims concern payment for the subcontractor's works, even though these two parties are usually not bound by a separate contract. For example, this is the case in Belgium[66] and France[67].

The subcontractor may well have an interest in multi-party arbitration if he has concluded a subcontract with the main contractor containing the so-called *pay when paid* clauses. These clauses envisage that the subcontractor will be paid for his work when the main contractor receives payment for the same work by the employer. Thus, they pass the risk of non-payment to the subcontractor[68]. In such a situation, the subcontractor's willingness to participate in an arbitration between the employer and the main contractor concerning payment of the subcontractor's work is understandable. At first sight, it may seem that such a multi-party arbitration will probably be longer and more expensive for the subcontractor than a single arbitration against the main contractor only. However, such a multi-party arbitration will have the potential of ensuring a faster recovery for the subcontractor. If the main contractor's claim for payment against the employer is successful, the main contractor will be obliged to transfer the respective amount to the subcontractor under the terms of the same arbitral award. Thus, there will be no need for the subcontractor to start separate arbitration if the main contractor refuses to pay the subcontractor.

The subcontractor may also prefer multi-party arbitration in case of main contractor's claims concerning defects resulting from the poor workmanship of a sub-subcontractor or defective materials supplied by a supplier chosen by the subcontractor. In these cases, the position of the subcontractor will be identical to that of the main contractor who is a respondent under an employer's claim concerning subcontractor's defective works.

3.4.4 Designer

The designer (or also sometimes called a design professional) is an architect or an engineer who prepares the design for the project. In practice, the role of the designer is often carried out by a firm offering design services, which includes in its staff qualified engineers and / or architects. The designer will be bound by a contract concluded either with the employer (in *build-only*, construction management or management contracting projects) or with the contractor (in turnkey and DBO projects). In partnering and alliancing,

---

[66] See Bernard Hanotiau (2005) *Complex Arbitrations: Multiparty, Multicontract, Multi-issue and Class Actions*, Kluwer Law International, The Hague, pp. 213–214 (§ 468–471).

[67] See Law on Subcontracting (n 75-1334) of 31 December 1975, as amended. An English translation of the law is available at www.legifrance.gouv.fr/content/download/1952/13689/version/4/file/Code_23.pdf&prev=search (accessed 25 July 2016).

[68] In England, 'pay when paid' clauses have been outlawed with the adoption of the HGCRA in 1996. Section 113 HGCRA declares that these clauses are ineffective, except in the case of insolvency of the payer. For more information about 'pay when paid' clauses, see John Adriaanse (2010) *Construction Contract Law. The Essentials*, 3rd edn, Palgrave Macmillan, Basingstoke, pp. 250–252.

the designer is often hired by the employer but there may also be situations where the appointment is made by the contractor. The contractual relation with the designer may be based on different standard forms, such as the FIDIC White Book, the NEC3 PSC or the IChemE Professional Services Contract but bespoke contracts are also commonly in use.

The rare situations where a designer may have an interest in multi-party arbitration comprise cases where the designer may have a recourse claim against a sub-designer or another consultant hired by the designer or in cases where these sub-designers or consultants have claims against the designer due to defaults attributable to the party that hired the designer. Apart from these cases, the designer will normally prefer to resolve his disputes with the client who appointed him in a bipolar arbitration. The participation of third parties in such arbitration will inflate the costs and increase the time involved in the resolution of these disputes. Moreover, the risk of inconsistent findings in parallel arbitrations will often work in favour of the designer. To take an example, the employer under a turnkey plant project initiates arbitration against the main contractor claiming a substantial amount of compensation due to a plant's failure to reach the required output. Having reviewed all the documentation and listened to the parties' pleas, the tribunal ascertains that the failure is due to a design that was unfit for its intended purpose. As a result, the main contractor is held liable because he is vicariously liable for the defaults of the designer in turnkey contracting. Then, the main contractor files a request for arbitration against the designer in an attempt to recover the compensation paid to the employer. A contradictory award in this second arbitration acknowledging that the design was fit for its purpose and denying the request will be to the benefit of the designer. For this reason, design professionals may sometimes have a strategic advantage to avoid multi-party arbitration until the arbitration involving the related dispute to which the designer is not a formal party is over[69]. If that arbitration results in a favourable ruling (e.g. that the design was flawless), the designer may try to use this ruling in his own favour later on. In case of an unfavourable ruling, the designer may argue that this ruling is not binding in the second arbitration involving the designer. Furthermore, the designer will have more time to prepare for the second arbitration and submit evidence that may eventually refute the findings that the design was incorrect.

3.4.5 Engineer

The word *engineer* has a twofold meaning in construction projects. First, the engineer can be the person who elaborates the design for the project. In this case, the engineer is actually the designer whose position was described in the previous subsection. However, the engineer may also mean a contract administrator – a third party authorized to perform certain contract administration functions under the construction agreement. It is exactly this second meaning that is used in the present subsection. However, the

[69] Mark Bloomquist (2004) 'Chapter 26, Consolidation and Joinder' in Daniel Brennan, Richard Lowe, Jennifer Nielsen and John Spangler (eds) *The Construction Contracts Book, How to Find Common Ground in Negotiating Design and Construction Contract Clauses*, American Bar Association, Forum of the Construction Industry, Chicago, IL, pp. 268, 270.

reader should bear in mind that often it is one and the same person who acts both as a designer and as a contract administrator.

The FIDIC Red Book and the FIDIC Yellow Book use the term *engineer* to designate such a contract administrator. Under these books, the engineer has manifold tasks, including, *inter alia*, certification of payments, certification of the works and determinations in respect of claims[70]. Under other construction agreements, the person performing the contract administration is known under different names such as an *architect*, a *project manager* and an *employer's representative*[71]. The engineer is not a party to the construction agreement and he is appointed by the employer. Under the FIDIC Conditions of Contract, this appointment can be made under the terms of the FIDIC White Book. Other standard forms, such as the NEC3 PSC or the IChemE Professional Services Contract can also be used for the same purpose.

When acting under the terms of the construction agreement, the engineer fulfils a dual role. On one hand, he is acting as an employer's agent who has to protect the interests of the employer[72]. In that respect, the role of the engineer is to secure the completion of the construction works in an economical and efficient manner[73]. On the other hand, the engineer must act impartially and fairly as between the parties when he is certifying payments to the contractor, determining claims under the contract or otherwise giving his professional opinion[74]. This dual role of the engineer has been criticized in the legal literature[75]. However, it will be outside the scope of this book to embark further on this topic.

In principle, the engineer has no interest in multi-party arbitration. His contractual obligations do not derive from the construction agreement, to which he is not privy, but from the separate consultancy agreement executed with the employer[76]. Therefore, he

---

[70] The role of the engineer (referred to as the 'Engineer') under these books is described in Clause 3 [The Engineer] but there are many other provisions throughout the FIDIC Red Book and the FIDIC Yellow Book that refer to the Engineer and his rights and duties.

[71] For example, the IChemE International Red Book uses the term 'Project Manager'. Under the FIDIC Gold Book, a reference is made to the '*Employer's Representative*' who has similar functions to those of the Engineer under the FIDIC Red Book and the FIDIC Yellow Book. Even though the FIDIC Silver Book also uses the term 'Employer's Representative', the contract administration under this contract is actually carried out by the employer himself.

[72] Sub-clause 3.1 [Engineer's Duties and Authority] of the FIDIC Red Book and the FIDIC Yellow Book.

[73] John Adriaanse (2010) *Construction Contract Law. The Essentials*, 3rd edn, Palgrave Macmillan, Basingstoke, pp. 102–103.

[74] Sub-clause 3.5 [Determinations] of the FIDIC Red Book and same sub-clause of the FIDIC Yellow Book envisage that whenever the engineer should determine any matter he shall consult with each party in an endeavour to reach an agreement. If such an agreement is not achieved, the Engineer 'shall make a fair determination in accordance with the Contract, taking due regard of all relevant circumstances'.

[75] About the role of the engineer, see Axel-Volkmar Jaeger and Götz-Sebastian Hök (2009) *FIDIC: A Guide for Practitioners*, Springer, New York, NY, pp. 221–230. See also John Adriaanse (2010) *Construction Contract Law. The Essentials*, 3rd edn, Palgrave Macmillan, Basingstoke, pp. 99–116.

[76] Under sub-clause 3.3.1 of the FIDIC White Book, the consultant (i.e. the engineer in the case at hand) shall have no other responsibility than to exercise reasonable skill, care and diligence in the performance of his contractual obligations. This position will be modified in the new edition of the FIDIC White Book expected to be published in 2017. Under the new edition, the services performed should satisfy the function and purpose specified in the contract. However, this increased 'fitness for purpose' liability will only apply 'to the extent achievable' using the general standard of reasonable care.

prefers to resolve his disputes only with the employer. The participation of third parties in the proceedings will protract the dispute resolution process and burden him with additional costs.

3.4.6 Suppliers

The materials put into the construction works are generally delivered by a multitude of suppliers. The contract price under the different supply contracts is in most cases trifling in comparison with the agreed price under the main contract. Therefore, suppliers have little interest in multi-party arbitration. The supplier would prefer to resolve his disputes only with the party to which he delivered the materials than engage in lengthy and costly multi-party arbitration where his relatively simple claims will be reviewed together with more complex claims accompanied by voluminous documentation.

3.4.7 Technical consultants

Technical consultants involved in construction projects may act in different capacities and perform different functions. They can be, for example, quantity surveyors, consultants preparing feasibility studies, geologists and so forth. Depending on the structure of the construction project, the technical consultants can be appointed either by the employer or the main contractor. Like suppliers, technical consultants have no interest in multi-party arbitration for the reasons discussed in the previous subsection.

In this way, their position will sometimes be at odds with the interest of the party that hired them. For example, the employer under a FIDIC Red Book might want to join the geologist appointed by him who prepared the report on the soil conditions in an arbitration commenced by a main contractor's claim for extension of time and additional compensation due to unforeseen ground conditions that were not indicated in the report.

3.4.8 Guarantors

There are two types of guarantors in construction projects. First, a guarantor may be a bank which has issued a bank guarantee in favour of one of the parties under the main contract. The issuance of these guarantees is a widely spread practice in large construction projects[77]. In the predominant number of cases, these guarantees are first-demand

[77] For example, the FIDIC Red Book envisages the issuance of two types of bank guarantees by the contractor. Under sub-clause 4.2 [Performance Security], the contractor should provide to the employer a performance security. The employer is allowed to claim for payment under the performance security in cases of contractor's defaults specified in that sub-clause. Furthermore, under sub-clause 14.2 [Advance Payment], the contractor is obliged to provide an advance payment bank guarantee which secures the repayment of the advance payment paid by the employer to the contractor. In addition, some of the FIDIC books contain a sample of a bank guarantee that may be provided to the contractor as a security for the payment obligations of the employer under the contract.

bank guarantees provided to the employer to secure the performance of all or some of the main contractor's obligations under the construction agreement. The guarantees represent unilateral statements in favour of their intended beneficiaries but there is always an underlying agreement between the bank and the party whose obligations are secured which regulates the terms for the issuance of the guarantee and the obligations of the parties in that respect. First demand guarantees are usually autonomous from the construction agreement.

The party under a surety agreement is also called a guarantor. This is a warranty agreement whereby one person, the guarantor, promises to pay a debt or perform a duty of another, debtor, in the event of default by the latter. In the construction industry, this agreement is often used in cases where the employer is a newly established subsidiary of a large company. The subsidiary will often not possess sufficient funds and therefore payments under the project will be made by the mother company. It is a common practice in these cases for the contractor to request the execution of a warranty agreement with the mother company under which the latter guarantees the employer's payment obligations under the contract. The liability of the guarantor could be either joint and several, meaning that the contractor may request payment directly from the mother company, or subsidiary, where the obligation of the guarantor arises only if and when the employer fails to pay.

Theoretically, the guarantor has a clear interest in multi-party arbitration. If he pays to the beneficiary under the bank guarantee or the surety agreement, as the case may be, the guarantor will have a recourse claim against the defaulting party. The obvious advantage of the guarantor of having multi-party arbitration involving both the debtor and the beneficiary will be the obviation of the risk of inconsistent findings in the different arbitrations, which could thwart the guarantor's recovery from the debtor. However, this advantage should not be overestimated and its weight will depend on the specific circumstances of the case and the content of the respective agreement between the guarantor and the debtor. Sometimes the guarantor's recourse claim against the debtor will be based solely on the agreement with the debtor and will be quite straightforward and easy to deal with. The arbitrators reviewing this claim may not even need to look at the construction agreement and determine the debtor's default thereunder. In order for the guarantor's claim to be successful it will often be sufficient for the guarantor to demonstrate that he has paid to the respective beneficiary. From that perspective, the guarantor may well prefer not to engage in a complex multi-party arbitration that will require, *inter alia*, a full substantiation of the debtor's default under the construction agreement. For these reasons, multi-party arbitrations with the participation of banks or other guarantors are highly unlikely.

The question of multi-party arbitration involving guarantors may also arise in the context of incorporation of arbitration clauses by reference. For example, there is an arbitration clause in a main contract and the issued bank guarantee, which does not contain an arbitration clause, refers to that contract. The question is whether the reference to the main contract can be construed broadly in a way incorporating the arbitration clause contained therein. It will be outside the scope of this book to deal with incorporation of arbitration clauses by reference and therefore this question will not be dealt with here[78]. It will suffice to mention that it is very unlikely that courts or arbitral tribunals will decide that a main contract arbitration clause has been incorporated by reference in a bank guarantee or a warranty agreement without an explicit wording in the guarantee or the warranty agreement to that effect[79].

3.4.9 Concluding remarks

It can be summarized that there is often a need for multi-party arbitration in the construction industry. However, it does not arise in respect of all the participants in construction projects. The need for multi-party arbitration will very much depend on the structure of the contractual relations with regard to the completion of the project and the interests of the different stakeholders[80].

It will often be the main contractor who is interested in multi-party arbitration, as it would enable him to pursue his recourse claims against his contracting parties (e.g. subcontractors and suppliers) within the same arbitration. The main contractor can also be interested in such a complex arbitration in case of claims pursued by subcontractors or suppliers hired by him, which are based on defaults for which the employer is ultimately responsible under the terms of the main contract.

In *build-only* contracting, the employer will be interested in multi-party arbitration to arbitrate his claims concerning defective works against the designer and the main contractor who may have both contributed to the occurrence of the defects. His position will be similar in construction management and management construction models, as well as in partnering and alliancing in cases where the designer is appointed by the employer. The employer will usually try to avoid multi-party arbitration in *design-build* and DBO projects. Under these projects, he has a single point of responsibility in the face of the

[78] On that point see Bernard Hanotiau (2005) *Complex Arbitrations: Multiparty, Multicontract, Multi-issue and Class Actions*, Kluwer Law International, The Hague, pp. 31–32 (§ 65), 81 (§ 165), 129–132 (§ 274–279), where the author has cited several court decisions and arbitral awards dealing with these issues. See also Bernard Hanotiau, 'Arbitration and Bank Guarantees. An Illustration of the Issue of Consent to Arbitration in Multicontract-Multiparty Disputes', in *16 Journal of International Arbitration*, no. 2 (1999), pp. 15–23. For a more recent analysis of some court cases by the same author, see Bernard Hanotiau, 'Non-signatories, Group of Companies and Group of Contracts in Selected Asian Countries: A Case Law Analysis', in *32 Journal of International Arbitration*, no. 6 (2015), pp. 571–619. See also Gary Born (2014) *International Commercial Arbitration, Volume I*, 2nd edn 2014, Kluwer Law International, Alphen aan den Rijn, pp. 1181–1184.

[79] See, on that point, Georg Naegeli and Chris Schmitz, 'Switzerland: Strict Test for the Extension of Arbitration Agreements to Non-Signatories' in *7 Zeitschrift für Schiedsverfahren*, no. 4 (2009), pp. 185–188. In this article, the authors have discussed a judgment (Decision no. 4A.128/2008 of 19 August 2008) where the Swiss Federal Tribunal decided that the reference to a subcontract in a guarantee was not sufficient to incorporate the arbitration agreement contained in the subcontract in order to allow single multiparty arbitration involving the parties under the subcontract and the guarantor. An explicit wording in the guarantee was required to that effect. See also Andrea Marco Steingruber (2012) *Consent in International Arbitration*, Oxford University Press, Oxford, para. 9.70.

[80] Dimitar Hristoforov Kondev, 'Do Recent Overhauls of Arbitration Rules Respond to the Need for Multi-Party Arbitration in the Construction Industry?', in *32 International Construction Law Review*, no. 1 (2015), pp. 66–67.

contractor. Regardless of the contractual model in use, the employer may also have an incentive to participate in multi-party arbitration if he has imposed nominated subcontractors on the main contractor or if there are third parties, such as subcontractors or suppliers, that have provided collateral warranties in favour of the employer.

Subcontractors are usually not interested in multi-party arbitration, except in cases of arbitration concerning payment of the subcontractors' works under subcontracts containing *pay when paid* clauses. Likewise, designers and engineers usually have no incentives to participate in multi-party arbitration. In general, the same holds true with regard to all parties that are involved in smaller portions of the construction works, such as technical consultants, suppliers, and subcontractors.

While multi-party arbitration is unlikely to serve the interests of all parties equally, it may nevertheless generally serve the interests of international commercial arbitration as a whole and increase its efficacy[81]. Multi-party arbitration allows related disputes to be resolved in a consistent manner within a single proceeding which usually requires less time and costs than the time and costs to be spent in separate arbitrations dealing with the same disputes.

[81] Ruth Stackpool-Moore (2014) 'Joinder and Consolidation – Examining Best Practice in the Swiss, HKIAC and ICC Rules', in Nathalie Voser (ed.) *10 Years of the Swiss Rules of International Arbitration*, ASA Special Series No. 44, JurisNet LLC, New York, NY, pp. 16–17.

Chapter 4

Multi-Party Arbitration Solutions under Arbitration Rules[1]

Contracting parties often refer to a certain set of arbitration rules in the arbitration clauses contained in their contracts. The parties' legitimate expectations are that arbitration rules in general introduce a balanced and flexible mechanism for resolution of disputes, which does not cause prejudice to any party. The reference to a certain set of arbitration rules constitutes the parties' consent to the conduct of arbitral proceedings in the way contemplated under these rules, including in respect of multi-party arbitration issues. Until recently, multi-party arbitration provisions were rarely seen in arbitration rules. Of late, however, we are witnessing a proliferation of these clauses as a result of overhauls of the major sets of institutional and *ad hoc* arbitration rules. Often one of the main purposes of these overhauls is to introduce more efficient dispute resolution mechanisms capable of handling multi-party disputes. However, even today there are some arbitration rules that do not contain provisions regulating multi-party arbitration[2].

The present chapter will focus on several sets of arbitration rules. The main criterion for the choice of the reviewed arbitration rules is their frequent application to construction disputes. The chapter starts with a review of the ICC Rules. These rules are the most popular arbitration rules chosen by parties under international commercial transactions. Besides the ICC Rules, parties sometimes prefer the rules of some other popular arbitral institutions in Europe, such as the LCIA in London, CEPANI in Belgium, the Swiss Chambers' Arbitration Institution, the Arbitration Institute of the Stockholm Chamber of Commerce and the Vienna International Arbitral Centre. The rules of these institutions have therefore also been reviewed.

[1] Parts of this chapter were first published in the article 'Do Recent Overhauls of Arbitration Rules Respond to the Need for Multi-Party Arbitration in the Construction Industry', in *32 International Construction Law Review*, no. 1 (2015), pp. 63–94.

[2] For example, the DIS-Rules adopted by the Deutsche Institution für Schiedsgerichtsbarkeit e.V. (discussed in Section 4.8) do not contain joinder and consolidation provisions. The most popular arbitration rules in the United Arab Emirates, such as the DIAC Arbitration Rules adopted by the Dubai International Arbitration Centre, in force as from 1 May 2007, and the Procedural Regulations of Arbitration of the Abu Dhabi Commercial Conciliation and Arbitration Centre, in force as from 1 September 2013, also do not address these matters.

Multi-Party and Multi-Contract Arbitration in the Construction Industry, First Edition.
Dimitar Kondev.

Considering that major construction projects take place throughout the world, a review of the arbitration rules published by arbitral institutions in Europe will be insufficient in its scope. Therefore, this book also analyses the arbitration rules of some nascent arbitral centres in the Asian region, which are often chosen by contracting parties operating in that part of the globe.

Furthermore, the review under this chapter also encompasses two sets of arbitration rules published by the American Arbitration Association, namely the Construction Industry Arbitration Rules and the ICDR Rules. Even though the former set of rules predominantly attracts disputes arising under domestic contracts in the United States, it has been included in the review because of its peculiar approach to multi-party arbitration.

Finally, international construction arbitration may also take the form of *ad hoc* arbitration conducted without the participation of an arbitral institution administering the proceedings. Therefore, the UNCITRAL Rules, the most widely used rules for *ad hoc* arbitrations, have also been discussed.

The main purpose of the review of the arbitration rules in this chapter is to examine whether they provide for workable solutions to multi-party arbitration that can be readily employed by the parties in case of need. In other words, the question is whether these rules provide for a self-contained mechanism for multi-party arbitration – a mechanism that can be put into operation without the need to obtain the explicit *ad hoc* parties' consent to multi-party arbitration. For that purpose, the chapter will analyse how efficient the solutions under the reviewed rules can be in situations in which the parties have neither included multi-party arbitration clauses in their contracts, nor agreed to the conduct of such proceedings once the arbitration has started. At the same time, a workable solution implies that the resulting arbitral award should be capable of being recognized and enforced internationally without any difficulties.

4.1 ICC Rules

It would be natural to start the review under this chapter with the ICC Rules[3]. The reason for this is twofold. First, these rules are the most popular set of institutional arbitration rules nowadays. Secondly, the ICC Rules are the default arbitration rules under most of the FIDIC Conditions of Contract[4] and also under the ICC Contracts[5]. Therefore, the

---

[3] Rules of Arbitration by the International Chamber of Commerce, in force as from 1 January 2012, http://www.iccwbo.org/Products-and-Services/Arbitration-and-ADR/Arbitration/Rules-of-arbitration/Download-ICC-Rules-of-Arbitration/ICC-Rules-of-Arbitration-in-several-languages/ (accessed 25 July 2016).

[4] See sub-clause 20.6 of the FIDIC Red Book, the FIDIC Yellow Book and the FIDIC Silver Book and also sub-clause 20.8 of the FIDIC Gold Book. It should be noted, however, that not all FIDIC contract forms refer to the ICC Rules. For example, the FIDIC Green Book (sub-clause 15.3) does not refer to the ICC Rules but to rules to be further specified by the parties in the Appendix to that contract. A similar approach has been adopted under the FIDIC White Book (sub-clause 44). The FIDIC Pink Book does not refer to the ICC Rules either. Instead, the FIDIC Pink Book envisages that the arbitral proceedings shall be administered by the institution specified in the Contract Data to the contract and conducted in accordance with the rules administered by this institution or the UNCITRAL arbitration rules, at the choice of the institution.

[5] See articles 66(4) and 66(5) of the ICC Turnkey Contract. See also article 66.3.3 and article 66.3.4 of Option A and article 66.4.5 of Option B, as well as article 67.7 of the ICC Subcontract.

ICC Rules will find application to all disputes arising under these standard forms, unless the parties decide to modify the arbitration clause contained thereunder.

The current version of ICC Rules has been in force from 1 January 2012. One of the main motives for the last revision of the rules was the attempt to provide for better solutions to multi-party problems and to systematize the practice developed by the ICC Court in this respect[6].

4.1.1 Multi-contract claims and prima facie assessment

The ICC Rules contain a new provision dealing with disputes arising under multiple contracts[7]. Article 9 of ICC Rules envisages that:

> Subject to the provisions of Articles 6(3)–6(7) and 23 (4), claims arising out of or in connection with more than one contract may be made in a single arbitration, irrespective of whether such claims are made under one or more than one arbitration agreement under the Rules.

Article 9 should always be read together with Articles 23(4) and 6(3)–6(7), which introduce certain limitations to the conduct of multi-contract arbitrations. Pursuant to the first article, no claims, including claims under Article 9, can be made after the signing of the Terms of Reference or their approval by the Court if these claims fall outside the limits of the Terms of Reference, unless the arbitral tribunal authorizes otherwise. Articles 6(3)–6(7) deal, *inter alia*, with pleas raised by a respondent objecting that all of the claims made in the arbitration may be determined together in a single arbitration. These pleas actually constitute jurisdictional objections to the conduct of multi-party arbitration. From the perspective of the construction industry, this could be a plea by an architect under a *build only* construction project objecting to the conduct of a single arbitration dealing with employer's claims against both the main contractor and the architect.

Upon the occurrence of such jurisdictional objections, the arbitration shall proceed and it will be up to the arbitral tribunal to take a decision, unless the Secretary General decides to refer the matter to the ICC Court[8]. This approach is compliant with the principle of *Kompetenz-Kompetenz* stating that the arbitral tribunal has the power to rule on

[6] Article 4(6) of the 1998 ICC Rules permitted consolidation in very limited circumstances. Consolidation was possible only prior to the signing or approval of the Terms of Reference by the ICC Court with regard to proceedings pending between the same parties. Furthermore, the 1998 ICC Rules did not address the question of joinder of third parties.

[7] Even though this provision appeared for the first time in the 2012 ICC Rules, it actually systematized the previous practice of the ICC Court, which acknowledged the possibility of single arbitration dealing with multi-contract claims under certain conditions.

[8] See Article 6(3) of the ICC Rules. This article is based on Article 6(2) of the 1998 ICC Rules, under which the Court also had the power to make a prima facie decision concerning the existence of an ICC arbitration agreement binding the parties upon raised jurisdictional objections. However, the new article has further elaborated the process by giving the Secretary General a new screening or *gatekeeping* function: the Secretary General decides which cases should be referred to the Court, and the rest are referred directly to the arbitral tribunal.

its own jurisdiction. However, in complex disputes, such as multi-party construction disputes, it can be anticipated that decisions on jurisdictional objections shall be taken by the ICC Court and not by the arbitral tribunal. There are two reasons for such a proposition. First, multi-contract disputes in most cases presuppose the existence of several parallel arbitration clauses binding parties that are not identical. In these cases, there is no single contract containing an arbitration clause signed by all parties, which creates doubt as to the existence of a prima facie basis for asserting ICC arbitral jurisdiction over the multiple claims. Therefore, the Secretary General would most likely refer such a jurisdictional objection to the ICC Court for consideration under Article 6(4). Secondly, jurisdictional objections are usually made at a relatively early stage of the arbitral proceedings before the constitution of the arbitral tribunal. The ICC Secretariat's practice has sometimes been to defer any steps towards the constitution of the arbitral tribunal until after the jurisdictional objection has been settled[9]. Therefore, in most cases there will be no tribunal to decide on the jurisdictional objection once it has been raised. For these reasons, it could be expected that the referral of the jurisdictional objection to the ICC Court will be the rule rather than the exception[10].

Once the plea has been referred to the Court, the latter should make a decision under Article 6(4), which states the following:

> In all cases referred to the Court under Article 6(3), the Court shall decide whether and to what extent the arbitration shall proceed. The arbitration shall proceed if and to the extent that the Court is prima facie satisfied that an arbitration agreement under the rules may exist. In particular:
>
> (i) where there are more than two parties to the arbitration, the arbitration shall proceed between those of the parties, including any additional parties joined pursuant to Article 7, with respect to which the Court is prima facie satisfied that an arbitration agreement under the Rules that binds them all may exist; and
> (ii) whether claims pursuant to Article 9 are made under more than one arbitration agreement, the arbitration shall proceed as to those claims with respect to which the Court is prima facie satisfied (a) that the arbitration agreements under which those claims are made may be compatible, and (b) that all parties to the arbitration may have agreed that those claims can be determined together in single arbitration.
>
> The Court's decision pursuant to Article 6(4) is without prejudice to the admissibility or merits of any party's plea or pleas.

---

[9] See Jason Fry, Simon Greenberg and Francesca Mazza (2012) *The Secretariat's Guide to ICC Arbitration*, ICC Publication No. 729, ICC Publishing SA, Paris, pp. 68–69 (§ 3-198 and § 3-205).

[10] See Nathalie Voser, 'Overview of the Most Important Changes in the Revised ICC Arbitration Rules', in 29 *ASA Bulletin*, no. 4 (2011), p. 789. See also Jason Fry, Simon Greenberg and Francesca Mazza (2012) *The Secretariat's Guide to ICC Arbitration*, ICC Publication No. 729, ICC Publishing SA, Paris, pp. 69–70 (§ 3-203 and § 3-207). It can be assumed on the basis of the cited paragraphs that questions concerning jurisdiction over claims arising under several contracts binding parties that are not identical would most likely be referred to the ICC Court for a prima facie decision. However, there are also some opinions that the Secretary General may decide not to refer these questions to the ICC Court. See in that regard Thomas Webster and Michael Bühler (2014) *Handbook of ICC Arbitration. Commentary, Precedents, Materials*, 3rd edn, Sweet & Maxwell, London, p. 111 (§ 6-34).

At first reading, because of the explicit reference in subparagraph (ii) to multiple arbitration agreements it may seem that multi-party disputes arising under multiple contracts will have to meet the threshold under subparagraph (ii) of Article 6(4) only. However, this is not the case. Multiple disputes arising under multiple contracts, such as the construction disputes within the scope hereof, will have to comply with both subparagraphs (i) and (ii) of Article 6(4) precisely because they involve both multiple parties and multiple contracts[11]. First, the Court should be prima facie satisfied that there is an arbitration agreement involving all multiple parties under subparagraph (i). Secondly, the Court should make the same prima facie assessment as regards the compatibility of the different arbitration agreements and the parties' consent to a single arbitration under subparagraph (ii). These two requirements are not necessarily contradictory. They neither represent alternatives to the prima facie assessment by the Court, nor provide different thresholds for such an assessment[12]. As has been observed in the Secretariat's Guide to ICC Arbitration ('**ICC Secretariat's Guide**') with respect to multi-party claims based on multiple arbitration agreements:

> In such circumstances, both subparagraphs (i) and (ii) will apply in the context of the prima facie assessment. In other words, when Article 6(4), subparagraph (ii), applies, it will almost always apply in conjunction with Article 6(4), subparagraph (i). Both subparagraphs (i) and (ii) are concerned with the same issue, namely to ensure that the prima facie assessment is conducted appropriately. In practice, this means that under each subparagraph of Article 6(4), the Court will be looking for prima facie consent to arbitrate – under subparagraph (i), consent of all parties; and under subparagraph (ii), consent to a single arbitration involving claims from more than one arbitration agreement. However, the Court will not apply the requirements of subparagraphs (i) and (ii) separately, but will rather make a holistic assessment of the case[13].

This situation should be distinguished from cases where there are multi-party disputes that have arisen under multiple contracts but under the same arbitration agreement. The latter agreement is sometimes referred to as an *umbrella* arbitration agreement or a framework arbitration agreement. It is a single agreement binding all or some of the parties participating in the economic transaction that regulates the terms under which the parties' disputes will be resolved through arbitration. Such framework arbitration agreements can sometimes be seen in the construction sector: for example, a single arbitration agreement binding an employer, a design professional, a main contractor and/or subcontractors. Apparently, upon the existence of such a framework agreement only subparagraph (i) of Article 6(4) will apply. Subparagraph (ii) of the same article will not come into play because it explicitly refers to disputes arising under more than one arbitration agreement.

---

[11] See Nathalie Voser, 'Overview of the Most Important Changes in the Revised ICC Arbitration Rules', in 29 *ASA Bulletin*, no. 4 (2011), pp. 794–795. See also Thomas Webster and Michael Bühler (2014) *Handbook of ICC Arbitration. Commentary, Precedents, Materials*, 3rd edn, Sweet & Maxwell, London, pp. 164–165 (§ 8-7).

[12] See Jason Fry, Simon Greenberg and Francesca Mazza (2012) *The Secretariat's Guide to ICC Arbitration*, ICC Publication No. 729, ICC Publishing SA, Paris, p. 72 (§ 3-212).

[13] Ibid., pp. 73 (§ 3-216), 84–85 (§ 3-253–254). See also Nathalie Voser, 'Overview of the Most Important Changes in the Revised ICC Arbitration Rules', in *29 ASA Bulletin*, no. 4 (2011), pp. 794–795.

As evident from the wording of Article 6(4), the latter article vests the ICC Court with a large degree of discretion when deciding on a plea concerning the joint review of disputes under several contracts. The assessment whether an arbitration agreement that binds all parties 'may exist' (under subparagraph (i)) and what the parties 'may have agreed' (under subparagraph (ii)) will be a subjective one and the criteria for such an assessment will depend on the circumstances of each specific case. Apparently, the use of the word 'may' (rather than 'does') presupposes that the threshold that should be met is fairly low. However, the ICC Court will normally require some evidence to be provided by the parties and would not base its decision solely on allegations made by one of the parties that the threshold has been met[14].

The ICC Secretariat's Guide suggests that certain factors may be taken into account by the ICC Court when making a decision under Article 6(4). It has been suggested there that none of these factors is decisive in itself and that all factors will be considered together. These factors include, *inter alia*, the identity of the parties to the different arbitration agreements, the nature of the relationship between the contracts, whether the contracts concern a single economic transaction, the dates of the contracts, the compatibility between the wording of the arbitration agreements, and so forth.[15] The consideration of the first three factors by the ICC Court, as described in the ICC Secretariat's Guide, sheds some light on the way in which the Court may make its prima facie decision under Article 6(4). It can be argued that the different contracts concluded in relation to a certain construction project concern a single economic transaction, namely, the completion of the project. However, in most cases the parties under these contracts are not identical. In such a scenario, it has been observed in the ICC Secretariat's Guide that:

> In general, it will be helpful to establish *prima facie* consent if at least one of the arbitration agreements binds all the parties. If not, the Court would look to see whether there is a close relationship between any parties not bound by a common arbitration agreement[16].

In construction disputes, such a close relationship could hardly be found because the different participants in the construction project are separate legal entities with their own internal organizational structure and management[17]. As regards the nature of the relationship between the parties, the ICC Secretariat's Guide distinguishes between horizontal and vertical relationships. According to the ICC Secretariat's Guide, the first relation comprises situations, for example, of two separate construction contracts

[14] See Jason Fry, Simon Greenberg and Francesca Mazza (2012) *The Secretariat's Guide to ICC Arbitration*, ICC Publication No. 729, ICC Publishing SA, Paris, p. 75 (§ 3-219).

[15] Ibid., pp. 82–83 (§ 3-249).

[16] Ibid.

[17] However, sometimes there are exceptions to this general position. Such exceptions can be found in the context of group of companies. Parent companies often operate in different jurisdictions through local subsidiaries incorporated in the country where the project is carried out. These situations may give rise to discussions whether an arbitration clause signed by the subsidiary company could be extended to the parent company. As pointed out in the introduction, the notion of extension of arbitration clauses to non-signatories is outside the scope of this book and therefore has not been discussed further.

concluded between the same parties (e.g. two main contracts with the same main contractor for different sections of the work). The ICC Secretariat's Guide suggests that in these cases the ICC Court is likely to find a prima facie indication of consent if the two agreements contain identical arbitration clauses[18]. The vertical relation involves a contractual scheme that gives rise to multi-party disputes as the ones examined in this book, for example related disputes arising under a main contract and a subcontract. With regard to this second category of contractual relations, the ICC Secretariat's Guide has observed:

> ... if the first contract is between the owner and a contractor, and the second is between the contractor and its subcontractor, such as may be found in a classic construction or engineering project, the legal relationships are usually entirely distinct, even though the economic transactions are closely related. In situations such as this involving a chain of contracts, the parties cannot generally be expected to arbitrate the disputes arising under different contracts together in a single arbitration, unless they have specifically provided otherwise in some way[19].

Hence, the mere existence of compatible arbitration clauses in two separate agreements between non-identical parties, which are silent on multi-party arbitration, will not be sufficient *per se* for the ICC Court to decide in favour of the joint review of the disputes. The overall application of both subparagraphs (i) and (ii) of Article 6(4) confirms such a conclusion. Subparagraph (i) will not be satisfied because there will be no single arbitration agreement binding all parties. Instead, there are separate arbitration clauses binding parties that are not identical. Subparagraph (ii) will not be satisfied either because there will usually be no consent by all parties that their related disputes may be reviewed in single arbitral proceedings. Consent to multi-party arbitration may also be given after the emergence of the disputes. However, it is unrealistic to expect that the parties may consent to multi-party arbitration at this stage. They will have conflicting interests and pursue different goals in the pending proceedings. Some parties will almost certainly prefer a single arbitration instead of multi-party proceedings.

As a result, it is more likely that the ICC Court will decide that an arbitral tribunal under the ICC Rules will not have jurisdiction to review multi-party claims made under multiple contracts in a single arbitration, unless there is an explicit agreement for such joint review from all parties or some other conduct manifesting the parties' unequivocal consent to be bound with a single arbitration award. Following a negative decision under Article 6(4), the disputes arising under each separate contract will have to be reviewed in separate proceedings.

As Nathalie Voser has stated:

> A case which was repeatedly discussed during the drafting process, and where it was however unmistakable that the test of Article 6(4)(ii) would not be met, relates to disputes arising in the construction industry: an owner...files claims against the general or main contractor who in

[18]Jason Fry, Simon Greenberg and Francesca Mazza (2012) *The Secretariat's Guide to ICC Arbitration*, ICC Publication No. 729, ICC Publishing SA, Paris, pp. 82–83 (§ 3-249).
[19]Ibid.

turn wishes to file claims against its subcontractor. In such circumstances, even if the arbitration agreements are compatible, it could not be assumed that the parties 'may have agreed that those claims can be determined together in a single arbitration' (Article 6(4)(ii)). Thus, the basic principle remains that if multiple parties want to join claims under several contracts in one arbitration they must themselves contractually provide for this possibility[20].

This position is also acknowledged in the ICC Secretariat's Guide. The latter gives an example which is similar to the one discussed above[21]. The authors of the ICC Secretariat's Guide conclude with regard to this example that:

> [In] the absence of other circumstances, the Court will more likely than not consider *prima facie* that the parties at either end of the chain should not arbitrate together, unless the circumstances suggest that the parties may have agreed otherwise (e.g. the owner signed the subcontract)[22].

In reality, it will be very rare to see cases where an employer signs a subcontract. As observed in Subsection 3.4.1 hereof, the general position of the employer will be to arbitrate his disputes with the main contractor without the participation of the main contractor's subcontractors.

Even if the ICC Court decides that there is a prima facie basis for arbitration of the multi-contract claims (which is highly unlikely), this decision is not binding on the tribunal reviewing the case. The decision of the ICC Court is administrative in its nature, and the tribunal may well decide that it does not have jurisdiction to deal with the multi-contract arbitration in single proceedings despite a positive prima facie decision[23]. However, if the ICC Court decides that there is no prima facie basis for arbitration with respect to the filed claims, the arbitration may not proceed with regard to these claims[24].

4.1.2 Joinder

Historically, the approach of the ICC Court was that only the claimant had the right to define the parties to the arbitral proceedings in the request for arbitration. If the claimant wanted to join an additional party as a defendant, this was considered possible by

---

[20] See Nathalie Voser, 'Overview of the Most Important Changes in the Revised ICC Arbitration Rules, in *29 ASA Bulletin*, no. 4 (2011), p. 792. See also Andreas Reiner and Christian Aschauer (2013) 'Chapter II, ICC Rules', in Rolf Schütze (ed.) *Institutional Arbitration, Article-by-Article Commentary*, C. H. Beck / Hart / Nomos, Munich, p. 54, where the authors have reached a similar conclusion.

[21] See Jason Fry, Simon Greenberg and Francesca Mazza (2012) *The Secretariat's Guide to ICC Arbitration*, ICC Publication No. 729, ICC Publishing SA, Paris, p. 85 (§ 3-255). Under the example, an employer signs a contract with a main contractor and the latter signs a separate contract with a subcontractor.

[22] Ibid.

[23] Thomas Webster and Michael Bühler (2014) *Handbook of ICC Arbitration. Commentary, Precedents, Materials*, 3rd edn, Sweet & Maxwell, London, pp. 112 (§ 6-40), 115–116 (§ 6-55). In the authors' opinion: 'it will be wrong for a Tribunal to take the ICC Court's *prima facie* decision as indicative for its arbitral jurisdiction. It is not, since the analysis of the ICC Court and that of a Tribunal is carried out at two different levels.'

[24] Andreas Reiner and Christian Aschauer (2013) 'Chapter II, ICC Rules', in Rolf Schütze (ed.) *Institutional Arbitration, Article-by-Article Commentary*, C. H. Beck / Hart / Nomos, Munich, p. 52.

amending the claim initially filed[25]. The respondent could file a counter claim only against the claimant and was not entitled to file a claim against other parties. It was argued that this approach gave certain procedural advantage to the claimant and violated the right of the respondent to be treated equally, as the latter (unlike the claimant) was not entitled to join additional parties in the proceedings. Gradually, the ICC Court changed its practice in order to allow a joinder of a third party upon the request of the respondent. This was possible under three cumulative conditions, namely: (i) the third party should be a signatory to the arbitration agreement, (ii) the respondent should have a claim against this third party, and (iii) the request for joinder should be made before the constitution of the arbitral tribunal.

The new Article 7 for the first time explicitly deals with joinder of third parties in pending arbitration under conditions similar to the ones observed above. Pursuant to Article 7(1):

> A party wishing to join an additional party to the arbitration shall submit its request for arbitration against the additional party (the 'Request for Joinder') to the Secretariat....Any such joinder shall be subject to the provisions of Articles 6(3)–6(7) and 9. No additional party may be joined after the confirmation or appointment of any arbitrator, unless all parties, including the additional party, otherwise agree...

The request for joinder may be submitted at any time after the filing of the request for arbitration but not later than the confirmation or appointment of an arbitrator. The purpose of this temporal restriction is to avoid any delay in the proceedings[26] and to ensure that the third party being joined has an equal influence on the constitution of the arbitral tribunal. Article 7 refers to Articles 6(3)–6(7), and therefore the above-mentioned prima facie control by the ICC Court will follow if there is a plea regarding the admissibility of the joinder request. In a multi-contract construction scenario, such a plea may be observed in cases where a main contractor tries to drag a subcontractor into his arbitration with the employer. The plea in this latter case may be filed by either the subcontractor or by the employer. The subcontractor may argue that he has not agreed to arbitrate his disputes under the subcontract with the participation of the employer. Similarly, the latter may claim that the resolution of his dispute with the main contractor does not require the participation of the subcontractor in the same arbitration. The above observations concerning the prima facie decision under Article 6(4) will also apply with respect to the joinder request. This means that the joinder request most likely will be denied, unless the parties have explicitly regulated the matter in their contracts.

---

[25] Anne Marie Whitesell (2009) 'Multiparty Arbitration: The ICC International Court of Arbitration Perspective', in the Permanent Court of Arbitration (ed.) *Multiple Party Actions in International Arbitration*, Oxford University Press, New York, NY, p. 206.

[26] Nathalie Voser, 'Overview of the Most Important Changes in the Revised ICC Arbitration Rules', in *29 ASA Bulletin*, no. 4 (2011), p. 793.

4.1.3 Consolidation

The ICC Rules contain a provision dealing with consolidation of two or more arbitrations pending under the ICC Rules – that is, two or more arbitrations with separate ICC case reference numbers.

Pursuant to Article 10:

> The Court may, at the request of a party, consolidate two or more arbitrations pending under the Rules into a single arbitration, where:
>
> (a) the parties have agreed to consolidation; or
> (b) all of the claims in the arbitrations are made under the same arbitration agreement; or
> (c) where the claims in the arbitrations are made under more than one arbitration agreement, the arbitrations are between the same parties, the disputes in the arbitrations arise in connection with the same legal relationship, and the Court finds the arbitration agreements to be compatible.
>
> In deciding whether to consolidate, the Court may take into account any circumstances it considers to be relevant, including whether one or more arbitrators have been confirmed or appointed in more than one of the arbitrations and, if so, whether the same or different persons have been confirmed or appointed.
> When arbitrations are consolidated, they shall be consolidated into the arbitration that commenced first, unless otherwise agreed by all parties.

The new consolidation provision is broader than Article 4(6) of the 1998 ICC Rules where consolidation was only deemed possible with regard to pending proceedings involving the same parties. Unlike the solutions under other institutional rules, the ICC Court is not entitled to order consolidation by its own volition[27]. There is no restriction as to when consolidation may be requested. This is another difference from the 1998 ICC Rules, which made clear that no consolidation is possible once the Terms of Reference have been signed. Therefore, consolidation may be possible even if the first arbitration has reached an advanced stage. In practice, however, the advanced stage of the proceedings will work against consolidation[28]. Furthermore, if the arbitrators in the different arbitrations have already been appointed or confirmed, the Court will be unable to consolidate the proceedings because it will be impossible to have a single tribunal in place, unless the already appointed or confirmed arbitrators are the same for the different arbitrations[29]. Therefore, consolidation should be requested as early as possible.

Only letters (a) and (b) of the consolidation provision are pertinent to the type of construction disputes discussed hereof. The parties' consent to consolidation under

---

[27] See, for example, Article 4(1) of the Swiss Rules where the arbitration court is allowed to order consolidation on its own motion.

[28] Nathalie Voser, 'Overview of the Most Important Changes in the Revised ICC Arbitration Rules', in *29 ASA Bulletin*, no. 4 (2011), p. 797.

[29] Stephen Bond, Marily Paralika and Matthew Secomb (2015) 'ICC Rules of Arbitration, 2012', in Loukas Mistelis (ed.) *Concise International Arbitration*, 2nd edn, Kluwer Law International, Alphen aan den Rijn, pp. 373–374.

letter (a) could be given beforehand in the form of a multi-party arbitration clause or later on at the stage when the disputes have arisen. However, as already mentioned, such consent will rarely be available because of the lack of multi-party arbitration clauses under standard form agreements and the parties' conflicting interests on the brink of arbitration. Thus, the availability of separate arbitration clauses in a main contract and a subcontract, which are silent on consolidation, will generally preclude the possibility for consolidation of parallel main contract and subcontract arbitrations[30]. Letter (b) of the same Article could be used as a basis for consolidation only if there is an umbrella arbitration agreement binding all parties. However, these agreements are rarely met in construction projects.

The ICC Rules do not explicitly envisage what is the interrelation between Article 9 and Article 10 in respect of multi-contract disputes. The wording of these two provisions differs with respect to the authority that is competent to decide on the issue and the preconditions for the joint review of the related disputes. Under Article 10 it is only the ICC Court that may decide to consolidate proceedings, while under Article 9 it is the arbitral tribunal that deals with the plea concerning the conduct of multi-contract arbitration, unless the matter has been referred for a decision to the ICC Court. Unlike the decision under Article 9, the ICC Court's decision under Article 10 is not a prima facie decision but a final procedural decision[31]. Whereas under Article 9 the arbitration shall continue if an arbitration agreement that binds all parties 'may exist' and all the parties to the arbitration 'may have agreed' for a joint review of the disputes in single proceedings, under Article 10 the pending proceedings may be consolidated only if 'the parties have agreed to consolidation' or 'all of the claims in the arbitrations are made under the same arbitration agreement'[32]. At first glance, it seems that the approach adopted under Article 9 is more lenient than the one in the consolidation provision. Considering the wording of these provisions, it could be assumed that Article 9 will find application to cases where the claims arising under more than one contract and / or arbitration agreement have been brought together in a single arbitration – that is, these claims have not resulted in separate arbitrations yet. This could be the case, for example, when an employer initiates arbitral proceedings by filing a single request for arbitration against both a design professional and a main contractor with whom the employer has contracted separately. However, if the employer has filed separate requests for arbitration against the

[30] Thomas Webster and Michael Bühler (2014) *Handbook of ICC Arbitration. Commentary, Precedents, Materials*, 3rd edn, Sweet & Maxwell, London, p. 173 (§ 10-3 and 10-4). According to the authors: 'If a subcontractor starts an arbitration against the general contractor, and the latter then decides to start arbitration against the owner (employer) of the project, these two cases could not be joined by the ICC Court, absent unanimous consent of all parties concerned.'

[31] Nathalie Voser, 'Overview of the Most Important Changes in the Revised ICC Arbitration Rules', in *29 ASA Bulletin*, no. 4 (2011), p. 796.

[32] See Article 10, letters (a) and (b). The third alternative under letter (c) deals with arbitrations between the same parties, and is therefore not applicable to multi-contract disputes involving different parties.

designer and the main contractor, which have resulted in separate arbitrations, then the question of joint review of these disputes will be decided by the ICC Court by applying Article 10 and not Article 9[33].

The review of the ICC Rules reveals that, irrespective of the way in which multi-party arbitral proceedings are initiated, and the particular provision applicable to such proceedings, the consent of all parties will be necessary for the joint review of their disputes. The reference to the ICC Rules in the parties' contracts is not sufficient because these rules do not provide for a self-contained regime for the conduct of multi-party arbitrations based on multiple contracts. The provisions of the ICC Rules on these matters can be applied only if the parties have given their consent to be involved in multi-party proceedings. However, such consent is usually not available because of the reasons already explained above. Hence, this results in the conduct of separate arbitrations on related disputes which brings forward the drawbacks pertaining to these arbitrations discussed in Section 2.3 above.

4.2 CEPANI Rules[34]

The CEPANI Rules have, from the outset, been inspired by the ICC Rules[35]. The new CEPANI Rules entered into force on 1 January 2013. They contain several provisions addressing multi-party arbitration.

4.2.1 Multiple parties and multi-contract claims

Article 9 of the CEPANI Rules acknowledges that arbitration may take place among multiple parties 'when they have agreed to have recourse under the CEPANI Rules'.

---

[33]See Simon Greenberg, Jose Ricardo Feris and Christian Albanesi (2010) 'Consolidation, Joinder, Cross-Claims, Multiparty and Multicontract Arbitrations: Recent ICC Experience', in Bernard Hanotiau and Eric Schwartz (eds) *ICC Dossiers VII, Multiparty Arbitration*, ICC Publication No. 701E, ICC Publishing SA, Paris, pp. 161–182. According to the co-authors: 'As a matter of ICC internal practice, "multicontract" arbitration means a single arbitration where claims have been brought on the basis of more than one contract. As noted above, some practitioners consider this as a form of consolidation. It is true that there is a close conceptual link between a request to consolidate two pending arbitrations that have been filed on the basis of different contracts, on the one hand, and a single arbitration that has been filed on the basis of more than one contract, on the other. For ICC purposes, however, the two situations are considered procedurally distinct.' See also Jason Fry, Simon Greenberg and Francesca Mazza (2012) *The Secretariat's Guide to ICC Arbitration*, ICC Publication No. 729, ICC Publishing SA, Paris, p. 111 (§ 3-347).

[34]Arbitration Rules of the Belgian Centre for Arbitration and Mediation, in force as from 1 January 2013, http://www.cepani.be/sites/default/files/images/hayez_reglement_arbitrage_cepani_en_dec2014_1.1.pdf (accessed 25 July 2016).

[35]Herman Verbist, 'New Belgian Arbitration Law of 24 June 2013 and New CEPANI Arbitration Rules of 1 January 2013', in *30 Journal of International Arbitration*, no. 5 (2013), p. 607.

Article 10 of the CEPANI Rules provides for the opportunity for joint review of claims arising under multiple contracts in a single arbitration:

> (1) Claims arising out of various contracts or in connection with same may be made in a single arbitration. This is the case when the said claims are made pursuant to various arbitration agreements:
> (a) if the parties have agreed to have recourse to arbitration under the CEPANI Rules and
> (b) if all the parties have agreed to have their claims decided with a single set of proceedings.
> (2) Differences concerning the applicable rules of law or the language of the proceedings do not give rise to any presumption as to the incompatibility of the arbitration agreements.
> (3) Arbitration agreements concerning matters that are not related to one another give rise to a presumption that the parties have not agreed to have their claims decided in a single set of proceedings...

The article does not set a requirement that the multiple contracts should be between the same parties and therefore it may be applied to disputes arising under contracts binding non-identical parties. If the claims are made pursuant to various arbitration agreements, as is usually the case, the consent of all parties for the joint review of their disputes is required. This follows from letter (b) of Article 10(1).

Articles 9 and 10 should be read in conjunction with Article 6 and Article 12 of the CEPANI Rules. Article 6 introduces a prima facie test similar to that under Article 6(4) of the ICC Rules. Pursuant to Article 6 of the CEPANI Rules, the arbitration may not proceed if there is a prima facie lack of an arbitration agreement and the respondent refuses arbitration or does not answer the claim within a certain period of time. Under Article 6, it is CEPANI that carries out the prima facie assessment. Article 12, on the other hand, stipulates that it is the arbitral tribunal that should rule on its own jurisdiction in multi-party arbitrations. The question may arise as to the interrelation between Article 6 and Article 12 in case of a party's objection to the conduct of multi-party arbitration. From one side, it may be argued that, in a multi-party arbitration based on multiple contracts, CEPANI may find that there is a prima facie lack of an arbitration agreement because there is no single agreement binding all parties, which would mean that the multi-party arbitration may not proceed. On the other hand, Article 12 stipulates that it is the arbitral tribunal that should decide on all disputes in connection with multi-party arbitrations under Articles 9 to 11, including on its own jurisdiction in these arbitrations. The explicit wording of the clause may serve as an argument that it is not CEPANI but the arbitral tribunal that should have the final say on the matter. This second view is supported by some scholars who assert that it is not for CEPANI but for the tribunal to decide whether arbitration may proceed in these cases[36]. Difficulties may arise in cases where the tribunal has not been constituted yet. In these cases, it has been suggested that the party objecting to multi-party arbitration will nevertheless be asked

[36] Herman Verbist, 'Multiparty and Multicontract Arbitration under the 2013 CEPANI Arbitration Rules', in *17 Vindobona Journal of International Commercial Law and Arbitration*, no. 1-24 (2014), pp. 7, 10, 16–17. See also Dirk De Meulemeester, *Multicontract Arbitration Under the CEPANI Arbitration Rules (Article 10)*, Kluwer Arbitration Blog, http://kluwerarbitrationblog.com/blog/2013/10/23/multicontract-arbitration-under-the-cepani-arbitration-rules-article-10/(accessed 25 July 2016).

to nominate an arbitrator or to participate in the constitution of the tribunal[37]. If they refuse to do so, the tribunal shall be constituted in accordance with the relevant provisions under the CEPANI Rules. Then, the CEPANI Secretariat will refer the matter to the constituted tribunal, which shall decide on its own jurisdiction by applying Article 12 of CEPANI Rules[38].

Like the ICC approach, the arbitration agreements under the different contracts should be compatible in order to allow the joint review of the multi-contract disputes. The CEPANI Rules go further into this question and provide some guidance on the criteria for the compatibility assessment in Articles 10(2) and 10(3). Of specific interest for the type of construction disputes discussed in this book is the presumption under Article 10(3). This Article introduces a negative presumption (namely, that the parties have not agreed on multi-party arbitration) in cases where the parties concluded different contracts that are not related to one another. In other words, these contracts do not concern the completion of a single economic transaction[39]. However, as already pointed out, contracts concerning one and the same construction project can arguably be treated as related to the completion of a single economic transaction. Hence, Article 10(3) leaves some leeway for the party that is willing to resolve its dispute in a multi-party arbitration to assert *per argumentum a contrario* that it may be presumed that the parties have agreed on the joint review of their disputes if the arbitration agreements are contained in related contracts[40]. It is rather debatable whether such an argument will be accepted by the arbitral tribunal when faced with a jurisdictional objection. In the author's opinion it is highly unlikely that the tribunal would assume jurisdiction solely on the basis of this argument. In any case, it will be much easier for the tribunal to decide that it has jurisdiction over disputes arising under two or more contracts signed by the same parties than in cases where the contracts are signed by parties that are not identical.

4.2.2 Joinder and intervention

Article 11 of the CEPANI Rules envisages:

> (1) A third party may request to intervene in the proceedings and any party to the proceedings may seek to have a third party joined.
> The intervention may be allowed when the third party and the parties to the dispute have agreed to have recourse to arbitration under the CEPANI Rules.

---

[37] Herman Verbist, 'Multiparty and Multicontract Arbitration under the 2013 CEPANI Arbitration Rules', in *17 Vindobona Journal of International Commercial Law and Arbitration*, no. 1-24 (2014), p. 7.

[38] See Dirk De Meulemeester, *Multicontract Arbitration Under the CEPANI Arbitration Rules (Article 10)*, Kluwer Arbitration Blog.

[39] Ibid. See also Herman Verbist, 'Multiparty and Multicontract Arbitration under the 2013 CEPANI Arbitration Rules', in *17 Vindobona Journal of International Commercial Law and Arbitration*, no. 1-24 (2014), p. 11.

[40] Dimitar Hristoforov Kondev, 'Do Recent Overhauls of Arbitration Rules Respond to the Need for Multi-Party Arbitration in the Construction Industry?', in *32 International Construction Law Review*, no. 1 (2015), p. 82.

(2) No intervention may take place after the Appointments Committee or the President has appointed or confirmed each of the members of the Arbitral Tribunal, unless all the parties, including the third party, have agreed otherwise…

(4) The Request for Intervention shall inter alia include the following information…
A copy of the agreements entered into and in any event of the arbitration agreement that binds the parties and the third party and other useful documents shall be enclosed with the Request for Intervention…'

The Article deals with both joinder and intervention. For the purposes of the CEPANI Rules, joinder is seen as a type of intervention. In any case, it seems that joinder and / or intervention will not be possible if there is no arbitration agreement binding the disputants and the third party. This follows from the second subparagraph of Article 11(1), as well as from Article 11(4) which requires a copy of such an agreement to be presented together with the request for joinder or intervention[41]. The joinder or the intervention should take place before the confirmation or appointment of the members of the arbitral tribunal, unless all parties, including the third party, agree otherwise. If no confirmations and appointments have been made at the time of the request and the disputes are to be reviewed by a three-member tribunal, the third party may nominate an arbitrator jointly with the claimant or the respondent, and in the absence of such a joint nomination the Appointments Committee or the President shall appoint each of the members of the tribunal[42]. Where the disputes are to be decided by a sole arbitrator, the latter will be appointed by the Appointments Committee or the President[43]. If the parties have agreed that the joinder or intervention request may be made after the confirmation or appointment of the members of the tribunal, then the Appointments Committee is empowered either to confirm the confirmations or nominations already made or to terminate these appointments and appoint the new members of the tribunal and its chairman[44]. These provisions aim at ensuring the parties' equal treatment in the constitution of the tribunal.

The above observations concerning the interrelation between Article 6 and Article 12 apply with regard to the joinder article as well. The more likely view is that any objection concerning the jurisdiction of the tribunal to proceed with the multi-party arbitration will be decided by the tribunal by applying Article 12[45].

[41] Herman Verbist, 'Multiparty and Multicontract Arbitration under the 2013 CEPANI Arbitration Rules', in *17 Vindobona Journal of International Commercial Law and Arbitration*, no. 1-24 (2014), p. 13. See also Koen De Winter and Michael De Vroey (2015) 'Belgium', in Liz Williams (ed.) *The Baker & McKenzie International Arbitration Yearbook 2014–2015*, JurisNet, LLC, New York, NY, p. 47.

[42] The first paragraph of Article 15(6) in relation to Article 15(5) of the CEPANI Rules.

[43] The second paragraph of Article 15(6) of the CEPANI Rules.

[44] Article 15(7) of the CEPANI Rules.

[45] Herman Verbist, 'Multiparty and Multicontract Arbitration under the 2013 CEPANI Arbitration Rules', in *17 Vindobona Journal of International Commercial Law and Arbitration*, no. 1-24 (2014), pp. 7, 10, 16–17.

4.2.3 Consolidation

Article 13, which deals with consolidation, stipulates as follows:

(1) When one or more contracts containing an arbitration agreement providing for the application of the Rules give rise to separate arbitrations, which are related or indivisible, the Appointments Committee or the President may order their consolidation. This decision is taken either, prior to any other plea, at the request of the most diligent party, or, at the request of the Arbitral Tribunals or any of them.
In any event no decision is taken without the parties and the Arbitral Tribunal or, as the case may be, the Arbitral Tribunals being invited to present their written observations within the time limit determined by the secretariat.
(2) The application for consolidation shall be granted when it is presented by all the parties and they have also agreed on the manner in which consolidation shall occur.
If this is not the case, the Appointments Committee or the President may grant the application for consolidation, after having considered, inter alia:
(a) whether the parties have not excluded consolidation in the arbitration agreement;
(b) whether the claims made in the separate arbitrations have been made pursuant to the same arbitration agreement;
(c) or, where the claims have been made pursuant to more than one arbitration agreement, whether they are compatible and whether the proceedings involve the same parties and concern disputes arising from the same legal relationship.
The Appointments Committee or the President shall take account, inter alia:
(a) of the progress made in each of the arbitrations and, inter alia, of the fact that one or more arbitrators have been appointed or confirmed in more than one of the arbitrations and, as the case may be, of the fact that the persons appointed or confirmed are the same;
(b) of the place of arbitration provided for in the arbitration agreements…

There is no requirement that the parties under the different proceedings should be the same. Furthermore, there is no time limit as to when consolidation can be requested. It has been stated, however, that if a party wishes to file a request for consolidation, it should do so before any other plea[46]. Consolidation of arbitrations could be admitted provided that the disputes are 'related or indivisible' but the CEPANI Rules do not determine when the disputes will satisfy this criterion[47]. The initiative for the consolidation

---

[46] Herman Verbist, 'Multiparty and Multicontract Arbitration under the 2013 CEPANI Arbitration Rules', in *17 Vindobona Journal of International Commercial Law and Arbitration*, no. 1-24 (2014), p. 19.

[47] Ibid. The author has suggested that certain provisions of the Belgian Judicial Code can be taken into account to clarify these concepts even though he has acknowledged that these provisions are not directly applicable to CEPANI arbitral proceedings. Thus, pursuant to Article 30 of the Belgian Judicial Code, claims can be considered to be related to one another, if they are so closely related that it is desirable to examine them together, so as to avoid solutions which would be incompatible if the claims were to be decided separately. Thus, the risk of inconsistent findings should be taken into account. Furthermore, Article 31 stipulates that a dispute is indivisible if it would turn out to be impossible to enforce together the different decisions that may arise out of the dispute.

could come not only from one of the parties but also from an arbitral tribunal. Pursuant to Article 13(2), the application for the consolidation shall be granted if it is presented by all the parties, and if they have also agreed on the manner in which the consolidation shall occur. It should be noted that this is a procedural requirement that demands an action from all parties involved irrespective of the availability of multi-party arbitration provisions in the parties' contracts. If the application for consolidation is not presented by all parties, consolidation could still be ordered by the competent authority (i.e. the Appointments Committee or the President of CEPANI), provided that the latter has given a careful consideration to a number of circumstances. In a multi-contract scenario, these circumstances will include, *inter alia*, whether consolidation has not been excluded in the parties' contracts, the compatibility of the arbitration agreements (including the place of arbitration), whether the disputes concern the same legal relationship and involve the same parties, the progress made in each of the arbitrations (including appointment of arbitrators). The CEPANI Rules also make clear that consolidation will not be possible with regard to arbitrations in which a decision has already been rendered with regard to preliminary measures, admissibility or as to the merits of a claim, unless the parties agree otherwise[48].

Difficulties may arise with the constitution of the arbitral tribunal in cases of consolidation. Article 15(8) of the CEPANI Rules stipulates that when the request for consolidation is granted, the Appointments Committee or the President will appoint each member of the tribunal. However, unlike the corresponding provision dealing with the constitution of the tribunal in cases of joinder or intervention, the provision in question does not envisage any termination of appointments or confirmations already made. In practice, this will mean that no consolidation will be possible if arbitrators have already been appointed or confirmed in the two arbitrations and if these arbitrators are different persons because the Appointments Committee or the President will not be in a position to constitute a three-member tribunal, unless the arbitrators resign or are replaced at the request of the parties[49].

The wording of the consolidation provision is quite flexible and does not explicitly require the consent of all parties for the purposes of consolidation. This has caused some scholars to liken the consolidation provision to the flexible approach under the Swiss Rules, which will be examined later on[50]. Thus, on the face of it, it seems that consolidation could be granted in cases where the parties' contracts are silent on this matter and some of the disputants object to it. However, it is very doubtful whether the proceedings will be consolidated in these cases. All other provisions in the CEPANI Rules dealing

[48] Article 13(3) of the CEPANI Rules.

[49] Herman Verbist, 'Multiparty and Multicontract Arbitration under the 2013 CEPANI Arbitration Rules', in *17 Vindobona Journal of International Commercial Law and Arbitration*, no. 1-24 (2014), p. 21.

[50] Bernard Hanotiau (2005) *Complex Arbitrations: Multiparty, Multicontract, Multi-issue and Class Actions*, Kluwer Law International, The Hague, p. 182 (§ 410). According to the author, 'Within the framework of the CEPANI Rules, consolidation is possible, even if the parties to the different disputes are not the same in whole or in part. All that is required is some link of connexity or indivisibility.' It should be mentioned that this observation concerned an earlier article of the CEPANI Rules (Article 12 of the 2005 CEPANI Rules) which, however, contained a similar flexible wording. See also Andrea Marco Steingruber (2012) *Consent in International Arbitration*, Oxford University Press, Oxford, § 10.37.

with multi-party arbitration require the parties' consent. The abandonment of the consent requirement for the purposes of consolidation may result in disparate outcomes in situations that are substantially identical[51]. This can be illustrated with an example under a *build-only* construction project where the employer has concluded two separate agreements with a designer and a main contractor. If the parties' contracts are silent on multi-party arbitration, the employer will not be allowed to join the designer in his pending arbitration with the main contractor because of the lack of a single arbitration agreement binding all three parties. However, if the employer initiates a second arbitration against the designer, he may then rely on the consolidation provision, which does not require the explicit parties' consent and merge the two proceedings into one. In this way, he would actually achieve the same effect as the one that he would have achieved if his joinder request had been granted.

4.3 LCIA Rules

Arbitrations under the LCIA Rules are administered by the London Court of International Arbitration (**'LCIA'**). The new LCIA Rules, in force since 1 October 2014, deal with joinder of third parties in pending arbitration and consolidation of parallel arbitrations[52].

The previous version of the LCIA Rules from 1998 did not contain a consolidation provision. Consolidation under the 1998 rules was deemed possible with the agreement of all parties involved[53]. The new LCIA Rules contain a consolidation clause. However, the scope of the provision is rather narrow because it requires that all the parties to the arbitrations to be consolidated agree to such consolidation in writing. If there is not such an agreement, the pending disputes can be consolidated only if there is a single arbitration agreement binding all parties or compatible arbitration agreements between the same parties[54]. In a multi-contract construction setting, neither of these requirements will typically be satisfied, unless the parties are bound by an umbrella arbitration agreement or have included multi-party arbitration clauses in their contracts.

Unlike the ICC approach with respect to joinder, the LCIA Rules embrace a different solution. Pursuant to Article 22(1)(viii) of the LCIA Rules, the arbitral tribunal shall

[51] Dimitar Hristoforov Kondev, 'Do Recent Overhauls of Arbitration Rules Respond to the Need for Multi-Party Arbitration in the Construction Industry?', in *32 International Construction Law Review*, no. 1 (2015), p. 84.

[52] LCIA Arbitration Rules, in force as from 1 October 2014, http://www.lcia.org/Dispute_Resolution_Services/lcia-arbitration-rules-2014.aspx (accessed 25 July 2016).

[53] Peter Turner and Reza Mohtashami (2012) *A Guide to the LCIA Arbitration Rules*, Oxford University Press, Oxford, pp. 151–152 (§ 6.55–6.59). The authors have stated that their research (as of 2012) showed that consolidation had been asked 48 times and 16 orders for consolidation had been made, in each case following the agreement of all parties.

[54] Article 22 (1) (ix) and Article 22 (1) (x) of the LCIA Rules.

have the power, but only upon the request of a party and after giving the parties a reasonable opportunity to state their views:

> to allow one or more third persons to be joined in the arbitration as a party provided any such third person and the applicant party have consented to such joinder in writing following the Commencement Date or (if earlier) in the Arbitration Agreement; and thereafter to make a single final award, or separate awards, in respect of all parties so implicated in the arbitration[55].

The above clause is based on Article 22 (1) (h) of the 1998 LCIA Rules and the differences between the two articles are not so significant[56]. Both the previous and the new joinder article allow for the joinder of a third party, including a party that is a non-signatory to the same arbitration agreement, into pending arbitration[57]. The provisions may find application, for example, where a main contractor asks for the joinder of a subcontractor in an arbitration between the employer and the main contractor. Literally read, joinder under the LCIA Rules may take place in cases where both the main contract and the subcontract are silent on the matter, provided that the main contractor and the subcontractor have agreed to the joinder in writing. Such a joinder can be ordered even over the objection of the employer. This position has also been confirmed by the LCIA[58]. It has also been argued that the joinder article is so far reaching that it may even allow a further joinder upon the request of a party that has already joined in the arbitration[59]. For example, a subcontractor joined in the main contract arbitration may require the joinder of his sub-subcontractor, and so forth. Furthermore, under the LCIA Rules, a third party may be joined even after a tribunal has been appointed. This situation should not give rise to any concerns regarding the parties' equal treatment in

---

[55] Reproduced with permission by the LCIA. Copyright LCIA.

[56] It has been clarified in the 2014 LCIA Rules that the consent of the party requesting the joinder and the party to be joined is not necessarily a procedural consent that should be given in the course of the proceedings, but can also be contained in the arbitration agreement binding the parties. Even though this was not explicitly stated under the earlier joinder article, it was asserted by some authors that the intention behind the latter clause was the same (see Richard Bamforth and Katerina Maidment, '"All join in or not"? How well does international arbitration cater for disputes involving multiple parties or related claims?', in *27 ASA Bulletin*, no. 1 (2009), p. 12, where the authors have stated that the consent to joinder under the 1998 LCIA Rules may be given either through the arbitration agreement or separately). Other authors, however, have expressed the opinion that the wording of the earlier joinder provision created the impression that the third party's consent could be construed as a posteriori consent, i.e. consent to be given in the course of the proceedings (see Paolo Marzolini (2012) 'Is the Parties' Consent Still an Overriding Principle for Joinder and Intervention of Third Parties in International Commercial Arbitration?, in Daniele Favalli, Xavier Favre-Bulle, Andreas Furrer *et al.* (eds) *Selected Papers on International Arbitration: Volume 2 Series on International Arbitration SAA*, Stämpfli Verlag, Bern, p. 121).

[57] Richard Bamforth and Katerina Maidment, '"All join in or not"? How well does international arbitration cater for disputes involving multiple parties or related claims?', in *27 ASA Bulletin*, no. 1 (2009), p. 12.

[58] This position was confirmed during an online webinar '*The LCIA Rules: what you need to know*', presented by Jacomijn van Haersolte-van-Hof and Paula Hodges on 24 September 2014.

[59] Peter Turner and Reza Mohtashami (2012) *A Guide to the LCIA Arbitration Rules*, Oxford University Press, Oxford, p. 150 (§ 6.53). According to the authors: '[In] theory, the cycle of joinder of further parties (say, a long chain of sub-contractors in a large construction dispute) could continue ad infinitum, or at least until the tribunal decided that to join further such parties came into conflict with its duty…to conduct the arbitration efficiently and avoid unnecessary delay and expense.'

the composition of the tribunal because by giving its consent to the joinder the third party is deemed to have accepted the already appointed tribunal[60].

The joinder solution under the LCIA Rules has been criticized and has given rise to different interpretations. According to one group of scholars, a reference to the LCIA Rules in the arbitration agreement is an indication about the anticipated consent of the non-requesting party (i.e. the employer in the abovementioned case) to such joinder[61]. Other scholars reckon that the mere reference to the LCIA rules cannot be construed as consent on behalf of the non-requesting party to arbitrate with the participation of the third party[62]. There is no absolute clarity as to which approach an arbitral tribunal will follow when faced with a joinder request like the one mentioned above. The abovementioned controversies show that parties involved in construction disputes subject to the LCIA Rules will face a certain risk of uncertainty; that is, they will not know what to expect if there is a joinder request from one of the disputants.

Notwithstanding the abovementioned, it is unlikely that the LCIA joinder provision will be applied in practice when it comes to the type of construction disputes examined here. First, tribunals conducting arbitrations under the LCIA Rules have traditionally been conservative when it comes to joinder requests. Statistics show that from 2010 until the end of 2014, 47 applications for joinder were filed and only eight applications were successful[63]. Earlier statistics show a similar tendency[64]. Furthermore, it has been stated that as of 2012 there has not yet been a case in which a third party had been joined against

---

[60] James Castello and Rocio Digon (2012) 'Maximizing Possibilities for Joinder in International Arbitration' in Arthur Rovine (ed.) *Contemporary Issues in International Arbitration and Mediation. The Fordham Papers 2011*, Martinus Nijhoff Publishers, Leiden, p. 112.

[61] This opinion has been shared by Julian Lew, Loukas Mistelis and Stefan Kröll (2003) *Comparative International Commercial Arbitration*, Kluwer Law International, The Hague, p. 390. See also Gary Born (2014) *International Commercial Arbitration, Volume II: International Arbitral Procedures*, 2nd edn, Kluwer Law International, Alphen aan den Rijn, p. 2601; Audley Sheppard (2010) 'English Arbitration Act 1996 (Chapter 23), 1996 – Arbitration Law in England, Wales and Northern Ireland', in Loukas Mistelis (ed.) *Concise International Arbitration*, Kluwer Law International, Alphen aan den Rijn, p. 774; Jean-Francois Poudret and Sébastien Besson (2007) *Comparative Law of International Arbitration*, 2nd edn, Sweet & Maxwell, London / Schulthess, p. 201; Stavros Brekoulakis (2010) *Third Parties in International Commercial Arbitration*, Oxford University Press, Oxford, p. 114 (§ 3.77), and Peter Turner and Reza Mohtashami (2012) *A Guide to the LCIA Arbitration Rules*, Oxford University Press, Oxford, p. 149 (§ 6.48–6.50).

[62] Anthony Diamond (1998) *The New (1998) LCIA Rules, Multi-Party Arbitrations – Formation of and Vacancies in the Tribunal – The Removal of Arbitrators – Truncated Tribunals*, London Court of International Arbitration, New Arbitration Rules 1998, Centre of Construction Law and Management Conference at King's College London, p. 2 (5 June).

[63] This statistical data has been communicated to the author in an e-mail sent by the LCIA on 19 February 2015.

[64] It has been reported that from the introduction of the joinder provision in the LCIA Rules in 1998 until 2010, approximately ten applications for joinder were filed and those applications were successful only on a few occasions. See, in that regard, Working Group II, *47th Session (10–14 September 2007, Vienna)*, UN Doc A/CN.9/WG.II/WP.147/Add.1, para. 8. See also Richard Bamforth and Katerina Maidment, '"All join in or not"? How well does international arbitration cater for disputes involving multiple parties or related claims?', in *27 ASA Bulletin*, no. 1 (2009), p. 12; Simon Nesbitt (2010) 'LCIA Arbitration Rules', in Loukas Mistelis (ed.) *Concise International Arbitration*, Kluwer Law International, Alphen aan den Rijn, p. 442; James Castello and Rocio Digon (2012) 'Maximizing Possibilities for Joinder in International Arbitration' in Arthur Rovine (ed.) *Contemporary Issues in International Arbitration and Mediation. The Fordham Papers 2011*, Martinus Nijhoff Publishers, Leiden, pp. 114–116.

the wishes of one of the original parties[65]. Secondly, the party to be joined usually does not have an incentive to participate in multi-party arbitration. For example, a subcontractor would normally not agree to be joined in a main contract arbitration concerning defective work allegedly caused by the same subcontractor where he would have to defend a recourse claim filed by the main contractor. The subcontractor would prefer to resolve his dispute with the main contractor in a separate arbitration where the tribunal might take a position that is more favourable to him. Therefore, the joinder provision has often been considered as unsatisfactory for main contractors[66]. Similarly, the architect or the engineer does not have an interest to be joined in an arbitration between the employer and the main contractor in case of doubts that the deviations in the construction works are due to alleged flaws in the drawings. Thus, the subcontractor, in the first case, and the architect or the engineer, in the second case, would try to thwart their participation in the pending proceeding by withholding their consent to the requested joinder[67].

The abovementioned issues will not occur if the parties agree on multi-party arbitration clauses in their contracts. These clauses can be in the form of either self-contained *ad hoc* multi-party arbitration clauses, which allow for the joinder of a third party and describe the circumstances under which such joinder will be effectuated, or clauses modifying the existing joinder article of the LCIA Rules by taking into account the individual circumstances of the case and the interests of the parties. For example, parties may clarify in their contracts that the joinder provision will be applied only in respect of certain parties (e.g. a certain subcontractor) and exclude its application in respect of other parties (e.g. sub-subcontractors and designers). In such cases, the joinder procedure, as described in the LCIA Rule will not apply as the parties will be deemed to have agreed on a different solution in their contracts.

4.4 UNCITRAL Rules[68]

The UNCITRAL Rules have been specially developed for *ad hoc* arbitrations – arbitrations that are not conducted under the auspices of an arbitral institution. Even though *ad hoc* arbitration has certain advantages[69], it is usually considered as unsuitable for handling complex arbitrations, such as those involving multiple parties and / or multiple contracts. Furthermore, the effectiveness of *ad hoc* arbitrations depends

[65] Peter Turner and Reza Mohtashami (2012) *A Guide to the LCIA Arbitration Rules*, Oxford University Press, Oxford, pp. 150–151 (§ 6.54).

[66] Jan Paulsson, Nigel Rawding and Lucy Reed (2011) *The Freshfields Guide to Arbitration Clauses in International Contracts*, 3rd edn, Kluwer Law International, Alphen aan den Rijn, p. 97.

[67] Dimitar Kondev (2015) 'Can Arbitral Rules Resolve Multi-Party / Multi-Contract Construction Disputes?', in Giovanni Iudica (ed.) *Construction Contract, Arbitration and ADR, Papers from the Annual Conference of the European Society of Construction Law (Milan, 10 October 2014)*, Editoriale Scientifica, Naples, pp. 78–79.

[68] The UNCITRAL Rules are available at http://www.uncitral.org/pdf/english/texts/arbitration/arb-rules-revised/arb-rules-revised-2010-e.pdf (accessed 25 July 2016). The UNCITRAL Rules were adopted by the United Nations Commission on International Trade Law (UNCITRAL).

[69] *Ad hoc* arbitration is usually cheaper than institutional arbitration. Furthermore, *ad hoc* arbitration is more apt to be tailored to the specific needs of the parties.

heavily on voluntary co-operation between parties and their ability to reach an agreement on procedural questions at a time when they are already in dispute[70]. However, at this stage the parties have divergent interests and are usually disinclined to cooperate. In addition, *ad hoc* arbitration usually requires a more intensive fallback on the arbitration law of the place of arbitration due to the lack of an arbitral institution administering the case. Thus, the settlement of controversies as to the appointment of arbitrators or their jurisdiction to review multi-party and / or multi-contract claims might require the assistance of local courts, which may result in protracted and costly proceedings. All these matters can be dealt with more easily and rapidly within institutional arbitration. For these reasons, the mere existence of multi-party arbitration provisions in the UNCITRAL Rules has been criticized by some authors[71].

The most recent revision of the UNCITRAL Rules took place in 2010. The inclusion of a joinder provision in the 2010 UNCITRAL Rules was seen as a *major modification* to the rules and was subject to thorough discussions within a specially established working group following an input from various arbitral institutions[72].

Joinder of third parties under the UNCITRAL Rules is regulated under Article 17.5[73]:

> The arbitral tribunal may, at the request of any party, allow one or more third persons to be joined in the arbitration as a party provided such person is a party to the arbitration agreement, unless the arbitral tribunal finds, after giving all parties, including the person or persons to be joined, the opportunity to be heard, that joinder should not be permitted because of prejudice to any of those parties. The arbitral tribunal may make a single award or several awards in respect of all parties so involved in the arbitration.

This approach has been followed by other arbitration rules suitable for *ad hoc* arbitrations. For example, the same provision can be found in the Arbitration Rules of the Chartered Institute of Arbitrators, also known as the CIArb Rules[74].

---

[70] Jan Paulsson, Nigel Rawding and Lucy Reed (2011) *The Freshfields Guide to Arbitration Clauses in International Contracts*, 3rd edn, Kluwer Law International, Alphen aan den Rijn, pp. 57–59.

[71] Nathalie Voser (2009) 'Multi-party Disputes and Joinder of Third Parties', in Albert Jan van den Berg (ed.) *50 Years of the New York Convention, ICCA International Arbitration Conference, ICCA Congress Series No. 14*, Kluwer Law International, Alphen aan den Rijn, p. 408.

[72] Working Group II, *47th Session (10–14 September 2007, Vienna)*, UN Doc A/CN.9/WG.II/WP.147/Add.1, para. 8.

[73] It has been reported that the working group updating the UNCITRAL Rules initially considered a draft joinder provision similar to the one under the LCIA Rules. However, the proposal was rejected because of concerns that it would run counter to the fundamental principle of consent of the parties in arbitration. See Clyde Croft, Christopher Kee and Jeff Waincymer (2013) *A Guide to the UNCITRAL Arbitration Rules*, Cambridge University Press, Cambridge, pp. 188–189.

[74] The CIArb Arbitration Rules entered into force on 1 December 2015. They are available at https://www.ciarb.org/docs/default-source/das/ciarb-arbitration-rules.pdf?sfvrsn=2 (accessed 25 July 2016). Unlike the previous version of the rules from 2000, which was suitable for domestic arbitrations under the English Arbitration Act 1996, the new rules can be used in both domestic and international arbitral proceedings. There was no joinder provision under the 2000 CIArb Rules. The latter rules, however, empowered an arbitrator who is appointed in two or more related arbitrations to order consolidation of these arbitrations under certain conditions. This provision is not present in the current CIArb Arbitration Rules. The 2000 CIArb Arbitration Rules are available at http://www.ciarb.org/docs/default-source/das/arbitration/ciarb-arbitration-rules-2000.pdf?sfvrsn=6 (accessed 25 July 2016).

Under the UNCITRAL Rules, the initiative for the joinder should come from one of the disputing parties. Only a person who is a party to the arbitration agreement can be joined in the pending proceedings. It is exactly for this reason that the drafters of the rules decided to use the phrase 'third persons' instead of 'third parties' because the latter term could indicate a person that stood completely outside the arbitration agreement[75]. The Working Group considered a proposal envisaging that the person to be joined should explicitly consent to the joinder but decided against this proposal because 'requiring additional agreement by the party to be joined would provide that party with a veto right, which might not be justified'[76]. Indeed, the requirement for such an additional consent was deemed to be unnecessary because the person to be joined had to be bound by the same arbitration agreement, which meant that he had agreed in advance to the application of the joinder position.

Despite the flexible position of the rules on the latter point, they remain very restrictive in their scope: only third parties – signatories to the arbitration agreement may be joined. As it has already been seen, in the construction sector there is often a need to join a party bound by a different arbitration agreement than the one on the basis of which the arbitration was initiated. Such a joinder will not be possible under the UNCITRAL Rules, unless all the relevant parties have provided otherwise in their arbitration clauses[77]. The joinder provision under the UNCITRAL Rules, as it stands, may only be applied to the type of construction disputes examined hereof in cases of an umbrella arbitration agreement binding all the multiple parties.

Interestingly, the joinder provision does not set a time limit for any joinder request. It follows from here that the joinder of a third person may be requested even after the constitution of the arbitral tribunal. In such a scenario, the third person in question may object that he was not given an opportunity to participate in the constitution of the tribunal[78]. This objection should be considered by the arbitral tribunal when hearing the parties on the joinder request. Under Article 17(5), the joinder should not be permitted if the arbitral tribunal finds that it would cause prejudice to any of the parties. Prejudice in this sense should be understood as a real prejudice to a party and not simply as the loss of the tactical advantage a party may have sought to gain by initiating a separate arbitration[79]. It is up to the tribunal to decide how to form its opinion on this question. Matters that should probably be taken into account would include the stage of the proceedings, the impact of the joinder on previous

[75] Peter Binder (2013) *Analytical Commentary to the UNCITRAL Arbitration Rules*, Sweet & Maxwell, London, pp. 185–186 (§ 17-052). See also Working Group II, *49th Session (15–19 September 2008, Vienna)*, UN Doc A/CN.9/665, para. 129.

[76] Working Group II, *49th Session (15–19 September 2008, Vienna)*, UN Doc A/CN.9/665, para. 130.

[77] David Caron and Lee Caplan (2013) *The UNCITRAL Arbitration Rules, A Commentary*, 2nd edn, Oxford University Press, Oxford, p. 56.

[78] Peter Binder (2013) *Analytical Commentary to the UNCITRAL Arbitration Rules*, Sweet & Maxwell, London, p. 187 (§ 17-060).

[79] Clyde Croft, Christopher Kee and Jeff Waincymer (2013) *A Guide to the UNCITRAL Arbitration Rules*, Cambridge University Press, Cambridge, pp. 191–192 (§ 17.26).

events, the risk of inconsistent rulings, language and geographical convenience.[80] Even if the tribunal finds that there is no prejudice to the parties, it is not obliged to join the third person in question because its powers are discretionary[81].

The Working Group discussed the question of intervention of third persons in pending arbitration but no explicit provision was included in the UNCITRAL Rules. From the report of the discussions it becomes clear that a suggestion was expressed that intervention could be allowed on the basis of Article 17(1) of the Rules, which authorized the tribunal to conduct the arbitration 'in such manner as it considers appropriate'[82]. It is the author's opinion, however, that this article cannot be construed in such a broad manner. Intervention could only be allowed on the basis of an explicit provision contained in the parties' arbitration agreements or the applicable arbitration rules. Furthermore, the suggestion that intervention is possible under Article 17(1) sits at odds with the approach under the joinder clause that only one of the main disputants may request the participation of third persons in the arbitration. It follows from here that a third person may not intervene in the proceedings upon its own initiative, unless all the parties have agreed otherwise. This opinion is shared by other scholars[83].

A consolidation provision was discussed by the Working Committee but was deleted from the final version of the rules[84]. It was acknowledged that such a clause would almost certainly appear to be unworkable in non-administered cases[85]. For example, under institutional arbitration rules containing consolidation provisions it is most often the arbitral institution that is authorized to order consolidation. In *ad hoc* arbitrations, however, there is often no such institution. Nonetheless, it has been suggested that an arbitral tribunal will not be precluded from consolidating two parallel cases if the parties have included in their arbitration clauses consolidation provisions and if the contemplated consolidation does not infringe the parties' rights to equal treatment with regard to the constitution of the arbitral tribunal[86].

---

[80] Ibid.

[81] David Caron and Lee Caplan (2013) *The UNCITRAL Arbitration Rules, A Commentary*, 2nd edn, Oxford University Press, Oxford, p. 57.

[82] Working Group II, *45th Session (11–15 September 2006, Vienna)*, UN Doc A/CN.9/614, para. 82.

[83] See Peter Binder (2013) *Analytical Commentary to the UNCITRAL Arbitration Rules*, Sweet & Maxwell, London, p. 184 (§ 17-046): 'It is…not possible for one or more third persons to unilaterally force their participation into an ongoing arbitration, even if such third person may be one of the parties to the underlying contract.'

[84] Working Group II, *47th Session (10–14 September 2007, Vienna)*, UN Doc A/CN.9/WG.II/WP.147/Add.1, para. 7. The draft consolidation clause had the following content: 'the arbitral tribunal may, on the application of any party assume jurisdiction over any claim involving the same parties and arising out of the same legal relation, provided that such claims are subject to arbitration under these Rules and that the arbitration proceedings in relation to those claims have not yet commenced'.

[85] Working Group II, *46th Session (5–9 February, New York)*, UN DOC A/CN.9/619, para. 116–120. See also Clyde Croft, Christopher Kee and Jeff Waincymer (2013) *A Guide to the UNCITRAL Arbitration Rules*, Cambridge University Press, Cambridge, pp. 195–196.

[86] Gary Born (2014) *International Commercial Arbitration, Volume II: International Arbitral Procedures*, 2nd edn 2014, Kluwer Law International, Alphen aan den Rijn, p. 2597.

4.5 Swiss Rules[87]

The Swiss Rules probably introduce the most flexible and liberal approach concerning multi-party arbitrations. Multi-party arbitration provisions were first included in the 2004 Swiss Rules, which were subsequently amended in 2012. The current version of the Swiss Rules came into force on 1 June 2012. Of particular interest for the questions examined in this book are the prima facie test on jurisdiction under Article 3(12), the consolidation provision under Article 4(1) and also Article 4(2) which deals with intervention and joinder of third persons in pending arbitration.

4.5.1 Prima facie test

The prima facie control under Article 3(12) is much more flexible than that under the ICC Rules. It applies if the respondent does not submit an answer to the notice of arbitration or if he raises an objection to the arbitration being administered under the Swiss Rules. The Arbitration Court established by the Swiss Chambers' Arbitration Institution ('**Arbitration Court**') will refuse to administer the case only if 'there is manifestly no agreement to arbitrate referring to these Rules'. It has been suggested by one of the members of the working group on the last revision of the Swiss Rules that any questions as to whether two or more claims involving more than two parties and more than two contracts may be determined in a single arbitration should be left to the arbitral tribunal and not the Arbitration Court[88].

Therefore, in case of doubt, the Arbitration Court will administer the case and transmit it for a decision to the tribunal. In that aspect, the approach under the Swiss Rules resembles the one under the CEPANI Rules.

4.5.2 Consolidation

Article 4(1), dealing with consolidation of a newly commenced case under the Swiss Rules with pending arbitration under the same rules, stipulates the following:

> Where a Notice of Arbitration is submitted between parties already involved in other arbitral proceedings pending under these Rules, the Court may decide, after consulting with the parties and any confirmed arbitrator in all proceedings, that the new case shall be consolidated with the pending arbitral proceedings. The Court may proceed in the same way where a Notice of Arbitration is submitted between parties that are not identical to the parties in the

[87] Swiss Rules of International Arbitration (Swiss Rules) of the Swiss Chambers of Commerce Association for Arbitration and Mediation, in force as from 1 June 2012, https://www.swissarbitration.org/sa/download/SRIA_english_2012.pdf (accessed 25 July 2016).

[88] See Philipp Habegger, 'The Revised Swiss Rules on International Arbitration – An Overview of the Major Changes', in *30 ASA Bulletin*, no. 2 (2012), p. 276.

pending arbitral proceedings. When rendering its decision, the Court shall take into account all relevant circumstances, including the links between the cases and the progress already made in the pending arbitral proceedings. Where the Court decides to consolidate the new case with the pending arbitral proceedings, the parties to all proceedings shall be deemed to have waived their right to designate an arbitrator, and the Court may revoke the appointment and confirmation of arbitrators and apply the provisions of Section II (Composition of the Arbitral Tribunal).

As is evident from the second sentence of this provision, there is no requirement that the parties under the separate arbitrations should be identical and therefore this clause may well find application to the type of construction disputes examined here. Furthermore, the fact that the two (or more) cases to be consolidated are not based on the same arbitration agreement should not in itself prevent consolidation[89]. There is no restriction as to when consolidation may be ordered but the progress in the existing proceedings is one of the circumstances that will be taken into account when deciding on consolidation[90]. The decision as to consolidation should be taken by the Arbitration Court, which shall consult the parties and any confirmed arbitrators and take into account any relevant circumstances[91]. Consolidation may be ordered by the Arbitration Court even on its own motion without a party's request for consolidation.

Consolidation of arbitral proceedings between parties that are not identical may raise issues concerning the constitution of the arbitral tribunal that will review the united proceedings. More particularly, consolidation can breach the principle of equality setting out that each party should have equal influence on the constitution of the arbitral tribunal. The arbitral tribunal reviewing the first arbitration should normally not review the consolidated arbitral proceedings because the parties in the second arbitration subject to consolidation were not involved in the constitution of that tribunal[92]. Therefore, the last sentence of the consolidation provision envisages that all parties shall be deemed to have waived their right to designate an arbitrator. This will enable the Arbitration Court to revoke any appointments already made and appoint all the members of the arbitral tribunal dealing with the consolidated

[89] Philipp Habegger, 'The Revised Swiss Rules on International Arbitration – An Overview of the Major Changes', in *30 ASA Bulletin*, no. 2 (2012), p. 277. See also Philippe Bärtsch and Angelina Petti (2013) 'Consolidation and Joinder (Article 4)' in Tobias Zuberbühler, Christoph Müller, and Philipp Habegger (eds) *Swiss Rules of International Arbitration: Commentary*, 2nd edn, Schulthess / JURIS, Zurich, p. 59.

[90] Philipp Habegger, 'The Revised Swiss Rules on International Arbitration – An Overview of the Major Changes', in *30 ASA Bulletin*, no. 2 (2012), p. 277. According to the author, 'Generally speaking,...the more advanced the pending proceedings are, the less justified a consolidation will be.'

[91] This approach is different from the 2004 Swiss Rules. Under the latter rules, any consolidation decision had to be taken by the Chambers that administered the new arbitral proceeding that was subject to consolidation with the pending proceeding.

[92] The parties under the second arbitration may, of course, accept the arbitral tribunal that has been constituted and confirmed under the first arbitration. In this case, no issues will arise and the tribunal may proceed with the review of the consolidated cases.

proceedings. The validity of such a waiver, however, might be influenced by the applicable national arbitration law, as evident from the well known *Dutco* case[93].

What is probably most remarkable about the consolidation clause is that it does not explicitly require the consent of the parties. The same applies to Article 4(2), which deals with joinder and intervention and is further examined below. There are very few equivalents of these clauses in other arbitration rules[94]. Literally read, the consolidation provision would allow the Arbitration Court to unite an arbitration between an employer and a design professional with another arbitration between the employer and a main contractor concerning the same construction project even if all the parties involved object to the consolidation. This flexible solution under the Swiss Rules has been extensively debated. Some scholars are of the opinion that Article 4 gives the arbitral tribunal far-reaching powers to disregard the lack of consent of the parties involved upon deciding on consolidation, joinder or intervention[95]. More particularly, they apprehend that consolidation, joinder and intervention are possible even in cases where consent thereto is not expressed by the parties in their agreements, as these legal mechanisms are envisaged under the arbitration rules to which the parties have referred in their arbitration agreements. Thus, by agreeing to apply the Swiss Rules, the parties have consented in advance to the possible multi-party arbitration solutions and the relevant consequences pertaining to these

[93] *Siemens AG and BKMI Industrienlagen Gmbh v. Dutco Construction Company*, Cour de Cassation, 7 January 1992 (*XVIII Yearbook Commercial Arbitration*, 1993, pp. 140–142). The court reached the conclusion that under French law 'the principle of the equality of the parties in the appointment of the arbitrators is a matter of public policy; one cannot therefore waive it until after the dispute has arisen'. For further details concerning the *Dutco* case and its potential implications, see Subsection 6.2.3.4. However, it has been stated that such a waiver will be valid under Swiss law as long as the principle of equality is preserved (see Philippe Bärtsch and Angelina Petti (2013) 'Consolidation and Joinder (Article 4)' in Tobias Zuberbühler, Christoph Müller, and Philipp Habegger (eds) *Swiss Rules of International Arbitration: Commentary*, 2nd edn, Schulthess / Juris, Zurich, p. 61).

[94] See, for example, the Construction Industry Arbitration Rules and the ICDR Rules in their part concerning joinder. An analysis of these rules is provided in Section 4.6.

[95] Philippe Bärtsch and Angelina M. Petti (2013) 'Consolidation and Joinder (Article 4)' in Tobias Zuberbühler, Christoph Müller, and Philipp Habegger (eds) *Swiss Rules of International Arbitration: Commentary*, 2nd edn, Schulthess / Juris, Zurich, pp. 58–59, Philippe Gilliéron and Luc Pittet (2005) 'Part 1: Introductory Rules', in Tobias Zuberbühler, Christoph Müller, and Philipp Habegger (eds) *Swiss Rules of International Arbitration: Commentary*, Kluwer Law International, Alphen aan den Rijn, pp. 36–44; Dorothée Schramm (2013) 'Chapter 3, Part II: Commentary on the Swiss Rules, Article 4 [Consolidation and Joinder]' in M. Arroyo (ed.) *Arbitration in Switzerland: The Practitioner's Guide*, Kluwer Law International, Alphen aan den Rijn, pp. 360–369. See also Richard Bamforth and Katerina Maidment, '"All join in or not"? How well does international arbitration cater for disputes involving multiple parties or related claims?', in *27 ASA Bulletin*, no. 1 (2009), p. 12; Jean-Francois Poudret and Sébastien Besson (2007) *Comparative Law of International Arbitration*, 2nd edn, Sweet & Maxwell, London, p. 201; Pierre Karrer (2013) 'Chapter V, Swiss Rules', in Rolf Schütze (ed.) *Institutional Arbitration, Article-by-Article Commentary*, C. H. Beck / Hart / Nomos, Munich, p. 378; Stavros Brekoulakis (2010) *Third Parties in International Commercial Arbitration*, Oxford University Press, Oxford, p. 118 (§ 3.96), and Christoph Brunner, 'The Swiss Rules of International Arbitration: An Overview for Prospective Users', in *8 Zeitschrift für Schiedsverfahren*, no. 5 (2010), pp. 250–251.

solutions[96]. Other authors suggest that the wording of Article 4 cannot be a substitute for the parties' consent and claim that such consent is still required[97]. The opinions of the parties will, of course, be one of the circumstances that the Arbitration Court is obliged to consider when deciding on consolidation. The Arbitration Court should also consult with any confirmed arbitrator(s) in the proceedings subject to consolidation[98]. Additionally, the Court should consider further circumstances, such as the link between the disputes (both in terms of substance and procedure), the progress in the pending proceedings, the possible delay in the proceedings resulting from the consolidation, the compatibility of the seats of arbitration in both proceedings, the risk of conflicting awards, and also other relevant factors[99].

It has been noted that the Arbitration Court has adopted a restrictive approach towards consolidation. Even though, theoretically speaking, consolidation may take place even over the objection of one or all parties, the Arbitration Court will generally allow consolidation only if it has been endorsed by the parties[100].

---

[96] Ruth Stackpool-Moore (2014) 'Joinder and Consolidation – Examining Best Practice in the Swiss, HKIAC and ICC Rules', in Nathalie Voser (ed.) *Ten Years of the Swiss Rules of International Arbitration*, ASA Special Series No. 44, JurisNet LLC, New York, NY, pp. 19, 28; Gary Born (2012) *International Arbitration: Law and Practice*, Kluwer Law International, Alphen aan den Rijn, pp. 228–229; Andrea Marco Steingruber (2012) *Consent in International Arbitration*, Oxford University Press, Oxford, § 10.17, 10-38.

[97] Andrea Meier (2007) *Einbezug Dritter vor internationalen Schiedsgerichten*, Schulthess, Zurich, p. 140, and Philipp Habegger, 'The Revised Swiss Rules on International Arbitration – An Overview of the Major Changes', in *30 ASA Bulletin*, no. 2 (2012), p. 280. See also Lara Pair (2012) *Consolidation in International Commercial Arbitration, The ICC and Swiss Rules*, International Commerce and Arbitration Volume 10, Eleven International Publishing, The Hague, p. 70, where the author has stated: 'The provision on consolidation permits only the procedural mechanism, but does not expand the original arbitration clause.'

[98] This consultation would enable the arbitrators to express their opinion about the appropriateness of the prospective consolidation and also to perform additional conflict checks, which are necessary because of the inclusion of new parties in pending arbitration. This is especially relevant if the same tribunal is going to deal with the consolidated proceedings.

[99] See Dorothée Schramm (2013) 'Chapter 3, Part II: Commentary on the Swiss Rules, Article 4 [Consolidation and Joinder]' in Manuel Arroyo (ed.) *Arbitration in Switzerland: The Practitioner's Guide*, Kluwer Law International, Alphen aan den Rijn, pp. 360–369. According to the author, the Arbitration Court should also take into account the risk of setting aside or non-recognition / non-enforcement of the award due to, among other considerations, revocation or upholding of arbitrators' appointments, the legitimate interests of the parties in not involving other parties and / or keeping aspects of their dispute confidential, as well as the additional costs that consolidation would cause to the resisting party. Other factors concerning the compatibility of the arbitrations should also be taken into account. These include: applicable procedure (expedited or non-expedited procedure), number of arbitrators, the language of the arbitration, existence of any specific arrangements regarding the arbitral procedure that may make consolidation practically burdensome or otherwise inappropriate, etc.

[100] Philipp Habegger 'The Revised Swiss Rules on International Arbitration – An Overview of the Major Changes', in *30 ASA Bulletin*, no. 2 (2012), p. 277. According to the author, 'Practice has shown that the Chambers ordered consolidation only in limited and justifiable circumstances, and usually only when this was endorsed by the parties concerned. It can be expected that the Court will continue to adopt a restrictive approach.' See also Philippe Bärtsch and Angelina Petti (2013) 'Consolidation and Joinder (Article 4)' in Tobias Zuberbühler, Christoph Müller, and Philipp Habegger (eds) *Swiss Rules of International Arbitration: Commentary*, 2nd edn, Schulthess / Juris, Zurich, pp. 58–59.

4.5.3 Joinder and intervention

Pursuant to Article 4(2) of the Swiss Rules:

> Where one or more third persons request to participate in arbitral proceedings already pending under these Rules or where a party to pending arbitral proceedings under these Rules requests that one or more third persons participate in the arbitration, the arbitral tribunal shall decide on such request, after consulting with all of the parties, including the person or persons to be joined, taking into account all relevant circumstances.

This article deals with both joinder and intervention of third parties in pending arbitration[101]. Unlike the case with consolidation, a decision on a request for joinder or intervention will be taken by the arbitral tribunal and not by the Arbitration Court. There is no time limit for making the request but any delay may be considered by the tribunal. The request for joinder can be made either by the claimant or the respondent. As mentioned above, the parties' consent is not explicitly required for the joinder or intervention. Thus, it seems that this article may find application to cases where the parties have not addressed multi-party arbitration in their contracts. Therefore, if a main contractor asks for the joinder of a subcontractor in his arbitration with the employer, the consent of both the employer and the subcontractor will not be necessary. Similarly, upon the subcontractor's request for intervention in an arbitration pending between the employer and the main contractor, the consent of the main disputants is not required either. It has already been mentioned that the opinion of scholars on this flexible approach is bifurcated[102]. Some are of the opinion that the mere reference to the Swiss Rules is tantamount to consent to joinder or intervention. Interestingly, one author has mentioned a case where an arbitrator acting under the Swiss Rules held that a third party could be joined under Article 4.2 over an opponent's objection even in the absence of an agreement to arbitrate because this article did not require such an agreement[103]. Other authors reckon that the reference to

[101] It has been stated that the clause is worded in a broad way, which could encompass both 'main intervention' and 'side intervention' (for the difference between these two forms, please see Subsection 2.2.3), as well as filing of *amicus curiae* briefs. See Dorothée Schramm (2013) 'Chapter 3, Part II: Commentary on the Swiss Rules, Article 4 [Consolidation and Joinder]' in Manuel Arroyo (ed.) *Arbitration in Switzerland: The Practitioner's Guide*, Kluwer Law International, Alphen aan den Rijn, pp. 364–365, and Philipp Habegger, 'The Revised Swiss Rules on International Arbitration – An Overview of the Major Changes', in *30 ASA Bulletin*, no. 2 (2012), p. 278.

[102] Please see the aforementioned analysis on the consolidation clause under the Swiss Rules. See also Philipp Habegger, 'The Revised Swiss Rules on International Arbitration – An Overview of the Major Changes', in *30 ASA Bulletin*, no. 2 (2012), p. 278.

[103] Christopher Koch, 'Judicial Activism and the Limits of Institutional Arbitration in Multiparty Disputes', in *28 ASA Bulletin*, no. 2 (2010), p. 391 (see footnote 23 in the article). The decision of the arbitrator to join the third party was referred to the Swiss Federal Tribunal. The parties settled the case and therefore no decision was taken on this matter.

Article 4.2 cannot serve as a substitute for consent[104]. To support the latter statement, an argument has been made that parties' consent is still required because Article 4(2) does not explicitly state that such consent is not necessary[105]. A third group of scholars adopt an intermediate position. They are of the opinion that joinder will be admissible against a resisting disputant if the latter could have foreseen at the time of conclusion of the contract that the party requesting the joinder would potentially have an interest in including the third person in the resolution of the subject matter of the dispute[106]. Thus, it could be asserted, for example, that the employer could have foreseen that the main contractor might have an interest in involving his subcontractors in the arbitration between the employer and the main contractor if that arbitration concerns subcontractors' works because of the recourse claim which the main contractor might have against his subcontractors. In any case, this *foreseeability* test rests on subjective assessment and the outcome of its application will be far from certain.

Upon deciding on a request for joinder or intervention, the arbitral tribunal will have to consult with all parties and take into consideration all relevant circumstances. These circumstances are similar to the ones considered by the Arbitration Court when deciding on consolidation.

It should also be noted that unlike Article 4(1), Article 4(2) does not envisage a waiver of parties' rights in the appointment of the arbitral tribunal and the possibility for revocation of appointments and confirmations of arbitrators. This raises additional issues when it comes to joinder of third parties against their will, as they do not have a say in the way the tribunal is constituted. Therefore, it seems that a joinder of such a reluctant third party will only be possible if the latter accepts the already appointed and confirmed tribunal[107]. Otherwise, if the arbitral tribunal proceeds and renders an award against this

---

[104] Philip Habegger, for example, belongs to this second group of scholars. See Philipp Habegger, 'The Revised Swiss Rules on International Arbitration – An Overview of the Major Changes', in *30 ASA Bulletin*, no. 2 (2012), p. 280, where the author has stated that 'Article 4(2) cannot serve as a substitute for the consent of either the parties to the arbitration or the third person' and also that 'the provision only sets out the procedural framework for joining a third person to a pending proceeding and does not in itself create a jurisdictional basis over the third person or persons concerned.' See also are Philippe Bärtsch and Angelina Petti (2013) 'Consolidation and Joinder (Article 4)' in Tobias Zuberbühler, Christoph Müller, and Philipp Habegger (eds) *Swiss Rules of International Arbitration: Commentary*, 2nd edn, Schulthess / Juris, Zurich, pp. 63–65, and Gary Born (2014) *International Commercial Arbitration, Volume II: International Arbitral Procedures*, 2nd edn, Kluwer Law International, Alphen aan den Rijn, pp. 2600–2601.

[105] Paolo Marzolini (2012) 'Is the Parties' Consent Still an Overriding Principle for Joinder and Intervention of Third Parties in International Commercial Arbitration?' in Daniele Favalli, Xavier Favre-Bulle, Andreas Furrer *et al.* (eds) *Selected Papers on International Arbitration: Volume 2 Series on International Arbitration SAA*, Stämpfli Verlag, Bern, pp. 126–127. According to the author: 'Article 4(2) does not state in so many words that consent is not required under the Swiss Rules with regard to intervention and joinder...The departure from such a general and fundamental principle [of parties' consent] would have called for an express reference to this effect by the provision under consideration.'

[106] Dorothée Schramm (2013) 'Chapter 3, Part II: Commentary on the Swiss Rules, Article 4 [Consolidation and Joinder]' in Manuel Arroyo (ed.) *Arbitration in Switzerland: The Practitioner's Guide*, Kluwer Law International, Alphen aan den Rijn, pp. 367–368.

[107] Philippe Bärtsch and Angelina Petti (2013) 'Consolidation and Joinder (Article 4)' in Tobias Zuberbühler, Christoph Müller, and Philipp Habegger (eds) *Swiss Rules of International Arbitration: Commentary*, 2nd edn, Schulthess / Juris, Zurich, p. 66.

recalcitrant third party, the risk of setting aside of the award or its non-recognition and / or non-enforcement will be imminent. Intervention should not give rise to similar concerns as the third party in question wants to participate in the proceedings on its own motion. Therefore, it can reasonably be assumed that the third party has accepted the appointed tribunal when making its request for intervention.

As can be seen from the above analysis, the Arbitration Court (in case of consolidation) and the arbitral tribunal (in case of joinder or intervention) enjoy broad discretion when deciding on multi-party arbitration matters. They should consider a significant number of factors in their assessment and take a decision that may vary widely depending on the particular circumstances of the case. The increased power of the Arbitration Court or the arbitral tribunal, as the case may be, inevitably results in a lesser degree of control by the parties over the way the arbitral proceedings are conducted. Hence, contracting parties will face some uncertainty when it comes to the prospective conduct of multi-party arbitration.

4.6 Rules adopted by the American Arbitration Association ('AAA')[108]

Two types of arbitration rules adopted by the AAA are examined in this section. These are the Construction Industry Arbitration Rules and the ICDR International Arbitration Rules.

4.6.1 Construction Industry Arbitration Rules ('CIAR')[109]

The CIAR are primarily designed for construction cases based on domestic standard forms used in the United States. It has been suggested that the rules can also be applied in international cases subject to parties' agreement to that effect[110]. In any case, the application of the CIAR remains limited to the domestic US construction industry. The CIAR are discussed in this book because of their novel and peculiar approach to multi-party arbitration.

Like the Swiss Rules, the CIAR also adopt a flexible approach because these rules do not explicitly require the parties' consent to multi-party arbitration. Clause 7 of the Regular Track Procedure (also known as 'R-7'), which deals with both consolidation and joinder, provides as follows:

> (a) If the parties are unable to agree to consolidate related arbitrations or to the joinder of parties to an ongoing arbitration, the AAA shall directly appoint a single arbitrator (hereinafter

[108] The American Arbitration Association (www.adr.org, accessed 25 July 2016) is a public service, non-profit organization that offers a broad range of dispute resolution services. It has its headquarters in New York, and it has offices in many major cities throughout the United States and around the world, including in Dublin, Mexico City and Singapore.

[109] Construction Industry Arbitration Rules and Mediation Procedures, Including Procedures for Large, Complex Construction Disputes, in force as from 1 July 2015, https://www.adr.org/aaa/ShowProperty?nodeId=/UCM/ADRSTG_004219&revision=latestreleased (accessed 1 August 2016).

[110] Patricia Galloway, Luis Martinez and Michael Marra, 'Dispute Resolution under FIDIC – The Parties' Options', in 9 *Transnational Dispute Management (TDM)*, no. 7 (December 2012), pp. 8, 11, https://www.adr.org/aaa/ShowPDF?doc=ADRSTAGE2009402 (accessed 25 July 2016).

referred to as the R-7 arbitrator) for the limited purpose of deciding whether related arbitrations should be consolidated or parties joined…

The single arbitrator who is appointed to decide on the consolidation or the joinder request is chosen from a panel of construction attorneys who have experience with these issues[111]. The request for joinder or consolidation should come from one of the parties involved in the proceedings. If the R-7 arbitrator decides that the separate arbitrations should be consolidated or that the additional party should be joined, that arbitrator may also establish a process for selecting arbitrators for any ongoing or newly constituted case[112].

R-7 also introduces certain time constraints as to the filing of consolidation and joinder requests. Any such requests must be submitted prior to the appointment of an arbitrator who is going to review the merits of the dispute(s) or within 90 days of the AAA's determination that all administrative filing requirements concerning the demand for arbitration have been complied with, whichever is later[113]. Any requests after this date will not be admitted, unless the arbitrator reviewing the merits of the dispute(s) determines that good cause was shown for such late request[114]. Furthermore, R-7 regulates the time frames within which the parties, including the party to be joined in the case of joinder, should provide their responses to any consolidation or joinder requests. These responses should be given within 10 days or 14 days, respectively, after the AAA's notice of the request[115]. If a party participating in the pending arbitration fails to object to the requested joinder, this party shall be deemed to have waived any objection which it may have in relation to such a request[116].

It should be mentioned that the above timing requirements were introduced with the amendments of the CIAR which took effect on 1 July 2015. These amendments aimed to streamline the process of filing multi-party arbitration requests so that any such requests are served at the outset of the arbitration. The earlier CIAR, from October 2009, did not provide for any time limits as to when requests for joinder or consolidation may be served. The principal position under the CIAR is that the 2015 amendments will apply to any arbitration subject to the CIAR initiated on or after 1 July 2015 regardless of the date when the relevant construction agreements were executed[117].

On the basis of the wording of R-7, it may be argued that the CIAR go a step further than the Swiss Rules in their flexibility to multi-party arbitration for two reasons. First, the clause does not set any criteria or circumstances that should be considered by the R-7 arbitrator when deciding on joinder or consolidation, and in this way it vests that arbitrator with a larger degree of discretion. Secondly, the CIAR explicitly provide that the clause may be invoked even if the parties (or some of them) disagree on joinder or

[111] R-7 (g) of the CIAR.
[112] R-7 (e) of the CIAR.
[113] R-7(a) of the CIAR.
[114] Ibid.
[115] R-7(b) and R-7(c) of the CIAR.
[116] R-7(c) of the CIAR.
[117] However, if the parties have explicitly stipulated in their arbitration clauses that the rules in effect at the time of execution of the respective contract are to be applied, the AAA will apply these rules.

consolidation. The reference to the CIAR therefore constitutes the parties' anticipatory consent for the conduct of multi-party arbitration. The comparison between the original and the current wording of R-7 further strengthens this conclusion. While R-7, as originally introduced in the CIAR, envisaged that 'all involved parties will endeavor to agree on a process to effectuate the consolidation or joinder' to the extent 'the parties' agreement or the law provides for consolidation or joinder of related arbitration', the current wording of R-7 has removed any references to parties' agreements. The purpose of this was to avoid any obstacles to the application of R-7 based on disputes concerning the question of whether the parties' contracts provided for multi-party arbitration[118]. However, some scholars in the United States have suggested that the power of the arbitrator to order consolidation or joinder should be limited only to cases where the parties' contracts explicitly authorize this[119].

4.6.2 ICDR Rules[120]

The International Centre for Dispute Resolution ('**ICDR**')[121] is the international division of the AAA with distinct international procedures, administration and panels of arbitrators. Recent statistics show that the ICDR has experienced a steady increase in the international cases that it administers and that construction cases are the leading type of disputes filed with the ICDR[122]. In 2014, the ICDR completed a comprehensive review of the ICDR Rules and issued a revised set of rules, which deal with multi-party arbitration for the first time.

---

[118] See AAA Construction Rules Updated: An Interview with Catherine Shanks, Vice President, Construction Division, American Arbitration Association, in *64 Dispute Resolution Journal*, no. 4 (November 2009–January 2010), p. 44.

[119] See James Butler, 'AAA Construction Rules', in *65 Dispute Resolution Journal*, no. 2/3 (2010), pp. 96–103. The author argues that the Supreme Court's Ruling in *Stort-Nielsen S.A. et al. v. AnimalFeeds Corporation* (*Stolt-Nielsen S.A. v. Animalfeeds Int'l Corp.*, 130 S.Ct. 1758, 1774 ((U.S. S.Ct. 2010)), http://www.supremecourt.gov/opinions/09pdf/08-1198.pdf (accessed 25 July 2016), might have a significant impact on the R-7 consolidation procedure. That case dealt with class arbitration and not with consolidation. It confirmed that arbitrators may not order class arbitration if the arbitration agreements are silent on the matter. The Supreme Court further stated that: 'An arbitration agreement must be enforced notwithstanding the presence of other persons who are parties to the underlying dispute but not to the arbitration agreement.' Therefore, if arbitrators order class arbitration without an explicit authorization from the parties, they will exceed their powers and their award may be set aside. The author has argued that the same considerations should apply to consolidation by analogy.

[120] International Dispute Resolution Procedures (Including Mediation and Arbitration Rules), in force as from 1 June 2014, https://www.icdr.org/icdr/ShowProperty?nodeId=/UCM/ADRSTAGE2020868&revision=latestreleased (accessed 25 July 2016).

[121] The ICDR was established in 1996. It maintains specialized administrative facilities in New York and has also offices in Mexico City and Singapore, as well as a senior executive domiciled in Europe serving Europe, the Middle East and Africa. More information about the ICDR may be found at www.icdr.org (accessed 25 July 2016).

[122] See The ICDR International Arbitration Reporter, September 2013/Volume 4, https://www.adr.org/cs/groups/international/documents/document/z2uy/mde1/~edisp/adrstage2015007.pdf (accessed 25 July 2016). According to the information disclosed therein, in 2012 the ICDR administered 996 international cases involving parties from 92 countries. The ICDR has experienced a constant increase in the number of its international cases since 2007. Furthermore, international construction cases are the leading type of dispute filed with the ICDR in recent years.

Joinder under the ICDR Rules is addressed in Article 7. Pursuant to the latter article:

> A party wishing to join an additional party to the arbitration shall submit to the Administrator a Notice of Arbitration against the additional party. No additional party may be joined after the appointment of any arbitrator, unless all parties, including the additional party, otherwise agree...Any joinder shall be subject to the provisions of Articles 12 and 19.

The function of the Administrator under the above clause is actually carried out by the ICDR itself. Like other institutional rules, such as the Swiss Rules and the CIAR, the ICDR Rules are very flexible because they do not require parties' consent to the joinder. The ICDR Rules introduce a time limit for making a joinder request; this should be before the appointment of any arbitrator. In this matter, the ICDR Rules closely resemble the approach under Article 7 of the ICC Rules and Article 11 of the CEPANI Rules. As mentioned above, the purpose of this limitation is to avoid a situation where a third party is joined in a pending arbitration with an already constituted tribunal. Thus, the restriction aims at avoiding the risk of setting aside, non-recognition or non-enforcement of the award due to unequal treatment of the parties in the constitution of the arbitral tribunal. Any joinder request shall also be subject to Article 19 of the ICDR Rules that deals with the arbitral jurisdiction. If a jurisdictional objection is raised by a party, the Administrator will administer the case and refer the objection to the arbitral tribunal. The latter shall have the power to decide whether the joinder is admissible once it has been constituted[123]. This solution resembles the approach under the Swiss Rules and the CEPANI Rules.

Article 8 of the ICDR Rules deals with consolidation:

> (1) At the request of a party, the Administrator may appoint a consolidation arbitrator, who will have the power to consolidate two or more arbitrations pending under these Rules, or these and other arbitration rules administered by the AAA or ICDR, into a single arbitration where:
> (a) the parties have expressly agreed to consolidation; or
> (b) all of the claims and counterclaims in the arbitrations are made under the same arbitration agreement; or
> (c) the claims, counterclaims, or setoffs in the arbitrations are made under more than one arbitration agreement; the arbitrations involve the same parties; the disputes in the arbitrations arise in connection with the same legal relationship; and the consolidation arbitrator finds the arbitration agreements to be compatible...

The provision continues and describes the procedure for appointment of the consolidation arbitrator[124], the circumstances that the latter should consider[125] and the

[123] Article 19(1) and Article 19(4) of the ICDR Rules.

[124] Under Article 8(2) of the ICDR Rules, the ICDR will first invite the parties to agree on a procedure for the appointment of the consolidation arbitrator, and will proceed with the appointment if an agreement is not reached within 15 days. The consolidation arbitrator should not be an arbitrator who is already appointed in one of the proceedings subject to consolidation, unless all parties agree otherwise.

[125] Under Article 8(3) of the ICDR Rules, these circumstances include the applicable law, the appointment of arbitrators in the pending proceedings, the progress in the arbitrations, the link between the proceedings, the interests of justice and efficiency.

appointment of the arbitrators who will conduct the consolidated proceedings. If the proceedings are consolidated, they shall be consolidated in the arbitration that commenced first, unless the parties have agreed otherwise or the consolidation arbitrator finds otherwise[126]. In the case of consolidation, each party shall be deemed to have waived its right to nominate an arbitrator and the consolidation arbitrator is empowered to revoke any appointments already made and select one of the previously appointed tribunals to serve in the consolidated proceedings[127]. If necessary, the ICDR will complete the appointment of the tribunal[128]. The consolidation arbitrator should not be appointed as an arbitrator in the consolidated proceedings, unless all parties agree otherwise[129].

The figure of the consolidation arbitrator is derived from the CIAR. However, the ICDR consolidation clause is narrower in scope than the consolidation clause under the CIAR. Under the ICDR Rules, consolidation of proceedings concerning construction disputes which are both multi-party and multi-contract in character will be possible on the rare occasions where the parties have included ad hoc multi-party arbitration agreements in their contracts or have agreed to consolidation in the course of the proceedings (where Article 8(1)(a) can be invoked) or are bound by an umbrella arbitration agreement (where Article 8(1)(b) could come into play). In fact, the three alternative scenarios for consolidation under letters (a), (b) and (c) almost literally repeat the wording of Article 10 of the ICC Rules.

Therefore, if a party is willing to arbitrate its claims in a multi-party setup under the ICDR Rules but has not addressed multi-party arbitration in its contract, it should make sure to request the joinder of any additional parties against which it may have claims under Article 7 of the ICDR Rules[130]. If the requesting party decides to start separate arbitrations against the respondents, the opportunity for multi-party arbitration will be lost because of the narrow scope of the consolidation clause[131].

4.7 *Vienna Rules*[132]

Arbitrations under the Vienna Rules are administered by the Vienna International Arbitral Centre of the Austrian Federal Economic Chamber ('**VIAC**')[133]. In recent years the number of international cases administered by VIAC has increased, which has

[126] Article 8(5) of the ICDR Rules.
[127] Article 8(6) of the ICDR Rules.
[128] Ibid.
[129] Ibid.
[130] Dimitar Hristoforov Kondev, 'Do Recent Overhauls of Arbitration Rules Respond to the Need for Multi-Party Arbitration in the Construction Industry?', in *32 International Construction Law Review*, no. 1 (2015), p. 93.
[131] Ibid.
[132] VIAC Rules of Arbitration and Mediation, in force as from 1 July 2013, http://www.viac.eu/en/arbitration/arbitration-rules-vienna (accessed 25 July 2016).
[133] For more information about VIAC, see http://www.viac.eu/en/(accessed 25 July 2016).

fortified VIAC as one of the leading centres for international arbitration in Central and Eastern Europe[134]. The majority of claims submitted to the VIAC concern disputes under construction and engineering contracts[135].

The Vienna Rules were recently revised and the current version of the rules entered into force on 1 July 2013. The earlier 2006 Vienna Rules contained a regime for multi-party proceedings that was considered fairly complicated and conceptually rooted more in the Austrian civil procedure than in international arbitration practice[136]. Therefore, this regime was revised in the new Vienna Rules. Joinder of third parties and consolidation are now regulated under Articles 14 and 15 of the new Vienna Rules.

4.7.1 Joinder

The 2006 Vienna Rules did not contain a joinder provision. Pursuant to Article 14 of the new Vienna Rules:

> (1) The joinder of a third party in an arbitration, as well as the manner of such joinder, shall be decided by the arbitral tribunal upon the request of a party or a third party after hearing all parties and the third party to be joined as well as after considering all relevant circumstances...
>
> (3) If a Request for Joinder of a third party is made within a Statement of Claim,
>
> 3.1 it shall be submitted to the Secretariat. The provisions of Article 7 et seqq shall apply by analogy. The Secretary General shall transmit the Statement of Claim to the third party to be joined as well to the other parties for their comments. If the joinder is requested by the third party, the Secretary General shall submit copies of the Request for Joinder to the parties to the pending arbitration for comments.
>
> 3.2 the third party may participate in the constitution of the arbitral tribunal pursuant to Article 18 if no arbitrator has yet been appointed.
>
> 3.3 the arbitral tribunal may return the Statement of Claim with a Request for Joinder of a third party to the Secretariat to be treated in separate proceedings. In this case, the Board may revoke any confirmed nomination or appointment of arbitrators and order the new constitution of the arbitral tribunal or arbitral tribunals in accordance with Article 17 et seqq.

---

[134] Franz Schwarz and Christian Konrad, 'The Revised Vienna Rules. An Overview of Some Significant Changes (and a Preview of the New Austrian Arbitration Law 2014)', in *31 ASA Bulletin*, no. 4 (2013), p. 791. According to the authors, the workload of VIAC has increased steadily since 2006, with the VIAC administrating some 70 to 90 international disputes each year, often with very significant amounts in dispute.

[135] Marguerita Sedrati-Müller (2013) 'Arbitration Rules and Country Reports: Austria', in Nicole Conrad, Peter Munch and Jonathan Black-Branch (eds) *International Commercial Arbitration, Standard Clauses and Forms Commentary*, Helbing Lichtenhahn / C. H. Beck / Hart / Nomos, Basel, p. 242 (§ 6.31). According to the author, roughly one-third (approximately 28%) of the submitted disputes are construction and engineering cases followed by general trade (18%), distribution (12%), etc.

[136] Franz Schwarz and Christian Konrad, 'The Revised Vienna Rules. An Overview of Some Significant Changes (and a Preview of the New Austrian Arbitration Law 2014)', in *31 ASA Bulletin*, no. 4 (2013), pp. 799–800. For a commentary on the 2006 Vienna Rules, see Franc Schwartz and Christian Konrad, 'The New Vienna Rules' in *23 Arbitration International*, no. 4 (2007), pp. 601–643.

The quoted provision covers both joinder and intervention and refers to them with the generic term *joinder*. Article 14(3) deals with the situation where the joinder of a third party is requested together with the statement of claim. The question may arise whether this article may be applied to situations comprising the filing of a single request for arbitration against multiple parties. For example, at the outset of the arbitration the employer under a *build-only* contractual model simultaneously files a statement of claim against both the main contractor and the designer. In the author's opinion, the application of Article 14(3) to those cases may be possible but this is debatable[137].

Any decision concerning joinder under the Vienna Rules should be taken by the arbitral tribunal after hearing all parties and considering all circumstances. It is up to the tribunal to decide what circumstances to consider. The tribunal has full discretionary power to decide whether to admit the joinder or not. Multi-party arbitration may take place if requested by one of the main disputants (in the case of joinder) or by a third party (in the case of intervention). Unlike the ICC Rules, there is no time limitation with regard to the filing of the joinder request.

Like the Swiss Rules and the ICDR Rules, the joinder provision is flexible. It does not demand the explicit consent of the parties to the joinder. The arbitral tribunal should hear the parties and the third party but is not bound by their opinions. Furthermore, there is no explicit requirement that the main disputants and the third party to be joined should be bound by a single arbitration agreement and therefore it seems that the clause may be applied in a multi-contract context. Some authors are of the opinion that the availability of compatible arbitration clauses providing for VIAC arbitration in the multiple contracts might constitute the parties' agreement to such joinder[138]. Not surprisingly, there are contrary opinions as well[139]. Furthermore, according to some authors, joinder under Article 14 may be possible only if there is a single arbitration agreement binding all parties[140]. It has also been stated that 'Article

[137] Paul Oberhammer and Christian Koller (2014) 'Article 14, Joinder of Third Parties and Consolidation' in Vienna International Arbitration Centre of the Austrian Federal Economic Chamber (ed.) *Handbook Vienna Rules, A Practitioner's Guide*, WKÖ-Service Gmbh, Bad Vöslau, p. 70 (§ 1). According to the authors: 'Art. 14 governs the joinder of third parties in an arbitration that has already been instituted between other parties according to the Vienna Rules.' Therefore, it seems that the authors exclude the application of this article to cases comprising the filing of a single request for arbitration against multiple parties.

[138] See Franz Schwarz and Christian Konrad, 'The Revised Vienna Rules. An Overview of Some Significant Changes (and a Preview of the New Austrian Arbitration Law 2014)', in *31 ASA Bulletin*, no. 4 (2013), p. 802. However, the authors have stated that the appropriateness of this solution may also depend on the applicable substantive law and on each party's ability to participate in the constitution of the tribunal.

[139] Paul Oberhammer and Christian Koller (2014) 'Article 14, Joinder of Third Parties and Consolidation' in Vienna International Arbitration Centre of the Austrian Federal Economic Chamber (ed.) *Handbook Vienna Rules, A Practitioner's Guide*, WKÖ-Service Gmbh, Bad Vöslau, pp. 74–75 (§ 18). The authors have stated with regard to situations where the parties and the third party are bound by separate agreements containing compatible VIAC arbitration agreement that 'reference to Art. 14 cannot be understood as a general advance consent to the joinder of third parties'.

[140] See Nikolaus Pitkowitz (2015) 'Chapter II: The Arbitrator and the Arbitration Procedure, Multi-Party Arbitrations – Joinder and Consolidation under the Vienna Rules 2013', in Christian Klausegger, Peter Klein, Florian Kremslehner *et al.* (eds) *Austrian Yearbook on International Arbitration*, Manz'sche Verlags- und Universitätsbuchhandlung, Vienna, pp. 310–311. According to the author: 'For a full joinder, the arbitration agreement must also be applicable to the third party. In other words, there must either be an arbitration agreement binding all parties or a submission of the third party to that arbitration agreement.'

14 constitutes no autonomous basis of jurisdiction but rather requires that the relevant arbitration agreement is applicable to the third party as well'[141]. In other words, these authors assert that Article 14 merely prescribes the procedure that should be followed upon joinder but that the reference to the rules cannot constitute the parties' consent if such consent is not expressed elsewhere.

The appointment of arbitrators in cases of joinder seems problematic. As evident from paragraph 3.2 of Article 14(3), the third party may participate in the constitution of the tribunal only if no arbitrator has yet been appointed. It has been stated that the provision must not be read to the adverse conclusion, i.e. that if the request for joinder is made after the constitution of the arbitral tribunal the third party will be deprived of its right to participate in the constitution of the tribunal[142]. But what should be the approach if one of the main disputants requests the joinder of a third party at a time when the arbitral tribunal has already been constituted? The third party may, of course, accept that tribunal but if the tribunal proceeds with the multi-party arbitration over the third party's objection, that party may later on resist the recognition and enforcement of the arbitral award on the ground that the principle of parties' equal treatment in the constitution of the tribunal has been breached[143].

In order to deal with this risk, the Vienna Rules might have envisaged, for example, that VIAC has the right to revoke any appointments already made and appoint all members of the tribunal on behalf of all parties. However, paragraph 3.3 of Article 14(3) provides that this power is available only in cases where the tribunal has decided that the claims cannot be reviewed in single proceedings and has returned the statement of claim with the request of joinder to the Secretariat, which should then administer the proceedings separately[144]. Because of this and in order to avoid the risk of setting aside, non-recognition and / or non-enforcement of the award, a joinder request against a third party following the constitution of the tribunal should normally be denied unless the third party confirms the already appointed tribunal[145].

---

[141] Paul Oberhammer and Christian Koller (2014) 'Article 14, Joinder of Third Parties and Consolidation' in Vienna International Arbitration Centre of the Austrian Federal Economic Chamber (ed.) *Handbook Vienna Rules, A Practitioner's Guide*, WKÖ-Service Gmbh, Bad Vöslau, p. 72 (§ 10).

[142] Ibid., p. 77 (§ 26).

[143] In the author's opinion, the intervention of a third party into a pending arbitration with an already constituted tribunal should not give rise to similar concerns. The third party may be deemed to have agreed on the way the tribunal has been constituted by filing its request for intervention.

[144] Paul Oberhammer and Christian Koller (2014) 'Article 14, Joinder of Third Parties and Consolidation' in Vienna International Arbitration Centre of the Austrian Federal Economic Chamber (ed.) *Handbook Vienna Rules, A Practitioner's Guide*, WKÖ-Service Gmbh, Bad Vöslau, pp. 79–81 (§ 32-38). The purpose of the revocation in this case is to reverse the constitution of the arbitral tribunal if this constitution is based on the basis of multi-party proceedings but it turns out later on that the joinder is inadmissible.

[145] On that point see Nikolaus Pitkowitz (2015) 'Chapter II: The Arbitrator and the Arbitration Procedure, Multi-Party Arbitrations – Joinder and Consolidation under the Vienna Rules 2013', in Christian Klausegger, Peter Klein, Florian Kremslehner *et al.* (eds) *Austrian Yearbook on International Arbitration*, Manz'sche Verlags- und Universitätsbuchhandlung, Vienna, pp. 311–312, who has stated that: 'If the tribunal has already been constituted and the joining party does or did not waive his right to participate in the appointment of the arbitrators…the tribunal must return the Statement of Claim to the Secretariat and request the treatment of the claim in a separate proceeding.'

4.7.2 Consolidation

Consolidation is regulated under Article 15 as follows:

(1) Upon a party's request two or more proceedings may be consolidated if
  1.1 the parties agree to the consolidation; or
  1.2. the same arbitrator(s) was / were nominated or appointed;
  and the place of arbitration in all of the arbitration agreements on which the claims are based is the same.

(2) The Board shall decide on Requests for Consolidation after hearing the parties and the arbitrators already appointed. The Board shall consider all relevant circumstances in its decision, including the compatibility of the arbitration agreements and the respective stage of the proceedings.

As far as the author is aware, this provision does not have an equivalent in any other set of arbitration rules. Unlike Article 14, where the arbitral tribunal decides on a request for joinder, Article 15 states that it is the Board (a special board at the VIAC) that should take a decision on consolidation. Consolidation may only be requested by one of the parties to the proceedings and therefore *ex officio* consolidation by the Board is not possible. Since the introduction of the new Vienna Rules in 2013 only one request for consolidation has been made, and this request was granted by the Board[146].

Any successful consolidation under the Vienna Rules will require the fulfilment of certain prerequisites: First, that the place of arbitration is the same in the parallel proceedings and, secondly, that one of the additional prerequisites under items 1.1 and 1.2 is present. Unlike the 2006 Vienna Rules[147], the conditions under items 1.1 and 1.2 above are provided alternatively.

Under item 1.1, the parties' agreement to consolidation is required. This agreement will rarely be available when it comes to construction disputes, unless the parties have addressed this matter in their contracts. An interesting situation may arise if the parties have agreed on consolidation in their contracts but different tribunals have been constituted to deal with each of the arbitrations. The Vienna Rules do not empower the Board to revoke any appointments or nominations of arbitrators and appoint the whole tribunal in these situations. Therefore, a consolidation request in this case can only be successful if the parties reach an agreement on how the tribunal reviewing the consolidated proceedings is to be constituted[148].

Item 1.2 does not require the parties' agreement to consolidation. This means that consolidation might be possible even if the parties have not agreed on consolidation in their contracts, provided that the same arbitrator or the same arbitral tribunal has been appointed in each of the arbitrations. However, it is very unlikely that

---

[146] This information has been confirmed by the VIAC in an e-mail dated 5 February 2016.

[147] Under Article 15(8) of the 2006 Vienna Rules, consolidation was admissible only if both proceedings involved the same arbitrators and all parties to such proceedings and the arbitrators agreed to the consolidation.

[148] Paul Oberhammer and Christian Koller (2014) 'Article 14, Joinder of Third Parties and Consolidation' in Vienna International Arbitration Centre of the Austrian Federal Economic Chamber (ed.) *Handbook Vienna Rules, A Practitioner's Guide*, WKÖ-Service Gmbh, Bad Vöslau, pp. 86–87 (§ 17).

parties bound by different bilateral contracts would agree to submit their related disputes to one and the same arbitrator or tribunal. As pointed out in Section 3.4, disputing parties often have divergent interests. Therefore, it is very likely that at least one party would object to having the same arbitrator or tribunal as the one reviewing the other dispute[149]. The consolidation provision under the Vienna Rules will thus hardly find any application to the construction disputes discussed in this book.

4.8 DIS Arbitration Rules[150]

Disputes conducted under the DIS Arbitration Rules are administered by the German Institution of Arbitration ('**DIS**')[151]. Article 13(3) of the DIS Rules stipulates that 'The arbitral tribunal decides on the admissibility of the multi-party proceedings.' However, the rules do not contain any consolidation or joinder provisions. Therefore, the conduct of multi-party arbitration will only be possible if authorized by all parties[152].

In May 2016, DIS announced that it will revise its arbitration rules. The new DIS Rules are expected to come into force in the second half of 2017. At the time of writing this book, it is still unclear whether the new rules will contain joinder and/or consolidation provisions.

---

[149] There may be several reasons for this. A party to the second arbitration may assert, for example, that the impartiality of the arbitrator will be questioned if that same arbitrator has participated in the first arbitration. This arbitrator might have listened to the parties' pleas and reviewed evidence in the first arbitration, which may have resulted in a bias towards a certain opinion that he would be likely to follow in the second arbitration. For example, a subcontractor against whom a claim concerning defects has been filed by the main contractor will not be willing to accept the tribunal reviewing the same question in the arbitration between the employer and the main contractor.

[150] DIS-Arbitration Rules 98, in force as from 1 July 1998, http://www.dis-arb.de/scho/16/rules/overview-id0 (accessed 25 July 2016).

[151] The abbreviation stands for Deutsche Institution für Schiedsgerichtsbarkeit e.V. More information about the DIS can be seen at http://dis-arb.de/(accessed 25 July 2016).

[152] See Christoph Benedict (2015) 'Part IV – Selected Areas and Issues of Arbitration in Germany, Construction Arbitration in Germany', in K. Böckstiegel, S. Kröll and P. Nacimiento (eds) *Arbitration in Germany: The Model Law in Practice*, 2nd edn, Kluwer Law International, Alphen aan den Rijn, p. 840. According to the author, 'two preconditions are generally recognized: There has to be a contractual basis for the introduction of multi-party proceedings and all parties must be in a position to equally influence the nomination process. The absence of one of these conditions renders multi-party proceedings impossible.' See also Jens Bredow and Isabel Mulder (2015) 'Part III – Commentary on the Arbitration Rules of the German Institution of Arbitration (DIS Rules), Section 13 – Multiple Parties on Claimant or Respondent Side', in K. Böckstiegel, S. Kröll and P. Nacimiento (eds) *Arbitration in Germany: The Model Law in Practice*, 2nd edn, Kluwer Law International, Alphen aan den Rijn, pp. 629–631; Jens Bredow (2013) 'Arbitration Rules and Country Reports: Germany', in Nicole Conrad, Peter Munch and Jonathan Black-Branch (eds) *International Commercial Arbitration, Standard Clauses and Forms Commentary*, Helbing Lichtenhahn / C. H. Beck / Hart / Nomos, Basel, pp. 455–498 (§ 10.78), where the author has stated: 'For the sake of securing the enforceability of the award the Arbitral Tribunal shall not decide upon consolidation or joinder unless all parties agree thereto.'

4.9 SCC Rules[153]

The Arbitration Institute of the Stockholm Chamber of Commerce ('**SCC**')[154] administers arbitrations of disputes in accordance with the SCC Rules. The SCC Rules do not contain a joinder clause. However, Article 11 deals with consolidation of parallel arbitrations[155]. Consolidation will be possible upon the request of one of the parties and any decision should be taken by the SCC's Board. The clause is narrow in its scope as it may be applied only to cases where the parties to both proceedings are the same. The clause cannot therefore be used to increase the number of parties in a pending arbitration[156]. Furthermore, the practice of the SCC has been very conservative when it comes to consolidation over the opposition of one of the parties[157]. Therefore, the consolidation clause has no practical application to the construction disputes examined in this book.

The SCC Rules are currently under revision. A draft of the new SCC Rules, which are expected to enter into force on 1 January 2017, was released for public consultation in May 2016. The draft introduces a number of noteworthy revisions, including in respect of multi-party and multi-contract arbitrations. Article 13 of the draft SCC Rules stipulates that the SCC Board may join additional parties to a pending arbitration. If the claims are made under more than one arbitration agreement, joinder will be possible provided that the SCC Board is preliminarily satisfied that the following conditions are met: (i) all the parties have agreed to arbitrate their disputes under the SCC Rules, (ii) the arbitration agreements are compatible, and (iii) 'it may be inferred, having regard to all relevant circumstances, that there is an agreement between all parties to the arbitration that the claims may be determined in a single arbitration'. Under draft Article 14, claims arising under multiple contracts can now be pursued in a single arbitration under similar conditions. The consolidation provision will also be amended but the approach to consolidation under the new Article 15 is likely to remain conservative. Absent agreement of the parties, consolidation in a multi-contract scenario will only be possible if the parties under the separate arbitrations are the same. At the time of writing this book, the final approved draft of the new SCC Rules has not been released yet.

---

[153] Arbitration Rules of the Arbitration Institute of the Stockholm Chamber of Commerce, in force as from 1 January 2010, http://sccinstitute.com/media/40120/arbitrationrules_eng_webbversion.pdf (accessed 25 July 2016).

[154] For more information about the SCC, see www.sccinstitute.com (accessed 25 July 2016). The majority of the caseload at the SCC comprises international disputes. In 2013, out of 203 cases, 58% (or 117 cases) involved international disputes with parties coming from 36 different countries. In 2014, out of 183 cases, 94 were international and 89 were domestic cases. See http://www.sccinstitute.com/statistics/(accessed 25 July 2016).

[155] Article 11 SCC Rules: 'If arbitration is commenced concerning a legal relationship in respect of which an arbitration agreement between the same parties is already pending under these Rules, the Board [of SCC] may, at the request of a party, decide to consolidate the new claims with the pending proceedings. Such decision may only be made after consulting the parties and the Arbitral Tribunal.'

[156] Karl Guterstam, Jakob Ragnwaldh and Fredrik Andersson (2015) 'SCC Arbitration Rules 2010', in Loukas Mistelis (ed.) *Concise International Arbitration*, 2nd edn, Kluwer Law International, Alphen aan den Rijn, pp. 721–722.

[157] Marie Öhrström (2013) 'Chapter XII, SCC Rules', in Rolf Schütze (ed.) *Institutional Arbitration, Article-by-Article Commentary*, C. H. Beck / Hart / Nomos, Munich, p. 826.

4.10 *DIA Rules*[158]

Arbitrations subject to the DIA Rules are administered by the Danish Institute of Arbitration ('**DIA**')[159]. Consolidation under the DIA Rules is dealt with under the first two paragraphs of Article 9[160]. The request for consolidation should come from one of the parties and should be dealt with by the DIA Chairman's Committee. The clause is very flexible because it neither requires the explicit parties' consent to consolidation, nor the identity of the parties under the cases subject to consolidation. Articles 9(1) and 9(2) almost literally repeat Article 4(1) of the Swiss Rules. Therefore, the reader is referred to the commentary on the Swiss Rules in Section 4.5.

Joinder and intervention under the DIA Rules are regulated under Article 9(3). Any decision as to joinder or intervention should be taken by the arbitral tribunal after considering all relevant circumstances[161]. Unlike the consolidation provision, Article 9(3) is narrower in its scope because it demands the existence of 'an arbitration agreement covering the third party / parties'. It is not absolutely clear whether this should be a single arbitration agreement binding all parties (i.e. the main disputants and the third party) or an agreement between the third party and one of the disputants only. This arguably leaves some leeway for an argument that the clause may be applied to multi-contract disputes stemming from bilateral contracts binding non-identical parties.

It seems that the practice of the Chairman's Committee (in case of consolidation requests) and the arbitral tribunals (in case of joinder and intervention requests) is rather conservative. The number of requests under Article 9 of the DIA Rules so far has been below five and none of the requests has been granted[162].

---

[158] Rules of Arbitration Procedure adopted by the Board of the Danish Institute of Arbitration, in force as from 1 May 2013, http://voldgiftsinstituttet.dk/wp-content/uploads/2015/01/rules_1_may_2013_-_pdf-uden-logo.pdf (accessed 25 July 2016).

[159] For more information about the DIA, see www.voldgiftsinstituttet.dk/en (accessed 25 July 2016).

[160] Article 9 of the DIA Rules:

'(1) Where a Statement of Claim is submitted in a dispute between parties already involved in other arbitral proceedings under the Rules, the Chairman's Committee may decide, upon the request of a party and after consulting with the other party and any confirmed arbitrators in all the above cases, that the new case shall be consolidated with the pending case. The Chairman's Committee may proceed in the same way where a Statement of Claim is submitted in a dispute between parties that are not identical to the parties in other arbitral proceedings pending under the Rules.

(2) When rendering its decision, the Chairman's Committee shall take into account all relevant circumstances, including the mutual connection between the cases and / or the parties and the progress already made in the pending case. Where the Chairman's Committee decides to consolidate the new case with the pending case, the parties to both cases shall be deemed to have waived their right to an arbitrator, and the Chairman's Committee may revoke the appointment of arbitrators already confirmed in order to confirm new arbitrators in accordance with Article 10-14 ...'

[161] Article 9(3) of the DIA Rules: 'Where one or more third parties request to join cases already pending under the Rules, or where a party to a pending case under the rules requests that one or more third parties join the arbitration case, the Arbitral Tribunal shall decide on such request, provided that an arbitration agreement covering the third party / parties exist, and after consulting with all of the parties, including the party / parties to be joined, taking into account all relevant circumstances, including the mutual connection between such third party / parties and the parties to the pending case and the progress already made in the pending case.'

[162] This information was communicated to the author by DIA in an e-mail dated 4 February 2016. However, it should be mentioned that DIA does not keep an official record of the number of applications under Article 9, and therefore this information does not have an official character.

4.11 Arbitration rules in Asia

The present section reviews the arbitration rules adopted by some arbitral institutions in Asia. More particularly, this section focuses on the arbitration rules of the most popular arbitral institutions in China, Singapore, Hong Kong and Japan. Parties engaged in construction projects in Asia often choose these rules as applicable to their contractual disputes for different reasons. These may include the proximity of the venue to the subject matter of the contract (for example, for the purposes of technical investigations, hearing of witnesses, etc.), the availability of support services by the relevant arbitral institutes, etc.

4.11.1 CIETAC Rules[163]

Arbitrations conducted under the CIETAC Rules are administered by the China International Economic and Trade Arbitration Commission ('**CIETAC**') or one of its sub-commissions / centres[164]. Most arbitrations under the CIETAC Rules concern domestic cases but the number of foreign-related cases is also substantial[165].

The CIETAC Rules were subject to two major revisions between 2012 and 2015. Multi-party arbitration was addressed for the first time in the 2012 CIETAC Rules[166]. The purpose of the introduction of the 2012 CIETAC Rules was to bring them more into line with internationally accepted arbitration practices. The 2012 Rules only dealt with consolidation of parallel proceedings and were silent on other types of multi-party arbitration. The 2015 CIETAC Rules introduced certain amendments to the consolidation provision and included articles dealing with the filing of a single request for arbitration based on multiple contracts and joinder of third parties. Each of these provisions is briefly discussed below. The commentary below is on the 2015 CIETAC Rules but, wherever relevant, certain references have been made to the 2012 CIETAC Rules as well.

(i) Single request for arbitration against multiple parties

The 2015 CIETAC Rules for the first time addressed the possibility for filing of a single request for arbitration based on multiple contracts under Article 14. The article merely

[163] China International Economic and Trade Arbitration Commission CIETAC Arbitration Rules, in force as from 1 January 2015, http://cn.cietac.org/rules/rule_E.pdf (accessed 1 August 2016).

[164] There is an ongoing dispute between CIETAC and two of its largest sub-commissions (CIETAC Shanghai and CIETAC South China). Following the introduction of the 2012 CIETAC Rules (which reduced the number of new cases referred to the sub-commissions), the two sub-commissions declared their independence from CIETAC and adopted their own rules. As a result, CIETAC withdrew its authorization to these sub-commissions and declared its intention to re-establish them. As of the date of this book, the status of the two sub-commissions, as well as that of the arbitrations that they handle, remains unclear.

[165] In 2013, CIETAC accepted a total of 1256 economic and trade dispute cases, including 375 foreign-related cases and 881 domestic cases. In 2014, the total number of cases was 1610, out of which 387 were foreign-related cases. This information is available at http://cietac.org/index.php?m=Page&a=index&id=40&l=en (accessed 25 July 2016).

[166] China International Economic and Trade Arbitration Commission CIETAC Arbitration Rules, effective as from 1 May 2012, http://cn.cietac.org/rules/rule_E.pdf (accessed 1 August 2016).

formalizes the existing practice of CIETAC which allowed claimants to do so even before the promulgation of the new rules[167]. Pursuant to Article 14:

> The Claimant may initiate a single arbitration concerning disputes arising out of or in connection with multiple contracts, provided that:
> (a) such contracts consist of a principal contract and its ancillary contract(s), or such contracts involve the same parties as well as legal relationships of the same nature;
> (b) the disputes arise out of the same transaction or the same series of transactions; and
> (c) the arbitration agreements in such contracts are identical or compatible.

All three conditions under letters (a), (b) and (c) should be satisfied when filing a single request for arbitration. The first condition under letter (a) contains two alternative sub-conditions. For the present analysis, the first sub-condition of letter (a) is of particular interest – that is, the contracts consist of a principal contract and its ancillary contract. CIETAC has not suggested any examples of such a relation[168]. It is debatable whether this condition can be satisfied with regard to the type of construction disputes examined here. Can, for example, a main contract be considered as a principal contract and a subcontract – as an ancillary contract? Similarly, can a professional services agreement with a designer be considered as an ancillary contract to the main contract? It may, for example, be argued that a professional services agreement entered into by a main contractor under a *design-and-build* project is ancillary to the main contract because it has been concluded in implementation of the main contract. Its scope concerns only part of the contractor's obligations under the main contract and the drawings that the designer will prepare will enable the contractor to fulfil his obligations under the main contract. On the other hand, it may be counterargued that such an agreement exists independently from the main contract. It is concluded by different parties and is not subordinate to the main contract. The present author shares this second line of reasoning. In any case, it will be difficult to give a definite answer to the above questions. It remains to be seen how this sub-condition under letter (a) will be applied.

It should not be forgotten, however, that a single request for arbitration should also satisfy the other two conditions: that the disputes arise out of the same series of transactions, and that the arbitration agreements in the different contracts are identical or compatible.

---

[167] Jingzhou Tao and Mariana Zhong, 'A Quick Read of the CIETAC Arbitration Rules 2015', in *31 Arbitration International*, no. 3 (2015), p. 458. See also Jingzhou Tao (2015) 'CIETAC Arbitration Rules 2015' in Loukas Mistelis (ed.) *Concise International Arbitration*, 2nd edn, Kluwer Law International, Alphen aan den Rijn, p. 639.

[168] Some scenarios where this sub-condition may be deemed fulfilled have been suggested by some practitioners. For example, it has been suggested that a claimant may commence a single arbitration where the dispute arises out of a loan agreement and an equity pledge agreement in the same transaction because the equity pledge agreement is ancillary in nature to the principal contract – the loan agreement. See Matthew Gearing and Matthew Hodgson, *CIETAC's New Arbitration Rules*, http://www.allenovery.com/publications/en-gb/Pages/CIETAC's-New-Arbitration-Rules-2015-.aspx (accessed 25 July 2016).

(ii) Consolidation

Traditionally, CIETAC has been very reluctant to consolidate separate arbitral proceedings[169]. Consolidation was first regulated under the 2012 CIETAC Rules whereunder the agreement of all parties was required[170]. The wording of the 2012 consolidation article implied that the agreement of the parties is actually a procedural consent, which should be given during the course of the proceedings[171]. Therefore, even if the parties had agreed on *ad hoc* multi-party arbitration clauses in their contracts, the existence of these clauses will most probably not have been sufficient *per se* for the consolidation of their related disputes under the 2012 CIETAC Rules. In the author's opinion, this approach was quite burdensome and conservative. Basically, it enabled any party, even a party which had agreed on multi-party arbitration in its contract beforehand, to use the requirement for such an additional procedural consent as a tactical tool to discomfit its contemplated participation in the proceedings and veto the prospective consolidation.

The position under the 2015 CIETAC Rules is different. The parties' consent is no longer the only circumstance under which consolidation can be granted. Consolidation is now dealt with under Article 19 which reads as follows:

> (1) At the request of a party, CIETAC may consolidate two or more arbitrations pending under these Rules into a single arbitration if:
> (a) all of the claims in the arbitrations are made under the same arbitration agreement;
> (b) the claims in the arbitrations are made under multiple arbitration agreements that are identical or compatible and the arbitrations involve the same parties as well as legal relationships of the same nature;
> (c) the claims in the arbitrations are made under multiple arbitration agreements that are identical or compatible and the multiple contracts involved consist of a principle contract and its ancillary contract(s), or
> (d) all the parties to the arbitrations have agreed to consolidation…

All conditions in Article 19, except for the condition under letter (c), closely resemble the conditions under the consolidation clause in the ICC Rules. None of these conditions will normally be fulfilled when it comes to multi-contract construction disputes. Letter (a) can only be invoked if the parties are bound by an umbrella arbitration agreement. Letter (b) is only applicable to disputes involving the same parties. Letter (d) requires parties' agreement to consolidation, which would also not be available, unless the parties have included consolidation clauses in their contracts or have consented to consolidation once the disputes have arisen. The question then arises of whether a party may rely

---

[169] Jingzhou Tao (2010) 'CIETAC Arbitration Rules, 2005', in Loukas Mistelis (ed.) *Concise International Arbitration*, Kluwer Law International, Alphen aan den Rijn, p. 538.

[170] Pursuant to Article 17 of the 2012 CIETAC Rules, '[at] the request of a party and with the agreement of all other parties, or where CIETAC believes it necessary and all the parties have agreed, CIETAC may consolidate two or more arbitrations pending under these Rules into a single arbitration.'

[171] See Song Lu, 'The New CIETAC Arbitration Rules of 2012', in *29 Journal of International Arbitration*, no.3 (2012), pp. 300–302. Pursuant to the author, consolidation under the 2012 CIETAC Rules 'requires separate agreement of all the parties concerned evidencing mutual intention favouring consolidation of the parallel pending proceedings.'

on letter (c) that does not explicitly require the parties' consent to consolidation. Like Article 14, letter (c) refers, among other things, to the existence of a principal contract and an ancillary contract. As mentioned above, it is debatable whether this condition can be satisfied when it comes to separate bilateral contracts concluded with a view to the implementation of a single construction project.

Consolidation may only be allowed if requested by a party to one of the proceedings and any decision will be made by the CIETAC by taking into account the parties' opinions and other relevant factors such as the correlations between the arbitrations, including the nomination and appointment of arbitrators in the separate arbitrations[172]. It has been stated that the CIETAC does not encourage consolidation of arbitrations where the arbitrators have already been nominated or appointed[173]. The arbitrations shall be consolidated into the arbitration that commenced first[174]. The conduct of the consolidated arbitration will be decided by the Arbitration Court (if the tribunal is not formed) or by the arbitral tribunal (if it has been formed)[175].

The scope of application of Article 19 should clearly be distinguished from that of Article 14. Article 14 applies if the claimant simultaneously pursues his claims against two or more respondents with which he has concluded separate contracts by filing of a single request for arbitration. This request then gives the start of the arbitration. Article 19 will apply, for instance, if the claimant has initiated separate arbitrations against each of the respondents and files a request for the merger of these two arbitrations[176].

(iii) Joinder

The joinder of third parties was addressed for the first time in the 2015 CIETAC Arbitration Rules. It is regulated under Article 18, which is one of the longest articles in the 2015 CIETAC Rules. The joinder article will have limited application to the construction disputes discussed here because it requires prima facie evidence for the existence of an arbitration agreement binding the main disputants and the party to be joined[177]. Such evidence will typically not be available, unless all the parties have entered into an umbrella arbitration agreement. Any jurisdictional objection by a party

---

[172] Article 19(2) of the 2015 CIETAC Rules.

[173] Jingzhou Tao and Mariana Zhong, 'A Quick Read of the CIETAC Arbitration Rules 2015', in *31 Arbitration International*, no. 3 (2015), p. 460.

[174] Article 19(3) of the 2015 CIETAC Rules.

[175] Article 19(4) of the 2015 CIETAC Rules.

[176] Jingzhou Tao and Mariana Zhong, 'A Quick Read of the CIETAC Arbitration Rules 2015', in *31 Arbitration International*, no. 3 (2015), p. 460, and Jingzhou Tao (2015) 'CIETAC Arbitration Rules 2015' in Loukas Mistelis (ed.) *Concise International Arbitration*, 2nd edn, Kluwer Law International, Alphen aan den Rijn, p. 640.

[177] Pursuant to Article 18(1) of the 2015 CIETAC Rules: 'During the arbitral proceedings, a party wishing to join an additional party to the arbitration may file a Request for Joinder with CIETAC, based on the arbitration agreement invoked in the arbitration that prima facie binds the additional party. Where the Request for Joinder is filed after the formation of the arbitral tribunal, a decision shall be made by CIETAC after the arbitral tribunal hears from all parties including the additional party if the arbitral tribunal considers the joinder necessary.'

as to the requested joinder will be decided by the CIETAC[178]. If the conditions under the article are fulfilled, a third party may be joined even after the tribunal has been constituted. In this case, the process of constitution of the tribunal should start anew if the third party does not want to accept the already constituted tribunal[179].

4.11.2 SIAC Rules[180]

The SIAC Rules are adopted by the Singapore International Arbitration Centre ('**SIAC**')[181]. The case workload of SIAC is growing, and it involves parties from around the world[182]. In 2013, SIAC issued the fifth edition of its rules. Before dealing with the 2013 SIAC Rules, the joinder provision in an earlier edition of the SIAC Rules will be examined. The application of this provision was subject to some court proceedings in Singapore, which ultimately ended in the denial of enforcement of an arbitral award.

According to Rule 24.1 (b) of the 2007 SIAC Rules, the arbitral tribunal was given power to 'allow other parties to be joined in the arbitration with their express consent, and make a single final award determining all disputes among the parties to the arbitration'[183]. Thus, the rule required the consent of the third party to be joined but did not explicitly require the consent of the party which had not requested the joinder. This approach closely resembled the one under the LCIA Rules.

The application of the joinder rule became a source of controversy in the *Astro v. Lippo* case[184]. In this case, disputes arose in relation to a contemplated execution of a joint venture agreement for the provision of multimedia and television services in Indonesia between certain companies belonging to the Astro Group and certain companies belonging to the Lippo group. The terms of the joint venture agreement were contained in a shareholders' agreement. Disputes arose as to the funding of the joint venture vehicle, and Astro initiated arbitration against the members of the Lippo group that had signed the shareholders' agreement. The 2007 SIAC Rules were applicable to this dispute and the seat of arbitration was in Singapore. Astro requested the joinder of several Astro affiliated companies that were non-signatories to the arbitration agreement contained in the shareholders' agreement. The arbitral tribunal permitted the joinder by applying Rule 24(1) (b) of the 2007 SIAC Rules. It construed the rule as allowing the joinder of entities that are not parties to the same arbitration agreement as the one invoked in the arbitration, provided

---

[178] Article 18(3) of the 2015 CIETAC Rules.

[179] Article 18(5) of the 2015 CIETAC Rules.

[180] Arbitration Rules of the Singapore International Arbitration Centre SIAC Rules (5th edn, 1 April 2013), http://www.siac.org.sg/our-rules/rules (accessed 25 July 2016).

[181] For more information about the SIAC, see http://www.siac.org.sg/(accessed 25 June 2016).

[182] Pursuant to the statistical information on the SIAC's web page, SIAC registered 259 cases in 2013, which was the largest number of cases ever registered in a single year at the SIAC. In 2014, the number of cases dropped down to 222. See http://www.siac.org.sg/2014-11-03-13-33-43/facts-figures/statistics (accessed 25 July 2016).

[183] Arbitration Rules of the Singapore International Arbitration Centre SIAC Rules (3rd edn, 1 July 2007). The article has been reproduced with permission. Copyright © 2007 Singapore International Arbitration Centre.

[184] *PT First Media TBK v. Astro Nusantara International BV & Others* [2013] SGCA 57 in *1 Singapore Law Reports* (2014), pp. 372–452, https://leeshih.files.wordpress.com/2013/11/judgment-ca150151.pdf (accessed 1 August 2016).

that the parties that were to be joined consented to the joinder[185]. Later on, the tribunal rendered an award against the Lippo companies and enforcement orders were obtained. One of the Lippo companies sought to set aside the enforcement orders on the grounds that there was no arbitration agreement between the company and the joined parties. The High Court refused to set aside the award. The matter was appealed to the Singapore Court of Appeal, which denied the enforcement of the award since the arbitral tribunal had been wrong to find that it had jurisdiction over the joined parties. The Court of Appeal held that the joinder rule in the 2007 SIAC Rules did not empower the tribunal to join non-parties to the arbitration agreement without the consent of the parties to the arbitration agreement. In other words, the court decided that the joinder rule was merely a procedural mechanism for the joinder and could not be used by the tribunal to extend its jurisdiction over non-signatories[186].

The above case is not from the construction sector but is very illustrative as to the type of issues that may potentially arise from the application of joinder provisions similar to Rule 24.1(b) of the 2007 SIAC Rules. Even though this rule did not explicitly require the consent of the party that had not requested the joinder, the Singapore Court of Appeal held that this consent was nevertheless required. Therefore, multi-party arbitration requests granted solely on the basis of broadly worded arbitration clauses, such as the one under the 2007 SIAC Rules, may turn out to be problematic.

The 2013 SIAC Rules also deal with joinder but under different conditions. Pursuant to Rule 24(1)(b) of the 2013 edition of the rules:

> In addition to the powers specified in these Rules and not in derogation of the mandatory rules of law applicable to the arbitration, the Tribunal shall have the power to:...
>
> b. upon the application of a party, allow one or more third parties to be joined in the arbitration provided that such person is a party to the arbitration agreement, with the written consent of such third party, and thereafter make a single final award or separate awards in respect of all parties...[187]

The scope of the joinder rule has been narrowed down. Only persons bound by the same arbitration agreement can be joined. Therefore, the rule may come into play with regard to the construction disputes discussed here only if the multiple parties are bound by an umbrella arbitration agreement. The rule does not prescribe any time limit as to when a joinder request should be made. This means that joinder can also be allowed after the constitution of the arbitral tribunal. In such a scenario, the joined party will have no influence in the constitution of the arbitral tribunal. In the context of the SIAC Rules, however, this should not give rise to any major concerns because the explicit written consent of the third party is required. Presumably, this means that by giving its written consent the third party accepts the constituted arbitral tribunal[188]. In other instances, however, the requirement for such a third party's written consent to the joinder can hardly be justified. This will be the case,

---

[185]Bernard Hanotiau, 'Non-signatories, Group of Companies and Group of Contracts in Selected Asian Countries: A Case Law Analysis', in *32 Journal of International Arbitration*, no. 6 (2015), pp. 584–585.

[186]Ibid., pp. 585–586.

[187]Reproduced with permission. Copyright © 2013 Singapore International Arbitration Centre.

[188]John Savage and Simon Dunbar (2015) 'SIAC Arbitration Rules 2013', in Loukas Mistelis (ed.) *Concise International Arbitration*, 2nd edn, Kluwer Law International, Alphen aan den Rijn, p. 803.

for example, if a party has already agreed to be joined in accordance with a multi-party arbitration clause in its contract. If this party is to be joined in an arbitration pending under the SIAC Rules, it will have to give its further written consent irrespective of the existence of a contractual multi-party arbitration clause in its contract.

At the final stage of writing this book, the sixth edition of the SIAC Rules was released[189]. The new rules, which introduced a major overhaul of the existing multi-party arbitration regime, entered into force on 1 August 2016.

The mechanism of joinder of additional parties is now regulated under Article 7. In fact, this article deals with both joinder and intervention. The requested joinder may be admitted if one of the following two criteria is satisfied: (i) the additional party to be joined is *prima facie* bound by the arbitration agreement that gave rise to the arbitration, or (ii) all parties, including the party to be joined, have consented to the joinder[190]. Thus, the SIAC Rules no longer require the third party's written consent if such party is bound by the same arbitration agreement, which is a positive development. However, the above criteria will hardly be met when it comes to construction disputes arising under multiple contracts, as these disputes typically arise under multiple arbitration agreements and there will be normally no unanimous agreement on the joinder.

For the first time, the SIAC Rules deal with disputes arising under multiple contracts. Pursuant to Article 6 of the new SIAC Rules, the claimant can either submit a separate request for arbitration in respect of each arbitration agreement and concurrently submit an application for consolidation or submit a single request for arbitration in respect of all the arbitrations agreements. In both cases, the applicable criteria under the consolidation provision (these are discussed below) should also be satisfied.

Consolidation of pending arbitrations is regulated under Article 8. The decision on consolidation will be taken either by the Court of Arbitration of SIAC (if the consolidation request is made prior to the constitution of any tribunal) or by an arbitral tribunal (if the consolidation request is made after the constitution of any tribunal)[191]. The Court's decision to reject a consolidation request does not deprive the requesting party from making that same application before the tribunal once the latter has been constituted. If consolidation is granted by the Court or the arbitral tribunal, the Court is empowered to revoke the appointment of any arbitrators made prior to the consolidation request in order to ensure parties' equality in the constitution of the tribunal[192].

Any of the following three criteria should be satisfied when a party requests consolidation:

(a) all parties have agreed to the consolidation;
(b) all the claims in the arbitrations are made under the same arbitration agreement; or
(c) the arbitration agreements are compatible, and (i) the disputes arise out of the same legal relationship(s); (ii) the disputes arise out of contracts consisting of a principal contract and its ancillary contract(s); or (iii) the disputes arise out of the same transaction or series of transactions.[193]

---

[189] Arbitration Rules of the Singapore International Arbitration Centre SIAC Rules (6th edn, 1 August 2016), http://www.siac.org.sg/our-rules/rules/siac-rules-2016 (accessed 7 November 2016).
[190] Article 7.1 and Article 7.8 of the 2016 SIAC Rules.
[191] Article 8.1 and Article 8.7 of the 2016 SIAC Rules.
[192] Article 8.6 and Article 8.10 of the 2016 SIAC Rules.
[193] Article 8.1 of the 2016 SIAC Rules. Reproduced with permission.

If the request for consolidation is made after the constitution of the tribunal there is a further requirement under letter (b) and letter (c), namely that the same tribunal has been constituted in each of the arbitrations or that no tribunal has been constituted in the other arbitrations[194].

As observed above, the first two criteria (i.e. those under letter (a) and letter (b)) will hardly be satisfied in a multi-contract setting. The third criterion under letter (c) above will be the one that contracting parties will most likely try to invoke when requesting consolidation of multi-contract disputes. The parties' consent is not a prerequisite for the satisfaction of this criterion. Among its other requirements, letter (c) introduces three subcriteria. It would suffice to satisfy any of these subcriteria. As discussed in the context of the CIETAC Rules, it may probably be argued that related multi-contract disputes in the construction sector arise out of contracts consisting of a principal contract and its ancillary contract. However, such a statement is debatable (see Section 4.11.1 about this point). Furthermore, it may be argued that related multi-contract disputes in the construction sector arise out of the same economic transaction, that is the particular construction project, and consequently that the third criterion is satisfied. It remains to be seen how these criteria will be applied to a request for consolidation of arbitrations arising in respect of multi-contract construction disputes.

4.11.3 HKIAC Rules[195]

The HKIAC Rules have been adopted by the Hong Kong International Arbitration Centre ('**HKIAC**'). HKIAC is one of the leading arbitral centres in South East Asia handling a significant number of international disputes[196]. A recent survey reveals that HKIAC is the most preferred arbitral institution outside of Europe[197]. The HKIAC Rules were last amended in 2013, with effect from 1 November 2013, and the new rules contain more elaborate provisions on joinder, consolidation and single arbitration based on multiple contracts.

(i) Single request for arbitration against multiple parties

Article 29 of the new HKIAC Rules acknowledges that a claimant may pursue his claims arising under two or more contracts within a single arbitration under certain conditions. Pursuant to Article 29.1:

---

[194] Article 8.7 of the 2016 SIAC Rules.

[195] Hong Kong International Arbitration Centre Administered Arbitration Rules, in force as from 1 November 2013, http://hkiac.org/arbitration/rules-practice-notes/administered-arbitration-rules (accessed 25 July 2016).

[196] In 2014, HKIAC handled 477 new disputes, of which 252 were arbitration matters. This represents a 36% growth from 2013 and a 62% increase from 2012. In 2014, 93% of the new administered arbitrations were international in nature featuring parties from 38 jurisdictions. The above information is available at http://220.241.190.1/en/hkiac/statistics/case-statistics. (accessed 1 August 2016).

[197] *2015 International Arbitration Survey: Improvements and Innovations in International Arbitration*, conducted by Queen Mary University of London and White & Case LLP. The survey is available at http://www.arbitration.qmul.ac.uk/docs/164761.pdf accessed 25 June 2016.

> Claims arising out of or in connection with more than one contract can be made in a single arbitration, provided that:
>
> (a) all parties to the arbitration are bound by each arbitration agreement giving rise to the arbitration;
> (b) a common question of law or fact arises under each arbitration agreement giving rise to the arbitration;
> (c) the rights to relief claimed are in respect of, or arise out of, the same transaction or series of transactions; and
> (d) the arbitration agreements under which those claims are made are compatible.

All four conditions should be fulfilled. The scope of application of this provision is rather narrow because of the first condition requiring that 'all parties to the arbitration are bound by each arbitration agreement giving rise to the arbitration'. In a multi-contract scenario, this would mean that there should be one or more arbitration agreements binding all the multiple parties. This condition will normally not be fulfilled in a typical construction project characterized by numerous bilateral contracts entered into between non-identical parties. Therefore, this provision has limited relevance to the construction disputes examined in this book.

(ii) Intervention and Joinder

Joinder of third parties in pending arbitration is not a new feature under the HKIAC Rules. There was a joinder provision under the 2008 HKIAC Rules which followed the approach under the LCIA Rules, i.e. that a third party might be joined provided that the party requesting the joinder and the third party had consented to the joinder in writing[198]. HKIAC diverted from this approach in its 2013 rules. Joinder of additional parties is now regulated under Article 27, which is probably the longest joinder provision available in institutional arbitration rules. Some of the article's paragraphs that are most relevant to the discussion in this book have been reproduced below:

> 27.1 The arbitral tribunal shall have the power to allow an additional party to be joined to the arbitration provided that, prima facie, the additional party is bound by an arbitration agreement under these Rules giving rise to the arbitration, including any arbitration under Article 28 or 29 ...
> 27.3 A party wishing to join an additional party to the arbitration shall submit a Request for joinder to HKIAC. HKIAC may fix a time limit for the submission of a Request for Joinder...
> 27.6 A third party wishing to be joined as an additional party to the arbitration shall submit a Request for Joinder to HKIAC...
> 27.8 Where HKIAC receives a Request for Joinder before the date on which the arbitral tribunal is confirmed, HKIAC may decide whether, prima facie, the additional party is bound by an arbitration agreement under these Rules giving rise to the arbitration, including any arbitration under Article 28 or 29. If so, HKIAC may join the additional party to the arbitration.

[198] Article 14(6) of the 2008 HKIAC Rules, http://220.241.190.1/en/arbitration/arbitration-rules-guidelines/hkiac-administered-arbitration-rules-2008/19-arbitration/arbitration-rules/26-hong-kong-international-arbitration-centre-administered-arbitration-rules-1#14 (accessed 1 August 2016).

Any question as to the jurisdiction of the arbitral tribunal arising from HKIAC's decision under Article 27.8 shall be decided by the arbitral tribunal once confirmed, pursuant to Article 19.1 …

27.11 Where an additional party is joined to the arbitration before the date on which the arbitral tribunal is confirmed, all parties to the arbitration shall be deemed to have waived their rights to designate an arbitrator, and HKIAC may revoke the appointment of any arbitrators already designated or confirmed. In these circumstances, HKIAC shall appoint the arbitral tribunal…

Several main observations can be made. First, the article covers both joinder (Article 27.3) and intervention (Article 27.6). Secondly, multi-party proceedings under this clause can only take place upon the request of a party. Thirdly, there is no time limit for submitting a request for joinder or intervention. In practice, however, it is unlikely that a request for joinder or intervention will be granted once the arbitral tribunal has been constituted, unless the party to be joined or to intervene in the proceedings accepts that tribunal. The decision on the request will be taken by HKIAC under Article 27.8 (if the arbitral tribunal has not been confirmed yet) or by the arbitral tribunal under Article 27.1 (if the tribunal has been constituted).

When it comes to the parties' consent to the joinder or intervention, there is no requirement that such consent should be given in the course of the proceedings. However, joinder or intervention under Article 27 may only be allowed if '*prima facie*, the additional party is bound by an arbitration agreement under these Rules giving rise to the arbitration'[199]. It follows from here that the HKIAC or the arbitral tribunal, as the case may be, should prima facie establish the existence of a single arbitration agreement binding all three parties[200]. As noted above, the construction disputes discussed hereof most often arise under separate arbitration clauses binding non-identical parties. Therefore, the HKIAC or the tribunal will most likely decide that the conditions under Article 27 have not been complied with with regard to those disputes. Hence, the joinder or intervention request will be denied, unless the parties have included multi-party arbitration clauses in their contracts or have given their *ad hoc* consent in the course of the proceedings.

Since the date of introduction of the new rules there have been three applications for joinder, two of which were granted[201].

(iii) Consolidation

Consolidation under the HKIAC Rules is regulated under Article 28. The consolidation article has been supplemented with a Practice Note on Consolidation with effect

---

[199] See Articles 27.1 and 27.8 of the HKIAC Rules.

[200] See also Peter Yuen, *The New HKIAC Arbitration Rules and how they compare to other institutional rules*, available at http://us.practicallaw.com/3-542-4605?q=&qp=&qo=&qe= (accessed 25 July 2016). When comparing the previous and the current wording of the joinder clause, the author observed: 'This change, removing the consent requirement for joinder, will be controversial to some, by granting the HKIAC and the arbitration tribunal broader powers…The author believes that the change brought about in the HKIAC Rules should not be at all that controversial, given that it still requires a valid arbitration agreement between all the parties, including the party to be joined.'

[201] This information was communicated to the author by the HKIAC in e-mails dated 25 February 2015 and 15 March 2016.

from 1 January 2016[202]. The Practice Note sets forth the content of the request for consolidation and the answer to such a request and does not change the content of the consolidation provision in a material way. Pursuant to Article 28:

> 28.1 HKIAC shall have the power, at the request of a party...and after consulting with the parties and any confirmed arbitrators, to consolidate two or more arbitrations pending under these Rules where:
> (a) the parties agree to consolidate; or
> (b) all of the claims in the arbitrations are made under the same arbitration agreement; or
> (c) the claims are made under more than one arbitration agreement, a common question of law or fact arises in both or all of the arbitrations, the rights to relief claimed are in respect of, or arise out of, the same transaction or series of transactions, and HKIAC finds the arbitration agreements to be compatible.

In deciding whether to consolidate, the HKIAC shall take into account the particular circumstances of the case, which may include the designation or confirmation of one or more arbitrators, whether the same or different arbitrators have been confirmed, and so forth.[203] The arbitrations will be consolidated into the arbitration that commenced first, unless the parties agree otherwise[204]. If the HKIAC decides to consolidate the arbitrations, the parties to these arbitrations shall be deemed to have waived their right to designate an arbitrator[205]. Furthermore, the HKIAC is empowered to revoke any appointments made so far and to appoint the arbitral tribunal in the consolidated proceedings[206]. This aims at ensuring the parties' equal treatment in the constitution of the arbitral tribunal. Literally read, the article could allow consolidation even if the arbitral tribunals in the separate arbitrations have already been constituted. However, consolidation in these cases can significantly delay the proceedings because of the revocation of appointments which may have to be made and the constitution of the new tribunal. Therefore, consolidation in these cases should only be allowed as a last resort. The HKIAC Rules also stipulate that the parties waive any objection, on the basis of any decision to consolidate proceedings, to the validity and / or enforcement of any award made by the tribunal, in so far as such a waiver can be validly made[207].

At first glance, it seems that Article 28.1 of the HKIAC Rules closely resembles Article of the 10 ICC Rules, and therefore the analysis in respect of the ICC Rules is relevant here as well (see Section 4.1.3). However, there is one significant difference between the ICC Rules and the HKIAC Rules concerning letter (c). While the ICC Rules limit the application of letter (c) only to cases where the parties under both proceedings are the same,

---

[202] The Practice Note on Consolidation is available at http://220.241.190.1/en/arbitration/arbitration-rules-guidelines/practice-note-on-consolidation-of-arbitrations (accessed 1 August 2016).

[203] Article 28.3 of the HKIAC Rules.

[204] Article 28.4 of the HKIAC Rules.

[205] Article 28.6 of the HKIAC Rules.

[206] Ibid.

[207] Article 28.8 of the HKIAC Rules. Article 27.13 contains a similar waiver with regard to the joinder provision.

there is no such restriction under the HKIAC Rules. Therefore, it seems that consolidation under letter (c) may also take place if the arbitration agreements in question are executed between different parties and these agreements are silent on consolidation[208]. This has also been confirmed by the HKIAC[209]. Some practitioners have stated that the consolidation provision creates a jurisdictional basis for consolidation even if there are no multi-party arbitration clauses in the parties' contracts[210]. This statement is supported by the fact that letter (c) of Article 28.1 does not explicitly require the parties' consent to consolidation. Article 28.1 read as a whole creates the impression that the parties' consent to consolidation is not a prerequisite for the operation of letter (c). Unlike letter (a) of the same article, which explicitly refers to the parties' agreement on consolidation, letter (c) omits such a reference. Hence, the parties are deemed to have agreed to a possible consolidation in advance by referring in their arbitration agreements to the HKIAC Rules.

As of March 2016, five requests for consolidation have been made under the 2013 HKIAC Rules and all requests have been granted[211]. It has been acknowledged by the HKIAC that in two cases letter (c) of Article 28.1 has been applied to consolidate arbitrations under contracts binding different parties[212]. In these two cases, the HKIAC requested comments from all parties to the separate arbitrations and in both matters consolidation was granted over a party's objection.

The approach of the HKIAC in respect of consolidation is compliant with the content of the consolidation clause. In the author's opinion, however, it is quite peculiar that the HKIAC has decided to adopt different stances to consolidation, on one side, and to joinder and a single request of arbitration against multiple parties on the other side, when it comes to parties' consent to multi-party arbitration. Whereas Articles 27.1 and 29.1 require the existence of a single arbitration agreement binding all parties, there is no such a requirement under Article 28.1. As a result, the application of these clauses to multi-contract situations involving non-identical parties could result in different treatment of situations that are substantially identical. This difference in treatment is reminiscent of the approach under the CEPANI Rules discussed in Subsection 4.2.3.

[208] See Ruth Stackpool-Moore (2014) 'Joinder and Consolidation – Examining Best Practice in the Swiss, HKIAC and ICC Rules', in Nathalie Voser (ed.) *Ten Years of the Swiss Rules of International Arbitration*, ASA Special Series No. 44, JurisNet LLC, New York, NY, p. 29. See also Peter Yuen, *The New HKIAC Arbitration Rules and how they compare to other institutional rules*, available at http://us.practicallaw.com/3-542-4605?q=&qp=&qo=&qe= (accessed 25 July 2016). According to the author, consolidation under HKIAC Rules does not require the consent of the parties, and the HKIAC may consolidate cases even when the parties and the arbitrators are different between the separate proceedings.

[209] See Karen Tan, *New Year, New Practice Note: HKIAC Issues Practice Note on Consolidation of Arbitrations*, available at http://www.ciarb.org.sg/new-year-new-practice-note-hkiac-issues-practice-note-on-consolidation-of-arbitrations/(accessed 1 August 2016). According to Joe Liu, a Deputy Managing Counsel at the HKIAC, 'HKIAC can order consolidation even if the parties to each arbitration are different, making consolidation possible for related disputes arising under a web or chain of contracts.'

[210] Ibid. According to Nils Eliasson, an international arbitration partner at Shearman & Sterling, 'The unique provisions on consolidation and joinder have largely replaced the need for drafting consolidation and joinder clauses in [multi-party and / or multi-contract] cases.'

[211] This information was communicated to the author by the HKIAC in e-mails dated 23 February 2015 and 16 March 2016.

[212] Ibid.

In the context of the HKIAC Rules, this would mean, for example, that an employer will refrain from pursuing his claims against both the designer and the main contractor within a single request for arbitration because of the lack of an arbitration agreement binding all three parties. However, the employer may then initiate separate arbitrations and request their consolidation on the basis of the more lenient Article 28(1)(c).

It should not be forgotten that consolidation of parallel arbitrations under letter (c) of Article 28(1) will require the fulfilment of the other conditions stipulated in that letter. These include the existence of a common question of law or fact in the arbitrations, the availability of a single transaction or series of transactions out of which the rights to relief claimed arise, and the compatibility of the different arbitration agreements. The fulfilment of these conditions will be ascertained on a case-by-case basis.

Any jurisdictional objection concerning the conduct of multi-party arbitration under the HKIAC Rules shall be decided by the arbitral tribunal itself[213]. If the objection is made before the constitution of the tribunal, the decision shall be taken by the HKIAC following a prima facie assessment[214]. This, however, would not preclude the tribunal from taking a decision on the matter once it has been constituted.

It should also be mentioned that the clauses dealing with consolidation and single request for arbitration do not apply to arbitration agreements concluded before the date of entry into force of the new HKIAC Rules, i.e. 1 November 2013, unless the parties agree otherwise[215]. The drafters of the HKIAC Rules considered that these clauses represent a substantial change, which should not be imposed on parties who negotiated their contracts at a time when these clauses were still non-existent. In the author's opinion, this approach is to be commended. There is no such limitation with regard to the joinder article, which may be applied to any arbitration where the notice of arbitration is submitted on or after 1 November 2013 regardless of the time of conclusion of the arbitration agreement. This can probably be explained by the fact that there was a joinder provision under the earlier edition of the HKIAC Rules, and therefore the drafters decided that such a limitation was not justified with regard to the joinder article.

4.11.4 JCAA Rules[216]

Arbitrations conducted under the JCAA Rules are administered by the Japan Commercial Arbitration Association ('**JCAA**'). Recently, the JCAA substantially revised its arbitration rules, and the new JCAA Rules entered into force on 1 February 2014. They contain detailed provisions concerning multi-party arbitrations.

Rule 15 of the JCAA Rules allows for the filing of a single request for arbitration comprising multiple claims if: (i) all parties have agreed in writing that all such claims shall be resolved in single arbitration, (ii) the claims arise under the same arbitration

---

[213] Articles 19.1 and 19.3 of the HKIAC Rules.

[214] Article 19.4 of the HKIAC Rules.

[215] Article 1.4 of the HKIAC Rules.

[216] Japan Commercial Arbitration Association Commercial Arbitration Rules, in force as from 1 February 2014, http://www.jcaa.or.jp/e/arbitration/docs/Arbitration_Rules_2014e.pdf (accessed 25 July 2016).

agreement, or (iii) the claims are between the same parties and some further conditions have been satisfied. Rule 53 reiterates the same three alternative conditions with regard to consolidation of parallel conditions. None of these conditions will normally be fulfilled in a multi-contract scenario, unless the parties have included multi-party arbitration agreements in their contracts or are bound by an umbrella arbitration agreement. Of course, the parties may also consent to multi-party arbitration in the course of the proceedings but such unanimous consent can hardly be achieved because of the parties' divergent interests at that stage.

Rule 52 refers to a third party's joinder but it actually covers both joinder and intervention. The third party may join the proceedings as a claimant or be joined as a respondent. Under the JCAA Rules, the joinder will be possible only if all parties, including the third party, agree in writing to the joinder or there is a single arbitration agreement binding all parties. Any jurisdictional objections regarding multi-party arbitration will be handled by the arbitral tribunal. If the tribunal has not been appointed, JCAA will proceed with its constitution and will refer the matter to it for a determination[217].

Thus, it can be summarized that the general approach under the JCAA Rules with regard to disputes that are both multi-party and multi-contract is that the parties should explicitly agree on the conduct of multi-party arbitration[218]. Therefore, if the parties' contracts are silent on multi-party arbitration and the parties cannot reach an agreement on the matter in the course of the proceedings, as would usually be the case, multi-party arbitration may not be conducted under the JCAA Rules.

4.12 Concluding remarks regarding arbitration rules

On the basis of the above synopsis of different arbitration rules, it can be seen that the approaches under these rules to multi-party arbitration in a multi-contract setting differ substantially. The available approaches have been summarized in Table 1 towards the end of this book. It should be mentioned, however, that this table should be read with caution. It only briefly summarizes the available solutions to multi-party and multi-contract arbitrations without describing in detail all the procedural requirements necessary for the conduct of such arbitrations. Therefore, the reader should always read the table in conjunction with the full text of the relevant articles in the arbitration rules and the analysis pertaining to these articles in the present Chapter 4. Furthermore, it should be noted that the table is drafted with a view to the type of construction disputes discussed hereof, that is, multi-party disputes arising under multiple contracts entered into between non-identical parties. For this reason, multi-party arbitration provisions in the rules that are irrelevant to these disputes are not reflected in the table. For instance, situations where the applicable arbitration rules allow for consolidation with regard to

[217] Articles 15(2), 17 42, and 52.5 of the JCAA Rules.

[218] See 'The Key Points of the 2014 Amendment to the Commercial Arbitration Rules', in *31 JCAA Newsletter* (2014), pp. 1–4, http://www.jcaa.or.jp/e/arbitration/docs/news31.pdf (accessed 25 July 2016), where it has been stated that the JCAA is of the opinion that multiple claims can be heard together in a single arbitration if all the respective claims arise under the arbitration agreement or if all parties have so agreed.

arbitrations pending between the same parties are not explicitly mentioned in the table because of their irrelevance to the present discussion. Finally, the table reflects the content of the most up-to-date editions of the reviewed arbitration rules.

The analysed arbitration rules can be distinguished on the basis of their approach to parties' consent. Three main approaches can be discerned. First, there are arbitration rules that require the consent of all parties for the purposes of multi-party arbitration. This is the position under the ICC Rules, the CEPANI Rules (in respect of joinder and intervention), the LCIA Rules (in respect of consolidation), the UNCITRAL Rules, and the ICDR Rules (in their part concerning consolidation). Most arbitral institutions in Asia have also followed this trend. These include the SIAC Rules (except for the consolidation provision), the JCAA Rules, the CIETAC Rules (in their part concerning joinder) and the HKIAC Rules (except for the consolidation provision). Secondly, some arbitration rules require the consent of some of the parties for the conduct of multi-party arbitrations. A notable example in that regard is the joinder article under the LCIA Rules, where a third party may be joined, provided that the party requesting the joinder and the third party consent to the joinder. A similar provision was also contained in an earlier edition of the SIAC Rules from 2007. Thirdly, and most controversially, there are arbitration rules that do not explicitly require the consent of the parties to multi-party arbitration. This is the approach under the Swiss Rules, the CIAR, the ICDR Rules (in their part concerning joinder), the Vienna Rules (concerning joinder only), and the DIA Rules[219]. From the arbitration rules in Asia, only the HKIAC Rules and the SIAC Rules follow this flexible approach in their part concerning consolidation. It may be argued that by choosing these rules as applicable to their disputes the parties have given their anticipatory consent to multi-party arbitration under these rules, if the need for such arbitration arises.

The reviewed arbitration rules also differ with regard to the form into which parties' consent, if required, should be materialized. In general, this consent can find expression in four main forms. First, parties may have addressed multi-party arbitration in the arbitration agreements contained in their contracts. Multi-party arbitration agreements are a direct expression of the principle of party autonomy and should be recognized by most arbitral institutions and arbitral tribunals. In some cases, however, the relevant authority competent to decide on multi-party arbitration will retain some discretion on the matter. Thus, it may refuse multi-party arbitration even if the parties have included multi-party arbitration agreements in their contracts. This could happen in cases where the contemplated multi-party arbitration is likely to cause material prejudice to some of the parties[220]. For example, consolidation of parallel arbitrations in which hearings on the merits have already commenced may be undesirable in view of the significant delay that

[219] Arguably, the consolidation provision in the CEPANI Rules can also be considered as belonging to this category of arbitration rules.

[220] Gary Born (2014) *International Commercial Arbitration, Volume II: International Arbitral Procedures*, 2nd edn, Kluwer Law International, Alphen aan den Rijn, p. 2092. According to the author, 'A party should not be permitted to exercise any consolidation or joinder right that it may have in a manner that unnecessarily or unreasonably delays the resolution of the claimant's claims, or that imposes unnecessary or unreasonable expense on the claimant or other parties.'

consolidation may cause and the complexities as to which tribunal is going to review the consolidated proceedings. Such constraints on the conduct of multi-party arbitrations are in principle justified.

Secondly, there are some arbitration rules that require the explicit *procedural* consent of the parties to multi-party arbitration. This consent has to be given in the course of the proceedings regardless of the availability of multi-party arbitration agreements in the parties' contracts. Under the 2013 SIAC Rules, for instance, the written consent of the party to be joined was necessary even if this party had contractually agreed to arbitrate its disputes in a multi-party setting. The same approach was adopted under the 2012 CIETAC Rules. In the author's opinion, this approach is very conservative and lacks a proper justification. Once arbitral proceedings commence, parties relations' enter into a contentious phase where they are usually no longer inclined to co-operate. Therefore, such a requirement for an additional procedural consent can be used by a recalcitrant third party as a tactical tool to bypass its contractual commitments to participate in a multi-party arbitration. The third party will be entitled to veto a request for multi-party arbitration, and in this way put a spoke into the wheel of what could otherwise be a workable contractual mechanism for multi-party arbitration. It is exactly for this reason that the Working Party on the UNCITRAL Rules refused to introduce such a requirement in the latest version of these rules[221]. The approach under the 2013 SIAC Rules illustrates how arbitration rules may sometimes create further impediments to the conduct of multi-party arbitration instead of suiting parties' mutual arrangements to arbitrate their disputes in a multi-party setting. With the recent amendments of the SIAC Rules and the CIETAC Rules, there is no longer a requirement for parties' explicit procedural consent to multi-party arbitration. This demonstrates a positive trend among arbitral institutions to dispose of these restrictive requirements.

Thirdly, parties' consent may also be incorporated in an agreement reached once the disputes have arisen. This type of agreement is often referred to as a submission agreement. This agreement should principally enable the relevant arbitral institution or tribunal to order multi-party arbitration, provided that the agreement binds all the multiple parties. It is not very realistic, however, to expect that parties with divergent interests will enter into such an agreement. As noted in Section 3.4, not all parties are interested in multi-party arbitration. Therefore, there will usually be at least one party that will refrain from acceding to such an agreement.

Fourthly, parties' consent to multi-party arbitration can also be derived from an arbitration agreement that is binding on all multiple parties. This will be the case, for instance, if all the multiple parties have entered into an umbrella arbitration agreement executed before the respective disputes have arisen. Many institutional arbitration rules would allow the consolidation of parallel arbitrations in cases where all the parties are bound by such a single arbitration agreement regardless of whether this agreement addresses the conduct of multi-party arbitrations in explicit terms[222]. In

---

[221] Working Group II, *49th Session (15–19 September 2008, Vienna)*, UN Doc A/CN.9/665, para. 130.

[222] See for example, letter (b) of Article 10 of the ICC Rules, Article 11 of the CEPANI Rules, Article 17.5 of the UNCITRAL Rules, letter (b) of Article 8 of the ICDR Rules, etc.

the author's opinion, this approach is justified. Once a party has entered into an arbitration agreement with two or more parties, it can reasonably be assumed that this party should have foreseen that it may be involved in multi-party arbitration with the participation of the other parties[223]. The single arbitration agreement creates a jurisdictional basis for the conduct of such a multi-party arbitration. In practice, however, umbrella agreements binding all multiple parties are rarely seen in the construction sector.

On the basis of the above observations it can be concluded that the majority of arbitration rules still require the parties' consent to multi-party arbitration in the form of multi-party arbitration agreements in the parties' contracts, a submission agreement or an umbrella arbitration agreement binding all parties. However, all these expressions of consent will rarely be available when it comes to disputes under complex construction projects. As will be seen in Chapter 6, relatively few international standard forms address the question of multi-party arbitration. Often the numerous contracts pertaining to a construction project contain different bilateral arbitration agreements that are silent on multi-party arbitration. Furthermore, in most cases the multiple parties will be unwilling to agree on a single submission agreement. In these scenarios, the majority of arbitration rules would not allow the conduct of multi-party arbitration because of the lack of parties' consent to this type of arbitration. Thus, these arbitration rules do not provide for a self-contained mechanism for multi-party arbitration that can be operated solely on the basis of the provisions contained in these rules. In other words, the parties' agreement to refer to a certain set of arbitration rules addressing multi-party arbitration will not be sufficient *per se* for the conduct of such arbitration. Consequently, these rules fail to provide workable solutions to multi-party arbitration that parties may readily employ in case of need.

It may probably be argued that such a self-contained mechanism is contained in those arbitration rules that do not explicitly require the parties' consent to multi-party arbitration. By agreeing to apply those rules the parties have also agreed in advance to the application of the multi-party arbitration articles contained in these rules[224]. However, as already observed in this chapter, the flexibility of these rules has split scholars and practitioners in their opinions. Whereas some are of the opinion that the provisions in these rules can be operated without parties' consent and that they create a jurisdictional basis for multi-party arbitration, others believe that these provisions only prescribe the procedure that should be followed and that they may not *create* consent if

[223] Jeffrey Waincymer (2012) *Procedure and Evidence in International Arbitration*, Kluwer Law International, Alphen aan den Rijn, p. 509. See also Andrea Marco Steingruber (2012) *Consent in International Arbitration*, Oxford University Press, Oxford, § 10.21, and Martin Platte (2008) 'Multi-Party Arbitration: Legal Issues Arising Out of Joinder and Consolidation', in E. Gaillard and D. di Pietro (eds) *Enforcement of Arbitration Agreements and International Arbitral Awards: The New York Convention in Practice*, Cameron May, London, pp. 485–486.

[224] Ruth Stackpool-Moore (2014) 'Joinder and Consolidation – Examining Best Practice in the Swiss, HKIAC and ICC Rules', in Nathalie Voser (ed.) *Ten Years of the Swiss Rules of International Arbitration*, ASA Special Series No. 44, JurisNet LLC, New York, NY, p. 19.

such consent is not expressed in other ways[225]. Statistical information reveals that, with the exception of the consolidation provision under the HKIAC Rules, requests for multi-party arbitration based on these flexible clauses are rarely granted[226]. Arbitral institutions and arbitral tribunals constituted under these rules will usually refrain from ordering multi-party arbitration in the absence of all parties' consent thereto. One reason for this cautiousness can be the fear that the arbitral award may be set aside or that its recognition or enforcement may be denied. The decision of the Singapore Court of Appeal in the *Astro v. Lippo* case concerning the joinder provision of the 2007 SIAC Rules reminds arbitrators that this risk should not be overlooked and that flexible multi-party arbitration provisions under arbitration rules should be applied with utmost caution.

Last but not least, there is always some degree of uncertainty about the outcome of the arbitration procedure following a request for multi-party arbitration from one of the parties. The increased power of arbitral tribunals and / or arbitral institutions to order multi-party arbitration under certain circumstances and the different factors that they should take into account in their assessment inevitably results in a lesser degree of parties' control over the way the arbitral proceedings are conducted[227]. The degree of uncertainty varies depending on the applicable arbitration rules and the solutions contained thereunder. This element of uncertainty is reinforced by the presence of transitional provisions in most sets of arbitration rules that envisage that the parties shall be deemed to have agreed on the application of the rules in effect on the date of commencement of the arbitration regardless of the date of conclusion of the contract containing the relevant arbitration agreement[228]. In the author's opinion, this approach is not appropriate. In recent years, we have seen substantial revisions in existing arbitration rules especially in respect of multi-party arbitration issues. Thus, there is a significant risk that the multi-party arbitration solution adopted in the arbitration rules chosen by the parties will be different from the one that the parties anticipated at the time of conclusion of their contracts. This uncertainty can be eliminating by including multi-party arbitration agreements in parties' contracts. The presence of such agreements will make arbitral proceedings

[225] See for example, the relevant discussion in Sections 4.5, 4.6 and 4.7.

[226] See Subsection 4.5.2. See also Section 4.3 concerning the LCIA Rules. Strictly speaking the LCIA do not belong to the arbitration rules that do not require parties' consent to multi-party arbitration (because they require the consent of some of the parties only). However, the statistics revealed in that section are indicative of the conservative approach undertaken by arbitral tribunals when it comes to ordering multi-party arbitration over the objection of some of the parties. The consolidation provision under the HKIAC Rules may be considered as an exception to this conservative approach (see Subsection 4.11.3) because all the consolidation requests made under these rules have been granted (in some cases even over a party's objection to consolidation). It remains to be seen whether the consolidation provision under the new SIAC Rules will be applied in the same liberal way.

[227] Dimitar Hristoforov Kondev, 'Do Recent Overhauls of Arbitration Rules Respond to the Need for Multi-Party Arbitration in the Construction Industry?', in *32 International Construction Law Review*, no. 1 (2015), pp. 90, 94.

[228] See, for example, Article 6 (1) of ICC Rules and Article 7 (1) of CEPANI Rules. An exception in that regard is the HKIAC Rules in their part concerning consolidation and single request of arbitration (see Subsection 4.10.3.2).

more predictable, whereas the lack of contractual solutions will increase 'the fear of the unknown'.

On the basis of the analysis presented above, it can be concluded that the current legal framework of multi-party arbitration, as contained in the analysed arbitration rules, does not respond to the need for multi-party arbitration in the construction industry[229]. The arbitration rules provide certain solutions but these solutions can only be put into operation subject to parties' consent.

[229] Dimitar Hristoforov Kondev, 'Do Recent Overhauls of Arbitration Rules Respond to the Need for Multi-Party Arbitration in the Construction Industry?', in *32 International Construction Law Review*, no. 1 (2015), p. 94.

Chapter 5
Multi-Party Arbitration Solutions under Arbitration Laws[1]

As pointed out in Section 4.12, arbitration rules do not provide for a self-contained mechanism for resolving multi-party construction disputes, which can be operated solely on the basis of the provisions contained in these rules. This raises the question whether national arbitration laws can provide for a workable solution to be applied to cases where parties' contracts are silent on multi-party arbitration.

Due to the inherent consensual nature of arbitration, national laws usually refrain from dealing with multi-party arbitration. The UNCITRAL Model Law is also silent on the matter. However, a few states have introduced statutory multi-party arbitration provisions allowing for consolidation of parallel arbitrations and / or joinder of third parties into pending arbitration under certain conditions.

A question may arise as to which law governs questions of joinder, intervention and consolidation. In scholarly writings, two possible answers are proposed[2]. First, it has been stated that because questions of multi-party arbitration are of purely procedural character, the law of the seat (*lex arbitri*) should probably apply to these matters[3]. Hence, statutory multi-party arbitration provisions may come into play if the place of arbitration is located in a state that has followed this statutory approach. The present author prefers this first view. Thus, for example, if the parties have chosen London as the seat of arbitration, the English Arbitration Act will apply as to the possibility of consolidation (subject, of course, to the content of the arbitration agreement and the applicable arbitration

[1] Parts of this chapter were first published in the article 'Statutory Approaches to Multi-Party / Multi-Contract Construction Arbitration', in *19 The Vindobona Journal of International Commercial Law and Arbitration*, no. 1 (2015), pp. 31–54.

[2] Edwin Tong Chun Fai and Nakul Dewan, 'Drafting Arbitration Agreements with Consolidation in Mind', in *5 Asian International Arbitration Journal*, no. 1 (2009), p. 89.

[3] Jeffrey Waincymer (2012) *Procedure and Evidence in International Arbitration*, Kluwer Law International, Alphen aan den Rijn, p. 564. See also ICC Case No. 12171, Award on Third Party Person Notice, 7 April 2004, an extract of which is published in *23 ASA Bulletin* no. 2 (2005), p. 271, where the arbitral tribunal made the following statement with regard to the requested joinder of a third party: 'The issue, however, whether a request for third person notice is to be admitted in arbitration proceedings is of a procedural nature and thus subject to the rules governing the proceedings.'

Multi-Party and Multi-Contract Arbitration in the Construction Industry, First Edition.
Dimitar Kondev.

rules). Secondly, it has been argued that the law applicable to the arbitration agreement should principally govern questions of multi-party arbitration[4]. Under this second view, questions of multi-party arbitration can be looked at within the prism of parties' consent given the predominant role of party autonomy on the subject[5]. Due to the autonomous character of the arbitration agreement, there is no uniform view as to which law governs the arbitration agreement itself[6]. In most cases, this would either be the *lex arbitri* or the governing law of the contract (the law applicable to the substance of the contract). For example, if there is a main contract governed by Dutch law and a seat of arbitration in London, the choice will be between the Dutch law and the law of England and Wales. Even if this second view is followed, however, the more likely outcome seems to be the application of the *lex arbitri*[7] (i.e. the English Arbitration Act in the given example).

This chapter contains an overview of some legislative approaches to multi-party arbitration. Since the majority of states have not provided statutory regulation on this matter, the focus in this chapter naturally falls on the arbitration laws of those states which address multi-party arbitration. Some of these laws are based on the UNCITRAL Model Law, subject to certain modifications, and therefore the position under the UNCITRAL Model Law is discussed first (Section 5.1). The chapter then continues with a discussion of the arbitration laws in the United Kingdom (Section 5.2), the Netherlands (Section 5.3), Belgium (Section 5.4), New Zealand (Section 5.5), Hong Kong (Section 5.6), Canada (Section 5.7) and Australia (Section 5.8). The arbitration laws of some other countries are also occasionally mentioned (Section 5.9). Section 5.10 is dedicated to multi-party arbitration in the United States, where court-ordered consolidation is sometimes ordered not only on the basis of statutes but also case law. After having reviewed the different legislative approaches to the topic, the appropriateness of the statutory approach to multi-party arbitration is discussed (Section 5.11) and some concluding remarks are made (Section 5.12).

5.1 UNCITRAL Model Law

Legislation based on the UNCITRAL Model Law has been adopted in 72 states and a total of 102 jurisdictions[8]. The UNCITRAL Model law does not regulate any forms of multi-party arbitration. Some countries following the UNCITRAL Model Law have

[4] Gary Born (2014) *International Commercial Arbitration, Volume II: International Arbitral Procedures*, 2nd edn, Kluwer Law International, Alphen aan den Rijn, p. 2076.

[5] Ibid.

[6] See on that point Martin Hunter and Alan Redfern with Nigel Blackaby and Constantine Partasides (2004) *Law and Practice of International Commercial Arbitration*, 4th edn, Sweet & Maxwell, London, pp. 124–130.

[7] Gary Born (2014) *International Commercial Arbitration, Volume II: International Arbitral Procedures*, 2nd edn, Kluwer Law International, Alphen aan den Rijn, p. 2076. According to the author, the application of the lex arbitri 'is consistent with the quasi-procedural character of questions of consolidation, intervention and joinder, as well as with the tendency of national arbitration legislation (when it addresses the issue) to be limited to locally-seated arbitrations.'

[8] Current information about the states that have adopted the UNCITRAL Model Law can be obtained at http://www.uncitral.org/uncitral/en/uncitral_texts/arbitration/1985Model_arbitration_status.html (accessed 25 July 2016).

introduced certain modifications to the draft proposed by UNCITRAL and have included consolidation provisions in their statutes[9]. The national arbitration laws of some of these countries will be examined later on in this chapter.

It has been suggested that Article 19(2) of the UNCTRAL Model Law may be used as a basis for an arbitral tribunal to order consolidation or joinder in cases where the applicable arbitration rules are silent on multi-party arbitration[10]. Article 19(2) envisages that failing parties' agreement regarding the procedural rules to be applied, the arbitral tribunal can conduct the arbitration in such manner as it considers appropriate. This position is debatable. In the author's opinion, it is very unlikely than an arbitral tribunal would allow the conduct of multi-party arbitration solely on the basis of the discussed article. The discretion of the tribunal under Article 19(2) to set procedural rules should be exercised only within the limits of the arbitration agreements in the parties' contracts. It is the author's opinion that Article 19(2) merely concerns ancillary procedural questions, such as, for example, rules on the taking of evidence, witness statements and the organization of hearings, and cannot be applied to core questions that may have a significant impact on the conduct of the proceedings, such as multi-party arbitration. Hence, if the relevant arbitration agreements are silent on multi-party arbitration and the parties cannot reach an agreement on the matter, the tribunal may not use Article 19(2) as a jurisdictional basis to order consolidation or joinder over a party's objection[11].

An additional argument against such a broad interpretation of Article 19(2) can be found in the preparatory works of the model law. They reveal that the drafters of the UNCITRAL Model Law considered the inclusion of a consolidation provision in the original 1985 version of the model law[12] and in the amended 2006 version[13]. These proposals, however, were ultimately rejected. Furthermore, the official explanatory note to the 2006 amendments in the UNCITRAL Model Law sets out that the question of consolidation is not regulated in the UNCITRAL Model Law[14].

The absence of specific provisions regulating multi-party arbitration matters in the UNCITRAL Model Law means that contracting parties cannot request joinder, intervention and / or consolidation solely on the basis of legislative provisions in countries

---

[9] Among these countries are Ireland, Australia, Scotland, Singapore, Malaysia and Peru.

[10] Kristina Maria Siig, 'Multi-party Arbitration in International Trade: Problems and Solutions', in *1 International Journal of Liability and Scientific Enquiry*, no. 1/2 (2007), p. 80.

[11] A similar opinion has been shared by Delaram Mehdizadeh Jafari (2012) *Resolution of Multiparty Construction Disputes under the Singapore International Arbitration Legal Framework*. Unpublished PhD thesis. National University of Singapore, pp. 47–48.

[12] See Working Group II, *3rd Session (16–26 February 1982, New York)*, UN Doc A/CN.9/216, pp. 36–37, para. 37. At this session it was discussed whether consolidation agreements should be given effect, or whether even without such agreements consolidation might be ordered. There was a general agreement that the model law should not deal with these questions.

[13] Matters concerning consolidation were given low priority and were not discussed further. See Commission Sessions, *32nd Session (17 May–4 June, 1999, Vienna)*, UN Doc A/54/17, p. 43, para. 356–357. See also Commission Sessions, *32nd Session (17 May–4 June, 1999, Vienna)*, UN Doc A/CN.9/460, pp. 15–17, para. 51–61.

[14] See para. 17 of the Explanatory Note by the UNCITRAL Secretariat on the 1985 Model Law on International Commercial Arbitration as amended in 2006, http://www.uncitral.org/pdf/english/texts/arbitration/ml-arb/MLARB-explanatoryNote20-9-07.pdf (accessed 25 July 2016).

which have adopted this law. Gary Born has stated that 'consolidation and joinder / intervention should be required – as an element of the parties' agreement to arbitrate – where that is what the parties have agreed, but not otherwise'[15]. Hence, contracting parties should generally address these issues in their arbitration agreements in an explicit manner. The parties' silence as to multi-party arbitration cannot be construed as consent to this type of arbitration. As mentioned in Subsection 2.4.1, the presence of separate arbitration clauses silent on multi-party arbitration, which are contained in two or more contracts binding non-identical parties, creates a strong presumption that each contracting party expects to resolve its dispute in a bipolar setting with its counterparty only.

On the other hand, if the parties have included multi-party arbitration clauses in their contracts, these provisions should be given effect. This stems from the basic requirement under the UNCITRAL Model Law that arbitration agreements should be recognized and enforced in accordance with the intentions of the parties[16]. Article II of the New York Convention also requires from each contracting state to recognize arbitration agreements concluded by the parties.

5.2 The United Kingdom

In *England*, the position has always been that multi-party arbitration cannot take place without parties' consent[17]. Prior to 1996, there was no statutory provision dealing with the different forms of multi-party arbitration[18]. In *Property Investments (Developments) Ltd. v. Byfield Building Services Ltd.*[19] it was stated:

> Much emphasis was placed on the fact that it will not be possible to join a third party in the present dispute. This is, however, a fact of life in a great many arbitrations...Plainly, when two parties enter into a commercial contract containing an arbitration clause they know, or ought to know, that in multi-party disputes they will be unable to join other parties. This is a risk of future inconvenience which they assume in the interest of the perceived benefits of arbitration.

Thus, the position was that courts had no power to join third parties in pending arbitration, which was something that the parties had to accept. The limited power of the courts can also be illustrated with the well-known case *Abu Dhabi Gas Liquefaction Co Ltd. v. Eastern Bechtel Corp*[20]. The case concerned the erection of tanks for the storage of liquefied natural gas in the Persian Gulf. The main contract was concluded with

[15] Gary Born (2014) *International Commercial Arbitration, Volume II: International Arbitral Procedures*, 2nd edn, Kluwer Law International, Alphen aan den Rijn, p. 2574.

[16] Ibid.

[17] Peter Sheridan (1999) *Construction and Engineering Arbitration*, Sweet & Maxwell, London, p. 314.

[18] For the position under English law prior to 1996 and the difficulties stemming from the court's inability to consolidate related proceedings, see V. V. Veeder, 'Multi-Party Disputes: Consolidation under English Law *The Vimeira* – a Sad Forensic Fable', in *2 Arbitration International*, no. 4 (1986), pp. 310–322.

[19] *Property Investments (Developments) Ltd. v. Byfield Building Services Ltd*, in *31 Building Law Reports* (1986), pp. 47–56.

[20] *Abu Dhabi Gas Liquefaction Co Ltd. v. Eastern Bechtel Corp.*, in *21 Building Law Reports* (1983), pp. 117–126.

a consortium of two contractors who had entered into two separate subcontracts with one and the same subcontractor. Cracks appeared in one of the tanks, which resulted in expensive repair works. The question arose as to who was responsible for the repair works. The employers claimed against the main contractors and the latter claimed against the subcontractor. The issue of causation was central to both disputes. The trial judge appointed a different arbitrator in each of the proceedings[21]. The main contractors maintained that the same arbitrator should be appointed in both proceedings and appealed before the Court of Appeal. It was stated by one of the judges at the latter court that the ideal solution would have been multi-party arbitration, which would have eliminated the risk of inconsistent findings in both proceedings. This was, however, not feasible, because of the lack of parties' agreement on such type of arbitration. Therefore, the Court of Appeal tried to propose a compromise solution in the appointment of one and the same arbitrator in both proceedings. This proposal was, however, made subject to the parties' consent. It was acknowledged that this approach could create problems[22]. For example, the subcontractor, who had no right to participate in the main contract arbitration, had reasons to fear that the arbitrator might form an opinion, during the main contract arbitration, which could be detrimental to him, and which could be difficult to dispel in the course of the subcontract arbitration[23]. This opinion might be formed on the basis of evidence that was to be presented in the first arbitration but not in the second arbitration[24]. Furthermore, there was no guarantee that the risk of inconsistent findings was fully eliminated[25]. Even though this result may appear unsatisfactory, there was nothing more that the court could have done given its limited powers to order multi-party arbitration.

---

[21] The parties could not agree on the appointment of arbitrators in the two proceedings. The main contractors wanted the same arbitrator for both arbitrations but the subcontractor disagreed. There was an agreement among all parties that the English High Court will have the power to appoint the arbitrators in default of agreement.

[22] For the issues arising out of the appointment of the same arbitrator(s) in two or more related proceedings, see Hans Van Houtte (1991) 'Due Process in Multi-Party Arbitration', in P. Bellet, P. Bernardini, G. Bernini *et al.* (eds) *Multi-Party Arbitration: Views from International Arbitration Specialists*, Publication No. 480/1, ICC Publishing SA, Paris, pp. 189–195.

[23] See the Commentary on *Abu Dhabi Gas Liquefaction Co Ltd. v. Eastern Bechtel Corp.*, in *21 Building Law Reports* (1983), p. 120. For that reason, the Court of Appeal stated that if there was any disadvantage to a party resulting from the appointment of one and the same arbitrator in both proceedings then this party was allowed to apply to the court and request the appointment of a different arbitrator.

[24] Chandra Mohan Rethman and Wee Teck Lim, 'Some Contractual Approaches to the Problem of Inconsistent Awards in Multi-Party, Multi-Contract Arbitration Proceedings', in *1 Asian International Arbitration Journal*, no. 2 (2005), pp. 165–166.

[25] Even though the appointment of the same tribunal in two or more proceedings is in principle capable of reducing the risk of inconsistent findings, this mechanism cannot fully eliminate this risk. The tribunal is bound to render an award on the basis of the submissions and evidence presented in the particular arbitration. If there is a significant difference in the evidence presented in the separate proceedings this may well result in inconsistent findings on similar points of law and / or fact despite the fact that it was the same arbitrator who conducted the proceedings. See, on that point, Fritz Nicklisch, 'Multi-Party Arbitration and Dispute Resolution in Major Industrial Projects', in *11 Journal of International Arbitration*, Issue 4 (1994), p. 66; Julian Lew, Harris Bor, Gregory Fullelove and Joanne Greenaway (eds) (2013) *Arbitration in England with Chapters on Scotland and Ireland*, Kluwer Law International, Alphen aan den Rijn, pp. 473–474 (para. 22.58).

The case of *Oxford Shipping Co Ltd. v. Nippon Yusen Kaisha (The Eastern Saga)*[26] is also illustrative of the inability of courts to order multi-party arbitration and other measures aiming at minimizing the risk of inconsistent findings, such as concurrent hearing of disputes. A vessel, owned by Oxford Shipping, was chartered to Nippon Kaisha, and the latter sub-chartered it to a third party. A dispute arose between the owner and the charterer, of which the dispute between the charterer and the sub-charterer was to be regarded as a mirror image. The same arbitrators were appointed in each of the two cases, and they ordered concurrent hearing of the disputes. The question arose as to whether such an order was within the powers of the arbitrators. The owners applied to the High Court to have the order set aside. The judge stated that the arbitrators had no such power:

> It seems to me that, as is graven on the heart of any commercial lawyer, arbitrators in the position of these arbitrators enjoy no power to order concurrent hearings, or anything of that nature, without the consent of the parties. The concept of private arbitrations derives simply from the fact that the parties have agreed to submit to arbitration particular disputes arising between them and only between them. It is implicit in this that strangers shall be excluded from the hearing and conduct of the arbitration and that neither the tribunal nor any of the parties can insist that the dispute shall be heard or determined concurrently with or even in consonance with another dispute, however convenient that course may be to the party seeking it and however closely associated the disputes in question may be.

The decisions in the abovementioned cases were made prior to the adoption of the English Arbitration Act 1996[27]. The new act is not based on the UNCITRAL Model Law but there is a close resemblance between some of the clauses of the act and the model law. The Arbitration Act is silent on the questions of joinder and intervention but it deals with consolidation of parallel proceedings in Section 35. This provision merely codifies the existing case law on the matter and does not change the English position as to multi-party arbitration[28].

Pursuant to Section 35:

> (1) The parties are free to agree –
> (a) that the arbitral proceedings shall be consolidated with other arbitral proceedings, or
> (b) that concurrent hearings shall be held,
> on such terms as may be agreed.
> (2) Unless the parties agree to confer such power on the tribunal, the tribunal has no power to order consolidation of proceedings or concurrent hearings.

---

[26] *Oxford Shipping Co Ltd. v. Nippon Yusen Kaisha (The Eastern Saga)*, in *2 Lloyd's Law Reports* (1984), ref. p. 373. See also 'England and Wales: Oxford Shipping Co Ltd. v Nippon Yusen Kaisha (The Eastern Saga)', in *2 Journal of International Arbitration*, no.1 (1985), pp. 79–81.

[27] Arbitration Act 1996, http://www.legislation.gov.uk/ukpga/1996/23/contents (accessed 25 July 2016).

[28] In *Great Ormond Street Hospital NHS Trust v. Secretary of State for Health*, His Honour Humphrey Lloyd has stated that: 'I do not think that one can infer from s 35 (consolidation and concurrent hearings) that the policy of the Act is positively to encourage multiplicity of proceedings although I would accept that the Act does nothing to assist the resolution of multi-party disputes by arbitration, other than to accord primacy to the parties' agreements...Section 35(1) is merely permissive (it could hardly have been otherwise); s 35(2) does no more than record existing law.' See *Great Ormond Street Hospital NHS Trust v. Secretary of State for Health and others*, in *56 Construction Law Reports* (1997), p. 28.

Under Section 35, consolidation will only be possible if all the parties vest the tribunal with the power to consolidate. In a multi-contract context, this means that arbitral tribunals and institutions may not trespass parties' expectations to resolve their disputes with their contractual party only if the parties' contracts are silent on consolidation and the chosen arbitration rules do not provide for a self-contained system for consolidation of parallel arbitrations.

Some criticism has been expressed against the approach under Section 35. It is true that the clause promotes the supremacy of party autonomy by leaving the decision on the conduct of multi-party arbitration to contracting parties. On the other side, the clause is too general in content and can hardly be of any guidance to users of the English arbitration regime[29]. Furthermore, if contracting parties want to agree on multi-party arbitration, they may do so regardless of the existence of such a declaratory clause. Other authors have expressed the opinion that the provision should have been replaced with a rule authorizing consolidation, which applies by default, unless the parties explicitly exclude its application[30].

The report of the Departmental Advisory Committee on Arbitration Law ('**DAC**') on the draft proposal of the Arbitration Act contains some useful information concerning the adoption of Section 35. The report indicates that different suggestions have been discussed during the consultation stage of the draft. One of the submissions called for a provision that would empower either a tribunal or a court (or both) to order consolidation or concurrent hearings[31]. The suggestion was considered carefully by the DAC but was rejected with the following reasoning:

> In our view it would amount to a negation of the principle of party autonomy to give the tribunal or the Court the power to order consolidation or concurrent hearings. Indeed it would to our minds go far towards frustrating the agreement of the parties to have their own tribunal for their own disputes...Accordingly we would be opposed to giving the tribunal or the Court this power. However, if the parties agree to invest the tribunal with such a power, then we would have no objection[32].

It was also stated in the report that questions concerning multi-party arbitration could be best solved by obtaining the agreement of the parties and not by legislating[33].

It addition, it was suggested that proper consolidation clauses may be proposed by those drafting standard forms of contract or by institutions that offer arbitration services[34]. This position seems to be understandable. It is widely accepted nowadays that the interference of national legislation and state courts in arbitral proceedings should be kept to the minimum because of the private and consensual character of arbitration.

---

[29] Dimitrios Athanasakis and Robert Morgan, 'Joinder of Arbitrations: an Overview of English and Hong Kong Construction Industry Practice', in *Asian Dispute Review* no. 1 (2008), p. 19,

[30] Michael Marks Cohen, 'A Missed Opportunity to Revise the 1996 Arbitration Act', in *23 Arbitration International*, no. 3 (2007), pp. 463–464.

[31] Lord Justice Saville *et al.*, 'The 1996 DAC Report on the English Arbitration Bill', in *13 Arbitration International*, no. 3 (1997), pp. 303–304 (para. 178). The report is also available at http://uk.practicallaw.com/6-205-5120 (accessed 25 July 2016).

[32] Ibid., p. 304 (para. 180).

[33] Ibid., p. 304 (para. 181).

[34] Ibid.

In England, the question of resolution of multi-party disputes has been closely intertwined with the authority of state courts to stay litigation in favour of arbitration whenever faced with a dispute subject to a valid arbitration clause. Under the legal regime prior to 1997, it was possible in some cases for the court to refuse to stay court proceedings in favour of arbitration in order to allow all of the multiple disputes to be litigated[35]. Exemplary in that regard is the case of *Taunton-Collins v. Cromie*[36]. In this case, an employer commenced court proceedings against an architect, alleging, among other things, that the architect was negligent in respect of the design of a house. In the course of the proceedings, the architect blamed the main contractors for the defects. In response to this, the employer claimed against the contractors, and they were joined as second defendants. The contractors applied for a stay of the court proceedings due to the presence of a valid arbitration clause in their contract with the employer. The Court of Appeal refused to stay the court proceedings and decided that the related disputes should be litigated because of the undesirability of having separate proceedings on the same subject matter and the possible risk of inconsistent findings[37]. This case was relied upon in several other construction cases with a similar outcome[38]. However, the courts' discretion to refuse to grant a stay was applicable only with regard to domestic arbitration agreements[39]. The Arbitration Act 1996 removed any distinction between domestic and non-domestic agreements and divested the courts of their power to refuse a stay. Thus, under the current regime, the courts are obliged to grant a stay in all cases where court proceedings are initiated in respect of a dispute that is subject to a valid arbitration agreement[40].

Unlike England, *Scotland* decided to base its legislation on the UNCITRAL Model Law and adopted a new arbitration Act in 2010[41]. Despite the different approach, Scots law broadly follows the Arbitration Act 1996, which applies in England. The approach to consolidation is not an exception in that regard. Like in England, the tribunal is entitled to issue a consolidation order only if it has been authorized by the parties to do so[42].

---

[35] This was possible on the basis of Section 4 of the Arbitration Act 1950. This provision gave competent courts the discretion (rather than the obligation) to stay court proceedings upon the application of a party against which court proceedings had been commenced in respect of a dispute that was subject to arbitration. For further details concerning the pre-1997 courts' discretion to refuse to grant a stay and relevant case law, see William Godwin (1998) 'Arbitration or Litigation? Multi-Party Disputes and Arbitration Clauses', in Anthony Thornton and William Godwin (eds) *Construction Law: Themes and Practice, Essays in Honour of I.N. Duncan Wallace Q.C.*, Sweet & Maxwell, London, pp. 245–272.

[36] *Taunton-Collins v. Cromie and Others*, in *1 The Weekly Law Reports* (1964), pp. 633–638.

[37] Ibid., pp. 635–636.

[38] See, for example, *Berkshire Senior Citizens Housing Association Ltd v. McCarthy E. Fitt Ltd and National Westminster Bank Ltd.*, in *15 Building Law Reports* (1981), pp. 27–36, and *Great Ormond Street Hospital NHS Trust v. Secretary of State for Health and others*, in *56 Construction Law Reports* (1997), pp. 1–30.

[39] Robert Merkin (2004) *Arbitration Law*, Informa, London, pp. 648–649.

[40] Section 9(4) of the Arbitration Act 1996.

[41] Arbitration (Scotland) Act 2010, http://www.legislation.gov.uk/asp/2010/1/contents (accessed 25 July 2016).

[42] Consolidation in Scotland is regulated under Rule 40 of Schedule 1 (Scottish Arbitration Rules) which is an inseparable part of the Arbitration (Scotland) Act 2010. Pursuant to this rule: 'Parties may agree –

(a) to consolidation the arbitration with another arbitration, or

(b) to hold concurrent hearings.

(2) But the tribunal may not order such consolidation, or the holding of concurrent hearings, on its own initiative.'

5.3 *The Netherlands*

In the Netherlands, consolidation of parallel arbitral proceedings was first introduced in 1986 with the adoption of Article 1046 of the Netherlands Code of Civil Procedure. This article was included as a result of lobbying exerted by the domestic construction industry[43]. It envisaged that arbitral proceedings on related issues, which were pending before different tribunals in the Netherlands, could be consolidated by virtue of an order issued by the President of the Amsterdam District Court following a party's request. The majority of consolidation requests as of 1997 concerned construction cases, and the president of the Amsterdam District Court almost always ordered consolidation following such requests[44].

On 27 May 2014, the Dutch Parliament adopted certain amendments in the Netherlands Code of Civil Procedure which also concerned Article 1046[45]. These amendments entered into force on 1 January 2015. Pursuant to the new Article 1046:

> 1. In respect of arbitral proceedings pending in the Netherlands, a party may request that a third person designated to that end by the parties order consolidation with other arbitral proceedings pending within or outside the Netherlands, unless the parties have agreed otherwise. In the absence of a third person designated to that end by the parties, the provisional relief judge of the district court of Amsterdam may be requested to order consolidation of arbitral proceedings pending in the Netherlands with other arbitral proceedings pending in the Netherlands, unless the parties have agreed otherwise.
> 2. Consolidation may be ordered insofar as it does not cause unreasonable delay in the pending proceedings, also in view of the stage they have reached, and the two arbitral proceedings are so closely connected that good administration of justice renders it expedient to hear and determine them together to avoid the risk of irreconcilable decisions resulting from separate proceedings...

The provisional relief judge of the district court of Amsterdam or the third party, as the case may be, shall decide on the request after he has given all the parties involved and also the arbitrators (if already appointed) an opportunity to express their opinions on the consolidation request[46]. Once the consolidation request has been granted, it is up to the parties to agree on the constitution of the arbitral tribunal and the procedural rules to be applied to the consolidated proceedings. If the parties are unable to reach an agreement, then it is the third party or the provisional relief judge who shall decide on these matters[47].

---

[43] Jacomijn van Haersolte-Van Hof, 'Consolidation Under the English Arbitration Act 1996: A View from the Netherlands', in *13 Arbitration International*, no. 4 (1997), p. 427.

[44] Ibid., pp. 427–428. The author has stated that the parties often gave up objecting to the consolidation requests and that they merely tried to co-operate in appointing mutually acceptable arbitrators and working out which rules should apply. Some parties even forewent the opportunity to attend the hearings scheduled to discuss a consolidation request, as a result of which the president of the district court often issued decisions by default.

[45] For an English translation of the Netherlands Code of Civil Procedure in its part concerning arbitration, see http://www.nai-nl.org/downloads/Text%20Dutch%20Code%20Civil%20Procedure.pdf (accessed 25 July 2016).

[46] Article 1046(3) of the Netherlands Code of Civil Procedure.

[47] Article 1046(4) of the Netherlands Code of Civil Procedure.

In its substance, the new consolidation article largely resembles the previous one. However, there are a few important differences. The main amendment is that consolidation can be ordered by a third person designated by the parties. This is a new feature of the legislation. In the absence of such a designation, consolidation can be ordered by the provisional relief judge of the district court of Amsterdam. Under the earlier consolidation article, the President of the Amsterdam District Court had the exclusive authority to decide on consolidation requests. Under the current regime, the third party has greater powers than the provisional relief judge. While the latter may only order consolidation of parallel arbitrations pending in the Netherlands, the third party may order consolidation of a pending proceeding in the Netherlands with another arbitral proceeding regardless of whether this second proceeding takes place in or outside the Netherlands.

The other important change concerns the second paragraph of Article 1046. This new paragraph provides some guidance to the deciding authority by outlining certain criteria that should be taken into account when deciding on a consolidation request. In this respect, the new paragraph is more elaborate than its predecessor, which only demanded the existence of a connection between the pending proceedings without requiring consideration of other factors.

Both the previous and the new consolidation articles have an *opt-out* character. In other words, the consolidation provision will apply by default, unless the parties agree to exclude its application. This solution has been criticized by some authors who consider that it violates the autonomy of the will of the parties because foreign contractors will often be unaware of the particularity of this law and will be unable to reach an agreement to exclude it once the dispute has arisen[48].

It seems that stakeholders from the Dutch construction sector have not been entirely satisfied with the application of the consolidation provision[49]. For that reason, contracting parties in the Netherlands typically opt out of Article 1046 by adopting institutional rules, such as those of the Court of Arbitration for the Building Industry[50]. Therefore, the statutory approach to consolidation in the Netherlands has become redundant as far as the Dutch construction industry is concerned.

The Netherlands consolidation provision will seldom find application to international construction disputes. If the parties have not explicitly designated a third person to decide on the consolidation request, the provision can be invoked only in respect of proceedings pending in the Netherlands. This, in itself, is a significant limitation of the scope of application of Article 1046. Furthermore, international standard forms often refer to the application of institutional arbitration rules. The parties' choice of

---

[48] Francois Poudret and Sébastien Besson (2007) *Comparative Law of International Arbitration*, 2nd edn, Sweet & Maxwell, London, p. 206. See also Pieter Sanders (1999) *Quo Vadis Arbitration? Sixty Years of Arbitration Practice, A Comparative Study*, Kluwer Law International, The Hague, p. 219, who has stated that an opt-in solution would have been more in line with the requirement of consent of the parties.

[49] Jacomijn van Haersolte-Van Hof, 'Consolidation Under the English Arbitration Act 1996: A View from the Netherlands', in *13 Arbitration International*, no. 4 (1997), p. 428.

[50] John Marrin (2009) 'Multiparty Arbitration in the Construction Industry', in the Permanent Court of Arbitration (ed.) *Multiple Party Actions in International Arbitration*, Oxford University Press, New York, NY, pp. 410–411.

these rules will constitute an opt-out of the statutory consolidation provision. Thus, if a main contract is based on some of the FIDIC Contracts, such as the FIDIC Red Book, the reference to the ICC Rules therein will constitute the parties' agreement to exclude the possibility for consolidation under Article 1046. The ICC Rules contain a different mechanism for consolidation, pursuant to which the ICC Court has the exclusive authority to decide on consolidation requests. Therefore, if a consolidation request is made, the consolidation article under the ICC Rules will apply in lieu of Article 1046[51].

Article 1045 of the Netherlands Code of Civil Procedure regulates joinder and intervention of third parties in pending proceedings[52]. This provision, however, requires the existence of an arbitration agreement binding all parties. Therefore, the article can find application to multi-contract situations only in cases where the parties are bound by an umbrella arbitration agreement.

5.4 *Belgium*

Belgium has a new arbitration law that introduces a framework for arbitration largely based on the UNCITRAL Model Law. The new Belgian arbitration law entered into force on 1 September 2013[53]. It does not address consolidation but it contains a clause dealing with both joinder and intervention. Pursuant to Article 1709 of the Belgian Judicial Code:

> § 1. Any interested third party may apply to the arbitral tribunal to join the proceedings. The request must be put to the arbitral tribunal in writing, and the tribunal shall communicate it to the parties.
> § 2. Any party may call upon a third party to join the proceedings.
> § 3. In any event, the admissibility of such joinder requires an arbitration agreement between the third party and the parties involved in the arbitration. Moreover, such joinder is subject to the unanimous consent of the arbitral tribunal.

As evident from the last paragraph, this article cannot be applied to join disputes based on multiple contracts, unless all the parties are bound by a single arbitration agreement.

---

[51] See Albert Jan van den Berg, 'Consolidation Arbitrations, the New York Arbitration Convention and the Dutch Arbitration Act 1986 – A Replique to Mr Jarvin', in 3 *Arbitration International*, no. 3 (1987), pp. 260–261.

[52] Article 1045, effective as from 1 January 2015: '1. Unless the parties have agreed otherwise, at the written request of a third person who has an interest in the arbitral proceedings, the arbitral tribunal may allow that person to join or intervene in the proceedings, provided that the same arbitration agreement as between the original parties applies or enters into force between the parties and the third person…'

[53] The new arbitration law is contained in Chapter 6 of the Belgian Judicial Code, in force from 1 September 2013. An English translation of Chapter 6 is available at http://www.cepani.be/en/arbitration/belgian-judicial-code-provisions (accessed 25 July 2016).

5.5 New Zealand

The New Zealand 1996 Arbitration Act is also based on the UNCITRAL Model Law[54]. It allows for consolidation of related arbitral proceedings under Subsection 2 of Schedule 2[55]. The clause distinguishes between situations where the same tribunal has been appointed in each of the arbitrations and those where the related arbitral proceedings do not have the same tribunal. In the first case, any party may apply for consolidation, and the request shall be dealt with by the tribunal itself[56]. If the tribunal refuses to admit consolidation, any of the parties can refer the matter to the High Court of New Zealand, which may issue a consolidation order[57]. In the second case, any party in the proceedings may request consolidation, and it is the tribunal dealing with the arbitration involving that same party that has the competence to decide on the question of consolidation[58]. Consolidation will be granted in the form of a provisional order. The order ceases to be provisional once the tribunal(s) reviewing the other related disputes issue provisional consolidation orders that are consistent with the first order[59]. If such orders are not issued by the other tribunal(s), any party may refer the question to the High Court, which may issue the order(s) instead[60]. Once the proceedings have been consolidated, it is up to the parties to agree on the tribunal which will review the consolidated arbitration. Failing such an agreement, the tribunal will be appointed by the High Court[61].

Even though the existence of a certain link between the related arbitrations is generally required as a precondition for the issuance of a consolidation order, the arbitral tribunal or the High Court, as the case may be, has a wide discretion to consolidate the proceedings[62]. Furthermore, in both situations examined above, there is no requirement that the parties under the different arbitral proceedings should be the same[63]. Therefore, theoretically speaking, the consolidation provision may find application to construction disputes arising under multiple contracts even if the parties have not envisaged multi-party arbitration in their contracts. However, the New Zealand statutory rule has a rather limited application when it comes to international arbitrations.

---

[54] New Zealand Arbitration Act 1996, http://www.legislation.govt.nz/act/public/1996/0099/latest/DLM403277.html (accessed 16 April 2016).

[55] Subsection 2 of Schedule 2 of the Arbitration Act 1996.

[56] Subsection 2(1)(a) of Schedule 2 of the New Zealand Arbitration Act 1996.

[57] Subsection 2(1)(b) of Schedule 2 of the New Zealand Arbitration Act 1996.

[58] Subsection 2(2)(a) of Schedule 2 of the New Zealand Arbitration Act 1996.

[59] Subsection 2(2)(b) of Schedule 2 of the New Zealand Arbitration Act 1996.

[60] Subsection 2(2)(d) of Schedule 2 of the New Zealand Arbitration Act 1996. The High Court will have similar powers if inconsistent provisional orders have been issued by the different tribunals. In this case, the court is empowered to amend the orders in order to make them consistent (Subsection 2(2)(e) of the New Zealand Arbitration Act 1996).

[61] Subsection 2(3) of Schedule 2 of the New Zealand Arbitration Act 1996.

[62] Pursuant to Subsection 2(4) of Schedule 2 of the New Zealand Arbitration Act 1996, consolidation should not be allowed unless: (a) common questions of law or fact exist in the related proceedings, (b) the claimed rights of relief arise out of the same transactions or series of transactions, or (c) 'for some other reason it is desirable to make the order or the provisional order'.

[63] This is explicitly specified in Subsection 2(7) of Schedule 2 of the New Zealand Arbitration Act 1996.

Unlike domestic arbitrations, where the clause applies as a default rule, the parties involved in international arbitrations have to opt-in for its application[64]. Anecdotal evidence suggests that there is no case law in New Zealand concerning the consolidation provision.

5.6 *Hong Kong*

Hong Kong's arbitration legislation is also based on the UNCITRAL Model Law. Hong Kong was one of the first countries that introduced a consolidation provision in its arbitration act. Consolidation was first dealt with under the 1982 Arbitration Ordinance, which gave courts a wide discretion to issue regulatory orders concerning related arbitrations, including consolidation orders[65]. The clause applied mainly to domestic arbitrations and rarely to international arbitrations[66]. It did not explicitly refer to parties' consent to consolidation, and therefore it was possible to apply that clause to multi-party disputes stemming from contracts containing arbitration agreements silent on consolidation[67]. Furthermore, the then effective legislation did not explicitly regulate whether the parties had the right to opt out of the consolidation clause. The application of this clause was considered in the well known *Shui On* cases[68].

The cases concerned a domestic project for the construction of two 34-storey buildings. Shui On was the main contractor on the site who had entered into numerous subcontracts. One of them was with Schindler Lifts. It concerned the supply and installation of lifts and

---

[64] Article 6 of the of the New Zealand Arbitration Act 1996.

[65] 1982 Hong Kong Arbitration Ordinance, Chapter 341, Section 6B, http://oelawhk.lib.hku.hk/items/show/3286 (accessed 1 August 2016). For a commentary about the application of Section 6B, see Geoffrey Ma and Neil Kaplan (eds) *Arbitration in Hong Kong: A Practical Guide*, Sweet & Maxwell Asia, Hong Kong, 2003, pp. 259–262.

[66] 1982 Hong Kong Arbitration Ordinance, Chapter 341, Section 2L. It was possible to apply the consolidation clause to international arbitrations if one of the following three alternative conditions had been fulfilled: (i) the parties had agreed that the part of the arbitration ordinance containing the consolidation clause was to apply, (ii) the arbitration agreement was or was treated as a domestic arbitration agreement under the ordinance, or (iii) the dispute was to be arbitrated as a domestic arbitration (see Chapter 231, Section 2M form the same ordinance). The 1982 Hong Kong Arbitration Ordinance defined a domestic arbitration agreement as any agreement that is not an international arbitration agreement. With regard to the latter, the ordinance referred to the definition under the UNCITRAL Model Law.

[67] See Geoffrey Ma and Neil Kaplan (eds) (2003) *Arbitration in Hong Kong: A Practical Guide*, Sweet & Maxwell Asia, Hong Kong, pp. 259–260.

[68] *Re Shui On Construction C. Ltd. And Schindler Lifts (HK) Ltd.* [1986] HKLR 1177. About this case see also Albert Jan van den Berg (1989) 'Shui On Construction Co. Ltd. V. Moon Yik Co. Ltd., Xipho Development Co. Ltd., High Court of Hong Kong, Not Indicated, 12 September 1986', in Albert Jan van den Berg (ed.) *Yearbook Commercial Arbitration 1989–Volume XIV*, Kluwer Law International, Alphen aan den Rijn, pp. 215–223, and Howard Miller, 'Consolidation in Hong Kong: the Shui On Case', in 3 *Arbitration International*, no. 1 (1987), pp. 87–90. See also *Shui On Construction Co. Ltd. v. Dah Chong Hong Ltd.* (Unreported, MP No. 1275 of 1987). For a commentary on this second Shui On case, see V. V. Veeder, 'More News from the Front-Line – The Second Shui On Case', in 3 *Arbitration International*, no. 3 (1987), pp. 262–266.

escalators for the project. The subcontract contained a pay-when-paid clause, which allowed progress payments to the subcontractor once the main contractor had been paid by the employer. There were no major differences between the main contract and the subcontract because they were drafted with reference to each other. Both contracts contained arbitration clauses.

The time for completion was delayed and the employer suspended the progress payments due to the main contractor. He argued that he was allowed to deduct these payments from the claim for delay damages that he had against Shui On. The latter suspended the progress payments due to Schindler by invoking the pay-when-paid clause in their contract. This resulted in two separate arbitrations. The first one was commenced by Shui On against the employer and the second one was commenced by Schindler against the main contractor. The same sole arbitrator was appointed in both proceedings. The main contractor then requested statutory consolidation of these proceedings on the basis of the then-effective legislation in Hong Kong[69]. The Supreme Court decided that consolidation was not appropriate in this case[70]. However, it admitted that there was an imminent risk of inconsistent findings[71]. Therefore, the court issued a regulatory order that the related proceedings should be heard together without formal consolidation[72]. The arbitrator had full discretion to arrange the proceedings in such manner as he deemed appropriate.

The second Shui On case again concerned two separate arbitrations. The first one was the abovementioned arbitration between Shui On and the employer. The second arbitration was between Shui On and Dah Chong Hong Limited – one of its other subcontractors. An architect was appointed as the sole arbitrator in both proceedings. Shui On once again

[69] Section 6B, Chapter 341, of the 1982 Hong Kong Ordination Ordinance.

[70] Two main reasons for the denial of the consolidation request were pointed out. The first concerned the different progress achieved in the two proceedings. While the arbitration with the subcontractor had reached an advanced stage, the first arbitration between Shui On and the employer was in its initial phase. Secondly, the judge decided that formal consolidation was not possible because there would be no single claimant in the consolidated proceeding, since Shui On was claimant in the first case and respondent in the second one.

[71] See Albert Jan van den Berg (1989) 'Shui On Construction Co. Ltd. V. Moon Yik Co. Ltd., Xipho Development Co. Ltd., High Court of Hong Kong, Not Indicated, 12 September 1986', in Albert Jan van den Berg (ed), Yearbook Commercial Arbitration 1989–Volume XIV, Kluwer Law International, Alphen aan den Rijn, p. 220. Pursuant to the order, which was cited there: 'Clearly, the prospect of two separate arbitrations, even before the same arbitrator, is intolerable, because of the possibility of inconsistent decisions. The witnesses on the common matters of fact might not give their evidence the same each time, and the submissions on the law might not be the same for the common points in the arbitrations. Hence inconsistent verdicts may occur…There is also the point that the claimant in the arbitration heard second might feel that the arbitrator had already prejudged the issues in the first arbitration without the claimant in the second arbitration having had any opportunity to influence him…'

[72] Another example of arbitrations being ordered to be heard concurrently can be found in *Chun Wo Building Construction Ltd. v. China Merchants Tower Co Ltd & Others* [2000] 2 HKC 255. In this case, there were three arbitrations arising out of a development project. The first was between the employer and the main contractor, the second was between the main contractor and the subcontractor and the third was between the latter and a sub-subcontractor. The court found that there was sufficient commonality between the arbitrations because the issue of delay was common to all arbitrations.

requested consolidation and this time the Supreme Court decided to allow formal consolidation of the proceedings[73].

It should be noted that in both Shui On cases there was no common consent from all parties to consolidation. In both proceedings, consolidation was requested by the main contractor and the employer did not object to it. However, the subcontractors opposed to the consolidation request. In the first case, Schindler admitted that there were some common points of law and fact in both proceedings but expressly opposed consolidation because of the different progress in the two proceedings. In the second case, the other subcontractor opposed any form of consolidation on the grounds that the request was premature because it was made at a very early stage of his arbitration with Shui On. Apparently, the subcontractors' opposition did not preclude the Supreme Court from granting the regulatory orders under the then-effective Hong Kong legislation.

However, the court had the practice of ordering consolidation only if it saw a real benefit or advantage from the consolidation[74]. This means that the court's discretion was not automatically exercised in favour of making a consolidation order just because there was some commonality of issues[75]. In some cases, the court refused to consolidate parallel arbitrations because of the lack of sufficient legal or factual connection between the two arbitrations and the material prejudice that such consolidation could cause to one of the parties[76].

The legislative approach to consolidation in Hong Kong changed when a new Arbitration Ordinance came into force on 1 June 2011[77]. One of the purposes of the new Act was to abolish the previous distinction in the treatment of domestic and international arbitration and to diminish the powers of state courts to intervene in the

---

[73] Another example of consolidation of arbitrations on the basis of Section 6B of the 1982 Hong Kong Arbitration Ordinance can be found in the case of *Linfield Ltd. v. Brooke Hillier Parker* [2003] 2 HKC 624. In this case, the assessment of whether consolidation should be granted was characterized as involving a three-stage process, including: (i) ascertainment of the existence of two or more arbitrations (which would normally require two or more references to arbitration), (ii) consideration of whether the commonality between the arbitrations was sufficient to justify consolidation, and (iii) consideration of other factors. These other factors included the risk of inconsistent decisions, the timing of the application, the link between the reliefs claimed, cost implications, confidentiality considerations, etc.

[74] Geoffrey Ma and Neil Kaplan (eds) (2003) *Arbitration in Hong Kong: A Practical Guide*, Sweet & Maxwell Asia, Hong Kong, pp. 259–260. See also the case *Linfield Ltd. v. Brooke Hillier Parker* [2003] 2 HKC 624.

[75] Dimitrios Athanasakis and Robert Morgan, 'Joinder of Arbitrations: an Overview of English and Hong Kong Construction Industry Practice', in *Asian Dispute Review* no. 1 (2008), pp. 19–20.

[76] See *Dickson Construction Co. Ltd. v. Schindler Lifts (HK) Ltd. & Another* (unreported, MP No. 545 of 1992). The case is described in Geoffrey Ma and Neil Kaplan (eds) (2003) *Arbitration in Hong Kong: A Practical Guide*, Sweet & Maxwell Asia, Hong Kong, pp. 516–517. The judge in this case found that a consolidation order would have significantly delayed the resolution of the subcontract dispute.

[77] 2011 Hong Kong Arbitration Ordinance (Chapter 609), http://www.legislation.gov.hk/blis_pdf.nsf/6799165D2FEE3FA94825755E0033E532/C05151C760F783AD482577D900541075/$FILE/CAP_609_e_b5.pdf (accessed 25 July 2016).

proceedings[78]. The new ordinance provides for the opportunity of consolidation of parallel arbitrations under Article 2 of Schedule 2:

> (1) If, in relation to 2 or more arbitral proceedings, it appears to the Court –
> (a) that a common question of law or fact arises in both or all of them;
> (b) that the rights to relief claimed in those arbitral proceedings are in respect of or arise out of the same transaction or series of transactions; or
> (c) that for any other reason it is desirable to make an order under this section,
> the Court may, on the application of any party to those arbitral proceedings –
> (d) order those arbitral proceedings –
> (i) to be consolidated on such terms as it thinks just; or
> (ii) to be heard at the same time or one immediately after another; or
> (e) order any of those arbitral proceedings to be stayed until after the determination of any of them…

This article almost literally repeats the wording of the clause under the previous ordinance. Initially, it was suggested that the consolidation clause should be fully abolished but it was kept in the final draft of the ordinance at the insistence of stakeholders from the construction industry in Hong Kong[79]. However, the scope of application of the clause has been significantly narrowed down. While the previous clause applied by default, the new clause can come into play only if the parties opt for its application. When it comes to domestic arbitrations, the clause retains its automatic application under certain conditions. More particularly, there is a transitional provision in the ordinance that specifies that the consolidation clause will apply in respect of any arbitration agreement entered before or within 6 years after the entry into force of the ordinance which provides that the arbitration is a *domestic arbitration*[80].

A peculiar feature of Hong Kong legislation is that it explicitly specifies that the consolidation provision will apply in respect of construction projects where the work assigned under the main contract is subcontracted to subcontractors[81]. More particularly, the consolidation provision will apply to subcontracts of any tier that also contain arbitration clauses, unless explicitly specified otherwise. The purpose of this provision is to make clear that related disputes arising under a main contract and a subcontract may be united in a single proceeding. However, there are two main hurdles to the application of this clause to international construction projects. First, the clause applies subject to the transitional provision mentioned above. This means, *inter alia*, that there should be a construction agreement containing an arbitration clause specifying that the arbitration is considered as *domestic arbitration*. Secondly, the clause is not applicable with regard to

---

[78] Kun Fan, 'The New Arbitration Ordinance in Hong Kong', in *29 Journal of International Arbitration*, no. 6 (2012), pp. 715–717.

[79] Ibid., p. 717. See also Dean Lewis, 'The Hong Kong Arbitration Ordinance – Proposed Changes', in 5 *Asian International Arbitration Journal*, no. 2 (2009), pp. 123–125.

[80] Section 100 of the 2011 Hong Kong Arbitration Ordinance (Chapter 609). The parties are allowed to opt out of the transitional clause (see in that regard Section 102).

[81] Section 101 of the 2011 Hong Kong Arbitration Ordinance (Chapter 609).

subcontractors which have been incorporated and / or have their central management or control outside Hong Kong[82]. Therefore, the application of the clause remains limited to cases of domestic subcontracting only.

5.7 Canada

Canadian arbitration legislation has some special features. There is no federal law regulating international commercial arbitration[83]. Therefore, parties that choose to arbitrate their international disputes in Canada should look at the specific local arbitration law in the province or territory that is the seat of arbitration[84]. This law will apply as *lex arbitri* to their disputes. Canada consists of ten provinces and three territories, and all of them have adopted international arbitration legislation that is based on the UNCITRAL Model Law. Furthermore, all provinces and territories, except for Quebec, have modified the UNCITRAL Model Law and have included statutory provisions addressing consolidation of parallel proceedings[85]. The approach followed in all provinces and territories is that all the parties should consent to consolidation. Most provincial laws require that the request for consolidation should come from all parties to the proceedings

[82] Section 101(2)(a)–(c) of the 2011 Hong Kong Arbitration Ordinance (Chapter 609). This limitation is known as the *international exception*. The discussions prior to the adoption of the ordinance reveal that there was a proposal that foreign subcontractors should not be excluded from the scope of application of the clause. However, the suggestion was rejected. Pursuant to the report prepared by the Hong Kong Department of Justice: 'given that the key objective of the Arbitration Bill is to enhance Hong Kong's standing as an international arbitration centre, we considered it essential to provide for the International Exception to avoid inadvertent imposition of domestic arbitration provisions on unwary non-local subcontractor.' There was also a suggestion that Section 101(2) should be a mandatory provision for all subcontractors. However, this proposal was also rejected on the ground that 'it is against the principle [to facilitate party autonomy] to impose the opt-in provisions in Schedule 2 of the Arbitration Bill on subcontractors on a mandatory basis'. For more details, see *Arbitration Bill Gazetted in June 2009, Automatic Opt-in for Subcontractors*, prepared by the Administration for the Bills Committee on Arbitration Bill, http://www.legco.gov.hk/yr08-09/english/bc/bc59/papers/bc590512cb2-1477-3-e.pdf (accessed 25 July 2016).

[83] There is a Federal Arbitration Act in Canada but it only deals with matters that involve the federal government. Therefore, it does not apply to commercial disputes involving private parties.

[84] Claude Thomson and Annie Finn, 'International Commercial Arbitration: A Canadian Perspective', in *18 Arbitration International*, no. 2 (2002), pp. 204–208. See also Brian Casey and Christina Doria (2012) 'Canada', in Karyl Nairn and Patrick Heneghan (eds) *Arbitration World, Jurisdictional Comparisons*, 4th edn, Sweet & Maxwell, London, p. 310.

[85] See Article 8 of the Alberta International Commercial Arbitration Act, Article 27(2) of the British Columbia International Arbitration Act, Article 8 of the Manitoba International Commercial Arbitration Act, Article 9 of the Newfoundland and Labrador International Commercial Arbitration Act, Article 9 of the New Brunswick International Commercial Arbitration Act, Article 7 of the Ontario International Commercial Arbitration Act, Article 9 of the Nova Scotia International Commercial Arbitration Act, Article 8 of the Prince Edward Island International Commercial Arbitration Act, Article 7 of the Saskatchewan International Commercial Arbitration Act, Article 10 of the International Commercial Arbitration Act (Northwest Territories), Article 10 of the Nunavut International Commercial Arbitration Act and Article 6 of the Yukon International Commercial Arbitration Act.

subject to consolidation[86]. Other laws permit the request to be made only by some of the parties but then all the other parties should express their consent to the contemplated consolidation[87]. The requirement for all parties' consent is reaffirmed in case law in some of the provinces[88]. In all cases, it is the superior court in the respective province or territory that decides on the request. If the court decides to consolidate the proceedings, it may do so on such terms as it deems just. The same court will appoint the arbitral tribunal to review the united proceedings if the parties cannot reach a common agreement on this matter. Furthermore, all the consolidation provisions contain a paragraph stating that nothing in these provisions will be construed as preventing the parties to the two or more arbitrations from agreeing to consolidate and take the necessary steps to effect that consolidation. In the author's opinion, this means that the court should be able to grant a consolidation order if the parties have envisaged consolidation in their contracts despite subsequent opposition from some of the parties in the course of the proceedings.

5.8 Australia

The principle laws that govern arbitration in Australia depend on the type of arbitration. Domestic arbitrations are regulated at state level, whereas international arbitration is regulated at federal level[89]. The federal International Arbitration Act 1974[90] was amended in 2010 and it contains a provision addressing consolidation[91]. Despite some suggestions to the contrary[92], the Australian legislator decided that the provision should have an *opt-in* character[93], which means that it does not apply automatically, unless the parties decide otherwise.

Any party to a pending arbitral proceeding may apply for the issuance of an order for the consolidation of that same proceeding with another related proceeding. If the

[86] This is the case in Alberta, Manitoba, Newfoundland and Labrador, New Brunswick, Ontario, Nova Scotia, Prince Edward Island, Saskatchewan and Yukon.

[87] British Columbia, Nunavut and Northwest Territories.

[88] See, for example, *Western Oil Sands Inc. Allianz Insurance Co. of Canada* [2004] A.J. No. 85, 2004 ABQB 79, https://wcart.files.wordpress.com/2012/03/western_oil_sands_inc_v_allianz_insurance_co_of_canada.pdf (accessed 25 July 2016). In this case, the Alberta Court of Queen's Bench, Judicial District of Calgary, confirmed that no consolidation is possible without the parties' consent.

[89] Peter Megens, Max Bonnell, Mark Darian-Smith and Beth Cubitt (2012) 'Australia', in Karyl Nairn and Patrick Heneghan (eds) *Arbitration World, Jurisdictional Comparisons*, 4th edn, Thomson Reuters, London, pp. 250–251.

[90] International Arbitration Act 1974 (Act no. 136 of 1974), https://www.comlaw.gov.au/Details/C2011C00342 (accessed 25 July 2016).

[91] Article 24 of the International Arbitration Act 1974.

[92] See Luke Nottage and Richard Garnett, 'Top 20 Things to Change in or around International Arbitration Act', in 6 *Asian International Arbitration Journal*, no. 1 (2010), p. 39. The authors have suggested that the consolidation clause should apply as a default 'opt-out' clause.

[93] Pursuant to Section 22(5) of the International Arbitration Act 1974: 'Section 24 applies to arbitral proceedings commenced in reliance on an arbitration agreement if the parties to the agreement agree (whether in the agreement or otherwise in writing) that it will apply.'

two arbitrations are being heard by the same arbitral tribunal, it is up to that tribunal to issue the order[94]. If the two or more proceedings are being reviewed by different tribunals, then the tribunal reviewing the arbitration whereunder the consolidation request was made should communicate this request to the other tribunals. In this case, the different tribunals should deliberate jointly on the application[95]. If they decide that a consolidation order is necessary, the order should be issued by the tribunals jointly[96]. However, if the tribunals cannot reach a joint position on the request, then the parallel proceedings will proceed as if no consolidation request has been made[97].

Unlike the approach in New Zealand, the party requesting the order is not allowed to refer the question to the competent court. This position has been criticized by some authors who argue that the clause should be amended in order to allow the competent court to resolve the impasse resulting from a tribunals' lack of a common approach to the consolidation request[98].

5.9 Other countries

In *Malaysia*, the approach to consolidation almost literally follows the approach under the English Arbitration Act 1996. The Malaysian Arbitration Act stipulates that consolidation can be ordered by the tribunal if the parties agree. Hence, the tribunal does not have the right to consolidate if the parties have not conferred such powers on it[99].

In *Singapore*, the legislation regulating international commercial arbitrations does not contain multi-party arbitration provisions. However, the legislation that applies to domestic arbitrations addresses consolidation. The clause resembles the English and the Malaysian approach[100].

Ireland adopted a new arbitration Act in 2010, which also deprives the tribunal from granting consolidation orders, unless the parties agree to the making of such orders[101].

---

[94] Article 24(4) of the International Arbitration Act 1974.

[95] Article 24(5) of the International Arbitration Act 1974.

[96] Article 24(6) of the International Arbitration Act 1974.

[97] Article 24(7) of the International Arbitration Act 1974.

[98] See Luke Nottage and Richard Garnett, 'Top 20 Things to Change in or around International Arbitration Act', in 6 *Asian International Arbitration Journal*, no. 1 (2010), p. 39.

[99] Article 40 of the Malaysian Arbitration Act 2005 (Act 646), http://www.newyorkconvention.org/11165/web/files/document/1/6/16298.pdf (accessed 25 July 2016).

[100] Article 26 of the Singapore Arbitration Act 2001 (No. 37 of 2001), http://statutes.agc.gov.sg/aol/search/display/view.w3p;page=0;query=DocId%3A%22e8687d02-1aae-42ff-9afa-92c086e168c0%22%20Status%3Apublished%20Depth%3A0%20TransactionTime%3A20151010000000;rec=0;whole=yes (accessed 25 July 2016).

[101] Article 16 of the Irish Arbitration Act 2010, http://www.irishstatutebook.ie/eli/2010/act/1/enacted/en/pdf (accessed 25 July 2016).

Italy has also introduced a statutory multi-party arbitration provision, which deals with joinder and consolidation. It requires the agreement of all parties and also the consent of the arbitrators (if they have already been appointed)[102].

5.10 *Multi-party arbitration in the United States*

Case law and legislation in the United States predominantly deal with consolidation of parallel arbitral proceedings. The US approach is peculiar and is very much influenced by the interplay among the federal legislation, the legislation of the different states and case law. An understanding of the US stance on multi-party arbitration requires some insight into the legal framework applicable to arbitration. Therefore, this section first explains the application of the Federal Arbitration Act ('**FAA**')[103] and the legislation of some states to multi-party arbitrations. On that basis, the relevant case law has been analysed with the purpose of identifying some general patterns in the handling of multi-party arbitrations in the United States.

5.10.1 Legal framework

5.10.1.1 Multi-party arbitration under the FAA

On a federal level, arbitral proceedings are governed by the FAA. The federal Act subjects most arbitrations in the United States to a single standard for judicial review, regardless of whether the dispute is domestic or international[104]. The FAA was enacted in 1925 to 'overrule the judiciary's longstanding refusal to enforce agreements to arbitrate' and to secure arbitration in accordance with the terms agreed by the parties[105]. Chapter 2 of the FAA creates jurisdiction for the federal district courts for cases falling under the scope of the New York Convention[106]. They can be removed from a state court and referred to the

---

[102] Article 816-*quinquies* of the Italian Civil Procedure Code (for an English translation of the article, see Paolo Marzolini (2012) 'Is the Parties' Consent Still an Overriding Principle for Joinder and Intervention of Third Parties in International Commercial Arbitration?' in Daniele Favalli, Xavier Favre-Bulle, Andreas Furrer *et al.* (eds) *Selected Papers on International Arbitration: Volume 2 Series on International Arbitration SAA*, Stämpfli Verlag, Bern, pp. 116–117). The abovementioned article also deals with some other forms of third party participation in pending proceeding where the parties' consent is not required. However, these other forms are not relevant to the present discussion.

[103] Federal Arbitration Act (USA), http://sccinstitute.com/media/37104/the-federal-arbitration-act-usa.pdf (accessed 25 July 2016).

[104] Omer Kesikli, *United States: International Arbitration and Arbitrability from the United States Perspective*, http://www.mondaq.com/unitedstates/x/309172/Arbitration+Dispute+Resolution/International+Arbitration+And (accessed 25 July 2016).

[105] Okuma Kazutake, 'Party Autonomy in International Commercial Arbitration: Consolidation of Multiparty and Classwide Arbitration', in 9 *Annual Survey of International & Comparative Law*, no. 1 (2003), p. 190, http://digitalcommons.law.ggu.edu/cgi/viewcontent.cgi?article=1077&context=annlsurvey (accessed 25 July 2016).

[106] Chapter 2, Section 203 of the FAA.

federal court 'at any time prior to trial'[107]. In other words, the FAA gives to state and federal courts a broad scope for subject matter jurisdiction over international commercial arbitrations[108].

The FAA does not address multi-party arbitration. There is nothing in the Act that directly permits tribunal-ordered or court-ordered consolidation, either with or without parties' agreement[109]. On the other hand, nothing in the FAA expressly forbids consolidation[110]. Pursuant to Section 2, Chapter 1, of the FAA, arbitration agreements 'shall be valid, irrevocable and enforceable, save upon such grounds as exist at law or in equity for the revocation of any contract'. Furthermore, pursuant to Section 4 of the FAA, if either party fails to arbitrate under the agreement, the aggrieved party may petition any district court to make an order summarily directing the parties to proceed with the arbitration 'in accordance with the terms of the agreement'. Therefore, if the parties have included a multi-party arbitration agreement in their contracts, this agreement should be recognized and enforced in accordance with what the parties have agreed.

Any international arbitration conducted in the United States falls within the framework of the FAA. This means that the FAA will pre-empt any US state arbitration law containing provisions inconsistent with the FAA. Other state law provisions consistent with the FAA may still apply. As it will be seen below, some states have adopted arbitration laws that envisage consolidation of parallel arbitrations. The intricate question is whether these consolidation provisions will be pre-empted as inconsistent with the FAA.

5.10.1.2 Multi-party arbitration under states' legislation

Several states have adopted international arbitration laws. It has been stated that these laws have only had a marginal effect so far because of the pre-empting effect of the FAA in respect of conflicting state arbitration laws[111].

Most of the international arbitration laws in the United States are based on the UNCITRAL Model Law. As of the date of this book, eight states have adopted the model law[112]. Some of these states, such as California, Texas and Georgia, have included consolidation provisions in their statutes.

---

[107] Chapter 2, Section 205 of the FAA.

[108] Dominique Hascher, 'Consolidation of Arbitration by American Courts: Fostering or Hampering International Commercial Arbitrations?', in *1 Journal of International Arbitration*, no. 2 (1984), p. 128.

[109] Gary Born (2014) *International Commercial Arbitration, Volume II: International Arbitral Procedures*, 2nd edn, Kluwer Law International, Alphen aan den Rijn, p. 2576.

[110] Ibid.

[111] Christopher Drahozal (2007) 'International Arbitration Law in the United States', in Nuray Eksi, Pedro Martinez-Fraga and William Sheehy (eds) *International Commercial Arbitration: A Comparative Survey*, ICOC Publication, No. 2007/45, Istanbul Chamber of Commerce, Istanbul, http://papers.ssrn.com/sol3/papers.cfm?abstract_id=1905702 (accessed 25 July 2016).

[112] These include California, Connecticut, Florida, Georgia, Illinois, Louisiana, Oregon and Texas.

Pursuant to Section 1297.272 of the California Code of Civil Procedure[113]:

> Where the parties to two or more arbitration agreements have agreed, in their respective agreements or otherwise, to consolidate the arbitrations arising out of those arbitration agreements, the superior court may, on the application by one party with the consent of all the other parties to those arbitration agreements, do one or more of the following:
>
> (a) Order the arbitrations to be consolidated on terms the court considers just and necessary.
> (b) Where all the parties cannot agree on an arbitral tribunal for the consolidated arbitration, appoint an arbitral tribunal in accordance with Section 1297.118.
> (c) Where all the parties cannot agree on any other matter necessary to conduct the consolidated arbitration, make any other order it considers necessary.

Thus, consolidation is possible only if agreed by the parties. Interestingly, the consolidation clause applicable to domestic arbitrations in California does not explicitly require parties' consent and it allows consolidation even in cases of inconsistent arbitration agreements[114]. The consolidation clauses in the international arbitration laws in Texas[115] and Ohio[116] largely resemble the Californian Section 1297.272 discussed above.

In 2012, Georgia introduced a new International Commercial Arbitration Code[117]. It contains a consolidation clause following the English legislative approach to consolidation. Pursuant to Section 9-9-46(d) from that same code:

> Unless the parties agree to confer such power on the tribunal, the tribunal shall not have the power to order consolidation of proceedings or concurrent hearings; provided, however, that the parties shall be free to agree:
>
> (1) That the arbitral proceedings shall be consolidated with other arbitral proceedings; or
> (2) That concurrent hearings shall be held, on such terms as may be agreed.

Unlike the abovementioned international arbitration laws, which require parties' consent to consolidation, other states have followed a different approach. A notable example is the Massachusetts legislation. It contains a mandatory consolidation provision intended to prevail over any arbitration agreement. Pursuant to Chapter 251, Section 2A of the General Laws of Massachusetts[118]:

> A party aggrieved by the failure or refusal of another to agree to consolidate one arbitration proceeding with another or others, for which the method of appointment of the

---

[113] California Code of Civil Procedure, http://www.leginfo.ca.gov/.html/ccp_table_of_contents.html (accessed 25 July 2016).
[114] Section 1281.3 of the California Code of Civil Procedure.
[115] Section 172.173 of the Texas Civil Practice and Remedies Code, http://www.statutes.legis.state.tx.us/?link=CP (accessed 25 July 2016).
[116] Section 2712.52 of the Ohio Revised Code, http://codes.ohio.gov/(accessed 25 July 2016).
[117] Georgia International Commercial Arbitration Code (Senate Bill 383), http://www.legis.ga.gov/Legislation/20112012/127687.pdf (accessed 25 July 2016).
[118] General Laws of Massachusetts, https://malegislature.gov/Laws/GeneralLaws (accessed 25 July 2016).

arbitrator or arbitrators is the same, or to sever one arbitration proceeding from another or others, may apply to the superior court for an order for such consolidation or such severance. The court shall proceed summarily to the determination of the issue so raised...No provision in any arbitration agreement shall bar or prevent action by the court under this section.

Thus, the competent court may order consolidation in the absence of parties' agreement on the matter. Furthermore, the clause might also find application in cases where the parties have explicitly excluded consolidation in their contracts. This approach is highly controversial and is in sharp contrast with the consensual nature of arbitration. In practice, this scenario may only occur in domestic arbitrations. As far as international commercial arbitrations are concerned, any mandatory consolidation clauses will be pre-empted by the provisions of the FAA demanding the recognition and enforcement of parties' arbitration agreements in accordance with their terms.

Legislation similar to that of Massachusetts may be found in New Jersey. Pursuant to Section 2A: 23A-3 of the Alternative Procedure for Dispute Resolution Act[119]:

> a. When parties have agreed to alternative resolution proceedings under separate agreements under this act, and the claims to be resolved may involve evidence, witnesses and testimony reasonably necessary to resolve issues and facts arising out of a related project or series of agreements, then these proceedings may be held in a consolidated alternative resolution proceeding. Whenever reasonably possible, the same umpire shall be designated to hear and determine these claims...
>
> c. The provisions of Subsections a. and b. of this Section shall be liberally construed to effectuate the remedial purpose of this act to provide for the expeditious resolution of disputes arising out of a related project or series of agreements.

The provision applies if the parties have chosen the law of New Jersey as applicable to their disputes. By this choice, they vest the court with a high degree of discretion to shape the arbitral proceedings in a consolidated manner even over the objection of some of the parties[120]. The court has full authority to determine the way in which the proceedings will be conducted. Like the Massachusetts consolidation clause, the New Jersey provision should also be deemed pre-empted by the FAA if the parties have excluded consolidation in their arbitration agreements. It is, however, less clear whether this pre-emption effect will occur in a situation where the parties' contracts are silent on consolidation and one or some of the parties oppose consolidation. Some authors argue that the explicit choice of a state law containing such a clause

---

[119]New Jersey Alternative Procedure for Dispute Resolution Act, http://www.mediationandarbitrationadr.com/the-new-jersey-alternative-procedure-for-dispute-resolution-act/(accessed 25 July 2016).

[120]This also follows from Section 2A: 23A-2 of the New Jersey Alternative Procedure for Dispute Resolution Act, which stipulates that any arbitration agreement referring to the Act shall be construed as an implied consent by the parties to the jurisdiction of the court to enforce that agreement pursuant to the provisions set forth in the Act.

will trump the pre-emptive effect of the FAA[121] but this position is far from certain. Therefore, for reasons of legal certainty it is recommendable that parties express their preferred approach to consolidation in a clear and explicit way in their arbitration agreements.

It should also be mentioned that in 2000 the Revised Uniform Arbitration Act ('**RUAA**') was introduced[122]. The act was based on its predecessor, the 1955 Uniform Arbitration Act, which had been adopted in 49 states. The purpose of both the old act and the RUAA is to harmonize the domestic arbitration laws of the different states. So far, the RUAA has been enacted by 19 states[123], and its enactment has been proposed in two more states[124].

The RUAA does not address international arbitration. However, domestic arbitration laws, including the RUAA, may find application to international cases in two, albeit rare, cases[125]. First, they may be applied if the parties have designated a specific state arbitration law to govern their international arbitration. Secondly, domestic laws may also find application if all parties to an international arbitration decide to proceed on a matter in state courts and do not exercise their right to remove the case from these courts and submit it to the federal courts[126]. In this second case, only those domestic arbitration provisions that are not pre-empted by the FAA will apply. In both cases examined above, the state courts will refer to the domestic arbitration law, including the RUAA, unless the state in question has also introduced an international arbitration law which will be applied instead[127].

Unlike its predecessor, the RUAA contains a consolidation provision. Pursuant to Section 10:

> (a) Except as otherwise provided in Subsection (c), upon [motion] of a party to an agreement to arbitrate or to an arbitration proceeding, the court may order consolidation of separate arbitration proceedings as to all or some of the claims if:
> (1) there are separate agreements to arbitrate or separate arbitration proceedings between the same persons or one of them is a party to a separate agreement to arbitrate or a separate arbitration proceeding with a third person;
> (2) the claims subject to the agreements to arbitrate arise in substantial part from the same transaction or series of related transactions;

[121] Ronald Ricketts, '*Judicial Review of Arbitral Awards*', http://gablelaw.com/wp-content/uploads/2015/06/2013-08-02-Judicial-Review-of-Arbitration-Awards.pdf (accessed 25 July 2016).

[122] National Conference of Commissioners on Uniform State Laws, *Uniform Arbitration Act with Preparatory Note and Comments*, http://www.uniformlaws.org/shared/docs/arbitration/arbitration_final_00.pdf (accessed 25 July 2016).

[123] These are Washington, Oregon, Nevada, Utah, Arizona, Colorado, New Mexico, North Dakota, Oklahoma, Minnesota, Arkansas, Michigan, Florida, New Jersey, District of Columbia, North Carolina, West Virginia, Alaska and Hawaii.

[124] Massachusetts and Pennsylvania.

[125] See National Conference of Commissioners on Uniform State Laws, *Uniform Arbitration Act with Preparatory Note and Comments*, p. 6.

[126] Ibid.

[127] Ibid.

(3) the existence of a common issue of law or fact creates the possibility of conflicting decisions in the separate arbitration proceedings; and

(4) prejudice resulting from a failure to consolidate is not outweighed by the risk of undue delay or prejudice to the rights of or hardship to parties opposing consolidation.

(b) The court may order consolidation of separate arbitration proceedings as to some claims and allow other claims to be resolved in separate arbitration proceedings.

(c) The court may not order consolidation of the claims of a party to an agreement to arbitrate if the agreement prohibits consolidation.

The provision acknowledges that consolidation may not be ordered if the relevant arbitration agreement prohibits consolidation. This means that consolidation can be ordered if the parties' agreements are silent on the matter. The lack of an explicit requirement for parties' consent under Section 10 has been criticized, in the author's opinion with justification, by some scholars[128]. The Drafting Committee was well aware that the above consolidation clause may be imposed on parties who did not envisage the conduct of multi-party arbitration. Pursuant to the official comments to the RUAA:

> A provision in the RUAA specifically empowering courts to order consolidation in appropriate cases makes sense for several reasons…[It] is likely that in many cases one or more parties, often non-drafting parties, will not have considered the impact of the arbitration clause on multiparty disputes. By establishing a default provision which permits consolidation…in the absence of a specific contractual provision, Section 10 encourages drafters to address the issue expressly and enhances the possibility that all parties will be on notice regarding the issue[129].

By including a statutory consolidation provision, it is the drafters' anticipation that they would encourage the drafting of multi-party arbitration provisions. In other words, if contracting parties do not want consolidated proceedings, they should explicitly exclude consolidation in their arbitration agreements. This reasoning may seem perplexing. By agreeing on a standard arbitration agreement, contracting parties will usually expect that any arbitration will take place only between parties that have signed the relevant arbitration agreement. One cannot assume that the parties' intention is to have their multi-contract disputes aggregated in a single proceeding simply because they have not excluded consolidation in their contracts[130].

---

[128]See Thomas Carbonneau (2007) *Cases and Materials on Arbitration Law and Practice*, 6th edn, American Casebook Series, Thomson West, St Paul, MN, p. 94. According to the author: 'It is difficult to understand why the provision is not anchored in the clear majority view that mutual party consent is a requisite to consolidation.'

[129]National Conference of Commissioners on Uniform State Laws, *Uniform Arbitration Act with Preparatory Note and Comments* p. 37.

[130]See also Thomas Carbonneau (2007) *Cases and Materials on Arbitration Law and Practice*, 6th edn, American Casebook Series, Thomson West, St Paul, MN, p. 95. According to the author, 'The Reporter's commentary seems to be saying that, by establishing an overly aggressive statutory rule on consolidation, parties will have a stronger incentive to address the matter of consolidation themselves in their agreement to avoid the rule's application. This peculiar rationalization for the rule and its content is unlikely to persuade anyone.'

Section 10 of the RUAA will apply by default, and consolidation may be ordered provided that the four preconditions outlined above are met. The first condition poses a relatively low threshold because it does not require the identity between the parties in the pending arbitrations. Therefore, it will be met in respect of disputes arising under multiple contracts binding non-identical parties, for example disputes under a main contract and a subcontract. The close link between these contracts and the related disputes will probably be sufficient to meet the second and the third condition. Thus, the fourth criterion, dealing with the prejudice caused to the party opposing consolidation, gains more significance. If this prejudice is higher than the prejudice resulting from the failure to consolidate, then consolidation should not be ordered[131]. The burden of proof is not only on the party requesting consolidation but also on the one resisting consolidation[132]. The court has a large discretion to decide whether the precondition has been met. It will make a subjective assessment based on the particular facts of the case.

If parties to international commercial transactions expressly address consolidation in their contracts, then this agreement should be respected as required under the FAA. Therefore, in case of a collision between the arbitration agreement and the consolidation clause in a legislation based on the RUAA, the arbitration agreement should prevail because of the pre-emptive effect of the FAA[133]. It is less clear whether the pre-emptive effect of the FAA will occur in cases where the parties have not addressed multi-party arbitration in their arbitration agreements but have explicitly referred to the law of the state which adopted the RUAA. In the author's opinion, the more likely approach, as evident from the case law examined below, seems to be that the FAA will pre-empt the application of the consolidation clause in these cases too.

5.10.2 United States' case law on multi-party arbitration

As mentioned above, if contracting parties explicitly address multi-party arbitration in their arbitration agreements (either by allowing or excluding such type of arbitration), then these agreements should be respected and enforced. This follows from

[131]The court will consider several factors in its assessment. These include the different progress achieved in the proceedings, the prejudice to a party's right to appoint an arbitrator, standards for the admission of evidence and rendition of the award. See Andrew Ness and David Peden, 'Arbitration Developments: Defects and Solutions', in *22 The Construction Lawyer*, no. 3 (2002), p. 11. See also National Conference of Commissioners on Uniform State Laws, *Uniform Arbitration Act with Preparatory Note and Comments*, pp. 38–39.

[132]The mere desire to have one's dispute heard in a separate proceeding is not in itself sufficient to avoid consolidation. In addition, there have been cases where consolidation was allowed despite allegations and proofs that consolidation will impose additional economic burdens on the party opposing it or that it will increase the complexity of the proceedings (See National Conference of Commissioners on Uniform State Laws, *Uniform Arbitration Act with Preparatory Note and Comments*, pp. 38–39).

[133]Gary Born (2012) *International Arbitration: Law and Practice*, Kluwer Law International, Alphen aan den Rijn, pp. 226–227.

the FAA which pre-empts any state legislation that impedes or precludes the enforcement of privately agreed arbitration clauses and also from the New York Convention to which the US have acceded. The question becomes more intricate in cases where parties' contracts do not address multi-party arbitration. Can the courts order consolidation in these cases? What if the applicable state law is also silent on the matter? And if such court-ordered consolidation takes place, would it be consistent with the FAA that requires enforcement of arbitral agreements in accordance with their terms? Unfortunately, all these questions lack a clear answer. United States' case law is far from uniform because the US courts have approached these matters in divergent ways.

There is an abundance of case law concerning consolidation in the United States. This necessitates the introduction of certain limitations as regards the cases reviewed in this book. The focus in the following subsections will be on the most important cases at a federal level and also on some construction cases that are illustrative of the different approaches adopted by courts when it comes to disputes arising under construction projects.

Historically, two trends can be observed in the courts' approach to multi-party arbitrations. These trends are inconsistent with each other and even contradictory. Relevant case law representing each trend has been examined below.

5.10.2.1 Consolidation when parties' contracts are silent on the matter

The seminal decision exemplifying this first trend was made by the US Court of Appeals for the Second Circuit in *Compania Espanola de Petroleos, S.A., v. Nereus Shipping, S.A.*[134]. In this case, the ship owner, Nereus Shipping, chartered its own vessel to the Venezuelan corporation HIDECA. Further, the company Compania Espanola guaranteed the fulfilment of all obligations of HIDECA under the charter agreement towards Nereus. Compania Espanola was not a signatory to the charter agreement. The latter agreement contained an arbitration clause, whereas the guarantee did not provide for arbitration[135]. A dispute arose between Nereus and HIDECA and Nereus requested multi-party arbitration with the participation of Compania Espanola. Despite the latter company's objection and the absence of contractual provisions addressing consolidation in both the charter agreement and the guarantee, the court decided to consolidate the two proceedings. It reasoned its decision by declaring that there was a broad judicial power to consolidate arbitral proceedings in the interests of efficiency: 'We think the liberal purposes of the Federal Arbitration Act clearly require that this Act be interpreted

[134] *Compania Espanola de Petroleos, S.A., v. Nereus Shipping, S.A.*, 527 F.2d 966 (2nd Cir. 1975), https://law.resource.org/pub/us/case/reporter/F2/527/527.F2d.966.75--7208.75--7207.75--7206.75--7069.241--244.html (accessed 25 July 2016).

[135] Although it lacked an arbitration clause, the guarantee contained a broad and abstract wording. Pursuant to the text of the guarantee, the guarantor would 'assume the rights and obligations of HIDECA on the same terms and conditions as contained in the Charter Party'.

so as to permit and even to encourage the consolidation of arbitration proceedings in proper cases'[136].

The US Court of Appeals for the First Circuit adopted a similar reasoning in *New England Energy Inc., v. Keystone Shipping Co*[137]. In this case, there was a joint-venture agreement between New England Energy Inc. ('**NEEI**') and Keystone Shipping ('**Keystone**'), whereunder the joint venture company NECCO was created. The latter company was the owner and operator of a coal carrying ship. Under a second agreement, New England Power Company ('**NEP**') chartered the ship from NECCO. The arbitration agreements in both contracts referred to arbitration in Boston and contained no explicit reference to consolidation. Two separate arbitrations started: the first was between the joint venturers (i.e. NEEI and Keystone), and the second one between NEP and NECCO. NEEI and NEP requested from the competent district court the consolidation of the proceedings by invoking the Massachusetts consolidation provision (discussed in Subsection 5.10.1.2). Even though the district court was of the opinion that the factual circumstances were appropriate for consolidation, it denied the application on the ground that it lacked the power to join the cases because of the lack of specific wording on consolidation in the two arbitration agreements. Thus, the district court found that the FAA pre-empted the Massachusetts statutory consolidation clause. The denial was appealed before the Court of Appeals for the First Circuit. The latter court reversed the decision of the district court and reached the opposite decision, i.e. that the Massachusetts law is not pre-empted and can be applied to consolidate the proceedings. Pursuant to the court's decision:

> Because the [Federal Arbitration] Act says nothing about consolidation, the Massachusetts statute...does not directly conflict with the Act's provisions...We disagree that ordering consolidation pursuant to a state statute when the contract is silent on the subject improperly modifies the agreement struck by the parties. We believe...that an order [for consolidation] not contradicting the contractual terms regarding arbitration is in 'accordance with [those terms]'. This is certainly true when the language of the arbitration clause is broad and in no way suggests limits on the subjects or the parties to the agreed-upon arbitration[138].

The Court further acknowledged that the lack of parties' consent to consolidation and the non-identity of the parties under the separate arbitrations do not constitute obstacles to consolidation under Massachusetts law. The Court also concluded that by referring to

---

[136] *Compania Espanola de Petroleos, S.A., v. Nereus Shipping, S.A.*, 527 F.2d 966 (2nd Cir. 1975), para. 42.

[137] *New England Energy Inc., v. Keystone Shipping Co.* 855 F.2d 1 (1st Cir. 1988) cert. denied 489 U.S. 1077, 109 S. Ct.1527, 103 L.Ed.2d 832, http://openjurist.org/855/f2d/1/new-england-energy-inc-v-keystone-shipping-company-keystone-shipping-company (accessed 25 July 2016).

[138] Ibid., para. 9–10.

the arbitration laws in Boston the parties had affirmatively agreed to the possibility of consolidation in Massachusetts.

It is interesting to note that there was a dissenting opinion in that judgement with which the author fully concurs. The dissenting opinion speaks for itself, and therefore a large part of it has been cited below:

> The Federal Arbitration Act cuts quite a precise pattern, leaving little room for judicial embroidery...Neither agreement provides for consolidation. Absent such a provision, the duty rigorously to enforce the agreements 'in accordance with the terms thereof'...does not allow us to substitute our judgement for that of the parties and order the proceedings consolidated. Nor can the happenstance that a state has a law allowing consolidation – or mandating it, for that matter – command a different result...By fashioning an arbitral clause which omits reference to consolidation, the parties have made a choice. By imposing consolidation ab extra, the majority trumps that choice. Rather than order the parties to hold the arbitration to which they consented, as the Act suggests, the court disrupts the negotiated risk / benefit allocation and directs them to proceed with a different sort of arbitration. Perhaps the consolidated arbitration will prove to be better conceived, or more efficient – but it is not what the parties agreed to undertake[139].

Furthermore, the dissenting judge stated that the FAA 'necessitate that we enforce the parties' bargain as they wrote it – nothing more. Neither the language of the statute nor the decisions of the Supreme Court leave the door ajar for reshaping the bargain based on state law'[140].

Some other courts, both at federal and state level, followed the reasoning in the *Nereus* and the *Keystone* cases. The following construction cases can be mentioned here because of their relevance to the issues discussed in this book: *County of Sullivan v. Edward L. Nezelek*[141],

---

[139] Ibid., para. 30–34.

[140] Ibid., para. 36.

[141] *County of Sullivan et al., v. Edward L. Nezelek, Inc., and Edward Durell Stone and Associates,* 42 N.Y.2d 123, 366 N.E.2d 72, 397 N.Y.S.2d 371 (1977), http://law.justia.com/cases/new-york/court-of-appeals/1977/42-n-y-2d-123-0.html (accessed 25 July 2016). The case concerned the construction of college buildings. The employer signed a contract with an architect, and the local sponsor of the construction, who was different from the employer, signed the main contract. The contracts gave rise to two parallel arbitrations. Both contracts contained broad arbitration clauses silent on consolidation. The court decided that the proceedings should be consolidated and made the following controversial statement: 'In recent times, given the decisions of our court and others, parties signing an agreement to arbitrate must be held to do so in contemplation of the announced authority of the courts in proper cases to direct consolidation. If it is now desired to avoid the possibility of consolidation, appropriate provisions to preclude or limit consolidation can be drafted for inclusion in the particular agreement.'

Litton Bionetics v. Glen Construction[142], *Polshek v. Bergen County Iron Works*[143], *Sparwick Contracting, Inc. v. Tomasco Corporation*[144], *Garden Grove v. Pittsburgh*[145], *Conejo Valley v.*

---

[142] *Litton Bionetics, Inc., v. Glen Construction Company, Inc., et. al,* 292 Md. 34 (1981) 437 A.2d 208, http://www.leagle.com/decision/1981326292Md34_1321/LITTON%20BIONETICS%20v.%20GLEN%20CONSTR (accessed 25 July 2016). The case concerned a 'build-only' construction project. The agreements with the main contractor and the architect contained identical arbitration clauses that did not address consolidation. Maryland state law was also silent on the matter. The court decided that it is appropriate to consolidate the arbitration between the main contractor and the employer with the one between the employer and the architect. Consolidation was possible, in the court's opinion, because each of the contracts did not confer an explicit right to arbitrate separately. After having reviewed the contradictory case law on the matter in the different US states, the court concluded: 'We are satisfied from our review of the cases that the better analysis is presented in those decisions which conclude that the power to order consolidation exists as an incident of the jurisdiction statutorily conferred on a court generally to enforce arbitration agreements. We hold that the power is not limited simply to enforcing a particular agreement which contains an express consent to consolidation with related arbitrations.' Furthermore, the court construed the FAA in a way that allowed consolidation. According to the dissenting opinion in this case, parties' silence in the contracts should have been interpreted in a way that precluded consolidation.

[143] *James Steward Polshek & Associates v. Bergen County Iron Works,* 142 N.J.Super. 516, 362 A.2d 63 (1976), http://law.justia.com/cases/new-jersey/appellate-division-published/1976/142-n-j-super-516-0.html (accessed 25 July 2016). The case concerned the construction of a building based on a 'build-only' contractual model. The contractor filed a request for arbitration against both the employer and the architect even though there was no direct contractual link between the contractor and the architect. Both the main contract and the design services agreement contained identical arbitration clauses silent on consolidation. Furthermore, there was no state law that authorized consolidation. The court concluded that consolidation can be ordered: 'In this case there is an uncontroverted common thread of issues and facts arising out of a single project. Absent specific language prohibiting joint or consolidated arbitration, and where there is no showing of prejudice, consolidation is a practical, economical, convenient and preferred method of proceeding in the matters before the court.' Furthermore, the court stated that the jurisdiction conferred upon it to enforce an arbitration agreement includes the power to regulate the method of enforcement. Even though consolidation was allowed, the contractor's claim against the architect was excluded because of the lack of a contractual link between these two parties.

[144] *Sparwick Contracting, Inc., v. Tomasco Corporation,* 335 N.J. Super. 73, 761 A.2d 90 (N.J. Super. App. Div. 2000), http://caselaw.findlaw.com/nj-superior-court-appellate-division/1372901.html (accessed 25 July 2016). The case concerned related disputes between an employer, a main contractor, a subcontractor and a sub-subcontractor. The sub-subcontract did not contain an arbitration clause. The sub-subcontractor initiated litigation against the three other parties. The main contractor stated that he would like to resolve his dispute with the subcontractor in arbitration as required under the subcontract. The court followed the reasoning in the *Polshek* case and allowed consolidation of all related proceedings. Furthermore, the court ignored the wording of the arbitration agreement in the subcontract, which required arbitration in Pittsburgh. The judge decided that the place of arbitration of the consolidated proceedings would be in New Jersey because this was the more convenient venue for the other parties and the witnesses. Even though the proceedings were consolidated, the sub-subcontractors claims against the employer and the main contractor were excluded because they were not within the authority of the arbitrators.

[145] *Garden Grove Community Church v. Pittsburgh-Des Moines Steel Co.* (1983) 140 Cal. App. 3d 251 [191 Cal. Rptr. 15], http://law.justia.com/cases/california/court-of-appeal/3d/140/251.html (accessed 25 July 2016). An employer had entered into several bilateral contracts with a project manager, a project architect and a main contractor. The main contractor started arbitration against the employer by claiming payment due to alleged defaults by the other two participants in the construction project. Both the agreement with the project architect and the one with the main contractor contained wording aimed at limiting consolidation. Despite this wording, the court decided that all the proceedings could be consolidated by applying retroactively the Californian law that allowed consolidation of domestic arbitrations absent parties' agreement. As stated by the

William Blurock[146], *The School District of Philadelphia v. Livingston-RosenWinkel*[147], *Children's Hospital Philadelphia v. AAA*[148], etc.[149].

court, consolidation was ordered for reasons of efficiency, judicial economy and avoidance of contrary results. The court acknowledged that 'a party may be forced into a coordinated arbitration proceeding in a dispute with a party with whom he has no agreement, before an arbitrator he had no voice in selecting and by a procedure he did not agree to'. Furthermore, the court was of the opinion that the Californian law could not be pre-empted by the FAA because the parties had explicitly chosen that law as applicable.

[146] *Conejo Valley Unified School District v. William Blurock & Partners, Inc.*, 169 Cal. Rptr. 102, Civ. 57894 (1980), http://law.justia.com/cases/california/court-of-appeal/3d/111/983.html (accessed 25 July 2016). An employer hired an architect and a main contractor under two separate agreements containing standard bipolar arbitration clauses. The main contractor started arbitral proceedings against the employer. The claim was based upon allegedly faulty architectural plans provided by the architect. The court decided that the arbitrations should be consolidated with regard to all three parties and applied retroactively the Californian statutory consolidation clause. The court concluded that consolidation was allowed to the extent the contractually agreed party's right to appoint an arbitrator is not impaired. The architect did not have such a right under his contract.

[147] *The School District of Philadelphia v. Livingston Rosenwinkel*, P.C., 690 A.2d 1321 (Pa. Commw. Ct. 1997), http://caselaw.findlaw.com/1974461231pa-commonwealth-court/1280458.html (accessed 25 July 2016). An employer hired an architect and the latter appointed a mechanical engineer. The agreement with the mechanical engineer excluded consolidation without either party's written consent. The court ignored this wording and ordered consolidation. The court stated: 'We conclude that the arbitration clause here is not enforceable because the underlying disputes involve entities which were not parties to the [agreement between the architect and the mechanical engineer] and because enforcement of the arbitration provision would frustrate the public policy interest in efficient dispute resolution.'

[148] *Children's Hospital of Philadelphia v. American Arbitration Association*, 231 Pa. Super. 230, 331 A.2d 848 (1974), http://www.leagle.com/decision/1974461231PaSuper230_1426/CHILDREN'S%20HOSP.%20of%20PHILA.%20v.%20AM.%20ARB.%20ASSN (accessed 25 July 2016). An employer signed four separate contracts with four prime contractors for different sections of the construction works. A dispute arose as regards the allocation of the contractors' responsibility for safety precautionary measures. The arbitration agreements in the separate contracts and the applicable state law were silent on multi-party arbitration. The court consolidated the proceedings because it considered that the issue was of common interest for all parties.

[149] *Vigo Steamship Corp. v. Marship Corp. of Monrovia*, 26 N.Y.2d 157, 309 N.Y.S.2d 165, cert. denied, 400 U.S. 819 (1970), http://www.leagle.com/decision/197018326NY2d157_1161/MATTER%20OF%20VIGO%20CORP.%20(MARSHIP%20CORP.%20OF%20MONROVIA) (accessed 25 July 2016) (Consolidation was ordered on the basis of the federal rules concerning civil procedure that allowed consolidation. At that time, it was considered that the statutory consolidation clause in the civil procedure rules had subsidiary application to arbitrations in cases where parties' contracts were silent on the matter. This interpretation was refuted later on in subsequent case law); *WM. C. Blanchard Co. v. Beach Concrete Co.*, 150 N.J. Super. 277, 375A.2d 675 (App. Div. 1977), http://www.leagle.com/decision/1977427150NJSuper277_1386/WM.%20BLANCHARD%20CO.%20v.%20BEACH%20CONCRETE%20CO.,%20INC (accessed 25 July 2016); *Travellers Casualty and Surety Company of America Inc. v. Long Bay Management Company,* 58 Mass. App. Ct 786 (2003), http://masscases.com/cases/app/58/58massappct786.html (accessed 25 July 2016) (Consolidation was allowed under Massachusetts law in the absence of specific wording in the contractual documentation.); *Hoover Group, Inc. v. Probala & Associates*, 710 F.Supp. 677,681 (N.D. Ohio 1989), http://law.justia.com/cases/federal/district-courts/FSupp/710/677/1462587/(accessed 25 July 2016) (Under the FAA, a court could compel consolidation of arbitrations when the agreements to arbitrate were embodied in separate contracts, none of which provided for consolidation); *Robinson v. Warner*, 370 F. Supp. 828 (D.R.I. 1974), http://law.justia.com/cases/federal/district-courts/FSupp/370/828/1801675/(accessed 25 July 2016) (The court compelled consolidation of arbitrations arising under two separate contracts which were silent on consolidation.); *Grover-Diamond Associates, Inc. v. AAA*, 297 Minn. 324, 211, N.W.2d 787 (Minn. 1973) (A demand for joint arbitration against the main contractor and the architect was accepted. However, the architect and the main contractor were not obliged to arbitrate their dispute with one another because there was no direct contractual link between them.); *Exber, Inc. v.*

What is common in all these cases is that the courts concluded that they have inherent power to order consolidation of arbitral proceedings even absent parties' explicit agreement, provided that there are common questions of law and / or fact in the separate proceedings. In some cases, the courts went even further by ordering consolidation without taking into account the contractual wording in parties' contracts aimed at limiting or excluding consolidation. For states that did not have consolidation provisions in their statures, the power to consolidate was deemed to derive from the statutory obligation of courts to enforce arbitration agreements, which allegedly included the power to direct the proceedings in the most efficient way, including by means of consolidation. For states with statutory consolidation provisions, the power to consolidate was based on these provisions. Most of the courts decided that the FAA did not pre-empt statutory consolidation provisions contained in US states' laws. The FAA was interpreted liberally to foster resolution of disputes in a speedy and economical manner. In most cases, the rationale for consolidation was public policy requiring judicial efficiency and avoidance of the risk of inconsistent findings.

5.10.2.2 No consolidation absent parties' contractual agreement to the contrary

The reasoning in the *Nereus* case was overruled in *Government of the United Kingdom v. Boeing Co*[150]. In this case, the UK Government, in its capacity of assignor, entered into two separate agreements with Boeing and Textron, respectively, concerning the manufacture of a helicopter. Both agreements contained identical arbitration clauses that were silent as to the conduct of multi-party arbitration. The UK Government filed separate requests for arbitration against its contracting parties claiming losses resulting from an unsuccessful ground test and requested consolidation of the two proceedings by relying on the reasoning in the *Nereus* case, which at that time was still considered as a precedent. The district court granted the petition and ordered consolidation. On appeal by Boeing, the US Court of Appeals for the Second Circuit reversed the district court by stating that the court was not empowered to order consolidation of parallel proceedings based on several contracts (even in cases when they involve the same questions of fact and law) without the parties' consent. More particularly, the court reasoned its decision with the following wording:

> a court is not permitted to interfere with private arbitration agreements in order to impose its own view of speed and economy. This is the case even where the result would be possibly

---

Sletten Construction Company, 92 Nev. 721, 558 P.2d 517 (1976), http://law.justia.com/cases/nevada/supreme-court/1976/8236-1.html (accessed 25 July 2016) (Consolidation was ordered for reasons of efficiency absent specific wording in the contracts and the applicable state law.); *Matter of Kallas v. Milberg Weiss LLP*, 61 A.D.3d 451 (2009), App. Div. N.Y.S.C., http://law.justia.com/cases/new-york/appellate-division-first-department/2009/2009-02683.html (accessed 25 July 2016).

150 *Government of the United Kingdom of Great Britain v. The Boeing Company*, 998 F.2d 68 (2nd Cir.1993), http://law.justia.com/cases/federal/appellate-courts/F2/998/68/48624/(accessed 25 July 2016).

inefficient maintenance of separate proceedings. If contracting parties wish to have all disputes that arise from the same factual situation arbitrated in a single proceeding, they can simply provide for consolidated arbitration in the arbitration clauses to which they are a party.

Thus, the Court of Appeals for the Second Circuit departed from its previous case law, pursuant to which consolidation was possible in the absence of parties' agreement on the matter. Afterwards, the majority of the circuit courts followed the reasoning in the *Boeing* case: the Second Circuit in *Glencore Ltd.* v. *Schnitzer Steel Products Co*[151], the Fifth Circuit in *Del E. Webb Construction v. Richardson Hospital Authority*[152], the Sixth Circuit in *American Centennial Ins. Co. v. National Casualty Co.*[153], the Ninth Circuit in *Weyerhauser Co. v. Western Shipping Co.*[154], the Eighth Circuit in *Baesler v. Continental*

[151] *Glencore Limited v. Schnitzer Steel Products Co.*, 189 F.3d 264 (2nd Cir. 1999), http://caselaw.findlaw.com/us-2nd-circuit/1011784.html (accessed 25 July 2016). The court held that consolidation was not possible in the absence of the parties' agreement. Furthermore, it stated that although duplication, delay and the risk of inconsistent decisions might be valid concerns, they did not provide courts with the authority to reform the private contracts that underlay a dispute.

[152] *Del E. Webb Construction v. Richardson Hospital Authority*, 823 F.2d 145 (5th Cir. 1987), http://law.justia.com/cases/federal/appellate-courts/F2/823/145/221658/(accessed 25 July 2016). The case concerned the construction of a medical centre based on a 'build-only' contractual model. The main contractor requested the consolidation of his arbitration with the employer with the one between the employer and the architect. The district court granted the order but the court of appeals reversed it by relying on the wording in one of the contracts, which excluded the architect from consolidated proceedings absent his consent: 'since under the grant of authority in § 4 [of the FAA] the district court was limited to enforcing arbitration agreements according to their terms, and since the parties agree that the architect has not consented in writing, the district court should not have ordered consolidation.'

[153] *American Centennial Ins. Co. v. National Casualty Co.*, 951 F.2d 107 (6th Cir. 1991), http://law.justia.com/cases/federal/appellate-courts/F2/951/107/258151/(accessed 25 July 2016). The court stipulated that where there was no consolidation provision concerning insurance and reinsurance contracts, the District Court was not empowered to circumvent the FAA and order consolidation.

[154] *Weyerhauser Co. v. Western Shipping*, 743 F.2d 635 (9th Cir. 1984), cert. denied 105 S.Ct. 544, 469 U.S. 1061, http://openjurist.org/743/f2d/635/weyerhaeuser-company-v-western-seas-shipping-co (accessed 25 July 2016). A ship charterer was a party under two charter agreements (i.e. a main charter contract and a sub-charter contract) concluded with different parties. The charterer tried to consolidate the related proceedings arising under the two contracts. The Ninth Circuit declined the request because the two contracts did not address consolidation. Furthermore, the court stated that the authority granted to courts under the FAA should be construed narrowly, i.e. courts should only 'determine whether a written arbitration agreement exists, and if it does, enforce it in accordance with its terms'.

Grain Co.[155], the Eleventh Circuit in *Protective Life Ins. Corp. v. Lincoln National Life Ins. Corp.*[156]. Many lower courts followed the same trend[157].

---

[155] *Baesler v. Continental Grain Co.*, 900 F. 2d 1193 (8th Cir. 1990), http://www.leagle.com/decision/199020939 00F2d1193_11904/BAESLER%20v.%20CONTINENTAL%20GRAIN%20CO (accessed 25 July 2016). Continental had entered into standard safflower contracts with several producers. The contracts contained arbitration agreements silent on consolidation. Disputes involving common issues of law and fact arose under the contracts and one of the producers requested consolidation. The court denied the request: 'We agree with the majority view that the Federal Arbitration Act precludes federal courts from ordering consolidation of arbitration proceedings…We read the [act] as requiring federal courts to enforce arbitration agreements as they are written. Accordingly, we hold that absent a provision in an arbitration agreement authorizing consolidation, a district court is without power to consolidate arbitration proceedings.'

[156] *Protective Life Insurance Corp. v. Lincoln National Life Insurance Corp.*, 873 F. 2d 281 (11th Cir. 1989), http://openjurist.org/873/f2d/281/protective-life-insurance-corporation-v-lincoln-national-life-insurance-corporation (accessed 25 July 2016). Lincoln National Life Insurance appealed the consolidation of its arbitration with Protective Life Insurance with an arbitration between the latter entity and a third party. The arbitrations had arisen under two separate contracts containing two distinct bipolar arbitration agreements. By following the reasoning in the *Weyerhauser Co. v. Western Shipping*, the court concluded that consolidation was not allowed if the parties had not provided for consolidation in their agreements. The court stated that 'parties may negotiate for and include provisions for consolidation of arbitration proceedings in their arbitration agreements, but if such provisions are absent, federal courts may not read them in.'

[157] *Gavlik Construction Co. v. H.F. Campbell Co.*, 389 F.Supp. 551 (W.D. Pa. 1975), http://law.justia.com/cases/federal/district-courts/FSupp/389/551/1591873/(accessed 25 July 2016) (A request by a main contractor for consolidation of arbitrations arising under a main contract and a subcontract was denied because of the lack of specific wording in the arbitration agreements); *The Stop & Shop Companies, Inc. vs. Gilbane Building Company*, 364 Mass. 325, 304 N.E.2d 429 (1973), http://masscases.com/cases/sjc/364/364mass325.html (accessed 25 July 2016) (In the absence of an agreement for multiparty arbitration, consolidation of employer-main contractor proceedings with employer-architect proceedings was not possible.); *J. Brodie & Son, Inc. v. George A. Fuller Co.*, 16 Mich. App. 137, 167 N.W.2d 886 (1969), https://www.courtlistener.com/opinion/1932977/j-brodie-son-inc-v-george-a-fuller-co/(accessed 25 July 2016) ('there is no basis for intervention or consolidation where they are separate and district contracts with different burdens and subject matter, and where the parties and proceedings have no privity or basis in fact.'); *Bay County Building Authority & Spence Brothers*, 140 Mich. App. 182 (1984), 326 N.W.2d 739, http://www.leagle.com/decision/1984322140 MichApp182_1299/BAY%20COUNTY%20BUILDING%20AUTH.%20v.%20SPENCE%20BROS (accessed 25 July 2016) ('The court should not meddle with [the parties'] contractual provisions even though we might fashion a more expedient, efficient and economical remedy.'); *Consolidated Pacific Engineering, Inc. v. Greater Anchorage Area Borough*, 563 P.2d 252 (Alaska 1977), http://www.leagle.com/decision/1977815563P2d252_1813/CONSOLIDATED%20PAC.%20ENG'G%20v.%20GREATER%20ANCHORAGE%20AREA%20BOROUGH (accessed 25 July 2016); *Balfour, Guthrie and Company, Limited v. Commercial Metals Co.*, 93 Wn.2d 199 (1980), 607 P.2d 856, http://law.justia.com/cases/washington/supreme-court/1980/46338-1.html (accessed 25 June 2016) (silence in parties' contracts excludes consolidation); *Matter of Chariot Textiles Corp.*, 21 A.D.2d 762 (N.Y. App. Div. 1964), https://casetext.com/case/matter-of-chariot-textiles-corp-1 (accessed 25 July 2016); *Atlas Plastering, Inc. v. Superior Court of Alameda County*, 72 Cal. App. 3d 63, 68, 140 Cal. Rptr. 59, 63–64 (1977), http://law.justia.com/cases/california/court-of-appeal/3d/72/63.html (accessed 25 July 2016) (the court decided that disputes between a main contractor and several subcontractors, who were not in contractual privity with each other, cannot be consolidated in single proceedings because this would have modified the agreed mechanism for the appointment of arbitrators. Furthermore, at that time there was no consolidation legislation in California); *Seretta Construction, Inc., v. Great American Insurance Co.*, 869 So. 2d 676 (Fla. Dist. Ct. App. 2004), https://www.courtlistener.com/opinion/1601984/seretta-const-inc-v-great-american-ins-co/(accessed 25 July 2016) (A main contractor tried to consolidate two arbitrations against two of his subcontractors. Consolidation was rejected because there was no agreement from the parties to authorize consolidation.); *Bateman Construction, Inc., v. Haitsuka Brothers, Limited*, 889 P.2d 58 (1995), 77 Haw. 481,

Pursuant to all cases examined in this Subsection, consolidation is only possible subject to parties' explicit agreement. Thus, more weight is attributed to the sphere of party autonomy which is gradually expanding[158]. These decisions acknowledge that the FAA should be construed narrowly – the power of the court to consolidate is not implied but should be conferred upon it by the parties in their agreements. The underlying rationale is that the FAA 'rigorously enforces agreements to arbitrate, even if the result is piecemeal litigation'[159]. In this way, the FAA gives the parties the freedom to structure their arbitrations as they think best[160]. Therefore, silence in parties' contracts should not be construed as an implied consent to consolidation but rather as a dissent. If the parties' intentions were to submit their disputes to multi-party arbitration, they would have provided so in their contracts[161].

The current trend in US case law is that consolidation may not be authorized without parties' agreement[162]. This is the prevailing view nowadays in the United States[163]. An exception to this is the decision of the US Court of Appeals for the First Circuit in the *Keystone* case, where it was held that courts have the power to consolidate arbitrations absent parties' agreement, especially in cases where the applicable US state arbitration act allowed for consolidation. Pursuant to the Keystone case, the FAA did not pre-empt the state arbitration act authorizing consolidation.

---

http://law.justia.com/cases/hawaii/supreme-court/1995/17745-2.html (accessed 25 July 2016) (the circuit court had no jurisdiction to consolidate arbitrations where the arbitration agreements were silent as to consolidation); *Louisiana Stadium and Exposition District v. Huber, Hunt & Nichols*, Inc., 349 So.2d 491 (La. App. 1977), http://www.leagle.com/decision/1977840349So2d491_1718/LA.%20STADIUM%20&%20EXPOSITION%20DIST.%20v.%20HUBER,%20HUNT%20&%20NICHOLS,%20INC. (accessed 25 July 2016); *Biber Partnership v. Diamond Hill Joint Venture LLC*, 404 N.J. Super. 96, 960 A.2d 774 (App. Div. 2008), http://law.justia.com/cases/new-jersey/appellate-division-published/2008/a1766-07-opn.html (accessed 25 July 2016) (consolidation under the RUAA was not allowed because of the inconsistent arbitral clauses concerning the appointment of arbitrators); *Georgia Casualty & Surety Co. v. Excalibur Reinsurance Corp.*, Case No. 1:13-CV-00456-JEC (ND Ga, 12 March 2014), http://02ec4c5.netsolhost.com/blog/data/20/1/142/136/1957625/user/2137514/htdocs/blog/wp-content/uploads/2014/03/Georgia-Casualty-v.-Excalibur-3.13.2014-Order-and-Opinion.pdf (accessed 25 July 2016).

[158] Okuma Kazutake, 'Party Autonomy in International Commercial Arbitration: Consolidation of Multiparty and Classwide Arbitration', in *9 Annual Survey of International & Comparative Law*, no. 1 (2003), p. 191.

[159] *Dean Witter Reynolds, Inc. v. Byrd*, 470 U.S. 213, 221 (1985), https://supreme.justia.com/cases/federal/us/470/213/case.html (accessed 25 July 2016).

[160] Gary Born (2014) *International Commercial Arbitration, Volume II: International Arbitral Procedures*, 2nd edn, Kluwer Law International, Alphen aan den Rijn, p. 2577.

[161] Dominique Hascher, 'Consolidation of Arbitration by American Courts: Fostering or Hampering International Commercial Arbitrations?', in *1 Journal of International Arbitration*, no. 2 (1984), p. 134.

[162] Richard Wallace, 'Consolidated Arbitration in the United States, Recent Authority Requires Consent of the Parties', in *10 Journal of International Arbitration*, no. 4 (1993), pp. 5, 17.

[163] Dimitar Hristoforov Kondev, 'Statutory Approaches to Multi-Party/Multi-Contract Construction Arbitration', in *19 The Vindobona Journal of International Commercial Law and Arbitration*, no. 1 (2015), p. 49; Christopher Stippl, 'International Multi-party Arbitration: The Role of Party Autonomy', in *7 The American Review of International Arbitration*, no. 1 (1996), p. 68; Gary Born (2014) *International Commercial Arbitration, Volume II: International Arbitral Procedures*, 2nd edn, Kluwer Law International, Alphen aan den Rijn, p. 2080.

Despite the conflicting case law in the different circuit courts, the US Supreme Court has not expressed an opinion on the matter yet[164]. Of the federal circuit court cases reviewed so far, some were appealed to the US Supreme Court, but all were denied certiorari. However, some decisions of the Supreme Court, albeit not directly related to consolidation, may serve as additional arguments that the FAA should be construed in a restrictive way, namely that it does not allow consolidation where parties' contracts contain no specific wording in that regard. Thus, in *Moses H. Cone Memorial Hospital v. Mercury Construction Corp.*[165] the Supreme Court held that under the FAA, an arbitration agreement should be enforced irrespective of the existence of a third party who is a party to the underlying contract disputes but is not a party to the arbitration agreement. Furthermore, in *Dean Witter Reynolds, Inc. v. Byrd*[166] the Supreme Court acknowledged that the purpose of the FAA was not to promote the expedited resolution of claims but to ensure judicial enforcement of privately negotiated arbitration agreements. Hence, public policy considerations aiming at consistent resolution of related disputes in a consolidated manner should not outweigh party autonomy. One of the most recent cases is *Stolt-Nielsen v. Animalfeeds*[167] where the Supreme Court held that imposing class arbitration on parties without their explicit consent constituted a violation of the FAA. The same reasoning may be applied by analogy to consolidation.

Contracting parties considering the United States as a possible venue for their arbitrations should be aware of the abovementioned developments in US legislation and case law. Parties willing to resolve their disputes through multi-party arbitration should make sure that appropriate arbitration agreements are included in their contracts. If the parties do not regulate these matters in their contracts, there would hardly be any prospect of consolidation. In addition, parties arbitrating their disputes in a jurisdiction falling within the domain of the US Court of Appeals for the First Circuit should bear in mind the reasoning in the *Keystone* case. These parties might find themselves involved in a consolidated arbitration which can frustrate their expectations to resolve their disputes in a bipolar context. Therefore, if the parties want to preserve these expectations, they should include specific clauses in their contracts which exclude the possibility for consolidation.

5.10.2.3 Who should decide on consolidation?

Another controversial issue in US case law concerns the authority competent to order consolidation. Some courts are of the opinion that issues of consolidation should be

[164] Okuma Kazutake, 'Party Autonomy in International Commercial Arbitration: Consolidation of Multiparty and Classwide Arbitration', in 9 *Annual Survey of International and Comparative Law*, no. 1 (2003), p. 210.

[165] *Moses H. Cone Memorial Hospital v. Mercury Construction Corp.*, 460 U.S. 1 (1983), 103 S.Ct. 927, 74 L.Ed.2d 765, https://www.law.cornell.edu/supremecourt/text/460/1 (accessed 25 July 2016).

[166] *Dean Witter Reynolds, Inc. v. Byrd*, 470 U.S. 213, 221 (1985).

[167] *Stolt-Nielsen S.A. v. Animalfeeds Int'l Corp.*, 130 S.Ct. 1758, 1774 (U.S. S.Ct. 2010), http://www.supremecourt.gov/opinions/09pdf/08-1198.pdf (accessed 26 July 2016).

decided by the arbitral tribunals and not by the courts[168]. Other courts, however, have adopted the opposite approach[169]. After the Supreme Court decision in *Green Tree Financial Corp. v. Bazzle*[170], it seems that the first standpoint will prevail. This case concerned class arbitration and the court acknowledged that it was for the arbitrator(s) to decide whether the arbitration agreement authorized class arbitration. By analogy, this reasoning may be applied to consolidated arbitrations. Indeed, several federal and state courts have later relied on the abovementioned Supreme Court decision and decided that, since the issue of consolidation was a matter of contract interpretation and arbitration procedures, it was not for the court but for the arbitrators to decide[171]. In any case, the general principles underlying the approach of the FAA to multi-party arbitrations should be considered as issues of substantive federal law that are binding on both US courts and arbitral tribunals seated in the United States[172].

---

[168] See, for example, *Pedcor Management Co., Inc. Welfare Benefit Plan v. Nations Personnel of Texas, Inc.*, 343 F.3d 355 (5th Cir. 2003), http://caselaw.findlaw.com/us-5th-circuit/1411299.html (accessed 26 July 2016); *Shaw's Supermarkets, Inc. v. United Food & Commercial Workers Union*, 321 F.3d 251, 254 (1st Cir. 2003), http://openjurist.org/321/f3d/251/shaws-supermarkets-inc-v-united-food-and-commercial-workers-union-local (accessed 25 July 2016); *Certain Underwriters at Lloyd's London v. Westchester Fire Ins. Co.*, 489 F.3d 580 (3rd Cir. 2007), http://law.justia.com/cases/federal/appellate-courts/F3/489/580/574065/(accessed 26 July 2016); *Dockser v. Schwartzberg*, 433 F.3d 421 (4th Cir. 2006), http://caselaw.findlaw.com/us-4th-circuit/1252061.html (accessed 26 June 2016); *Bay County Building Authority & Spence Brothers*, 140 Mich. App. 182 (1984), 326 N.W.2d 739, http://www.leagle.com/decision/1984322140MichApp182_1299/BAY%20COUNTY%20BUILDING%20AUTH.%20v.%20SPENCE%20BROS. (accessed 26 June 2016).

[169] *Del E. Webb Construction v. Richardson Hospital Authority*, 823 F.2d 145 (5th Cir. 1987); *Connecticut General Life Insurance Co. v. Sun Life Assurance Co. of Canada*, 210 F.3d 771, 775 (7th Cir. 2000), http://caselaw.findlaw.com/us-7th-circuit/1281923.html (accessed 26 July 2016); *The North River Ins. Co. v. Philadelphia Reinsurance Corp.*, 63 F.3d 160 (2nd Cir. 1995), http://openjurist.org/63/f3d/160/north-river-insurance-company-v-philadelphia-reinsurance-corporation (accessed 26 June 2016).

[170] *Green Tree Fin. Corp. v. Bazzle*, 539 U.S. 444 (U.S. S.Ct. 2003), https://supreme.justia.com/cases/federal/us/539/444/case.pdf (accessed 26 July 2016). See Irene Ten Cate, 'Multi-party and Multi-contract Arbitrations: Procedural Mechanisms and Interpretation of Arbitration Agreements under U.S. Law', in *15 The American Review of International Arbitration*, no. 1 (2004), pp. 146–148.

[171] Philip Bruner, 'Dual Track Proceedings in Arbitration and Litigation: Reducing the Peril of "Double Jeopardy" by Consolidation, Joinder and Appellate Arbitration', in *31 International Construction Law Review*, part 4 (2014), p. 542; Shawn Aiken, *2009 Private Arbitration Update, Consolidation of Separate Arbitration Proceedings*, pp. 2–3, http://www.ashrlaw.com/dox/SKA-arb-consolidation.pdf (accessed 26 July 2016); Bernard Hanotiau (2005) *Complex Arbitrations: Multiparty, Multicontract, Multi-issue and Class Actions*, Kluwer Law International, The Hague, p. 186 (§ 415). See also *Blimpie International Inc. v. Blimpie of the Keys*, 371 F.Supp.2d 469 (S.D.N.Y. 2005), http://www.leagle.com/decision/2005840371FSupp2d469_1784/BLIMPIE%20INTERN.,%20INC.%20v.%20BLIMPIE%20OF%20THE%20KEYS (accessed 26 July 2016); *Yuen v. The Superior Court of Los Angelis County*, 121 Cal. App. 4th 1133 (2004), http://caselaw.findlaw.com/ca-court-of-appeal/1010328.html (accessed 26 July 2016); *Employers Insurance Co. of Wausau v. Century Indemnity Co.*, 443 F 3d 573 (2006), http://openjurist.org/443/f3d/573/employers-insurance-company-of-wausau-v-century-indemnity-company (accessed 26 July 2016) and *Nath v. Merrill Lynch, Pierce, Fenner & Smith Inc.*, WL 2438435, 4 (NY Sup, 21 May 2014), http://www.leagle.com/decision/In%20NYCO%2020140530361/NATH%20v.%20LYNCH (accessed 26 July 2016).

[172] Gary Born (2014) *International Commercial Arbitration, Volume II: International Arbitral Procedures*, 2nd edn, Kluwer Law International, Alphen aan den Rijn, p. 2578.

5.11 Should arbitration laws deal with multi-party arbitration?

At first sight, the legislative approach to multiparty arbitration may seem as a convenient and efficient tool to overcome the problems pertaining to this type of arbitration. It has been observed in Chapter 4 that arbitration rules generally do not provide for a self-contained mechanism for the conduct of multi-party arbitrations, which can be put into operation solely on the basis of provisions contained in these rules. Furthermore, as will be seen in Chapter 6, most standard form agreements suitable for international use do not propose a solution to multi-party arbitration problems and *ad hoc* multi-party arbitration agreements are not commonplace in construction projects. Therefore, national arbitration laws may seem to be the only remaining source to regulate multi-party arbitration. They can provide a straightforward and uniform legal framework to the problems on a state level. For this reason, some authors have encouraged the statutory approach to multi-party arbitration[173]. It may even be stated that for contracting parties aware of this framework, the dispute resolution process will be more predictable. If they are satisfied with the statutory regulation of multi-party disputes, they will not have to address these issues in their contracts, which saves negotiation time and costs.

Furthermore, certain public policy arguments may also be stated to support the introduction of statutory multi-party arbitration provisions. From a public policy perspective, it may be argued that states are not interested in hosting arbitrations that lead to irreconcilable arbitration awards on common legal and / or factual matters. This can be considered as a hurdle to states' ambitions to attract more international arbitrations, especially by states trying to strengthen their position as popular arbitration hubs. Therefore, states might be tempted to introduce legislation that avoids this undesired result. Furthermore, it may also be argued that legislative multi-party arbitration provisions are necessary from a public policy perspective for reasons of procedural economy because they would encourage the resolution of multi-contract disputes in a faster and more cost-efficient way[174].

Despite all arguments described above, the author is of the opinion that there are convincing arguments against the introduction of statutory provisions dealing with

[173] Pieter Sanders (1999) *Quo Vadis Arbitration? Sixty Years of Arbitration Practice, A Comparative Study*, Kluwer Law International, The Hague, p. 213. In the author's opinion, while other forms of multi-party arbitration can be regulated in parties' contracts or applicable arbitration rules, consolidation will require assistance from the courts: 'the arbitration world itself cannot solve the issues of consolidation of connected arbitral proceedings pending before different tribunals and to be decided under different Arbitration Rules. This issue can, in my opinion, only be solved by statutory regulation'. See also Dimitrios Athanasakis and Robert Morgan, 'Joinder of Arbitrations: an Overview of English and Hong Kong Construction Industry Practice', in *Asian Dispute Review* no. 1 (2008), p. 20. When analysing the objections against the earlier mandatory consolidation provision in Hong Kong and its likely breach of the consensual nature of arbitrations, the authors stated 'party autonomy cannot be used as a means of preventing the just and expeditious conduct of separate but related arbitrations'.

[174] Jean-Francois Poudret and Sébastien Besson (2007) *Comparative Law of International Arbitration*, 2nd edn, Sweet & Maxwell, London, pp. 883–884.

multi-party arbitration. First of all, it is rather difficult to reconcile these legislative provisions with the consensual nature of arbitration, unless the provisions constitute *opt-in* clauses[175]. Consent is one of the cornerstones of arbitration. In the context of construction disputes, consent to arbitration means not only consent to arbitrate in general but rather consent to arbitrate specific disputes arising under a specific contract against a specific party – the contractual counterparty under the same contract[176]. The type of multi-party arbitrations examined in this book necessitates the participation of a third party or parties who are not in contractual privity with at least one of the main disputants. Therefore, consent to the bringing of such third parties in the pending arbitration is usually something that should be *agreed* among the parties and *not legislated* by states. This agreement should be expressed by the parties in those legal sources over which they have some influence. More particularly, the parties' agreement to multi-party arbitration may be materialized either in the arbitration agreements contained in the parties' contracts or in the arbitration rules chosen by the parties as applicable to their disputes[177]. These are the two sources where the parties' autonomy can be expressed in its full extent. By drafting an arbitration agreement or choosing a certain set of arbitration rules, the parties usually have the full discretion to shape the arbitration as they think fit. While the parties are usually aware of the content of the arbitration rules to which they refer, the same is not always true with regard to arbitration laws. These are outside the domain and sphere of influence of the parties. Multi-party arbitration in the form of statutory court-ordered consolidation or other forms should not therefore be imposed on the parties absent their consent[178].

As Thomas Carbonneau has stated on this matter:

> Court-ordered consolidation of separate arbitral proceedings creates issues about the boundaries of the contract for arbitration. In effect, courts rewrite material provisions of the agreement and force parties to arbitrate with parties who were not included in the original agreement. Parties, therefore, are bound by an implied duty to arbitrate imposed by an entity outside

[175] The same opinion is shared by Julian Lew, Loukas Mistelis and Stefan Kröll (2003) *Comparative International Commercial Arbitration*, Kluwer Law International, The Hague, p. 400. See also ICC Commission on International Arbitration, 'Final Report on Multi-Party Arbitrations', in *6 ICC International Court of Arbitration Bulletin*, No. 1 (1995), pp. 30–31, where it is stated that the introduction of statutory consolidation clauses, such as the provision in the Netherlands law, leads to the infringement of the principle of mutual consent in arbitration.

[176] Gary Born (2014) *International Commercial Arbitration, Volume II: International Arbitral Procedures*, 2nd edn, Kluwer Law International, Alphen aan den Rijn, p. 2072.

[177] Parties' agreement to multi-party arbitration may also be in the form of a submission agreement given once the related disputes under the multiple contracts have already arisen. However, because of the parties' divergent interests, a submission agreement on multi-party arbitration is unlikely to be achieved.

[178] See also CIArb Practice Guideline 15: Guidelines for Arbitrators on how to approach issues relating to Multi-Party Arbitration, https://www.ciarb.org/docs/default-source/practice-guidelines-protocols-and-rules/international-arbitration-guidelines-2011/2011multipartyarbitrations.pdf?sfvrsn=6 (accessed 26 July 2016). Pursuant to Section 1.3 of this guideline, 'There is in general no justification for any intervention by the Court to require the dispute to be determined otherwise than in accordance with parties' agreement.'

> the boundaries of the contract. Court consolidation violates parties' autonomy and their sovereign authority over their transaction. The court intrudes upon a private transaction for no public reason.[179]

The public policy arguments in favour of statutory multi-party arbitration solutions can hardly be maintained[180]. Unlike litigation, which is regulated in detail in state civil procedure codes, arbitration is based on parties' consent and is predominantly regulated by private sources of law. Arbitration laws, as public sources of law, provide the legal framework within which the private sources of law, such as arbitration agreements and arbitration rules, operate. Arbitration laws should aim at facilitating the parties to resolve their disputes in their chosen forum and in accordance with their agreed procedure rather than to prescribe solutions that are not addressed in the private sources of regulation. Because of the consensual nature of arbitration, the interests of the stakeholders using arbitration should prevail over public policy reasons. Public policy arguments, such as procedural economy, the avoidance of irreconcilable awards on common legal or factual matters, and preservation of resources have much weight in the context of litigation but they are not directly relevant to private dispute resolution mechanisms, such as arbitration[181]. In the context of arbitration, what the parties actually want is important and not what the state feels desirable. As it has been stated by Dominique Hascher:

> The submission of the disputes to a court-directed arbitration panel is injurious to the psychological climate of arbitration…The role of the courts is to enforce the expectations of the trade community by advancing its aims, not to surprise it by rulings based on an ideology not germane to that of the business world[182].

Have the parties actually agreed to multi-party arbitration if both their contracts and the applicable arbitration rules do not allow such arbitration but the applicable state law permits it? As pointed out by William Craig in respect of court-ordered consolidation:

> the issue is whether the effect of the law at the place of arbitration, when it permits such consolidation, overcomes the lack of contractual intent on the grounds that the contractors must be deemed to have contracted in knowledge of, and subject to, provisions of such law[183].

---

[179] Thomas Carbonneau (2007) *Cases and Materials on Arbitration Law and Practice*, 6th edn, American Casebook Series, Thomson West, St Paul, MN, p. 35.

[180] Emmanuel Gaillard, 'The Consolidation of Arbitral Proceedings and Court Proceedings', in *14 ICC International Court of Arbitration Bulletin, Complex Arbitrations – Special Supplement 2003*, p. 42.

[181] Stavros Brekoulakis (2010) *Third Parties in International Commercial Arbitration*, Oxford University Press, Oxford, 2010, pp. 124–125 (para. 3.119). According to the author: '[The] stakes in multiparty disputes in arbitration are hardly linked to public interests, mandatory laws, or general state policies…Any relevant interests that should be taken into account in this discussion are first the private interests of the parties to an arbitration agreement, and second the private interests of third parties with a legitimate financial and legal interest in the outcome of the dispute pending before a tribunal between two parties in arbitration.'

[182] Dominique Hascher, 'Consolidation of Arbitration by American Courts: Fostering or Hampering International Commercial Arbitrations?' in *1 Journal of International Arbitration*, no. 2 (1984), pp. 142–143.

[183] William Craig (1991) 'Means of Recourse and Enforcement of Awards', in P. Bellet, P. Bernardini, G. Bernini *et al.* (eds) *Multi-Party Arbitration: Views from International Arbitration Specialists*, Publication No. 480/1,

The answer to this question will depend on the specific circumstances of the case. If the parties have decided to choose a certain state with the full knowledge that the law of that state regulates multi-party arbitration, then this choice might be considered as an agreement to multi-party arbitration. In this case, however, there is no 'lack of contractual intent' because this intent has presumably been expressed in the choice of the specific arbitration law. This, however, requires that the law had already been in existence at the time when the parties negotiated their contracts. Only under these circumstances may it be argued that the parties have contracted in the knowledge of that law[184]. Apparently, this will not be true if the statutory regulation of multi-party disputes was introduced after the parties had signed their contracts. The same will be true if the existing legislative framework, of which the parties were aware at the time of negotiation, was subsequently changed after the conclusion of their contracts. In the latter two cases, the parties could not be deemed to have contracted in the knowledge of law that did not exist. Therefore, it cannot be maintained that parties have agreed to multi-party arbitration just because they have chosen a certain seat of arbitration.

There are also other cases in which the application of a certain arbitration law providing for multi-party arbitration will not be in compliance with the parties' agreement. Often parties do not specify a seat of arbitration in their arbitration agreements either because they do not have any special preferences or they cannot agree on the matter during the negotiations. In these cases, the place of arbitration will be fixed by the arbitral institution or the competent arbitral tribunal once the disputes have arisen. The choice of the seat will trigger the application of *lex arbitri* of the state where the seat is located. However, the parties do not have a say in this choice. As a result, an unknown state law allowing court-ordered consolidation may be imposed on them thus frustrating their expectations to resolve their disputes in a bipolar setting[185]. In these cases, the parties will not be aware of the applicable arbitration law at the time when they conclude their contracts. Some scholars, with whom the author does not concur, raise the counterargument that by not agreeing on the place of arbitration, the parties have entrusted the

ICC Publishing SA, Paris, p. 231. The author has asserted that consolidation by courts may frustrate at least two contractual intentions of the parties: the intent of a party to arbitrate only with its contractor and the intent to respect an agreed arbitration procedure and, most particularly, a procedure for the appointment of arbitrators.

[184]However, this statement is not beyond any doubt. In many cases, the choice of that law would be a consequence of having chosen a certain city as the place of arbitration. This choice might have been dictated by reasons of convenience only, such as proximity to the construction site, residence of witnesses, etc., which does not necessarily imply that the parties were fully aware of the content of the applicable arbitral law. On that point, see Julian Lew, Loukas Mistelis and Stefan Kröll (2003) *Comparative International Commercial Arbitration*, Kluwer Law International, The Hague, p. 400, where it has been stated that the selection of a certain place of arbitration can hardly be seen as an expression of consent to multi-party arbitration because few parties will be aware of the existence of multi-party arbitration provisions in local arbitration laws.

[185]Cristian Conejero Roos (2009) 'Multi-party Arbitration and Rule Making: Same Issues, Contrasting Approaches', in Albert Jan van den Berg (ed.) *Fifty Years of the New York Convention, ICCA International Arbitration Conference, ICCA Congress Series No. 14*, Kluwer Law International, Alphen aan den Rijn, p. 417.

designation of this place to the arbitrators or the arbitral institution, and therefore the choice of the seat in these cases is legally tantamount to a designation by the parties themselves[186]. Hence, court-ordered consolidation forms part of the parties' agreement. In the author's opinion, this assertion is quite contentious. Contracting parties that cannot agree on a place of arbitration should not be overburdened with expectations to foresee any and all possible aspects of the arbitral proceedings which might follow from the choice of that seat by the arbitral tribunal or institution, especially when it comes to problems such as multi-party arbitration, which rarely find legislative regulation[187]. Furthermore, accepting this argument will mean that parties not willing to participate in a multi-party arbitration should explicitly exclude this type of arbitration in their arbitration agreements. This, in fact, constitutes an agreement not to arbitrate in a specific manner, which will be at odds with well established arbitration-drafting practices.

Moreover, arbitration laws allowing for joinder or consolidation often empower competent courts to decide on these issues, which is contrary to contracting parties' willingness to submit their disputes to arbitration and not to state courts. As professor Emmanuel Gaillard has stated 'it would certainly be illusion to believe that arbitration, without losing its soul, could find a remedy for all its defects in the systematic intervention of state courts'[188].

Another issue related to court-ordered forms of multi-party arbitration is the likely risk of setting aside of the award in the country where it is rendered and of non-recognition and/or non-enforcement of the award in third countries. Pursuant to Article V of the New York Convention, recognition and enforcement of an arbitral award may be refused if the composition of the arbitral tribunal or the arbitral proceedings was not in accordance with the agreement of the parties or, failing such an agreement, with *lex fori* – the law of the country where arbitration took place (Article V(1)(d)). An analogous ground for setting aside of an award is contained in the UNCITRAL Model Law[189]. Can an award be set aside or denied recognition and enforcement on the ground that parties' arbitration agreements did not address multi-party arbitration but such arbitration was ordered on the basis of a statutory clause that did not require parties' consent? Different opinions have been expressed on this matter. Pursuant to one group of scholars, the agreement of the parties should prevail over the law of the seat[190]. They support this argument with the explicit wording of Article V (1)(d) which gives priority to arbitration agreements over

---

[186] Albert Jan van den Berg, 'Consolidated Arbitrations, the New York Arbitration Convention and the Dutch Arbitration Act 1986 – A Replique to M Jarvin', in *3 Arbitration International*, no. 3 (1987), pp. 257–258.

[187] On this point, see also Jeffrey Waincymer (2012) *Procedure and Evidence in International Arbitration*, Kluwer Law International, Alphen aan den Rijn, p. 564, who has stated: 'If…the tribunal or an institution selected the Seat, it is more problematic to attempt an original consent logic based on broad discretion in those laws.'

[188] Cited by V. V. Veeder,' Consolidation: More News from the Front-Line – The Second Shui On Case', in 3 *Arbitration International*, no. 3 (1987), p. 264. For a similar position, see W. Michael Reisman, W. Laurence Craig, William W. Park and Jan Paulsson (1997) *International Commercial Arbitration. Cases, Materials and Notes on the Resolution of International Business Disputes*, The Foundation Press, New York, NY, p. 482.

[189] Article 34(2)(a)(iv) of the UNCITRAL Model Law.

[190] Sigvard Jarvin, 'Consolidated Arbitrations, the New York Arbitration Convention and the Dutch Arbitration Act 1986 – a Critique of Dr. van den Berg', in *3 Arbitration International*, no. 3 (1987), pp. 254–255; Gary Born (2009) *International Commercial Arbitration*, Kluwer Law International, Alphen aan den Rijn, pp. 2075–2076;

the law of the seat. Thus, in the case of judicially ordered consolidation of arbitral proceedings without the consent of all parties, the non-consenting party may try to resist the enforcement of the award by claiming that the award was not made in compliance with the parties' arbitration agreement that did not envisage multi-party arbitration. Furthermore, where the relevant arbitration agreements envisage the appointment of a three-member arbitral tribunal in whose constitution the party may participate, the aggrieved party may also claim that the consolidation deprived it of its right to designate an arbitrator. Pursuant to a second group of scholars, court-ordered consolidation in these cases will not endanger the recognition and enforcement of the arbitral award[191]. They are of the opinion that the arbitration law of the seat may restrict the contractual liberty of the parties in certain cases by introducing mandatory rules. If so, these mandatory rules will override the parties' agreement on the matter. Accordingly, consolidation ordered on the basis of a statutory clause is compatible with the New York Convention even if the parties' arbitration agreements do not say anything about consolidation.

It is difficult to judge with certainty which of these two positions will prevail. In any case, the mere existence of contentiousness on this matter indicates that the risk of non-recognition and non-enforcement of an award in these cases should not be overlooked. For contracting parties, the finality and enforceability of the outcome of the chosen by them dispute resolution method is of vital importance. For that reason, even the slightest uncertainties concerning the enforcement of the resulting arbitral award are highly undesirable. Therefore, arbitrators or judges should proceed with utmost caution if they decide to order consolidation on the basis of statutory provisions. The Chartered Institute of Arbitrators, for example, has advised arbitrators not to order consolidation solely on the basis of legislative provisions[192]. In the author's opinion, this risk will probably not be so significant if the parties have chosen the applicable law with the knowledge that it provides for multi-party arbitration. However, at the stage of arbitration there will most likely be at least one party arguing that this was not the case. The risk will substantially

---

Martin Platte (2008) 'Multi-Party Arbitration: Legal Issues Arising Out of Joinder and Consolidation', in E. Gaillard and D. di Pietro (eds) *Enforcement of Arbitration Agreements and International Arbitral Awards: The New York Convention in Practice*, Cameron May, London, pp. 491–492.

[191] Albert Jan van den Berg, 'Consolidated Arbitrations and the 1958 New York Arbitration Convention', in *2 Arbitration International*, no. 4 (1986), pp. 367–369, Albert Jan van den Berg, 'Consolidated Arbitrations, the New York Arbitration Convention and the Dutch Arbitration Act 1986 – A Replique to M Jarvin', in *3 Arbitration International*, no. 3 (1987), pp. 257–261. See also Jean-Francois Poudret and Sébastien Besson (2007) *Comparative Law of International Arbitration*, 2nd edn, Sweet & Maxwell, London, pp. 209–210; Irene Ten Cate, 'Multi-party and Multi-contract Arbitrations: Procedural Mechanisms and Interpretation of Arbitration Agreements under U.S. Law', in *15 The American Review of International Arbitration*, no. 1 (2004), p. 145, and Andreas Austmann, 'Commercial Multi-Party Arbitration: A Case-By-Case Approach', in *1 The American Review of International Arbitration*, no. 3 (1990), p. 355.

[192] See CIArb Practice Guideline 15: Guidelines for Arbitrators on how to approach issues relating to Multi-Party Arbitration. Pursuant to Section 5.1 of the guideline: 'It is vital that [arbitrators] do not make orders for consolidation or concurrent hearings unless the arbitration agreement (including any rules incorporated in it) permits this. Arbitrators should be very wary of making any order in this area that the parties have not explicitly addressed. If an issue of this kind arises, arbitrators should first explore the possibility of agreement before going further.' Furthermore, the guideline warns that any consolidation that is not authorized in the parties' agreements or applicable arbitration rules could imperil the enforceability of the award (Section 5.4 of the guideline).

increase in cases where multi-party arbitration statutory provisions are applied retroactively to arbitration agreements concluded before the entry into force of the respective legislation.

Due to the above arguments, national arbitration laws should refrain from regulating multi-party arbitration. Otherwise, the notion of the consensual character of arbitration will be seriously undermined as the parties might be *forced* to agree on consolidation they have never foreseen. The contractual basis of arbitration should remain untouched and should not be blurred with the incorporation of legislative provisions into the parties' agreements.

Finally, a few remarks have to be made with regard to those statutory multi-party arbitration provisions that have an opt-in character. These provisions can come into play only if the parties have expressed consent to their application. That is why some authors have referred to these solutions as 'false' legislative solutions[193]. Opt-in statutory provisions are in consonance with the consensual nature of arbitration. However, in the author's opinion these provisions are not particularly useful[194]. Multi-party arbitration requires all parties' consent. Contracting parties do not need legislation that tells them that they may agree on multi-party arbitration. They may well reach an agreement on the conduct of such type of arbitration regardless of the existence of statutory opt-in clauses[195]. Hence, the only impact of these laws is that they underline the necessity of parties' agreement on the matter[196]. In addition, the parties are principally better able to address multi-party arbitration problems. Unlike statutory clauses, which are of general nature and often have a declaratory effect, the parties may agree on multi-party arbitration clauses that are suited to the specifics of the particular construction projects and their needs.

5.12 Concluding remarks regarding arbitration laws

The statutory approaches to multi-party arbitration reviewed here have been summarized in Table 2 towards the end of this book. This table has been drafted for ease of reference only. It should always be read in conjunction with the full content of the statutory provisions mentioned in the table and the analysis in the present Chapter 5.

---

[193] Andrea Marco Steingruber (2012) *Consent in International Arbitration*, Oxford University Press, Oxford, § 10.42.

[194] See also Pieter Sanders (1999) *Quo Vadis Arbitration? Sixty Years of Arbitration Practice, A Comparative Study*, Kluwer Law International, The Hague, p. 222. When discussing the approach under the English Arbitration Act 1996, the author has stated: 'The reference [in the legislation] to the freedom of the parties to agree on consolidation of arbitral proceedings, although in itself a declaration which can only be welcomed, will not lead to consolidation in spite of how desirable it would be.'

[195] Thomas Bevilacqua, 'Voluntary Intervention and Other Participation of Third Parties in Ongoing International Arbitrations: A Survey of the Current State of Play', in *1 World Arbitration & Mediation Review*, no. 4 (2007), p. 521.

[196] Andrea Marco Steingruber (2012) *Consent in International Arbitration*, Oxford University Press, Oxford, § 10.23.

Unlike domestic arbitrations, where mandatory court-ordered consolidation is often observed, especially in the United States and Hong Kong, national arbitration laws have been much more cautious when it comes to international commercial arbitrations. Only a few states have proposed legislative solutions to multi-party arbitration that are applicable to international commercial transactions. In approaching the problem, most states have acknowledged the consensual nature of arbitration and adopted the view that multi-party arbitration may not be imposed absent parties' agreement. Therefore, the majority of the reviewed states have introduced provisions the application of which depends on the parties' will. Thus, some states, such as England, Scotland, Ireland, Malaysia, Canada, and some US states (e.g. California, Texas, Georgia and Ohio), recognize the power of courts or tribunals to issue consolidation orders only to the extent the parties have authorized them to do so. Other states have achieved the same result by either introducing 'opt-in' multi-party arbitration provisions (such as Hong Kong, Australia and New Zealand) or by making multi-party arbitration contingent on the existence of a single arbitration agreement binding all parties (such as the Netherlands as to joinder and intervention, and Belgium). The Netherlands has diverted from this approach by adopting an 'opt-out' consolidation clause, which applies by default, unless the parties agree otherwise. It is arguable whether this clause is in consonance with the consensual nature of arbitration. In practice, however, the parties' choice of institutional arbitration rules, which is commonplace under international construction agreements, will trigger the clause inapplicable.

The only deviations from the consensually oriented statutory approach to consolidation can be found in some US states, such as Massachusetts and New Jersey, where statutory consolidation clauses may be applied over the objection of some or all of the parties to the pending proceedings. However, these clauses will be pre-empted by the FAA to the extent they contradict parties' arbitration agreements. Mandatory consolidation clauses in the United States can also be found in some domestic arbitration statutes based on the RUAA. However, these clauses may find application to international commercial arbitrations only in exceptional cases. In addition, the prevailing case law in the United States suggests that multi-party arbitration may not be ordered in cases where the arbitration agreements in the parties' contracts are silent on this type of arbitration. An exception in that regard is the case law in jurisdictions falling within the domain of the US Court of Appeals for the First Circuit.

On the basis of the above, it can be concluded that the reviewed arbitration laws do not offer a self-contained mechanism for resolution of multi-party disputes, which can be operated in cases where the parties' agreements are silent as to the conduct of this type of arbitration. The author is of the opinion that states should refrain from introducing such a mechanism for the reasons discussed in Section 5.11. Therefore, arbitration laws are not in a position to respond adequately to the need for multi-party arbitration in the construction industry.

The recent trend is that fewer and fewer states adopt default statutory multi-party arbitration clauses which may be applied regardless of parties' agreement on the matter. Court-ordered consolidation was an emerging trend in the 1980s, and some authors stated at that time that 'it appears to be a fashion whose time has come'[197]. However, consolidation absent parties' agreement is not the rule any more. The current arbitration Act in Hong Kong, which converted the initially default consolidation clause into an 'opt-in' clause, as well as the recent developments in the US case law, which forbids court-ordered consolidation absent parties' agreement, exemplify the reverse trend. Thus, court-ordered consolidation may well have turned into an anachronism whose time has irretrievably gone[198].

[197] See Howard Miller, 'Consolidation in Hong Kong: the Shui On Case', in *3 Arbitration International*, no. 1 (1987), p. 90.

[198] Dimitar Hristoforov Kondev, 'Statutory Approaches to Multi-Party/Multi-Contract Construction Arbitration', in *19 The Vindobona Journal of International Commercial Law and Arbitration*, no. 1 (2015), p. 54.

Chapter 6

Contractual Solutions to Multi-Party Arbitration

As demonstrated in Chapters 4 and 5, the reviewed arbitration laws and institutional and *ad hoc* arbitration rules do not provide for self-contained multi-party arbitration solutions. Arbitration is based on consent, so undoubtedly the best way in which contracting parties can deal with multi-party arbitration is to provide relevant solutions in their arbitration agreements or, if such solutions are not available, to consent to multi-party arbitration once the respective disputes have arisen. However, once it becomes clear that the parties are going to arbitrate their disputes, they are usually no longer inclined to co-operate to the extent they were willing to at the time when they entered into their contracts. As a result, it is very unlikely that a common position on multi-party arbitration will be reached at this stage. Hence, parties' consent to multi-party arbitration expressed in their contracts remains the only feasible alternative for those willing to engage in this type of arbitration.

The presence of multi-party arbitration clauses in the parties' contracts increases the predictability of the dispute resolution process and eliminates the risk of non-recognition or non-enforcement of the award on the grounds listed under the New York Convention. The contractual approach to multi-party arbitration may take two main forms. It may either be in the form of a standardized solution available under standard form agreements or an *ad hoc* multi-party arbitration agreement. The majority of contracting parties still do not include *ad hoc* multi-party arbitration clauses in their contracts. Because of time constraints or other considerations, sometimes parties intentionally refrain from losing too much time on negotiating a multi-party arbitration agreement[1]. Instead, they often focus on the commercial aspects of the deal, such as contract price, time for completion and amount of liquidated damages payable upon default[2]. At such an early stage, contracting parties tend to concentrate upon how and on what terms the project is to be

[1] Parties often adopt available boilerplate arbitration clauses, which are often unworkable in a multi-party arbitration context.

[2] See W. Michael Reisman, W. Laurence Craig, William W. Park and Jan Paulsson (1997) *International Commercial Arbitration. Cases, Materials and Notes on the Resolution of International Business Disputes*, The Foundation Press, New York, NY, p. 483. According to the authors: 'In areas of trade where business has to be conducted quickly because profit margins are relatively slight, the multi-partite clause is often a waste of money to prepare.' See also Mark Huleatt-James and Nicholas Gould (1999) *International Commercial Arbitration. A Handbook*, 2nd edn, LLP Reference Publishing, London, p. 40.

Multi-Party and Multi-Contract Arbitration in the Construction Industry, First Edition.
Dimitar Kondev.

brought to a successful conclusion, rather than upon what will happen if things go wrong[3]. Even if contracting parties are diligent in the negotiation phase and are willing to subject their future disputes to multi-party arbitration, it is often difficult to foresee all issues that may arise during the conduct of such an arbitration. For these reasons, *ad hoc* multi-party arbitration clauses are not commonplace.

The present chapter focuses on the first form of contractual solutions to multi-party arbitration, namely, standard form multi-party arbitration agreements. More particularly, the chapter discusses the approaches to multi-party arbitration under international standard forms, such as the FIDIC Conditions of Contract (Section 6.1), NEC3 (Section 6.5), the IChemE Contracts (Section 6.6), the ICC Contracts (Section 6.7), the PPC and SPC International (Section 6.8), and the ENAA Model Forms (Section 6.9). Some domestic standard forms are also discussed. The emphasis is on domestic forms published in England, such as the CECA Form of Sub-Contract, also known as the Blue Form (Section 6.2), the JCT Contracts (Section 6.3), and the ACA forms (Section 6.4). Even though domestic construction contracts are in principle not within the main scope of this book, the abovementioned contracts have been reviewed for several reasons. First, England is a leading publisher of standard form construction agreements. Some of the most famous international standard forms are either published in England or they derive from domestic English forms. The domestic forms listed above have contained multi-party arbitration clauses for several decades and have been litigated from time to time before local courts and / or have been subject to arbitral proceedings. Therefore, the provisions contained in these contracts, together with the case law pertaining to them, represent a fruitful ground for research in the field of construction multi-party arbitration. In addition to the domestic forms mentioned above, the chapter provides an overview of some multi-party arbitration clauses contained in several other domestic forms. These include the AIA Forms (Section 6.10) and the Consensus Docs (Section 6.11), both published in the United States, and some standard forms used in Denmark (Section 6.12). These suites have been included in the chapter because of their peculiar approach to multi-party arbitration. Together with the other domestic forms, they might serve as an inspiration for the finding of solutions on an international level.

As will be seen in this chapter, some of the most popular international standard forms have not addressed the question of multi-party arbitration. This is especially true with regard to the standard forms of the main contract. Accordingly, a question may arise as to why drafters of the standard forms have not included multi-party arbitration provisions thereunder. There may be several reasons for this. First, standard forms are commonly drafted by construction professionals, such as engineers and architects. As analysed in Section 3.4, engineers and architects are usually not interested in multi-party arbitration. Hence, provisions envisaging the participation of these parties in such type of arbitration are often not considered in the drafting process. Secondly, it is often assumed that employers are not interested in multi-party arbitration as they will hold main contractors liable for any defects in the works and leave the main contractors to pursue their claims further down the contractual chain. As it is commonplace that employers choose the particular

---

[3] John Marrin (2009) 'Multiparty Arbitration in the Construction Industry', in the Permanent Court of Arbitration (ed.) *Multiple Party Actions in International Arbitration*, Oxford University Press, New York, NY, p. 398.

standard form when contracting with main contractors, it is often thought that it is not necessary to include a multi-party arbitration clause in standard forms of main contract.

In any case, the lack of multi-party arbitration agreements in some of the most widely used international standard forms does not mean that there is no need for multi-party arbitration solutions. The case law examined in this chapter reveals that multi-party arbitration clauses, in cases where such clauses are available, have been relied upon by contracting parties. The abundance of case law on this topic in the United States (discussed in Section 5.10) is also indicative of the need for multi-party arbitration solutions. Furthermore, the assumption that employers are not interested in multi-party arbitration is only partly true. The analysis in Section 3.4 revealed that the need for multi-party arbitration might arise in respect of employers and main contractors alike. These parties are the main users of standard form construction agreements, so drafters of these agreements should be prepared to respond to such need by including multi-party arbitration clauses in their forms or, at least, by suggesting draft clauses in the guidance notes to these forms, which contracting parties may decide to adopt.

6.1 FIDIC Conditions of Contract[4]

The FIDIC Conditions of Contract do not contain multi-party arbitration provisions. Moreover, it has recently been stated by the FIDIC's Contracts Committee that multi-party arbitration provisions have not been considered in the new editions of the FIDIC Red Book, the FIDIC Yellow Book and the FIDIC Silver Book, which are expected to be released in 2017[5].

The Old FIDIC Subcontract anticipated that the parties may wish to agree on a multi-party arbitration clause[6]. Furthermore, it provided a list of matters to be considered when drafting a multi-party arbitration clause[7]. However, FIDIC refrained from introducing such a clause in the Old FIDIC Subcontract. This was partly explained by the lack of employers' consent for multi-party arbitration under the Old Red Book. The recently introduced FIDIC Subcontract, which is intended for use with the FIDIC Red Book, does

[4] See Section 3.2.1 for a brief description of the FIDIC Conditions of Contract. The commentary on the alternative clause in the FIDIC Subcontract contained in this Section 6.1 was first published in the article 'Do Recent Overhauls of Arbitration Rules Respond to the Need for Multi-Party Arbitration in the Construction Industry?', in *32 International Construction Law Review*, no. 1 (2015), pp. 63–94, published by Informa Law.

[5] This information was disclosed by the FIDIC Contracts Committee at the 28th Annual FIDIC International Contract Users' Conference held in London on 1–2 December 2015.

[6] See the Guidance for the Preparation of Conditions of Particular Application to the Old FIDIC Subcontract in its part concerning Clause 19.2.

[7] The list comprised the following matters: the parties' consent, the compatibility of the dispute resolution procedures under the two contracts, the link between the disputes, the party deciding on the link, the timing of a request for multi-party arbitration, and the number of parties. This list was similar to the one posed by His Honour Humphrey Lloyd in his article (see Humphrey Lloyd (1991) 'A National Experience', in P. Bellet, P. Bernardini, G. Bernini *et al.* (eds) *Multi-Party Arbitration: Views from International Arbitration Specialists*, Publication No. 480/1, ICC Publishing SA, Paris, pp. 66–74). See also Christopher Seppälä, 'The New FIDIC International Civil Engineering Subcontract', in *12 International Construction Law Review*, part 1 (1995), pp. 18–22, http://fidic.org/sites/default/files/red_subcon_intro.pdf (accessed 26 July 2016).

not contain such a provision either. Instead, the latter contract contains an alternative clause that aims at dealing with related disputes pertaining to more than one contract[8]. Even though this is not a true multi-party arbitration clause, it has been examined below because it is the first attempt undertaken by FIDIC to deal with multi-contract disputes. The alternative clause, if adopted by the parties, will replace the default resolution clause[9]. The alternative clause was proposed by FIDIC 'on a trial basis only'. It introduces a complex and rather lengthy procedure which intends to make the subcontractor bound by any decision of the dispute adjudication board ('**DAB**') and / or an arbitral award, both rendered under the FIDIC Red Book, which concern claims related to FIDIC Subcontract's claims. The alternative clause is reproduced in full in Appendix 1 to this book.

There are two separate procedures under the alternative clause. The first one concerns claims and the second one concerns disputes. The second procedure comes into play once the claim has crystallized into a dispute – a claim that has been rejected and which the claiming party has decided to pursue further (for further explanation of the difference between claims and disputes under the FIDIC Conditions of Contract, see Subsection 6.2.1.1 below). Claims and disputes are divided into two categories: Related and Unrelated Claims and Related and Unrelated Disputes. Related Claims are those claims that arise from circumstances also giving rise to a claim under the FIDIC Red Book or which concern issues subject to existing claims and / or disputes thereunder. Unrelated Claims are all other claims. Related Disputes are disputes based on Related Claims and Unrelated Disputes are all other disputes.

When the subcontractor gives a notice of claim under the FIDIC Subcontract, the contractor must notify the subcontractor of whether the claim constitutes a Related Claim[10]. Any disputes as to the nature of the claim shall be decided by a pre-arbitral referee under the ICC Rules for Pre-arbitral Referee Procedure[11]. The Related Claims are of particular interest for the discussion in this book[12]. When a Related Claim is notified by the subcontractor, the contractor has to submit a notice of claim to the engineer under the Red Book and pursue that claim with the support of the subcontractor. It is stated that the contractor 'shall use all reasonable endeavours' to secure any additional payment and / or extension of time from the employer to the benefit of both the contractor and the subcontractor[13]. The subcontractor has the right to attend the meetings with the engineer

[8] Second Alternative of Clause 20 contained in the Guidance for the Preparation of Particular Conditions of the FIDIC Subcontract. All references under this section 6.1, unless explicitly indicated otherwise, are references to this second alternative clause.

[9] The default Clause 20 under the FIDIC Subcontract envisages a multi-tier system for resolution of disputes similar to the one under the FIDIC Red Book. It includes the following main steps: giving notice of dispute, a referral of the dispute to the Subcontract DAB, a decision by the DAB, giving notice of dissatisfaction against the decision, an attempt to reach an amicable settlement, and finally ICC Arbitration. The main difference from the FIDIC Red Book is that the main contractor is allowed to defer the referral of the subcontract dispute to the subcontract DAB by a period of 112 days, or as otherwise agreed, in order to refer the same dispute to the main contract DAB. However, the subcontractor is neither bound by the main contract DAB decision, nor by the arbitral award rendered under the FIDIC Red Book.

[10] See sub-clause 20.2 [Sub-contractor's Claims]. If the contractor does not notify the subcontractor about the nature of the claim, the latter will be treated as an Unrelated Claim.

[11] The same procedure will apply to any dispute concerning the nature of the dispute based on that claim (i.e. whether it constitutes a Related or Unrelated Dispute).

[12] See sub-clause 20.4 [*Related Claims*].

[13] Sub-clause 20.4(2). Similar provisions apply to Related Disputes (sub-clause 20.8(2) and 20.8(15)).

during which the Related Claim is discussed but the exercise of this right will be thwarted if the engineer and / or the employer object to it[14]. Therefore, the contractor is not allowed to reach an agreement with the engineer on the Related Claim without any prior consultation with the subcontractor if the latter was not able to participate in the discussions with the engineer. If the engineer determines that the contractor is entitled to additional payment and / or extension of time under the FIDIC Red Book, the contractor shall pass on the subcontractor an appropriate share of that benefit. A subcontractor's dissatisfaction with the allocated share will give rise to a dispute between the parties[15].

When a dispute arises under the FIDIC Subcontract, either party may give *a Notice of Dispute* to the other party. In case of Unrelated Disputes, the general dispute resolution procedure under the FIDIC Subcontract applies[16]. If the subcontractor's notice concerns a Related Dispute, the contractor must refer it for a decision to the main contract DAB with the assistance of the subcontractor[17]. The subcontractor must be given reasonable opportunity to participate in the proceedings before the FIDIC Red Book DAB. However, like the case with Related Claims, there is nothing in the Red Book that obliges the employer or the DAB to allow such subcontractor's participation. Similarly, if the subcontractor is prevented from participating in the main contract DAB proceedings, the contractor is not entitled to reach any settlement with the employer without prior consultation with the subcontractor. Any main contract DAB decision is binding on the subcontractor, unless the latter expresses his dissatisfaction[18]. Following the subcontractor's dissatisfaction, the contractor may either concur with the subcontractor's dissatisfaction or disagree with the subcontractor. In the former case, the contractor should serve a notice of dissatisfaction against the main contract DAB decision[19]. In the latter case, the dispute shall be treated as an Unrelated Dispute[20].

---

[14] See sub-clause 20.4, paragraph (6). The FIDIC Red Book does not contain clauses envisaging the subcontractor's participation in the dispute resolution process under this contract.

[15] Any such dispute will be treated as an Unrelated Dispute, which shall be finally resolved in arbitration. See sub-clause 20.4, paragraph 8.

[16] See sub-clause 20.7 [Unrelated Disputes]. Unrelated Disputes should be referred for a decision to the subcontract DAB. If either party serves a notice of dissatisfaction against the decision, the parties should attempt to reach an amicable settlement, and thereafter proceed to arbitration.

[17] See sub-clause 20.8 [Related Disputes]. Pursuant to paragraph (1) of the latter clause, the dispute must be referred to the main contract DAB within 28 days of the Notice of Dispute (if there is a DAB in place) or within 56 days (if no main contract DAB is yet in place). Any failure of the contractor to refer the dispute to the main contract DAB would result in the treatment of the dispute as an Unrelated Dispute.

[18] See sub-clause 20.8, paragraph (7). If the main contract DAB entitles the contractor to any benefit, the contractor should pass on the subcontractor the appropriate share of that benefit (sub-clause 20.8, paragraph (10)). Any dispute as regards what constitutes an appropriate share is considered an Unrelated Dispute (sub-clause 20.8, paragraph (11)).

[19] Sub-clause 20.8, paragraph (8). See Emma Kratochvilova and Michael Mendelblat, 'Testing the Water – A New FIDIC Subcontract', in *28 International Construction Law Review*, part 1 (2011), p. 63. The authors have noted that this sub-clause is silent as to what would happen if the subcontractor delays in issuing the notice of dissatisfaction so that the contractor misses the deadline for issuing a notice of dissatisfaction under the main contract, which would preclude the contractor from starting arbitration. Therefore, the authors recommend that the users of the clause should explicitly specify therein that any delay on behalf of the subcontractor will have the result that the subcontractor will be bound by the main contract DAB decision.

[20] See sub-clause 20.8, paragraph (9). The dispute will also be treated as an Unrelated Dispute if the contractor does not respond to the subcontractor's notice or fails to serve a notice of dissatisfaction against the main contract DAB decision.

If an amicable settlement is not reached[21] the dispute reaches its final stage, and the contractor should refer that dispute to arbitration under the FIDIC Red Book. The arbitral proceedings shall be conducted between the contractor and the employer. The subcontractor should be given the opportunity to participate in the proceedings, unless the employer and / or the arbitral tribunal object to that. However, even if the subcontractor participates in the arbitration, he is not considered as a formal party to the proceedings[22]. The arbitration award is deemed to be binding on the subcontractor to the same extent that it is binding on the contractor and the appropriate share of any benefit to be paid to the contractor should be passed on to the subcontractor[23].

All of the abovementioned procedures concern situations where the subcontractor has a claim under the FIDIC Subcontract for additional payment and / or extension of time. The alternative clause under discussion also deals with cases where the employer may have claims against the contractor related to the subcontractor's work or performance[24]. The procedure that applies to these claims is largely similar to the one discussed above regarding Related Claims and Related Disputes. A DAB decision and an arbitral award under the FIDIC Red Book will be binding on the subcontractor to the same extent as they are binding upon the contractor.

It is not the intention of the author to discuss in detail all the advantages and disadvantages concerning the alternative clause. One of the merits of the clause is that it provides for a comprehensive mechanism that deals not only with related disputes but also with related claims arising under the FIDIC Red Book and the FIDIC Subcontract. The clause tries to synchronize the joint review of any matters of controversy at a very early stage and in this way encourages dispute prevention[25]. Thus, the clause also ensures that the proposed mechanism is compatible with any pre-arbitral stages of dispute resolution, such as, for example, dispute adjudication. However, there are several drawbacks which may hinder the useful application of the clause. While some of these drawbacks are of purely commercial nature, others raise legal issues as well.

At first glance, it seems that it is mainly the contractor who might want to opt for this clause. However, there are some elements in the clause that might deter him from insisting on its adoption. For example, the final decision of whether a certain claim or a dispute constitutes a Related or Unrelated Claim, respectively Related or Unrelated Dispute, rests with the pre-arbitral referee and not the contractor. The result is that the

[21] Since the participation of the subcontractor in these settlement attempts will depend on the good will of the employer, the clause precludes the contractor from reaching a settlement without prior consultation with the subcontractor (sub-clause 20.8, paragraph (12)).

[22] If the subcontractor is not able to participate in the proceedings, the contractor is not allowed to reach any settlement agreement with the employer without prior consultation with the subcontractor.

[23] Any dispute as regards the subcontractor's share shall constitute an Unrelated Dispute.

[24] These situations often arise in case of existence of defects in the subcontractor's works for which the main contractor is responsible towards the employer under the terms of the FIDIC Red Book. In this case, the main contractor will have a recourse claim towards the subcontractor for the sums which the main contractor paid to the employer.

[25] Delaram Mehdizadeh Jafari (2012) Resolution of Multiparty Construction Disputes under the Singapore International Arbitration Legal Framework. Unpublished PhD thesis. National University of Singapore, pp. 86–87.

contractor may have to resolve claims filed against him under a single contract through two different procedures. The Related Claims and Related Disputes will follow the dispute resolution procedure under the main contract, whereas the Unrelated Claims and Unrelated Disputes will have to be resolved under the FIDIC Subcontract. This is not problematic from a legal point of view but might appear to some contractors to be a rather protracted, burdensome and expensive mechanism for resolution of disputes, especially when it comes to claims of insignificant amount.

In addition, there are some uncertainties concerning the impact of the pre-arbitral referee's order on the jurisdiction of the arbitrator reviewing the related disputes (for more details on this point see Subsection 7.3.3.5). What if, for example, the pre-arbitral referee has found that a link between the disputes exists but the arbitrator later on finds no link between the disputes? If the arbitrator revisits the question concerning the link and declines jurisdiction over the related subcontract dispute, this would mean that both the contractor and the subcontractor have lost significant time and efforts by trying to keep to the contractual mechanism under the alternative clause. Furthermore, even if the contractor manages to pursue the Related Claim through the mechanisms under the main contract successfully, any dispute concerning the exact share of the benefit due to the subcontractor will constitute an Unrelated Dispute, which will trigger a separate dispute resolution procedure under the FIDIC Subcontract[26]. As a result, the contractor may face the risk of passing on the subcontractor the whole benefit that he received from the employer, even though a certain part of that benefit was due to the contractor. Lastly, when it comes to subcontractor's defective works resulting in employer's claims against the contractor, the position of the contractor under sub-clause 20.8 is not well protected. The main interest of the contractor will be to pass on the subcontractor the total compensation that he paid to the employer. Pursuant to the alternative clause, any payment by the contractor to the employer constitutes a precondition to the subcontractor's liability to the contractor[27]. However, once the contractor pays the employer, the subcontractor may object to the share which he should pay. This may finally result in arbitration between the contractor and the subcontractor[28]. If the arbitral tribunal decides that the share that the subcontractor should pay is less than the one paid to the employer or that the subcontractor should not pay at all, the contractor will face the outcome of having paid compensation for the subcontractor's defects which he may not fully recover from the subcontractor.

Apart from this, there are some uncertainties regarding the binding effect of a DAB decision or an arbitral award made under the FIDIC Red Book on the subcontractor. The clause does not provide clear guidance on the consequences of a subcontractor's failure to comply with the main contract DAB decision or award. As the subcontractor is not a formal party to these proceedings, their outcome cannot be directly enforced against the subcontractor. Any failure of the subcontractor to comply with the DAB decision or the arbitral award will constitute a contractual breach, which may require the conduct of further arbitral proceedings. In these proceedings, it remains uncertain if the tribunal will consider all the facts and submissions related to the dispute again or will just

[26] See sub-clause 20.4, paragraph (8), sub-clause 20.8, paragraphs (11), (13) and (18).

[27] See sub-clause 20.9, paragraph (10), items (ii) and (iv).

[28] See sub-clause 20.9, paragraph (10), in conjunction with sub-clause 20.8, paragraph (11).

acknowledge the subcontractor's default and reiterate the content of the main contract DAB decision or arbitral award that were not complied with by the subcontractor[29].

From the contractor's perspective, all these drawbacks can be avoided by agreeing on a properly drafted multi-party arbitration clause, which may ensure a faster and more cost efficient dispute resolution process and avoid the risk of non-recovery of sums paid to the employer due to subcontractor's default. It should be acknowledged, however, that the drafters of the alternative clause under the FIDIC Subcontract were not in a position to propose a workable multi-party arbitration solution because there was nothing in the FIDIC Red Book that could allow for such type of arbitration.

The alternative clause might also appear unappealing to some subcontractors for at least four reasons. First, the clause provides that the contractor 'shall use all reasonable endeavours' to secure from the employer any additional payment and / or extension of time to the benefit of both the contractor and the subcontractor. In its essence, such a clause resembles a technique that is known as a 'pass-through claim'. In other words, under this clause the subcontractor has delegated the pursuit of these claims to the main contractor. The application of these clauses often results in unjust outcomes for subcontractors. In practice, subcontractors are often invited by main contractors to drop some of their claims as the price for effective pursuit of their pass-through claims[30]. Furthermore, the mechanism of 'pass-through' claims does not fit in well with cases where the main contractor and the subcontractor have opposing interests[31]. For example, there are defects in the subcontractor's works but the main contractor has also contributed to these defects by giving inaccurate instructions to the subcontractor. In this situation, it is hard to imagine that the main contractor would use all reasonable endeavours to act for the benefit of the subcontractor. He would rather try to put all the blame for the defects on the subcontractor. Secondly, even though the subcontractor should be given the opportunity to participate in the dispute resolution proceedings under the FIDIC Red Book, this opportunity will not be available if the employer or the decision maker under the main contract objects to that. In these cases, the contractor is precluded from reaching settlement on the dispute without prior consultation with the subcontractor. The extent to which the contractor should consult with the subcontractor is unclear. Certainly, subcontractors would prefer the binding effect of any settlement agreement to be conditioned on their written consent[32]. Thirdly, the alternative clause introduces a mechanism for resolution of Related Disputes, which is rather lengthy and usually more expensive than the default resolution procedure. Apart from that, the contractor may further delay the procedure by leaning on some of the alternative clause provisions. Thus, in the case of a Related Dispute, the contractor may bring the dispute before the main

[29] There is no provision under the alternative clause similar to sub-clause 20.7 of the Red Book that allows the aggrieved party to refer the other party's failure itself to arbitration without having to go through dispute adjudication and an attempt for amicable settlement again. Therefore, it is doubtful whether this solution may be applied by analogy to the case at hand.

[30] John Marrin (2009) 'Multiparty Arbitration in the Construction Industry', in the Permanent Court of Arbitration (ed.) *Multiple Party Actions in International Arbitration*, Oxford University Press, New York, NY, p. 406.

[31] Delaram Mehdizadeh Jafari (2012) *Resolution of Multiparty Construction Disputes under the Singapore International Arbitration Legal Framework*. Unpublished PhD thesis. National University of Singapore, p. 87.

[32] See Emma Kratochvilova and Michael Mendelblat, 'Testing the Water – A New FIDIC Subcontract', in *28 International Construction Law Review*, part 1 (2011), p. 61.

contract DAB. If the subcontractor expresses his dissatisfaction to the DAB decision, the contractor may decide not to serve a notice of dissatisfaction under the FIDIC Red Book. This will qualify the dispute as an Unrelated Dispute, which then should be referred to the subcontract DAB for a decision. Thus, two dispute adjudication proceedings will have to be carried out in respect of one of the same dispute. Lastly, the fact that any payment to the subcontractor under a Related Dispute is conditional on the contractor receiving this payment may also be considered as controversial by some subcontractors.

As the above analysis shows, the alternative clause may be found unacceptable by both contractors and subcontractors, which can dissuade them from making this clause part of their contracts.

6.2 *Blue Form*

A popular form of subcontract in England is the subcontract that was previously published by the Federation of Civil Engineering Contractors ('**FCEC**') and now by the Civil Engineering Contractors Association ('**CECA**'). The subcontract forms published by FCEC and CECA are commonly known as the '**Blue Form**'. The Blue Form was drafted for use in conjunction with the civil engineering contracts published by the Institution of Civil Engineers ('**ICE Contract**')[33].

The Blue Form has been considered in this section in more detail for several reasons. First, multi-party arbitration clauses were introduced in the Blue Form several decades ago. These clauses have been kept in the current editions of the Blue Form, albeit with a different wording. Secondly, the Blue Form has often been used in conjunction with the FIDIC Conditions of Contract. For that reason, the Blue Form appears in the present analysis right after the section dealing with the FIDIC Conditions of Contract. Thirdly, there is some case law in the form of court cases and arbitral awards on the multi-party party arbitration provisions contained in the Blue Form. This case law is very instructive about the application of these clauses and also about the pitfalls and areas of controversy that should be avoided when attempting to draft a multi-party arbitration clause.

One of the earlier editions of the Blue Form containing multi-party arbitration provisions was the Blue Form, published in 1984. This form was updated on several occasions, including in 1987, 1991, 1998, 2008 and 2011. The content of these provisions developed over time supposedly as a result of case law that revealed some flaws in the operation of the provisions. This section contains a chronological review and analysis of the multi-party arbitration clauses contained in the Blue Form from 1984 until today. A compiled draft of all these clauses is provided in Appendix 2.

6.2.1 Clause 18(2) of the 1984 Blue Form

Clause 18(1) of the 1984 Blue Form provided in clear and straightforward terms that any disputes under the subcontract should be referred to an arbitrator to be appointed under that subcontract. The type of arbitration envisaged under this clause was a bipolar

[33] These contracts are now replaced by the Infrastructure Conditions of Contract.

arbitration with the participation of the main contractor and the subcontractor. A similar clause can be found in all the later editions of the Blue Form. Clause 18(2) of the 1984 Blue Form is of more interest for the present discussion. The clause provided as follows:

> If any dispute arises in connection with the Main Contract and the Contractor is of the opinion that such dispute touches or concerns the Sub-Contract Works, then provided that an arbitrator has not already been agreed or appointed in pursuance of the preceding sub-clause, the Contractor may by notice in writing to the Sub-Contractor require that any such dispute under this Sub-Contract shall be dealt with jointly with the dispute under the Main Contract in accordance with the provisions of Clause 66 thereof. In connection with such joint dispute the Sub-Contractor shall be bound in like manner as the Contractor by any decision of the Engineer or any award by an arbitrator.[34]

The wording of the clause was not very clear and it gave rise to several questions. What did a 'dispute' mean in the context of the clause and when did such a dispute arise under the main contract? How was the main contractor's opinion to be formed? What did it mean that the related disputes would be dealt with 'jointly'? When should a main contractor, who had given a notice for the joint review of the disputes, invoke the contractual mechanism provided under the main contract (i.e. in clause 66)?

Clause 18(2) was considered in several English cases, which shed some light on its operation. These cases are *Erith Contractors Ltd. v. Costain Civil Engineering Ltd.*[35], *M J Gleeson Group PLC v. Wyatt of Snetterton Ltd.*[36] and *Lafarge Redlands Aggregates Ltd. v. Shephard Hill Civil Engineering Ltd.*[37]. The analysis below addresses the questions posed above with a view to the legal reasoning contained in these three cases.

6.2.1.1 What did a 'dispute' mean?

Before answering this question, it should be noted that in construction projects the words 'dispute' and 'claim' are often not equivalent. It is true that, in most cases, a dispute arises on the basis of a claim. However, the mere existence of a claim filed by either party is rarely sufficient for such a claim to be qualified as a dispute. In the construction sector, a dispute usually occurs when a party files a claim which has been rejected, in whole or in part, and the same party wishes to pursue that claim further[38].

---

[34] Reproduced with permission of CECA.

[35] *Erith Contractors Ltd. v. Costain Civil Engineering Ltd.*, in *The Arbitration and Dispute Resolution Law Journal* (ADRLJ) (1994), pp. 123–128.

[36] *M J Gleeson Group Plc v. Wyatt of Snetterton Ltd.*, in *72 Building Law Reports* (1995), pp. 15–25. See also *M J Gleeson Plc v. Wyatt of Snetterton Ltd.*, An Editorial Case Note, in *12 International Construction Law Review*, part 2 (1995), pp. 341–346.

[37] *Lafarge Redlands Aggregates Ltd (Formerly Redland Aggregates Ltd) v. Shephard Hill Civil Engineering Ltd*, Judgment by the House of Lords, http://www.publications.parliament.uk/pa/ld199900/ldjudgmt/jd000727/lafarg-1.htm (accessed 26 July 2016).

[38] Dimitar Hristoforov Kondev, 'Is Dispute Adjudication under FIDIC Contracts for Major Works Indeed a Precondition to Arbitration?', in *31 International Construction Law Review*, Part 3 (2014), p. 257.

There is no definition of the word 'dispute' under the 1999 FIDIC suite of contracts[39]. However, the dispute resolution clauses under the FIDIC Conditions of Contract exemplify the distinction between claims and disputes. Under these clauses, whenever a party considers itself to be entitled to a certain remedy, it has to give a notice of its claim. When it comes to contractor's claims, the notice should be given to the engineer appointed under the main contract within the contractually prescribed period of time[40]. As regards the employer's claims, the notice should be given to the contractor by either the employer or the engineer[41]. However, it will usually be the contractor who is claiming under the contract. Following the giving of the notice of claim, the engineer is required to make a fair determination of the claim after having consulted the parties and taken due regard of all relevant circumstances[42]. The engineer then notifies his determination to the parties, and either party can express its dissatisfaction with it. The aggrieved party can then refer the dispute to the DAB constituted, or to be constituted, under the contract for a decision[43]. Thus, it is not until the party has expressed its dissatisfaction with the engineer's determination of the claim, when the claim crystallizes into a 'dispute'. The above mechanism outlines the procedure under the 1999 FIDIC suite of contracts. In the pre-1999 FIDIC Conditions of Contract[44], the engineer had a more prominent role in the resolution of disputes. There were no DABs under these earlier contractual forms, and it was the engineer who was to make a decision on the disputes in the pre-arbitral phase[45]. With the introduction of the 1999 contract suite, this role is now overtaken by the DAB but the engineer is still involved in the earlier phase of the dispute resolution procedure when he has to make determinations on claims before they have crystalized into disputes.

In any case, under both the 1999 and the pre-1999 FIDIC Conditions there should be a rejection by the engineer of the contractor's claim and the contractor should pursue this claim further in order to trigger a 'dispute'. This means that the contractor should have referred the rejected claim to the engineer (under the earlier FIDIC Conditions)[46] or to the DAB (under the 1999 Conditions of Contract). Illustrative of this approach was

---

[39] However, this might change in the near future. It was disclosed by the FIDIC's Contracts Committee at the 28th Annual FIDIC International Contract Users' Conference held on 1–2 December 2015 in London that such a definition is discussed for the purposes of the second editions of the FIDIC Red Book, FIDIC Yellow Book and FIDIC Silver Book. A definition of a 'dispute' can be found in the FIDIC Gold Book.

[40] Sub-clause 20.1 of the FIDIC Red Book.

[41] Sub-clause 2.5 of the FIDIC Red Book. Unlike sub-clause 20.1, which serves as a time-bar in respect of claims not submitted within the contractually determined deadline, sub-clause 2.5 only requires that the notice should be given 'as soon as practicable'.

[42] Sub-clause 3.5 in relation to sub-clause 2.5 and sub-clause 20.1 of the FIDIC Red Book.

[43] Sub-clause 20.4 of the FIDIC Red Book.

[44] FIDIC Conditions of Contract, 4th edn 1987.

[45] Clause 67 of the FIDIC Conditions of Contract, 4th edn 1987.

[46] In this case, there were actually two referrals to the engineer. With the first referral, the engineer reviewed the claim acting in his capacity as an agent of the employer. If the engineer rejected the claim, the contractor could once again refer the dispute that arose on the basis of the rejected claim for a decision to the engineer under Clause 67. See Christopher Seppälä, 'International Construction Contract Disputes: Commentary on ICC Awards Dealing with the FIDIC International Conditions of Contract', in 9 *ICC International Court of Arbitration Bulletin*, no. 2 (1998), pp. 34–35.

the position taken in ICC case No. 6535 of 1992[47] in which the arbitral tribunal denied jurisdiction to review claims submitted by the contractor under clause 67 of the dispute resolution clause under the pre-1999 FIDIC Contracts because these claims had not been rejected by the engineer. Hence, they did not constitute disputes:

> before a claim or contention can constitute a dispute to be referred under Clause 67, it must first have been submitted and rejected under the contract. It follows that if the matters submitted to the Engineer are claims which have not previously been rejected, they cannot be regarded as submitted under Clause 67 whatever language is used in the submission.

The main contract referred to in clause 18(2) of the Blue Form is the ICE Contract. The first edition of the FIDIC contracts published in 1957 was based on an earlier version of the ICE Contract. This explains some of the common features between these two forms. Clause 66 of the ICE Contract, which was also referred to in clause 18(2) of the Blue Form, envisaged a dispute resolution procedure, which was largely similar to the one under the pre-1999 FIDIC Conditions of Contract. Any dispute or difference arising under the ICE Contract was to be referred to and resolved by the engineer. The engineer had to take a decision that was final and binding, unless the party dissatisfied with it required the matter to be referred to arbitration within the contractual time limits. The parties were also allowed to proceed to arbitration in cases where the engineer failed to make a decision within the prescribed period.

It is against the backdrop of this discussion that the posed question should be answered. The denotation of a 'dispute' under clause 18(2) was of great importance, since the lack of any dispute under the main contract would render the whole clause 18(2) inoperative. The meaning of the word was considered in *Erith v. Costain* and *Gleeson v. Wyatt of Snetterton*. In the latter case, the subcontractor submitted his final account to the main contractor who passed it to the employer. Afterwards, the engineer under the main contract identified areas of dispute between the employer and the main contractor, which were largely related to the subcontractor's final account and claim for payment. Therefore, the main contractor invoked clause 18(2) and required the subcontract dispute to be dealt with jointly with the main contract dispute. However, at the time of the main contractor's notice under clause 18(2) there was neither a decision of the engineer under clause 66 of the ICE Contract, nor even a request for such a decision. The main contractor demanded such a decision but only after the notice under clause 18(2) had been given. The subcontractor, in his attempts to secure a separate arbitration of his claims under clause 18(1) of the subcontract, asserted that the word 'dispute' in the first sentence of clause 18(2) of the Blue Form should be given a special meaning. More particularly, the subcontractor claimed that there could be no dispute between the main contractor and the employer until at least the engineer's decision had been requested

[47] Final Award in ICC Case 6535 of 1992 (Extract), in *9 ICC International Court of Arbitration Bulletin*, no. 2 (1998), pp. 60–61. See also Christopher Seppälä, 'International Construction Contract Disputes: Commentary on ICC Awards Dealing with the FIDIC International Conditions of Contract', in *9 ICC International Court of Arbitration Bulletin*, no. 2 (1998), p. 35.

under clause 66 and clause 66 had been invoked[48]. The judge disagreed with this submission. He stated that the word 'dispute' should be given its ordinary meaning, which covered any cases where a claim had been put forward and rejected regardless of whether clause 66 had been formally invoked. According to the judge, the existence of a main contract dispute was not necessarily dependent on the engineer's decision on the matter. The judge further stated that there was nothing mentioned in the Blue Form that hinted that the word 'dispute' should be given some special meaning. Therefore, it was held that a dispute was in existence on the date when the engineer identified areas of dispute between the employer and the contractor even though there was no explicit rejection on behalf of the engineer in the form of an engineer's decision under clause 66[49].

In *Erith v. Costain*, a subcontractor claimed for payment under the Blue Form and tried to ensure the appointment of an arbitrator under the terms of clause 18(1). In the correspondence that followed, the main contractor contended that the subcontract dispute was related to the main contract and refused to concur in the appointment of an arbitrator under the subcontract. The main contractor requested the engineer to give his decision under clause 66 of the main contract, and afterwards invoked clause 18(2) and requested the subcontract dispute to be dealt with jointly with the main contract dispute that touched and concerned the subcontractor's works. The legal counsel for the subcontractor asserted that there was no dispute in existence under the main contract by raising arguments similar to the ones asserted by the subcontractor in *Gleeson v. Wyatt of Snetterton*. The judge decided that there was a dispute in existence at the date when the contractor requested the engineer's decision under clause 66 of the ICE Contract. However, the judge emphasized that the moment when the dispute had arisen was more a question of fact, which did not necessarily have to be defined in general terms by reference to the dispute resolution clause under the main contract. Hence, a dispute might be in existence even before the date of serving of the request under clause 66 of the main contract. In the particular case, it was accepted that the date of the dispute was the date of the contractor's request for a decision by the engineer just because there was no other evidence pointing to an earlier date in time.

Therefore, the decision in *Erith v. Costain* followed the same approach as the one in *Gleeson v. Wyatt of Snetterton* – that the word '*dispute*' in clause 18(2) should be given an ordinary meaning rather that a special meaning implying the explicit serving of a main contractor's notice requiring an engineer's decision on the matter. This interpretation was confirmed later on in *Lafarge v. Shephard Hill.*

It should be noted, however, that the position adopted by the English courts concerning the meaning of a 'dispute' was not universally accepted. In ICC case No. 5333[50] and ICC case

---

[48] *M J Gleeson Group Plc v. Wyatt of Snetterton Ltd.*, in *72 Building Law Reports* (1995), pp. 15–25.

[49] This interpretation is in line with other case law, such as the *Channel Tunnel Group Ltd. v. Balfour Beatty Construction Ltd. And others*, in *56 Building Law Reports* (1991), pp. 19–42, and *Enco Civil Engineering Ltd. v. Zeus International Development Ltd.*, in *56 Building Law Reports* (1991), ref. p. 43. In these two cases it was held that a dispute might arise under Clause 66 of the ICE Contract even before an engineer's decision had been given.

[50] Partial award in ICC case No. 5333, in *4 International Construction Law Review* (1987), pp. 320–333.

No. 5898[51], the arbitral tribunals adopted a different interpretation of clause 18(2). These two cases concerned the international application of the Blue Form in conjunction with the FIDIC Conditions of Contract, and they are discussed in more detail in Subsection 6.2.2 below. It will suffice to mention here that the tribunals deviated from the view that the word 'dispute' in the first sentence of clause 18(2) should be given an ordinary meaning. The tribunals construed its meaning in the context of the meaning of the same word ascribed in the main contract. Hence, a dispute that had not been referred to the engineer for a decision could not be considered as a dispute under the meaning of clause 18(2).

6.2.1.2 Contractor's opinion that the main contract dispute 'touches or concerns Sub-Contract Works'

Clause 18(2) of the Blue Form vested the main contractor with the discretion to decide whether the dispute arising under the main contract 'touches or concerns the Sub-Contract Works'. The contractor was one of the main disputants, so it was very likely that his opinion would be a subjective one rather than one based on objective assessment of the facts. But how was the contractor supposed to form this opinion and was such an opinion subject to any control? This question was discussed in *Erith v. Costain* where it was argued by the main contractor that the opinion could be wholly unqualified and even capricious. It was further asserted that it did not have to be reasonable and that, once formed, it was not challengeable. The judge did not accept this argument and stated that 'there must be some ground, however tenuous, to enable the contractor to form such an opinion'[52]. Both counsel in that case agreed that the main contract dispute should be regarded as touching or concerning the subcontract works if it had even the slightest connection with these works. However, in *Lafarge v. Shephard Hill*, it was suggested that the contractor had a very wide discretion when forming his opinion because 'he need not consult any commercial interest but his own'[53].

It should also be mentioned that there was a restriction concerning the timing when the main contractor had to give a notice under clause 18(2). The clause could only be operated if an arbitrator reviewing the subcontract dispute had not been agreed or appointed under the subcontract. After the appointment of such an arbitrator, the subcontract dispute could not be reviewed jointly with the main contract dispute.

6.2.1.3 When should the contractor set clause 66 of the main contract in motion?

This was one of the main questions discussed in *Lafarge v. Shephard Hill*. In this case, a local authority had employed a main contractor to construct a bypass. The main contractor

[51] Interim Award in ICC case No. 5898 of 1989, in *9 ICC International Court of Arbitration Bulletin*, no. 1 (1998), ref. p. 83. See also Christopher Seppälä, 'International Construction Contract Disputes: Commentary on ICC Awards Dealing with the FIDIC International Conditions of Contract', in *9 ICC International Court of Arbitration Bulletin*, no. 2 (1998), pp. 38–41, and Christopher Seppälä, 'International Construction Contract Disputes: Commentary on ICC Awards Dealing with the FIDIC International Conditions of Contract', in *International Construction Law Review*, no. 3 (1999), pp. 347–353.

[52] *Erith Contractors Ltd. v. Costain Civil Engineering Ltd.*, in *The Arbitration and Dispute Resolution Law Journal* (ADRLJ) (1994), p. 126.

[53] Opinion of Lord Hobhouse of Woodborough in *Lafarge Redlands Aggregates Limited (Formerly Redland Aggregates Limited) v. Shephard Hill Civil Engineering Limited.*

engaged a subcontractor to supply and lay the asphalt surfacing. There was delay under both the main contract and the subcontract, which gave rise to claims for extension of time and additional payment. The disputes that arose were mostly related to the causes of the delay. The subcontractor required the appointment of a subcontract arbitrator under clause 18(1) of the Blue Form. The main contractor opposed to the request and by invoking clause 18(2) requested the subcontract disputes to be dealt with jointly with the main contract dispute in accordance with clause 66 of the main contract. Clause 66 required that the dispute should be referred to the engineer for a decision and that either party could then proceed to arbitration if it was dissatisfied with the decision or if the engineer failed to make such a decision. At the time of the clause 18(2) notice, however, the related main contract disputes had not been referred for a decision to the engineer. The main contractor entered into protracted negotiations with the employer, which delayed this referral. The subcontractor then challenged the validity of the notice given under clause 18(2) and sought a declaration that the main contractor was no longer entitled to rely on that notice.

The question arose as regards the period of time within which the contractor had to initiate the procedure under clause 66. It was accepted by the court that by invoking clause 18(2) the main contractor had an implied obligation to set clause 66 in motion in reasonable time and with all deliberate speed. The rationale behind this was that the clause introduced an exception to the general dispute resolution procedure under clause 18(1). This exception deprived the subcontractor of his right to have his dispute decided under the subcontract and dragged his dispute into the main contract dispute resolution mechanism. Since the subcontractor was not a party to the main contract, he did not have any control over the timing of this mechanism. Therefore, the main contractor was not entitled to defer the operation of clause 66 while he negotiated with the employer. It was stated in that case that:

> a contractor who seeks to take advantage of the power under clause 18(2) is not entitled to have regard only to his own interests in selecting a means of resolving its disputes with the employer. It must have regard also to the interests of the sub-contractor, which is being deprived of its power to make use of the procedures set out in clause 18(1)…Clause 18(2) of the sub-contract does not give the contractor the right to deprive the sub-contractor of the benefit of the procedure in clause 18(1) while he attempts to settle the main contract dispute by negotiation with the employer.

The court stated that the process of negotiations was different from the procedure stipulated in clause 66. Furthermore, clause 18(2) provided that the subcontractor was to be bound by any decision of the engineer or an award by an arbitrator, but there was nothing mentioned in the clause about negotiations. Therefore, if the main contractor had reached a settlement agreement with the employer on the main contract dispute, the effect of this agreement would not have been binding on the subcontractor. Furthermore, the result of the negotiations might not have been acceptable to the subcontractor. In this case, the subcontract dispute, which would have otherwise gone to subcontract arbitration under clause 18(1), would have remained unresolved, and the subcontractor would have waited in vain. The court confirmed that this was not the situation that clause 18(2) contemplated. Hence, it found that the main contractor had failed to put clause 66 of the main contract in motion within reasonable time and that any delay attributable to the negotiations process was unjustified. For this reason, the main contractor was no longer entitled to rely on the clause 18(2) notices.

6.2.1.4 What did joint review of disputes mean?

Clause 18(2) enabled the main contractor to request a subcontract dispute to be dealt with 'jointly' with the main contract dispute under the terms of the main contract. It was not quite clear whether the word 'jointly' denoted a form of multi-party arbitration or something else. This was one of the main questions addressed in the *Lafarge v. Shephard Hill*. The opinion of the judges was bifurcated on this issue. Some were of the opinion that the clause did not contemplate multi-party arbitration because there was no equivalent clause in the main contract that obliged the employer to participate in such arbitration[54]. In the absence of such a clause, it was suggested that the Blue Form clause should be read in a way that made it operable even without the consent of the employer. A further argument raised by one of the judges in support of this view was that multi-party arbitration was not possible where only some of the parties – the employer and the main contractor – participated in the constitution of the arbitral tribunal[55]. Therefore, it was suggested that clause 18(2) envisaged a procedure where the contractor should represent the interests of the subcontractor before the engineer and the arbitrator under the main contract. This required that the subcontractor should be kept informed about the progress of the procedures pending before the engineer and the arbitral panel and also that the subcontractor should have an opportunity to provide the necessary information to the contractor in support of the subcontractor's claims, which should then be used by the main contractor in the above proceedings. The wording at the end of clause 18(2) that the subcontractor 'shall be bound in like manner as the contractor by any decision of the engineer or any award by an arbitrator' was interpreted to mean not that the tribunal was empowered to render a binding award against the subcontractor, who was not a party to the proceedings, but that the subcontractor was bound by the results of the award because of the contractual arrangement under the subcontract.

The other judges in the same case, as well as the judges in the court of appeal, were of the opposite opinion[56]. They stated that clause 18(2) contemplated a tripartite arbitration – multi-party arbitration where the subcontractor had the right to appear as a formal party in the arbitration under the main contract. In this way, the subcontractor was to be bound by the award itself. It was admitted, however, that the machinery under clause 18(2) could fail for various reasons and these included, among others things, the employer's lack of consent to participate in an arbitration involving the subcontractor[57]. If such a failure occurred, clause 18(2) could not be operated any longer

[54] Opinions of Lord Hope of Craighead and Lord Clyde in *Lafarge Redlands Aggregates Limited (Formerly Redland Aggregates Limited) v. Shephard Hill Civil Engineering Limited.*

[55] Opinion of Lord Hope of Craighead in *Lafarge Redlands Aggregates Limited (Formerly Redland Aggregates Limited) v. Shephard Hill Civil Engineering Limited.* According to Lord Hope of Craighead: 'I do not think that there can be such a thing as a tripartite arbitration that does not have as its starting point a tripartite method of conferring jurisdiction on the arbitrator. Clause 18(2) does not address this difficulty.'

[56] Opinions of Lord Cooke of Thorndon, Lord Hobhouse of Woodborough and Lord Millett in *Lafarge Redlands Aggregates Limited (Formerly Redland Aggregates Limited) v. Shephard Hill Civil Engineering Limited.*

[57] The court decision mentioned some other examples where the operation of the joint review procedure under clause 18(2) could fail. For example, the engineer may not be willing to determine the dispute arising under the subcontract or the main contractor may negotiate a settlement with the employer, and therefore decide not to refer the engineer's decision to arbitration. A further obstacle to the operation of the clause might arise if the main contract arbitrator is unwilling to deal with the subcontract dispute.

and the contractor would be free to pursue the subcontract arbitration under the terms of clause 18(1). By a majority, this second opinion prevailed.

6.2.2 Use of the Blue Form in conjunction with the FIDIC Conditions of Contract

The Blue Form has been widely used not only in the domestic market in England, for which it was initially intended, but also in the international construction industry[58]. It was often adopted as a subcontract in conjunction with the FIDIC Conditions of Contract and more particularly with the FIDIC Red Book[59]. This was especially the case prior to 1994 when FIDIC decided to publish its own subcontract form. The international application of the Blue Form was the subject matter of two ICC awards: ICC case No. 5333 and ICC case No. 5898. Both cases concerned a main contractor's request that the subcontract dispute should be dealt with jointly with the main contract dispute. The ground for such a request was clause 18(2) of the Blue Form, albeit in a different wording from the one discussed in the previous section[60]. The provision analysed in the two awards was the following:

> If any dispute arises in connection with the Main Contract and the Contractor is of the opinion that such dispute touches or concerns the Sub-Contract Works, then provided that an arbitrator(s) has not already been agreed or appointed in pursuance of the preceding sub-clause, the Contractor may by notice in writing to the Sub-Contractor require that any dispute under this Sub-Contract shall be referred to the arbitrator(s) to which the dispute under the Main Contract is referred and if any such arbitrator(s) (hereinafter called the 'joint arbitrator(s)') be willing so to act such dispute under this Sub-Contract shall be so referred. In such event the joint arbitrator(s) may subject to the consent of the Employer give such directions for the determination of the two said disputes either concurrently or consecutively as he may think just and convenient and provided that the Sub-Contractor is allowed to act as a party to the dispute between the Employer and the Contractor, the joint arbitrator(s) may in determining the dispute under this Sub-Contract take account of all material facts proved before him in the dispute under the Main Contract.

6.2.2.1 ICC Case No. 5333[61]

ICC case No. 5333 concerned two subcontracts, the first entered into by the subcontractor and the main contractor, and the second one between the same subcontractor and a company to which the main contractor had assigned the construction and maintenance of the building to be developed. The two subcontracts contained clause 18(2) as cited immediately above. The main contract with the employer was based on an earlier draft

---

[58] *M J Gleeson Plc v. Wyatt of Snetterton Ltd.*, An Editorial Case Note, in *12 International Construction Law Review*, part 2 (1995), p. 341.

[59] Christopher Seppälä, 'International Construction Contract Disputes: Commentary on ICC Awards Dealing with the FIDIC International Conditions of Contract', in *9 ICC International Court of Arbitration Bulletin*, no. 2 (1998), p. 38. See also Christopher Seppälä, 'The New FIDIC International Civil Engineering Sub-Contract', in *12 International Construction Law Review*, part 1 (1995), p. 9.

[60] The relevant clause in the two subcontracts was closely modelled on the 1973 edition of the Blue Form, which was intended for use with the 1973 ICE Contract, whereas Clause 18(2) discussed in the *Erith v. Costain* and *Wyatt v. Snetterton* cases was based on the 1984 edition of the Blue Form.

[61] Partial Award in ICC case No. 5333, in *4 International Construction Law Review* (1987), pp. 320–333.

of the FIDIC Conditions of Contract. Clause 67 of that contract contained a dispute resolution provision that was largely similar to the one contained in the pre-1999 FIDIC Conditions of Contract (discussed in Subsection 6.2.1.1 above). In short, the clause envisaged that any dispute under the main contract should first be referred to the architect who should give his decision within 90 days. If the architect failed to give a decision or if the employer or the contractor were dissatisfied with the decision, then the employer or the contractor could refer the matter in dispute to arbitration within further 90 days from receiving the notice of the architect's decision or of the architect's failure to issue such a decision, as the case might be.

The subcontractor claimed against the main contractors who included this claim in the main contractors' claims against the employer. The main contractors served a formal notice under clause 67 and required the architect's decision on the submitted claims. Shortly afterwards, the main contractors informed the subcontractor that they considered themselves to be in dispute with the employer and that this dispute touched or concerned the subcontract works. Therefore, the main contractors argued that the subcontract claim should be subject to arbitration under the main contract on the ground of clause 18(2). Several letters were exchanged between the main contractors and the architect concerning the claims submitted for a decision to the architect. The architect wrote to the main contractors on several occasions and stated that the claims submitted for decision were normal claims that had not been previously rejected by the architect. Therefore, the architect asserted that the claims did not amount to disputes and that clause 67 of the main contract, which was only applicable to disputes, could not be invoked. Eventually, the architect considered the main contractor's claims but refused to issue a decision under clause 67.

In the meantime, the subcontractor initiated arbitration on the ground of clause 18(1) of the Blue Form, which provided for a straightforward arbitration of the subcontractor's claims under the terms of the subcontract without any recourse to the dispute resolution mechanisms under the main contract. The main contractors objected to the jurisdiction of the arbitral tribunal by arguing that a valid notice under clause 18(2) had been served to the subcontractor before the constitution of the tribunal, which precluded the subcontractor from pursuing a separate arbitration under the subcontract.

The main contractors raised arguments regarding the meaning of the word 'dispute' that were similar to the ones discussed in *Erith v. Costain* and *Wyatt v. Snetterton*. More particularly, they argued that the word 'dispute' in the first line of clause 18(2) should be read widely and that a dispute could arise at any time under the main contract if it was clear that the submitted claim would not be accepted regardless of whether a reference to the architect as required under clause 67 had been made. The subcontractor argued that there should be a claim that had been rejected and thereafter referred to the architect for a decision. Moreover, the subcontractor asserted that for the purposes of clause 18(2) there should be either an architect's decision on the dispute or a failure to render such a decision and also a notice of dissatisfaction with it.

The arbitral tribunal accepted the arguments advanced by the subcontractor. By pointing at the recitals of the subcontract, which stipulated that the subcontractor was to be treated as having read the main contract, the tribunal decided that the word 'dispute' should be given a meaning that was consistent with the dispute resolution provision in the main contract. In this way, the tribunal deviated from the interpretation adopted in

Erith v. Costain and *Wyatt v. Snetterton* cases. The tribunal stated that there were four preconditions that should be complied with before a tribunal under the main contract could be seized of a dispute. These were as follows:

- a dispute should have arisen under the main contract, which meant a claim which had already been rejected;
- the dispute should have been referred to the architect for a decision under clause 67 of the main contract;
- the dispute should then have been decided by the architect under clause 67 or there had to be a failure on behalf of the architect to decide the dispute within the contractually prescribed period of 90 days;
- a dissatisfaction should have been expressed with the architect's decision or the failure to decide within a further period of 90 days by requiring that the matter in dispute should be referred to arbitration.

The introduction of the fourth precondition was necessitated because of the wording of clause 18(2), which explicitly required that the main contract dispute 'is referred' to the arbitrators under the main contract. There was no such an additional requirement in the clause discussed in *Erith v. Costain* and *Wyatt v. Snetterton*, which only required the existence of a dispute under the main contract but not the constitution of a tribunal thereunder. Thus, in ICC case No. 5333 the word 'dispute' had to be read not only as a rejected claim, which had been submitted to the architect for a decision, but also as a dispute that was referred to arbitration.

As a result, the tribunal confirmed that it had jurisdiction to review the subcontractor's claims. It found that the main contractors did not have the right to invoke clause 18(2) because the four preconditions had not been complied with. The main contractors could have relied on the clause only if they had followed all the stages outlined above, provided that no tribunal had been constituted under the subcontract. Furthermore, the tribunal stated that the words 'is referred' to the arbitrator under the main contract should be construed as 'is presently referred' or 'has been referred' rather than 'is to be referred'. This meant that the tribunal under the main contract should already be in existence or at least in the process of being formed. Otherwise, the tribunal stated, the clause might open the door to an abusive behaviour on behalf of the main contractor who could protract the resolution of disputes under the subcontract by claiming that these disputes were related to the main contract and might be referable to arbitration under the main contract in the future[62]. In such a case, the subcontractor would have had no other option but to wait for the main contractor to trigger the dispute resolution clauses under the main contract.

When it comes to the nature of the subcontract dispute, it should be mentioned that there is a difference between the wording of clause 18(2) in the English cases discussed in Subsection 6.2.1 above and the one in the arbitral award under review. In the former

[62] This, in the words of the tribunal, would mean that 'the normal method of resolving disputes under the contract by means of Clause 18(1) could easily be blocked by a contractor by reference to a supposed dispute or a dispute in respect of which there was no need or intention to seek arbitration'.

case, the clause referred to 'any such dispute under this Sub-Contract', where in the latter case the reference was to 'any dispute under this Sub-Contract'. On the face of it, this was a minor difference in the wording, which, however, could have important consequences. Even though it was not explained in *Wyatt v. Snetterton* and *Erith v. Costain* to what the word 'such' referred to, it could be reasonably assumed that it referred to a subcontract dispute, which concerned the subcontract works which, on their side, were touched or concerned by the main contract dispute. The lack of 'such' in the clause discussed in the arbitral award created the impression that such qualification was not required, and more particularly, that the main contractor could request the joint review of all subcontract disputes under the dispute resolution procedure under the main contract – even those that were not touched or concerned by the main contract dispute. Thus, if there were multiple subcontract disputes comprising disputes that were both related and unrelated to the main contract it could be argued that all of these disputes had to be submitted for review to the tribunal under the main contract.

6.2.2.2 ICC Case No. 5898[63]

ICC Case No. 5898 of 1989 also dealt with an arbitration initiated by the subcontractor against the main contractor under clause 18(1) of the Blue Form. As in ICC case No. 5333, the main contractor objected to the jurisdiction of the subcontract arbitral tribunal by claiming that he had validly invoked clause 18(2)[64]. The interim award in this case presented a detailed analysis of clause 18(2).

The tribunal stated that clause 18(2) was principally made to the benefit of the contractor who had the unilateral right to invoke the clause provided that all the conditions stated therein were met[65]. Clause 18(2) had to be read in conjunction with clause 18(1), which entitled the subcontractor to refer any dispute under the Blue Form to ICC Arbitration initiated under the subcontract. The tribunal stated that the principal dispute resolution mechanism was provided under clause 18(1) and that clause 18(2) was the exception to that mechanism[66]. Therefore, clause 18(2) had to be construed narrowly, subject to the strict fulfilment of all conditions stated therein, because it deprived the subcontractor of his right to initiate an arbitration under the subcontract and to participate in the constitution of the tribunal thereunder. It logically followed from there that the party to whose benefit clause 18(2) was created (i.e. the main

---

[63] Interim Award in ICC case No. 5898 of 1989, in *9 ICC International Court of Arbitration Bulletin*, no. 1 (1998), ref. p. 83.

[64] The main contractor requested consolidation of the subcontract arbitration with the main contract arbitration. However, the ICC Court refused to effect the consolidation by stating that the conditions of Article 18 of the then applicable 1975 ICC Internal Rules were not met. Pursuant to this article, the ICC Court of Arbitration was allowed to include new claims in the existing arbitration provided that these new claims were in connection with a legal relationship already submitted to arbitral proceedings between the same parties. In the case at hand, there was neither a single legal relationship (but instead two distinct contracts), nor were the same parties involved.

[65] Interim Award in ICC case No. 5898 of 1989, in *9 ICC International Court of Arbitration Bulletin*, no. 1 (1998), ref. p. 83, Sections 4–5.

[66] Ibid., section 8.

contractor) had to bear the burden to prove the fulfilment of all the conditions stipulated in the clause when relying on it[67].

Furthermore, the tribunal stated that there were six conditions precedent to the operation of clause 18(2)[68]. These were:

- there had to be a dispute under the main contract;
- the contractor had to be of the opinion that the main contract dispute touched or concerned the subcontract works;
- the main contract dispute had to be one that was referred to arbitration;
- the contractor ought to have given written notice that any subcontract dispute was to be referred to the arbitrator(s) to whom the main contract dispute had been referred;
- the written notice had to be given to the subcontractor before an arbitrator had been agreed or appointed under clause 18(1); and
- the main contract arbitrator was willing to act in the subcontract dispute as well.

As regards the first precondition, the tribunal referred to the award in ICC case No. 5333 and confirmed that the preconditions stipulated in that award with regard to clause 67 of the main contract should have been fulfilled before the contractor was entitled to give notice under clause 18(2) of the Blue Form. As a result, the tribunal found that this first precondition was not fulfilled as there was no 'dispute' at the time when the contractor gave his notice under clause 18(2).

When it came to the second precondition (i.e. the main contractor's opinion that the main contract dispute touched or concerned the subcontract works), the tribunal in ICC case No. 5898 stated that this opinion should be determined in good faith and that the contractor should not act abusively. The main contract dispute should touch or concern the subcontract works, which meant that it should be related to the manner in which the subcontract works were to be performed or were performed. The tribunal also gave some examples of cases where the main contract dispute would not touch or concern the subcontract works. This would be the case, for example, where the employer was in bankruptcy proceedings, and therefore he was unable to pay to the contractor even though he did not deny the debt. In this case, the main contractor would start an arbitration against the employer to recover his claim. However, this was not necessarily a main contract dispute that touched or concerned the subcontract works. Even though the tribunal had some doubts whether the main contract dispute touched or concerned the subcontract works, it refrained from ascertaining whether this second precondition was complied with because it was within the discretion of the contractor to form such an opinion, and there was some evidence that (at least) part of the main contract dispute might touch or concern the subcontract works.

On the third condition, requiring that the main contract dispute 'is referred' to arbitration, the tribunal accepted the reasoning in ICC case No. 5333 that the dispute should have been presently referred to arbitration. Furthermore, the tribunal stated that the

---

[67] Ibid.

[68] Ibid., Sections 10–16.

term '*referral*' was not very precise because its meaning could differ depending on the type of arbitration pursued[69]. The tribunal acknowledged that, for the purposes of ICC arbitration, the date when the request for arbitration is received by the ICC Court is decisive. On that point, the tribunal stated that 'the sub-contractor may not be left in limbo, following the giving of a Clause 18(2) notice, while the contractor debates what remedy it intends to pursue'[70]. This condition might appear problematic in cases where the subcontract dispute referral under clause 18(1) was made prior to the referral of the main contract dispute to arbitration. If the subcontractor had already filed his request for arbitration under clause 18(1) and the main contract dispute had not yet been referred to arbitration, then the ICC Court had no other option but to process the subcontractor's request notwithstanding any attempts of the main contractor to stop it[71]. This was what actually happened in the case at hand. The main contractor had given notice under clause 18(2) before he had submitted his request for arbitration and therefore the tribunal held that the third condition had not been fulfilled.

With respect to the fourth condition (i.e. that the main contractor had to give written notice that the subcontract dispute should be referred to the arbitrators to whom the main contract dispute had been referred), the tribunal held that the main contractor should at least commence arbitration under the main contract and nominate one arbitrator[72].

As required under the fifth condition, a subcontract dispute should be referred to the main contract arbitral panel before an arbitrator had been agreed or appointed in the arbitration under the subcontract. The condition caused some controversy between the parties as to the latest date when such a referral may take place. The main contractor argued that this should be the date when the ICC Court of Arbitration had appointed all members of the subcontract tribunal. The subcontractor maintained that an earlier date should be given preference and, more particularly, that the date of the request for arbitration containing the nomination of the arbitrator by the claimant should be decisive. The tribunal held that the main contractor's notice under clause 18(2) should be given before the date of confirmation by the ICC Court of the subcontract arbitrator.

On the last condition concerning the main contract arbitrators' willingness to act in the subcontract dispute, the main contractor was required to present some evidence to demonstrate such willingness.

Finally, the subcontract tribunal confirmed its jurisdiction to deal with the subcontract dispute because some of the six conditions outlined above were not fulfilled.

---

[69] For example, in *ad hoc* arbitration there is no institution administering the case, and therefore there may be a referral on the date when one of the parties requests from the other to agree on the appointment of an arbitrator. This is not the case in institutional arbitration where normally a serving of a request of arbitration with the arbitral institution is required.

[70] Interim Award in ICC case No. 5898 of 1989, in *9 ICC International Court of Arbitration Bulletin*, no. 1 (1998), ref. p. 83, Section 13.

[71] Ibid., Section 13.

[72] Christopher Seppälä, 'International Construction Contract Disputes: Commentary on ICC Awards Dealing with the FIDIC International Conditions of Contract', in *9 ICC International Court of Arbitration Bulletin*, no. 2 (1998), p. 41.

6.2.3 Commentary on clause 18(2)

Clause 18(2) of the Blue Form was one of the first contractual attempts to provide for joint review of related disputes arising under a main contract and a subcontract. The court cases and arbitral awards discussed above revealed some of the issues resulting from main contractors' attempts to bring this clause into operation. This commentary aims to elaborate on the drawbacks that might preclude or impede the operation of the clause.

6.2.3.1 The requirement for the existence of a 'dispute'

The meaning of the word 'dispute' in clause 18(2) has already been scrutinized in Subsections 6.2.1.1 and 6.2.2.1 above. Regardless of the different interpretations of this word, the clause required the existence of something that was disputed, i.e. a '*lis*', under both the main contract and the subcontract. In practice, however, there may be cases where a joint review might be needed even though there is no true dispute under one of the contracts[73]. For instance, the subcontractor claims extension of time and additional payment against the main contractor because of the late delivery of drawings that were in the custody of the employer. The main contractor is well aware that the fault in this case is attributable to the employer. Therefore, the main contractor does not challenge the subcontractor's claim and files an equivalent claim against the employer, which triggers a main contract dispute. The main contractor will have an obvious interest in requesting multi-party arbitration in order to avoid inconsistent outcomes under the two contracts. But is there really a dispute under the subcontract in this case? The answer is probably 'no'. Therefore, if this scenario had occurred under the Blue Form, the employer would have been precluded from invoking clause 18(2). Particular guidelines as to how to avoid this situation when drafting multi-party arbitration clauses are given in Subsection 7.3.3.

6.2.3.2 Lack of employer's consent

A major obstacle to the successful operation of clause 18(2) was the lack of employer's consent to its application. This clause was contained in a subcontract drafted for use in conjunction with a main contract – the ICE Contract. However, there was nothing in the main contract that envisaged that the arbitral tribunal constituted thereunder could review subcontract disputes with the participation of the subcontractor. The conduct of multi-party arbitration requires the consent of all parties, and clause 18(2) was an expression of the consent of two of the parties only, namely the main contractor and the subcontractor. Clause 18(2) did not create any privity of contract between the subcontractor and the employer and therefore the employer

---

[73] Humphrey Lloyd (1991) 'A National Experience', in P. Bellet, P. Bernardini, G. Bernini *et al.* (eds) *Multi-Party Arbitration: Views from International Arbitration Specialists*, Publication No. 480 / 1, ICC Publishing SA, Paris, pp. 66–67.

could well object to the participation of the subcontractor in the main contract arbitration. As discussed in Subsection 3.4.1 hereof, the employer is usually not willing to arbitrate his disputes under the main contract with the participation of subcontractors. Therefore, a main contractor using the Blue Form had to obtain the consent of the employer in order to ensure the successful operation of clause 18(2). This consent could be given contractually at the time when the main contract was signed. However, the lack of standard form provisions on multi-party arbitration in the main contract required bespoke drafting, which was hard to achieve having in mind that it was usually the employer who determined the content of the main contract. Alternatively, the main contractor could ask for the *ad hoc* consent of the employer. If the employer did not provide his consent, the contractor had no other option but to arbitrate the related disputes under the main contract and the subcontract in two different arbitrations, where the risk of inconsistent findings would be present. Thus, the main contractor had to invest additional costs and time in participating in two separate arbitrations concerning wholly or partially the same issues of fact and / or law.

6.2.3.3 Nature of the procedure under clause 18(2)

It has already been stated in connection with *Lafarge v. Shephard Hill* that the nature of the procedure under clause 18(2) was subject to different interpretations. Some of the judges in that case reckoned that the clause envisaged multi-party arbitration, whereas the other judges were of the opinion that the contemplated arbitration was only between the employer and the main contractor, where the latter had to represent the interests of the subcontractor as well. However, this second interpretation did not take into account situations where the contractor and subcontractor had conflicting interests. Such a conflict may often be observed in case of employer's claims concerning defects in the subcontract works. The main contractor will usually blame the subcontractor for the defects. The main contractor will most likely adopt the same stance even if he himself has contributed to the subcontract defects. In this case, the main contractor and the subcontractor have opposing interests and it is hard to imagine that the main contractor would objectively represent the interests of the subcontractor in the main contract arbitration.

Furthermore, the interpretation that clause 18(2) contemplated a bipolar arbitration was at variance with the overall purpose of clause 18(2), which was to avoid the risk of inconsistent findings in separate arbitral awards on related claims. If the second interpretation were correct, this would have meant that the award rendered by the main contract tribunal would not have been directly enforceable against the subcontractor. The subcontractor would have been bound by the result of the award by reason of his contractual obligation under the subcontract. Thus, any failure of the subcontractor to comply with the award would have been considered as a contractual breach, which in itself was also capable of triggering a separate subcontract dispute referable to arbitration. This second arbitration also brought the risk of inconsistent findings because there was no guarantee that the arbitral tribunal would confirm the breach.

6.2.3.4 Unequal treatment of the parties in the constitution of the arbitral tribunal

If all the preconditions for the application of clause 18(2) were present and the main contractor had exercised his option under this clause, a subcontract dispute concerning the subcontract works, which were touched or concerned by the main contract dispute, was to be submitted to the arbitrator or arbitral tribunal constituted under the main contract. This tribunal was constituted in accordance with the arbitration clause in the main contract to which the subcontractor was not a party. The parties influencing the constitution of the tribunal were actually the employer and the main contractor and the subcontractor did not participate in this process. The subcontractor had voluntarily waived his right to participate in the constitution of the tribunal in respect of subcontract disputes falling within the scope of clause 18(2) by way of signing the subcontract containing clause 18(2). Notwithstanding this waiver, there could be an argument that the machinery under clause 18(2) did not offer equal treatment of the parties and that an award rendered in such circumstances might be set aside or its recognition and enforcement refused on grounds listed under the domestic arbitration law and / or the New York Convention.

Nowadays, similar arguments can be raised with regard to other clauses envisaging a referral of a subcontract dispute to a main contract arbitrator. The problem becomes particularly visible in cases where the main contract arbitration agreement envisages a three-member arbitral tribunal where each of the main contractor and the employer are entitled to designate one arbitrator and the third arbitrator is to be appointed by mutual agreement of the two other arbitrators or by the arbitral institution administering the case. The subcontractor is not entitled to make his own nomination. The situation might become even more problematic in cases where the arbitral tribunal under the main contract has already been constituted at the time when the related subcontract dispute arises. In this case, the subcontractor does not even have a right to challenge the appointment of the arbitrators on the ground of their alleged lack of impartiality or independence at the time when the appointment is made (on that point see Subsection 6.2.3.5). It has also been suggested that other factors than independence of the arbitrator may also play to the subcontractor's disadvantage[74].

It is true that the unequal treatment of the parties in the process of constitution of the arbitral tribunal might raise obstacles in the stage of enforcement of the award in the country where it was rendered or in third countries. This concern is particularly valid in France following the decision in the well known *Dutco* case[75]. The *Dutco* case did not concern multi-contract disputes but its outcome may be relevant for the present

---

[74] See the commentary of Sigvard Jarvin on Partial Award in ICC Case No. 5333, published in *4 International Construction Law Review* (1987), p. 331. The author gave the following example: an employer and a main contractor, both companies incorporated in England, enter into a contract subject to English law. The subcontractor is neither incorporated in England nor English speaking. In this case, the subcontractor and his foreign lawyer may feel at a disadvantage to explain their case before a tribunal consisting of three Englishmen.

[75] *Siemens AG and BKMI Industrienlagen Gmbh v. Dutco Construction Company, Cour de Cassation*, 7 January 1992 (*XVIII Yearbook Commercial Arbitration*, 1993, pp. 140–142). See also Christopher Seppälä, 'Multi-party arbitrations at risk in France', in *12 International Financial Law Review* (1993), pp. 33–35, and Eric Schwartz, 'Multi-Party Arbitration and the ICC: in the Wake of Dutco', in *10 Journal of International Arbitration*, no. 3 (1993), p. 10.

discussion[76]. The arbitral award in the *Dutco* case was set aside in France exactly on the ground of parties' unequal treatment in the constitution of the arbitral tribunal. The parties in that case had divergent interests in the arbitration. Pursuant to the court decision, 'the principle of the equality of the parties in the appointment of the arbitrators is a matter of public policy; one cannot therefore waive it until after the dispute has arisen'. It has been suggested that the French court went too far when it made this statement because, literally read, it would bar any contractual solution to the appointment of arbitrators that did not prescribe the same rights to the parties in the process of constitution of the arbitral tribunal[77]. According to some scholars, the effect of the *Dutco* case on arbitration agreements that do not attribute parties' equal treatment in the constitution of the arbitral tribunal may be summarized as follows:

> In other words, the Cour de cassation ruled that any procedure for designating an arbitral tribunal set out in a pre-dispute arbitration agreement that does not ensure the strict equality of all parties in constituting that tribunal may not be implemented against a party unless, after the dispute has arisen, all parties confirm their earlier-agreed designation method[78].

The *Dutco* decision had a great echo in the international arbitration community and resulted in the adoption of amendments in the ICC Rules and also other institutional rules ensuring that the arbitral institution will appoint all members of the tribunal if the parties disagree on the method for its constitution[79].

In the author's opinion, it is rather questionable whether the conclusion of the *Cour de Cassation* may be applied to the situation envisaged under the Blue Form or to similar multi-party arbitration clauses. It is true that the employer, the main contractor and the subcontractor often have divergent interests in the main contract arbitration and this divergence of interests was also observed in the *Dutco* case. However, the *Dutco* case concerned a situation in which the parties failed to address the conduct of multi-party arbitration in their agreement. A boiler-plate arbitration clause was inserted in a consortium agreement, which envisaged that each party would have the right to nominate an

---

[76] In this case, a consortium was formed between three companies BKMI, Siemens and Dutco for the construction of a cement factory. The arbitration agreement referred to the ICC Rules and envisaged the appointment of three arbitrators. Dutco brought proceedings against the other two members of the consortium and appointed one arbitrator. The respondents were requested to appoint jointly one arbitrator despite their objection. They claimed that such a request contradicted the principle of equality, which required that each of the two defendants had the right to appoint its own arbitrator. Finally, BKMI and Siemens jointly appointed one arbitrator and later on initiated proceedings to set aside the award. Ultimately, their claim was respected by the *Cour de cassation*. In its decision, the latter pointed out that the principle of equality should be assessed with regard to each of the disputants irrespective of the number of claimants or respondents.

[77] Christopher Seppälä, 'Multi-party arbitrations at risk in France', in *12 International Financial Law Review* (1993), p. 34. See also W. Michael Reisman, W. Laurence Craig, William W. Park and Jan Paulsson (1997) *International Commercial Arbitration. Cases, Materials and Notes on the Resolution of International Business Disputes*, The Foundation Press, New York, NY, pp. 475–476.

[78] Ricardo Ugarte and Thomas Bevilacqua, 'Ensuring Party Equality in the Process of Designating Arbitrators in Multi-Party Arbitration: An Update on the Governing Provisions', in *27 Journal of International Arbitration*, no. 1 (2010), p. 11.

[79] See, for example, Article 12(8) of the 2012 ICC Rules and Article 10(2) of the 1998 ICC Rules.

arbitrator (without taking into account that the parties were actually three) where the third arbitrator was to be appointed by the ICC Court. On the other hand, the Blue Form explicitly aimed at regulating the joint review of related multi-contract disputes. The subcontractor did not participate in the constitution of the tribunal but this was what the subcontractor had agreed when signing the subcontract. This paved the argument that the parties – the main contractor and the subcontractor – had provided for a specific mechanism for the constitution of the arbitral tribunal, which in principle should be respected regardless of whether the subcontractor had actually participated in the constitution or not[80]. Thus, the constraint on party autonomy suggested by the *Dutco* case can hardly be justified when it comes to specific contractual arrangements concerning the composition of a tribunal in multi-party arbitration. Furthermore, as argued by some scholars, there seems to be no valid reason to distinguish between a pre-dispute waiver and a post-dispute waiver[81]. An additional argument that such a contractual arrangement should be upheld can also be found in the New York Convention, which stipulates in Article II(1) that each contracting state should recognize an agreement in writing under which the parties undertake to submit certain disputes to arbitration[82]. Respectively, it is an obligation of the contracting states to recognize multi-party arbitration agreements that contain a specifically agreed mechanism for the constitution of the tribunal in a multi-party setting.

In order to fully assess the risk of setting aside, non-recognition and / or non-enforcement of an award resulting from the application of clause 18(2), one should also look at the grounds stipulated in the applicable arbitration laws and the New York Convention upon the occurrence of which such a risk may be materialized. Pursuant to one of the grounds, recognition and enforcement may be denied if the composition of the arbitral tribunal was not in accordance with the parties' agreement[83]. However, the subcontractor may not invoke this ground because the tribunal has been constituted exactly in the way agreed by the subcontractor. A second ground which might be invoked by a subcontractor in his attempts to block the enforcement of the award is that he was not given a proper notice

---

[80] See also Bernard Hanotiau (2005) Complex Arbitrations: Multiparty, Multicontract, *Multi-issue and Class Actions, Kluwer Law International*, The Hague, p. 206 (§ 456), where the author has suggested that the *Dutco* case may lead to difficulties in France if the parties have not included an appropriate multi-party arbitration provision dealing with the appointment of arbitrators in a multi-party setting. For a similar opinion, see also Richard Bamforth and Katerina Maidment, '"All join in or not"? How well does international arbitration cater for disputes involving multiple parties or related claims?', in *27 ASA Bulletin*, no. 1 (2009), p. 19.

[81] Jeffrey Waincymer (2012) *Procedure and Evidence in International Arbitration*, Kluwer Law International, Alphen aan den Rijn, p. 511. According to the author: 'Either the mandatory due process argument prevails or not. There is no reason to argue that it operates differentially in the two scenarios.'

[82] See Gary Born (2014) *International Commercial Arbitration, Volume II: International Arbitral Procedures*, 2nd edn, Kluwer Law International, Alphen aan den Rijn, pp. 2101–2102, where the author has stated: 'There is a serious argument that the Dutco rationale, and particularly its invalidation of advance waivers of rights to participate in constitution of the arbitral tribunal, cannot be reconciled with the effect given to the parties' agreed arbitral procedures under Articles II and V(1)(d) of the New York Convention. At a minimum, where sophisticated commercial parties have expressly agreed to arbitral procedures that may deny them the opportunity to participate in selecting an arbitral tribunal, then an automatic invalidation of all such advance waivers arguably invites non-recognition of an award under article V(1)(d).'

[83] Article 36(1)(a)(iv) of the UNCITRAL Model Law and Article V(1)(d) of the New York Convention.

of the appointment of an arbitrator[84]. It is highly questionable whether such a plea will be successful. The subcontractor has agreed on the appointment procedure under the main contract and has thus tacitly accepted that no such notice should be served to him. The third possible ground concerns cases where the recognition or enforcement of the award would be contrary to the public policy in the country where such recognition and enforcement is sought[85]. Pursuant to the *Dutco* decision, it is exactly this ground which might come into play if the procedure for the composition of the tribunal does not ensure the parties' equal treatment. In the author's opinion, however, it is difficult to see how a contractual arrangement which explicitly regulates the constitution of the tribunal in a multi-party setting can be considered as contrary to public policy[86]. Moreover, the arbitrators should be independent from the parties, which means that the constitution of the tribunal in the way contemplated under the Blue Form should not result in any bias against the party that did not participate in its constitution.

In addition, the *Dutco* decision concerned an arbitration with a seat in France and 'it is by no means certain that other national jurisdictions would decide in the same way if the problem came before them'[87]. For example, it has been stated that in Switzerland an arbitration agreement that provides for unequal treatment of the parties in the appointment of arbitrators will be recognized and respected[88]. Moreover, clause 18(2) of the Blue Form and similar clauses are unlikely to give rise to any concerns in situations where a sole arbitrator has to be appointed under the main contract and the appointment is made by the ICC Court. In this case, none of the parties has influenced the appointment of the arbitrator and therefore there can be no argument of unequal treatment of the parties.

Because of the above, the author is of the opinion that it is rather unlikely that the application of clause 18(2) or similar clauses may result in the setting aside, non-recognition or non-enforcement of an arbitral award rendered under the main contract. The outcome of the *Dutco* case should not be considered as a universal stumbling block for the enforcement of such an award. However, contracting parties choosing arbitration with a seat in France should approach this matter cautiously, and they might want to agree on a procedure for the constitution of the arbitral tribunal which avoids any similarities with the *Dutco* case. For particular drafting suggestions, the reader is referred to Subsection 7.3.3.6.

---

[84] Article 36(1)(a)(ii) of the UNCITRAL Model Law and Article V(1)(b) of the New York Convention.

[85] Article 36(1)(b)(ii) of the UNCITRAL Model Law and Article V(2)(b) of the New York Convention.

[86] See also Kristina Maria Siig, 'Multi-party Arbitration in International Trade: Problems and Solutions', in *1 International Journal of Liability and Scientific Enquiry*, no. 1/2 (2007), p. 79. According to the author: 'As construing a multi-party arbitration clause due to a specific contractual structure or company set-up would hardly amount to public policy or lack of arbitrability, recognition and enforcement cannot be refused under Article V(2) of the New York Convention.'

[87] Bernard Hanotiau (2005) *Complex Arbitrations: Multiparty, Multicontract, Multi-issue and Class Actions*, Kluwer Law International, The Hague, pp. 200–201 (§ 444). See also Olivier Caprasse, 'The Setting up of the Arbitral Tribunal in Multi-Party Arbitration', in *International Business Law Journal*, no. 2 (2006), pp. 206–207.

[88] See Pierre Karrer and Peter Straub (2009) 'Switzerland', in Frank Bernd Weigand (ed.) *Practitioner's Handbook on International Commercial Arbitration*, 2nd edn, Oxford University Press, Oxford, pp. 822–823 (§ 12.25).

6.2.3.5 Challenge of the arbitrators by the subcontractors

As explained in Subsection 6.2.3.4, under the Blue Form the subcontract dispute was to be referred to an arbitrator or a tribunal appointed under the main contract in whose constitution the subcontractor did not participate. One of the consequences of this mechanism was that the subcontractor was precluded from challenging the appointment of an arbitrator on the ground of alleged lack of impartiality or independence at the time of the appointment. At that time, challenges could be made by either the employer or the main contractor. Strangely enough, the ICE Arbitration Procedure, the default arbitration procedure under the Blue Form, did not deal (and still does not deal) with challenges of arbitrators on the grounds of lack of impartiality or independence. Nowadays, these questions are addressed in most modern sets of international arbitration rules and also in arbitration laws. As a starting point, most arbitration rules envisage that challenges against arbitrators are admissive only if raised within a certain period of time. Thus, for example, under Article 14(2) of the ICC Rules any challenge should be made within 30 days from the date of receipt of the notification for the appointment or confirmation of the arbitrator. Similar provisions can also be found in other sets of arbitration rules[89]. However, these rules also contain a fallback option for challenges at a later stage of the proceedings on the basis of facts and circumstances that have occurred after the appointment of the arbitrator[90]. The bringing of a third party in the proceedings can be ascribed to one of these facts and circumstances. Thus, a subcontractor may use these fallback provisions to challenge an appointed arbitrator. Moreover, challenges at this later stage can also be raised by the other two parties whose perception about the impartiality or independence of the appointed arbitrator may have changed as a result of the introduction of the third party in the arbitration. For example, an arbitrator may have advised the subcontractor on a point related to the subject matter of the subcontract disputes, which may result in allegations that he might be biased towards the subcontractor.

If the parties in their arbitration agreement have referred to arbitration rules that deal with these challenges, the procedures prescribed in the rules should be followed. If the applicable rules are silent on the matter, then the applicable arbitration laws may come into play. In England, for example, any party to the proceedings is allowed to request the court to remove an arbitrator with regard to whom circumstances exist that give rise to justifiable doubts as to his impartiality[91]. Arbitration laws of countries based on the UNCITRAL Model Law also contain provisions regulating the challenge procedure against arbitrators that apply if the parties have not agreed otherwise[92]. Therefore, regardless of whether the applicable arbitration rules regulate these matters, all parties should be given an opportunity to raise challenges against an arbitrator in case a third

---

[89] Article 16(2) of the CEPANI Rules requires that any challenges should be made within one month as of the date of the receipt of the notice for the arbitrator's appointment. Under Article 10(3) of the LCIA Rules, this period is set to 14 days.

[90] Article 14(2) of the ICC Rules, Article 16(2) of the CEPANI Rules, Article 10(3) of the LCIA Rules.

[91] Section 24(1) of the English Arbitration Act 1996.

[92] Pursuant to Article 13 of the UNCITRAL Model Law, any challenge should be raised within 15 days after the party has become aware of the constitution of the tribunal or of the circumstances giving rise to doubts as regards the arbitrator's impartiality.

party has been brought into the proceedings. Depriving a party of this right can have serious consequences. It may result in the setting aside of the arbitral award[93] or its non-recognition and / or non-enforcement[94].

If a challenge against an arbitrator is upheld, this will result in his replacement. The replacement procedure can be prescribed either in the applicable arbitration rules or arbitration law. Under most rules, upon replacement the arbitral institutions have the discretion to decide whether or not to follow the original process for nomination. Under most arbitration laws, however, the original nomination process should be followed[95].

The replacement of an arbitrator against whom a challenge has been raised changes in a material way the procedure contemplated under the Blue Form and under contracts containing similar multi-party arbitration clauses. Furthermore, the replacement is likely to cause a significant delay in the procedure, especially in cases where it is the court that has to decide on the removal of an arbitrator or if the challenge has been raised at a late stage of the proceedings. A main contractor using the Blue Form in one of its editions (or another contract containing similar multi-party arbitration provisions) has an interest that the replacement procedure is completed as swiftly as possible in order to ensure that the benefits of multi-party arbitration are not outweighed by the disadvantages pertaining to the delay that a replacement might cause. Generally, a replacement of an arbitrator under institutional arbitration rules that regulate such a replacement is likely to be done more quickly than under rules that are silent on this matter. In the latter case, parties will often have to have recourse to local courts, which might significantly disrupt the expedition of the proceeding[96].

6.2.3.6 Application of the clause to subcontract disputes arising prior to main contract disputes

Another drawback pertaining to clause 18(2) was that it did not fit in well when it came to subcontract disputes arising prior to the related main contract disputes. The clause started with the opening words 'if a dispute arises in connection with the main contract'. Later on, the clause stipulated the main contractor's right to request 'any such dispute under this sub-contract' to be dealt with jointly with the main contract dispute. Thus, it was clear that there should be two separate disputes – one under the main contract and one under the subcontract. But did it matter which of the two disputes arose first in time? On the face of it, the opening words of the clause could create the impression that there should be a main contract dispute, which was first in time and which resulted in a related dispute under the subcontract – disputes down the contractual chain. For example, this could be a main contract dispute based on an employer's claim against the

[93] Article 34 (1)(a)(iv) of the UNCITRAL Model Law could be used as grounds for requesting the setting aside of the award.

[94] Recognition and enforcement of an award in this case may be refused on the grounds of Article V(1)(d). The public policy exception under Article V(2)(b) can arguably also be invoked.

[95] Article 15 of the UNCITRAL Model Law. See also Section 27(3) of the English Arbitration Act 1996 in relation to Article 16 thereto.

[96] See, for example, Section 24(1) of the English Arbitration Act 1996.

main contractor for defects attributable to the subcontractor, which then resulted in a main contractor's claim (and respectively dispute) against the subcontractor. But what about subcontract disputes that thereafter led to disputes under the main contract? For example, the subcontractor claimed extension of time and/or additional costs against the main contractor because of late delivery of drawings for which the employer was responsible. In this second example, the subcontract dispute based on the subcontractor's claim would probably result in a second claim under the main contract whereunder the main contractor would claim the same remedy against the employer. Were these types of subcontract disputes also encompassed by clause 18(2) of the Blue Form? The *Erith v. Costain* case suggested that these disputes were also covered. The case dealt with a subcontract dispute that arose before the related main contract dispute. It was not until the subcontractor demanded that the main contractor concur in the appointment of an arbitrator under the subcontract that the main contractor requested the engineer's decision under the main contract. Therefore, the case suggested that there was no predetermined sequence of the two disputes and that the clause could be applied to both disputes up and down the contractual chain. In the author's opinion, however, the opening words of the clause created ambiguity, which called into question the application of the clause to disputes arising up the contractual chain – subcontract disputes resulting in main contact disputes. Therefore, further clarity was necessary in order to ensure that these disputes were also covered by the clause. It will be seen later on that this ambiguity has been resolved in later editions of the Blue Form[97].

6.2.3.7 Subcontractor's race to refer to arbitration

Clauses, such as the one in the Blue Form, are mainly to the benefit of the main contractor and to the disadvantage of the subcontractor. The operation of these clauses may result in a subcontractor's race to refer a certain dispute to arbitration.

Under the Blue Form, there had to be two disputes in order for clause 18(2) to be operated – one under the subcontract and the other one under the main contract. However, if the subcontract dispute arose first in time and the subcontractor referred it to arbitration under clause 18(1), i.e. subcontract arbitration without the participation of the employer, it would be very difficult for the main contractor to ensure the operation of clause 18(2). As noted above, the clause could not come into play if an arbitrator had been agreed or appointed under the subcontract. Certain stages had to be passed under the main contract in order for a dispute to be referred to arbitration thereunder. These include a claim, a rejection of the claim, a referral of the resulting dispute to an engineer, and the serving of a notice of dissatisfaction against the engineer's decision. The procedure under the Blue Form was much simpler because there was no separate engineer under the subcontract. This meant that the intermediate steps in the dispute resolution procedure (i.e. the referral to the engineer and the notice of dissatisfaction against his decision) were not required when it came to subcontract disputes. This allowed the subcontractor to ensure the appointment of an arbitrator under the subcontract more

[97] See Subsection 6.2.5 below.

quickly than the main contractor was able to do so under the main contract. Therefore, once the subcontractor had given notification of a dispute under the subcontract to be referred to arbitration, the main contractor had to promptly make up his mind and set the dispute resolution procedure under the main contract in motion in order to bring the two disputes together[98]. Even if the main contractor did so with all due speed, it was very likely that the subcontractor could ensure the appointment of an arbitrator earlier than the main contractor and in this way block the operation of clause 18(2). This analysis is also relevant for more up-to-date contracts containing dispute resolution provisions similar to the Blue Form and the main contract used in conjunction with it.

6.2.3.8 *Main contractor's opinion that the main contract dispute touches or concerns the subcontract works*

Under the Blue Form, it was the main contractor who had to determine the link between the two disputes. Similar clauses are also contained in the subsequent editions of the Blue Form and some other contracts (see, for example, Section 6.4 hereof). The first question that arises here is whether it is appropriate that the main contractor should be the person competent to determine this link. It may be argued that the main contractor will not be able to form an objective opinion on the matter and therefore that the link between the disputes should be determined by an independent party, such as an arbitrator or a judge. Even though such a criticism is in principle justified, it is the author's opinion that the involvement of an arbitrator or a judge in such an early stage of the dispute resolution procedure may result in significant delays. Therefore, a subjective approach, namely that the main contractor should form an opinion on the matter, may be the better workable solution for commercial reasons[99]. Clauses similar to clause 18(2) of the Blue Form aim at avoiding inconsistent results in cases where the main contractor sits in the middle of the contractual chain. Therefore, the main contractor, as a party to both the main contract and the subcontract, is in the best position to ascertain whether there is a link between the claims and disputes arising under these two contracts, which justifies their joint review. Furthermore, the main contractor's action on the matter is likely to take less time than cases where the decision has to be taken by an arbitrator or a judge.

The answer to the question whether the main contractor's opinion is subject to any control is of great importance because it may have a material impact on the conduct of the arbitration. One of the approaches to this question was that the main contractor's opinion can be unqualified and not subject to any control. If this view is followed, the subcontractor will not be allowed to argue that the multi-party arbitration clause is inapplicable on the ground that the subcontract disputes are unrelated to the main contract. As a result, the subcontractor cannot raise a jurisdictional objection against the

---

[98] See the commentary by Sigvard Jarvin on Partial Award in ICC Case No. 5333, in *4 International Construction Law Review* (1987), pp. 332–333.

[99] Humphrey Lloyd (1991) 'A National Experience', in P. Bellet, P. Bernardini, G. Bernini *et al.* (eds) *Multi-Party Arbitration: Views from International Arbitration Specialists*, Publication No. 480/1, ICC Publishing SA, Paris, p. 72.

arbitrator or the tribunal constituted under the main contract on that ground. However, if the main contractor's opinion is subject to control, any such argument on behalf of the subcontractor may develop into a jurisdictional objection[100]. Following such an objection, the arbitrator should decide on his own jurisdiction following the doctrine of *Kompetenz-Kompetenz* and the relevant provisions in the applicable arbitration rules that enshrine this doctrine.

The degree of connection required between the disputes can cause much controversy in cases of multiple subcontractor's claims if only some of these claims are touched or concerned by the main contract dispute. For instance, the subcontractor may have two main claims against the main contractor. The first one is for delayed drawings which have to be provided by the employer. This claim can give rise to a claim under the main contract as well, and the resulting subcontract dispute will be considered as one that is touched or concerned by the corresponding main contract dispute. The second subcontractor's claim is for additional payment because of a variation instructed by the main contractor under the subcontract. It may be argued that this claim and the resulting dispute are unrelated to the main contract. Therefore, this second claim will fall outside the scope of application of clauses, such as clause 18(2) of the Blue Form, and should be resolved in a separate subcontract arbitration[101].

The scenarios described in the preceding paragraph will ultimately result in a situation where both the main contractor and the subcontractor will have to resolve their disputes arising under a single contract in two different forums, which, for commercial reasons, might be unappealing to either party. For example, if the subcontractor's claim which is touched or concerned by the main contract dispute, constitutes a relatively small share of the total of the subcontractor's claims, the main contractor might prefer to arbitrate all these disputes under the subcontract only without invoking the multi-party arbitration clause. If he invokes the clause and requires the related subcontractor's claim to be dealt with under the main contract, this may result in additional costs and time pertaining to the separate main contract arbitration, which can well outweigh the advantages that multi-party arbitration clauses, such as clause 18(2) of the Blue Form, give to the main contractor. In addition, the main contractor will have to pursue a related claim against the employer in order to require the joint review of the disputes – something that the main contractor may want to avoid in order not to poison his relationship with the employer, especially when it comes to the subcontractor's claims for a small amount.

Similar observations may be made as regards the position of the subcontractor. If most of his claims and the resulting disputes are related to the main contract and the disputes arising thereunder and the main contractor invokes the subcontract multi-party arbitration clause, the subcontractor may prefer to resolve also his unrelated claims

---

[100] The position on this issue under English law has been discussed by Peter Sheridan. See Peter Sheridan (1999) *Construction and Engineering Arbitration*, Sweet & Maxwell, London, pp. 328–329, 580–581.

[101] However, this would probably not have been the case if the subcontract contained a multi-party arbitration clause similar to the one discussed in ICC case No. 5333 and ICC case No. 5898 because of the different qualification of the nature of the subcontract dispute in these two awards. (See Subsection 6.2.2.1 hereof and the analysis in respect of the reference to 'any dispute under this Sub-Contract'.)

under the main contract arbitration for the same reasons. Starting a separate arbitration under the subcontract, something that otherwise is to the benefit of the subcontractor, may not be so beneficial in this particular case because of the additional time and costs involved in this subcontract arbitration.

Apart from the nature of the main contractor's opinion, the reference to the 'sub-contract works' also deserves more attention. As mentioned in Subsection 6.2.2.2, with regard to ICC case No. 5898, the required link between the two disputes was the subcontract works themselves – the manner in which these works were performed – and not the subcontract. Perhaps this was not the best solution because it was likely to leave certain subcontract disputes related to disputes arising under the main contract outside the scope of application of clause 18(2). One such example was given by the arbitral tribunal in ICC case No. 5898. The tribunal expressed doubts about whether a claim for payment by the main contractor against the employer (which claim may include an amount due to the subcontractor) constituted a claim that touched or concerned the manner in which the subcontract works were provided. In addition, a common question of interpretation of a contractual provision for valuation that gave rise to disputes under both contracts might also fall outside the scope of application of clause 18(2) for the same reason[102]. Hence, a reference to the '*sub-contract works*' was not very appropriate. Therefore, when drafting multi-party arbitration clauses, contracting parties may consider a reference to the subject matter of the two contracts rather than to the works[103]. This will ensure a wider scope of application of the multi-party arbitration clause, which also covers the type of claims discussed above.

6.2.3.9 Employer's inability to join in the subcontract arbitration

In certain limited cases, the employer may also have an interest in participating in multi-party arbitration with subcontractors. Such an interest may be present if the subcontractors have provided collateral warranties to the employer or if the employer has imposed certain nominated subcontractors on the main contractor[104]. For example, the employer may want to intervene in a subcontract arbitration dealing with the main contractor's claims for defective work against the subcontractor if the latter has provided a direct collateral warranty in favour of the employer.

However, this situation was not addressed in the Blue Form and the main contract. The employer would often not be cognizant of the procedures conducted under the subcontract, including of arbitrations taking place thereunder, because the Blue Form did not envisage that notices for any such subcontract procedures should be served to the employer.

---

[102] See Humphrey Lloyd (2004) *Multi-Party Clauses and Agreements*, a paper for use by the University of London LLM students, p. 8 (the paper is based on an earlier version of the same article: see Humphrey Lloyd (1991) 'A National Experience', in P. Bellet, P. Bernardini, G. Bernini *et al.* (eds) *Multi-Party Arbitration: Views from International Arbitration Specialists*, Publication No. 480/1, ICC Publishing SA, Paris).

[103] See Humphrey Lloyd (2004) *Multi-Party Clauses and Agreements*, a paper for use by the University of London LLM students, p. 8.

[104] See in that regard Subsection 3.4.1.1 of this book.

6.2.4 Clause 18(8) of the 1991 Blue Form

In 1991, certain amendments were introduced in the Blue Form. Some of these concerned clause 18(2) discussed under the previous subsections. The numbering of the latter clause was changed to 18(8), and the new wording of the clause was as follows:

> If any dispute arises in connection with the Main Contract and the Contractor is of the opinion that such dispute touches or concerns the Sub-Contract Works and the dispute is referred to a conciliator or an arbitrator under the Main Contract the Contractor may by notice in writing require that the Sub-Contractor provide such information and attend such meetings in connection therewith as the Contractor may request. The Contractor may also by notice in writing require that any such dispute under this Sub-Contract be dealt with jointly with the dispute under the Main Contract and in like manner. In connection with any such joint dispute the Sub-Contractor shall be bound in like manner as the Contractor by any recommendation of the conciliator or any award by an arbitrator[105].

The new clause differed from clause 18(2) in two main aspects. The first sentence of the clause, which required the subcontractor's assistance in certain cases, was an entirely new clause. Secondly, there was no longer a requirement under the clause that there should be no arbitrator agreed or appointed under the subcontract as a condition precedent for the operation of the clause.

The new clause brought further uncertainties in the procedure contemplated thereunder, which can be seen from the decisions in *Dredging & Construction Co Ltd v. Delta Civil Engineering Co Ltd*[106] and *Dredging & Construction Co Ltd v. Delta Civil Engineering Co Ltd (No.2)*[107].

In these cases, the subcontractor requested arbitration of his disputes with the main contractor under the terms of the subcontract. Several days later, the main contractor formally requested a decision of the engineer under the main contract and served a notice on the subcontractor requiring the subcontract disputes to be dealt with jointly with the related main contract dispute under the terms of the main contract. In the meantime, the subcontractor managed to ensure the appointment of a sole arbitrator under the subcontract. The main contractor objected to his jurisdiction and claimed that he was not empowered to review the subcontractor's claims because of the notice served under clause 18(8). The arbitrator confirmed his jurisdiction. He ascertained that the notice given by the main contractor was not a valid one because the main contract dispute had not been referred to arbitration at the time of the notice. Afterwards, the engineer made his decision on the main contract dispute. The main contractor notified his dissatisfaction with the decision and referred the main contract dispute to arbitration. Then the main contractor gave a second notice under clause 18(8) by arguing that

---

[105] Reproduced with permission of CECA.

[106] *Dredging & Construction Co Ltd & Delta Civil Engineering Co Ltd.*, in *68 Construction Law Review*, pp. 87–95, http://www.nadr.co.uk/articles/published/ArbitrationLawReports/Dredging%20v%20Delta%201999.pdf (accessed 26 July 2016).

[107] *Dredging & Construction Co Ltd & Delta Civil Engineering Co Ltd. (No. 2)*, in *72 Construction Law Review*, pp. 99–117.

this time all the preconditions for the operation of the clause were fulfilled. The arbitrator then decided that his jurisdiction was revoked on the ground of the second notice.

The issue that came before the court was whether the referral of the main contract dispute to arbitration was a precondition to the joint review of the disputes under clause 18(8). The court decided that it was not. It stressed that clause 18(8) consisted of two distinct parts[108]. The first part dealt with the main contractor's right to require the subcontractor's assistance in the form of provision of documents and other information and also attendance at meetings. This right could be requested in respect of specific types of disputes, namely subcontract disputes arising in connection with the main contract and with regard to which the main contractor was of the opinion that the related main contract dispute touched or concerned the subcontract works. Then the clause provided for the timing when the contactor's request might be given – after the referral of the main contract dispute to an arbitrator or conciliator under the main contract. The second sentence dealt with the joint review of 'any such dispute under this Sub-Contract' with 'the dispute under the Main Contract'. The subcontractor argued that this second sentence referred not only to the nature of the disputes – related subcontract and main contract disputes – but also to the manner in which the contractor had dealt with the main contract dispute[109]. Hence, the argument that a pre-existing reference to arbitration was a necessary prerequisite for the notice under clause 18(8). This argument was not accepted by the court, which decided that the reference to the disputes referred to their nature only but not to the timing prescribed in the first sentence of the clause – the referral of the main contract dispute to arbitration. Thus, the court held that even the first notice given by the main contractor under clause 18(8) was a valid notice, which deprived the arbitrator of his jurisdiction to deal with the subcontract disputes that were the subject matter of this notice.

In the first *Dredging v. Delta* case, it became clear that the arbitrator did not have jurisdiction to deal with the subcontract disputes related to the main contract. Therefore, the award of the arbitrator was remitted to him to determine which disputes remained to be dealt with in the subcontract arbitration. Those were disputes that had arisen solely under the subcontract and were unrelated to the main contract. In the course of the proceedings, however, the arbitrator expressed the view that the main contractor was not in a position to secure the employer's consent to the '*tripartite arbitration*' required under clause 18(8) as elaborated in *Lafarge v. Shephard Hill* (see Subsections 6.2.1.4 and 6.2.3.3)[110]. If a tripartite arbitration was not possible, this meant that the machinery envisaged under the latter clause had failed, and respectively that all subcontract disputes subject to the notice under clause 18(8) could be reviewed in the subcontract arbitration. This, according to the arbitrator, meant that he had jurisdiction to review all disputes arising under the subcontract and therefore it had become irrelevant to categorize between purely domestic disputes under the subcontract and those related to the main

[108] *Dredging & Construction Co Ltd v. Delta Civil Engineering Co Ltd*, in *68 Construction Law Review*, para. 35.
[109] Ibid., para. 33.
[110] *Dredging & Construction Co Ltd & Delta Civil Engineering Co Ltd. (No. 2)*, in *72 Construction Law Review*, paras 17, 21, 22, 26 and 33.

contract[111]. The court confirmed that clause 18(8) envisaged tripartite arbitration, which in principle required the consent of the employer:

> Joint dealing under the FCEC Form (1984 edn) means a tripartite arbitration, namely an arbitrator adjudicating in relation to the main contract and sub-contract disputes with each party given the right to make representations and the right to participate in the proceedings. Joint dealing in the FCEC Blue Form (1991 edn) has the same meaning...The contractor who has served a valid notice requiring joint dealing must diligently pursue his remedies under cl. 66. In the event that the main contract arbitration ensues, the contractor must take all reasonable steps to procure a tripartite arbitration. This will involve, amongst other things, securing the employer's consent to such an arbitration...[112]

However, it held that the arbitrator's opinion, that he had jurisdiction over all disputes, was premature. It was up to the main contract arbitrator to decide whether a tripartite arbitration was possible and desirable and only when the latter arbitrator had decided that such an arbitration could not take place, then the subcontract arbitrator might review all the subcontract disputes[113]. Moreover, the court held that a tripartite arbitration was possible even without the consent of the employer in this particular case because of the reference in both the main contract and the subcontract to the Institution of Civil Engineers Arbitration Procedure (1983) ('**ICE Arbitration Procedure**')[114]. Rule 9 thereunder provided for an opportunity for concurrent hearing of related disputes under several contracts upon the request of a party that was common to these contracts (i.e. the main contractor in the case at hand). It was up to the main contractor arbitrator to decide whether to apply Rule 9.

Commentary on Clause 18(8)

To the extent that clause 18(8) had the same wording as clause 18(2) of the 1984 Blue Form, the analysis in respect of clause 18(2) in Subsection 6.2.3 remains relevant. Therefore, the present commentary will only focus on these issues concerning the application of clause 18(8) which resulted from its amended wording.

The question concerning the nature of the procedure contemplated under clause 18(2) of the 1984 Blue Form, and respectively clause 18(8) of the 1991 Blue Form, continued to be an ongoing problem. In *Dredging v. Delta (No.2)*, the court confirmed that the procedure contemplated under the clause was a tripartite arbitration. The definition provided by the court on this type of arbitration hinted that it was a single multi-party arbitration in which each party had the right to participate in the proceedings and make submissions. After having said that, the court concluded that tripartite arbitration might also take the form of concurring hearings in the way envisaged under Rule 9 of the ICE

---

[111] Ibid., paras 17, 22, 26, 33 and 35.

[112] Ibid., paras 37 and 38.

[113] Ibid., paras 43 and 65.

[114] The current version of this document is from 2010. However, the clause that is discussed hereunder, i.e. Rule 9, has similar wording in both the 1983 and the 2010 ICE Arbitration Procedure. As regards the specific comments on the rules in the case, see *Dredging & Construction Co Ltd & Delta Civil Engineering Co Ltd. (No. 2)*, in *72 Construction Law Review*, para. 39–43, 50, 56, 61.

Arbitration Procedure. However, Rule 9 did not envisage a true multi-party arbitration. In principle, multi-party arbitration entails the conduct of proceedings which result in the issuance of a single arbitral award binding on all parties. However, an arbitrator acting under Rule 9 was not allowed to render such a single award, unless he was authorized to do so by all parties[115]. Instead, he had to issue separate awards. Even though the mechanism of concurrent hearing of disputes was in principle capable of diminishing the risk of inconsistent findings, it could not fully eliminate this risk because of the separate awards that had to be issued. Furthermore, the scope of application of Rule 9 was rather limited. The rule was to be applied to situations where 'the resulting arbitrations have been referred to the same Arbitrator' – there were two separate arbitral proceedings referred to the same arbitrator. First of all, there was no guarantee that the same arbitrator would be appointed to review the related disputes. For example, if the subcontractor managed to ensure the appointment of an arbitrator under the subcontract, it was far from certain that the main contractor would agree on the appointment of the same arbitrator for his dispute with the employer. Secondly, the clause required the existence of two separate arbitrations. This was not required under clause 18(8). There have been several occasions where main contractors tried to invoke the clause in cases where there was a pending arbitration under the main contract only. The opposite scenario could also occur – a subcontract arbitration without a main contract arbitration. In these two cases, Rule 9 could not be operated because of the requirement for the existence of two arbitrations.

It was debatable whether the examined Rule 9 could be applied to clause 18(2) of the 1984 Blue Form. The reason for this was that the last sentence of 18(2) referred to 'any award by an arbitrator'. Read in conjunction with the rest of the clause, this wording might create the impression that there was only one arbitration and one arbitrator. If so, the requirement under Rule 9 for the existence of two arbitrations would not be satisfied.

While clause 18(2) of the 1984 Blue Form envisaged that the clause could not be operated once an arbitrator had been agreed or appointed under the subcontract, clause 18(8) of the 1991 Blue Form was silent on the matter. This created the impression that the clause might be put into operation even if an arbitrator had been appointed under the subcontract to deal with the subcontract dispute. However, such a situation would create unsurmountable difficulties. If the main contractor tries to drag the related subcontract disputes under the main contract arbitration, this would probably require the revocation of the appointment of the subcontract arbitrator. Any such revocation should be made on the basis of explicit provisions contained either in the applicable arbitration rules or in the arbitration laws. However, the ICE Arbitration Procedure does not provide for any mechanism for the revocation of the authority of the arbitrator in those situations. Likewise, arbitration laws rarely address this issue. Thus, the appointment of a subcontract arbitrator under the Blue Form would often preclude the main contractor from putting the multi-party arbitration clause into motion even though no such restriction was stipulated in the clause.

[115] Rule 9(2) of the ICE Arbitration Procedure.

Furthermore, unlike clause 18(2) which explicitly stipulated that the joint review of the disputes should be made in accordance with the main contract, no such requirement was found in clause 18(8). This gave rise to further questions concerning the operation of the clause. Could, for example, the main contractor request that the disputes should be decided jointly by the arbitrator appointed under the subcontract? This might seem as an unusual situation but perhaps the only option for the main contractor if a subcontract arbitrator had already been appointed due to the reasons mentioned above. Strictly read, clause 18(8) did not exclude such a scenario.

6.2.5 Clause 18(10) of the 1998 Blue Form

The provision for the joint review of disputes under the Blue Form was amended once more in 1998. A new clause 18(10) was introduced. Paragraphs (a) and (b) of this clause referred to conciliation and adjudication of related subcontract and main contract disputes, and paragraphs (c) and (d) to arbitration.

Pursuant to clause 18(10)(c):

> If the Contractor is of the opinion that a Main Contract Dispute has any connection with a dispute in connection with the Sub-Contract (hereinafter called a Related Sub-Contract Dispute) and the Main Contract Dispute is referred to an arbitrator under the Main Contract, the Contractor may by notice in writing require that the Sub-Contractor provide such information and attend such meetings in connection with the Main Contract Dispute as the Contractor may request. The Contractor may also by notice in writing require that any Related Sub-Contract Dispute be dealt with jointly with the Main Contract Dispute and in like manner. In connection with any Related Sub-Contract Dispute the Sub-Contractor shall be bound in like manner as the Contractor by any award by an arbitrator in relation to the Main Contract Dispute[116].

This clause was largely similar to clause 18(8) of the 1981 Blue Form, and therefore the analysis in Subsection 6.2.4 applies to this clause as well. One point deserves more attention here. The phrase that the main contract dispute 'touches or concerns the Sub-Contract Works' had been replaced with 'has any connection with a dispute in connection with the Sub-Contract'. This was an appropriate amendment which encompassed a broader category of situations. It has already been mentioned in Subsection 6.2.3.8 that a reference to the subcontract works was not very satisfactory because it could exclude from the scope of application of the clause certain disputes that were connected with the subcontract but not with the manner in which the subcontract works were to be performed.

Clause 18(10)(d) was an entirely new clause with no analogue in the previous editions of the Blue Form. It dealt with main contract disputes that had not yet been referred to arbitration. Pursuant to the clause:

> If a dispute arises under or in connection with the Sub-Contract (hereinafter called a Sub-Contract Dispute) and the Contractor is of the opinion that the Sub-Contract Dispute raises a

[116] Reproduced with permission of CECA.

> matter or has any connection with a matter which the Contractor wishes to refer to arbitration under the Main Contract, the Contractor may by notice in writing require that the Sub-Contract Dispute be finally determined jointly with any arbitration to be commenced in accordance with the Main Contract. In connection with the Sub-Contract Dispute, the Sub-Contractor shall be bound in like manner as the Contractor by any award by an arbitrator concerning the matter referred to arbitration under the Main Contract[117].

This clause eliminated one of the issues identified with regard to the earlier drafts of the clause. It has already been discussed in Subsection 6.2.3.6 above, that the wording of the clause in existence before 1998 did not fit in well with subcontract disputes arising prior to the related main contract disputes – to disputes arising up the contractual chain. A typical example will be the case where the subcontractor claims against the main contractor for extension of time and additional payment due to late delivery of drawings by the employer. If the subcontractor's dispute arises first in time, it will be followed by a related dispute under the main contract. The new clause aimed to cover exactly these types of disputes. It could give the main contractor sufficient time to trigger the dispute resolution procedure under the main contract without, however, causing any delay in the process.

The clause did not specify what would happen if an arbitrator or a tribunal had already been appointed under the subcontract to deal with the subcontract dispute. If the main contractor's notice for the joint review of the disputes was given prior to the appointment of the subcontract arbitrator, then the logical interpretation of the clause was that the appointed subcontract arbitrator would have no jurisdiction to deal with the subcontract dispute under clause 18(10)(d). However, if the notice was given after the appointment of the subcontract arbitrator, then, in the author's opinion, the arbitrator would have jurisdiction to deal with the subcontract dispute and his appointment could not be revoked.

6.2.6 Clause 18C(4) of the 2008 Blue Form

The latest amendments to the Blue Form, which affected the provision for joint review of disputes, were those implemented in 2008. Paragraphs (c) and (d) of clause 18C(4) are of direct relevance for the present discussion. Pursuant to clause 18C(4)(c):

> If the Contractor is of the opinion that a Main Contract Dispute has any connection with a dispute in connection with the Sub-Contract (hereinafter called a Related Sub-Contract Dispute) and the Main Contract Dispute is referred to an arbitrator under the Main Contract, the Contractor may by notice in writing require that the Sub-Contractor provide such information and attend such meetings in connection with the Main Contract Dispute as the Contractor may request. The Contractor may also by notice in writing require that any Related Sub-Contract Dispute be determined by the arbitrator appointed to determine the Main Contract Dispute consistently with the determination of the Main Contract

[117] Reproduced with permission of CECA.

> Dispute. In the event of such a notice, the arbitrator appointed to determine the Main Contract Dispute shall conduct a tripartite arbitration between the Employer, Contractor and Sub-Contractor if the Employer agrees. If the Employer does not agree, the arbitrator appointed to determine the Main Contract Dispute shall conduct the arbitration of the Related Sub-Contract Dispute concurrently with but separately from the arbitration of the Main Contract Dispute[118].

The first sentence of the clause is identical to the opening sentence of clause 18(10)(c) discussed in Subsection 6.2.5 above. The differences are to be identified in the rest of the clause. Clause 18C(4)(c) makes clear that the joint review of the related disputes takes place under the main contract and that it should be conducted by the arbitrator appointed under the main contract. In this way, the new clause eliminates some of the uncertainties in the application of some of its predecessors as regards the arbitrator who was empowered to deal with the joint review of the disputes (see the commentary in Subsection 6.2.4).

The clause stipulates that the subcontract dispute will be determined 'by the arbitrator appointed to determine the Main Contract Dispute' – there had to be an appointment of an arbitrator under the main contract as a precondition for the application of the clause. Clause 18C(4)(c) does not differentiate between situations where a subcontract arbitrator has been appointed and those where such an appointment has not taken place yet. This arguably means that the clause is broad enough to cover situations where the appointment of a subcontract arbitrator has taken place. However, as explained in Subsection 6.2.4 above, such a situation will give rise to material difficulties, which could block the operation of the clause.

One of the merits of the new clause 18C(4)(c) is that it clarifies the nature of the procedure that is contemplated thereunder. The type of arbitration to be conducted under the clause is a tripartite arbitration provided that the employer agrees to it. If the employer does not agree, then the clause should be read as authorizing concurring hearing of disputes. Considering that the default arbitration procedure under the Blue Form is the ICE Arbitration Procedure, the reference to concurrent hearings should be read in conjunction with Rule 9 of this procedure, which allows the conduct of concurrent hearings upon the application of one of the parties only. By differentiating between tripartite arbitration and concurrent hearings it becomes clear that the tripartite arbitration is a procedure that should not be equated with the concurrent review of the disputes. In this way, the drafters of the Blue Form departed from the view expressed in *Dredging v. Delta (No.2)* that a tripartite arbitration may be in a form of concurrent hearings under the ICE Arbitration Procedure (see Subsection 6.2.4 above). Hence, the tripartite arbitration is a procedure that contemplates a closer integration of the related disputes than in cases of concurrent hearing of disputes. This argument is further supported by the fact that the employer should give his consent to the conduct of this type of arbitration. It follows from here that the tripartite arbitration envisaged under the latest edition of the Blue Form is a true multi-party arbitration – a single arbitration where each party is a formal party to the proceedings.

---

[118] Reproduced with permission of CECA.

Clause 18C(4)(d) deals with subcontract disputes arising prior to the related main contract dispute:

> If a dispute arises under or in connection with the Sub-Contract (hereinafter called a Sub-Contract Dispute) and the Contractor is of the opinion that the Sub-Contract Dispute raises a matter or has any connection with a matter which the Contractor wishes to resolve under the Main Contract (hereinafter called a Related Main Contract Issue), the Contractor may by notice in writing require that the Sub-Contractor provide such information and attend such meetings in connection with the Related Main Contract Issue as the Contractor may request. In the event that the Related Main Contract Issue develops, or in the opinion of the Contractor may develop, into a Main Contract Dispute, the Contractor may also by notice in writing require that the Sub-Contract Dispute be determined by the arbitrator appointed or to be appointed to determine the Main Contract Dispute consistently with the determination of the Main Contract Dispute. In the event of such a notice, the arbitrator appointed to determine the Main Contract Dispute shall conduct a tripartite arbitration between the Employer, Contractor and Sub-Contractor if the Employer agrees. If the Employer does not agree, the arbitrator appointed to determine the Main Contract Dispute shall conduct the arbitration of the Related Sub-Contract Dispute concurrently with but separately from the arbitration of the Main Contract Dispute[119].

When compared with clause 18(10)(d) of the 1998 Blue Form, clause 18C(4)(d) is more elaborate and has a much wider scope of application. First, the clause now explicitly envisages that the main contractor may request that the subcontractor attends meetings and provides documents in respect of subcontract disputes that may result in main contract disputes. This is stipulated in the first sentence of the new clause, which did not have an analogue under the previous clause 18(10)(d). Secondly, while clause 18(10)(d) was to be applied to cases where the main contract dispute had not yet been referred to arbitration, the new clause 18C(4)(d) can also be applied to cases where a main contract arbitrator has already been appointed. Otherwise, the purpose of the new clause is the same as that of the preceding clause 18(10)(d): to deal with disputes arising up the contractual chain. Therefore, the commentary in Subsection 6.2.5 on the latter clause also applies to the clause discussed here.

6.3 JCT Contracts

The contracts published by the Joint Contracts Tribunal ('**JCT**'), or also known as the JCT Contracts, are among the most popular domestic standard forms used in England[120]. The JCT suite contains both contracts for major works and subcontracts. The approach of the JCT to multi-party arbitration has developed over time. The contract suite published in 1980, known also as JCT 80, contained explicit provisions dealing with multi-party arbitration. This approach was abandoned in the newer editions

---

[119] Reproduced with permission of CECA.

[120] For more information about the JCT and the contracts published by it, see http://www.jctltd.co.uk (accessed 26 July 2015).

of the contracts published from 1998 on, where the multi-party arbitration provisions were deleted and replaced with a reference to the Construction Industry Model Arbitration Rules ('**CIMAR**')[121]. Therefore, this section is subdivided into several subsections. The first two outline the JCT 80 multi-party arbitration regime and provide a commentary thereon. The last subsection discusses the new regime as regulated under the CIMAR.

6.3.1 JCT 80 approach to multi-party arbitration[122]

The arbitration clause under the JCT 80 Standard Form of Building Contract, a form of main contract, was contained in clause 41[123]. Clause 41.1 was a straightforward provision outlining the procedure to be followed when a dispute or difference under the main contract was to be referred to arbitration. Such a dispute or difference had to be referred to an arbitrator appointed under the terms of the main contract. Of more importance for the present discussion was the proviso that followed:

> 41.2.1. Provided that if the dispute or difference to be referred to arbitration under this Contract raises issues which are substantially the same as or connected with issues raised in a related dispute between:
> the Employer and Nominated Sub-Contractor under Agreement NSC/2 or NSC/2a as applicable, or
> the Contractor and any nominated Sub-Contractor under Sub-Contract NSC/4 or NSC/4a as applicable, or
> the Contractor and/or the Employer and any Nominated Supplier whose contract of sale with the Contractor provides for the matters referred to in clause 36.4.8.2,
> and if the related dispute has already been referred for determination to the Arbitrator, the Employer and the Contractor hereby agree
> that the dispute or difference under this Contract shall be referred to the Arbitrator appointed to determine the related dispute;
> that the JCT Arbitration Rules applicable to the related dispute shall apply to the dispute under this Contract;
> that such Arbitrator shall have power to make such directions and all necessary awards in the same way as if the procedure of the High Court as to joining one or more defendants or joining co-defendants or third parties was available to the parties and to him…;

[121] The first edition of the CIMAR was issued in 1998 by the English Society of Construction Arbitrators (www.constructionarbitrators.org, accessed 26 July 2016). This edition, known as CIMAR 1998, is available at http://www.constructionarbitrators.org/sites/default/files/local/browser/documents/cimar_final.pdf (accessed 26 July 2016). The CIMAR used in conjunction with the JCT Contracts are based on a JCT edition of these rules, known as JCT/CIMAR Construction Industry Arbitration Rules 2011 (JCT/CIMAR 2011), http://www.jctltd.co.uk/docs/JCT_CIMAR_2011.pdf (accessed 26 July 2016).

[122] Access to the superseded editions of the JCT Contracts has been obtained through earlier volumes of *Emden's Construction Law by Crown Office Chambers* published by LexisNexis.

[123] The JCT 80 Standard Form of Building Contract existed in different versions. These included, for example, the JCT Local Authorities Form of Contract with Quantities, 1980 edition, and the JCT Local Authorities Form of Contract Without Quantities, 1980 edition.

41.2.2 Save that the Employer or the Contractor may require the dispute or difference under this Contract to be referred to a different Arbitrator (to be appointed under this Contract) if either of them reasonably considers that the Arbitrator appointed to determine the related dispute is not appropriately qualified to determine the dispute or difference under this Contract.

41.2.3 Clauses 41.2.1 and 41.2.2 shall apply unless in the Appendix the word 'clauses 41.2.1 and 41.2.2 apply' have been deleted.

The abovementioned proviso was kept in some of the 1992 JCT editions with some slight modifications[124]. In short, the clause allowed for a main contract dispute that had not yet been referred to arbitration to be referred for review to an arbitrator seized with a related dispute under another contract. Thus, depending on the contract whereunder the related dispute had arisen, the main contract dispute could be determined by an arbitrator appointed under a subcontract or an agreement with a nominated supplier. In order to be operated, the clause required a certain link between the two disputes, which was determined in a broad and abstract way. Under the clause, the related disputes had to raise issues that were substantially the same or connected with each other. The existence of this link had to be ascertained on a case-by-case basis.

Clauses identical or largely similar to the one discussed above were also contained in two categories of subcontracts, which were used in conjunction with the JCT 80 contracts. First, these clauses could be found in the JCT 80 subcontracts for nominated subcontractors – subcontractors designated by the employer but hired by the main contractor to complete certain works. The JCT scheme of nominated subcontractors envisaged that they entered into direct contracts with the main contractor and in some cases also with the employer[125]. Secondly, multi-party arbitration clauses were also contained in some standard form subcontracts for domestic subcontractors – subcontractors appointed by the main contractor that were not nominated subcontractors. These contracts were not part of the JCT 80 suite but were drafted for use with the JCT family of

[124] See, for example, Clauses 9.2.1 and 9.2.2 of the JCT Standard Form of Prime Cost Contract, 1992 edn, and Clause 9.2 from the JCT Management Contract, 1987 edn.

[125] Prior to 1991, there were two systems for nomination of subcontractors under the JCT contracts. Under the basic system, the subcontractors entered into contracts with both the main contractor (Sub-Contract NSC/4) and the employer (Employer/Sub-Contract Agreement NSC/2). Under the alternative system, the execution of a subcontract with the employer (Employer/Sub-Contract Agreement NSC/2a) was optional but there was always a direct contract between the main contractor and the nominated subcontractor (Sub-Contract NSC/4a). The multi-party arbitration clauses were contained in clause 38.2 of these subcontracts. From 1991 on, there was only one system for nomination of subcontractors, pursuant to which nominated subcontractors entered into contracts with both the employer (Employer/Nominated Sub-Contractor Agreement NSC/W) and the main contractor (Articles of Nominated Sub-Contract Agreement NSC/A incorporating the Standard Conditions of Nominated Sub-Contract NSC/C). These contracts superseded the previous subcontract forms but the multi-party arbitration clauses were kept in clause 9.2. See also clause 11.2 from the 1992 JCT Standard Form of Employer/Nominated Sub-Contractor Agreement, known as NSC/W(PCC), which was intended for use with the JCT Standard Form of Prime Cost Contract 1992 edition.

contracts, and therefore contained similar multi-party arbitration provisions[126]. Under the terms of the subcontracts, the subcontractor and the main contractor, respectively the employer when it came to some nominated subcontractors, agreed that a subcontract dispute that was related to a dispute arising under another contract (a main contract, another subcontract or an agreement with a nominated supplier) could be referred to an arbitrator appointed under that other contract.

The JCT 80 provisions on multi-party arbitration were the subject matter of several English cases, which clarified their meaning and the preconditions for their operation. The problems discussed in these cases can be summarized in four main questions. Did the JCT 80 provisions provide for a self-contained mechanism that could be put into operation regardless of parties' objections? When could the provisions be applied? How is the link between the disputes to be determined? Who was to determine whether there was such a link if the parties disagreed? All these questions are dealt with below in the sequence in which they have been posed.

6.3.1.1 Did the JCT 80 provisions provide for a self-contained mechanism for multi-party arbitration?

In other words, this question deals with the matter whether the JCT 80 provisions incorporated the consent of all parties to multi-party arbitration. Unlike the Blue Form, which regulates multi-party arbitration on the level of the subcontract only, the old JCT contractual provisions on multi-party arbitration introduced identical provisions that were spread throughout the whole JCT suite. This created the impression that all parties had agreed in advance to multi-party arbitration by signing the relevant contracts. It followed from this that once one of the clauses had been put into operation upon the request of a party, all the other parties could not object to its application because of their advanced consent given at the time of execution of the contracts. However, a close analysis of the contractual provisions reveals that such an argument is not beyond doubt.

Strictly speaking, each of the discussed contractual provisions contained the consent to multi-party arbitration of the parties – signatories to the respective contract only.

[126] Even though the JCT 80 main contract allowed for the hiring of domestic subcontractors, there was no such subcontract form drafted by the JCT. This led to the occurrence of several subcontract forms intended for use with the JCT 80 suite, which were drafted by organizations different from JCT. See, for example, article 3 of the BEC/FASS/CASEC Domestic Sub-Contract DOM/1 1980 (in its version prior to Amendment 3:1987) and clause 38.2.1 of the Sub-Contract Conditions incorporated in the latter contract (as inserted by Amendment 3: 1987). See also article 3 of the BEC/FASS/CASEC Domestic Sub-Contract DOM/2 1981, which was to be used in conjunction with the JCT Standard Form of Building Contract with Contractor's Design, 1981 edn, and also clause 38.2.1 of the Domestic Sub-Contract DOM/1 incorporating DOM/2 amendments (in its version prior to 1998). These two subcontract forms were drafted by the National Federation of Building Trades Employers (later known as the Building Employers Confederation and the Construction Confederation), the Federation of Associations of Specialists and Sub-Contractors and the Confederation of Associations of Specialist Engineering Sub-Contractors. See also clause 35.4 (before Amendment 3: 1989) and clause 35.5 (after Amendment 3: 1989) of the BEC Domestic Sub-Contract IN/SC Articles of Agreement published in 1985 by BEC, which was later known as the Construction Confederation, for use with the JCT Intermediate Form IFC84.

Thus, the main contract provision contained the consent of the main contractor and the employer that their dispute could be referred to a subcontract arbitrator reviewing a related subcontract dispute. However, the subcontractor was not a party to this contract, and therefore his consent to this type of arbitration could not be derived from the terms of the main contract. Moreover, the subcontractor's consent could hardly be derived from the subcontract either. The reason for that was that the subcontract arbitration clause contemplated a different scenario; it envisaged a situation where a subcontract dispute could be referred to an arbitrator appointed under a contract different from the subcontract and not, as in the main contract, cases where a main contract dispute could be referred to a subcontract arbitrator.

The same reasoning could be applied to the subcontract multi-party arbitration clause, which incorporated the consent of the main contractor and the subcontractor that their dispute could be reviewed by an arbitrator appointed under another contract. This clause, however, was not directly binding on the employer who was not privy to the subcontract[127]. The employer's consent could not be derived from the main contract arbitration clause either, because the latter addressed a different scenario.

The above mentioned gap in the JCT multi-party arbitration clauses was likely to cause serious obstacles to their operation. The adoption of the strict interpretation posed above meant that whenever one of the multi-party arbitration clauses had to be applied, the *ad hoc* consent of the party non-signatory to the contract containing this clause should always be obtained. This point was discussed in detail in *Trafalgar House Construction Ltd v. Railtrack Plc*[128]. In this case, two nominated subcontractors claimed extension of time and additional payment against the main contractor. The latter served a notice of arbitration against the employer in which the main contractor repeated the subcontractors' claims and also sought some additional sums. The main contractor gave notice to the two subcontractors under the terms of the subcontracts requiring the subcontract disputes, which were related to the dispute under the main contract, to be reviewed by the arbitrator appointed under the main contract. Afterwards, the main contract arbitrator issued several procedural orders, one of which was made on the basis that there was a quadripartite arbitration between all parties. The employer sought a declaration that that the arbitrator did not have jurisdiction to issue such an order. One of the questions before the court was whether the arbitration in question was only between the employer and the main contractor or whether it was a multi-party arbitration with the participation of the two subcontractors as well. The employer argued that he had the right of bipolar arbitration under the terms of the main contract and that any arbitration with the participation of the subcontractor required the employer's consent because the employer was not privy to the subcontract containing the arbitration clause that was invoked. The judge reviewing the case developed an interpretation whereunder the arbitration clauses under the main contract and the subcontract should be read in conjunction with each other in a way that gave effect to the arrangements that they had in common:

[127] This was also confirmed in *Higgs & Hill Building Ltd v. Campbell Denis Ltd*, in *28 Building Law Reports* (1982), pp. 59–60.

[128] *Trafalgar House Construction (Regions) Ltd. v. Railtrack plc*, in *76 Building Law Reports* (1995), pp. 55–90.

> Although both clause 41.2.1 [from the main contract] and clause 38.2.1 [from the subcontract] should have been much clearer, as a matter of construction and if necessary implication they must in my judgment be read together as part of a group of contracts which are on their face commercially directly related to each other and as a matter of law to be read in conjunction with each other so that, whilst recognising that they remain separate agreements, effect is nevertheless to be given to the arrangements that they have in common. Thus the agreement in clause 41.2.1 means, first, that neither the employer, nor the contractor can object if, at the instance of the other, a third party is introduced with whom there is a related dispute which by reason of the provision of NSC/4 [the subcontract](for example) is to be referred for determination by the same arbitrator as appointed under the main contract, and secondly, that each consents to the dispute under the main contract and the related dispute being linked with the other if the arbitrator were to decide to treat a party as a co-defendant or third party in the other arbitration[129].

In this way, it was held that the employer could not object to a quadripartite arbitration under the main contract with the participation of the subcontractors. One of the arguments for this interpretation was based on the fact that under the JCT contractual schemes the employer obliged the main contractor to engage nominated subcontractors under the terms of the JCT subcontract forms. Therefore, the employer had knowledge of the arbitration clause contained in the subcontracts that allowed for the referral of a related subcontract dispute to the main contract arbitrator. Thus, the employer should have assumed that a subcontractor might be dragged into the main contract arbitration, and therefore was not allowed to object to his participation[130]. Similarly, the subcontractor could not object to multi-party arbitration with the participation of the employer conducted by an arbitrator appointed under the subcontract because the subcontractor tendered for the works on the basis of his knowledge of the main contract, including the arbitration clause contained therein[131]. A further argument strengthening this interpretation was found in the overall purpose of the clauses discussed. They aimed to avoid substantial injustice resulting from cases where different tribunals reached different conclusions on the same facts. An interpretation that required the *ad hoc* consent to multi-party arbitration was found to be incompliant with the purpose of the multi-party arbitration clauses to avoid multiplicity of proceedings on related matters[132].

6.3.1.2 When should the clause be invoked?

The answer to this question required consideration of two temporal aspects. The first was related to the requirement for the existence of a related dispute at the time when the clause was invoked. The second concerned the appointment of an arbitrator under the contract containing the multi-party arbitration clause. In other words, did such an appointment preclude the clause from being put into operation?

---

[129] Ibid., pp. 85–86.
[130] Ibid., p. 86.
[131] Ibid., p. 79.
[132] Ibid., p. 85.

The first point did not give rise to any concerns under the JCT 80 system. The wording of the multi-party arbitration clauses requiring that 'the related dispute has already been referred for determination to the Arbitrator' clearly required the presence of a dispute under the other contract that was in existence at the time when the clause was relied upon. Thus, a subcontract dispute could be referred to an arbitrator appointed under the main contract provided that two preconditions were fulfilled: first, there was a main contract dispute in existence and, secondly, this main contract dispute had been referred to an arbitrator appointed under the main contract. It should be mentioned that this second condition was arguably inserted to improve the multi-party arbitration regime contained in the predecessors of JCT 80 subcontracts, known as the NFBTE/FASS Sub-Contract Forms, which were used in conjunction with pre-1980 editions of the JCT Contracts[133]. These subcontracts included the following proviso in their arbitration clauses:

> provided that if the dispute or difference between the Contractor and Sub-Contractor is substantially the same as a matter which is in dispute or difference between the Contractor and the Employer under the Main Contract, the Contractor and Sub-Contractor hereby agree that such dispute or difference shall be referred to an Arbitrator appointed, or to be appointed, pursuant to the terms of the Main Contract...

The second precondition was not addressed under the terms of this clause. The use of the present tense 'is in dispute or difference...under the main contract' created the impression that the first precondition was still required. This was also confirmed in *Higgs & Hill Building Ltd v. Campbell Denis Ltd*[134]. However, the decision in *Multi-Construction Ltd v. Stent Foundations Ltd*[135] brought some uncertainty on this point. In that case, a subcontractor argued that in order for the proviso to be exercisable there had to be a main contract dispute at the date of the subcontractor's request to the main

[133] These forms were published by the then existing Building Employers Confederation and the Federation of Associations of Specialists and Sub-Contractors. The subcontracts were used in conjunction with the JCT 63 contracts, and with the introduction of the JCT 80 they were superseded by the subcontracts drafted for use with the JCT 80 main contract (i.e. NSC/4 and NSC4/a for nominated subcontractors and DOM/1 for domestic subcontractors). Two NFBTE/FASS Sub-Contract Forms existed: the Green Form, and the Blue Form. The Green Form, first issued in 1963, was to be used for nominated subcontractors under the JCT 63 suite and the Blue Form (to be distinguished from the Blue Form discussed in Section 6.2) was issued in 1971 and was to be used for the appointment of domestic subcontractors.

[134] See *Higgs & Hill Building Ltd v. Campbell Denis Ltd and Another*, in *28 Building Law Reports* (1982), p. 62. According to the judge: 'It seems to me that clause 24 provides alternatives, and that the relative suitability of these alternatives must be judged when an arbitrator is to be appointed under the sub-contract. If at that time (1) a dispute exists between the contractor and the employer, which, or part of which, is substantially the same as the dispute now sought to be submitted to arbitration, and (2) an arbitrator has been or is to be appointed under the main contract the sub-contract arbitration must be referred to him. In my judgment if either of those conditions is absent, the machinery provided for by the proviso cannot be brought into play and the appointment must be made in accordance with the first part of clause 24 [which required the appointment of a subcontract arbitrator to deal with the dispute].'

[135] *Multi-Construction (Southern) Ltd v. Stent Foundations Ltd and Others*, in *41 Building Law Reports* (1988), pp. 98–109.

contractor for the appointment of an arbitrator under the subcontract. The judge reached the decision that the proviso could be invoked by the main contractor even though there was 'no outward manifestation' of a main contract dispute on that date. This arguably left some leeway for main contractors facing subcontractors' claims without themselves being in dispute with the employer to trigger the dispute resolution mechanism under the main contract in order to benefit from the subcontract multi-party arbitration clause. However, as mentioned above, any uncertainty regarding the application of these clauses was removed with the introduction of the JCT 80 contracts for nominated subcontractors, which explicitly required that the main contract dispute had to be one referred to arbitration; hence, this meant a referral of an existing dispute.

The JCT 80 multi-party arbitration clauses did not mention anything about the appointment of an arbitrator under the contract where the clause was contained. This left some leeway for different interpretations. A question arose in the *Trafalgar v. Railtrack* case whether the main contract multi-party arbitration clause can be applied to cases where an arbitrator under the main contract had already been appointed. This question was answered in the negative. It was emphasized that the clause referred to a main contract dispute that is 'to be referred to arbitration under this Contract'. This wording was contrasted with the qualification of the related subcontract dispute 'which has already been referred for determination to the Arbitrator'. Therefore, a dispute 'to be referred to arbitration' was interpreted to mean a dispute that had not yet been referred to arbitration – a dispute with regard to which an arbitrator had not been appointed yet[136]. Thus, a party that intended to invoke clause 41.2.1 of the main contract ought to have done so before an arbitrator was appointed under the main contract. Once such an appointment was made, the provision could no longer be applied. This followed from the wording of the clause and also from the lack of contractual provisions envisaging the revocation of the appointment of an arbitrator[137]. The same can be said about the subcontract multi-party arbitration clause. The party trying to invoke this clause should do it before an arbitrator is appointed under the subcontract.

The same conclusion was reached in *Higgs & Hill Building Ltd v. Campbell Denis Ltd.* The arbitration clause discussed in that case was identical to the clause contained in the NFBTE/FASS Sub-Contract Forms cited above. There was no reference to 'to be referred to arbitration' with regard to the subcontract dispute that, on the face of the matter, created the impression that the subcontract multi-party arbitration clause could also be applied in cases where an arbitrator under the subcontract had already been appointed. In *Higgs & Hill v. Campbell*, the subcontractor was not admitted to the site in time due to an employer's default, which led to a failure to meet the contractual day of completion. The subcontractor submitted his final account for the delay and other matters to the main contractor, who claimed against the employer. The main contractor first tried to resolve his dispute with the employer before reverting to the subcontractor. This delayed the resolution of the subcontract dispute. Upon the request of the subcontractor, a subcontract arbitrator was appointed to review the subcontract dispute. Afterwards, a

[136] *Trafalgar House Construction (Regions) Ltd. v. Railtrack plc*, in *76 Building Law Reports* (1995), p. 82.
[137] Ibid., p. 83.

main contract arbitrator was also appointed to deal with the main contract dispute. The main contractor challenged the jurisdiction of the subcontract arbitrator by arguing that the subcontract dispute should be referred to the main contract arbitrator as envisaged under the subcontract multi-party arbitration clause. There was clearly a link between the two disputes which dealt with common causes of delay under the contracts. There was a controversy as to when the multi-party arbitration clause could be invoked. The main contractor argued that he was allowed to invoke the clause at any time – even after an arbitrator had been appointed under the subcontract. The subcontractor contended that the decision to rely on the clause had to be made at the stage when one of the parties applied for the appointment of an arbitrator under the subcontract. The judge agreed with the subcontractor's arguments[138]. In other words, at that stage the main contractor had to decide whether to resolve his dispute through subcontract arbitration or request that the subcontract dispute ought to be referred to the arbitrator under the main contract. Once a subcontract arbitrator had been appointed there was no longer an opportunity to rely on the subcontract multi-party arbitration clause. In these circumstances, the subcontract arbitrator was deemed to be properly appointed, and he had jurisdiction to proceed with the subcontract dispute.

6.3.1.3 How is the link between the related disputes to be determined?

The JCT 80 clauses were not very lucid concerning the link between the two disputes that justified their joint review. Pursuant to the clauses, the dispute or difference arising under the contract where the clause was contained should raise 'issues which are substantially the same as or connected with issues raised in a related dispute'. This wording comprised a broader category of disputes than the one covered under the pre-1980 subcontracts (i.e. the NFBTE/FASS Sub-Contract Forms) where the words '*or connected with*' were missing. It was clear that the required link was a matter of factual interpretation. But how exactly was this link to be determined? Did '*substantially*' refer to the phrase '*or connected with*' as well? In other words, if the dispute was not substantially the same but was connected with issues raised in the related dispute, what was the degree of the required connection? Did the dispute have to be substantially connected or merely connected with issues raised in a related dispute?[139] This was a point that lacked a clear answer.

City & General (Holborn) Ltd. v. AYH Plc[140] shed light on some of the above questions. In this case, an employer entered into a main contract, based on the JCT Standard Form of Building Contract, 1998 Edition, with a contractor and a separate contract with a project manager. The project management contract contained a multi-party arbitration clause, which was substantially the same as the one discussed in this section. Disputes arose under both the main contract and the project management contract and the

---

[138] *Higgs & Hill Building Ltd v. Campbell Denis Ltd and Another*, in *28 Building Law Reports* (1982), p. 62.

[139] Peter Sheridan (1999) *Construction and Engineering Arbitration*, Sweet & Maxwell, London, p. 324.

[140] *City & General (Holborn) Ltd. v. AYH Plc.*, in *56 Building Law Reports* (2006), pp. 55–65, http://www.nadr.co.uk/articles/published/AdjudLawR/City%20&%20General%20v%20AYH%202005.pdf (accessed 26 July 2016).

employer requested the disputes under the latter contract to be referred to the main contract arbitrator by invoking the multi-party arbitration clause contained in the project management contract. The main contract dispute concerned claims for additional payments due to, *inter alia*, variations and additional works, as well as claims for extension of time. The dispute under the project management contract comprised, among others, claims arising out of alleged project manager's underestimation of the likely costs at the outset of the project, his failure to monitor various programmes and to submit information to the contractor on time. The project manager contested the joint review of the disputes by stating that the issues raised in his contract with the employer were neither substantially the same, nor connected with the issues under the main contract dispute. Therefore, he asserted that the threshold required under the multi-party arbitration clause was not met. The judge in the case considered the principal question of the degree of convergence of the issues in the two disputes required for their joint review and reached the following conclusion:

> It is not necessary in my judgment for every single issue in dispute B to be substantially the same or connected with an issue in dispute A...Bearing in mind the commercial objective [to avoid multiplicity of proceedings], I do not think that the threshold of [the multi-party arbitration clause] should be set too high. It is not necessary that the majority of issues in dispute B should be the same as or connected with issues in dispute A. In my judgment, it is sufficient if a material portion of the issues in dispute B have that characteristic. Once a material portion of the issues in dispute B are the same as, or are connected with, issues in dispute A, then it makes obvious commercial sense for both disputes to be dealt with by the same tribunal.[141]

In this particular case, the judge decided that the required threshold was met. According to the judge, the issues that were common to both disputes were the actual costs of the executed works, the alleged late provision of information to the contractor and its impact on the construction works[142]. The fact that there were a number of other issues in the dispute between the employer and the project manager, which were unrelated to the main contract dispute, was not sufficient to change this conclusion[143].

6.3.1.4 Who was to decide whether the disputes were related?

Unlike the Blue Form, which vested the main contractor with the authority to decide this matter, the old JCT multi-party arbitration provisions were silent on this question. In *Higgs & Hill Building Ltd v. Campbell Denis Ltd*[144], it was stated that it is for the parties to operate the machinery provided by an arbitration clause contained in a subcontract. It was further held that it was particularly the main contractor, as a party to both the main contract and the subcontract, who was best placed to ascertain whether there were

---

[141] Ibid., para. 46–47.

[142] Ibid., para. 52.

[143] Ibid., para. 53.

[144] *Higgs & Hill Building Ltd v. Campbell Denis Ltd and Another*, in *28 Building Law Reports* (1982), pp. 47–75.

matters that were substantially the same under the two disputes[145]. The main contract clause could be invoked not only by the main contractor but also by the employer who, in certain cases, could have an interest in participating in multi-party arbitration with nominated subcontractors (see Subsection 3.4.1.1).

However, there were cases where the parties disagreed with each other as to whether the disputes in question were related or not. Who was then to decide whether the disputes were related? This was the subject matter in *Hyundai Engineering and Construction Co Ltd. v. Active Building and Civil Construction Pte Ltd*[146]. The case was based on an arbitration clause contained in NFBTE/FASS Sub-Contract Form. Even though the arbitration clause contained in that contract differed from the one in the JCT 80 subcontracts, the wording of the clause in its part concerning the present question was almost identical to the JCT clause (see Subsection 6.3.1.2). In *Hyundai v. Active Building*, the main contractor argued that the subcontractor's claims were part of one single composite dispute, which had to be referred to the arbitrator appointed under the main contract. The subcontractors asserted that there was a large number of separate disputes some of which were purely domestic with no link to the main contract. The judge rejected the argument that there was one single dispute. He underlined that the arbitration clauses contained two separate unequivocal submissions. The first part of the clause, which was determined as the dominant one, envisaged the referral of all disputes to subcontract arbitration, subject only to those disputes covered by the proviso (i.e. the multi-party arbitration clause)[147]. It was furthermore stated that the word 'dispute' in its natural meaning referred to a difference on a specific item. Therefore, it was held that there were separate disputes and not a single one. An interpretation to the contrary would have deprived the dominant part of the clause of its effect. Such an interpretation would have meant that whenever there were multiple disputes, some of which were related and some unrelated to a main contract, all these disputes would have fallen within the scope of the proviso, which would have made the dominant part of the arbitration clause meaningless[148]. As a result, a dispute arose as regards the particular disputes that fell within the scope of the multi-party arbitration provision. The subcontractor asserted that it is the subcontract arbitrator who had to decide the disputes falling within his jurisdiction – those of purely domestic nature. The court held that an arbitrator was entitled to decide on his own jurisdiction only in exceptional cases when there was a clear contractual wording to that effect[149]. Such wording was not contained in the arbitration clause, and therefore it was held that the court should decide which disputes fell within the contractual clause[150]. It was also mentioned that a full disclosure of information was required in order to enable the court to make a comprehensive analysis of the nature of the disputes and to

[145] Ibid., p. 62.

[146] *Hyundai Engineering and Construction Co Ltd. v. Active Building and Civil Construction Pte Ltd*, in 45 *Building Law Reports* (1989), pp. 62–71.

[147] Ibid., pp. 69–70.

[148] Ibid.

[149] Ibid., pp. 63, 65.

[150] Ibid., pp. 63, 65.

establish whether there was a link justifying their joint review. It was up to the party that invoked the clause – the main contractor in this case – to substantiate that there was such a link[151].

6.3.2 Commentary on the JCT 80 approach

The JCT 80 multi-party arbitration provisions were among the first tested successfully in English courts. This was evident from the decision in *Trafalgar House Construction Ltd v. Railtrack Plc*. The reasoning in that case, that these provisions contained a self-contained mechanism for multi-party arbitration that did not require the *ad hoc* consent of the parties for its operation, was authoritative and convincing. However, there is no guarantee that the same reasoning will be adopted in international arbitral proceedings based on arbitration clauses similar to those discussed above. Therefore, contracting parties using such clauses should formulate them in a way that ensures that their application is not thwarted by a party's argument that multi-party arbitration is not possible because the provision contemplating it is contained in a contract to which this party is a non-signatory.

Hyundai v. Active Building was very illustrative of a situation where a court had to decide a substantive point of law – to review comprehensively the merits of the disputes and decide on the existence of a link between them, despite the clear intention of the parties to submit their disputes to arbitration. Nowadays, the doctrine of *Kompetenz-Kompetenz*, according to which it is the arbitrator who should decide on his own jurisdiction, is stipulated in most modern sets of arbitration rules. Therefore, if an arbitration clause similar to the one discussed in the *Hyundai v. Active Building* contains a reference to one of these rules, it will be the arbitrator to decide the scope of disputes falling with the multi-party arbitration clause and not the court. This approach, however, may cause difficulties when arbitral proceedings are underway under both the subcontract and the main contract. Then jurisdictional objections regarding the connection between the disputes may be raised in both proceedings. The main contractor may object in the subcontract arbitration that the arbitrator does not have jurisdiction to deal with the dispute because the latter is related to a main contract dispute and therefore should be referred to the main contract arbitrator. Likewise, in the main contract arbitration, the subcontractor may claim, as in the *Hyundai* case, that some disputes have to be decided under the subcontract because they are not related to the main contract dispute. The arbitrators under both proceedings will have to decide on the jurisdictional objections but there is no guarantee that they will decide these matters consistently. However, such a scenario was unlikely to occur under the JCT 80 multi-party arbitration provisions, which were intended to be applied to situations where there was only one pending arbitration (see Subsection 6.3.1.2).

As mentioned above, the JCT 80 multi-party arbitration provisions could be applied, provided that there was a related dispute that had already been referred to arbitration.

---

[151] Ibid., p. 65.

It may be argued whether this was a good approach. On one side, such a requirement undoubtedly brought some clarity in the operation of the clauses as regards the temporal preconditions for the operation of the clause. As indicated in Subsection 6.3.1.2, it was unclear under the pre-1980 subcontracts (i.e. the NFBTE/FASS Sub-Contract Forms) whether there had to be a related dispute in existence at the time when the clause was invoked. On the other hand, it seemed that the clause left some disputes with regard to which multi-party arbitration might be needed outside its scope of application. For example, the subcontractor notified the main contractor of a dispute that was also related to the main contract. This could be a dispute based on a subcontractor's claim concerning late delivery of the design which was in the custody of the employer. Even though the main contractor could have been aware that this might also trigger a dispute under the main contract, he might not want to serve a notice of dispute to the employer immediately after receiving the subcontractor's notice of dispute. For example, he might not want to spoil his relations with the employer at an early stage of the project or he might have been in possession of a sufficient float of time which would enable him to complete the works with no further costs and within the completion date. However, if the main contractor did not notify the employer of the related main contract dispute and did not refer that dispute to arbitration under the main contract, he could not rely on the subcontract multi-party arbitration clause to refer the subcontract dispute to the main contract arbitrator (because of the requirement that the main contract dispute should be one already referred to arbitration). The most likely outcome in this case would be the appointment of a subcontract arbitrator to deal with the subcontract dispute. However, this would not preclude the possibility of having multi-party arbitration if the employer decided to pursue the related main contract dispute at a later stage. After having lost the option to rely on the subcontract multi-party arbitration provision, the main contractor could invoke the main contract multi-party arbitration provision that allowed for a related main contract dispute to be referred to a subcontract arbitrator who had already been seized with the related subcontract dispute. Therefore, even though it seemed that there were some gaps in the JCT 80 provisions as regards the practical scenarios covered by these clauses, the latter actually covered a wide variety of situations. One of the few scenarios that were clearly excluded from the scope of application of the multi-party arbitration provisions were those where two pending arbitrators or tribunals had already been appointed under the contracts whereunder the related disputes had arisen – for example, where a main contract arbitrator had been appointed to review the main contract dispute and a subcontract arbitrator had been appointed to deal with the subcontract dispute. The appointment of an arbitrator under the contract where the respective multi-party arbitration clause was contained precluded either party bound by that contract from relying on the clause. Therefore, none of the multi-party arbitration provisions could be invoked in the scenario described above and the two arbitrations would proceed separately.

The application of the JCT 80 arbitration provisions was also likely to give rise to issues similar to those discussed in relation to the Blue Form. First, the JCT 80 multi-party arbitration clauses required the existence of a 'dispute or difference' under one of the contracts and a 'dispute' that had already been referred to an arbitrator under the other contract. However, as observed in Subsection 6.2.3.1, this wording was likely to exclude from the scope of application of the proviso cases where there was no pure dispute under one of the contracts, even though there was a need for multi-party arbitration. For example, a subcontractor's claim against the main contractor due to some employer's default (e.g. late delivery of drawings or a failure to provide timely access to the site) does not necessarily constitute a matter that is disputed by the main contractor if both the subcontractor and the main contractor agree that the fault lies with the employer. Secondly, the application of the JCT 80 multi-party arbitration clauses could result in situations where disputes arising under one agreement were referred to an arbitrator or an arbitral tribunal appointed under another contract in whose constitution the party not privy to the second contract did not participate. Thus, a subcontract dispute was to be referred to the main contract arbitrator or tribunal in whose appointment the subcontractor did not have a say. Similarly, the main contract dispute could be referred to a subcontract arbitrator or a tribunal in whose constitution the employer did not take part. This mechanism was likely to give rise to arguments of unequal treatment of the parties, which, in the light of the *Dutco* case, might result in the setting aside of the award or its non-recognition and non-enforcement. This issue has been discussed in detail in Subsection 6.2.3.4. Thirdly, the party that did not participate in the constitution of the tribunal was precluded from challenging the members of that tribunal on the grounds of alleged lack of impartiality or independence at the time of its composition, which was also likely to hamper the enforcement of the award. Generally, this party should always have the right to challenge the members of the tribunal at a later stage (i.e. once its dispute has been referred to that tribunal) either on the basis of the applicable arbitration rules or, if these rules are silent, on the basis of the applicable arbitration law. The replacement of an arbitrator as a result of a successful challenge could significantly delay the proceedings and change the contemplated multi-party arbitration regime under the JCT 80 contracts. Such a replacement was likely to deprive the party invoking the multi-party arbitration clause of one of its main benefits – that is, saving time and costs. This matter has been discussed in Subsection 6.2.3.5 above. Finally, the JCT 80 provisions were likely to result in parties' race to refer existing disputes to arbitration. More particularly, a party wishing to avoid multi-party arbitration had an incentive to give a prompt notice to its contractual counterparty that it intended to refer its dispute to arbitration and require from that party to concur in the appointment of an arbitrator. The appointment of an arbitrator in this case could be achieved within a relatively short period because of the default mechanism under the JCT 80 contracts, which provided that the person named in the contract was to appoint an arbitrator upon the parties' failure to agree on the appointment within a period of 14 days. Thus, the party that managed to ensure the appointment of an arbitrator in respect of a dispute was effectively allowed to block the possible referral of that same dispute to an arbitrator appointed under another contract. This outcome was supported by the reasoning in the *Trafalgar v. Railtrack* and *Higgs & Hill Building v. Campbell* (see Subsection 6.3.1.2 above). In this way, a subcontractor could try to ensure the appointment of a subcontract arbitrator in order to obstruct the main contractor's attempts to refer a subcontract dispute to an arbitrator appointed under the main contract.

6.3.3 New JCT approach

In 1998, the JCT introduced substantial amendments to the then-existing regime of multi-party arbitration. The multi-party arbitration provisions contained in JCT 80 and analysed in Subsections 6.3.1 and 6.3.2 above were deleted and replaced with a reference to the CIMAR[152]. The CIMAR address multi-party arbitration in Rule 3. Rules 3.1–3.6 of the CIMAR deal with disputes between the same parties under the same arbitration agreement and are therefore not relevant to the present discussion. Multi-party and multi-contact situations are covered under Rules 3.7–3.12. Rules 3.7–3.8 deal with concurrent hearing of related disputes and Rules 3.9–3.10 with consolidation of disputes. Both mechanisms can take place only if 'the same arbitrator is appointed in two or more related arbitral proceedings…each of which involves some common issue'. Such an arbitrator may order concurrent hearing of the proceedings or of some of the claims or issues arising in these proceedings[153]. The explicit consent of the parties is not required under the rules. The parties are deemed to have given their implied consent to the concurrent hearing by agreeing that the CIMAR will apply to the arbitral proceedings[154]. In concurrent hearing of disputes, the arbitrator is allowed to give such orders and directions as are necessary or desirable for the purpose of such a hearing[155]. However, a concurrent hearing of disputes does not constitute multi-party arbitration in the strict sense of the term. Each of the two proceedings remains distinct, which results in separate arbitral awards.

Pursuant to Rule 3.9:

> Where the same arbitrator is appointed in two or more arbitral proceedings each of which involves some common issue, whether or not involving the same parties, the arbitrator may, if all the parties so agree, order that any two or more such proceedings shall be consolidated.

If the arbitrator consolidates the proceedings, he is allowed to give any directions that he thinks appropriate for the purpose of these proceedings, and should issue a single award that is binding on all parties, unless the parties agree otherwise[156].

The new JCT approach is substantially different from the old self-contained multi-party arbitration regime under the JCT 80. Under the new approach, as regulated under the CIMAR, consolidation of related disputes requires the consent of all parties. However, the parties' consent to consolidation is not incorporated in the newer editions of the JCT suite. Thus, any party may veto the conduct of multi-party arbitration by withholding its consent. Furthermore, the new JCT regime applies only to the extent

---

[152] See, for example, Section 9B.6 of the JCT Nominated Sub-Contract Conditions NSC/C, as amended by Amendment 7: 1998, and Clause 11.2 of the JCT Employer/Nominated Sub-Contract Agreement NSC/W, as amended by Amendment 2: 1998.

[153] Rule 3.7 of JCT/CIMAR 2011.

[154] Peter Sheridan (1999) *Construction and Engineering Arbitration*, Sweet & Maxwell, London, pp. 320–321.

[155] Rule 3.8 of JCT/CIMAR 2011.

[156] Rule 3.10 of JCT/CIMAR 2011.

that the same arbitrator has been appointed in the related proceedings, which is in itself a significant limitation in the scope of application of the CIMAR consolidation provision. Having the same arbitrator in related proceedings involving different parties is not very common in construction projects. Therefore, this limitation will, in practice, result in the cases in which the power to consolidate is exercised being few in number[157]. The CIMAR make an attempt in tackling this problem in Rules 2.6–2.7. Under Rule 2.6, the authority appointing the arbitrators in the related arbitral proceedings based on different arbitration agreements should consider whether to appoint the same arbitrator in those proceedings. The appointment of the same arbitrator should be given preference, unless sufficient grounds exist for not doing so[158]. If the arbitrators have to be appointed by different persons, they have to consult with each other and, if an arbitrator has already been appointed in one proceeding, they should consider whether to appoint the same arbitrator in the other proceeding[159]. These clauses, which are uncommon for institutional arbitration rules, vest the appointing authority with a discretion (rather than an obligation) to appoint the same arbitrator in the related proceedings. If the authority refuses to appoint the same arbitrator, then the consolidation provision cannot be applied.

The reasons for the change in the JCT multi-party arbitration regime remain unclear. It has been suggested that one of these reasons appears to have been a desire for a uniform approach in the construction industry[160]. In the author's opinion, the new regime does little to solve problems pertaining to multi-party arbitrations. It does not go further than the statutory approach under the English Arbitration Act, pursuant to which consolidation of proceedings is possible only if the parties have agreed to confer on the arbitrator the power to consolidate (see Section 5.2). Therefore, the consolidation provision under the CIMAR has limited practical effect.

6.4 ACA standard forms

The UK Association of Consulting Architects ('**ACA**') has issued several standard forms for domestic use within the United Kingdom. These are the ACA Form of Building Agreement 1982 ('**ACA Main Contract**')[161] and the ACA Form of Sub-Contract 1982 ('**ACA Subcontract**')[162]. These two forms are intended to be applied in different scenarios, and they contain alternative clauses between which the parties may select the one(s) most appropriate to their relationship. Both contracts contain multi-party arbitration provisions which are briefly discussed below.

---

[157] John Marrin (2009) 'Multiparty Arbitration in the Construction Industry', in the Permanent Court of Arbitration (ed.) *Multiple Party Actions in International Arbitration*, Oxford University Press, New York, NY, p. 405.

[158] Rule 2.6 of JCT/CIMAR 2011.

[159] Rule 2.7 of JCT/CIMAR 2011.

[160] Peter Sheridan (1999) *Construction and Engineering Arbitration*, Sweet & Maxwell, London, p. 325.

[161] This contract is currently in its third edition, which was issued in 1998, last revised in 2003.

[162] This subcontract is also currently in its third edition, which was issued in 1998, last revised in 2003.

The ACA Main Contract arbitration clause contains the following proviso:

> Provided always that if, in the Employer's opinion, any dispute or difference to be referred to arbitration under this Agreement raises matters which are connected with matters raised in another dispute between the Contractor and any of his sub-contractors or suppliers and provided that such other dispute has not already been referred to an arbitrator, the Employer and the Contractor agree that such other dispute shall be referred to the arbitrator appointed under this Agreement and such arbitrator shall have power to deal with both such disputes as he thinks most just and convenient.[163]

Unlike other contractual clauses, such as the JCT 80 main contract provisions envisaging that the main contract dispute could be referred to an arbitrator appointed under another contract, the ACA Main Contract addresses the question from a different angle. Any multi-party arbitration under the clause is to be conducted under the main contract where the clause is contained. The clause incorporates the consent of the contracting parties that third parties with whom the main contractor has contracted with may be joined in the main contract arbitration under certain circumstances. It seems debatable whether the intended effect of the clause is to create true multi-party arbitration or some other form of dispute resolution[164]. In the author's opinion, however, the clause is broad enough to authorize the joinder of subcontractors or suppliers as formal parties in the main contract arbitration[165].

A novel approach in this clause is that its operation depends on the discretion of the employer. The clause may come into play if 'in the Employer's opinion' the main contract dispute or difference is related to matters in a subcontract and/or supply agreement. It seems open to discussion whether this approach is appropriate. The employer is usually not interested in multi-party arbitration with the participation of subcontractors and suppliers, which can be a disincentive for him to form an objective opinion. However, as explained in Subsection 3.4.1.1, the employer may be willing to arbitrate in a multi-party setting when it comes to subcontractors nominated by the employer or subcontractors and suppliers who have provided collateral warranties in favour of the employer. In addition, the employer is usually not a party to the subcontracts and the supply agreements, and therefore he is often not cognizant of the disputes arising under these agreements. Hence, it will be difficult for him (if at all possible) to form an opinion about whether these disputes are related to his disputes with the main contractor. In order to be able to form an opinion about such a link, the employer should be given a notification whenever disputes arise under the subcontracts or supply agreements concluded by the main contractor, together with some further information concerning the subject matter of these disputes.

---

[163] Clause 25.9 of Alternative 2 of the ACA Main Contract (2003 Revision).

[164] For example, it may be argued that the clause authorizes the conduct of two separate arbitrations by the same arbitrator who has to render separate awards on the disputes.

[165] This follows from the wide discretion granted to the main contract arbitrator who is empowered to deal with the two disputes 'as he thinks most just and convenient'.

Despite the above, some arguments in favour of this approach may also be found. As an assignor under the main contract, the employer is the party that is paying the contractual price and therefore he has a legitimate interest to determine the content of the contract and on that basis to invite bids from interested parties. Therefore, the employer may well want to maintain his discretion to decide whether to be involved in a multi-party arbitration at the time when the disputes arise. From that perspective, the clause in the ACA Main Contract may seem appealing to employers.

The multi-party arbitration provision under the ACA Subcontract is as follows:

> Provided always that if, in the Contractor's opinion, any dispute or difference to be referred to arbitration in accordance with Clause 15.8 raises issues which are substantially the same as or connected with issues raised in a related dispute between the Contractor and the Employer under the Agreement and an arbitrator has already been appointed to determine such related dispute, then the Contractor may elect by notice in writing to the Sub-Contractor to require that any dispute under this Sub-Contract shall be referred to the arbitrator appointed to determine the related dispute and if such arbitrator shall be willing so to act, such dispute under this Sub-Contract shall be referred so to him. In such event, the arbitrator shall have the power to make such directions and all necessary awards in the same way as if the procedure of the High Courts as to joining one or more defendants or co-defendants or third parties was available to the parties and to him[166].

Unlike the ACA Main Contract clause, here it is the main contractor who will decide whether there is a link between the main contract and the subcontract disputes. The subcontract clause requires that the main contract dispute has already been referred to a main contract arbitrator. In this way, the main contract and subcontract clauses deal with the same situation, i.e. how a subcontract dispute can be referred to an arbitrator who has already been appointed under the main contract[167]. The clauses read in conjunction with each other provide the consent of all three parties to their prospective participation in a multi-party arbitration. However, it is far from certain that such an arbitration will take place even if there is a link between the multi-contract disputes. If the main contractor notifies the subcontractor that the subcontract dispute should be referred to the main contract arbitrator, the employer may veto the contemplated joinder by refuting the existence of a link between the two disputes. Moreover, multi-party arbitration will not be possible if an arbitrator under the subcontract has already been appointed to deal with the subcontract dispute.

It should also be mentioned that the ACA has not published a standard form that governs the relations between contractors and suppliers. Therefore, multi-party arbitration

[166] Clause 15.9 of Alternative 2 of the ACA Subcontract (2003 Revision).

[167] However, it should be admitted that the main contract clause is not very precise in this aspect. At the beginning, the clause requires that the main contract dispute is one 'to be referred to arbitration', i.e. a dispute that has not yet been referred to arbitration. Later on, the clause specifies that the related disputes under the subcontract or the supply agreement 'shall be referred to the arbitration appointed under [the main contract]', which creates the impression that the main contract dispute has already been referred to arbitration. In the author's opinion, the second view should be adopted. It is also in compliance with the content of the subcontract clause.

with the participation of suppliers will only be possible if *ad hoc* clauses are included in the supply agreements providing for the suppliers' consent to be involved in such type of arbitration, or if the suppliers give their consent thereto in the course of the proceedings.

6.5 NEC3[168]

The NEC3 suite of contracts does not contain multi-party arbitration provisions. However, these contracts provide for joint adjudication of disputes arising under two or more contracts under certain circumstances. Among other international standard form agreements, the NEC3 is the first suite which addresses this question on a contractual level. Clauses addressing joint dispute adjudication can be found in the Engineering and Construction Contract ('**ECC**'), the Engineering and Construction Subcontract ('**ECS**') and the Professional Services Contract ('**PSC**')[169]. The presence of multi-party adjudication provisions is not a novelty in the NEC3. Provisions for joint adjudication of related disputes first appeared in the NEC3 predecessor, the NEC2[170].

Even though dispute adjudication is in principle outside the scope of this book, the NEC3 clauses on the matter have been discussed for several reasons. Despite the different nature of arbitration and adjudication, clauses for joint adjudication of related multi-contract disputes may serve as a useful source of inspiration when drafting multi-party arbitration clauses. Adjudication of multi-party and multi-contract disputes raises procedural challenges and questions that are largely similar to those observed in multi-party arbitrations. These include, *inter alia*, the timing for giving of notices, the party deciding on the link between the disputes justifying their joint review and the conduct of the decision maker. In addition, the rationale behind the institute of joint adjudication is the same as in multi-party arbitration. It aims to avoid inconsistent findings and also to reduce the time and costs involved in the resolution of disputes.

The major contracts within the NEC3 family contain two alternative dispute resolution procedures. The first is Option W1, which is drafted for use mostly in international projects where the governing law is not English law. Option 2 is intended for domestic projects in the United Kingdom where the process of adjudication is also regulated by statute[171]. The analysis below concerns the international use of NEC3 and is therefore confined only to Option W1.

In general, the dispute resolution procedure under NEC3 involves three main stages: a notification of a dispute, a referral of the dispute to an adjudicator and arbitration or litigation. The meaning of the word 'dispute' has caused much controversy both in the

[168] This Section 6.5 was first published in the article 'Joint Adjudication of Related Disputes under NEC3' in *10 Construction Law International*, no. 4 (2015), pp. 13–18, and is reproduced with permission from the International Bar Association, UK. © International Bar Association.

[169] Clause W1.3(4) of the ECC, clauses W1.3(4a) and W1.3(4b) of the ECS and the same clauses from the PSC.

[170] Clause 91.2 of the NEC2 Engineering and Construction Contract and the same clause of the NEC2 Professional Services Contract.

[171] Option W2 contains provisions that are in compliance with the 1996 Housing Grants, Construction and Regeneration Act.

United Kingdom and internationally (see Subsection 6.2.1.1). Nowadays, it is well established that the mere submission of a claim does not amount to a dispute. However, a claim that is not admitted by its addressee may qualify as a dispute[172]. Once a dispute has arisen, a notice of the dispute should be made to the other party within contractual timeframes. The position under NEC3 is that any dispute arising under or in connection with the contract in question should be referred to an adjudicator for a decision under that contract[173]. The adjudication stage is mandatory and cannot be bypassed by the parties[174]. In other words, only disputes submitted to adjudication may proceed to litigation or arbitration. A decision by an adjudicator becomes final and binding, unless either party notifies the other party that it is dissatisfied with the decision and refers the matter to arbitration or litigation.

6.5.1 Main contract provisions

Pursuant to clause W1.3(4) of the ECC:

> If a matter disputed by the Contractor under or in connection with a subcontract is also a matter disputed under or in connection with this contract and if the subcontract allows, the Contractor may refer the subcontract dispute to the Adjudicator at the same time as the main contract referral. The adjudicator then decides the disputes together and references to the Parties for the purposes of the dispute are interpreted as including the Subcontractor[175].

The clause requires the existence of two disputes (a subcontract dispute and a main-contract dispute) which the main contractor may refer to the adjudicator appointed under the main contract. The requirement for the existence of disputes under both contracts may appear to be problematic. There are cases where joint review might be needed even though there is no true dispute under one of the contracts[176]. An example in this regard has already been given in Subsection 6.2.3.1 above. A subcontractor's claim for additional payment and / or extension of time against the main contractor because of the late delivery of the design for which the employer is responsible does not necessarily result in a subcontract dispute if the main contractor does not challenge the subcontractor's claim. In this case, the main contractor will have an equivalent claim against the employer under the main contract. However, in order to ensure the joint adjudication of these two claims the main contractor will have to challenge the claim of the subcontractor

[172] The non-admittance of the claim may take different forms: an explicit rejection of the claim, a failure to reply to the claim within the contractually determined deadlines, etc. See Richard Anderson (2001) *Adjudication under the NEC*, Thomas Telford Publishing, London, pp. 51–54.

[173] Clause W1.1 of the ECC.

[174] See clause W1.3(2) and clause W1.4(2) of the ECC. Identical provisions can be found in the ECS and PSC.

[175] Reproduced with permission of the copyright holders of NEC3.

[176] See Humphrey Lloyd (1991) 'A National Experience', in P. Bellet, P. Bernardini, G. Bernini *et al.* (eds) *Multi-Party Arbitration: Views from International Arbitration Specialists*, Publication No. 480/1, ICC Publishing SA, Paris, pp. 66–67. The comments of the author concern multi-party arbitration but may well be applied to multi-party adjudication as well.

to ensure that a subcontract dispute arises and then claim the same remedy against the employer as the one that the subcontractor sought against the main contractor. Such an approach will be far from consistent, but the main contractor will have no other alternatives if he wants to have the same adjudicator deal with the two related claims.

The subcontract dispute under this clause is described as follows: 'a matter disputed by the Contractor under or in connection with a subcontract'. But what does 'disputed by the Contractor' mean? This wording is equivocal, giving rise to different interpretations. One possible interpretation is that the clause covers a main contractor's claim not admitted by the subcontractor in respect of which the main contractor has given a notification of a dispute to the subcontractor. Hence, this is a matter disputed under the subcontract by the main contractor. This could be, for example, a claim for delay damages against the subcontractor because of the subcontractor's failure to complete the works by the completion date[177], or a claim for defects not rectified by the subcontractor[178]. The main contractor has the right to refer the disputes that have arisen on the basis of these claims to adjudication in compliance with the terms under the adjudication table in clause W1.3 of the ECS – between two and four weeks after the notification of the dispute has been given to the subcontractor.

A second possible interpretation is that the clause has a wider scope of application, which can also cover subcontractor's claims against the main contractor. More particularly, these are subcontractors' claims whose existence and / or scope are disputed by the main contractor. For example, where the contractor has failed to provide access to the site[179] or to deliver the design for the subcontract works for which the employer was responsible[180]. The main contractor may reject these claims by arguing, among other things, that the delay in completion was not due to the events asserted by the contractor but the subcontractor's fault[181]. This will trigger a dispute between the parties, which can also be construed as a 'matter disputed by the Contractor' even though it is not based on a main contractor's claim.

If the second interpretation prevails, clause W1.3(4) of the ECC may be applied to a wide range of disputes under the subcontract regardless of which party made the claims. Some support for this interpretation may be found in the NEC3 Guidance Notes on the ECC, which refer to the existence of a subcontract dispute in rather broad terms[182]. However, there are also arguments against this second interpretation. First, the predecessor to clause W1.3(4), namely clause 91.2 of the NEC2 ECC, referred to the subcontract dispute as 'a matter disputed under or in connection with a subcontract'.

---

[177] Under the ECS, such a claim can be made under Option Clause X7.

[178] Such a claim will be based on clause 45 of the ECS.

[179] Clause 33.1 in relation to clause 60.1(2) of the ECS.

[180] Such a failure will constitute a compensation event under clause 60.1(3) of the ECS.

[181] In this case, the main contractor should notify the subcontractor under clause 61.4 of the ECS that there will be no changes in the subcontract price and the completion date.

[182] On clause W1.3(4) the Guidance Notes state: 'Where a dispute which affects work which has been subcontracted arises, and which may constitute a dispute between the Contractor and a Subcontractor as well between the Contractor and the Employer, there is a provision for the matter to be resolved between the three parties by the main contract adjudicator. This saves time and expense and prevents a dispute being dealt with by different adjudicators who may take different decisions.'

There was no reference to the contractor in this case, which created the impression that the clause could be applied to any subcontract dispute. It can be argued that by adding 'disputed by the Contractor', the drafters of NEC3 intended to deviate from the previous broad wording of the clause. Otherwise, the amended wording would add no further value if both the NEC2 and NEC3 clauses were intended to have the same meaning. Secondly, it has been argued by some authors that clause W1.3(4) of the ECC cannot be applied to disputes starting from the bottom of the contractual chain – disputes based on subcontractor's claims[183]. With regard to these disputes, it is the subcontractor who should serve a notification of a dispute under the ECS and refer the dispute to adjudication within the contractually prescribed terms. This seems to be at variance with clause W1.3(4), which envisages that the main contractor may refer the subcontract dispute to adjudication at the same time as the referral under the main contract. Such a simultaneous referral of the two disputes may take place only in cases where it is the same party referring the disputes to the adjudicator[184]. Therefore, it seems, according to these authors, that the clause may not be applied to disputes that should be referred to adjudication by the subcontractor.

It is questionable which of the two interpretations is correct. The first interpretation leaves many disputes based on subcontractors' claims outside the scope of clause W1.3(4) of the ECC. This is a matter of regret because the main contractor may well have an interest in joint adjudication of these disputes in order to avoid inconsistent findings concerning matters pertinent to both contracts. For example, disruption of the subcontract works that is attributable wholly or partially to the employer will result in a subcontract dispute (based on a subcontractor's claim against the main contractor) and a main contract dispute (based on an equivalent claim of the main contractor against the employer). The contractor will try to refer both disputes to a single adjudicator in order to avoid a situation where he is to pay the subcontractor without being able to pass on this payment to the employer. However, he cannot do so if the first interpretation prevails. It is true that the main contractor may bring the matter further before a judge or an arbitral tribunal if he is dissatisfied with the decisions of the adjudicators. However, it will be in the interest of the main contractor to avoid any risk of inconsistent findings in the dispute resolution process as early as possible.

6.5.2 Subcontract provisions

Clause W.1.3(4) of the ECC only operates to the extent the 'subcontract allows' so. The ECS contains two clauses dealing with joint adjudication. The first is clause W1.3(4a), which, apart from the references to the parties, reiterates clause W1.3(4) of the ECC. The main difference is that clause W1.3(4a) applies to disputes that are one step further down in the contractual chain – that is, it envisages joint review of sub-subcontract disputes

---

[183] Brian Eggleston (2015) *The NEC3 Engineering and Construction Contract, A Commentary*, 2nd edn, Wiley Blackwell, Chichester, p. 325.

[184] Ibid.

with subcontract disputes[185]. It is clause W1.3(4b), which is intended to be applied in conjunction with clause W1.3(4) of the ECC. Pursuant to clause W1.3(4b):

> Within two weeks of the notification of the dispute by the Subcontractor to the Contractor, the Contractor notifies the Subcontractor if the matter disputed is a matter disputed under or in connection with the main contract.
> The Contractor may then:
> Submit the subcontract dispute to the main contract Adjudicator at the same time as the main contract submission and
> Instruct the Subcontractor to provide any information which the Contractor may require.
> The main contract Adjudicator then decides the disputes together[186].

Broadly, once the contractor is notified of a subcontract dispute, he has two weeks to decide whether the dispute in question is related to a main contract dispute. If so, the main contractor may request that the subcontract dispute be referred to the main contract adjudicator for a decision together with the main contract dispute. The same clause is also contained in the PSC and applies in cases where the PSC is used as a subcontract[187].

It should be stressed that clause W1.3(4b) concerns only disputes that are notified by the subcontractor. According to the adjudication table in clause W1.3(1) of the ECS, these disputes are related, *inter alia*, to actions or inactions of the contractor. These disputes could concern, for example, a subcontractor's claim due to the main contractor's failure to provide access to the site or to deliver the design on the basis of which the subcontract works are to be performed. Clause W1.3(4b) of the ECS does not address disputes that are to be notified by the main contractor to the subcontractor. These are disputes arising from the main contractor's claims against the subcontractor, for example for defects in the subcontractor's works.

6.5.3 Do NEC3 provisions create a self-contained mechanism for joint adjudication?

A self-contained mechanism for joint adjudication would be one where the respective contractual provisions can be put into operation without the need to obtain the *ad hoc* parties' consent for the application of these provisions. The above analysis shows that the ECC deals with disputes arising out of main contractors' claims against a subcontractor, and, if the second interpretation is to be followed, also with the subcontractors' claims disputed by the main contractor. Alternatively, the subcontract only addresses the latter category of disputes. This discrepancy may cause severe obstacles to the operation of the joint adjudication clauses. Like multi-party arbitration, multi-party adjudication

---

[185] A similar clause is to be found also in the PSC. Clause W1.3(4a) thereunder deals with the joint review of disputes under a subcontract (to which the consultant is a party) and the agreement between the employer and the consultant.

[186] Reproduced with permission by the copyright holders of NEC3.

[187] For example, the main contractor subcontracts the design work (which he is to procure under the main contract) to a designer under the terms of PSC. See clause W1.3(4b) of the PSC.

requires the consent of all parties. However, is this consent contained in the NEC3 provisions discussed above? In the author's opinion, this question should be answered in the negative. In order to explain this position, the author has analysed the application of the abovementioned clauses in two situations that typically necessitate joint review of related disputes from the point of view of the contractor. The first situation concerns a main contract dispute based on an employer's claim against the main contractor for defects in the subcontractor's works. The second situation concerns subcontract disputes arising under a subcontractor's claim against the main contractor due to the late delivery of the design for the works.

In the first case, the main contract dispute will trigger a related subcontract dispute under the subcontract where the main contractor will claim against the subcontractor. The subcontract dispute may either precede or follow in time the main contract dispute. The main contractor will likely require the joint review of the disputes by the main contract adjudicator on the basis of the provisions contained in the ECC and the ECS. As mentioned, clause W1.3(4) of the ECC covers the type of dispute discussed, and therefore the employer's consent for the joint review of the disputes is in fact incorporated in this clause. The main contractors' notice to the subcontractor for the joint adjudication is to be given under the terms of clause W1.3(4b) of the subcontract. However, the latter clause does not explicitly address disputes based on main contractor's claims towards the subcontractor. Therefore, the subcontractor may argue that his consent for the joint review of the disputes is not contained in the ECS, and respectively that his *ad hoc* consent for such a joint review should be obtained.

In the second situation, the subcontractor notifies the main contractor about a subcontract dispute due to the late delivery of drawings. Under the subcontract, it is the contractor that should provide the drawings but the procurement obligation and delivery may ultimately rest with the employer under the main contract. The subcontract dispute will most likely result in a main contract dispute based on the main contractor's claim towards the employer. The main contractor's attempt to ensure joint adjudication of the two disputes in this case will give rise to issues similar to the ones described in the previous paragraph. Even though the subcontract dispute in question falls within the scope of clause W1.3(4b) of the ECS, it is rather doubtful whether this dispute falls within the ambit of the corresponding clause of the main contract, which is subject to different interpretations. If the employer is not interested in joint adjudication of disputes with the participation of subcontractors, he may assert that the first interpretation of clause W1.3(4) of the ECC should be followed, that is, that the clause only covers disputes originating from main contractors' claims against the subcontractor. Since the subcontract dispute discussed here is different, it follows that the employer's consent for a joint adjudication is not contained in the main contract. Hence, the joint adjudication will require the employer's *ad hoc* consent.

Thus, depending on the specific situation either the subcontractor or the employer may block the operation of the clauses for joint adjudication of multi-contract disputes. An argument may be put forward that the withholding of the consent of the party opposing the joint adjudication might be at variance with the parties' duty of co-operation under the NEC3. It is true that under clause 10.1 of ECC the parties are obliged to act 'in a spirit of mutual trust and co-operation'. It has also been stated that this clause may be inferred to apply also with regard to the dispute resolution provisions[188]. However, it is rather doubtful that a party's refusal to give its *ad hoc* consent for joint adjudication may be measured against an obligation to co-operate. First of all, a party's decision to withhold its consent may not be construed as a breach under the contract because it rests on the wording of the joint adjudication provisions. In the author's opinion, by refusing to give its consent the party is pursuing its legitimate interests under its contract to adjudicate its disputes, to the extent these disputes fall outside the scope of the joint adjudication clauses in the contract, with the participation of its counterparty only. Furthermore, even if a party's decision to withhold its consent to participate in multi-party adjudication were to be interpreted as incompliant with the general obligation to co-operate under NEC3, further uncertainties would arise as regards the particular remedy which could be claimed as a result of that breach. In any case, such remedy, if available at all, would not be sufficient to overcome the lack of party's consent to multi-party adjudication.

6.5.4 Compatibility between the joint adjudication provisions and the dispute notification requirements

Another issue that may arise as regards the operation of the multi-party adjudication clauses relates to the timing within which the notifications for the disputes should be given and the referrals to adjudication should be made. A party's failure to notify a dispute or to refer a notified dispute to adjudication within the contractually prescribed terms will generally preclude that party's rights to pursue the dispute further[189]. Thus, for example, under the adjudication table under the ECC the contractor has to notify any disputes about an action or inaction of the project manager or the supervisor within four weeks after the contractor became aware of the action or inaction. The subcontractor has the same obligations under the ECS when it comes to actions or inactions of the main contractor. When it comes to other matters, there is no deadline for a notification to be made. In all cases, however, once a notification has been made, a separate deadline for the referral of the notified dispute to adjudication starts to run. Such a referral should be made between two and four weeks following the notification of the dispute. The three main contracts within the NEC3 suite – the ECC, ECS and PSC – have adjudication tables containing identical periods of time within which a notification of a dispute, and respectively, a referral to adjudication should be made. In the author's opinion, these identical contractual deadlines do not sufficiently accommodate cases where joint adjudication of disputes has been requested.

The issues that arise in this regard can be illustrated with the two types of disputes discussed in Subsection 6.5.3 above. In the first case, the employer serves a notification of a dispute to the main contractor relating to defects discovered in the subcontract

---

[188] Richard Anderson (2001) *Adjudication under the NEC*, Thomas Telford Publishing, London, p. 43.

[189] Pursuant to clause W1.3(2) of the ECC, last sentence, neither party may refer a dispute to adjudication or arbitration, unless such a dispute has been notified within the contractual time limits. Identical clauses can be found in the ECS and the PSC.

works. Then, the employer has to refer the dispute to adjudication between 2 and 4 weeks after the dispute notification date, otherwise his claim will be time barred. On receiving the notification, the main contractor will have to decide whether the main contract dispute is related to a subcontract dispute. The main contractor will have to notify the subcontractor about the dispute under the main contract. The subcontractor may, for example, admit that there are indeed defects and undertake the obligation to rectify them within the correction notification period[190]. In this context, it would not be commercially viable to adjudicate the main contract dispute given the subcontractor's commitment to rectify the defects. However, what if the subcontractor changes his mind later on and refuses to rectify the defects because he denies their existence? This will definitely trigger a dispute under the subcontract that is related to the main contract dispute previously notified by the employer. However, at that later stage the deadline for referral of the main contract dispute to adjudication – four weeks as of the dispute notification date – will have expired already. This will have two consequences. First, the employer will lose his right to refer the dispute to adjudication, and also to litigation or arbitration. Second, joint adjudication of the related disputes will be time barred under the main contract. This example illustrates that the presence of identical time-bar clauses in the adjudication tables under the related contracts is not appropriate when it comes to disputes that should be adjudicated jointly. In the above example, it would have been more logical if the main contract had provided for a longer deadline for referral to adjudication in order to take into account the progress on the related matter under the subcontract.

Similar issues may arise in the context of disputes starting from the bottom of the contractual chain, namely, disputes based on subcontractor's claims, which may result in related main contract disputes. If the subcontractor serves a dispute notification to the main contractor because of the late delivery of the design, the subcontractor will have to refer this dispute to adjudication within 2 and 4 weeks of the dispute notification date. Then, under clause W1.3(4b) of the ECS, the main contractor will have two weeks to notify the subcontractor as to whether the matter is also disputed under the main contract. Assuming that the main contractor notifies the subcontractor at the end of the 2-week period that there is a related dispute under the main contract, the main contractor will have to wait at least 2 weeks before being able to refer the related disputes to the adjudicator under the main contract. Thus, the subcontract deadline for referral of the subcontract dispute to subcontract adjudication will already have expired at the time when the main contractor becomes entitled to refer the main contract dispute to adjudication. What if the main contractor does not refer the subcontract dispute to adjudication under the main contract despite his notice to the subcontractor that the two disputes are related?[191] The literal wording of clause W1.3(4b) of the ECS creates the impression that the main contractor has the option (but not the obligation) to make such a referral to joint adjudication[192]. The logical outcome in this case seems to be that the

[190] This is commonly set to 2 weeks from the completion date.

[191] The main contractor may decide not to refer the dispute because, for example, he has reached a settlement with the employer within the 2-week grace period before the referral to the adjudicator.

[192] Clause W1.3(4b) of the ECS uses the word 'may' instead of 'shall' when it comes to the referral of the subcontract dispute to an adjudicator.

subcontractor will still be allowed to refer his dispute to the subcontract adjudicator regardless of the lapse of the contractually determined period. The subcontract, however, does not address such a scenario.

The above analysis reveals that the NEC3 contracts do not provide a self-contained mechanism for adjudication of multi-party disputes arising under several contracts[193]. The application of these clauses will often require the *ad hoc* consent of one of the parties, which hinders their useful operation. Some of the NEC3 clauses on joint adjudication are ambiguous, which gives rise to difficulties in their interpretation and application. In addition, the contractual deadlines for notification of disputes and their referral to adjudication often fail to take into account situations where joint adjudication of related disputes may be needed. Therefore, the drafters of the NEC3 should reconsider the current wording of these contractual provisions. They may also consider whether to go one step further and to introduce multi-party arbitration provisions in the next edition of the contracts. Even though the mechanism of joint adjudication of related disputes is, in principle, capable of removing the risk of inconsistent findings pertaining to separate adjudications, the overall benefit of such a mechanism will be significantly decreased if the disputes subject to adjudication proceed to the next level of the dispute resolution process, namely arbitration[194]. There the related disputes will be reviewed in separate arbitrations, which would bring the risk of inconsistent findings and the other drawbacks pertaining to the running of parallel arbitrations to the fore.

6.6 IChemE contracts

The International IChemE Subcontract, which can be used in conjunction with all international main contract forms published by IChemE, contains a clause dealing with main contract disputes related to the subcontract. Sub-clause 46.1 provides that the subcontractor should assist the contractor in the preparation and submission of information in support of main contract claims touching or concerning matters under the subcontract. Sub-clause 46.2 contains a multi-party arbitration clause with the following wording:

> In the event that any dispute arising between the Contractor and the Subcontractor which is referable to arbitration is substantially the same as a dispute arising or which has arisen between the Contractor and the Purchaser (and / or the Project Manager) and which is also referable to arbitration under the Main Contract, then, subject to an arbitrator not having been appointed under the Subcontract, the Contractor shall be entitled to require the Subcontractor to be joined as a party to such reference and such Subcontract dispute shall be referred to the arbitral tribunal appointed or to be appointed pursuant to the provisions of the Main Contract[195].

[193] Dimitar Hristoforov Kondev, 'Joint Adjudication of Related Disputes under NEC3', in *10 Construction Law International*, no. 4 (2015), pp. 16–17.
[194] Ibid., p. 18.
[195] Reproduced with permission by the IChemE.

There are certain similarities between this clause and the JCT 80 subcontract multi-party arbitration provisions. First, the requirement for the existence of two disputes under the subcontract and the main contract, which are 'substantially the same' is the same. Secondly, the IChemE clause may not be applied if a subcontract arbitrator has been appointed. Even though this was not explicitly stated in the JCT 80 clauses, the same condition applied there as well. The main difference concerns the referral of the main contract dispute to arbitration. The JCT 80 subcontract provisions required that the main contract dispute should have already been referred to arbitration but no such requirement is introduced under the IChemE Subcontract. In that regard, the IChemE approach is similar to that under clause 18C(4)(d) of the Blue Form (see Subsection 6.2.6).

It should be mentioned that the term 'dispute' has a special meaning under the IChemE Contracts[196]. In this aspect, the IChemE Contracts resemble the approach under the FIDIC Conditions (see Subsection 6.2.1.1). Under the international IChemE main forms of contract, if a party is dissatisfied with any matter under the contract it should first refer that matter for a decision to the project manager appointed under the contract[197]. The project manager should notify the parties of his decision within 28 days as of the date of the referral. It is only when the project manager fails to give his decision within the prescribed term or his decision is unacceptable to either party or has not been implemented within 21 days, when either party is allowed to serve a notice of dispute[198]. Therefore, the existence of a 'dispute' presupposes a prior referral of the matter to the project manager and the serving of a notice of dispute by the aggrieved party. Identical clauses are contained in the IChemE Subcontract[199]. However, the existence of disputes is not sufficient for the operation of the subcontract multi-party arbitration clause. The latter requires that the disputes are 'referable to arbitration'. Pursuant to clause 44.6 of the IChemE main forms of contract, the parties should make a good-faith attempt to negotiate a settlement of the dispute as a precondition to its referral to arbitration. This also follows from the arbitration clauses in the IChemE contracts, which stipulate that 'any dispute which has not been settled' will be referred to arbitration.

Therefore, it can be summarized that the multi-party arbitration clause requires the existence of disputes in respect of which three main steps have been pursued:

- a referral for a decision has been served to the project manager;
- a notice of dispute has been given following the project manager's decision or his failure to give a decision; and
- an attempt for settlement of the dispute has been made.

The multi-party arbitration clause uses different wording in respect of the timing of occurrence of the disputes. While the subcontract dispute should be 'arising' under the contract, the main contract dispute is one that is 'arising or which has arisen'. Thus, it is clear that a main contract dispute may arise prior to a related subcontract dispute. But is

[196] See last sentence of clause 44.3 of the international IChemE main forms of contract.

[197] Clause 44.3 of the international IChemE main forms of contract.

[198] Clause 44.4 of the IChemE international main forms of contract.

[199] Clauses 44.3 and 44.4 of the IChemE International Subcontract. Under the subcontract, the role of the project manager is performed by a contract manager.

the opposite also true? Does the clause cover cases where the main contract disputes follow in time the related subcontract disputes? For example, the subcontractor serves a notice of dispute to the main contractor for a reason attributable to the employer, and then the main contractor decides to invoke the main contract dispute resolution provisions in order to serve a notice of dispute to the employer. It is hard to give an unequivocal answer to this question. A strict interpretation of the wording of the clause may create the impression that the clause may not be applied to main contract disputes that have arisen after the related subcontract disputes. Even if it is assumed that the clause covers these disputes as well, the main contractor will have very limited time to put the main contract dispute resolution provisions in motion in order to invoke the subcontract multi-party arbitration clause. If the subcontractor refers the dispute to arbitration, he will be able to ensure the appointment of a subcontract arbitrator within a relatively short period[200]. Once such an arbitrator is appointed, the multi-party arbitration clause may not be applied. Therefore, if the main contractor wants to invoke the clause, he may not just wait for the subcontractor's claims or notices of disputes in order to decide whether to pursue the dispute resolution mechanisms under the main contract. If he does so, he will probably lose his right to rely on the clause because it would take him longer to ensure the existence of a main contract dispute that is 'referable to arbitration' than the time that the subcontractor would need to ensure the appointment of a subcontract arbitrator. It follows from here that the main contractor will have to pursue promptly all his claims against the employer and serve notices of disputes in respect of these claims in order to retain his right to invoke the multi-party arbitration clause. It might be argued whether this is an appropriate approach. Sometimes the main contractor will prefer to postpone his decision to serve a notice of dispute against the employer for several reasons. He might, for example, not want to spoil his relations with the employer, especially when it comes to claims of small value.

The clause does not envisage any period within which the main contractor should refer the main contract dispute to arbitration. However, having in mind the decision in *Lafarge Redlands Aggregate v. Shephard Hill*, which dealt with a similar question, it may be concluded that the main contractor should do so within a reasonable period of time[201]. Furthermore, the main contractor does not have an incentive to procrastinate the process because, in the meantime, the subcontractor may succeed in ensuring the appointment of a subcontract arbitrator, which will block the operation of the clause.

Like the multi-party arbitration clause in the Blue Form, the main obstacle to the operation of the IChemE Subcontract clause is that there is no equivalent clause in the IChemE main contracts. This raises the question of whether the joinder envisaged under the subcontract could take place on the basis of the arbitration rules applicable to the

---

[200] Unlike the default clauses of the IChemE main contracts, which envisage that the disputes will be reviewed by a three-member tribunal, clause 45.1 of the IChemE Subcontract stipulates that subcontract disputes are to be reviewed by a sole arbitrator. Pursuant to clause 45.2, if the parties are unable to agree on an arbitrator within one month, either party may request from the President of the IChemE to appoint the arbitrator. Pursuant to the arbitration rules applicable to the contract, the default appointment should normally be made within 28 days.

[201] See *Lafarge Redlands Aggregates Ltd (Formerly Redland Aggregates Ltd) v. Shephard Hill Civil Engineering Ltd*, and Subsection 6.2.1.3.

disputes. Under both the IChemE Subcontract and main contracts, any arbitration shall be conducted in accordance with the Arbitration Rules published by the IChemE ('**IChemE Rules**')[202]. However, the IChemE Rules do not address the type of joinder contemplated in the subcontract multi-party arbitration clause. Rule 9 deals with the joint review of disputes but not in the form of a formal joinder but of concurrent hearing of the two disputes[203]. Concurrent hearings under the IChemE Rules will be possible either with the agreement of all parties or upon the request of the party that is bound by all the contracts (i.e. the main contractor). Unlike multi-party arbitration, the concurrent hearing of disputes normally results in the issuance of separate arbitral awards[204]. Therefore, the joinder mechanism envisaged under the IChemE Subcontract may not be put into operation, unless the employer gives his *ad hoc* consent thereto.

Several other issues may be pointed out. These have already been commented on with regard to multi-party arbitration clauses already discussed, and therefore they will be reiterated here without further discussion. These include: the inability of the subcontractor to participate in the appointment of the main contract arbitrator or tribunal and to raise challenges concerning the alleged lack of impartiality or independence of the arbitrator or the members of the tribunal (see Subsections 6.2.3.4 and 6.2.3.5). Furthermore, the requirement for the existence of two disputes might leave certain situations where multi-party arbitration may be needed outside the scope of application of the discussed clause (see Subsection 6.2.3.1). Finally, the multi-party arbitration clause might cause a subcontractor's race to refer his disputes to arbitration because the clause may not be operated once a subcontract arbitrator has been appointed (see Subsection 6.2.3.7).

Except for the International IChemE Subcontract, none of the other IChemE forms addresses multi-party arbitration. The Professional Services Contract – Short Form Agreement does not contain a multi-party arbitration clause. The Professional Services Contract – Long Form Agreement is still in the process of drafting and is expected to be released in 2017. It has been stated by the IChemE that the drafting committee will discuss the question of inclusion of a joinder clause in the latter contract but that it is unlikely that such a clause will be adopted[205].

6.7 *ICC contracts*[206]

The ICC contracts contain multi-tier dispute resolution provisions, which are similar to the ones under the FIDIC Conditions of Contract. Thus, under the ICC Turnkey Contract, any disputes should be first referred to a combined dispute board, which,

---

[202] These rules are known as the IChemE Pink Book. They are currently in their fourth edition, which was published in 2005.

[203] The Guidance on compiling the Particular Conditions, which is attached to the IChemE main contracts, wrongly refers to Rule 9 as a joinder clause.

[204] Under Rule 9.1 of the IChemE Rules, separate awards shall be rendered, unless all the parties agree otherwise. However, the arbitrator may decide to prepare one combined set of reasons to cover all the awards.

[205] This information was communicated to the author by the IChemE in an e-mail dated 17 November 2015.

[206] The ICC Contracts are published by the International Chamber of Commerce in Paris. Please see Subsection 3.2.3 hereof for a brief description of these contracts.

depending on the circumstances of the case, may issue either a recommendation or a decision[207]. If a party expresses its dissatisfaction with the recommendation or the decision, as the case may be, or if the combined dispute board fails to issue a recommendation or a decision, then either party may refer the dispute for final resolution to arbitration under the ICC Rules[208]. The ICC Turnkey Contract does not say anything about multi-party arbitration.

The ICC Subcontract, which is to be used in conjunction with the ICC Turnkey Contract, contains two options for dispute resolution. The first is largely similar to the procedure under the ICC Turnkey Contract[209]. Under the second option, the function of a dispute board is replaced with the requirement for a meeting between representatives of the parties who are competent to resolve the dispute[210]. As in the ICC Turnkey Contract, any arbitral proceedings are subject to the ICC Rules.

The ICC Subcontract contains certain provisions that regulate the interface between main contract disputes and the subcontract works. On the one hand, the main contractor may request the subcontractor's assistance in case of a main contract dispute that is related to the subcontractor's works or the subcontractor's rights[211]. Such assistance may take difference forms, for example, provision of documents, participation as a witness and so forth. On the other hand, if the main contractor has received some extensions of time or additional payments, which also concern the subcontractor's works or rights, then he should share these benefits with the subcontractor to the extent they accrue to the latter[212]. The ICC Subcontract is also silent on multi-party arbitration. As already analysed in Section 4.1, multi-party arbitration will not be possible on the basis of the provisions in the ICC Rules, unless the parties consent to it on an *ad hoc* basis.

6.8 PPC and SPC International

As mentioned in Subsection 3.2.6, PPC International is a form of partnering contract that tries to join all major participants in construction projects, such as the employer, the main contractor, the different consultants and specialists, into a single document as partnering team members. The consultant appears as a defined term under the PPC International. The consultant is usually the designer of the project hired by the employer but can also be a person or an entity providing other services to the employer[213]. The

[207] Clauses 66.2 and 66.3 of the ICC Turnkey Contract. The ICC Dispute Board Rules shall apply to disputes referred to the board. However, under clause 67.6 a dispute that has arisen after the taking over of the works may be referred directly to arbitration.

[208] Clause 66.5 of the ICC Turnkey Contract.

[209] Option A in clause 66.3 of the ICC Subcontract.

[210] Option B in clause 66.4 of the ICC Subcontract.

[211] Clause 67.8 of the ICC Subcontract.

[212] Ibid.

[213] Pursuant to Appendix 1 to PPC International, the consultant is defined as a party that provides services (including design services) in relation to the project.

specialist is also a defined term that commonly covers subcontractors and suppliers hired by the main contractor[214].

The dispute avoidance and resolutions provisions in the PPC International involve a multi-tier procedure, the final step of which is either litigation or arbitration, with litigation being the default option[215]. If arbitration is selected, the arbitral proceedings shall be conducted in accordance with Part 2 of Appendix 5 which contains the following provision:

> If, in the opinion of any Partnering Team member in dispute, any difference or dispute to be referred to arbitration under the Partnering Terms raises matters which are connected with matters raised in another difference or dispute between the same and / or other Partnering Team members already referred to arbitration under the Partnering Terms, the Partnering Term Members in dispute shall arrange for their difference or dispute to be referred to the arbitrator first appointed and such arbitrator shall have the power to deal with all such connected differences or disputes as he or she thinks most just and conventional[216].

The clause does not explicitly mention multi-party arbitration but is formulated in broad terms, which could allow the joinder of a third party to existing arbitration[217]. The temporal preconditions for the operation of the clause are relatively clear. There should be a dispute that is not yet referred to arbitration (this follows from the phrase 'to be referred to arbitration') and another dispute that has already been referred to arbitration. In this aspect, the approach resembles the one under the JCT 80 contracts (discussed in Subsection 6.3.1).

The exact form of the multi-party arbitration depends on the way the contractual relations are structured. Two situations should be distinguished. In the first case, all the participants in the construction project, including the specialists contracted under the SPC International, are bound by the terms of PPC International. The purpose of the partnering agreement is to join all the parties in a single document. Normally, all the construction participants known at the time of execution of the PPC International should sign this document. However, there may be other parties, such as subcontractors and suppliers, who are hired by the contractor under the terms of the SPC International after the date of execution of the PPC International. There is a commitment for these other parties to sign a joining agreement and thus become partnering team members bound by the terms of the PPC International[218]. If they have done so and arbitration is the preferred option under the PPC International, the arbitral proceedings among all

---

[214] In Appendix 1 to PPC International, the specialist is defined as a party providing works, services or supplies to the contractor. It follows from this broad definition that a designer can also be considered as a specialist if he is hired by the contractor to provide design services in relation to the project.

[215] Clause 27.6 of the PPC2000 Partnering Terms.

[216] Paragraph 2 of Appendix 5, Part 2, of PPC International.

[217] John Marrin (2009) 'Multiparty Arbitration in the Construction Industry', in the Permanent Court of Arbitration (ed.) *Multiple Party Actions in International Arbitration*, Oxford University Press, New York, NY, p. 403.

[218] Clause 1.2 of the SPC 2000 Specialist Agreement.

multiple parties shall be conducted in accordance with the above quoted clause[219]. The conduct of multi-party arbitration in this case should be possible on the basis of the multi-party arbitration provision in the PPC, which is binding on all parties. Issues related to parties' consent to multi-party arbitration are unlikely to arise in this case, because all the parties have agreed in advance that they may be involved in multi-party arbitration by signing the PPC International. The exact procedural requirements relating to the joinder will depend on the applicable arbitration rules.

The second situation comprises those cases where the subcontractors and / or suppliers hired by the contractor under the terms of SPC International have not acceded to the PPC International. In this case, the multi-party arbitration provision in the PPC International cannot be invoked against these parties. A provision with a similar content is contained in the SPC International but it only concerns related disputes arising between the same contractual parties, i.e. between the main contractor and the respective specialist[220]. The clause does not deal with SPC disputes that are related to the PPC International or to another subcontract or supply agreement. Therefore, multi-contract arbitration in respect of related disputes arising under the PPC International and the SPC International will generally not be possible in this second case.

6.9 ENAA Model forms

The third edition of the ENAA Process Plant Model addresses multi-party arbitration. The Guide Notes to this contract suggest that the parties may regulate multi-party arbitrations in two ways: by way of an arbitral protocol to which all parties that might be involved in these proceedings should adhere or by inserting multi-party arbitration clauses in the separate bilateral agreements. For this second approach, the Guide Notes propose two draft multi-party arbitration clauses that can be used by the parties[221]. The first provision is drafted for use with a main contract and the second one with a subcontract or a supply agreement. The draft clauses are reproduced in full in Appendix 3 towards the end of this book. Before analysing these provisions, it should be reiterated that these provisions are just drafts. They do not have any legal effect, unless the relevant parties decide to incorporate them in their contracts.

The draft multi-party arbitration clauses provide for a mechanism where a dispute or difference arising under a subcontract or a supply agreement which is related to a main contract dispute or difference can be referred for a decision to an arbitral tribunal constituted or to be constituted under the main contract. On this aspect, the mechanism reminds the reader of some of the contractual solutions under the Blue Form (discussed in Section 6.2), the ACA standard forms (Section 6.4) and the IChemE Contracts (Section 6.6). Accordingly, this approach raises similar issues related to the unequal treatment of the subcontractor in the constitution of the main contract arbitral tribunal

[219] See also Clause 27.1 of the SPC 2000, Specialist Terms.

[220] Paragraph 2 of Appendix 4, Part 2 of SPC International.

[221] The draft clauses are contained in the Attachment 'Draft Joinder Clauses for Multi-Party Arbitration' to the Guide Notes, pp. 73–75.

and the subcontractor's inability to raise objections at the time of appointment of the main contract arbitrators on the ground of their alleged lack of impartiality or independence. These problems have already been discussed in Subsections 6.2.3.4 and 6.2.3.5.

The scope of the multi-party arbitration clauses is very broad and encompasses a wide range of scenarios for the reasons mentioned below. First, the clauses aim to cover not only 'disputes' arising under the main contract and the subcontract but also 'differences'. This allows the clauses to be applied to cases where there is a difference in the parties' positions on certain matters but no formal dispute has arisen yet. However, this differentiation seems to be of little practical significance since the ENNA Process Plant Model refers to 'disputes' and 'differences' interchangeably throughout the different provisions and unlike other forms, such as FIDIC Conditions of Contract and the IChemE Contracts, does not ascribe any special meaning to the word 'dispute'. Secondly, the link between the related disputes or differences that justifies their joint review is also determined in a very broad way. The issues raised in the main contract dispute or difference should be 'substantially the same as, or connected with, or touch upon, or concern' issues raised in the related subcontract dispute or difference, or the main contract dispute or difference should 'arise out of, or touch upon, or concern substantially the same facts' as the ones subject to the subcontract dispute or difference[222]. Thirdly, the draft clauses may be operated regardless of the sequence in which the related disputes or differences have arisen and regardless of whether and when these disputes have been referred to arbitration. In other words, it does not matter which of the two disputes has arisen first in time. Likewise, it does not matter whether the main contract dispute or the subcontract dispute has already been referred to arbitration under the main contract, respectively the subcontract.

Notwithstanding the abovementioned resemblance to other forms envisaging referral of subcontract disputes to main contract arbitration, the approach under the ENAA Process Plant Model is novel when it comes to the appointment of a subcontract arbitrator under the subcontract. Would the appointment of such an arbitrator preclude the referral of the subcontract dispute, which is related to the main contract, to a main contract arbitrator or a tribunal? The contractual solutions discussed so far have addressed this question in divergent ways. Under an earlier edition of the Blue Form[223], the multi-party arbitration clause could only be put into operation if a subcontract arbitrator had not yet been agreed or appointed. The same approach can be found in the International IChemE Subcontract. Later editions of the Blue Form removed this precondition, which left the impression that a subcontract dispute may be referred to a main contract arbitrator or arbitrators even if a subcontract arbitrator had already been appointed to deal with the same dispute[224]. However, these contracts did not envisage any mechanism for the revocation of the authority of the subcontract arbitrator in these cases. This created uncertainty and a risk that both arbitrations may proceed and end up with two separate

---

[222] Draft clause GC 6.1.6, letters (a) and (b) and sub-clause 2.1, items (i) and (ii) from Appendix 10, both clauses from Attachment 'Draft Joinder Clauses for Multi-Party Arbitration' to the Guide Notes.

[223] Clause 18(2) of the 1984 Blue Form.

[224] Clause 18(8) of the 1991 Blue Form and clause 18C(4) of the 2008 Blue Form. An analysis of the Blue Form multi-party arbitration provisions can be found in Section 6.2.

awards on the same subcontract dispute. The ENAA Process Plant Model goes a step further in comparison with other standard forms. The draft subcontract multi-party arbitration clause explicitly stipulates that the subcontract arbitrator's authority will be revoked[225]. For that purpose, the contractor's notice that the subcontract dispute should be referred to the main contract tribunal should also be served on the subcontract arbitrator(s). The clause also regulates how the subcontract arbitration costs will be dealt with and also ensures that any claims or defences made by a party in the subcontract arbitration will not be lost because of the expiration of limitation periods[226]. The ENAA Process Plant Model recognizes that the revocation of the authority of the subcontract arbitrator(s) is not justifiable in all cases. This is especially true if the subcontract arbitration has reached an advanced stage of the proceedings. Therefore, pursuant to the ENAA Process Plant Model, multi-party arbitration will not be possible if a hearing on the merits has already commenced in the subcontract arbitration[227]. This approach is reasonable. The revocation of the subcontract arbitrator's authority after this date may result in significant delays in the resolution of the subcontract dispute.

Under the draft multi-party arbitration clauses, it is in principle the contractor who has the discretion to request that the related subcontract dispute is referred to main contract arbitration[228]. The clauses do not envisage who should decide on an eventual dispute concerning the link between the two disputes. In the author's opinion, this dispute should be resolved by the arbitral tribunal which should decide on its own jurisdiction by applying the doctrine of *Kompetenz-Kompetenz.*

The clauses envisage one peculiar situation in which the contractor has an obligation to refer a subcontract dispute to the main contract arbitration. This will be the case where both the employer and the contractor have agreed that the subcontract dispute or difference is of interest to them in connection with the resolution of a main contract dispute or difference. This scenario might comprise situations, for example, where the disputes arise out of or are connected with the same events, such as a *force majeure* clause invoked under a subcontract if the same force majeure event has also affected the parties' obligations under the main contract.

6.10 AIA standard forms

The AIA forms are the leading standard forms in the United States and are published by the American Institute of Architects ('**AIA**')[229]. The forms are primarily designated for domestic use. However, parties who are familiar with the AIA forms tend to use contracts

[225] Sub-clause 2.1 in relation to clause 2.3 of Appendix 10 to the Guide Notes.

[226] Sub-clauses 2.3 and 2.4 of Appendix 10 to the Guide Notes.

[227] Sub-clause 2.2 of Appendix 10 to the Guide Notes.

[228] This follows from the wording of the clauses, which stipulate that 'the Contractor may' request the joint review of the disputes by the main contract arbitral tribunal.

[229] For more information about the AIA, see http://www.aia.org/(accessed 26 July 2016). An explanation of the AIA Contract Document Families is available at http://www.aia.org/contractdocs/referencematerial/aiab099118 (accessed 26 July 2016).

based on these forms in their international operations[230]. The approach of the AIA forms to multi-party arbitration has undergone significant changes over time and is very illustrative of how a major publisher of standard forms may change its opinion about multi-party arbitration as a result of criticism expressed by construction stakeholders.

Prior to 2007, the AIA forms contained provisions that limited consolidation. This approach is exemplified in the 1997 edition of the AIA General Conditions of Contract for Construction, also known as AIA A201-1997, the most commonly used form suitable for conventional *build-only* contracting. Pursuant to § 4.6.4:

> No arbitration arising out of or relating to the Contract shall include, by consolidation or joinder or in any other manner, the Architect, the Architect's employees or consultants, except by written consent containing specific reference to the Agreement and signed by the Architect, Owner, Contractor and any other person or entity sought to be joined. No arbitration shall include, by consolidation or joinder or any other manner, parties other than the Owner, Contractor, a separate contractor as described in Article 6 and other persons substantially involved in a common question of fact or law whose presence is required if complete relief is to be accorded in arbitration. No person or entity other than the Owner, Contractor or a separate contractor as described in Article 6 shall be included as an original third party or additional third party to an arbitration whose interest or responsibility is unsubstantial. Consent to arbitration involving an additional person or entity shall not constitute consent to arbitration of a Claim not described therein or with a person or entity not named or described therein...[231]

Identical clauses were also contained in other AIA forms, such as those intended to regulate the relations between an employer and an architect[232], an architect and the consulting engineer hired by the latter, and also in AIA subcontracts. The first sentence of the clause excludes joinder or consolidation with the participation of the architect without the latter's and the other parties' consent. In other words, the employer (called the 'Owner' in the AIA forms) was neither entitled to request the joinder of the architect in the employer–main contractor arbitration, nor to consolidate the latter arbitration with a separate employer–architect arbitration. This restrictive provision was to be applied regardless of the existence of a common question of fact or law in the separate arbitrations. The provision was mainly to the benefit of architects who, as explained in Subsection 3.4.4, generally do not have interest in multi-party arbitration. This restrictive approach was not surprising considering that the AIA is a professional organization of architects. The AIA's stance on consolidation was explained with the eventual complexity of multi-party arbitration and also with the different subject matter of the disputes arising under a main contract and a professional services agreement[233].

[230] John Hinchey and Troy Harris (2008) *International Construction Arbitration Handbook*, Thomson West, Eagan, MN, pp. 147–148.

[231] Reproduced with permission of the AIA.

[232] See, for example, subparagraph 1.3.5.4 of the AIA B141-1997 – the standard form agreement between the employer and the architect. See also Commentary on AIA Document B141-1997, p. 26, http://www.umich.edu/~cee431/AIA/B141-1997Commentary.pdf (accessed 26 July 2016).

[233] Commentary on AIA Document A201-1997, pp. 47–48, http://www.umich.edu/~cee431/AIA/A201-1997Commentary.pdf (accessed 26 July 2016).

Main contract disputes concerned the completion of the work in conformity with the specified requirements, whereas disputes involving the designer concerned the professional standard of care due by architects in common law countries.

It should be noted, however, that § 4.6.4 did not exclude consolidation in all cases. The second sentence of the provision excluded consolidation and joinder of parties, other than the employer, the contractor, other contractors and 'other persons substantially involved in a common question of fact or law whose presence is required if complete relief is to be accorded in arbitration'. *Per argumentum a contrario*, multi-party arbitration with the participation of the persons listed in this second sentence was allowed, provided that the other requirements in the same sentence were met. Subcontractors can be considered as belonging to the 'other persons' referred to in the clause[234]. Thus, consolidation and joinder of these parties could take place and there was no need to obtain their *ad hoc* consent. For example, a main contractor was allowed to join a subcontractor in his arbitration with the employer over the objection of the latter, provided that the subcontract also contained the discussed provision.

Notwithstanding the abovementioned, the phrase 'other persons' was to be interpreted restrictively because of the overall purpose of § 4.6.4, which was to exclude consolidation and joinder[235]. Thus, for instance, it was not possible to interpret this second sentence to cover multi-party arbitrations with 'other persons' who had never signed an arbitration agreement[236].

The last sentence of the provision made clear that whenever a party had given its consent to joinder and consolidation, this consent applied only to the dispute in respect of which the joinder or consolidation was requested, and could not be extended to other disputes involving that same party. Thus, the additional *ad hoc* consent of the party was necessary for multi-party arbitration concerning these other disputes.

The discussed § 4.6.4 was severely criticized, especially by employers[237]. The provision was favouring architects by precluding employers from joining architects in their main contract arbitrations and was considered unfair to employers. Thus, employers often had to arbitrate related claims arising under a main contract and a professional services agreement separately which exposed them to costly proceedings and the risk of inconsistent findings. For this reason, employers often decided to delete the whole arbitration clause contained in the AIA forms and submit their disputes to litigation where they

---

[234] Ibid., p. 47. See also Gail Kelley (2012) *Construction Law: An Introduction for Engineers, Architects and Contractors*, John Wiley & Sons, Inc., Hoboken, NJ, p. 255.

[235] §4.6.4 of the AIA A201-1997, where the provision was contained, had the title 'Limitation on Consolidation and Joinder'.

[236] For example, in *Bay Hotel & Resort Ltd. v. Cavalier Construction Co. Ltd.* [2001] APP.L.R. 07/16, http://www.nadr.co.uk/articles/published/ArbLR/Bay%20Hotel%20v%20Cavalier%202001.pdf (accessed 26 July 2016), the Privy Council decided that the arbitral tribunal did not have jurisdiction to join a third party – non-signatory to the arbitration agreement, which was a subsidiary of the contractor performing the construction works on the site.

[237] James Jankowski, Suzanne Harness, Michael Bomba, '*AIA 2007 Update: How does it affect Architects?*', pp. 19–23, http://www.aia.org/groups/aia/documents/pdf/aiab078767.pdf (accessed 1 August 2016). See also Suzanne Harness, *2007 Revisions to AIA Contract Documents*, pp. 6–7, http://www.aia.org/groups/aia/documents/document/aiab078763.pdf (accessed 1 August 2016).

were able to benefit from the available joinder rules[238]. As a result of the above criticism and in order to preserve arbitration as a viable option for resolution of construction disputes involving multiple parties, the AIA decided to liberalize its approach to multi-party arbitration in the 2007 editions and introduced new provisions on more permissive terms. Pursuant to § 15.4.4 of AIA A201-2007:

> § 15.4.4.1 Either party, at its sole discretion, may consolidate an arbitration conducted under this Agreement with any other arbitration to which it is a party provided that (1) the arbitration agreement governing the other arbitration permits consolidation, (2) the arbitrations to be consolidated substantially involve common questions of law or fact, and (3) the arbitrations employ materially similar procedural rules and methods for selecting arbitrator(s).
> § 15.4.4.2 Either party, at its sole discretion, may include by joinder persons or entities substantially involved in a common question of law or fact whose presence is required if complete relief is to be accorded in arbitration, provided that the party sought to be joined consents in writing to such joinder. Consent to arbitration involving an additional person or entity shall not constitute consent to arbitration of any claim, dispute or other matter in question not described in the written consent.
> § 15.4.4.3 The Owner and Contractor grant to any person or entity made a party to an arbitration conducted under this Section 15.4, whether by joinder or consolidation, the same rights of joinder and consolidation as the Owner and Contractor under this Agreement[239].

Provisions on identical terms were also included in the AIA standard forms between the employer and the architect[240] and also in the AIA subcontract forms[241].

Under the new consolidation provision, only the entity that is a party to both arbitrations is entitled to request consolidation. This, for example, means that the main contractor may request the consolidation of his separate arbitrations with the employer and the subcontractor. Likewise, the employer is given the right to consolidate his separate arbitrations with the architect and the main contractor. The main contractor is not allowed to request consolidation in the latter scenario because he is a party to the arbitration with the employer only. However, once the employer–architect and employer–main contractor arbitrations are consolidated, the main contractor becomes a party to the consolidated arbitration. This means that the main contractor may then request the consolidation of another arbitration to which he is a party, for example arbitration between the main contractor and a subcontractor, with the already consolidated arbitration. This is achieved on the basis of § 15.4.4.3, which aims to ensure that a third party who is joined in a pending arbitration or that becomes a party to the proceedings as a result of consolidation may on its turn also request joinder or consolidation of other parties. In this way, the AIA consolidation provisions create the potential for all disputes

---

[238] James Jankowski, Suzanne Harness, Michael Bomba, '*AIA 2007 Update: How does it affect Architects?*', p. 21, http://www.aia.org/groups/aia/documents/pdf/aiab078767.pdf (accessed 1 August 2016).
[239] Reproduced with permission of the AIA.
[240] See § 8.3.4 of the AIA B101-2007 (which replaced AIA B141-1997).
[241] See § 6.3.3, 6.3.4 and 6.3.5 of the AIA A401-2007. Moreover, the AIA 201-2007 general conditions, including the consolidation clause, are incorporated in AIA A401-2007 by virtue of § 1.2 of the AIA A401-2007.

which share the same common issues to be resolved in one arbitration[242]. Another consequence of the application of § 15.4.4.3 is that a party to a pending arbitration may not object to a request for multi-party arbitration on the ground that such a request is based on a joinder or consolidation provision contained in another contract to which it is not privy. In this way, any party is deemed to have given its consent to the operation of the AIA multi-party arbitration clauses contained in contracts not signed by that party[243].

The new consolidation provision requires three preconditions for its operation. First, the arbitration agreement governing the other arbitration should also permit consolidation. This condition will be easily satisfied if the contractual relations between the different stakeholders are regulated by using the AIA forms. Most of these forms contain consolidation clauses that are identical or largely similar to the one discussed above. The third condition, requiring the availability of similar procedural rules and methods for selecting arbitrators in the two arbitrations, will also be readily met if the relevant AIA forms are used. These forms refer to the CIAR (discussed in Subsection 4.6.1). The application of identical arbitration rules will most likely be sufficient to satisfy the condition. The second condition requires that the arbitrations involve substantially common questions of law and fact. Whether this condition has been satisfied will have to be ascertained on a case-by-case basis. For example, an investigation of the causes of delay which is common to both contracts will satisfy the condition. The same holds true for employer's claims concerning subcontractors' works. In case of a dispute concerning the link between the arbitrations, Rule 7 of the CIAR will come into play. This is a broadly worded provision that provides for the appointment of an arbitrator for the limited purpose to decide on consolidation or joinder if the parties are unable to agree. When exercising his power the arbitrator will have to consider all the criteria for consolidation as provided under the AIA forms[244].

In the author's opinion, the AIA provisions on consolidation together with the application of the CIAR create a workable regime where all parties whose disputes raise similar points of fact or law may be brought together in a single multi-party arbitration. However, there is one drawback in the application of these provisions: they do not limit the number of parties that may participate in the consolidated arbitration. For example, the employer consolidates his separate arbitrations with the main contractor and the architect. Then, the main contractor consolidates the already consolidated proceeding with his arbitration with the subcontractor. The latter may also require consolidation

---

[242] Suzanne Harness and Kenneth Cobleigh, *2007 AIA Contract Documents: Key Issues of Interest to Owners*', p. 12, http://www.aia.org/groups/aia/documents/pdf/aiab078725.pdf (accessed 1 August 2016).

[243] This also follows from § 15.4.3 of the AIA A201-2007, which envisages that the arbitration agreement contained in the latter standard form and any other arbitration agreement entered into by a party to that same form will be enforceable in any court. It has been suggested that the meaning of this clause is that any contractual commitment to arbitrate also means that parties to this commitment consent to having a third party in their arbitration, provided that this third party has an arbitration agreement with at least one of the parties to the commitment. For interpretation of this clause, see Adrian Bastianelli and Charles Sink (eds) (2014) *ADR Construction*, American Bar Association, Forum on the Construction Industry, Chicago, p. 89.

[244] Unlike the AIA forms, the CIAR do not set any criteria or circumstances that should be considered by the arbitrator when deciding on joinder or consolidation. However, since the reference to the CIAR is contained in the AIA Forms, the arbitrator's discretion in that regard is limited by the content of the arbitration clause and the preconditions to consolidation set therein.

with a sub-subcontract arbitration, etc. This may result in a single arbitration with a multitude of parties, which will be very cumbersome and difficult to handle. Therefore, contracting parties may consider limiting the operation of the multi-party arbitration provision to some parties only.

In contrast with the consolidation provision, which does not demand the consent of the parties, the joinder provision in § 15.4.2 allows the joinder of a third party subject to the latter's written consent. This means, for example, that the employer may not join the architect in the employer–main contractor arbitration, unless the architect gives his consent thereto. From the employer's perspective, there may often be a need to join a third party in the same arbitration. For example, the employer may have started arbitration against the main contractor because of deviations in the construction works that are allegedly due to the poor workmanship of the contractor. In the course of the proceedings, however, it becomes clear that the architect's design might have caused or at least contributed to the deviations. In this case, the architect will be allowed to veto his contemplated joinder by withholding his consent. Hence, the employer will have no other choice but to start a separate arbitration against the architect and require the consolidation of the proceedings on the basis of the AIA consolidation clause. In the author's opinion, this difference in the treatment of joinder and consolidation is not justified. In the above example, the employer's considerations for requesting multi-party arbitration are the same regardless of the exact form of the proceedings. These include saving of time and costs and avoiding the risk of inconsistent findings. The types of claims and disputes among the parties are also the same regardless of whether these disputes are to be reviewed in a consolidated arbitration or an arbitration where a third party has been joined.

6.11 *ConsensusDocs*

The ConsensusDocs, a new US family of contracts first published in 2007, are drafted by a consortium of general and specialty contractors, architects, engineers, and employers[245]. Nowadays, the ConsensusDocs emerge as a main competitor of the AIA forms discussed in Section 6.10. Like the AIA forms, the ConsensusDocs foster multi-party arbitration but in a somewhat different way. The ConsensusDocs 200, the traditional 'build-only' main contract within the family, contains the following meagre provision in clause 12.6:

> All parties necessary to resolve a matter agree to be parties to the same dispute resolution proceeding. Appropriate provisions shall be included in all other contracts relating to the Work to provide for the joinder or consolidation of such dispute resolution procedures[246].

The same clause with some minor modifications is also contained in the standard agreement between the employer and the design professional[247]. It seems that the purpose

---

[245] The ConsensusDocs family consists of approximately 70 documents which are divided into six series. More information about the ConsensusDocs is available at https://www.consensusdocs.org/(accessed 26 July 2016).

[246] The clause is reproduced with permission of ConsensusDocs® under License No. 0639.

[247] Clause 9.6 of ConsensusDocs 240.

of these clauses is to acknowledge that all parties which are somehow implicated into the resolution of a certain matter, including parties that are non-signatories to the contract containing the clause, should be able to resolve this matter in a single dispute resolution procedure. Thus, if there is a main contract dispute concerning the subcontract works, this dispute may be resolved in the same procedure with the participation of the subcontractor. By signing the main contract containing the clause in question, the employer shall be deemed to have given his consent for such participation.

The abovementioned multi-party arbitration clause raises many questions. First of all, the phrase 'all parties necessary' is likely to cause controversy because of its vagueness. This phrase is not defined in the ConsensusDocs. It has been suggested that the phrase covers any project participant who has performed work in relation to the project[248]. However, some limitations should be introduced for practical reasons. For example, parties that have not agreed to arbitrate cannot be considered as parties to the same arbitration absent their consent. Secondly, the clause envisages that all necessary parties shall be parties 'to the same dispute resolution proceeding'. This wording also creates some uncertainty. Does the clause cover only the final step of the dispute resolution process, such as arbitration, or also the pre-arbitration dispute resolution steps? Under the ConsensusDocs, these steps include direct discussions, mitigation (if selected by the parties) and mediation[249]. Some authors assert that the clause covers any type of alternative dispute resolution and not only arbitration[250]. Thirdly, the multi-party arbitration clause does not regulate how exactly the joinder and consolidation will take place. Presumably, any disagreement on the procedure will have to be decided by an R-7 arbitrator to be appointed under the CIAR, which are the default arbitration rules under the ConsensusDocs, unless the parties agree otherwise[251]. Finally, the workability of the provision depends on 'appropriate provisions' providing for joinder and consolidation being included in the other contracts. This requirement acknowledges that a provision in one of the contracts is only binding on the signatories to that contract[252]. But what does 'appropriate provisions' mean? Would it be sufficient to include clauses identical to

[248] See Jeffrey Alitz and Ben Dunlap, *The New AIA and ConsensusDOCS: Beware of the Differences – The Professional Services Agreements*, p. 88, http://www.nspe.org/sites/default/files/resources/pdfs/Professional_Services_Docs.pdf (accessed 25 July 2016). See also Mark McCallum, *Getting Directly to the Point of the Contested Matter: Dispute Mitigation and Resolution in ConsensusDocs Construction Forms*, pp. 21–22, https://www.consensusdocs.org/News/Download/fbb7a767-bf76-4f3d-8447-9fb400e5f768?name=Dispute%20Mitigation%20and%20Resolution%20in%20ConsensusDOCS%20Construction%20Forms.pdf (accessed 26 July 2016).

[249] Article 9 of the ConsensusDOCS240, article 12 of the ConsensusDOCS200.

[250] See Adrian Bastianelli and Charles Sink (eds) (2014) *ADR Construction*, American Bar Association, Forum on the Construction Industry, Chicago, pp. 125–126. According to the authors: 'The ConsensusDocs approach contemplates that all necessary parties "shall" be included in whatever ADR process unfolds.'

[251] For more details about CIAR and the R-7 arbitrator, please see Subsection 4.6.1 hereof.

[252] See Adrian Bastianelli and Charles Sink (eds) (2014) *ADR Construction*, American Bar Association, Forum on the Construction Industry, Chicago, pp. 91–92. According to the authors: 'For an owner-constructor agreement to state that "all parties necessary to resolve a matter agree to be parties to the same dispute resolution proceeding" accomplishes nothing but to state an unenforceable good intention. The missing parties, such as an architect or a supplier, are not bound by what the owner and constructor agree themselves. Meaningful implementation of this concept then falls on the two parties to provide "appropriate provisions…in all other contracts relating to the Work".'

clause 12.6 in the other contracts, or should these clauses be more elaborate as to the terms and conditions of the contemplated multi-party arbitration? If the latter approach is to be given preference there is a risk that the joinder or consolidation provisions included in the different contracts are with different terms. For example, the different provisions may envisage different preconditions to multi-party arbitration or a different degree of relatedness between the disputes. In these cases, it is very likely that the multi-party arbitration system envisaged under the ConsensusDocs will collapse[253].

The conduct of multi-party proceedings is also addressed in the ConsensusDocs subcontract forms. Clause 11.4 of ConsensusDocs 750, the standard subcontract agreement, stipulates:

> All parties necessary to resolve a matter agree to be parties to the same dispute resolution proceeding. To the extent disputes between the Constructor and Subcontractor involve in whole or in part disputes between the Constructor and the Owner, disputes between the Subcontractor and the Constructor shall be decided by the same tribunal and in the same forum as disputes between the Constructor and the Owner[254].

Thus, if there are subcontract disputes involving either partially or fully main contract disputes, the subcontract disputes will have to be decided together with the main contract disputes by the same tribunal. But which tribunal? The one under the main contract or the one under the subcontract? The first option seems to be more likely, even though the wording of the clause allows an alternative interpretation.

If the main contract does not contain a joinder or consolidation provision for some reason, the employer may well object to the participation of the subcontractor in the main contract arbitration because the employer is not bound by the subcontract multi-party arbitration clause. Under the previous editions of the subcontract, it was clear that in these cases the subcontractor was allowed to pursue the resolution of his subcontract disputes under the subcontract dispute resolution procedure[255]. This situation is not explicitly addressed under the current subcontract form. However, in the author's opinion, the same approach should be followed if the employer fails to give his *ad hoc* consent to multi-party arbitration within a reasonable period of time[256].

There are also some uncertainties concerning the link justifying the joint review of the disputes[257]. First, what does it mean that the subcontract disputes 'involve in whole or in part' main contract disputes? If there are numerous subcontract disputes and only some of these involve a matter disputed under the main contract, which disputes should be referred to the main contract arbitration? All disputes, including those unrelated to

---

[253] Ibid., p. 126.

[254] The clause is reproduced with permission of ConsensusDocs® under License No. 0639.

[255] See Paragraph 11.4 of ConsensusDocs 750, in its version issued in 2007, in relation to Paragraph 11.5 of the same contract.

[256] See also Adrian Bastianelli and Charles Sink (eds) (2014) *ADR Construction*, American Bar Association, Forum on the Construction Industry, Chicago, p. 649.

[257] See Leonard Ruzicka and Andrew Scavotto, *A Review of the New Family of Construction Agreements, ConsensusDocs*, pp. 10–11, https://www.consensusdocs.org/News/Download/0a100c49-8b27-4946-ae0f-9fb400de4d49?name=ConsensusDocs-042009.pdf (accessed 26 July 2016).

the main contract, or only those related to the main contract? Furthermore, who is to decide whether there is such a link if the parties disagree? It seems that all these matters will have to be decided by the R-7 arbitrator under the CIAR.

6.12 AB 92 and ABT 93

Construction projects in Denmark are largely based on the following domestic standard forms:

- General Conditions for the Provision of Works and Supplies within Building and Engineering, known as AB 92;
- General Conditions for Turnkey Contracts, known as ABT 93; and
- General Conditions for Consulting Services, known as ABR 89.

The AB 92 is a standard form intended for use for construction projects based on the conventional 'build-only' model[258]. The AB 92 may also be used as a subcontract[259]. The ABT 93 is to be used for turnkey projects where the contractor undertakes, among others things, to design and build the works[260]. The ABR 89 regulates the relations between an employer and a technical advisor hired by the latter, e.g. an architect or an engineer[261]. Disputes arising under these three contracts are to be referred for a decision to the Danish Arbitration Board for Building and Construction (*Voldgiftsnævnet for bygge- og anlægsvirksomhed* or '**VBA**')[262] in accordance with the arbitration rules of this specialized arbitral institution[263].

There is a peculiar clause in the AB 92 and ABT 93 which may be used as a basis for the conduct of multi-party arbitrations. Pursuant to § 47, subs. 8 of the AB 92:

> 'Where the present general conditions apply to the relationship between the employer and several parties (contractors, suppliers), the provisions of subs. 1–7 shall also apply to the inter-relations between such parties.'

Subsections 1–7 referred to in the clause relate to the referral of disputes to the VBA, the required content of the statement of claim, and the constitution of the arbitral tribunal. An almost identical clause is contained in the ABT 93[264]. The ABR 89 does not contain such a provision.

[258] An English translation of the AB 92 is available at http://voldgift.dk/wordpress/wp-content/uploads/2014/09/AB-92-Engelsk.pdf (accessed 26 July 2016).

[259] § 47, subs. 2 of the AB 92.

[260] An English translation of the ABT 93 is available at http://voldgift.dk/wordpress/wp-content/uploads/2014/09/ABT-93-Engelsk.pdf (accessed 26 July 2016).

[261] An English translation of the ABR 89 is available at http://voldgift.dk/wordpress/wp-content/uploads/2014/09/ABR-89-Engelsk.pdf (accessed 26 July 2016).

[262] More information about this arbitral institution is available at www.voldgift.dk (accessed 26 July 2016).

[263] § 47, subs. 1 and 7 of the AB 92 and ABT 93, and § 9.0.1 of the ABR 89.

[264] § 47, subs. 8 of the ABT 93. The only difference is that instead of 'the present general conditions', the clause uses the phrase 'the present general conditions – or similar conditions'. The purpose of this is that the clause can find operation not only with regard to parties bound by the ABT 93 but also to those bound by the AB 92.

The AB 92 and ABT 93 provisions aim at creating a basis for arbitration between parties that are not directly bound by a contract. One of the purposes of these provisions is to create an opportunity for the employer for consistent resolution of his disputes against multiple parties through arbitration. In that regard, it should be mentioned that the AB 92 and ABT 93 admit direct employer's claims against suppliers and/or subcontractors[265]. This is a peculiar feature of these contracts, which is rarely available in other standard forms. With regard to those claims, § 47, subs. 8, could allow the employer to initiate arbitral proceedings against these parties even though these is no direct contractual link between them and the employer.

It has been stated that § 47, subs. 8, also provides a sufficient contractual basis for multi-party arbitration[266]. If the employer may arbitrate both his claims against the main contractor and the subcontractor, he may bring these two parties in a multi-party arbitration. Likewise, if the employer has hired two or more main contractors who are arguing among themselves about which party has caused the defects, the employer may pursue his claims against all the main contractors in a single arbitration[267]. As regards the parties' consent to this type of arbitration, it is deemed given in advance by signing the relevant contract. For example, § 47, subs. 8, contains the consent of the employer and the main contractor that there may be third parties who can participate in the main contract arbitration. If the AB 92 is used as a subcontract, it incorporates the consent of the main contractor and the subcontractor that other parties, such as the employer, may also participate in the same arbitration. In this way, all the parties have agreed that they may participate in a multi-party arbitration. It has even been stated that 'the parties have not only adopted the same arbitration clause, they are in effect parties to the same arbitration agreement'[268]. Other authors suggest that the technical consultant hired under the ABR 89 may also participate in such multi-party arbitration[269]. However, in the author's opinion multi-party arbitration involving technical advisors is not possible over their objection because of the lack of contractual wording addressing this matter in the ABR 89. If a multi-party arbitral award is rendered against these parties, they may request its setting aside or resist its recognition and enforcement.

It has already been established that § 47, subs. 8, ensures the parties' consent to multi-party arbitration (except for the consent of the technical consultant). But what would this multi-party arbitration look like? Would it take place in the form of consolidation,

---

[265] Pursuant to § 5, subs. 5 of the AB 92 and ABT 93, the employer may pursue direct claims for defects against the responsible suppliers or subcontractors in case his claim against the main contractor 'cannot, or can only with greatest difficulty, be successful'. See also § 10, subs. 4 of the same contracts.

[266] See Kristina Maria Siig (2006) 'Multi-Party Arbitration in International Trade: Problems and Solutions', in Sylvia Mercado Kierkegaard (ed.) *Business, Law and Technology: Present and Emerging Trends*, Volume 2, International Association of IT Lawyers, pp. 27–28.

[267] Mogens Hansen, Jan Eske Schmidt, Niels Sørensen *et al.* (1993), *AB 92 for Praktikere, En Kommentar til AB 92*, Byggecentrum, p. 172.

[268] Kristina Maria Siig (2006) 'Multi-Party Arbitration in International Trade: Problems and Solutions', in Sylvia Mercado Kierkegaard (ed.) *Business, Law and Technology: Present and Emerging Trends*, Volume 2, International Association of IT Lawyers, pp. 27–28.

[269] Holger Schöer, '"Something is rotten in the state of Denmark" – was Shakespeare right?', in *4 Construction Law International*, no. 2 (2009), p. 8.

joinder or both? Who is to decide on a request for multi-party arbitration? Are there any preconditions or criteria that should be taken into account when deciding on such a request? Neither the AB 92, nor the ABT 93 provides guidance on these questions. Given the lack of a contractual guidance, one would normally expect to find some regulation of consolidation or joinder in the arbitration rules chosen by the parties. However, the VBA Arbitration Rules 2010[270] do not regulate multi-party arbitrations at all. It has been stated that arbitral tribunals acting under these rules widely consolidate cases and allow intervention of third parties despite the lack of codification on this matter in the rules[271]. This approach may seem puzzling to international practitioners and has been subject to some criticism[272]. It may probably be explained with the specifics of domestic construction arbitrations in Denmark where there is a tradition of consolidation of construction disputes in both litigation and arbitration. Furthermore, one of the arbitrators participating in the tribunal is very often a High Court or a Supreme Court judge[273] who brings with him the knowledge of consolidation from the procedural rules applicable to litigation.

It seems that multi-party arbitrations based on the AB 92 and ABT 93 work well in practice in Denmark. However, in the author's opinion, this approach is unlikely to work in an international context because of the lack of explicit regulation of multi-party arbitrations in the applicable arbitration rules.

6.13 Concluding remarks regarding contractual approaches

In this chapter the author has analysed the contractual approaches to multi-party arbitration as contained in some standard form construction agreements. Some of the most popular international standard forms, such as the FIDIC Conditions of Contract, NEC3 and the ICC Contracts, still do not have multi-party arbitration provisions in their contracts. The FIDIC Subcontract contains an alternative opt-in clause, which aims to deal with related disputes arising under a main contract and a subcontract. However, this clause suffers from several drawbacks, which may dissuade contracting parties from

---

[270] Rules of Arbitration Procedure for Disputes Relating to Building and Construction, known as VBA Arbitration Rules, adopted on 15 November 2010 and in effect from 1 January 2011. An English version of the rules is available at http://voldgift.dk/wordpress/wp-content/uploads/2014/09/C-Voldgiftbehandling-2010-Engelsk.pdf (accessed 26 July 2016).

[271] Morten Nielsen, Kim Christian Thomsen, *A Greener Pasture*, http://www.cdr-news.com/categories/expert-views/5245-a-greener-pasture (accessed 26 July 2016). Arbitrators acting under these rules may arguably rely on the broad wording of Article 8 of the rules, which stipulates: 'The arbitral tribunal may conduct the arbitral proceedings in such manner as it considers appropriate.'

[272] Ibid. According to the authors: 'the absence of rules consolidating claims can still have potentially detrimental effects on the massive number of contracts concluded with a [VBA] clause in Denmark and elsewhere, as its use is very common' and also 'given a web of interconnected construction contracts, it is a severe detriment to clients that the rules do not contain a clause solving the issue of parallel proceedings, which leads to the possibility of conflicting decisions and problems in enforcement...'

[273] Steffen Pihlblad, Christian Lundblad and Claus Søgaard-Christensen (2014) *Arbitration in Denmark*, Djøf Publishing, Copenhagen, p. 17.

opting for its application. The other international standard forms reviewed address multi-party arbitration but they do not provide for a self-contained mechanism for resolution of multi-party construction disputes that can be operated solely on the basis of the provisions contained therein. The International IChemE Subcontract contains a multi-party arbitration clause. However, there is no equivalent clause in the main contract IChemE forms which means that the employer should give his *ad hoc* consent for the application of the subcontract clause. The PPC International allows for multi-party arbitration of multi-contract disputes only in cases where all the participants in the construction project, including subcontractors, designers and suppliers appointed under the terms of the SPC International, have either signed the PPC International at the time of its execution or adjoined to it at a later stage. Hence, multi-party arbitration will generally not be possible with regard to project participants that have not acceded to the PPC International. As regards the ENAA Model Forms, the Guide Notes to the ENAA Process Plant Model contains drafts of multi-party arbitration clauses, which can be inserted in the main contract and also in the subcontracts or supply agreements to be used together with the main contract. These drafts probably represent the most elaborate provisions on multi-party arbitration contained in standard forms suitable for international use. However, they will have no legal effect, unless the parties explicitly insert them in their contracts.

Because of the lack of self-contained solutions in most international standard forms, the author has analysed some multi-party arbitration provisions contained in domestic forms. Some of these forms, especially those used in the United Kingdom, share some common features. Most of these forms, such as the Blue Form, the JCT Contracts (in their wording prior to 1998) and the ACA Subcontract, envisage the joint review of multi-contract disputes in the form of a referral of a subcontract dispute to an arbitrator appointed under another contract (most frequently a main contract). While workable in the United Kingdom, this approach is likely to give rise to some issues if applied internationally. These include, *inter alia*, problems related to the subcontractor's unequal treatment in the composition of the main contract tribunal and the subcontractor's inability to challenge an arbitrator on the grounds of his alleged lack of impartiality or independence at the time when his appointment is made. As a matter of fact, the same issues can also be discerned under some international standard forms, such as the International IChemE Subcontract and the draft multi-party arbitration clauses under the ENAA Process Plant Model.

A second common feature is that most UK standard forms, such as the Blue Form, the JCT Contracts and the ACA standard forms, require the existence of 'disputes' under the different contracts in order for the multi-party arbitration clauses to be operated. This approach may arguably leave some matters, with regard to which multi-party arbitration may be needed, outside the scope of application of the multi-party arbitration clauses (e.g. with regard to subcontractor's claims attributable to employer's default which are not challenged by the main contractor).

Apart from the abovementioned resemblances, the multi-party arbitration provisions in the UK standard forms follow divergent approaches when it comes to other matters. The first such matter concerns the person who is to decide whether the disputes should be reviewed jointly. Some contracts, such as the Blue Form and the ACA Subcontract, follow the approach that it is the main contractor who should form an opinion in that regard. Other contracts, such as the ACA Main Contract, vest the employer with such discretion. A third group of contracts, such as the JCT Contracts, is silent on the matter. Furthermore, the UK domestic standard forms differ with regard to the exact link between the related disputes which justifies their joint review and also with regard to the preconditions for the operation of the multi-party arbitration clauses (such as the appointment of an arbitrator under some or all contracts, the actual referral of a dispute to arbitration, etc.).

Some standard forms published in other countries have also been considered because of their peculiar approach to multi-party arbitrations. These include the AIA standard forms and the ConsensusDocs, both published in the United States, as well as the standard forms published in Denmark. The AIA forms are very illustrative of how drafters of standard form agreements may change their approach to multi-party arbitration following a criticism by construction stakeholders using these forms. Whereas the earlier versions of the AIA forms contained a provision that limited joinder and consolidation, the newer editions permit consolidation and joinder under more flexible terms. The ConsensusDocs also allow for multi-party arbitration without however giving any guidance on the form of such arbitration. The workability of the multi-party arbitration provisions contained in the US standard forms is ensured by way of reference to CIAR (discussed in Subsection 4.6.1), which are very flexible in their wording concerning joinder and consolidation. However, since CIAR are designed primarily for domestic construction cases in the United States, it is doubtful whether the multi-party arbitration solutions contained in the AIA forms and the ConsensusDocs can be applied internationally.

As regards the Danish AB 92 and ABT 93, they contain a provision that creates a basis for multi-party arbitrations. However, this provision does nothing more than to ensure parties' consent to multi-party arbitration. It neither regulates the exact form of multi-party arbitration, nor the procedural requirements that should be taken into account. The arbitration rules referred to in the Danish standard forms are also silent on the matter. Nevertheless, it seems that multi-party arbitrations are conducted successfully in Denmark. However, the Danish approach is unlikely to work in an international context.

The contractual approaches to multi-party arbitration examined here are very instructive in two aspects. First, these approaches disclose some issues in the application of the reviewed multi-party arbitration clauses. In this way, the clauses hint at possible areas of controversy that should be avoided by those drafting multi-party arbitration clauses. Secondly, the reviewed contractual solutions reveal some elements of the clauses discussed that appear to be workable or at least cause least problems in practice. These elements can serve as useful tips to both drafters of standard form construction agreements and contracting parties in their attempts to construct workable multi-party arbitration clauses.

Chapter 7
Proposed Solutions

Consent is one of the cornerstones of arbitration. Multi-party arbitration may only take place if all parties consent to having their disputes reviewed in a multi-party setting. Therefore, any solutions as to how to conduct multi-party arbitration should take into account the consensual nature of arbitration. Only in this way the recognition and enforcement of the resulting multi-party arbitration award will not be threatened, which is of vital importance for contracting parties under international construction transactions. In this chapter the author has proposed some solutions that adhere to this nature.

As explained in Section 1.3, regulation of multi-party arbitration can be found in three different types of legal sources: the arbitration agreements contained in parties' contracts, the arbitration rules referred to in these agreements, and the law of the seat of arbitration. The parties' agreement on the application of one or more of the above sources may provide their consent to multi-party arbitration. Thus, if the arbitration agreements contained in the parties' contracts envisage multi-party arbitration, all the parties have consented to this type of arbitration and such arbitration should take place in accordance with what has been stipulated in these agreements. If the parties' arbitration agreements are silent on multi-party arbitration but refer to arbitration rules providing for a self-contained mechanism for multi-party arbitration, parties' consent to this type of arbitration may be derived from these rules. Likewise, multi-party arbitration in this latter case will be conducted subject to the regime contained in these rules. A similar conclusion, albeit with less certainty, may be drawn from cases where both parties' arbitration agreements and the applicable arbitration rules are silent on multi-party arbitration but the chosen seat of arbitration results in the application of a national arbitration law (*lex arbitri*) that provides for multi-party arbitration.

As explained in Section 5.11, it is the author's opinion that arbitration laws should not regulate multi-party arbitration. Statutory regulation seems to be at odds with the consensual nature of arbitration. The type of multi-party arbitrations examined in this book necessitate the participation of one or more third parties that are not in contractual privity with at least one of the main disputants. Therefore, bringing such third parties to the pending arbitration should usually be *agreed* by the parties rather than *legislated* by states. Furthermore, there are occasions where the application of a national arbitration law does not directly result from a parties' choice of a certain seat of arbitration. If the parties have not chosen a certain seat, the latter will be fixed by the relevant arbitral tribunal or institution. This might result in a situation where a state law regulating multi-party arbitration,

Multi-Party and Multi-Contract Arbitration in the Construction Industry, First Edition.
Dimitar Kondev.

which is unknown by the parties at the time they conclude their contracts, is applied to the parties' disputes. In these situations, it can hardly be said that the parties have consented to multi-party arbitration. The same observation holds true in situations where the applicable arbitration law is subsequently changed to introduce regulation of multi-party disputes. In this case, the parties cannot be deemed to have contracted in the knowledge of law that did not exist at the time when they entered into their contracts.

Because of the above, the proposed solutions to multi-party arbitration should target the other two sources where legal regulation can be found, that is, the arbitration agreements in parties' contracts and the arbitration rules referred to by the parties in these agreements. However, before elaborating on these solutions, the author will first discuss some alternative solutions that have been proposed by some scholars and the suitability of these solutions to the problems discussed in this book. These alternative solutions are different in nature but what they have in common is their deviation from the traditional perception that multi-party arbitration requires all parties' consent. The first such solution is known as the *jurisdictional approach*. The second rests on a broad understanding of the word *consent*, and is therefore referred to by the author as the *abstract consensual approach*.

This chapter is organized as follows. Section 7.1 discusses the *jurisdictional approach*, and Section 7.2 focuses on the *abstract consensual approach*. The next sections reveal the author's suggestions as to how the current regulation of multi-party arbitration can be improved in order to accommodate in a better way the construction disputes examined in this book. Section 7.3 addresses the contractual regulation of multi-party disputes. In this section, the author endeavours to provide some guidelines on the parties' regulation of multi-party arbitration in their contracts. The guidelines try to identify certain good practices that are likely to cause least problems in a legal context. Furthermore, in order to illustrate how a workable multi-party arbitration clause can be constructed on the basis of these guidelines, the author introduces an exemplary multi-party arbitration clause that can be suitable for use with the FIDIC Red Book. Section 7.4 calls for amendments in the regulation of multi-party arbitrations at the level of the arbitration rules.

7.1 Jurisdictional approach

The jurisdictional approach has been introduced by Stavros Brekoulakis[1]. This new approach has been proposed as an alternative to the theories for extension of the arbitration agreement to non-signatories, such as, for example, the group of companies

[1] Professor in International Arbitration and Commercial Law at Queen Mary University of London. The jurisdictional approach has been introduced in a monograph published by Brekoulakis in 2010. See Stavros Brekoulakis (2010) *Third Parties in International Commercial Arbitration*, Oxford University Press, Oxford. See also Stavros Brekoulakis, 'The Relevance of the Interests of Third Parties in Arbitration: Taking a Closer Look at the Elephant in the Room', in *113 Penn State Law Review*, no. 4 (2009), pp. 1165–1188. Ideas resembling the jurisdictional approach have also been shared by Karim Youseff. See Karim Youssef (2009) *Consent in Context: Fulfilling the Promise of International Arbitration. Multi-Party, Multi-Contract and Non-Contract Arbitration*, West Thomson, Eagan, MN. See also Keechang Kim and Jason Mitchenson, 'Voluntary Third-Party Intervention in International Arbitration for Construction Disputes: A Contextual Approach to Jurisdictional Issues', in *30 Journal of International Arbitration*, no. 4 (2013), pp. 407–430.

doctrine[2]. However, when discussing this approach Stavros Brekoulakis has drawn some examples from the construction sector that leave the impression that the approach has a wider scope of application. Therefore, the approach has been explained in this section in order to analyse whether it may be applied to the construction disputes examined here.

Even though the proposed jurisdictional approach does not aim at abolishing the consensual premises of arbitration, it intends to be a corrective to these premises. According to Brekoulakis:

> While [the traditional contractual approach] focuses on peripheral issues such as 'signature' and 'evidence of putative consent', the jurisdictional approach focuses on what really matters in an arbitration, namely the dispute. Therefore it allows the tribunal to determine its jurisdiction on a basis closer to commercial reality...Otherwise, parties with an important role in the commercial aspect of the dispute might be left outside the scope of arbitration for lack of sufficient evidence of consent[3].

The jurisdictional approach provides a new theoretical basis for tribunals to assume jurisdiction over third parties. Third parties are understood as 'parties that have neither signed nor consented to arbitration; not merely non-signatories'[4]. Under this approach, an arbitral tribunal dealing with a dispute arising under a contract containing an arbitration clause may in certain cases assume jurisdiction over a third party that is not bound by that arbitration clause. It has been suggested that when deciding whether to assume jurisdiction over such a third party, the tribunal should focus not on the parties' consent as expressed in the arbitration agreement but on the nature of the dispute and its repercussions on third parties[5]. The question is not so much whether the third party is bound by the contractual boundaries of the arbitration agreement but whether the dispute in question strongly implicates such a third party[6]. Hence, the tribunal may assume jurisdiction over a party whose claim is strongly implicated in the dispute before a tribunal regardless of whether there is sufficient evidence that this party has consented to be involved in multi-party arbitration[7]. It will be to the discretion of the tribunal whether to exercise its extended jurisdiction or not[8].

Stavros Brekoulakis has drawn an example to illustrate how the jurisdictional approach may be applied in the construction sector[9]. Under the example, there is a main contract containing an arbitration clause and a subcontract without such a clause. Under the

---

[2] Stavros Brekoulakis (2010) *Third Parties in International Commercial Arbitration*, Oxford University Press, Oxford, pp. 12 (§ 1.58), 16 (§ 1.77).

[3] Ibid., p. 17 (§ 1.83).

[4] Ibid., p. 200.

[5] Ibid., pp. 17 (§ 1.80), 21 (§ 1.101), 228–229 (§ 8.37). According to the author: 'tribunals may need to focus less on contractual purism and more on business and economic reality'.

[6] Ibid., pp. 17 (§ 1.82), 198 (§ 6.94).

[7] Ibid., p. 206 (§7.44).

[8] Ibid., p. 17 (§ 1.80).

[9] Ibid., pp. 207–208 (§ 7.29–7.31). See also Stavros Brekoulakis, 'The Relevance of the Interests of Third Parties in Arbitration: Taking a Closer Look at the Elephant in the Room', in *113 Penn State Law Review*, no. 4 (2009), p. 1180.

terms of the main contract, the employer is directly liable to the subcontractor for payment of the subcontractor's work. The subcontract contains a clause that empowers the employer to request modifications or variations of the work directly from the subcontractor. The subcontractor brings a request for arbitration against the employer concerning payment of his work either alongside the main contractor or separately. In these circumstances, Brekoulakis argues that there are good reasons for the arbitral tribunal under the main contract to look into the subcontractor's claim against the employer because this claim arises directly out of the construction contract.

The example is based on the premise that the subcontractor files a request for arbitration against the employer despite the fact that there is no arbitration clause in the subcontract and that the subcontractor is not privy to the main contract containing the arbitration clause. The present author agrees that the arbitral tribunal may indeed consider assuming jurisdiction over the subcontractor's claim. However, there is a much more straightforward way for the tribunal to justify its decision to deal with the subcontractor's claim than to rely on the jurisdictional approach. By filing a request for arbitration against the employer, the subcontractor has clearly expressed its willingness to arbitrate his claim despite the lack of an arbitration clause in the subcontract. In other words, the subcontractor has consented to arbitration as a result of his conduct. Therefore, this example should not raise any difficulties when it comes to the position of the subcontractor. In the author's opinion, the more intricate problem here concerns the position of the employer and the main contractor. If there is a pending arbitration between the employer and the main contractor and the subcontractor introduces his claim again the employer, the main contractor may object to the tribunal's jurisdiction on the ground that he expected arbitration with the employer only. Similar objections may be raised by the employer. Even though the subcontractor has a direct claim against the employer, there is no arbitration agreement binding these two parties. Accordingly, the employer may insist that the subcontractor's claim should be dealt with in litigation rather than in the pending arbitration. If such objections are raised, it is the author's opinion that the arbitral tribunal should decline jurisdiction to review the subcontractor's claim.

The example above is very specific and relatively uncommon in the construction sector. Therefore, it will be useful to analyse whether the jurisdictional theory can be applied to a broader category of cases that are directly pertinent to the disputes examined in this book. Can, for example, a main contract arbitral tribunal, which is seized with an employer's claim for defects, review the main contractor's claim against the subcontractor if the defects have been caused by the latter? It seems that Brekoulakis assumes that the jurisdictional approach may be applied to these cases as well[10]. This would mean that the tribunal may assume jurisdiction to review the subcontract claim regardless of whether the subcontract contains an arbitration clause or not.

It is the author's firm opinion that the proposed jurisdictional approach cannot and should not be applied to the type of construction disputes examined here. A major obstacle to the adoption of the approach is its incompatibility with the consensual nature

[10] Stavros Brekoulakis (2010) *Third Parties in International Commercial Arbitration*, Oxford University Press, Oxford, p. 227 (§8.31).

of arbitration[11]. The application of the jurisdictional approach results in a situation where a third party is brought into proceedings between two other parties regardless of the third party's opinion on this matter. The consensual nature of arbitration is widely recognized by both scholars and practitioners. Therefore, any approach that is incongruent with this lacks the potential to be widely accepted by the international arbitration community. Moreover, as Brekoulakis has stated, the jurisdictional approach has rather limited application. It may be employed by arbitral tribunals 'only in extremely exceptional cases and with particular caution'[12]. Moreover, it is very likely that the application of this approach may result in the setting aside of the award or its non-recognition and non-enforcement (see Subsection 2.4.4).

The rationale behind the jurisdictional approach, as explained by Brekoulakis, is to rectify the artificial discrepancy between commercial reality, which is often characterized by a network of interlinked rights and obligations among multiple parties, and the scope of arbitral proceedings, which are generally confined only to the parties that signed a contract, notwithstanding its repercussions on third parties[13]. In the abovementioned examples, the employer, the main contractor and the subcontractor are considered as an intertwined substantive group forming a common network of contractual rights and duties, which is wider than the boundaries of the arbitration agreement(s) binding only their signatories[14]. Thus, the jurisdictional approach aims at setting a functional equilibrium between the arbitral proceeding and its multi-party substantive background[15].

But is it not part of commercial reality that parties may decide against whom to arbitrate their disputes and to make dispute resolution arrangements that suit them best? By including an arbitration clause in a bilateral contract that is silent on multiparty arbitration the parties have made a conscious decision to submit disputes arising under *that* contract to arbitration involving the parties to *that* contract. This is a legitimate choice, which is an expression of the principle of procedural party autonomy and the principle of contractual freedom. Moreover, such a choice does not contravene any notions of public policy. There is no reason to overwrite the parties' choice on the matter by applying approaches, such as the jurisdictional approach, which deviate from the consensual premises of arbitration and do not take into account individual parties' expectations.

---

[11] Brekoulakis has acknowledged that the proposed approach deviates from the consensual nature of arbitration: 'it is not self-evident… why allowing a tribunal to deviate under exceptional circumstances from the consensual principle would cause unmitigated damage to arbitration.' See Stavros Brekoulakis (2010) *Third Parties in International Commercial Arbitration*, Oxford University Press, Oxford, pp. 223 (§ 8.10), 224–225 (§ 8.13–8.17).

[12] Ibid., p. 17 (§ 1.81). According to the author: 'Even in cases where a third party claim is essentially part of the dispute that is the main subject of the arbitration, the tribunal should carefully take into account various factors, such as confidentiality for example, before deciding whether to exercise its discretion and examine the third party claim.' See also pp. 200, 222 (§ 805), 226 (§ 8.23).

[13] Ibid., p. 209 (§ 7.37–7.39).

[14] Stavros Brekoulakis, 'The Relevance of the Interests of Third Parties in Arbitration: Taking a Closer Look at the Elephant in the Room', in *113 Penn State Law Review*, no. 4 (2009), p. 1180.

[15] Ibid., pp. 1179–1183.

In addition to the jurisdictional approach, Brekoulakis has also suggested that arbitral awards should have certain legal effects against third parties. An example has been given that an award rendered in an arbitration between an employer and a main contractor that has ascertained defects in the construction works should produce legal effects against the subcontractor who has actually caused the defects in a subsequent arbitration between the subcontractor and the main contractor[16]. It has been suggested that it is not the award as such but the determination in the award concerning the existence of defects that is binding on the subcontractor[17]. The second tribunal should take that determination into account when dealing with the subject matter of the subcontract dispute and should render an award which is in line with this determination[18]. According to Brekoulakis, it is the first tribunal that has an exclusive jurisdiction to determine these issues and the latter should not be open to a fresh determination in subsequent proceedings because of their conclusive character[19].

Notwithstanding the above statement, the same author has later on suggested that the second tribunal has the discretion whether to follow the determination of the first tribunal. Brekoulakis has suggested several criteria that should be considered by the second tribunal when deciding whether to follow a determination from a previous award. According to one of these criteria:

> the arbitral award could and should be relied upon in subsequent proceedings against the party that rejected the possibility of multiparty proceedings in the first place. This could either be the third party or one of the parties to the first arbitration. A party that wastes the opportunity of multiparty proceedings, choosing to stand by and adopt the wait-and-see tactic, should have to accept any adverse consequences arising from such tactic[20].

Applied to the example given above, this would mean that if the subcontractor's joinder was requested in the arbitration between the employer and the main contractor but the subcontractor refused to be joined, then the second tribunal dealing with the related subcontract dispute should be bound by the first tribunal's determination that the works are defective.

The abovementioned statements concerning the legal effects of arbitral awards on third parties are highly controversial. Brekoulakis has supported his statements with a selection of several cases[21]. These cases indeed reveal circumstances under which the findings in a previous award were taken into account in subsequent proceedings. However, the quoted cases are not sufficient to show that there is a general trend in international commercial arbitration that arbitral awards should produce certain effects on third parties. It is the author's opinion that a previous award has no binding effect in

---

[16] Stavros Brekoulakis (2010) *Third Parties in International Commercial Arbitration*, Oxford University Press, Oxford, p. 246 (§ 10.05–10.06).

[17] Ibid., pp. 246 (§ 10.05–10.06), 253 (§ 10.34), 259 (§ 10.61–10.63).

[18] Ibid., p. 246 (§ 10.06).

[19] Ibid., p. 246 (§ 10.08–10.09).

[20] Ibid., pp. 256–257 (§ 10.51–10.54). Similar arguments can be found on p. 260 (§ 10.67).

[21] Ibid., pp. 248–252.

subsequent proceeding involving different parties. There are no convincing arguments in favour of a statement that an arbitral award and / or the determinations contained therein should bind a party that did not participate in the proceedings and also an arbitral tribunal in a subsequent arbitration. This view is supported by several scholars and practitioners[22]. Furthermore, most arbitrators would be reluctant to accept the binding effect of such determinations because this would significantly limit their ability to arrive at their own conclusion[23]. If the award is disclosed to the tribunal in subsequent proceedings, its content can probably be considered as an argument substantiating the position of the party that relies on the award but nothing more[24]. There might be some fresh evidence and / or new arguments in the second case not known or presented during the first proceeding, which may refute the determination contained in the first award.

Furthermore, the observations concerning the specific example posed by Brekoulakis (i.e. that a subcontract tribunal should be bound by the determination of the first tribunal that there are defects in the work) are not necessarily true. The meaning of the word 'defect' should be examined in the context of the specific contract. Often main contracts and related subcontracts are governed by different substantive laws, which may impose different perceptions of defective work. Furthermore, the existence of defects is often established with a reference to certain technical standards, being either

---

[22] See Nigel Blackaby and Constantine Partasides with Alan Redfern and Martin Hunter (2015) *Redfern and Hunter on International Arbitration*, 6th edn, Oxford University Press, Oxford, pp. 33–34 (para. 1.116), where the authors have stated that: 'There is no system of binding precedents in international arbitration – that is, no rule that means that an award on a particular issue, or a particular set of facts, is binding on arbitrators confronted with similar issues or similar facts. Each award stands on its own.' See also Robert Merkin (2004) *Arbitration Law*, Informa, London, pp. 654, 656, 664. According to the author: 'the factual findings in an award cannot be used as evidence in proceedings involving third parties, whether or not a party to the arbitration is affected by those proceedings, unless the parties to the arbitration agree, the arbitrators in the second arbitration so order or the court gives permission.' See also Geoffrey Ma and Neil Kaplan (eds) (2003) *Arbitration in Hong Kong: A Practical Guide*, Sweet & Maxwell Asia, Hong Kong, p. 517, where it is stated that '[the] arbitrators are not compelled (and arguably are not permitted) to take account of the views of any outsider to their particular arbitration including other arbitrators'. See also Andrew Tweeddale and Karen Tweeddale (2007) *Arbitration of Commercial Disputes, International and English Law and Practice*, Oxford University Press, Oxford, pp. 572–574 (§ 19.71–19.74).

[23] Mark Huleatt-James and Nicholas Gould (1999) *International Commercial Arbitration. A Handbook*, 2nd edn, LLP Reference Publishing, London, p. 41.

[24] See Nigel Blackaby and Constantine Partasides with Alan Redfern and Martin Hunter (2015) *Redfern and Hunter on International Arbitration*, 6th edn, Oxford University Press, Oxford, pp. 33–34 (para. 1.116). See also Bernard Hanotiau, 'The Res Judicata Effect of Arbitral Awards', in *14 ICC International Court of Arbitration Bulletin, Complex Arbitrations – Special Supplement 2003*, pp. 49–50 (para. 36–37). In his article, the author has mentioned an ICC case (Award of 28 November 1997 in ICC case 7061 (unpublished)) in which one of the parties submitted to the tribunal a previous arbitral award resulting from an arbitration that took place between different parties but concerning the same project. Unsurprisingly, the tribunal stated that it was not bound by the previous award because it did not concern the same parties and the same contract. Furthermore, the tribunal made clear that it could not be assumed that the same evidence was equally available to both tribunals. The tribunal acknowledged that the award contained a helpful analysis of the common factual background, which could principally be borne in mind without, however, affecting the tribunal's discretion to reach its own conclusion on the basis of the materials submitted by the parties.

international or domestic standards. If the main contract adheres to an international standard and the subcontract to a more lenient domestic standard, it may well be the case that the construction works are considered defective in the context of the main contract but without any deviations in the context of the subcontract. In this case, the second tribunal cannot and should not adhere to the determination of the first tribunal.

The statement that the party that has thwarted the multi-party arbitration should bear the adverse consequences arising from its behaviour is also highly controversial. A subcontractor bound by a subcontract arbitration agreement silent on multi-party arbitration clause has a legitimate interest to insist on a bipolar arbitration with the main contractor. The subcontractor's stake in the construction project is usually much smaller than the amounts disputed in the main contract arbitration. Participation in the latter arbitration will almost certainly result in delay and additional costs for the subcontractor. Should the subcontractor be punished just because he has decided to pursue his legitimate interests not to be involved in a costly and lengthy multi-party arbitration with the employer? In the author's opinion, this question should be answered in the negative.

For the reasons discussed in the present section, the author believes that the jurisdictional approach is incapable of offering an adequate multi-party arbitration solution to the type of construction disputes examined hereof.

7.2 Abstract consensual approach

Anecdotal evidence suggests that the abstract consensual approach has been proposed by some practitioners in Switzerland and the United Kingdom.

This approach implies a broad understanding of the parties' consent to arbitrate where 'consent' is understood in an abstract way. If a party has agreed to arbitrate under an arbitration agreement, the introduction of a third party in the arbitration does not necessarily contradict the party's consent to arbitrate as long as that party does not have to arbitrate directly against the third party. For example, if both a main contract and a subcontract contain standard arbitration clauses, all the three parties can be brought together in a single arbitration, provided that the arbitration does not deal with claims by or against parties that are not privy to each other (i.e. with subcontractor's claims against the employer or *vice versa*). This type of arbitration, according to the supporters of this approach, should not breach the consensual nature of arbitration as the arbitration will only encompass claims with regard to which the parties have expressed their consent to arbitrate. In the resulting multi-party arbitration, the tribunal will deal with both the employer's claim against the main contractor, which is based on the main contract arbitration agreement, and the main contractor's related claim against the subcontractor, which is based on the subcontract arbitration agreement. Thus, consent to this type of arbitration can be derived from the two arbitration agreements and it is up to the tribunal to follow a procedure that excludes claims by or against parties that are not privy to each other.

In order to ensure the workability of this type of multi-party arbitration, whenever a dispute arises under one of the agreements, either party to this agreement should give a notice to its contractual party under a related agreement, that is, a party, which is not privy to the first agreement. Thus, the main contractor should notify the employer when a subcontract dispute arises if this dispute may trigger a main contract dispute. Similarly, the main contractor should notify the subcontractor in case of a main contract dispute that is linked to the subcontractor's works (e.g. a dispute based on an employer's claim for defects).

Even though the proposed approach is intriguing and not devoid of legal logic, there are certain issues that may arise if the approach is applied in practice. The first, and probably the most material issue, is related to the broad understanding of parties' *consent to arbitrate*. On the face of it, the proposed approach does not directly contradict the consensual nature of arbitration. It assumes that once a party has agreed to arbitrate, this party can be involved in arbitration with other parties with whom it is not privy as long as that party is not forced to arbitrate claims against or by these other parties. However, this assertion is debatable. It is the author's opinion that the meaning of 'consent to arbitrate' cannot be construed in such a broad and abstract way. Consent to arbitration should be viewed as consent in the context of a specific agreement. In other words, when a party includes a conventional arbitration agreement in a bipolar contract it expects to arbitrate its disputes arising under that contract *with its counterparty only*. The introduction of a third party in the pending proceeding will most likely increase the expenses and the time for resolution of the disputes between the contracting parties. The latter may have to comment on some additional evidence provided by the third party which would not have been introduced in a bipolar arbitration. Furthermore, the hearings will last longer because of the participation of the third party. This would also result in additional expenses. Besides, the organization of hearings with participation of multiple parties poses an additional logistical challenge, which may further delay the dispute resolution process.

For the above arguments, the author believes that the party's 'consent to arbitrate' should be given an interpretation with a view to the specific contract containing the arbitration agreement (on that point see also Subsection 2.4.1). A similar opinion has been stated by Brekoulakis who has stated that: 'for an arbitration agreement to exist it is not enough that a party has agreed to arbitrate *in abstracto*. It is required that a party has agreed to arbitrate with a specific person'[25]. Therefore, it is unlikely that arbitral tribunals acting, including but not only, under the auspices of the ICC, will adopt the proposed approach.

Another obstacle related to the application of the abstract consensual approach is related to the notices that should be given under the related contracts. Neither arbitration laws nor arbitration rules deal with such notice requirements. Therefore, parties should insert relevant provisions in their contracts implementing the above notice requirements. Without these provisions, the proposed multi-party arbitration can hardly be put into place because the party that is not privy to the respective contract

---

[25] Stavros Brekoulakis (2010) *Third Parties in International Commercial Arbitration*, Oxford University Press, Oxford, p. 189 (§ 6.52).

will be unable to obtain information about related disputes arising under that contract. As a result, it may be unable to participate in the constitution of the arbitral tribunal thereunder and to raise arguments as regards the alleged lack of independence and / or impartiality of that tribunal.

In addition, the adoption of the abstract consensual approach may result in difficulties related to the recognition of arbitration agreements and the recognition and enforcement of arbitral awards rendered as a result of the application of this approach. Under Article II(1) of the New York Convention, contracting states are obliged to 'recognize an agreement in writing under which the parties undertake to submit to arbitration all or any differences which have arisen or which may arise between them in respect of a defined legal relationship, whether contractual or not...' Furthermore, Article II (2) clarifies what the term 'agreement in writing' means. It is either an arbitral clause in a contract or an arbitration agreement that is signed by the parties or contained in an exchange of letters or telegrams. These two provisions reveal that the New York Convention was written on the basis of a strict understanding of an agreement to arbitrate. It should concern 'a defined legal relationship' between parties. Therefore, a broad understanding of parties' consent to arbitrate seems to be at odds with the text of the convention. As regards the grounds upon the occurrence of which the recognition and enforcement of an award can be denied, the reader is hereby referred to Subsection 2.4.4. The most obvious grounds that may be invoked in this case are Article V(1)(c) (that the award deals with a difference not contemplated by or not falling within the terms of the submission to arbitration, or that it contains decisions on matters beyond the scope of the submission to arbitration) or Article V(1)(d) (that the composition of the arbitral tribunal or the arbitration procedure was not in accordance with the agreement of the parties).

For the above reasons, it is the author's opinion that the abstract consensual approach is not capable of offering a viable solution to the problems discussed in this book.

7.3 Proposed contractual solutions

Many scholars and practitioners share the view that the best way to deal with multi-party arbitration is by way of regulation provided in the parties' contracts[26]. The advantages of this contractual approach are manifold. First, contractual regulation of multi-party arbitration is in full consonance with the consensual premises of arbitration. As a result, the contractual approach to multi-party arbitration is unlikely to raise any risks of setting aside of an award or the denial of its recognition and / or enforcement. Secondly, the availability of multi-party arbitration solutions increases the predictability of the dispute resolution process as a whole, which leaves little leeway for recalcitrant parties to

---

[26] Jan Paulsson, Nigel Rawding and Lucy Reed (2011) *The Freshfields Guide to Arbitration Clauses in International Contracts*, 3rd edn, Kluwer Law International, Alphen aan den Rijn, p. 98. See also Julian Lew, Loukas Mistelis and Stefan Kröll (2003) *Comparative International Commercial Arbitration*, Kluwer Law International, The Hague, p. 392 (no. 16–51), and Mark Huleatt-James and Nicholas Gould (1999) *International Commercial Arbitration. A Handbook*, 2nd edn, LLP Reference Publishing, London, p. 40.

vary their positions due to tactical reasons depending on the circumstances of the case. This facilitates the maintaining of good relations among the parties throughout the dispute resolution phase of construction projects.

Despite all these advantages, multi-party arbitration clauses are still rarely seen. The arbitration clause, often facetiously called 'the midnight clause', is located at the end of the contract, and contracting parties either do not have the time to negotiate it or they prefer to focus on the commercial aspects of the transaction. However, this is only one of the reasons explaining why these clauses are rarely used. Another (and probably the main) reason is that little has been done so far to propose workable solutions to the need for multi-party arbitration in the international construction sector. As observed in Chapter 6, most international standard form construction agreements do not provide for a standardized solution. Besides, most of the contributions in the legal literature confine themselves to identifying the issues related to multi-party arbitrations at a theoretical level, such as the lack of consent from all parties, potential infringement of the confidentiality of the proceedings, etc. There are relatively few articles that deal with the practical challenges involved in writing multi-party arbitration clauses[27]. The Working Party on Multi-Party Arbitration set up by the ICC provided some drafts of multi-party arbitration clauses in its final report[28]. However, these clauses were reproduced for informative purposes only without any further discussion. There is no doubt that the theoretical debate concerning multi-party arbitration is of material importance, but for the practitioners in the field these discussions are of limited avail.

In the author's opinion, the full-value benefit of the present work requires full consideration of the practical challenges involved in drafting multi-party arbitration clauses. Given the current lack of appropriate solutions at the level of the institutional arbitration rules and the absence of standardized approaches on the matter in international standard forms, *ad hoc* clauses in parties' agreements remain the only feasible solution for the time being. Drafting multi-party arbitration clauses is a complex exercise and is often considered a daunting task[29]. Notwithstanding the abovementioned, it

---

[27] Humphrey Lloyd (1991) 'A National Experience', in P. Bellet, P. Bernardini, G. Bernini *et al.* (eds) *Multi-Party Arbitration: Views from International Arbitration Specialists*, Publication No. 480/1, ICC Publishing SA, Paris, pp. 61–79, and Paul Friedland (2007) *Arbitration Clauses for International Contracts*, 2nd edn, JurisNet, New York, NY, pp. 129–141. See also Gary Born (2013) *International Arbitration and Forum Selection Agreements: Drafting and Enforcing*, 4th edn, Kluwer Law International, Alphen aan den Rijn, pp. 106–110, and Jan Paulsson, Nigel Rawding and Lucy Reed (2011) *The Freshfields Guide to Arbitration Clauses in International Contracts*, 3rd edn, Kluwer Law International, Alphen aan den Rijn, pp. 96–100, 157–160. The latter two sources contain short drafts of *ad hoc* multi-party arbitration clauses.

[28] See ICC Commission on International Arbitration, 'Final Report on Multi-Party Arbitrations', in 6 *ICC International Court of Arbitration Bulletin*, no. 1 (1995), Appendix # 1 to the report.

[29] See Geoffrey Ma and Neil Kaplan (eds) (2003) *Arbitration in Hong Kong: A Practical Guide*, Sweet & Maxwell Asia, Hong Kong, pp. 173–174. See also Julian Lew, Loukas Mistelis and Stefan Kröll (2003) *Comparative International Commercial Arbitration*, Kluwer Law International, The Hague, p. 393 (no. 16-44), Michael McIlwrath and John Savage (2010) *International Arbitration and Mediation, A Practical Guide*, Kluwer Law International, Alphen aan den Rijn, pp. 74–75, and W. Michael Reisman, W. Laurence Craig, William W. Park and Jan Paulsson (1997) *International Commercial Arbitration. Cases, Materials and Notes on the Resolution of International Business Disputes*, The Foundation Press, New York, NY, p. 483.

is perfectly feasible to construct a proper multi-party arbitration clause having in mind the specifics of the contract where the clause is to be inserted and the interests of the parties at stake[30]. The present section provides a list of matters that should be considered by drafters when embarking on this complex task. In this way, the section aims to bridge the gap between theoretical proposals regarding multi-party arbitration and their practical application.

Despite the difficulties involved in drafting these clauses, it is the author's expectation that parties' awareness of multi-party arbitration issues will increase, which will result in the more frequent use of *ad hoc* multi-party arbitration clauses in the near future. These clauses deserve much more attention during the negotiation stage of the respective contract than they are currently attributed. Multi-party arbitration clauses have the potential to reduce the time and costs involved in dispute resolution, especially for parties interested in multi-party arbitration. These parties should not rely on boilerplate arbitration clauses that appear to be unworkable in a multi-party arbitration setting. It is true that the parties may also agree on multi-party arbitration after the execution of the contracts at the stage when disputes have already arisen. However, this is highly unlikely. As already mentioned, multi-party arbitration requires the consent of all parties. At the stage of dispute resolution, parties usually have conflicting interests and are unable to reach a common agreement on multi-party arbitration. It is therefore much easier to agree on a proper multi-party dispute resolution clause at the time when the respective contracts are negotiated than in cases when a dispute has already arisen and some of the contracting parties have begun to see the tactical advantage of separate arbitrations[31].

This section comprises several parts. First, it considers some authoritative soft law instruments that might be useful for drafters of multi-party arbitration agreements on a more general basis. These instruments comprise the Guidelines for Drafting International Arbitration Clauses drafted by the International Bar Association, discussed in Subsection 7.3.1, and the Guide to Drafting Alternative Dispute Resolution Clauses for Construction Contracts drafted by the American Arbitration Association, discussed in Subsection 7.3.2. Subsection 7.3.3 poses a list of questions that should be taken into account by the draftsman of multi-party arbitration clauses. Finally, Subsection 7.3.4 contains an exemplary multi-party arbitration agreement suitable for use in conjunction with the FIDIC Red Book. It should be mentioned that the latter clause does not purport to be a universal solution which can be readily adopted by parties using the FIDIC Conditions of Contract. Instead, the proposed clause merely serves to illustrate how a multi-party arbitration clause can be constructed on the basis of the questions considered in Subsection 7.3.3.

---

[30] Gary Born (2013) *International Arbitration and Forum Selection Agreements: Drafting and Enforcing*, 4th edn, Kluwer Law International, Alphen aan den Rijn, p. 12.

[31] Jan Paulsson, Nigel Rawding and Lucy Reed (2011) *The Freshfields Guide to Arbitration Clauses in International Contracts*, 3rd edn, Kluwer Law International, Alphen aan den Rijn, p. 97.

7.3.1 IBA guidelines for Drafting International Arbitration Clauses

The IBA Guidelines for Drafting International Arbitration Clauses ('**IBA Guidelines**') were published in 2010 by the International Bar Association[32]. They aim at reflecting the best current international practices and providing both a framework and detailed provisions for drafters of international arbitration clauses[33].

The IBA Guidelines contain recommended drafts of both multi-party and multi-contract arbitration clauses[34]. However, none of these drafts can be directly applied to the type of construction disputes examined hereof, that is, multi-party disputes arising under two or more contracts binding different parties. The draft multi-party arbitration clause in Section V of the IBA Guidelines deals with single-contract situations only – cases where the multiple parties are bound by a single contract (e.g. a main contract between an employer and a consortium consisting of two or more contractors). The draft arbitration clause for consolidation of related arbitrations based on multi-contract disputes in Section VI of the IBA Guidelines concerns situations where two or more contracts bind the same parties (e.g. two main contracts between the employer and the same main contractor). Thus, the IBA Guidelines do not suggest a full-blown draft clause that can be applied to multi-party disputes arising under several contracts[35]. With regard to this category of disputes, the guidelines warn that the parties should be treated equally with respect to the appointment of arbitrators[36]. It has been suggested that a workable but less-than-ideal solution is to provide for all appointments of arbitrators to be made by the respective arbitral institution or the appointing authority[37]. Therefore, the IBA Guidelines call into question the mechanism envisaged under some of the standard forms discussed in Chapter 6, such as the Blue Form, the JCT 80 Contracts, the ACA Standard Forms, the IChemE Contracts and the ENAA Process Plant Model, where a dispute can be referred to a tribunal that has already been constituted under a contract different than the one under which the dispute has arisen.

The guidelines also specify that the arbitration clauses should make clear that a tribunal appointed under one of the contracts has the jurisdiction to consider and

---

[32] The IBA Guidelines were drafted by the Task Force on Drafting International Arbitration Clauses, established by the Arbitration Committee within the International Bar Association's Legal Practice Division. The IBA Guidelines are available at http://www.ibanet.org/ENews_Archive/IBA_27October_2010_Arbitration_Clauses_Guidelines.aspx (accessed 26 July 2016).

[33] See IBA Guidelines, p. 1.

[34] Ibid., Section V and Section VI.

[35] With regard to this category of disputes, the IBA Guidelines suggest on p. 41 (para. 112): 'Specialized advice is required when the related contracts also involve more than two parties. Drafting consolidation provisions in a multiparty context is especially intricate.'

[36] The same comment is reiterated in the section of the guidelines dealing with multi-party arbitrations arising under a single contract (see IBA Guidelines, p. 35, para. 98–99). In that regard, it has been stated that if there is a sole arbitrator, he should be appointed jointly by the parties or, absent agreement, by the relevant arbitral institution or appointing authority. Likewise, in case of a three-member tribunal, the members should be appointed jointly by the parties or, in the absence of agreement, by the arbitral institution or appointing authority.

[37] IBA Guidelines, p. 41 (para. 112).

decide issues related to the other related contracts[38]. In order to ensure this, the IBA Guidelines have proposed a short provision that should be inserted in each related contract. The provision reads as follows: 'The parties agree that an arbitral tribunal appointed hereunder or under [the related agreement(s)] may exercise jurisdiction with respect to both this agreement and [the related agreement(s)]'[39]. Even though this short provision can be a good starting point for those trying to draft a multi-party arbitration clause, it is not a proper multi-party arbitration clause in itself. As will be seen in Subsection 7.3.3, such a clause should deal with a wider spectrum of questions in order to be tailored to the specifics of the construction project and the contracts pertaining to it.

Notwithstanding the lack of an appropriate multi-party arbitration clause dealing with the type of construction disputes discussed here, the IBA Guidelines contain three comments of a more general nature that are also pertinent to these disputes. First, the IBA Guidelines specify that there are two main forms of contractual regulation of multi-contract disputes. It is suggested that the most straightforward solution is to establish a stand-alone dispute resolution protocol, often called an *umbrella* or a *master* arbitration agreement, which is signed by all the parties and incorporated in all bilateral contracts. Alternatively, if the execution of such an agreement is not feasible, the parties should ensure that the arbitration clauses in the related clauses are compatible[40]. This would mean, in the sense implied in the IBA Guidelines, that the arbitration clauses are identical or complementary. The Guidelines give some examples of situations that might result in incompatibility of the arbitration clauses, such as choice of different sets of arbitration rules, different places of arbitration or a different number of arbitrators.

A second comment in the IBA Guidelines, which may be relevant to the construction disputes examined hereof concerns the notice requirement in case of arbitrations involving multiple parties. The relevant section of the IBA Guidelines specifies that, whenever arbitration has been commenced, notice of the proceedings should be given to the other parties regardless of whether these parties are involved in the arbitration as respondents[41]. The purpose of this notice is to allow the non-participating party to consider whether to intervene in the existing proceeding or to ensure that the non-participating party may be joined therein upon the request of a party participating in the arbitration. This requirement seems to be relevant also to disputes that are both multi-party and multi-contract. Multi-party arbitration will not be possible if the party that is not participating in the arbitration has no knowledge of such arbitration. In practice, however, this notice requirement is more relevant to cases of intervention. When it comes to the joinder of a party in an existing arbitration, the party to be joined would undoubtedly be notified about the pending arbitration by the request for joinder.

Thirdly, the IBA Guidelines also suggest that there should be a clear time period following the notice for the non-participating party to intervene or to be joined in the

[38] Ibid., p. 39 (para. 108).
[39] Ibid., p. 40 (para. 109).
[40] Ibid., p. 39 (para. 107).
[41] Ibid., p. 36 (para. 103).

proceedings and that no arbitrator should be appointed before the expiry of that time period[42]. This latter requirement is at odds with the mechanism in some of the analysed standard forms, such as the Blue Form, the JCT 80 Contracts, the ACA Standard Forms, the IChemE Contracts and the ENAA Process Plant Model, whereunder the tribunal may often have been appointed at the time when the third party (most often a subcontractor) is joined in the proceedings.

Commentary on the IBA Guidelines

The IBA Guidelines provide little help to those seeking a readily available multi-party arbitration clause covering the construction disputes discussed in this book. Despite this, the guidelines are useful because they prescribe in general terms the different forms of contractual multi-party arbitration solutions. Furthermore, they remind drafters of multi-party arbitration clauses to address certain matters therein such as the mechanism for appointment of the tribunal and its jurisdiction, as well as the notices that should be given to parties not involved in the pending arbitration. These questions will be discussed in more detail in Subsection 7.3.3 below. However, for the purposes of this section the reader's attention is drawn to the following two matters: the umbrella agreement, which is the first proposed contractual form of regulation of multi-party arbitration, and the compatibility of the arbitration agreements in two or more contracts.

(i) The Umbrella Arbitration Agreement

The umbrella arbitration agreement is a stand-alone document binding all parties. It is true that such a document is probably the most straightforward way to deal with multi-contract arbitration issues. The existence of an umbrella agreement can be very useful, especially for the employer, when it comes to projects based on the *construction management* model and the *management contracting model*[43]. Under the former model, the employer enters into separate bilateral contracts with a design team, a project manager and one or more main contractors, and under the latter model, the employer enters into bilateral agreements with a management contractor and a design team. In these cases, the employer is often in a position to impose on the contracting parties the content of the different bilateral contracts, which may also incorporate the terms of the umbrella agreement. Thus, the employer may rely on this agreement to bring all these parties into single multi-party arbitration, which may be wanted in case of, for example, defective works caused by multiple parties.

An umbrella agreement may prescribe in detail the procedure that should be followed if related disputes arise under the different agreements. Arbitration may be initiated by any party to the umbrella agreement and notices of such arbitration should be given to all other parties. A sample of such an umbrella agreement has been suggested by

---

[42] Ibid., p. 36 (para. 103).

[43] See Subsections 3.3.3 and 3.3.4 hereof.

some practitioners[44]. The author does not intend to embark on a detailed discussion about the content of such an agreement. The reader is referred to the questions discussed in Subsection 7.3.3, most of which are also relevant for drafting umbrella arbitration agreements. The main benefit of having an umbrella arbitration agreement is that it incorporates all parties' consent to multi-party arbitration. Most modern sets of arbitration rules would allow such a multi-party arbitration even if one or some of the parties to the umbrella agreement object to it. For example, if the ICC Rules are the arbitration rules chosen under the umbrella agreement and a party raises an objection to the jurisdiction of the tribunal, the arbitral tribunal would be entitled to assume jurisdiction over all the disputes arising under the contracts covered by the umbrella agreement. Similarly, if the matter has been referred for a prima facie decision to the ICC Court, the ICC Court would almost certainly reach a decision that there is a prima facie basis for the conduct of multi-party proceedings under Article 6(4) of the ICC Rules because of the existence of a single arbitration agreement among all parties (see Subsection 4.1.1).

Even though the execution of a single umbrella agreement is a feasible option to ensure multi-party arbitration involving all parties – signatories to that agreement, these agreements are rarely seen in the construction sector. At the time of execution of the umbrella agreement there is often no clarity about the identity of all parties to be involved in the specific construction project. The umbrella agreement is commonly executed together with the main contract. Subcontractors are usually hired by the main contractor following the execution of the main contract. Thus, it may be the case that some of these subcontractors are not known at the time when the umbrella agreement is executed. As a result, these subcontractors will not be parties to this stand-alone document. This will exclude their participation in a contemplated multi-party arbitration. Similarly, under the *design-and-build* model, the engineer or the architect who is to prepare the drawings may be hired by the main contractor after the execution of the main contract. Thus, there will be no professional services agreement with the designer at the time when the umbrella agreement is entered into. As a result, the main contractor will be unable to rely on the umbrella agreement in order to request the joinder of the designer into the pending main contract arbitration. In order to avoid these situations, the main contract or the umbrella agreement would sometimes contain a provision that obliges the main contractor to ensure that any engineer, architect or a subcontractor hired by the main contractor accedes to the umbrella agreement[45]. There is, however, no guarantee that these parties

---

[44] Jan Paulsson, Nigel Rawding and Lucy Reed (2011) *The Freshfields Guide to Arbitration Clauses in International Contracts*, 3rd edn, Kluwer Law International, Alphen aan den Rijn – see Appendix 5, pp. 157–160. Martin Bartels, 'Multiparty Arbitration Clauses', in *2 Journal of International Arbitration*, no. 2 (1985), pp. 60–66. The drafting objectives concerning umbrella arbitration agreements have been discussed by Paul Friedland (see Paul Friedland (2007) *Arbitration Clauses for International Contracts*, 2nd edn, New York: JurisNet, pp. 136–137).

[45] For an example of a similar clause, see Jan Paulsson, Nigel Rawding and Lucy Reed (2011) *The Freshfields Guide to Arbitration Clauses in International Contracts*, 3rd edn, Kluwer Law International, Alphen aan den Rijn, p. 160. The suggested clause constitutes a part of the sample multi-party umbrella agreement and reads as follows: 'If any new agreement is entered into between any of the parties or between any party to this Agreement and a third party, the parties shall procure that this Agreement is amended to: (a) add such third party as a signatory to this Agreement; and/or (b) incorporate such new agreement in the list of Transaction Documents.'

would actually do so. For example, the main contractor may forget to include a clause in his subcontract stipulating that the subcontractor should accede to the umbrella agreement or the subcontractor may simply refuse to do so. Parties that have not acceded to the umbrella agreement cannot be dragged into multi-party arbitration.

(ii) Compatible Arbitration Agreements

This question only arises under the second form of contractual regulation of multi-party arbitration – that is, separate arbitration agreements inserted in each of the related contracts. Compatible arbitration clauses in the sense of the IBA Guidelines mean clauses that are either identical or complementary. In the author's opinion, multi-party arbitration provisions, such as those in the ACA Main Contract and the ACA Subcontract, are examples of the second type of clauses. Even though these provisions are not identical, they complement each other because they prescribe the conditions under which a certain subcontract dispute may be referred to an arbitral tribunal constituted under a main contract. The draft multi-party arbitration clauses in the ENAA Process Plant Model follow a similar approach.

As a matter of fact, most multi-party arbitration clauses to be found in contracts concerning the same construction project would not be identical *sensu stricto*. Therefore, the question of arbitration clauses with identical wording does not arise in these cases. This question is more relevant in cases where the separate arbitration clauses are silent on multi-party arbitration. The problem that arises then is whether the arbitral tribunal may assume jurisdiction over all the parties on the basis of the fact that the parties have included identical clauses in the different contracts. It may be argued that the parties' consent to multi-party arbitration in these situations may be presumed on the basis of the identical wording of the clauses. In the author's opinion, this observation may be true only when it comes to multiple contracts binding the same parties. If the contracts are concluded by different parties, consent to multi-party arbitration may not be presumed on the basis of the identical arbitration clauses *per se* (see Subsection 2.4.1). However, if these clauses refer to arbitration rules that vest the arbitral tribunal with a wide discretion to consolidate proceedings without the explicit agreement of the parties, the reference to the rules as such might be considered as the parties' consent to be involved in multi-party arbitration. It is exactly in this latter case that it matters whether the separate arbitration clauses are compatible in the sense that they have identical wording or at least non-contradictory wording. Therefore, the author discusses the question of the compatibility in more detail in Subsection 7.4.2 in the context of the proposed solution to multi-party arbitration at the level of the applicable arbitration rules.

7.3.2 AAA Guide to Drafting Alternative Dispute Resolution Clauses for Construction Contracts

The AAA Guide to Drafting Alternative Dispute Resolution Clauses for Construction Contracts ('***AAA Guide***')[46] is drafted by the American Arbitration Association. As its name suggests, the focus in the guide is on construction disputes. Even though the AAA

---

[46] *The AAA Guide to Drafting Alternative Dispute Resolution Clauses for Construction Contracts*, last revised on 1 July 2015, https://www.adr.org/aaa/ShowPDF?doc=ADRSTG_002542 (accessed 26 July 2016).

Guide is written with reference to certain rules primarily designed for domestic arbitrations in the United States, such as, for example, the CIAR, it is intended to assist parties in drafting alternative dispute resolution clauses for both domestic and international cases. The AAA Guide acknowledges that some standard construction industry documents, such as the AIA forms and the ConsensusDocs, contain certain joinder and consolidation provisions and if the parties agree to use these forms they should follow these provisions. Nevertheless, the AAA Guide also contains an optional multi-party arbitration clause, which reads as follows:

> The owner, the contractor, and all subcontractors, specialty contractors, material suppliers, engineers, designers, architects, construction lenders, bonding companies and other parties concerned with the construction of the structure are bound, each to each other, by this arbitration clause, provided that they have signed this contract or a contract that incorporates this contract by reference or signed any other agreement to be bound by this arbitration clause. Each such party agrees that it may be joined as an additional party to an arbitration involving other parties under any such agreement. If more than one arbitration is begun under any such agreement and any party contends that two or more arbitrations are substantially related and that the issues should be heard in one proceeding, the arbitrator(s) selected in the first-filed of such proceedings shall determine whether, in the interests of justice and efficiency, the proceedings should be consolidated before that (those) arbitrator(s).[47]

The wording of the clause suggests that it may be part of either an umbrella arbitration agreement or an arbitration clause contained in a bilateral contract. In the latter case, all the related contracts should contain the same clause in order to enable the multi-party arbitration envisaged thereunder. The clause is illustrative of how a multitude of parties involved in a construction project may all give their consent to multi-party arbitration.

Despite the merits of the clause, it raises many questions. The scope of the clause is very broad, as it encompasses not only the main participants in construction projects, such as employers, main contractors, designers, project managers, subcontractors and suppliers, but also 'any other parties concerned with the construction of the structure'. Is it not reasonable to limit the number of parties that may participate in a multi-party arbitration? The clause generally states that a party may be joined in existing arbitration. The clause, however, does not prescribe under what circumstances such a joinder may take place and at what point of time the joinder should be requested. Consolidation will be possible if 'two or more arbitrations are substantially related', but there is no similar text regarding the link between the disputes in cases concerning joinder. As regards consolidation, the provision envisages that the arbitrators in the arbitration that was first in time should decide whether the disputes should be consolidated or not. But is it the same tribunal that would review the consolidated cases or should it be a different one? And what would happen with the jurisdiction of the arbitrators sitting in the second arbitration and the costs incurred in the latter?

[47] The AAA Guide, p. 15. The same clause is contained in *Drafting Dispute Resolution Clauses – A Practical Guide*, last revised in 2013, American Arbitration Association, https://www.adr.org/aaa/ShowPDF?doc=ADRSTG_002540 (accessed 26 July 2016).

The provision does not give answers to the above questions. Presumably, the reason for this is that the clause has been drafted to correspond with the CIAR and Rule R-7 contained therein. In other words, it may have been the expectation of the drafters that the provision will be applied in conjunction with Rule R-7. As discussed in Subsection 4.6.1, Rule R-7 allows for the appointment of a single arbitrator who should decide on the joinder or consolidation request if the parties cannot reach an agreement on the matter. Among his other powers, that arbitrator is also entitled to establish a process for selecting arbitrators to deal with the consolidated arbitration and to allocate the responsibility for the arbitrators' compensation among the parties. Thus, some of the questions raised above can find their answer in the application of Rule R-7. However, this will not necessarily be the case if the clause is applied in conjunction with other institutional rules that do not contain a provision similar to R-7 of the CIAR.

7.3.3 Drafting Multi-Party Arbitration Clauses

Ad hoc multi-party arbitration clauses are often the result of the exercise of bargaining power between contracting parties when negotiating their contracts. While multi-party arbitration clauses will be beneficial to some parties, they may be undesired by other parties involved in the project. For example, the employer will often be in a position to impose the content of the proposed multi-party arbitration clause on the main contractor. A draft of the construction contract often forms part of the tender documentation submitted to prospective contractors. Therefore, contractors often have to make their bids on a *take-it-or-leave-it* basis, and their power to request amendments in the draft contract is limited[48]. Thus, for example, a main contractor bidding for the project will have to accept in his contract a multi-party arbitration clause envisaging his participation in arbitration with an engineer appointed by the employer, even though the main contractor is not interested in such arbitration. This reflects the stronger bargaining power of the employer who has the legitimate discretion to choose the party he wants to contract with. Similarly, the employer is generally in a position to impose the content of the professional services agreement on other parties with which he contracts, such as architects, engineers and / or project managers. The same can be said about the relations between a main contractor and a subcontractor, where the subcontract is commonly based on a contract proposed by the main contractor, which is drafted 'back-to-back' to the terms of the main contract.

Thus, multi-party arbitration agreements under construction contracts frequently reflect situations where the party that has proposed the clause has a superior bargaining power over the party that has accepted such a clause. This in itself should not raise any issues concerning the validity of contractual multi-party arbitration clauses. Unlike other types of contracts, for example consumer contracts, provisions resulting from

[48] Even though this statement is generally true, there might be some exceptions. For example, the case could be different if the construction project requires the exercise of a particular workmanship which few contractors possess. These few contractors may well have higher bargaining power, which would entitle them to introduce some material amendments in the proposed draft contract.

unequal bargaining power are generally tolerated under laws applicable to international commercial transactions. It is commonplace in these transactions that one of the parties (usually the party paying the contract price) has a higher influence in the negotiation process, and this reflects normal commercial practices.

Before embarking on drafting a multi-party arbitration clause, the draftsman should keep his mind on three main postulates. These postulates should guide him through the drafting process in order to facilitate the creation of a clause that is workable from both a theoretical and a practical perspective.

The first postulate is that there is no one-size-fits-all clause. Even if one succeeds in constructing a proper multi-party arbitration clause, this clause will not be suitable for universal use. It was exactly for this reason that the Working Party on Multi-Party Arbitration at the ICC refrained from introducing a draft multi-party arbitration clause[49]. Such a clause should always be tailored to the specifics of the construction project at stake, the content of the chosen contract and the needs of the party for whose benefit the clause is created.

Secondly, drafting multi-party arbitration clauses requires significant foresight and drafting skills. In order to construct a proper multi-party arbitration clause, the drafter should have a complete understanding of the dispute resolution mechanisms in the contracts whereunder related disputes may arise and to consider a number of factors that may affect the conduct of the proceedings. The drafter should diligently foresee the type of claims that may arise depending on the particularities of the construction project and their implications for parties not bound by the contract under which the claims have arisen. Then, the drafter should try to apply the clause he has created to the possible scenarios and check whether the clause is operative. If the drafter identifies some stumbling blocks in the operation of the clause, he should think how to overcome these and make the necessary amendments in the clause.

Finally, multi-party arbitration clauses should not be viewed in isolation from the overall regulative framework applicable to arbitration. Arbitration agreements, including multi-party arbitration clauses, do not exist in legal vacuum. They should be drafted and read in the light of both the applicable arbitration rules and the applicable arbitration law. In principle, a direct conflict between a multi-party arbitration clause and the chosen arbitration rules is unlikely. Most provisions in modern sets of arbitration rules are non-mandatory. Therefore, parties are normally allowed to deviate in their arbitration agreements from the solutions adopted in the arbitration rules. For example, if the parties have provided for a mechanism for the constitution of the tribunal in the arbitration clause, such a mechanism should generally be accepted even if it does not conform to the mechanism stipulated in the applicable arbitration rules[50]. In most cases, however,

[49] The working party was set up by the Commission of International Arbitration at the ICC. The work of the working party was materialized in a final report, which was submitted to the ICC in 1994. See ICC Commission on International Arbitration, 'Final Report on Multi-Party Arbitrations', in 6 *ICC International Court Arbitration Bulletin*, no. 1 (1995), pp. 26–50. Pursuant to Appendix 1 to this report: 'The Working Group has decided not to propose any standard multi-party arbitration agreement, due to the diversity of possible situations.' However, the report contains a list of several multi-party arbitration clauses published for informative and illustrative purposes only.

[50] See, for example, Article 11 (6) of the ICC Rules.

a multi-party arbitration clause will not regulate in detail any and all aspects of the arbitration. Often such a clause regulates only some aspects of the procedure, whereas the arbitration rules find application to other aspects that are not explicitly addressed in the multi-party arbitration clause. For example, if the multi-party arbitration clause allows for a joinder of a party but does not provide for a time frame within which the joinder request should be made, this does not mean that there is no time limit for such a request. The applicable arbitration rules may contain provisions that can preclude the joinder of a party after the expiry of a certain period or the occurrence of certain events. For example, under the ICC Rules the principal position is that no joinder will be possible after the confirmation or appointment of any arbitrator[51]. Furthermore, the Secretariat with the ICC Court of Arbitration may fix a time limit for the submission of a request for joinder[52]. In cases where the respondent tries to join an additional party to the arbitration, the Secretariat will typically require that the joinder request should be made in the respondent's answer to the request for arbitration[53]. Likewise, if the period of submission of claims among the multiple parties is not prescribed in the multi-party arbitration clause, the applicable rules will often contain a provision precluding claims after a certain date[54]. Therefore, the draftsman should always take into account the applicable arbitration rules and consider how the multi-party arbitration clause can be operated in conjunction with these rules. If a certain procedural solution under the rules (e.g. a time period for a joinder request or submission of claims or an institutionally prescribed mechanism for appointment of arbitrators) is at variance with what the drafter anticipates, he should try to address these matters explicitly in the multi-party arbitration clause.

The draftsman's task may seem easier when it comes to national arbitration laws. Arbitration laws usually give full credit to the principle of party autonomy in arbitral proceedings as a result of which they do not typically impose any requirements as to the validity of multi-party arbitration clauses[55]. This also follows from Article II of the New York Convention whereunder contracting states are obliged to recognize arbitration clauses in parties' contracts. Therefore, multi-party arbitration clauses should be capable of being operated without causing any tension with applicable arbitration laws[56].

---

[51] Article 7(1) of the ICC Rules.

[52] Ibid.

[53] Jason Fry, Simon Greenberg and Francesca Mazza (2012) *The Secretariat's Guide to ICC Arbitration*, ICC Publication No. 729, ICC Publishing SA, Paris, p. 100 (§ 3-305–306).

[54] For example, Article 8 of the ICC Rules, which concerns claims between multiple parties, states that no new claims can be made after the Terms of Reference are signed and approved.

[55] This statement has been based on the information contained in the country arbitration guides prepared by the Arbitration Committee with the International Bar Association, www.ibanet.org/Article/Detail.aspx?ArticleUid=a646cf32-0ad8-4666-876b-c3d045028e64 (accessed 26 July 2016). One of the standard questions posed in the guide is: 'What are the requirements for a valid multi-party arbitration agreement?' Out of the available 53 country guides, 49 stipulate that there are no particular requirements concerning the validity of multi-party arbitration agreements. See also Ricardo Ugarte and Thomas Bevilacqua, 'Ensuring Party Equality in the Process of Designating Arbitrators in Multi-Party Arbitration: An Update on the Governing Provisions', in *27 Journal of International Arbitration*, no. 1 (2010), pp. 9–49.

[56] Gary Born (2012) *International Arbitration: Law and Practice*, Kluwer Law International, Alphen aan den Rijn, pp. 222–223.

However, some states have occasionally introduced limitations in respect of multi-party arbitration clauses. These limitations are contained either in local arbitration laws or case law. It would be beyond the scope of this book to embark on a detailed review of local arbitration laws in order to identify any and all limitations that may affect the validity of properly agreed multi-party arbitration clauses. These limitations predominantly concern cases where the arbitration agreements do not guarantee parties' equal influence in the constitution of the arbitral tribunal. Such limitations exist, for example, in France[57], Germany[58], Italy[59], the Netherlands[60], Spain[61], Poland[62] and Lebanon[63]. Therefore, the draftsman should check carefully the content of the applicable arbitration law and any relevant case law that may impose similar restrictions. If such restrictions are identified, the drafter should try to construct the multi-party arbitration clause in

[57] These limitations result from the decision in the *Dutco* case (discussed in Subsection 6.2.3.4).

[58] See Article 1034(2) of the German Arbitration Act, http://arbitrationlaw.com/files/free_pdfs/German%20Arbitration%20Act.pdf (accessed 26 July 2016). Pursuant to this article, if an arbitration agreement grants preponderant rights to one party with regard to the composition of the arbitral tribunal, which places the other party at a disadvantage, that other party may request the court to appoint the arbitrator or arbitrators in deviation from the agreed nomination procedure. The request should be submitted within 2 weeks of that other party becoming aware of the constitution of the tribunal. See also Richard Kreindler, Thomas Kopp and Nicole Rother (2013) *Arbitration Guide, IBA Arbitration Committee, Germany*, pp. 4–5, http://www.ibanet.org/Document/Default.aspx?DocumentUid=72111D60-6585-412C-B239-189ABF22108F (accessed 26 July 2016).

[59] Mauro Rubino-Sammartano (2009) 'Italy', in Frank Bernd Weigand (ed.) *Practitioner's Handbook on International Commercial Arbitration*, 2nd edn, Oxford University Press, Oxford, p. 550. According to the author, if the arbitration agreement does not allow each party to be on an equal footing when it comes to the appointment of the tribunal, the agreement may not give rise to valid proceedings.

[60] See Article 1028 of the Netherlands Code of Civil Procedure. Pursuant to this article, if a party is given a privileged position with regard to the appointment of an arbitrator or arbitrators under the terms of an arbitration agreement or otherwise, the other party may, despite the pre-agreed method of appointment, request the competent provisional relief judge at the District Court to appoint the arbitrator or the arbitrators. Such a request should be made within 3 months from commencement of the arbitration. See also Ricardo Ugarte and Thomas Bevilacqua, 'Ensuring Party Equality in the Process of Designating Arbitrators in Multi-Party Arbitration: An Update on the Governing Provisions', in *27 Journal of International Arbitration*, no. 1 (2010), pp. 26–27.

[61] See Article 15(2) of the Spanish Arbitration Law (Act 60/2003 on Arbitration), pursuant to which: 'The parties are able to freely agree on the procedure for the appointment of the arbitrators, provided that there is no violation of the principle of equal treatment.' For an English translation of the Spanish Arbitration Law, see David Cairns and Alejandro Lopez Ortiz, *Spain's New Arbitration Act*, http://www.voldgiftsforeningen.dk/Admin/Public/Download.aspx?file=Files%2FFiler%2F2011%2FNationale_love%2FSpanien.pdf (accessed 26 July 2016).

[62] See Bartosz Kruzewski and Monika Diehl (2013) *Arbitration Guide, IBA Arbitration Committee, Poland*, p. 5, http://www.ibanet.org/Document/Default.aspx?DocumentUid=DE8F3274-8525-432D-9118-88300110F445 (accessed 1 August 2016). See also Article 1169 § 3 of the Polish Code of Civil Procedure, http://sakig.pl/uploads/upfiles/pdf/kpc-ang.pdf (accessed 26 July 2016), pursuant to which provisions granting one of the parties more rights in the procedure of appointment of the arbitral tribunal are ineffective.

[63] See Nayla Comair-Obeid (2012) *Arbitration Guide, IBA Arbitration Committee, Lebanon*, pp. 5–6, http://www.ibanet.org/Document/Default.aspx?DocumentUid=9D05A58F-F3E7-4585-A3F9-C69B8309D42D (accessed 5 August 2016). Pursuant to the guide, the Court of Appeal in Lebanon has confirmed in a recent decision from 19 October 2010 that the principle of equality of the parties in the appointment of arbitrators is a fundamental principle in arbitration that concerns public policy and can only be waived after the dispute has arisen. Thus, this decision substantially resembles the decision in the *Dutco* case.

such a way that it is not affected by these limitations. Alternatively, the drafter may give preference to a seat of arbitration that results in the application of a national arbitration law which does not impose similar restrictions.

This Subsection continues with a detailed list of matters that the draftsman should consider when constructing multi-party arbitration clauses. These matters can be considered as the main components of a proper multi-party arbitration clause. The list tries to identify certain good practices with regard to each of these matters which are likely to cause least problems in legal practice. The list can also be considered as a checklist by drafters of these clauses. The author has tried to be as explicit and detailed as possible in the proposed list. Some matters in the proposed list derive from a stimulating article written by His Honour Humphrey Lloyd[64]. The proposed list goes into further detail and also considers additional matters which have not been addressed in the abovementioned article.

The section will deal with each of the following questions in the sequence given below:

1. How to draft the clause in a way that incorporates all parties' consent?
2. How to describe the disputes to be submitted to multi-party arbitration?
3. How to ensure the compatibility of the clause with contractual preconditions to arbitration?
4. What should be the required link between the disputes which would justify their joint review?
5. Who is to decide whether such a link exists?
6. How is the tribunal to be constituted?
7. What type of multi-party arbitration should the clause envisage?
8. Should there be any limit on the number of parties involved in multi-party arbitration?
9. How to exclude or limit multi-party arbitration?

7.3.3.1 How to draft the clause in a way that incorporates all parties' consent?

This question deals with the knotty problem of how to create a self-contained contractual multi-party arbitration mechanism that can be put into operation solely on the basis of contractual provisions without the need to obtain any party's *ad hoc* consent. The drafter should bear in mind that an arbitration clause in a bilateral contract is binding only on the parties that have signed that contract. If such a clause envisages the joinder of a third party, the clause cannot be directly invoked against the third party who is non-privy to the contract containing the clause. Hence, if the main contractor wants to join the subcontractor into his arbitration with the employer, he should ensure that separate multi-party arbitration clauses are inserted in both the main contract and the subcontract[65]. If the multi-party arbitration clause is present in the main contract only, the subcontractor is

---

[64] See Humphrey Lloyd (1991) 'A National Experience', in P. Bellet, P. Bernardini, G. Bernini *et al.* (eds) *Multi-Party Arbitration: Views from International Arbitration Specialists*, Publication No. 480/1, ICC Publishing SA, Paris, pp. 66–74. In his article, His Honour Humphrey Lloyd poses a list of questions which should be considered by drafters of multi-party arbitration clauses.

[65] The same applies to cases where the employer wants to join a nominated subcontractor into his arbitration with the main contractor.

entitled to object to the joinder because he is not privy to the main contract. Similarly, if the multi-party arbitration clause is contained in a subcontract only (as, for example, in the case of the Blue Form and the International IChemE Subcontract examined in Chapter 6 above), the employer may object to the joinder because he is not privy to the subcontract. The same considerations apply with regard to *build-only* contractual models where the employer may want to conduct multi-party arbitration with the participation of the main contractor and the designer. In these cases, the employer should ensure that appropriate multi-party arbitration clauses are inserted in both the main contract and the professional services agreement executed with the designer.

In addition, the draftsman should carefully distinguish between situations where the arbitration clauses in the related agreements contemplate the same type of multi-party arbitration from those envisaging different types of multi-party arbitration. Examples of the first type are the multi-party arbitration clauses in the ACA Main Contract and the ACA Subcontract (discussed in Section 6.4). These clauses determine how a subcontract dispute can be referred to an arbitrator appointed under the main contract. In the same vein, the draft multi-party arbitration clauses in the ENAA Process Plant Model (discussed in Section 6.9) contemplate a situation where a dispute under a subcontract or a supply agreement can be referred to an arbitrator appointed (or to be appointed) under the main contract and reviewed together with a related main contract dispute. This type of multi-party arbitration clauses can principally be put into operation without the need to obtain the parties' *ad hoc* consent. In other words, these clauses are capable of constituting a self-contained mechanism for resolution of multi-party disputes because the related clauses can be construed as providing all parties' consent to multi-party arbitration. For example, under the terms of the main contract multi-party arbitration clause, the employer has agreed that a subcontractor could be joined in the main contract arbitration. Similarly, the subcontractor has also provided his consent to the joinder under the terms of the subcontract multi-party arbitration clause. The main contractor, as a party to both arbitration clauses, has also agreed to the contemplated joinder.

The situation is more complex when it comes to the second type of clause – clauses that anticipate different types of multi-party arbitration. The approach under the JCT 80 suite (discussed in Section 6.3) is exemplary in that regard. The main contract addressed a situation where a main contract dispute could be referred to an arbitrator appointed under a subcontract or a supply agreement, whereas the subcontract and the supply contract addressed cases where a subcontract dispute, or respectively a dispute under a supply contract, could be referred to an arbitrator under the main contract. It is debatable whether these types of clauses constitute a self-contained mechanism for resolution of related multi-contract disputes. As already mentioned, an arbitration clause is in principle only binding on the parties signatories to the clause. For example, under the terms of a main contract multi-party arbitration clause the employer has agreed that his dispute under the main contract may be referred to a subcontract arbitrator, and respectively that the employer may be joined in the subcontract arbitration under certain conditions. This, however, does not necessarily mean that the employer has consented that a subcontract dispute may be referred to a main contract arbitrator. The latter type of multi-party arbitration, which is generally anticipated under a subcontract to which the employer is not privy, is different from that envisaged under the main contract.

Similarly, the subcontractor has agreed under the subcontract arbitration clause that his dispute may be referred to a main contract arbitrator but has not necessarily agreed that a main contract dispute may be referred to a subcontract arbitrator. Again, the latter scenario is regulated only under the main contract to which the subcontractor is not privy.

The abovementioned multi-party arbitration clauses envisage different types of multi-party arbitration, which gives rise to arguments that the parties bound by an arbitration clause have agreed only to the type of multi-party arbitration under that clause but not to the other type of multi-party arbitration under the related contract containing the other arbitration clause. The parties sitting at the end of the chain (in the case of the JCT 80 suite these would be the employer and the subcontractor) may always object to the type of multi-party arbitration envisaged under a related contract to which they are not parties. For example, the employer may object to the joinder of the subcontractor in the main contract arbitration because this joinder is not explicitly anticipated in the main contract arbitration clause. As a result, the employer's *ad hoc* consent will be required for the joinder. *Trafalgar House Construction Ltd. v. Railtrack Plc.*[66] dealt exactly with these questions. The judge in the case acknowledged that the wording of the multi-party arbitration clauses in the JCT 80 suite could have been much clearer[67]. Regardless, he reached the conclusion that the clauses might be interpreted in a way that created a self-contained mechanism for resolution of disputes. The conclusion was reached, *inter alia*, by reason of the overall purpose of the discussed clauses, which was to avoid inconsistent findings on the same facts, and the JCT 80 contractual scheme where the employer was assumed to have knowledge of the multi-party arbitration clause contained in the JCT 80 subcontract. Despite the authoritative nature of this decision and the convincing arguments contained therein, it is far from certain that the same reasoning will be followed by arbitrators or judges interpreting multi-party arbitration clauses similar to the clauses contained in the JCT 80 suite. Therefore, contracting parties using such clauses should formulate them in a way ensuring that their application is not thwarted by a party's argument that multi-party arbitration is not possible because the provision contemplating it is contained in a contract to which this party is non-signatory. Such a risk can be avoided, for example, by the mechanism of cross-referencing to the arbitration clauses in the respective contracts. For example, the main contract can refer to the multi-party arbitration clause in the subcontract, which will generally ensure the employer's consent to the type of arbitration contemplated under the subcontract. Similarly, the subcontract can refer to the main contract arbitration clause. In this way, each party will have knowledge of the multi-party arbitration clauses contained in the two contracts, which can ensure their smooth operation.

7.3.3.2 How to describe the disputes to be submitted to multi-party arbitration?

When constructing multi-party arbitration clauses, the drafter should think of the subject matter of the referral to arbitration. Arbitration clauses typically stipulate that the subject matter of referral is a *dispute*. Hence, in the context of multi-party arbitration

---

[66] See Subsection 6.3.1.1 above

[67] *Trafalgar House Construction (Regions) Ltd. v. Railtrack plc*, in *76 Building Law Reports* (1995), pp. 85–86.

clauses discussed here, there should be two or more *disputes* arising under two or more related contracts. Before using this conventional wording, the drafter should peruse whether the contract into which the multi-party arbitration clause is to be incorporated ascribes some special meaning to the word *dispute*.

As discussed in Subsection 6.2.1.1, the words *claim* and *dispute* are not equivalent in the construction sector. Disputes are commonly based on claims but not all claims progress into disputes. It is generally accepted that a dispute occurs when a party files a claim that has been rejected, in whole or in part, and the same party wishes to pursue that claim further. However, the exact meaning of *dispute* might differ depending on the specific contract that is used. Often standard form agreements attribute a special connotation to the word *dispute*, which requires the fulfilment of certain procedural requirements. Thus, under the 1999 FIDIC suite of contracts, a contractor's claim filed in compliance with the contractual requirements, which has been rejected by the engineer, will qualify as a dispute, provided that the contractor expresses his dissatisfaction with the engineer's determination by way of referral to the DAB[68]. The position is similar under the IChemE Contracts[69]. Other standard forms, such as the Blue Form, the ENAA Process Plan Model, the ICC Contracts and NEC3, do not prescribe any such special meaning to the word *dispute* and therefore the emergence of a dispute is not necessarily contingent on the compliance of a certain procedure or the issuance of a certain act, such as, for example, an engineer's determination or a decision[70].

The process of drafting multi-party arbitration clauses is especially intricate when it comes to the first category of contracts – those implying a special meaning of a *dispute*. Whenever the drafter refers to a *dispute* in the multi-party arbitration clause, this means that he also sets forth certain procedural requirements before the multi-party arbitration clause can be put into operation. The drafter should consider carefully if this is what he is aiming for. For example, if a main contractor wants to join a subcontractor into his pending arbitration with the employer because of discovered defects in the subcontract works, the main contractor should first claim against the subcontractor under the subcontract. It is not until the subcontractor rejects the main contractor's claim or otherwise fails to acquiesce with the claim that a dispute arises[71]. Therefore, it is exactly at this

[68] Dimitar Hristoforov Kondev, 'Is Dispute Adjudication under FIDIC Contracts for Major Works Indeed a Precondition to Arbitration?', in *31 International Construction Law Review*, Part 3 (2014), p. 257. See also Subsections 6.2.1.1 and 6.2.2.

[69] Clause 44.4 of the international IChemE main forms of contract. See also Section 6.6 hereof.

[70] See the discussion on *M J Gleeson Group Plc v. Wyatt of Snetterton Ltd.* and *Erith Contractors Ltd. v. Costain Civil Engineering Ltd.* in Subsection 6.2.1.1.

[71] Under subcontracts, there is commonly no engineer who makes a determination on parties' claims. For example, sub-clause 3.3 of the FIDIC Subcontract envisages that the main contractor should give notice to the subcontractor of his claim and detailed particulars of the claim. Thereafter, the main contractor should consult with the subcontractor in an endeavour to reach an agreement on the amount claimed. If agreement is not reached, the contractor should himself make a fair determination of his own claim. However, the approach under the IChemE Subcontract is different. Under sub-clause 44.3 of the latter subcontract, there is a contract manager who should take a decision with regard to any matter arising under the subcontract with which either party is dissatisfied. Under sub-clause 44.4, a subcontract dispute arises if: (i) such a decision is not acceptable for either party or if the contract manager has failed to give his decision within the prescribed time, and, as a consequence, (ii) either party has given a notice of dispute.

point of time when the multi-party arbitration clause can be put into operation. If the subcontractor admits the claim there is no dispute and the precondition for the existence of a subcontract dispute in the multi-party arbitration clauses will not be fulfilled. The situation is similar with regard to claims starting from the bottom of the contractual chain, that is, subcontractor's claims that may trigger related main contractor's claims under the main contract and finally result in main contract disputes. If the subcontractor is claiming against the main contractor for a reason attributable to the employer (e.g. the employer was late in giving access to the site), the main contractor may have an interest in the conduct of multi-party arbitration with both the employer and the subcontractor. However, if the multi-party arbitration clause refers to the existence of a main contract dispute, the relevant procedural requirements should be complied with. In the context of the 1999 FIDIC suite of contracts, this would mean that the main contractor should first claim against the employer, wait for the engineer's decision on the claim and express his dissatisfaction with it before invoking the multi-party arbitration clause[72].

The very last example hints at another problem regarding the use of the word *dispute* in multi-party arbitration clauses. There are cases where multi-party arbitration may be needed even though there is no true dispute under one of the agreements. Subsection 6.2.3.1 touched upon this issue briefly. If the employer has given late access to the site, this may trigger a subcontractor's claim for extension of time and / or additional costs against the main contractor. Let us assume that the main contractor agrees that the employer's default has caused delay and therefore files an equivalent claim against the employer under the terms of the main contract. In this situation it may be argued that there is no dispute under the subcontract because the main contractor has not challenged the subcontractor's claim as such. As a result, the multi-party arbitration clause cannot be applied by reason of the lack of a subcontract dispute.

With regard to the abovementioned problem, it has been recommended that some other wording should be used in multi-party arbitration clauses so as to avoid situations where the clause becomes non-workable just because there is no *dispute* under one of the contracts. For example, His Honour Humphrey Lloyd has suggested that the following wording may be more appropriate instead of the conventional referral to a dispute: *some question or issue which has to be determined not only between (A) and (B) but also between (B) and (C)*[73]. This wording is indeed capable of eliminating the abovementioned risk. In the author's opinion, the suggested wording may be more appropriate for contracts that do not ascribe a special meaning to the word *dispute* but it may be problematic if adopted in contracts giving a special connotation to this word, such as the FIDIC Conditions and the IChemE Contracts. One of the central features of these contracts is their consistent claim management and dispute resolution procedures. A claim under

---

[72] See, for example, sub-clause 2.5 and sub-clause 3.5 from the FIDIC Red Book.

[73] Humphrey Lloyd (1991) 'A National Experience', in P. Bellet, P. Bernardini, G. Bernini *et al.* (eds) *Multi-Party Arbitration: Views from International Arbitration Specialists*, Publication No. 480/1, ICC Publishing SA, Paris, pp. 66–67. See also Dimitrios Athanasakis (2007) 'Has Multi-Party Arbitration Failed in Construction Disputes? Legal and Practical Issues in Drafting Joinder Provisions', in D. Boyd (ed.) *Procs 23rd Annual ARCOM Conference*, 3–5 September, Belfast, Association of Researchers in Construction Management, p. 111, http://www.arcom.ac.uk/-docs/proceedings/ar2007-0107-0116_Athanasakis.pdf (accessed 26 July 2016), who is also of the opinion that broader language is preferable in order to cover a variety of circumstances.

these contracts should first be referred to a third party for determination[74]. The claim crystalizes into a dispute if either party is dissatisfied with the third parties' determination (or if the third party has failed to give its determination within the prescribed time) and decides to pursue the matter further. The introduction of the alternative wording might cause much disturbance to this mechanism. If a certain common *question or issue* can be referred to multi-party arbitration, does this mean that any matter, including a matter that has not yet escalated into a dispute, may be referred to arbitration? If so, it follows that the multi-party arbitration clause creates an opportunity for contracting parties to bypass some of the mandatory requirements with regard to claims, for example the referral of the claim to a third party for determination. This would have a negative effect on the workability of the claim management provisions, especially for those contracting parties who find themselves bogged down in a multi-party arbitration with regard to claims that have not yet escalated into disputes. Therefore, the adoption of the suggested wording is not preferable with regard to the abovementioned category of contracts. If the drafter decides to introduce such wording, he should do so with utmost caution.

There are alternative ways to avoid the problem of certain matters falling short from the scope of the multi-party arbitration clause due to the lack of a proper dispute. Thus, for example, the main contractor may decide to challenge the subcontractor's claim concerning the late access to the site (for which the employer was ultimately responsible), even though he does not disagree with the subcontractor. In this way, the main contractor will ensure that there is a dispute under the subcontract. In the arbitration that will follow, the main contractor may still file his claim against the employer and this claim may well be identical with the subcontractor's claim against the main contractor. It is true that such an approach will be far from consistent from the main contractor's point of view but in this way the main contractor will preserve his right to invoke the multi-party arbitration clause. It is the author's opinion that this approach is likely to cause fewer practical problems than the issues which might otherwise occur from the adoption of the alternative wording proposed above.

7.3.3.3 How to ensure compatibility of the clause with contractual preconditions to arbitration?

The previous question has dealt with the meaning of the word *dispute* and the procedural requirements under some standard forms that have to be complied with in order to have a *dispute*. However, many standard forms pose further procedural requirements concerning dispute resolution in the form of multi-tier dispute resolution clauses. These requirements should not be confused with the former ones. Whereas the procedural requirements under the previous question address the period from the date of emergence of the claim until the date when the claim crystalizes into a dispute, this question will focus on the requirements applicable to the post-dispute phase of dispute resolution – the period from the emergence of the dispute until the date when the dispute is to be referred to arbitration.

---

[74] Under the FIDIC Conditions of Contract, this would be the Engineer. Under the IChemE Contracts, similar functions are to be carried out by the Project Manager.

In construction agreements, it is commonplace to find complex multi-tier dispute resolution clauses. Under these clauses a dispute should typically pass through several tiers before it is finally submitted to arbitration. The nature of these interim stages can have a significant impact on the admissibility and conduct of multi-party arbitration. Therefore, a brief discussion of the nature of some multi-tier dispute resolution clauses is necessary before embarking on a more elaborate analysis of their effect on multi-party arbitration.

Generally, the interim tiers in a dispute resolution clause have a mandatory character – a dispute cannot proceed to the next tier without first passing through the filter of a previous tier. Thus, a dispute should generally pass through all interim tiers before it is finally submitted to the final stage, which is arbitration or litigation. The 1999 FIDIC suite of contracts can exemplify this approach. Pursuant to these contracts, there is a three-step dispute resolution procedure, encompassing the following stages: (i) dispute adjudication by a DAB, (ii) an attempt to reach an amicable settlement and (iii) arbitration. Despite some different opinions on the matter, the prevailing view among scholars and practitioners nowadays is that the first two phases are preconditions to the commencement of arbitration[75]. Several parts of clause 20 of the 1999 FIDIC suite of contracts support this opinion. First, sub-clause 20.2 stipulates that 'Disputes shall be adjudicated by a DAB in compliance with Sub-Clause 20.4 [Obtaining Dispute Adjudication Board's Decision].' This means that all claims that turn into disputes should be subject to review by a DAB. Furthermore, the sixth paragraph of sub-clause 20.4, which deals with the notice of dissatisfaction against a DAB decision, contains probably the most cogent argument. This sub-clause states the general position that neither party shall be entitled to commence arbitration of a dispute unless a notice of dissatisfaction has been given against the DAB's decision in respect of that dispute[76]. Furthermore, sub-clause 20.5 specifies that prior to arbitration the parties should try to reach an amicable settlement of their dispute in relation to which a notice of dissatisfaction has been served. Thus, the sub-clause outlines in a clear way the sequence of steps that should be undertaken before

[75] Christopher Seppälä, 'The Arbitration Clause in FIDIC Contracts for Major Works', in *22 International Construction Law Review*, part 1 (2005), pp. 6–7. See also Dyalá Jiménez Figueres, 'Multi-Tiered Dispute Resolution Clauses in ICC Arbitration: Introduction and Commentary', in *14 ICC International Court of Arbitration Bulletin*, no. 1 (2003), p. 71; Götz-Sebastian Hök, 'Dispute Adjudication in Civil Law Countries – Phantom or Effective Dispute Resolution Method?', in *28 International Construction Law Review*, part 4 (2011), pp. 422–423, 426; Jane Jenkins (2013) *International Construction Arbitration Law*, 2nd revised edn, Kluwer Law International, Alphen aan den Rijn, pp. 398–399. However, it should be noted that an alternative interpretation of the FIDIC contractual provisions is followed in some countries in Central and Eastern Europe, which allows parties to bypass the dispute adjudication stage of the dispute resolution process. For an explanation of this alternative interpretation, see Dimitar Hristoforov Kondev, 'Is Dispute Adjudication under FIDIC Contracts for Major Works Indeed a Precondition to Arbitration?' in *31 International Construction Law Review*, part 3 (2014), pp. 256–268.

[76] Any deviations from this rule are exceptional, and, as evident from the wording of sub-clause 20.4, should satisfy either the conditions of sub-clause 20.7 or those of sub-clause 20.8. Sub-clause 20.7 only concerns cases where a DAB's decision has become final and binding and one of the parties fails to comply with it. In such a case, the other party may refer this failure directly to arbitration without having to go through dispute adjudication and amicable settlement a second time. The second exception under sub-clause 20.8 allegedly deals with cases where the DAB's appointment has expired.

the commencement of arbitration, namely, adjudication of the dispute, serving of a notice of dissatisfaction, and finally an attempt to reach an amicable solution. A further argument supporting the mandatory character of the DAB stage of the dispute settlement process is contained in sub-clause 20.6 which provides that 'Unless settled amicably, any dispute in respect of which the DAB's decision (if any) has not become final and binding shall be finally settled by international arbitration.' As Christopher Seppälä has noted, it follows from this sentence that only a dispute that has been referred to the DAB for a decision and which has not become the subject of a DAB's final and binding decision may be submitted to arbitration[77]. The content of some arbitral awards rendered under the auspices of the ICC International Court of Arbitration further emphasizes the importance of the pre-arbitral stages of dispute resolution under the FIDIC Contracts. It should be mentioned, however, that most of these awards dealt with disputes under earlier editions of the FIDIC Contracts in which there was no DAB and the engineer fulfilled the role of a dispute adjudicator instead[78]. Most of the known ICC awards were consistent in their approach towards the pre-arbitral procedure and concluded that a decision of the engineer was a precondition to the commencement of arbitration[79].

Similarly, more recent case law addressing the 1999 editions of the FIDIC Conditions of Contract confirms that the dispute adjudication phase of the dispute resolution mechanism under these editions has a mandatory character that cannot be bypassed by the parties[80].

On the basis of the above contractual provisions and arbitral awards, it can be concluded that a dispute that has not been referred to a DAB is premature and cannot proceed to arbitration. The arbitral tribunal will lack jurisdiction to review such a dispute. If it does so, it risks its award being set aside in the country where arbitration took place and / or its recognition and enforcement being denied in third countries[81].

---

[77] Christopher Seppälä, 'The Arbitration Clause in FIDIC Contracts for Major Works', in *22 International Construction Law Review*, part 1 (2005), pp. 6–7.

[78] The awards dealt with disputes that had arisen under the second (1969), third (1977) and fourth (1987) editions of the FIDIC Contracts.

[79] See Final award in ICC Case 6535 of 1992 (Extract), in *9 ICC International Court of Arbitration Bulletin*, no. 2 (1992), p. 60. In this case, the tribunal decided that it did not have jurisdiction to review a contractor's claim that had been previously referred to the engineer but not rejected by the latter. See also Partial Award in Cases 6276 and 6277 (Extract), in *9 ICC International Court of Arbitration Bulletin*, no. 2 (1998), p. 58, where the tribunal concluded that the contractor's claim was premature because it had not satisfied the prerequisites for arbitration set forth under the contract, as it had not been submitted for a decision to the engineer. See also ICC Case 12048 of 2003, cited by Christopher Seppälä, 'International Construction Contract Disputes: Third Commentary on ICC Awards', in *23 ICC International Court of Arbitration Bulletin*, no. 2 (2012), p. 27. In this latter case, the tribunal refused to consider counterclaims filed by the employer that had not been submitted to the engineer.

[80] See the ICC arbitral awards and the commentary on these awards in Christopher Seppälä, 'Commentary on Recent ICC Arbitral Awards dealing with Dispute Adjudication Boards under FIDIC Contracts', in *ICC Dispute Resolution Bulletin*, no. 1 (2015), pp. 28–30. See also *Peterborough City Council v. Enterprise Managed Services Ltd* [2014] EWHC 3193 (TCC), http://www.bailii.org/ew/cases/EWHC/TCC/2014/3193.html (accessed 6 November 2016), and the Swiss Federal Court's Decision 4A_124/2014 of 07 July 2014, http://www.servat.unibe.ch/dfr/bger/140707_4A_124-2014.html (accessed 6 November 2016).

[81] Christopher Seppälä, 'The Arbitration Clause in FIDIC Contracts for Major Works', in *22 International Construction Law Review*, part 1 (2005), pp. 6–7.

Dispute adjudication, as an interim stage in multi-tier dispute resolution clauses, can be found in other contracts. NEC3 envisages the following three-stage procedure: (i) notification of dispute, (ii) referral of the dispute to an adjudicator, and (iii) arbitration or litigation. As with the FIDIC Conditions of Contract, the adjudication stage is mandatory and cannot be bypassed by the parties[82]. The position is similar under the ICC Turnkey Contract. Pursuant to the latter, all disputes should be submitted, in the first instance, to a combined dispute board, and it is only afterwards that the party dissatisfied with the board's decision or recommendation, as the case may be, can refer the dispute to arbitration for final resolution[83].

Other contracts introduce different types of pre-arbitral steps. For example, the international IChemE main forms place a duty on the parties to make an attempt to negotiate a settlement[84]. The dispute can be referred to arbitration if it has not been settled[85]. The wording of the clauses creates the impression that the obligation to negotiate a settlement constitutes a precondition to arbitration[86]. Under the PPC2000, any difference or dispute should pass through numerous stages, which normally include giving notice, referral to senior individuals representing the partnering team members, meeting among the core group members, conciliation or mediation, adjudication, and finally litigation or arbitration[87]. The FIDIC White book introduces a three-stage dispute resolution system: (i) an attempt to settle the dispute by negotiation, (ii) mediation, and (iii) arbitration. Neither party may refer the dispute to arbitration without trying to settle it through mediation[88].

The draftsman should carefully consider the content of the multi-tier dispute resolution clauses under the respective contracts and the compatibility of the latter clauses with the relevant multi-party arbitration clause. More particularly, the drafter should try to foresee the impact of the multi-tier dispute resolution clause on the arbitration clause he is trying to construct. In principle, multi-tier dispute resolution clauses do not allow parties to leapfrog certain procedural steps and refer the dispute directly to arbitration. Thus, if the multi-party arbitration clause refers to disputes arising under two or more contracts, this means that all pre-arbitral steps with regard to each dispute should be exhausted before these disputes can be subject to multi-party arbitration. For example, let us assume that the employer wants to join the

---

[82] See clauses W1.3 (2) and W1.4 (1), W1.4 (2), W2.4 (1) and W2.4 (2) of the ECC. Similar clauses are contained in the ECS and the PSC.

[83] Articles 66.3 and 66.5 of the ICC Turnkey Contract. Similar provisions are to be found in the ICC Subcontract: see article 63 (Option A) and article 64 (Option B). Option A is substantially similar to the clause in the ICC Turnkey Contract. Option B envisages the referral of the dispute to parties' representatives. If this does not lead to a resolution of the dispute, either party has the option to ask for the appointment of an independent person who is to assist in the amicable resolution of the dispute. Finally, the dispute may be referred to arbitration.

[84] See, for example, sub-clause 44.6 from the International IChemE Red Book.

[85] See sub-clause 45.1 from the International IChemE Red Book.

[86] An argument in favour of this statement can also be found in the guidance on contractual issues appended to the International IChemE main forms. Pursuant to Guide Note P: Dispute Resolution, a failure to comply with the requirements stated in the dispute resolution clauses 'may lead to legal problems later when a particular form of dispute resolution has been chosen'.

[87] See clause 27 of PPC2000. Similar provisions can be found in the SPC2000, PPC International and SPC International.

[88] However, arbitration may be commenced if the dispute has not been settled within 90 days reckoned from the notice requesting the start of the mediation. See sub-clause 8.2.2 of the White Book.

engineer in his arbitration with the main contractor. The contract between the engineer and the employer is based on the FIDIC White Book, and the one between the employer and the main contractor – on the FIDIC Red Book. Let us further assume that both contracts contain multi-party arbitration clauses but there is nothing in these clauses that deals with the pre-arbitral stages of dispute resolution. In such a scenario, multi-party arbitration will only be possible if both disputes are referable to arbitration. The dispute under the main contract should first have been referred to a DAB, either party should have served a notice of dissatisfaction against the DAB's decision, and tried to reach an amicable settlement under the terms of sub-clause 20.5 from the FIDIC Red Book. The main contract dispute will fall within the scope of the multi-party arbitration clause once it has passed through all these steps. Similarly, the dispute under the White Book would fall outside the scope of the multi-party arbitration clause if it has not passed through the pre-arbitral phases envisaged thereunder, that is, an attempt to settle the dispute through negotiation, and, if negotiation was unsuccessful, mediation.

In practice, there are often cases where multi-party arbitration may be preferred by one of the parties at an earlier stage. For example, if in the course of the main contract arbitration regarding claims for defective works it becomes clear that the engineer may have contributed to the defects with his inaccurate design, the employer may want to join the engineer as soon as possible without having to wait for the fulfilment of all pre-arbitral steps under the professional services agreement. In the same vein, if in the course of the same proceedings it becomes evident that the subcontractor has also contributed to the defects, the main contractor may want to join him in the proceeding without waiting for the subcontract dispute to pass through all pre-arbitral steps envisaged under the subcontract. Furthermore, it could be too late to request such a joinder once all these steps have been completed. At that time, the main contract arbitration may have progressed too far, which could make the joinder unjustified because of the delay it would cause.

There are several options for the drafter to address this matter. The first option can only be employed when it comes to pre-arbitral steps from the same type. For example, both the main contract and the subcontract contain dispute adjudication provisions. In such a situation, the drafter may try to modify the existing adjudication clauses in such a way that the related disputes are submitted to a single adjudicator who takes a decision binding on all three parties. As far as the author is aware, the NEC3 suite is the first suite of contracts that has addressed this matter on a contractual level. It would go beyond the scope of this book to embark on a detailed analysis of how to draft these clauses. However, the analysis in Section 6.5 might serve as an indication for the type of issues that may arise in the context of NEC3, which the drafter might want to avoid. Furthermore, the considerations in Subsections 7.3.3.1 and 7.3.3.2 above are also relevant for the drafting of multi-party adjudication clauses.

Secondly, in the multi-party arbitration clause, the drafter may envisage that a dispute, which has not yet passed through all pre-arbitral stages, may nevertheless be referred to arbitration under certain conditions. An arbitrator would generally not have jurisdiction to review such a dispute, unless this is explicitly stated in the arbitration clause. The exact wording would very much depend on the specific contract in use and the interests of the party whose position the drafter is trying to protect. The CIMAR contain an innovative approach in that regard, which might serve as a source of inspiration. Pursuant to Rule 3.5 of the CIMAR:

In relation to a notice of arbitration in respect of any other disputes under Rules 3.2 or 3.3, the arbitrator is empowered to:

(i) decide any matter which may be a condition precedent to bringing the other dispute before the arbitrator;
(ii) abrogate any condition precedent to the bringing of arbitral proceedings in respect of the other dispute.

In the context of the CIMAR, Rule 3.5 applies only to multi-party arbitrations concerning disputes arising under the same arbitration agreement. Regardless, some contracting parties might consider introducing a similar wording in multi-party arbitration clauses intended to be operated in a multi-contract setting. Rule 3.5 empowers an arbitrator to abrogate the requirement that a certain dispute should pass through a pre-arbitral stage of dispute resolution. The wording of the rule is broad enough to encompass not only dispute adjudication but also other mandatory pre-arbitral stages, such as mediation and attempts to reach an amicable settlement. However, it should be emphasized that the power of an arbitrator to abrogate a condition precedent concerns only the dispute that is subsequently joined in a pending arbitration. In other words, the dispute that gives the start of the arbitration should have passed through all the required pre-arbitral stages, and the arbitrator can only abrogate a pre-arbitral stage concerning the related dispute, which is joined to the pending arbitration later on. In the author's opinion, this approach is reasonable. Generally, there should be at least one dispute that has complied with the general contractual requirements – that is, a dispute that has passed through all the required stages and is referable to arbitration, and this should normally be the dispute which initiates the arbitration.

The application of the above approach to the hypothetical situations discussed in this subsection can be illustrative of how the CIMAR approach can be applied in practice. If the employer tries to join the engineer into the pending main contract arbitration, he may be allowed to do so regardless of the fact that the pre-arbitral steps under the White Book may not have been fulfilled. The arbitrator will be allowed to abrogate the requirements that the parties should first try to settle the dispute through negotiation and thereafter submit it to mediation. In the same vein, if the main contractor tries to drag a subcontractor into the main contract arbitration, he may be able to do so without having to pass through all the pre-arbitral steps under the subcontract if the main contract arbitrator decides to abrogate these steps. It should be mentioned that, in both cases, the powers of the arbitrator are discretionary.

An additional issue concerning the compatibility of multi-party arbitration clauses with contractual pre-arbitral steps arises in the context of disputes starting from the bottom of the contractual chain. For instance, a subcontractor claims extension of time and additional costs against a main contractor due to an employer's failure to give timely access to the site, which results in an equivalent dispute under the main contract based on a main contractor's claim against the employer. The main contractor will typically require that the subcontract dispute should be reviewed in the main contract arbitration. In order to initiate such an arbitration, the main contractor should ensure that there is a main contract dispute referable to arbitration – that the main contractor's claim has been rejected and the resulting dispute has passed through all the pre-arbitral steps, such as dispute adjudication. However, subcontracts often envisage a quicker notification of claims and a less sophisticated dispute resolution procedure than main contracts. This often results in a situation where a subcontract dispute crystalizes and is referable to arbitration much faster than a related main contract dispute[89]. For this reason, subcontracts sometimes contain clauses that allow the main contractor upon the receipt of the subcontractor's claim to notify the subcontractor that his claim is related to the main contract and to defer the referral of the subcontract dispute to subcontract adjudication for a period of time that is necessary for the main contractor to complete the required steps under the main contract[90]. In these cases, drafters should make sure that the period with which the main contractor is entitled to defer the referral of the subcontract dispute is not less than the time that the main contractor would need to go through all the required stages under the main contract. In this way, the employer will have some leeway to initiate the main contract arbitration and then request the joinder of the subcontractor.

7.3.3.4 What should be the required link between the disputes which would justify their joint review?

If there is no link between the disputes arising under two or more agreements, there is no reason why these disputes should be reviewed together in a single multi-party arbitration[91]. Thus, if a certain subcontract dispute has no link with a dispute under a main contract, the subcontract dispute should be resolved in accordance with the dispute resolution provision under the subcontract. If, however, there is a link between the disputes, multi-party arbitration may be preferable. The intricate question is how exactly to determine the link that would justify the joint review of the disputes. It was observed in Chapter 6 that different standard forms employ different wording to deal with this question. An earlier edition of the Blue Form required that the main contract dispute be one that 'touches or concerns the Sub-Contract Works' which was interpreted to mean that the related disputes should concern the manner in which the subcontract works were performed[92]. It has already been mentioned that such wording is not very appropriate because it may leave certain related disputes outside the scope of the multi-party arbitration clause just because the relatedness concerns some other matter but not the manner in which the works are performed[93]. On that point, His Honour Humphrey Lloyd has

[89] For example, the FIDIC Subcontract provides for a shorter period of time within which the subcontractor should give a notice of his claim than the period of time within which the main contractor should do so under the FIDIC Red Book (see sub-clause 20.2 of the FIDIC Subcontract). Furthermore, there is no separate engineer under the FIDIC Subcontract. Thus, upon the receipt of a notice of claim it is the main contractor himself who should decide on the claim. The period of time within which the parties should reach an amicable settlement under the FIDIC Subcontract is also shorter in comparison with the FIDIC Red Book (see the penultimate paragraph of sub-clause 20.6 of the FIDIC Subcontract and sub-clause 20.5 of the FIDIC Red Book).

[90] See, for example, sub-clause 20.4 of the FIDIC Subcontract.

[91] See W. Michael Reisman, W. Laurence Craig, William W. Park and Jan Paulsson (1997) *International Commercial Arbitration. Cases, Materials and Notes on the Resolution of International Business Disputes*, The Foundation Press, New York, NY, p. 478. See also Fritz Nicklisch, 'Multi-Party Arbitration and Dispute Resolution in Major Industrial Projects', in *11 Journal of International Arbitration*, no. 4 (1994), pp. 69, 72.

[92] See ICC Case No. 5898 discussed in Subsection 6.2.2.2 hereof.

[93] See the discussion in Subsections 6.2.2.2 and 6.2.3.8.

suggested that the link should be determined with reference to the subject matter of the related contracts and not to the works[94]. The present author concurs with this suggestion. Such reference may be formulated in several ways. In some of the reviewed standard forms, the reader can commonly come across phrases, such as: 'if a certain dispute [under one agreement] raises issues and/or matters which are (substantially) the same or (substantially) connected with issues and or matters raised in a dispute [under another agreement].' The meaning of this wording was the subject matter of *City & General (Holborn) Ltd. v. AYH Plc*, which concerned the application of the multi-party arbitration clauses under the JCT 80 suite[95]. Identical or similar wording can be found in other contracts, such as the ACA standard forms, the IChemE Contracts, the PPC and SPC International, and the FIDIC Subcontract[96]. Another possible option is to stipulate that joint review of the disputes will be possible if the disputes '(substantially) involve common questions of law and/or fact' or 'arise out of, or touch upon, or concern substantially the same facts.' A similar approach can be found in the AIA forms[97]. The most elaborate wording regarding the required link between the disputes can be found in the ENAA Process Plant Model, which combines the two approaches mentioned above[98]. Apparently, there are different ways to formulate the required link between two or more multi-contract disputes but the abovementioned phrases are the most common ones[99].

There is no single right answer as to which wording would work best. When drafting multi-party arbitration clauses, it will not be feasible to enlist in detail any and all practical scenarios where a link between the related disputes may occur. Therefore, the drafter should use abstract phrases, such as those mentioned above.

The word '*substantially*' has been put in parentheses on purpose. The drafter should carefully consider the degree of required connectedness between the disputes. In other words, the drafter should consider the threshold that should be met in order for the disputes to be reviewed jointly. Would any connection between the disputes justify their joint review, or should such a connection be qualified by the use of words, such as '*substantially*' or '*materially*'?[100] When deciding on this matter, the drafter should take into account, among others things, the interests of the party whose position he is trying to protect. Parties interested in multi-party arbitration

[94] See Humphrey Lloyd (2004) *Multi-Party Clauses and Agreements*, a paper for use by the University of London LLM students, p. 8 (the paper is based on an earlier version of the same article: see Humphrey Lloyd (1991) 'A National Experience', in P. Bellet, P. Bernardini, G. Bernini *et al.* (eds) *Multi-Party Arbitration: Views from International Arbitration Specialists*, Publication No. 480/1, ICC Publishing SA, Paris).

[95] See Subsection 6.3.1.3 hereof.

[96] See sub-clause 20.4 of the FIDIC Subcontract, which addresses cases where 'the [subcontract dispute] involves an issue or issues which is/are also involved in a dispute between the Contractor and the Employer under the Main Contract'.

[97] See, for example, § 15.4.4 under AIA A201-2007 (discussed in Section 6.10).

[98] See Section 6.9 and Appendix # 3 hereof.

[99] See also Dimitrios Athanasakis (2007) 'Has Multi-Party Arbitration Failed in Construction Disputes? Legal and Practical Issues in Drafting Joinder Provisions, in D. Boyd (ed.) *Procs 23rd Annual ARCOM Conference, 3–5 September, Belfast, UK, Association of Researchers in Construction Management*, p. 112, http://www.arcom.ac.uk/-docs/proceedings/ar2007-0107-0116_Athanasakis.pdf (accessed 26 July 2016). In his paper, the author suggests a checklist of keywords about the required link between related disputes.

[100] See Subsection 6.3.1.3 on this point in the context of the wording used in the JCT 80 suite.

will prefer wording that requires a relatively tenuous connection between the disputes. In this way, the multi-party arbitration clause can be put into operation even if there is only a slim link between the disputes. In these cases, the multi-party arbitration clause may start with the following wording: 'if a dispute [under one contract] has any connection with a dispute [under another contract]'. Conversely, parties not willing to participate in multi-party arbitration would prefer the link to be qualified in some way so that the multi-party arbitration clause cannot be easily operated to their detriment.

7.3.3.5 Who is to decide whether such a link exists?

The standard forms examined in Chapter 6 reveal two main approaches to this question. Under the first approach, the answer to the question is explicitly contained in the multi-party arbitration clause whereunder it is usually one of the parties that should form an opinion on the required link. In most cases, this would be the main contractor as the party that is most often in the middle of the contractual chain and is best able to ascertain on the relatedness of disputes arising under two or more contracts. This approach can be seen under the majority of the reviewed standard forms, such as the Blue Form, the ACA Subcontract, the PPC International and SPC International[101].

In the author's view, the requirement that one of the parties should form an opinion about the link is sensible from a commercial point of view. This approach is likely to take less time than in cases where an arbitrator or a judge has to decide on the same matter. Furthermore, this approach allows the contracting party forming the opinion to retain its discretion to decide whether to be involved in a multi-party arbitration. If this party takes the position that such a link does not exist or refuses to express an opinion on the matter, it would veto the application of the multi-party arbitration clause.

On the other side, this approach has given rise to some controversy as regards the nature of the party's opinion and whether it is subject to control by an arbitrator[102]. In the author's view, a party's opinion should not be considered as an ultimate and binding evidence for the existence of a link between the disputes in question. Therefore, the draftsman should avoid wording that attributes such a meaning to this opinion. In the author's view, a party's opinion on this matter should be subject to control by the arbitrator reviewing the disputes if some of the other contracting parties controvert the existence of such a link[103]. Otherwise, the multi-party arbitration clause may be open to abuse, which may cause substantial injustice. For example, a main contractor may state that a subcontract dispute is related to a main contract dispute even though no such

[101] Under the ACA Main Contract, it is the employer who should be of the opinion that there is a link between the related disputes.

[102] See the discussion in Subsections 6.2.1.2 and 6.2.3.8.

[103] For a similar opinion, see Dimitrios Athanasakis and Robert Morgan, 'Joinder of Arbitrations: an Overview of English and Hong Kong Construction Industry Practice', in *Asian Dispute Review* no. 1 (2008), pp. 18–19. According to the authors: 'The opinion of the requesting party is only the starting point in ascertaining whether there is linkage between separately referred disputes. It is for the arbitrator, having considered the request and submissions against joinder, to break down and marshal the issues and to reach his own conclusions on any commonalities between the disputes, and how substantial those commonalities are.'

link exists. In this way, the subcontract would be unjustly bogged down in a time- and cost-consuming arbitration with the participation of the employer and the main contractor, where he would have to resolve his subcontract dispute that has nothing to do with the main contract. Therefore, in case of disagreement among the parties, the arbitrator should take a jurisdictional decision by following the doctrine of *Kompetenz-Kompetenz* and the relevant provisions in the applicable arbitration rules. An arbitrator's control on the matter would incentivize the party forming the opinion not to act frivolously and abusively. It will be in the interests of this party to take a well considered decision on the existence of the link, because if its opinion turns out to be ungrounded it may develop into a jurisdictional objection. This may delay the proceeding and result in a situation where the tribunal declines to exercise jurisdiction in respect of some of the disputes.

Under the second approach, the multi-party arbitration clauses require a certain link between the disputes but do not explicitly stipulate that a party should form an opinion on the matter. In these cases, it would normally be either party to the contract containing the multi-party arbitration clause that may assert that the necessary link exists. In case of a dispute about the link, it would finally be the arbitrator who should make sure that such a link exists in order to confirm his jurisdiction to deal with the related disputes. Thus, it actually seems that the differences between the first and the second approach are not so substantial as, in both cases, it will be the arbitrator who would finally determine whether there is a commonality between the disputes. Therefore, the drafter may give his preference for any of the two approaches mentioned above. In the author's personal view, the first approach is preferable because of its greater clarity on the question of who is to decide on the link between the disputes.

When it comes to these two approaches, one more point should be clarified. Certain arbitration agreements may allow for multi-party arbitration in cases where the related disputes have resulted in two separate arbitrations[104]. For example, a main contract arbitration agreement envisages that a subcontract dispute may be referred to a main contract arbitrator regardless of the fact that a subcontract arbitrator may have already been appointed to deal with the subcontract dispute. In these cases, the parties' disagreement about the existence of a link between the disputes may result in jurisdictional objections in both arbitrations[105]. For instance, the main contractor would challenge the jurisdiction of the subcontract arbitrator in respect of a subcontract dispute that is allegedly related to the main contract and the subcontractor would challenge the main contract arbitrator's jurisdiction over the same subcontract dispute by contesting its link with the main contract. In these situations, there is a risk that the arbitrators in the separate proceedings may reach inconsistent decisions on the same matter, which may result in a deadlock. It is therefore recommendable that the draftsman explicitly designate in the multi-party arbitration clause who is to decide on the relatedness of the disputes in case of any controversies.

The FIDIC Subcontract has introduced a third approach in the second alternative dispute resolution clause (see Section 6.1). Under this clause, any dispute as to whether

[104] Such a situation can arise, for example, in the context of the ENAA Process Plant Model.

[105] See Subsection 6.3.2.

a certain subcontract claim or dispute is related to a main contract claim or dispute should be decided by a pre-arbitral referee in accordance with the ICC Rules for a Pre-Arbitral Referee Procedure ('**ICC Pre-Arbitral Rules**')[106].

The main purpose for the introduction of the ICC Pre-Arbitral Rules in 1990 was to enable parties to apply for urgent provisional or protective measures in the context of a dispute. Under the ICC Pre-Arbitral Rules, any application in that regard is to be decided by a pre-arbitral referee who issues an interim binding order. In other words, the principal position is that the order has a provisional binding effect and should be carried out by the parties. The matters addressed in the order may be revisited subsequently by the arbitrator reviewing the merits of the case, who is empowered to reverse the order and / or grant a different order[107]. The ICC Pre-Arbitral Rules were introduced more than 20 years before the publication of the FIDIC Subcontract and therefore they were not initially intended to be applied in the situation contemplated under the FIDIC Subcontract. Furthermore, the list of referee's powers in Article 2.1 of the rules did not provide for a power that matched the pre-arbitral referee's role under the FIDIC Subcontract. Therefore, the drafters of the second alternative clause in the FIDIC Subcontract decided to introduce therein certain amendments to the ICC Pre-Arbitral Rules, which changed in a material way the nature of the pre-arbitral procedure as initially envisaged under these rules. First, the powers of the referee were modified. All his powers, as envisaged in Article 2.1, were revoked and instead he was vested with only one power: the authority to decide on the link between the claims and / or the disputes arising under the main contract and the subcontract[108]. Secondly, the referee's order was stipulated to be final and binding for the parties. The drafters' intention, as expressed in the alternative clause in the FIDIC Subcontract, seems to be that the arbitral tribunal that would review the merits of the case would not be allowed to revisit the subject matter of the referee's order[109].

One of the merits of this pre-arbitral mechanism is its speediness. The referee should issue the order within 21 days from the date on which he receives the file from the ICC Secretariat[110]. This feature may appear attractive to contracting parties for commercial reasons. However, there are certain uncertainties surrounding the pre-arbitral referee's procedure that may dissuade parties from choosing this mechanism. First, there has been a lack of clarity as regards the exact nature of the referee's order – that is, whether this order may be characterized as an arbitral award or merely as an act with no more

---

[106] The ICC Rules for a Pre-Arbitral Referee Procedure are available at http://www.iccwbo.org/products-and-services/arbitration-and-adr/pre-arbitral-referee/rules-for-a-pre-arbitral-referee-procedure/(accessed 26 July 2016).

[107] See the introduction to the ICC Pre-Arbitral Rules, as well as Articles 2.4.1, 6.3 and 6.6.

[108] This was achieved on the basis of Article 2.1.1 of the ICC Pre-Arbitral Rules, which stipulated that the referee's powers under Article 2.1 can be altered by express agreement between the parties. The purpose of sub-clauses 20.2 and 20.6(c) of the second alternative clause of the FIDIC Subcontract was to incorporate the parties' express agreement on the matter.

[109] Sub-clauses 20.2 and 20.6(c) of the second alternative clause of the FIDIC Subcontract in relation to Article 6.3 of the ICC Pre-Arbitral Rules.

[110] Sub-clauses 20.2 and 20.6(c) of the second alternative clause of the FIDIC Subcontract.

authority than a contract[111]. The answer on this matter will determine, for example, whether the order can be subject to judicial review in an action for annulment of an arbitral award. The prevailing opinion seems to be that the referee's order is not an arbitral award and one of the main arguments for such an opinion is the lack of finality of the order[112]. However, the FIDIC Subcontract has explicitly stipulated that the order shall be final, which calls the above opinion into question. Nevertheless, the explicit wording of the alternative dispute resolution clause under the FIDIC Subcontract supports the view that the pre-arbitral referee's order is not an arbitral award[113]. Secondly, the inability of the arbitral tribunal reviewing the merits of the dispute to revisit the subject matter of the referee's order does not seem justified in all cases. For example, the pre-arbitral referee may have issued an order that there is a link between the subcontract and the main contract dispute and it becomes clear later on in the course of the arbitration that there was actually no link between the disputes. Would it not be justified in this case to allow the tribunal to decline jurisdiction to review the disputes jointly? Thirdly, the ICC Pre-Arbitral Rules have been referred to by contracting parties only on rare occasions[114] and, on the basis of these cases, it is difficult to conclude whether the application of these rules produce satisfactory results. Besides, the author is not aware of any cases where the pre-arbitral referee's procedure was used in the way contemplated under the second alternative dispute resolution clause of the FIDIC Subcontract.

7.3.3.6 How is the tribunal to be constituted?

This is one of the most intricate questions when it comes to multi-party arbitrations. One of the main principles in arbitration is that the parties should be treated equally in the process of constitution of the arbitral tribunal. It is relatively easy to observe this principle if the arbitration is to be conducted by a sole arbitrator. The relevant arbitration clause or the applicable arbitration rules will often provide that the sole arbitrator will be appointed jointly by the parties or, if such joint appointment is not possible, by the arbitral institution administering the case[115]. In this way, neither party will have a preponderant

---

[111] Christine Lécuyer-Thieffry, 'First Court Ruling on the ICC Pre-Arbitral Referee Procedure', in *20 Journal of International Arbitration*, issue 6 (2003), pp. 599–607. See also Emmanuel Gaillard and Philippe Pinsolle, 'The ICC Pre-Arbitral Referee: First Practical Experiences', in *20 Arbitration International*, no. 1 (2004), pp. 13–37, and Ian Meredith and Marcus Birch, 'The ICC's pre-arbitral referee procedure. How valuable is it?, in *Cross-border Quarterly*, January–March 2008, pp. 52–53, http://www.klgates.com/files/Publication/ab0be67f-01ef-4206-9c12-6e91f5b4837e/Presentation/PublicationAttachment/bae41c65-1f1b-43c3-b963-7de5c496b5bc/article_meredith_icc_0108.pdf (accessed 26 July 2016).

[112] Emmanuel Gaillard and Philippe Pinsolle, 'The ICC Pre-Arbitral Referee: First Practical Experiences', in *20 Arbitration International*, no. 1 (2004), pp. 22–23. The authors have stated that, for the French courts, the requirement of finality is a generally accepted test for the characterization of a decision as an arbitral award. However, they admit that this requirement may be applied differently in different legal systems.

[113] See the penultimate paragraph of sub-clause 20.2 and letter (c) of sub-clause 20.6 of the second alternative dispute resolution clause under the FIDIC Subcontract.

[114] See Ian Meredith and Marcus Birch, 'The ICC's pre-arbitral referee procedure. How valuable is it?', in *Cross-border Quarterly*, January–March 2008, pp. 51, 53.

[115] In *ad hoc* arbitration, the appointment will be made by the local court or the appointing authority agreed upon the parties.

influence in the appointment process. The situation becomes more complex in cases of three-member tribunals. Arbitration clauses envisaging a three-member tribunal will typically grant each contracting party the right to nominate one arbitrator. The third arbitrator, who is usually the presiding arbitrator, will normally be agreed by the two already appointed members or will be appointed by the arbitral institution administering the case. These clauses operate smoothly when it comes to bipolar arbitrations but they often appear to be unworkable in a multi-party context. To give each of the multiple parties the right to appoint an arbitrator will often result in arbitration conducted by a tribunal consisting of more than three members. This scenario is unpractical and should be avoided. An arbitral tribunal consisting of more than three members is likely to cause additional costs and delay and may also lead to operational difficulties without necessarily providing any additional benefit in terms of the quality of decisions[116].

Therefore, alternative mechanisms should be employed to deal with multi-party arbitrations arising under two or more contracts. One of these mechanisms can be discerned from the multi-party arbitration clauses under some of the standard forms reviewed in Chapter 6, such as the Blue Form, the JCT 80 suite, the ACA standard forms, the IChemE Contracts and the ENAA Process Plant Model. Under these contract forms, a dispute under one contract can be referred to an arbitral tribunal constituted or to be constituted under another contract whereunder a related dispute has arisen. This may result in a situation where a party (most often a subcontractor) is joined in an arbitration conducted under another contract (most often a main contract) without that party having the opportunity to participate in the constitution of the arbitral tribunal reviewing the related disputes. This mechanism may result in two types of problems that have already been examined in previous sections. First, it may be argued that the principle of equal treatment of the parties in the process of appointment of the arbitrators has been breached. This problem has been examined in detail in Subsection 6.2.3.4. The problem is particularly visible where a subcontract dispute has to be referred to an already-appointed three-member main contract tribunal where the employer and the main contractor have nominated one arbitrator and the subcontractor was not allowed to make a separate nomination. Theoretically, parties' unequal treatment might result in an award that is annulled in the country where it was rendered or its recognition and enforcement is denied in third countries. Such a risk is particularly imminent in France in the light of the *Dutco* case (also discussed in Subsection 6.2.3.4), where the *Cour de Cassation* stipulated that the principle of equality of the parties upon the constitution of the arbitral tribunal constitutes a matter of public policy that cannot be waived by the parties before the respective dispute has arisen. In the author's opinion, it is doubtful whether the outcome of the *Dutco* case, which dealt with a principally different situation than the one discussed here, will render contractually agreed mechanisms for the appointment of arbitrators inoperative on the ground that these mechanisms do not ensure parties' equal treatment. However, drafters of multi-party arbitration clauses should proceed with caution if the chosen

---

[116] Jason Fry, Simon Greenberg and Francesca Mazza (2012) *The Secretariat's Guide to ICC Arbitration*, ICC Publication No. 729, ICC Publishing SA, Paris, p. 138 (§ 3-432).

seat of arbitration is in France or if the recognition and enforcement of an award rendered elsewhere is to be sought in France. The same would be true if the chosen seat of arbitration or the likely place of enforcement of the award is in a country that has introduced similar restrictions. As mentioned in Subsection 7.3.3, Germany, Italy, the Netherlands, Spain, Poland and Lebanon have introduced limitations similar to those in the *Dutco* case.

The second problem stems from the inability of the joined party to challenge the arbitrators on the grounds of their alleged lack of impartiality or independence at the time when the tribunal is constituted. This issue has been elaborated in Subsection 6.2.3.5. The principle that the arbitrators should be impartial and independent of the parties is one of the main tenets in international commercial arbitration. Generally, parties are entitled to challenge the appointment of arbitrators if they have doubts about the impartiality or independence of these arbitrators. This right stems from provisions contained in either the applicable arbitration rules or the national arbitration laws. These provisions have a mandatory character and therefore parties may not waive their corresponding rights by contractual arrangements[117]. This position is also reflected in the IBA Guidelines on Conflicts of Interest in International Arbitration[118]. These guidelines contain a list of facts and circumstances, described in the so-called *Non-waivable Red List* in Part II of the guidelines, regarding conflicts of interest that cannot be waived by the parties. Any parties' agreement to waive these material conflicts of interest will be regarded as invalid[119]. Even though the IBA Guidelines are a soft law instrument, arbitral institutions and arbitral tribunals have often drawn inspiration from their content on matters regarding conflicts of interest. Therefore, parties should have the right to challenge an arbitrator on the grounds of his lack of independence or impartiality regardless of the stage at which the joinder is admitted. Any drafters' attempts to limit or exclude this right will be of no avail. A successful challenge against an arbitrator will result in his replacement and the appointment of another arbitrator, which could disrupt the pending arbitration. The earlier such a challenge is raised, the less likely it is that the procedure will be delayed significantly. Therefore, multi-party arbitration clauses allowing for a third party's joinder in arbitration that is well under way are generally not recommendable. The better approach is that the opportunity for joinder should lapse if not requested within a short period of time following the initiation of the arbitration.

The abovementioned problems predominantly concern situations where the joinder of a party is requested into an arbitration that is already afoot. However, the situation is not much different in case of consolidation of two or more pending arbitrations. Which tribunal is going to review the consolidated arbitration? Would that be one of the tribunals dealing with the separate arbitrations subject to consolidation or a new tribunal?

---

[117] See, for example, Article 11(1) of the ICC Rules, according to which 'every arbitrator must be and remain impartial and independent of the parties involved in the arbitration'.

[118] IBA Guidelines on Conflicts of Interest in International Arbitration (2014), Adopted by a Resolution of the IBA Council on 23 October 2014, http://www.ibanet.org/Publications/publications_IBA_guides_and_free_materials.aspx (accessed 26 July 2016).

[119] See General Standard 4(b) of the IBA Guidelines on Conflicts of Interest in International Arbitration.

The answer to this question may sometimes be contained in the applicable arbitration rules[120] but the draftsman may prefer to address this matter explicitly in the arbitration clause. If the multi-party arbitration clause stipulates that the consolidated proceedings will be conducted by a new tribunal, the clause should also envisage a procedure for the revocation of the authority of the existing tribunals. Identical issues to the ones discussed above will arise if the merged arbitrations are to be conducted by a tribunal that has dealt with one of the pending arbitrations subject to consolidation. One of the parties – the party that has not participated in the separate arbitration conducted by that same arbitral tribunal – has not had an opportunity to participate in the constitution of that tribunal. Furthermore, the same party has not had an opportunity to challenge the arbitrators in that tribunal on the ground of their alleged lack of impartiality or independence at the time of their appointment. This party will still be entitled to raise challenges but only after it has been notified that the tribunal in question will conduct the consolidated arbitration.

Those drafting multi-party arbitration clauses may think of alternative wording regarding the constitution of the arbitral tribunal in order to avoid the abovementioned problems. Such wording might be particularly necessary if the seat of arbitration is in France, Germany, Italy, the Netherlands, Spain, Poland or Lebanon, or if the arbitration award is to be enforced in one of these countries. The standard form multi-party arbitration clauses examined in Chapter 6 would offer little inspiration in the search for an alternative wording. In any case, the draftsman should keep in mind the outcome of the *Dutco* case and should try to formulate the multi-party arbitration clause in a way that does not conflict with the principle of equality.

There are different ways to construct such a wording. For example, the parties may agree on arbitration to be conducted by a tribunal, consisting of a sole arbitrator or three arbitrators, which will be appointed directly by the arbitral institution. Alternatively, the arbitral institution may be empowered to revoke any appointments of arbitrators made so far in the proceedings and appoint the whole tribunal in parties' stead. This second option, however, might give rise to further difficulties, especially if the subcontract dispute is joined in a main contract arbitration that is well under way, as the revocation of the arbitrator's appointment may delay the proceedings significantly. Finally, the draftsman may think of constructing a multi-party arbitration clause, pursuant to which no multi-party arbitration would be allowed following the appointment of the arbitrators. Such an approach has also been recommended in the IBA Guidelines for Drafting

[120] See, for example, Article 28(6) of the HKIAC Rules and Article 4(1) of the Swiss Rules, which provide that the arbitral institution may revoke the appointment of any arbitrators already made and appoint the whole tribunal, which is going to review the consolidated procedure. See also the last sentence of Article 10 of the ICC Rules, pursuant to which when arbitrations are to be consolidated, they shall be consolidated in the arbitration that commenced first, unless the parties have agreed otherwise. However, it will be highly unlikely for the ICC Court to consolidate arbitrations where different tribunals have already been appointed in the separate arbitrations. Pursuant to the ICC Secretariat's Guide, the ICC Court will be unable to consolidate the arbitrations as it will be impossible to constitute a single arbitral tribunal, unless the different arbitrator(s) resign or are removed by the Court at the parties' request (see Jason Fry, Simon Greenberg and Francesca Mazza (2012) *The Secretariat's Guide to ICC Arbitration*, ICC Publication No. 729, ICC Publishing SA, Paris, p. 114 (§ 3-358)).

International Arbitration Clauses (see Subsection 7.3.1)[121]. In order to be workable, such a multi-party arbitration clause should stipulate time limits within which any joinder and / or intervention requests can be made. Following the expiry of these periods, the arbitral institution may proceed and appoint all the members of the arbitral tribunal. In this way, no party will have a superior position in the process of appointment of the arbitral tribunal and the principle of equality will be observed. Furthermore, even if an arbitrator has to be replaced as a result of a successful challenge raised by a party, this is likely to cause less delay than the delay that may otherwise be caused upon the replacement of an arbitrator in case of a third party's joinder after the constitution of the tribunal. The reason for this is that all challenges will have to be made by all the parties from the outset – within a certain period following the appointment or nomination of an arbitrator – and all decisions on the admissibility of such challenges will be made at an early stage of the procedure.

The conduct of multi-party arbitrations poses significant organization challenges for arbitrators. It is neither possible nor recommendable to regulate contractually every single detail pertinent to the conduct of these proceedings (e.g. how hearings are to be conducted, how evidence is to be collected). Therefore, it is recommendable that the arbitral tribunal is vested with wide discretion to organize the proceedings in the way it thinks fit and just within the limits permitted by the clause. If the applicable arbitration rules do not contain a clause granting such powers to the tribunal, the draftsman should address this matter in the multi-party arbitration clause. If the arbitration is seated in a country that has adopted the UNCITRAL Model Law, Article 19(2) of the latter may serve as a basis for the tribunal's discretion in that regard.

7.3.3.7 What type of multi-party arbitration should the clause envisage?

As explained in Section 2.2, multi-party arbitration may be initiated in different ways. These comprise filing a single request for arbitration against multiple parties, joinder or intervention of third parties and consolidation of parallel arbitrations. In theory, multi-party arbitration clauses can address all these legal techniques. In practice, however, a multi-party arbitration clause will only deal with some of them. The question may arise as to which of the above legal techniques should be given preference in the clause. It is the author's opinion that multi-party arbitration agreements addressing joinder and single request of arbitration should be given preference over consolidation and intervention provisions for the reasons explained below.

As observed in Chapter 6, most standard form agreements containing multi-party arbitration clauses have predilection for the joinder of a third party into existing arbitration. Undoubtedly, joinder provisions are one of the best ways to introduce multi-party arbitration and should definitely be among the first choice for those drafting multi-party arbitration clauses. Most considerations contained in the questions discussed so far in this Subsection 7.3.3 are also relevant in the drafting of joinder provisions. In addition,

---

[121] See also Joachim Goedel (1991) 'Examination of the Issues Involved in Drafting Arbitral Clauses', in P. Bellet, P. Bernardini, G. Bernini *et al.* (eds) *Multi-Party Arbitration: Views from International Arbitration Specialists*, Publication No. 480/1, ICC Publishing SA, Paris, p. 111.

it is also recommendable to stipulate a certain period of time in the joinder clause within which any joinder request should be made so as to preclude any joinder requests after the expiry of this period[122]. The purpose of this time period is to avoid delays resulting from a late joinder and the complexities that might occur following challenges against the arbitrators raised by the joined party.

Even though the legal technique of filing a single request for arbitration against multiple parties is not addressed in the reviewed standard forms, it can be a useful tool, especially for employers under *build-only* or *construction management* contractual models who want to pursue their claims against the design team and the main contractor or against multiple main contractors at one and the same time. Drafters, and especially those acting for the employer, may therefore well consider that their arbitration clauses address this legal technique.

Unlike joinder clauses, contractually agreed consolidation provisions are rarely seen in the construction sector. Of the standard forms examined, only the AIA forms contain a consolidation provision[123]. However, some of the discussed joinder provisions produce an effect that is similar (but not identical) to consolidation. For, example the draft multi-party arbitration clauses in the ENAA Process Plant Model are formulated in very broad terms, which would allow, among others, that a subcontract dispute with regard to which a subcontract arbitration is already initiated to be referred to a pending main contract arbitration. Even though these two pending arbitrations are not consolidated *sensu stricto* as in the case of consolidation, they nevertheless result in a situation where two disputes, which are initially the subject matter of two separate arbitrations, are ultimately reviewed by a single tribunal as in the case of consolidation. Therefore, the considerations below regarding consolidation provisions will also apply to this type of joinder clause.

One of the aims of multi-party arbitration is procedural efficiency, which finds expression in the overall saving of time and costs. In order to achieve this aim, any request for multi-party arbitration should be made as early as possible. Preferably, this would be the period of time when there is no arbitration or the pending arbitration is still in its initial stage. Once the related disputes have resulted in two or more separate arbitrations it is generally more complex and difficult (even though not impossible) to merge these arbitrations into a single proceeding. At that time, certain costs have already been incurred in both arbitrations. Moreover, some progress may have been made in the separate arbitrations. The merger of the two arbitrations into one will normally result in additional cost and further delay in the resolution of the disputes[124]. Additional consideration should be paid to the constitution of the arbitral tribunal to conduct the consolidated proceeding. This should either be a new tribunal or one of the existing tribunals. The latter approach, however, is risky because of the complications discussed in Subsection 7.3.3.6. In these

[122] See ICC Commission on International Arbitration, 'Final Report on Multi-party Arbitrations', in *6 ICC International Court Arbitration Bulletin*, no. 1 (1995), pp. 40–41. See also Paul Friedland (2007) *Arbitration Clauses for International Contracts*, 2nd edn, New York: JurisNet, pp. 130–134.

[123] See § 15.4.4 of AIA A201-2007, § 8.3.4 of AIA B101-2007 and § 6.3.3–6.3.5 of AIA A401-2007.

[124] See Geoffrey Ma and Neil Kaplan (eds) (2003) *Arbitration in Hong Kong: A Practical Guide*, Sweet & Maxwell Asia, Hong Kong, pp. 173–174.

situations, the overall benefit of having multi-party arbitration may well be outweighed by the prejudice that consolidation may cause to the parties. This prejudice will be in the form of inflated costs, overall delay in the dispute resolution process and disruption of each of the separate arbitrations. For the above reasons, the author is of the opinion that multi-party arbitration may be conducted more swiftly and efficiently if it is initiated by way of a joinder request or a single request for arbitration against multiple parties. This is, of course, a statement that might not be true in every single case. For example, a multi-party arbitration clause allowing for the joinder of a third party at a late stage of the proceedings might cause similar prejudice to the parties.

If the draftsman would like to construct a consolidation provision, all the questions discussed in this subsection should be taken into account. However, he should also bear in mind some special considerations. The consolidation clause should clarify how the contemplated consolidation should be carried into effect – who will decide on the consolidation, what procedure should be complied with, what would be the allocation of costs made in the arbitrations prior to consolidation, what would be the validity of acts done in the separate arbitrations prior to consolidation and the evidence submitted in these arbitrations and so forth. The draftsman may want to check the proposed consolidation clause in the IBA Guidelines, even though this clause concerns related arbitrations between the same parties[125]. The draft multi-party arbitration clause under the ENAA Process Plant Model Form can also provide some inspiration. In general, the clause should stipulate that any consolidation will not affect the validity of any acts or orders made in the separate arbitrations conducted prior to consolidation. In addition, any documents and / or evidence that have been disclosed in one of the pending arbitrations prior to consolidation should be considered admissible in the consolidated arbitration and also made available to the party that did not participate in the arbitration where the documents and / or evidence were initially disclosed. Any defences and / or claims raised in the separate arbitrations should also be recognized as valid and made on the dates when they were made in order to avoid any prejudice to a party resulting from the applicability of statutory or contractual limitations periods concerning the making of such claims or defences[126].

It is also very important that the consolidation clause introduces certain time limits within which consolidation may be requested[127]. Consolidation of arbitrations that have reached an advanced stage of proceedings is not desirable. Therefore, consolidation should not be allowed after the expiry of these time limits. In the context of ICC arbitrations, for example, it may be stipulated that no consolidation will be possible once the terms of reference in one of the pending arbitrations have been drawn up. The passing of a hearing on the merits in one of the arbitrations might also serve as an appropriate yardstick to preclude consolidation requests made after this date. Moreover, the consolidation clause should stipulate which tribunal will review the consolidated proceeding

---

[125] IBA Guidelines for Drafting International Arbitration Clauses, pp. 41–42.

[126] See the draft multi-party arbitration clause, which is to be inserted in subcontracts used in conjunction with the ENAA Process Plant Model Form (sub-clause 2.4 of Appendix 3 to this book).

[127] Richard Bamforth and Katerina Maidment, ' "All join in or not"? How well does international arbitration cater for disputes involving multiple parties or related claims?', in *27 ASA Bulletin*, no. 1 (2009), p. 20.

and what would happen with existing tribunals if those tribunals have already been appointed. Normally, their authority will have to be revoked. One possible way to approach the question of consolidation is to allow each party to a pending arbitration to request from the tribunal reviewing its dispute the issuance of a consolidation order by serving notices to all parties involved in the separate arbitral proceedings. Similar consolidation clauses have to be inserted in all the related agreements. However, in this case there is a risk that consolidation requests may be made before more than one tribunal. As a result, different consolidation orders may be issued by the different tribunals. Therefore, the drafter should clarify in the clause which consolidation order will prevail. Normally, this should be the order that was issued first in time. If the arbitral tribunal refuses to issue a consolidation order, then the parties may consider vesting a competent court with the discretion to decide on the consolidation request[128]. Consolidation provisions following a similar approach have been proposed by some practitioners and scholars and drafters may use these clauses as a source of inspiration in their attempts to draft a workable consolidation provision[129].

Like consolidation provisions, contractual arrangements envisaging the intervention of third parties are rare. One explanation for this is that there are relatively few circumstances where a party might want to intervene in pending proceedings on its own motion. For example, an employer may want to intervene in an arbitration between a main contractor and a subcontractor if he has a direct claim against the subcontractor, which he may pursue in the pending arbitration. This could be the case if the subcontractor has provided a collateral warranty in favour of the employer. By this intervention, the employer may try to obtain a faster recovery for the defective works caused by that subcontractor. Due to the rare occasions where intervention might be useful, intervention clauses should not be among the preferred options for the draftsman. This would, of course, depend on the specific circumstances of the case. In the author's opinion, intervention should only be allowed if the intervening party accepts the already appointed tribunal. In the above example, the employer would have to accept the jurisdiction of the subcontract tribunal to deal with the claim arising under the collateral warranty. This should be reflected in the multi-party arbitration clauses in both the main contract and the subcontract. One further particularity regarding intervention concerns the notices that should be given in order to make intervention possible. The party that might have an interest in intervening should have knowledge of any pending arbitration under the related contract. In the above example, the main contractor or the subcontractor, as the

[128] Grant Hanessian and Lawrence Newman (eds) (2009) *International Arbitration Checklists, Baker & McKenzie*, 2nd edn, JurisNet, LLC, New York, NY, pp. 236–237.

[129] See Paul Friedland (2007) *Arbitration Clauses for International Contracts*, 2nd edn, JurisNet, New York, pp. 137–140; Nicole Conrad, Barbara Baumann and Ömer Cilingir (2013) 'Sample Clauses for International Arbitration Agreements', in Nicole Conrad, Peter Munch and Jonathan Black-Branch (eds) *International Commercial Arbitration, Standard Clauses and Forms Commentary*, Helbing Lichtenhahn/C. H. Beck/Hart/Nomos, Basel, pp. 11–34, and Geoffrey Ma and Neil Kaplan (eds) (2003) *Arbitration in Hong Kong: A Practical Guide*, Sweet & Maxwell Asia, Hong Kong, p. 763 (the second consolidation clause in the latter source (see pp. 641–642) is not commendable because its application may result in the appointment of an arbitral tribunal consisting of more than three members). See also Gary Born (2013) *International Arbitration and Forum Selection Agreements: Drafting and Enforcing*, 4th edn, Kluwer Law International, Alphen aan den Rijn, pp. 106–110.

case may be, should be obliged to notify the employer once a subcontract arbitration is initiated. The purpose of the notice is to make the employer cognizant of the pending arbitration and to enable him to ascertain whether to intervene in the arbitration.

7.3.3.8 Should there be any limit on the number of parties in multi-party arbitration?

Multi-party arbitration clauses formulated in broad terms as regards the parties that may participate in such arbitration may result in a situation where an unlimited number of parties is brought within single proceedings[130]. For example, a multi-party arbitration clause may stipulate that a subcontractor may be joined in an arbitration pending under the main contract. If the main contractor has contracted with numerous subcontractors, this means that all these subcontractors may potentially participate in the multi-party arbitration, provided that appropriate multi-party arbitration clauses are inserted in the relevant subcontracts as well. Similarly, if a main contract multi-party arbitration clause stipulates that the employer may join technical consultants in the main contract arbitration, this implies that the employer may drag any engineers, architects and other technical consultants he has contracted with into the main contract arbitration, provided that this joinder is also envisaged in the relevant consultancy agreements. Similar issues can be observed in the context of the consolidation clause in the AIA forms[131]. As discussed in Section 6.10, the clause is formulated in a way that could allow numerous consolidation requests, including by a party partaking in the arbitration as a result of a previous consolidation request made by some other party.

Multi-party arbitration with the participation of a large number of parties leads to a high degree of complexity. It requires tremendous coordination efforts from both the arbitral tribunal and the disputants, which may make the conduct of arbitral proceedings impracticable. Therefore, those drafting multi-party arbitration clauses may think of introducing certain limitations as to the number of parties involved in such arbitration.

These limitations can be formulated in different ways. For instance, the multi-party arbitration clause should avoid broad references to 'any party substantially involved in the construction project' or 'any person substantially involved in a common question of fact or law whose presence is required if complete relief is to be accorded in arbitration'[132]. Instead, the clause should refer to contracting parties in the context of the specific function that they perform in the project (e.g. a supplier, subcontractor, engineer, etc.). In addition, the multi-party arbitration clause can go into further detail and refer to a specific legal entity by designating the name of that legal entity. This can be particularly useful in projects where there are multiple parties performing one and the same function (e.g. numerous subcontractors hired by the main contractor or numerous designers appointed by the employer). For the same purpose, a reference to a specific contract by designating the type of contract, the signatories and the date of execution can also be

---

[130] On this question, see also Humphrey Lloyd (1991) 'A National Experience', in P. Bellet, P. Bernardini, G. Bernini *et al.* (eds) *Multi-Party Arbitration: Views from International Arbitration Specialists*, Publication No. 480/1, ICC Publishing SA, Paris, p. 74.

[131] See § 15.4.4 of AIA A201-2007, § 8.3.4 of AIA B101-2007 and § 6.3.3–6.3.5 of AIA A401-2007.

[132] A similar clause existed in an earlier version of the AIA forms. See, for example, § 4.6.4 of AIA A201-1997.

appropriate. In a multi-party arbitration clause, it should be also possible to stipulate that the clause binds only the signatories to a specific agreement but shall not be binding on any assignees or successors of these signatories.

7.3.3.9 How to exclude or limit multi-party arbitration?

In principle, for a contracting party the best defence against multi-party arbitration is not to agree on a multi-party arbitration clause in its contract. However, there are a few occasions where contracting parties may have to stipulate explicitly in their contracts that multi-party arbitration is excluded. These are predominantly cases where either case law or national arbitration laws provide for court-ordered multi-party arbitration without the explicit parties' consent. For example, the Netherlands has introduced an *opt-out* consolidation provision in its legislation (see Section 5.3). Parties that have decided to arbitrate their disputes in a jurisdiction falling within the domain of the US Court of Appeals of the First Circuit may also want to introduce contractual wording excluding multi-party arbitration in the light of the *Keystone* case, where it was confirmed that consolidation may take place even in cases where the parties' contracts are silent on multi-party arbitration. Similarly, explicit wording excluding multi-party arbitration may be needed if parties have referred to arbitration rules that do not explicitly require the parties' consent to multi-party arbitration[133]. In all of the above cases, parties might find themselves involved in arbitration with the participation of third parties, which can frustrate the parties' expectations to resolve their disputes in a bipolar context. Therefore, if the latter type of arbitration is preferred by these parties, they should make the effort and include relevant clauses in their agreements stating that no intervention, joinder or consolidation will be permitted without their consent[134].

Sometimes contracting parties use clauses that exclude consolidation and joinder conditionally. These clauses stipulate, for example, that no multi-party arbitration shall take place absent parties' written consent, except with regard to parties substantially involved in the completion of the project. Thus, the consent of these parties to multi-party arbitration is incorporated in the clause, provided that the required threshold is fulfilled. An example of such a clause is the clause in the AIA forms prior to 2007 (see Section 6.10). A similar clause has also been quoted in the final report on multi-party arbitrations prepared by the ICC Working Committee on Multi-Party Arbitrations[135].

---

[133] See, for example, Article 4 of the Swiss Rules and Article 28.1(c) of the HKIAC Rules.

[134] For possible wording of such a clause, see Mark Bloomquist (2004) 'Chapter 26, Consolidation and Joinder' in Daniel Brennan, Richard Lowe, Jennifer Nielsen and John Spangler (eds) *The Construction Contracts Book, How to Find Common Ground in Negotiating Design and Construction Contract Clauses*, American Bar Association, Forum of the Construction Industry, Chicago, IL, p. 270.

[135] ICC Commission on International Arbitration, 'Final Report on Multi-party Arbitrations', in *6 ICC International Court Arbitration Bulletin*, no. 1 (1995), pp. 42–43. See draft clause 3 of Appendix 1 to the report, which states as follows: 'Except by written consent of the person or entity sought to be joined, no arbitration arising out of or relating to the Contract Documents shall include, by consolidation, joinder or any other manner, any person or entity not a party to the Agreement under which such arbitration arises, unless it is shown at the time the demand for arbitration is filed that such person or entity is substantially involved in a common question of fact or law.'

These clauses are not recommendable because of the uncertainty that they may produce. The parties' consent to multi-party arbitration under these clauses will depend on the degree of their involvement in the particular construction project that is likely to be a source of controversy.

There might also be cases where contracting parties do not want to exclude multi-party arbitration altogether. Multi-party arbitration may take place in diverse scenarios. Some contracting parties may not be able to foresee whether a multi-party arbitration clause would be beneficial to them or not. Generally, these parties would not mind the inclusion of a multi-party arbitration clause in their contracts. However, they would prefer to retain their discretion to decide whether to participate in such arbitration once the need for multi-party arbitration arises. They may want to veto the application of the clause if multi-party arbitration would be to their detriment. These techniques are usually employed by parties that have stronger bargaining power. For example, this would normally be the employer when negotiating with the main contractor, and the main contractor when negotiating with a subcontractor.

Wording appropriate for this purpose may be drafted in several ways. First, drafters may stipulate in the clause that it is one of the parties that would determine whether there is a common link between the disputes. This is the approach followed under the Blue Form, the ACA Main Contract, ACA Subcontract, the PPC International and the SPC International. Thus, the multi-party arbitration clause cannot be put into operation if the party does not express its opinion about the existence of such a link. Secondly, multi-party arbitration clauses may contain wording stipulating that the joinder or consolidation contemplated by the clause can be requested by one of the contracting parties only. In their essence, these clauses vest the party in question with the option (but not the obligation) to invoke the clause. Thus, if another party requests multi-party arbitration, such motion should be denied as it comes from a party that is not authorized to do so. This is the approach under the Blue Form, the ACA Subcontract, the IChemE Subcontract, the ENAA Process Plant Model and the NEC3 (in the context of multi-party adjudication). Finally, the entry into force of the multi-party arbitration clause could be postponed until a contracting party has stipulated that the clause should produce legal effect[136].

7.3.4 Sample multi-party arbitration clause

As mentioned above, there is no one-size-fits-all multi-party arbitration clause that can be used as a universal solution. Such a clause should always be drafted with a view to the specific contract into which it is to be inserted. The author has decided to introduce an exemplary multi-party arbitration clause that can be suitable for use with the FIDIC Red Book[137]. The ICC Rules are the default arbitration rules under most of the FIDIC

[136] For example, the following wording can be used: 'Clause [•] shall produce legal effect only subject to [employer]'s explicit written notice in that regard.'

[137] Some elements of the proposed clause have been inspired by an *ad hoc* multi-party arbitration clause sent to the author by an internationally renowned construction arbitrator.

Conditions of Contract, including the FIDIC Red Book. Therefore, the draft clause has been constructed in a way that would allow its application in arbitration subject to the ICC Rules.

The FIDIC Red Book is based on the traditional *build-only* model where the employer has hired a main contractor who is supposed to build the works in compliance with specifications and drawings prepared by or on behalf of the employer. As mentioned on several occasions, a need for multi-party arbitration in *build-only* contracting may arise on a number of occasions. For example, the employer may want to resolve his disputes against both the main contractor and the design team if there are deviations in the completed works attributable to both parties. Similarly, multi-party arbitration may be preferable if the main contractor is claiming against the employer due to an employer's default for which the design team is ultimately responsible (e.g. the designer has not provided the requested drawings in due time). The main contractor, on his side, will generally be interested in multi-party arbitration with the participation of his subcontractors if the employer's claim for defects in the works concerns the subcontractors' works, or if the subcontractors' claims against the main contractor concern a default attributable to the employer (e.g. the employer was late in giving access to the site to the main contractor, which resulted in the latter's failure to provide timely access to the site to the subcontractor). The author has tried to accommodate all these situations in the proposed draft clause. However, it should be emphasized that the proposed clause does not aim to be a panacea for all problems related to the conduct of multi-party arbitrations in the construction sector. Instead, the intention of the clause is merely to illustrate how a multi-party arbitration clause can be properly constructed by taking into account all the matters discussed in Subsection 7.3.3 hereof.

The proposed clause is based on the existing wording of the arbitration clause in the FIDIC Red Book – that is, sub-clause 20.6. Therefore, most elements of sub-clause 20.6 have been retained[138]. Those willing to adopt the proposed clause in the FIDIC Red Book should stipulate in the Special Conditions to the FIDIC Red Book that the existing sub-clause 20.6 is deleted and replaced with the following sub-clause:

20.6.1. Unless settled amicably, any dispute in respect of which the DAB's decision (if any) has not become final and binding shall be finally settled by international arbitration. Unless otherwise agreed by both Parties:

(a) the dispute shall be finally settled under the Rules of Arbitration of the International Chamber of Commerce ('Rules'),
(b) the dispute shall be settled by three arbitrators appointed in accordance with the terms set forth in Sub-Clauses 20.6.5 and 20.6.6;
(c) the place of arbitration shall be [•].
(d) the language shall be conducted in the language for communications defined in Sub-Clause 1.4 [Law and Language].

20.6.2. A party wishing to have recourse to arbitration under the Rules shall submit its Request for Arbitration with the Secretariat of the ICC without nominating an arbitrator.

[138] Sub-clauses 20.6.1, 20.6.11 and 20.6.12 of the draft clause largely correspond to the original wording of sub-clause 20.6 of the FIDIC Red Book.

20.6.3. Within [30] days from the receipt of the claimant's Request for Arbitration, the respondent shall submit an Answer to the Request for Arbitration with the Secretariat of the ICC, together with any counterclaim which he might have, without nominating an arbitrator.

20.6.4. Any multi-party arbitration shall only take place if requested in compliance with the procedures and within the time limits stipulated below. Other forms of multi-party arbitration which are not envisaged herein are explicitly excluded.

(i) In case of any arbitration initiated by the Contractor against the Employer or by the Employer against the Contractor, the Employer shall be entitled to join any third party with which the Employer has concluded a contract in relation to the designing and / or completion of the Works as a party to such arbitration by filing an Employer's Request for Arbitration against such third party, provided that the dispute under the main contract raises an issue which is substantially the same as, or connected with, or concern issues raised in a dispute between the Employer and such third party, or arises out of, or concerns substantially the same facts as are the subject of a dispute between the Employer and such third party. The joinder request shall be made either at the time when the Employer files his Request for Arbitration against the Contractor, or not later than [60] days after the receipt by the Employer of the Contractor's Request for Arbitration, or not later than [60] days after the receipt by the Employer of the Contractor's Answer to the Employer's Request for Arbitration and any counterclaim, as the case may be. The arbitral tribunal to be constituted in compliance with Sub-Clause 20.6.6 shall be empowered to abrogate any condition precedent to the bringing of arbitral proceedings in respect of the dispute between the Employer and such third party in order to allow for this dispute to be reviewed in the initiated arbitration.

(ii) In case of any arbitration initiated against the Employer by a third party pursuant to a contract concluded with the Employer in relation to the designing and / or completion of the Works or in case of any arbitration initiated by the Employer against any such third party, the Employer shall be entitled to join the Contractor as a party to such arbitration by filing an Employer's Request for Arbitration against the Contractor, provided that the dispute under the contract with such third party raises an issue which is substantially the same as, or connected with, or concern issues raised in a dispute between the Employer and the Contractor, or arises out of, or concerns substantially the same facts as are the subject of a dispute between the Employer and the Contractor. The joinder request shall be made either at the time when the Employer files his Request for Arbitration against the third party, or not later than [60] days after the receipt by the Employer of the third party's Request for Arbitration, or not later than [60] days after the receipt by the Employer of the third party's Answer to the Employer's Request for Arbitration and any counterclaim, as the case may be. The arbitral tribunal to be constituted under Sub-Clause 20.6.6 shall be empowered to abrogate any condition precedent to the bringing of arbitral proceedings in respect of the dispute between the Employer and the Contractor in order to allow for this dispute to be reviewed in the initiated arbitration.

(iii) In any arbitration under paragraph (i) or paragraph (ii) above, the Contractor shall be entitled to join a subcontractor to such arbitration by filing a Contractor's Request for Arbitration against the subcontractor, provided that a dispute between the Contractor and the subcontractor raises an issue which is substantially the same as, or connected with, or concern issues raised in the dispute between the Employer and the Contractor under paragraph (i) and / or paragraph (ii) above, or arises out of, or concerns substantially the same facts as are the subject of such dispute. The joinder request shall be made either at the time when the Contractor files his Request for Arbitration against the Employer, or not later than [60] days after the receipt by the Contractor of the Employer's Request for Arbitration against the Contractor, or not later than [60] days after the receipt by the Contractor of the Employer's Answer to the Contractor's Request for Arbitration and any counterclaim, as the case may be. The arbitral tribunal to be constituted under Sub-Clause 20.6.6 shall be empowered to abrogate any condition precedent to the bringing of arbitral proceedings in respect of the dispute between the Contractor and the subcontractor in order to allow for this dispute to be reviewed in the initiated arbitration.

20.6.5 If no joinder request has been filed within the time periods envisaged in Sub-Clause 20.6.4, each party should nominate one arbitrator for confirmation within a period of [15] days following the expiry of the last date when any such joinder requests should have been made. The third arbitrator, who will act as a president of the tribunal, shall be appointed by the ICC Court.

20.6.6 If one or more joinder requests have been made under Sub-Clause 20.6.4, all parties involved in the multi-party arbitration shall nominate unanimously all the three members of the tribunal, including the president of the tribunal, for confirmation within a period of [30] days reckoned from the last date when all the joinder requests under Sub-Clause 20.6.4 should have been made. Failing such an agreement, the ICC Court shall appoint each member of the tribunal and shall designate one of them to act as president.

20.6.7. All parties to the arbitration, including any multi-party arbitration, explicitly consent to the joinder provisions under Sub-Clause 20.6.4 above, and to the appointment of arbitrators upon the terms set forth under Sub-Clause 20.6.5 and Sub-Clause 20.6.6.

20.6.8. Any award arising out of any arbitration under Sub-Clause 20.6 shall be final and binding on the parties. The parties hereby waive any right to any form of recourse against the award, including any right to such recourse resulting from the constitution of the tribunal under Sub-Clause 20.6.5 and Sub-Clause 20.6.6, insofar as such waiver can be validly made.

20.6.9. The arbitral tribunal constituted under Sub-Clause 20.6.6 shall have full authority to adopt any procedural measures and / or rules which may be necessary, appropriate and / or desirable for the purpose of giving full effect to the provisions of this Sub-Clause 20.6 with a view to the multi-party nature of the proceedings.

20.6.10. Nothing in this Sub-Clause 20.6 shall allow any party to bring a claim against any other party with which it has not entered into a contract.

20.6.11. The arbitrators shall have full power to open up, review and revise any certificate, determination, instruction, opinion or valuation of the Engineer, and any decision of the DAB, relevant to the dispute. Nothing shall disqualify the Engineer from being called as a witness and giving evidence before the arbitrators on any matter whatsoever relevant to the dispute. Neither party shall be limited in the proceedings before the arbitrators to the evidence or arguments previously put before the DAB to obtain its decision, or to the reasons for dissatisfaction given in its notice of dissatisfaction. Any decision of the DAB shall be admissible in evidence in the arbitration.

20.6.12. Arbitration may be commenced prior to or after completion of the Works. The obligations of the Parties, the Engineer and the DAB shall not be altered by reason of any arbitration being conducted during the progress of the Works.

In general, the draft multi-party arbitration clause contemplates the following types of joinder:

- the joinder of a third party in an arbitration pending between the employer and the main contractor;
- the joinder of the main contractor in an arbitration pending between the employer and a third party;
- the joinder of a subcontractor in an arbitration pending between the employer and the main contractor.

The third party referred to in the first two types of joinder can be the engineer or the architect who has prepared the drawings for the contemplated works. However, the reference to such third party is not confined to the design team only. It comprises any third parties that have contracted with the employer in relation to the designing and / or the completion of the works. Therefore, these third parties may also comprise other technical consultants hired by the employer. The third party could also be a nominated subcontractor who has entered into direct contractual relations with the employer or a subcontractor who has provided a collateral warranty to the employer in the form of a contract.

Under the draft clause, the main contractor may request the joinder of a subcontractor only. If the main contractor undertakes to design some parts of the works for which he hires a designer, the main contractor may want to expand the scope of the clause so that he can also join the designer in the main contract arbitration in case of need. In this case, appropriate amendments should be introduced in paragraph (iii) of sub-clause 20.6.4.

Below, the author has briefly discussed how the proposed draft multi-party arbitration clause addresses the questions raised in Subsection 7.3.3.

(i) How to draft the clause in a way that incorporates all parties' consent?

The present clause is to be inserted in the FIDIC Red Book – in a main contract. It incorporates the consent to multi-party arbitration of the employer and the main contractor only. In order for the clause to be operational, it also requires the consent of the relevant third parties mentioned in the clause and the subcontractor. Therefore, multi-party arbitration provisions with identical or similar wording should also be inserted in the contracts between the employer and the relevant third party and also in the subcontracts.

In this way, the clauses read in conjunction with each other will create a self-contained mechanism for resolution of multi-contract disputes in single multi-party arbitration as these clauses will incorporate all parties' consent to such type of arbitration (see Subsection 7.3.3.1). If the clauses contain wording that is identical or substantially similar (this will in any case require that the same seat of arbitration is chosen in the separate clauses), these clauses will be considered as compatible in the context of the ICC Rules. Consequently, if a party raises a jurisdictional objection to the contemplated multi-party arbitration and such matter is referred to the ICC Court, the latter will almost certainly decide that there is a *prima facie* basis for the joint review of the multi-contract disputes under Article 6(4) of the ICC Rules because both criteria stated in this article will be satisfied (see Subsection 4.1.1).

In principle, the employer does not contract directly with subcontractors and he has no direct control over the content of the subcontracts. Therefore, the employer may consider including a provision in the main contract that obliges the main contractor to include a joinder provision with wording that is substantially similar to the proposed one in the subcontracts which he concludes. Furthermore, the main contract may even stipulate that the main contractor's failure to do so would be a contractual breach that could trigger certain consequences[139]. However, in most cases the employer is not interested

[139] Jan Paulsson, Nigel Rawding and Lucy Reed (2011) *The Freshfields Guide to Arbitration Clauses in International Contracts*, 3rd edn, Kluwer Law International, Alphen aan den Rijn, p. 99.

in multi-party arbitration with subcontractors hired by the main contractor. Therefore, the abovementioned technique should be employed mostly in cases of nominated subcontractors or subcontractors who have provided collateral warranties in favour of the employer.

(ii) How to describe the disputes to be submitted to arbitration?

The clause refers to the existence of *disputes* (about the meaning of this word see Subsections 6.2.1.1 and 7.3.3.2). The author has decided to keep the reference to *disputes*. The FIDIC Red Book contains a very consistent and structured claim management and dispute resolution procedures. The use of an alternative wording (such as, for example, 'an issue and / or matter') can create the impression that a certain matter, including a matter that has not yet escalated into a dispute, can be submitted directly to arbitration without complying with the claim management provisions. In the author's opinion, this is an undesired solution that can cause much disturbance to these provisions.

As already mentioned, the word 'dispute' has a special connotation when used in the context of the FIDIC Red Book. The clause, as drafted, presupposes that there is one dispute that has already been referred to arbitration. However, in order for the clause to be applied there should also be a dispute under the contract with regard to which the joinder is requested. For example, in the context of the joinder contemplated under paragraph (i) of draft sub-clause 20.6.4, there should be a main contract dispute referred to arbitration. In the context of the FIDIC Red Book, this means that the claims procedure has been followed, the engineer has made a determination on that claim under sub-clause 3.5, and the party dissatisfied with the determination has decided to pursue the matter further. In addition, the dispute that has arisen as a result of this claim should have been referred to a DAB, the DAB should have issued a decision on the dispute against which either party has expressed its dissatisfaction, and the parties should have tried to reach an amicable settlement. There should also be a dispute under the contract concluded between the third party and the employer. What is to constitute a dispute under that contract depends on its content. The employer may request the joinder of a third party either at the same time when he files his request for arbitration against the contractor or within a period of 60 days after receiving the contractor's answer to the request for arbitration and counterclaim or the contractor's request for arbitration (in cases where the arbitration has been initiated by the contractor). This period of 60 days should allow the employer to ensure, among other things, that a dispute has arisen under the contract with the third party. This is especially relevant in cases where the employer acquires knowledge of his claim against the third party at the time of receiving the contractor's request for arbitration or the contractor's answer to the employer's request for arbitration.

Under the joinder contemplated under paragraph (ii) of sub-clause 20.6.4, there should be a dispute under the contract concluded between the employer and the third party, which has already been referred to arbitration, and also a dispute under the main contract. Similarly, there might be cases where the employer acquires knowledge of his claim under the main contract once the arbitration with the third party is initiated. The period of 60 days within which the joinder request should be made should be sufficient for the employer to ensure the emergence of a dispute under the main contract. For example, the employer has initiated arbitration against the engineer because of the inaccurate design prepared by the engineer, which has led to deviations in the construction works. In the engineer's answer to the employer's request for arbitration the engineer blames the contractor for the deviations and provides documents to substantiate this statement. Then, it becomes clear to the employer that the contractor might indeed have caused or at least contributed to these deviations. However, there is no main contract dispute at this time because the employer has not pursued his claim in compliance with the claim management procedure. In this case, the employer will have 60 days from the date of receipt of the engineer's answer to the employer's request for arbitration to request the joinder of the main contractor. In the author's opinion, it should be possible for the employer to ensure that a main contract dispute arises within these 60 days. For that purpose, the employer should give a notice of his claim against the contractor under sub-clause 2.5 as soon as possible and then wait for the engineer's determination on that claim under sub-clause 3.5[140]. Either party's dissatisfaction with that determination will trigger a dispute. However, sub-clause 3.5 does not specify a time period within which the Engineer should make a determination. Therefore, employers might want to address this matter in the FIDIC Red Book and stipulate that a dispute will arise if the Engineer has failed to issue a determination within a certain period of time (e.g. 28 days) and the claiming party has expressed its dissatisfaction against this failure.

In addition to a dispute that has already been referred to arbitration, the joinder under paragraph (iii) of sub-clause 20.6.4 requires the existence of a subcontract dispute. The period of 60 days would probably be sufficient for the main contractor to ensure the existence of a subcontract dispute in cases where the main contractor acquires knowledge of his claim against the subcontractor once the arbitration involving the employer and the main contractor has been initiated. This would ultimately depend on the content of the subcontract. If the subcontract is based on the FIDIC Subcontract, the main contractor should give his notice of a claim and detailed particulars as early as possible, consult the subcontractor in an endeavour to reach an agreement and, if such agreement is not reached, make a fair decision on that claim[141]. However, it is very likely than some or all of these steps would have already been completed by the time of commencement of the main contract arbitration. For example, if the pending arbitration between the employer and the contractor concerns defects in the subcontractor's works, the main contractor would have probably acquired knowledge of his potential claim against the

[140] This may be the same engineer as the one who is respondent in the pending arbitration (i.e. the one who prepared the design) or a different engineer (in cases where the engineer who prepared the design is not the same as the one referred to as Engineer under the FIDIC Red Book).

[141] See sub-clause 3.4 in relation to sub-clause 3.3 of the FIDIC Subcontract. Sub-clause 3.3 stipulates that the Contractor should give his notice of claim as soon as practicable and not later than 28 days after the contractor became aware of the event or circumstance giving rise to the claim. The same sub-clause stipulates that the Contractor should send the detailed particulars of the claim as soon as practicable and not later than 28 days after giving the notice. Thus, the longest period within which the Contractor is obliged to send the particulars of his claim is 56 days. However, the Contractor should react much more quickly in order to preserve his right to join the subcontractor under the proposed clause.

subcontractor much earlier in time than the time when the arbitration was commenced. By that time the main contractor would have already received an employer's claim that had been determined by an engineer, and which had also probably been referred to a DAB for a decision. Therefore, the main contractor would have had sufficient time to undertake the necessary steps required for a claim to crystalize into a subcontract dispute before the commencement of the arbitration between the employer and the contractor.

(iii) Compatibility of the multi-party arbitration clause with contractual preconditions to arbitration

While the period of 60 days should normally be sufficient for the party requesting the joinder to ensure the emergence of a dispute between itself and the party to be joined (if such a dispute is not already present), this period may be insufficient for the requesting party to comply with all the pre-arbitral steps required under the respective contract with the party to be joined. A detailed discussion of these pre-arbitral steps is contained in Subsection 7.3.3.3. The author has therefore introduced wording empowering the arbitral tribunal to abrogate a condition precedent to arbitration concerning a dispute with regard to which the joinder is sought. Thus, if the employer finds himself in arbitration with the main contractor he may request the joinder of a third party under paragraph (i) of sub-clause 20.6.4, and the tribunal may abrogate any precondition to arbitration under the contract with such third party in order to allow for the joint review of the disputes in a single arbitration. For example, if the employer has requested the joinder of the engineer and the contract between these two parties is based on the FIDIC White Book, the arbitral tribunal will be empowered to abrogate the precondition under the FIDIC White Book that any dispute thereunder should be referred to mediation. On the other hand, if the pending arbitration is between the employer and the engineer, the employer may ask for the joinder of the main contractor under paragraph (ii) of sub-clause 20.6.4, in which case the tribunal will be empowered to abrogate any pre-arbitral step required under the FIDIC Red Book, such as the referral of the dispute to a DAB and / or the parties' attempts to reach an amicable settlement. Similarly, if the main contractor requires the joinder of a subcontractor, the arbitral tribunal may abrogate any pre-arbitral step under the subcontract under the terms of paragraph (iii) of sub-clause 20.6.4.

Special attention should be attributed to subcontract disputes based on the subcontractor's claims. For example, a subcontractor claims extension of time and additional costs against a main contractor due to an employer's failure to give timely access to the site, which results in an equivalent dispute under the main contract based on a main contractor's claim against the employer. As already mentioned in Subsection 7.3.3.3, subcontracts often envisage a quicker notification of claims and also a less sophisticated dispute resolution procedure than main contracts. This often results in a situation where a subcontract dispute crystalizes and is referable to arbitration much faster than a related main contract dispute. As a result, there is a danger for the main contractor that the subcontract dispute is referred to arbitration before he is able to initiate arbitral proceedings against the employer in which to join the subcontractor. If this happens, it may not be possible for the main contractor to invoke the draft multi-party arbitration clause. In order to preserve this right, the main contractor should address this question in the subcontract. One way to do this is to insert a provision in the subcontract whereunder the main contractor will be entitled to defer the referral of the subcontract dispute to dispute adjudication and / or arbitration with a period of time that is necessary for the main contractor to start arbitration against the employer[142]. Once such an arbitration is initiated, the main contractor will be able to join the subcontractor on the basis of paragraph (iii) of sub-clause 20.6.4.

(iv) The required link between the disputes

The draft clause refers to the subject matter of the disputes. One of these disputes should: (i) concern 'an issue which is substantially the same as, or connected with, or concern issues' raised in the other dispute, or (ii) arise out of or concern 'substantially the same facts as are the subject matter' of the other dispute. The wording of the ENAA Process Plant Model has been used as a source of inspiration when determining the required link between the disputes. The employer may broaden the scenarios in which the joinder provision can be invoked by deleting the word 'substantially' from the joinder provision. In this case, even a tenuous link between the subject matter of the disputes should be able to meet the required threshold (see on this point Subsection 7.3.3.4).

(v) Who is to decide whether such a link exists?

Even though the clause does not explicitly address this question, it would normally be the party requesting the joinder that would ascertain whether the required link between the disputes exists. Any dispute concerning the existence of such a link should be ultimately resolved by the arbitral tribunal when deciding on its jurisdiction (see Subsection 7.3.3.5).

(vi) How is the tribunal to be constituted?

Whenever contracting parties have agreed on a three-member tribunal, the ICC Rules envisage that a party should nominate in the request for arbitration, and the answer to the request, one arbitrator for confirmation[143]. However, this mechanism has been modified in the draft multi-party arbitration clause. The parties are allowed to deviate from the provisions concerning the constitution of the tribunal under the ICC Rules and therefore the modified mechanism should be respected by the ICC Court[144]. The

[142] The FIDIC Subcontract contains a similar clause under sub-clause 20.4. Under sub-paragraph (i) of this clause, the main contractor may defer the referral of a subcontract dispute, which is related to the main contract, to a subcontract DAB with a period of 112 days. However, it should be mentioned that the period of 112 days covers only the period from the referral of the related main contract dispute to a main contract DAB to the final date when a party may express dissatisfaction with main contract DAB's decision. Therefore, main contractors may consider extending this period in order to cover all the pre-arbitral stages required under the main contract.

[143] Article 12(4) of the ICC Rules in relation to Article 4(3)(g) and Article 5(1)(e).

[144] See Article 11(6) of the ICC Rules. See also Ricardo Ugarte and Thomas Bevilacqua, 'Ensuring Party Equality in the Process of Designating Arbitrators in Multi-Party Arbitration: An Update on the Governing Provisions', in *27 Journal of International Arbitration*, no. 1 (2010), p. 14.

purpose of the proposed wording is to obviate the risks identified in some already analysed multi-party arbitration clauses whereunder a third party is to be joined in a pending arbitration that is already afoot without the opportunity to participate in the constitution of the tribunal and to challenge the members of that tribunal at the time of their appointment.

The draft clause envisages that the claimant and the respondent will not make any appointment of an arbitrator at the time of filing the request for arbitration, and respectively the answer to the request. Any parties' nominations of arbitrators are to be made after the lapse of the time period within which any joinder requests should have been made. In this way, the tribunal will be constituted only after it becomes clear whether the forthcoming arbitration will be a bi-party or a multi-party arbitration. In a bipolar arbitration each party will nominate one arbitrator for confirmation, and the third arbitrator will be appointed by the ICC Court. In a multi-party arbitration, all the multiple parties should jointly agree on all the members of the tribunal. Pursuant to sub-clause 20.6.6, the ICC Court will appoint each member of the tribunal if the parties cannot unanimously agree on such a joint nomination. In this way, the draft clause ensures that the principle of parties' equality in the constitution of the arbitral tribunal is observed in a multi-party setting. Therefore, the proposed clause can be applied without any concerns in France and other countries that consider the principle of equality in the appointment of arbitrators as part of their public policy, which cannot be waived by parties in advance. A detailed discussion of the limitations in those countries is contained in Subsections 6.2.3.4 and 7.3.3.6.

In addition, the draft clause allows any challenges against the members of the tribunal to be made right after the appointment or confirmation of these members. The principal position under the ICC Rules is that any challenges should be submitted within 30 days from the receipt of the notification for appointment or confirmation of the arbitrators[145]. If the parties have jointly nominated all the members of the tribunal, the period for challenges would run from the date when the parties are notified about the confirmation of the tribunal. However, challenges in that instance are highly unlikely since the members would have been unanimously agreed upon by all parties. If the ICC Court is to appoint all the members of the tribunal, the period for challenges would run from the notification of their appointment. In both cases, however, all parties should make their challenges right after the constitution of the tribunal. Any replacement of an arbitrator upon a successful challenge will be done swiftly at a very early stage of the arbitration without materially delaying the arbitration[146].

(vii) Type of multi-party arbitration

The proposed provision is a joinder clause. However, in certain cases the clause also covers the legal technique of filing a single request for arbitration against multiple parties. For example, paragraph (i) of sub-clause 20.6.4 entitles the employer to ask for

---

[145] See Article 14(2) of the ICC Rules.

[146] See also Jason Fry, Simon Greenberg and Francesca Mazza (2012) *The Secretariat's Guide to ICC Arbitration*, ICC Publication No. 729, p. 179 (§ 3-592).

the joinder of a third party simultaneously with the filing of the employer's request for arbitration against the main contractor. In the same vein, paragraph (ii) of sub-clause 20.6.4 allows the employer to serve a joinder request against the contractor at the same time when serving his request of arbitration against the third party.

Intervention of third parties in pending arbitration and consolidation of parallel arbitrations are excluded under draft sub-clause 20.6.4.

(viii) Number of parties

The draft clause does not put an explicit limit on the number of parties that may be joined. The clause recognizes that employers often have superior bargaining power over main contractors with regard to the terms of the main contract. Generally, employers will not be interested in putting a limit on the number of parties that they may join. In this way, employers retain discretion to decide whether to join a third party and, if so, how many parties to join depending on the specific circumstances of the case. Therefore, paragraph (i) in sub-clause 20.6.4 generally refers to third parties that have contracted with the employer as parties that may be joined.

There is no limit on the number of subcontractors that may be joined under paragraph (iii) of sub-clause 20.6.4. The clause generally refers to subcontractors, which may also include nominated subcontractors. If the employer is not interested in the joinder of subcontractors into his arbitration with the main contractor, he may simply delete the suggested paragraph (iii) of sub-clause 20.6.4. Furthermore, the application of the joinder provision may be confined to specific subcontractors only by inserting the names of these subcontractors and / or the details of the executed subcontracts.

Finally, one last remark should be made with regard to the place of arbitration under letter (c) of draft sub-clause 20.6.1. In order to ensure the workability of the proposed multi-party arbitration regime, the same place of arbitration should be chosen in the arbitration clauses in the separate agreements. The clauses will be considered incompatible if different places of arbitration are chosen, which will make multi-party arbitration impossible. The author has endeavoured to draft the sample multi-party arbitration clause in a way that would ensure its workability even in jurisdictions that impose certain limitations on multi-party arbitration agreements. In any case, contracting parties are advised to choose a seat of arbitration in a country that is a signatory to the New York Convention and has a modern arbitration law that is supportive of arbitration.

7.4 Institutional approach

In Section 7.3, the author has suggested some guidelines as to how parties can regulate multi-party arbitration issues at a contractual level. The contractual approach is to be given preference because of its full consonance with the consensual nature of arbitration and the predictability it brings to the dispute resolution process. At the same time, the author recognizes that it may not always be possible for contracting parties to include multi-party arbitration agreements in their contracts. In these cases, the question arises whether arbitral institutions are in a position to respond to the need for multi-party arbitration in the construction industry. Given the possible lack of contractual multi-party arbitration solutions and the inherent inappropriateness of statutory solutions to the problem, the author is of the opinion that arbitral institutions have the potential to respond to such need by adopting arbitration rules containing appropriate multi-party arbitration provisions. As stated by one author:

> By inserting careful provisions into the respective rules, the arbitration institutions can put into operation a true 'contractual system of consolidation and/or harmonisation', therefore filling the gap created by the contractual foundation of arbitration, as opposed to the coercive measures available at the level of procedural law.[147]

However, as observed in Section 4.12, the current regulation of multi-party disputes under the different sets of arbitration rules has failed to provide for a self-contained mechanism for multi-party arbitrations which can be operated solely on the basis of provisions contained in these rules. Most arbitration rules require parties' consent to multi-party arbitration expressed in the form of contractual multi-party arbitration provisions, an umbrella or a submission arbitration agreement.

There are some arbitration rules that do not explicitly require parties' consent to multi-party arbitration. This is the position under Swiss Rules, the Vienna Rules (in their part concerning joinder) and the DIA Rules. The CIAR, the ICDR Rules (in their part concerning joinder), the SIAC Rules (concerning consolidation only) and the HKIAC Rules (concerning consolidation only) follow a similar approach. One might argue that workable solutions to multi-party arbitration problems are to be found in these arbitration rules. By choosing them as applicable to their disputes, the parties have given their anticipatory consent to multi-party arbitration under the terms of these rules, including to the joinder of third parties or consolidation of parallel arbitrations over the objection of some of the parties. However, if one looks at the statistics concerning the application of these provisions (in cases where such statistics are available)[148], one would notice that with the exception of the consolidation provision under the HKIAC Rules these clauses are sparingly operated absent all parties' consent. Therefore, it seems that these rules have also failed to provide for a workable solution.

The above mentioned observations reveal some shortcomings in the current regulation of multi-party disputes at the level of the arbitration rules. In the author's opinion, such regulation can be improved in order to meet the increasing demands for a workable resolution of multi-party disputes. Such improvements may take the form of adoption of new arbitration rules or amendment of existing ones with the purpose of introducing workable multi-party arbitration solutions, which can come into play in cases where the parties have not explicitly regulated multi-party arbitration in their arbitration agreements.

---

[147] Andrea Marco Steingruber (2012) *'Consent in International Arbitration'*, Oxford University Press, Oxford, para. 10.35. See also Mihajlo Dika (1985) 'The Problem of Multi-Party Arbitration from the Standpoint of Yugoslav Law', in Cornelis Voskuil and John Wade (eds) *Hague-Zagreb Essays 5 on the Law of International Trade, Reservation of Title, Multiparty Arbitration*, Martinus Nijhoff, The Hague, pp. 135, 138.

[148] See, for example, Subsection 4.5.2.

In this section, the author will try to present his ideas as to what such a workable solution may look like. In most cases, such a solution will require the existence of two or more compatible arbitration agreements. Therefore, this section also deals with such compatibility assessment. Finally, the author has briefly summarized some other relevant factors that should be considered by tribunals and institutions when deciding on requests for multi-party arbitration.

7.4.1 How to create a workable multi-party arbitration mechanism under arbitration rules?

The reader may ask why the flexible provisions which do not explicitly require parties' consent to multi-party arbitration have not been operated over a party's objection to such type of arbitration. Is it because of the notion of anticipatory consent, which has caused some controversy among legal scholars and practitioners, or for some other reason? In the author's opinion, the notion of anticipatory consent to multi-party arbitration is not so problematic as such. If the parties have referred in their contracts to certain arbitration rules allowing for multi-party arbitration absent parties' consent, the reference to these rules incorporates parties' consent to multi-party arbitration under these terms. Therefore, the reason for the sparing application of these flexible provisions should be sought somewhere else.

If one were to take a closer look at the wording of these provisions, one would notice that most provisions do not deal with parties' consent as such. This especially applies to the Swiss Rules, the DIA Rules, the Vienna Rules and the ICDR Rules. It is true that these clauses do not explicitly require parties' consent to multi-party arbitration. However, it is also true that they do not explicitly acknowledge that such consent is not necessary. In other words, the rules are silent as to the question of whether consent is required or not. This has caused some uncertainty as to whether the availability of consent is a necessary element for the operation of the discussed provisions. This question has split the opinion of scholars and practitioners. Some are of the opinion that consent is still required, whereas others share the view that the clauses can be operated even absent parties' consent[149]. If the former opinion is followed, the provisions should be construed as prescribing the relevant procedure to be followed upon a request for multi-party arbitration but not as creating a jurisdictional basis for the conduct of such arbitration. Hence, upon such a request, the respective tribunal or institution should obtain the endorsement of the request by all parties before instructing multi-party arbitration. If the latter opinion is followed such endorsement is not required because the provisions create a jurisdictional basis for the conduct of multi-party arbitration even over the objection of some of the parties.

In the author's opinion, the above uncertainty is the main reason for the cautiousness of tribunals and institutions when faced with a request for multi-party arbitration. Understandably, in case of doubt these tribunals and institutions tend to follow the more

[149] See the discussion in Sections 4.5 and 4.3 and Subsections 4.6.1 and 4.7.1.

conservative approach – that is, that the relevant provisions regulate procedural questions but cannot be used as a substitute for parties' consent if this consent is not expressed in other ways. Hence, this often precludes the opportunity for multi-party arbitration because parties with divergent interest will typically not be able to reach unanimous consent on the matter in the course of the proceedings.

The abovementioned uncertainties hint at how the current legal framework can be improved in order to provide for workable multi-party arbitration solutions. In the author's opinion, such a solution should comply with two main conditions. First, multi-party arbitration provisions under arbitration rules should not explicitly require the parties' consent to multi-party arbitration. This first condition mostly concerns arbitration rules that still require parties' consent in the form of multi-party arbitration agreements or a single arbitration agreement binding the multiple parties. The first condition is often not sufficient in itself. As has been seen, some rules comply with this condition but are nevertheless not operated if a party objects to their application. Therefore, arbitration rules should go one step further. They should also comply with the second condition – that is, they should create a jurisdictional basis for the conduct of multi-party arbitration. Unequivocal wording is required in that respect.

As a source of inspiration of how to construct such wording, one might want to look at some examples of provisions that create such a jurisdictional basis. One such example can be found in the consolidation provision under the HKIAC Rules (discussed in Subsection 4.11.3). The consolidation provision under the new SIAC Rules (discussed in Subsection 4.11.2) seems to follow a similar approach. Another example can be found in string arbitrations in commodity trades. For instance, the Arbitration Rules of the Grain and Feed Trade Association (**'GAFTA'**) stipulate that in cases of disputes concerning the quality or condition of goods sold under a string of contracts with materially identical terms, a single arbitration may be held between the first seller and the last buyer as though they were bound by a contract[150]. The resulting award is binding on all the parties in the string. A similar clause is contained in the Arbitration Rules of the Federation of Oils, Seeds and Fats Associations Ltd (**FOSFA**)[151]. These clauses are exemplary as to how a jurisdictional basis for multi-party arbitration can be created between parties not bound by a contract. In this way, the rules essentially entitle the parties to ignore the lack of a contractual relationship between the end buyer and the original vendor of the goods in order to resolve their disputes in a single forum[152].

A further example of a clause creating a jurisdictional basis for multi-party arbitration is to be found in the JAMS Engineering & Construction Arbitration Rules and

[150] See Rule 7.1 of GAFTA Arbitration Rules No. 125, effective for contracts dated from 1 June 2014, http://www.gafta.com/write/MediaUploads/Contracts/2014/125_2014.pdf (accessed 26 July 2016).

[151] See Rule 6(c) of the FOSFA Rules of Arbitration and Appeal, effective as from January 2012, and the same rule from the FOSFA Rules for Small Claims Single Tier, in force as from September 2008. Both sets of rules are available at http://www.fosfa.org/arbitration/guide-and-rules/(accessed 26 July 2016).

[152] CIArb Practice Guideline 15: Guidelines for Arbitrators on how to approach issues relating to Multi-Party Arbitrations, para. 4.2.1.

Procedures[153]. These rules are primarily designated for resolution of construction disputes in the United States. Pursuant to Rule 6 (e): 'Unless the Parties' agreement or applicable law provides otherwise, JAMS, if it determines that the Arbitrations so filed have common issues of fact or law, may consolidate Arbitrations in the following circumstances...'[154]

Unlike other provisions examined in this book, this clause explicitly touches upon the question of whether consent is required. It stipulates that consolidation may be ordered, unless the parties have agreed otherwise in their arbitration agreements. Thus, it becomes clear that if the parties' arbitration agreements are silent on multi-party arbitration, consolidation can be ordered solely on the basis of the abovementioned provision. For that reason, it has been stated that the quoted Rule 6(e) contains the broadest consolidation rights when compared with other arbitration rules that are less definitive in their wording[155]. The JAMS International Rules, which are suitable for international use, also contain a multi-party arbitration provision but with wording that closely resembles the solution under the Swiss Rules[156]. Hence, it is not clear whether consent is a required element for the operation of this provision.

The above mentioned clauses indicate possible wording that arbitral institutions may want to adopt if they decide to implement joinder or consolidation provisions containing a self-contained mechanism for multi-party arbitrations. For example, arbitration rules may stipulate that joinder and / or consolidation may be possible, unless the parties have excluded multi-party arbitration in their arbitration agreement(s). Such wording may eliminate the uncertainties discussed stemming from broadly worded multi-party arbitration clauses contained in arbitration rules. If such wording is used, any fears regarding the eventual setting aside, non-recognition and / or non-enforcement of an arbitral award rendered in a multi-party setting will be dispersed because of the coherent wording, which has made clear that the deciding authority is vested with the explicit jurisdiction to order multi-party arbitration. Hence, tribunals and institutions deciding on multi-party arbitration requests will have more confidence to grant such requests, provided, of course, that the other conditions stipulated in the relevant arbitration rules are fulfilled.

As already observed, the proposed institutional approach will not breach the consensual nature of arbitration. However, one important clarification should be made here. The consonance of this approach with the consensual nature of arbitration is subject to the condition that the respective multi-party arbitration provisions were in existence at

---

[153] JAMS (formerly known as Judicial Arbitration and Mediation Services) is a large private alternative dispute resolution provider and one of the major arbitration administration organizations in the United States. The JAMS Engineering and Construction Arbitration Rules and Procedures, effective as from 15 November 2014, are available at http://www.jamsadr.com/rules-construction-arbitration/(accessed 26 July 2016).

[154] Reprinted with permission. Copyright 2016 JAMS. All rights reserved.

[155] Philip Bruner, 'Dual Track Proceedings in Arbitration and Litigation: Reducing the Peril of "Double Jeopardy" by Consolidation, Joinder and Appellate Arbitration', in *31 International Construction Law Review*, part 4 (2014), p. 543

[156] JAMS International was established in 2011 by JAMS and the ADR Centre in Italy and has its headquarters in London. See Article 6 of the JAMS International Arbitration Rules, effective as from 1 August 2011, http://www.jamsinternational.com/arbitration-rules (accessed 1 August 2016).

the time when the parties concluded their contracts. As discussed in Section 4.12, most arbitration rules stipulate that the parties shall be deemed to have agreed on the application of the chosen set of rules that is in effect on the date of commencement of the arbitration. However, these rules may be different from the ones that were in force at the time when the parties concluded their contracts. This creates a risk that multi-party arbitration that has not been (and could not have been) anticipated by the parties is imposed on them as a result of multi-party arbitration provisions introduced after the date of conclusion of parties' contract(s). For instance, a revision of the arbitration rules chosen by the parties, which were previously silent on multi-party arbitration, may have resulted in the introduction of a self-contained mechanism for multi-party arbitration under these rules. It is questionable whether the conduct of multi-party arbitration over a party's objection in this case is compliant with the consensual nature of arbitration. Therefore, when arbitral institutions adopt self-contained multi-party arbitration provisions they should make clear that these provisions will not apply to arbitration agreements concluded prior to the date of entry into force of the amended rules containing these provisions. An example of this approach can be found in the HKIAC Rules discussed in Subsection 4.11.3 above. Alternatively, arbitral institutions may introduce such provisions in the form of opt-out clauses. In other words, the provisions could be operated even if introduced after the execution of the respective arbitration agreement on condition that none of the parties objects to their application in the course of the proceedings. An objection raised by any party will trigger the provision inapplicable which will result in the application of the corresponding provision (if any) in existence at the time of conclusion of the respective arbitration agreement.

In addition to the question of parties' consent, discussed above, a workable multi-party arbitration solution may have to address some other matters. Many consolidation provisions in popular sets of arbitration rules contain a requirement that consolidation in respect of claims made under multiple arbitration agreements is possible only if the pending arbitrations are between the same parties[157]. This mechanism is unworkable in a multi-contract context where the different bilateral contracts are signed by different parties. Accordingly, a workable mechanism for resolution of multi-party disputes arising under two or more contracts should dispense from this requirement.

Furthermore, such a mechanism should also cater for any mandatory pre-arbitral dispute resolution steps under the different agreements, such as dispute adjudication, which are commonplace in construction projects. As observed in Subsection 7.3.3.3, there may be cases where multi-party arbitration may be needed before the exhaustion of all such pre-arbitral phases. Moreover, these pre-arbitral steps are often not identical under the contracts in respect of which the need for multi-party arbitration may arise. For instance, the pre-arbitral steps under the FIDIC White Book include an attempt to settle the dispute by negotiation and mediation, whereas the FIDIC Red Book requires dispute adjudication and an attempt to reach an amicable settlement. In these cases, arbitral institutions may consider vesting tribunals with the jurisdiction to review a dispute that has not yet passed through all required pre-arbitral stages and, respectively,

[157] See Article 10(c) of the ICC Rules, Article 8(1)(c) of the ICDR Rules, Article 22.1(x) of the LCIA Rules, Article 11 of the SCC rules, and Article 19(1)(b) of the CIETAC Rules.

to abrogate any contractual precondition to arbitration in certain cases. As mentioned under Subsection 7.3.3.3, the CIMAR contain a provision that may serve as a source of inspiration as to how to deal with this matter.

The adoption of a self-contained multi-party arbitration mechanism under arbitration rules will eventually depend on the willingness of the respective arbitral institution to introduce such an approach. This would be the result of a policy decision to be taken by the institution. There may be institutions which will not be willing to go so far in their approach to multi-party disputes arising under two or more contracts. At the same time, however, it is the author's expectation that other institutions may be willing to introduce this approach and thus fill in a gap in the current regulation of multi-party disputes. For these institutions, the introduction of the discussed self-contained approach will be a good chance to attract users of arbitration who are in need of institutional multi-party arbitration solutions or are dissatisfied with the conservative approach to multi-party arbitration under other arbitration rules.

7.4.2 Compatibility of arbitration agreements

Most arbitration rules would allow multi-party arbitration comprising disputes under different contracts only if the arbitration agreements contained in these contracts are compatible[158]. In the author's opinion, this approach is justified. The incompatibility of the different arbitration agreements is a strong indication for the parties' dissent to multi-party arbitration. In these cases, a dispute arising under one contract should be resolved in compliance with the arbitration agreement contained in *that* contract alone.

If two or more arbitration agreements contain identical wording, they will be considered as compatible. However, compatibility does not necessarily presuppose arbitration agreements worded in identical terms. There may be cases where two or more arbitration agreements have different wording but are nevertheless compatible. On the other hand, there are some clear-cut cases where incompatibility may be presumed. This will be the case, for example, where a main contract contains an arbitration agreement, whereas the subcontract contains a clause giving jurisdiction to local courts. In addition, two or more arbitration agreements will be incompatible if the parties under each contract have chosen different types of arbitration, such as institutional and *ad hoc* arbitration, or have referred to different arbitration rules. Multi-party arbitration in all these cases will not be possible.

However, the assessment of whether two or more arbitration agreements are compatible, or respectively incompatible, is not always so straightforward. Different factors should be considered in such assessment. These include, among other things, the seats of arbitration, the method for the constitution of the arbitral tribunal, the language of the proceedings, the governing law and the preconditions for arbitration. These are briefly examined below.

---

[158] Articles 6(4) and 10(c) of the ICC Rules, Articles 10 and 13(2)(c) of the CEPANI Rules, Article 8(c) of the ICDR Rules, Article 15(2) of the Vienna Rules, Articles 14 and 19 of the CIETAC Rules, etc.

(i) Seats of Arbitration

The arbitration agreements will clearly be incompatible if they specify different seats of arbitration[159]. The question concerning compatibility is more difficult when one arbitration agreement provides for a certain city as the place of arbitration whereas the other arbitration agreement is silent as to the place of arbitration. Any potential incompatibility in these cases can be rectified if the tribunal or institution fixes the place of arbitration under the second arbitration agreement in the same city. Such a decision, however, should be taken with utmost caution by taking into account all the facts pertaining to the case. The arbitral tribunal or institution should refrain from fixing the place of arbitration under the second arbitration agreement in the same city if the sole reason for such a decision is the efficiency that multi-party arbitration may bring to the dispute resolution process.

(ii) Method for the constitution of the arbitral tribunal

A different number of arbitrators under the different arbitration agreements (e.g. a sole arbitrator and a three-member tribunal) will trigger their incompatibility. The situation will be more complex if the different arbitration agreements specify the same number of arbitrators but different methods for their appointment. For example, both agreements refer to a three-member tribunal. Under the first agreement, each party should nominate one arbitrator and the presiding arbitrator should be selected by the two nominated arbitrators. Under the second agreement, the so-called *list method* is used whereunder the arbitral institution sends identical lists of arbitrators to the parties. Each party has to strike out the names objected to, and the arbitral institution will choose the arbitrators among the remaining names on the list. It is debatable whether the different methods will result in the incompatibility of the agreements. In the author's opinion, such a difference will not trigger incompatibility in all cases. The same will be true in cases where one of the agreements specifies a number of arbitrators, whereas the other one is silent on this matter. In all these cases, however, the authority making the compatibility assessment should be wary of deciding in favour of compatibility for reasons of procedural efficiency alone.

(iii) Language of the proceedings

Different opinions have been expressed on the question whether different languages of arbitration in the different arbitration agreements result in incompatibility. Some authors and the ICC Secretariat's Guide suggest that the different languages of arbitration lead to incompatibility, which prevents multi-party arbitration[160]. The CEPANI Rules suggest that such differences do not give rise to any presumption as to such incompatibility[161].

---

[159] Jason Fry, Simon Greenberg and Francesca Mazza (2012) *The Secretariat's Guide to ICC Arbitration*, ICC Publication No. 729, ICC Publishing SA, Paris, pp. 81–82 (§ 3-243). Bernard Hanotiau (2005) *Complex Arbitrations: Multiparty, Multicontract, Multi-issue and Class Actions*, Kluwer Law International, The Hague, p. 114 (§ 248–249).

[160] Lara Pair (2012) *Consolidation in International Commercial Arbitration, The ICC and Swiss Rules*, International Commerce and Arbitration Volume 10, Eleven International Publishing, The Hague, pp. 54–55, and Jason Fry, Simon Greenberg and Francesca Mazza (2012) *The Secretariat's Guide to ICC Arbitration*, ICC Publication No. 729, ICC Publishing SA, Paris, p. 82 (§ 3-245).

[161] Article 10(2) of the CEPANI Rules.

In its decision of 11 April 2002, the Paris Court of Appeals was confronted with this question[162]. Disputes arose out of a framework agreement and four addenda concerning a licence to use software and various services to be provided in that regard. Whereas the agreement and the first three addenda provided for arbitration in the French language, the fourth addendum provided for arbitration in English. In a preliminary award, the arbitral tribunal decided that this difference did not render the agreements incompatible. It respected the parties' choice of different languages as to the different contractual instruments but allowed the parties to express themselves both in French and in English in their written and oral submissions. The respondent's action for setting aside of the award was unsuccessful. The Paris Court of Appeals decided that the arbitral tribunal had not exceeded its mandate when allowing the parties to express themselves in both languages.

It is difficult to generalize on the basis of this case as to whether differences in the language of the proceedings will make the arbitration agreements incompatible[163]. If, for example, a main contract provides for arbitration in English, and a subcontract envisages arbitration in Chinese, the more likely outcome is that this difference will render the arbitration agreements incompatible even if these agreements refer to the same arbitration rules and seat of arbitration.

(iv) Governing law

It is commonplace in construction projects that the different bilateral contracts are governed by different laws. For example, a subcontract is often governed by a law different from the one applicable to the main contract. The prevailing view is that differences in the laws applicable to the merits in the different contracts should not in itself render the arbitration agreements incompatible[164]. However, there are also opinions to the contrary[165]. The arbitral tribunal should in principle be in a position to apply one governing law to the claims brought under one arbitration agreement and a different law to the claims brought under the other arbitration agreement[166]. However, arbitral tribunals and institutions should not take this stance for granted and should make a careful assessment of all the circumstances of the case before ordering multiparty arbitration.

---

[162] First Ch. C., 2003 *Rev. Arb.*, 1252, commented by Bernard Hanotiau (see Bernard Hanotiau (2005) *Complex Arbitrations: Multiparty, Multicontract, Multi-issue and Class Actions*, Kluwer Law International, The Hague, pp. 137–138 (§ 292–296)).

[163] Bernard Hanotiau (2005) *Complex Arbitrations: Multiparty, Multicontract, Multi-issue and Class Actions*, Kluwer Law International, The Hague, p. 138 (§ 296).

[164] Jason Fry, Simon Greenberg and Francesca Mazza (2012) *The Secretariat's Guide to ICC Arbitration*, ICC Publication No. 729, ICC Publishing SA, Paris, p. 82 (§ 3-245). See also Article 10(2) of the CEPANI Rules and Bernard Hanotiau (2005) *Complex Arbitrations: Multiparty, Multicontract, Multi-issue and Class Actions*, Kluwer Law International, The Hague, p. 138 (§ 296).

[165] Stavros Brekoulakis (2010) *Third Parties in International Commercial Arbitration*, Oxford University Press, Oxford, p. 100 (§ 3.16), and Lara Pair (2012) *Consolidation in International Commercial Arbitration, The ICC and Swiss Rules*, International Commerce and Arbitration Volume 10, Eleven International Publishing, The Hague, pp. 54–55.

[166] Jason Fry, Simon Greenberg and Francesca Mazza (2012) *The Secretariat's Guide to ICC Arbitration*, ICC Publication No. 729, ICC Publishing SA, Paris, p. 82 (§ 3-245).

(v) Preconditions to arbitration

In the author's opinion, different preconditions to arbitration under the different contracts (e.g. dispute adjudication under one contract and mediation under the other contract) should not result in incompatibility of the arbitration agreements. As suggested in Subsection 7.4.1, if arbitral institutions are willing to introduce a self-contained mechanism for resolution of multi-party disputes in the construction sector, they should introduce a specific wording in their arbitration rules empowering arbitral tribunals to abrogate any condition precedent to arbitration. The availability of such wording will further strengthen the argument that any differences as to the preconditions to arbitration are not decisive in the compatibility assessment.

The abovementioned factors should not be considered as a definite list of all circumstances that tribunals and institutions should consider in such an assessment. There may be other circumstances, which may play an important role, such as differences in the law applicable to the arbitration agreements and time limits within which an award should be rendered.

7.4.3 Other circumstances

In addition to the compatibility assessment described above, arbitral tribunals and institutions should also consider other factors when deciding on multi-party arbitration. These factors typically include the link between the disputes, the appointment or confirmation of arbitrators, the identity of the appointed arbitrators (in case of separate proceedings subject to consolidation), the progress of the proceedings and so forth.

It is not the intention of the author to discuss in detail each of these factors. In principle, the tribunal or the institution deciding on multi-party arbitration should have the widest possible discretion to consider as many factors as it deems appropriate. Therefore, if a certain arbitral institution has decided to introduce a certain list of factors in its arbitration rules, that list should be considered as non-exhaustive. In principle, it would be sufficient if the relevant articles in the arbitration rules state that the deciding authority will consider all relevant circumstances without listing explicitly what these circumstances can be. In any case, the powers given to tribunals and institutions should be discretionary. This means that they should have the authority to deny a motion for multi-party arbitration even in cases where the rules provide for a self-contained mechanism for resolution of multi-party disputes and the arbitration agreements are compatible. There may be other circumstances in these cases that may make multi-party arbitration undesirable.

The CIArb Practice Guideline 15 provides some useful guidance to arbitrators as to what circumstances to consider when deciding on multi-party arbitration. Pursuant to the guidelines, 'the tribunal should attempt to balance the advantage of joinder against the disadvantages likely to result from it'[167]. The advantages of multi-party arbitration are well known. These comprise avoiding the risk of inconsistent findings and overall saving of

[167] CIArb Practice Guideline 15: Guidelines for Arbitrators on how to approach issues relating to Multi-Party Arbitrations, para. 5.5.

time and costs. The CIArb guideline contains a useful list of some of the disadvantages pertaining to multi-party arbitration. A material prejudice to some of the parties stemming from some of these disadvantages can serve as an argument against multi-party arbitration. The disadvantages may include the following matters: the proceedings in multi-party arbitration may become unwieldy or unduly prolonged (for some of the parties), there may be difficulties in selecting hearing dates, the claimant may suffer greater delay in enforcing his legal rights than if the dispute is decided on its own, and one or more parties (especially those involved in smaller claims) may incur higher legal costs[168].

Arbitral tribunals or institutions should also take into account the timing of the joinder or consolidation request. It has been suggested that if the applicant for joinder or consolidation has delayed unduly without unjust excuse, that alone may be a ground for denial, especially if there would be some prejudice to another party[169]. The deciding authority should also consider the impact of relevant evidence, which is already heard in the pending arbitration(s) on the multi-party arbitration[170].

Some special comments have to be made with regard to the constitution of the arbitral tribunal. In cases of consolidation, the appointment of arbitrators in the separate proceedings will be one of the circumstances to be considered by the deciding authority (typically the arbitral institution administering the arbitrations). The appointment of arbitrators in the separate arbitrations should not in itself preclude the possibility of consolidation. In order to preserve the parties' equal treatment in the constitution of the tribunal that is going to review the consolidated proceeding, the arbitration rules should provide that the arbitral institution will be empowered to revoke any appointments already made and appoint all members of the new tribunal. This approach can be found in the Swiss Rules and the DIA Rules. Potential delay in the resolution of the disputes subject to the separate arbitrations should also be one of the circumstances to be considered by the institution. If consolidation will cause material delay to the proceedings, it should not be allowed.

The problem concerning the appointment of the arbitral tribunal looks differently in cases of joinder of third parties. A reoccurring condition under many of the joinder provisions of the reviewed arbitration rules is that a third party may not be joined after the appointment of the arbitral tribunal[171]. Accordingly, arbitration rules dealing with joinder do not envisage the revocation of the authority of the already appointed tribunal in such cases. This restriction seems to be justified in most cases. Regardless, there may sometimes be compelling reasons to join a third party after the appointment of the tribunal. For example, if in the course of an arbitration between an employer and a main contractor concerning a subcontractor's default it becomes clear that the main contractor is endangered of entering into insolvency proceedings, the employer may want to join a subcontractor who has provided a collateral warranty in order to increase his chances of recovery. Similarly, if in the main contract arbitration some evidence is presented

---

168 Ibid.

169 Jeffrey Waincymer (2012) *Procedure and Evidence in International Arbitration*, Kluwer Law International, Alphen aan den Rijn, pp. 563, 575–576.

170 Ibid., p. 575.

171 See, for example, Article 7(1) of the ICC Rules, Article 11 of the CEPANI Rules and Article 7 of the ICDR Rules.

pointing to a design error that has contributed to the defects in the works, the employer may want to join the architect in the arbitration that is under way. Because of the abovementioned restriction, a joinder of a third party in these cases will not be possible if a main contract tribunal has already been appointed. The restriction seems to be too rigid in these cases. Arbitral institutions should think of how to accommodate these situations under their arbitration rules. One possible way can be to allow the joinder on condition that the third party accepts the already appointed tribunal. Otherwise, issues of due process may arise because of the third party being denied the right to participate in the selection of the tribunal which may endanger the enforcement of the award. Arbitration rules may also provide that the authority of the tribunal may be revoked in which case the institution will be empowered to appoint all members of the tribunal. It should be acknowledged, however, that such revocation is likely to cause more practical challenges in the context of joinder than in cases of consolidation. Whereas it is typically the arbitral institution that decides on consolidation, any requests concerning joinder after the constitution of the tribunal should normally be decided by the arbitral tribunal itself. However, it would be peculiar to vest that same tribunal with the power to revoke its own authority in order to allow for the joinder of a third party and preserve the third party's equal treatment in the constitution of the tribunal. Therefore, any decision concerning revocation of arbitrators' authority should be taken by the institution administering the case. Alternatively, such decision may also be taken by a specially designated arbitrator who is appointed by the institution for the limited purpose of deciding on the joinder request. If the arbitrator decides that the request should be granted, he should also be entitled to revoke the authority of the appointed arbitrators and establish a process for selecting a new tribunal. R-7 of the CIAR follows a similar approach and may serve as a source of inspiration to arbitral institutions willing to introduce a similar mechanism.

From the perspective of contracting parties, a self-contained approach to multi-party arbitration under the applicable arbitration rules could be a welcome solution to their needs for dispute resolution in a multi-party setting. However, it should be recognized that the proposed institutional approach does not have the same degree of predictability as the contractual approach discussed in Chapter 7. The large discretion granted to tribunals and institutions to order multi-party arbitration and the many factors that they may consider in that respect inevitably result in some uncertainty about the outcome of the arbitration following a request for multi-party arbitration. Whereas contractual multi-party arbitration solutions ensure greater predictability in the dispute resolution process, the institutional solution results in a lesser degree of parties' control over the way the arbitral proceedings are conducted. Notwithstanding this, the institutional approach has the potential to provide a workable mechanism for resolution of multi-party disputes in cases where the parties have failed to agree on a multi-party arbitration solution in their contracts[172]. On the other hand, if the parties are unwilling to participate in multi-party arbitration, they can always exclude or limit the self-contained institutional mechanism when drafting their arbitration agreements.

---

[172] See also Stavros Brekoulakis (2010) *Third Parties in International Commercial Arbitration*, Oxford University Press, Oxford, p. 135 (§ 3.121–3.123).

Chapter 8
Conclusion

This book has dealt with multi-party construction disputes arising under two or more bilateral contracts binding different parties. In the construction industry, there is often a need for these disputes to be resolved in a single multi-party arbitration. Such a need will ultimately depend on the structure of the contractual relations with regard to the completion of the project, the types of claims and the interests of the different contracting parties. Multi-party arbitration avoids the risk of inconsistent or conflicting arbitral awards stemming from the conduct of separate arbitrations on identical or similar questions of law and / or fact. From an overall perspective, multi-party arbitration also has the potential to reduce the time and costs in the dispute resolution process, thus making the proceedings more efficient.

The author has perused the current legal regulation of multi-party arbitrations, as contained in the parties' arbitration agreements, applicable arbitration rules and arbitration laws, with the purpose of identifying whether this framework provides for workable solutions that can be applied to the type of construction disputes examined in this book. The analysis reveals that the current legal framework has largely failed to provide such solutions for the reasons explained below.

Undoubtedly, the best way to deal with multi-party arbitration is to include appropriate multi-party arbitration clauses in the parties' contracts. Contractual regulation of multi-party arbitration is compliant with the consensual nature of arbitration. It increases the predictability of the dispute resolution process as a whole and eliminates the risk of setting aside, non-recognition and non-enforcement of an arbitral award rendered in a multi-party setting. However, multi-party arbitration agreements in international construction projects remain a rare phenomenon. To this date, the most popular international standard forms have still not provided for standardized multi-party arbitration clauses. Some of the other international standard forms reviewed in this book have addressed multi-party arbitration but not in the form of a self-contained mechanism for resolution of multi-party construction disputes that can be operated solely on the basis of the proposed contractual provisions.

The operation of the multi-party arbitration provisions under the reviewed arbitration rules is in most cases contingent on some form of expression of parties' consent to multi-party arbitration. This consent can be materialized in the form of multi-party arbitration agreements, an umbrella agreement or a submission agreement reached in the course of

Multi-Party and Multi-Contract Arbitration in the Construction Industry, First Edition.
Dimitar Kondev.

the proceedings. However, these expressions of consent will rarely be available when it comes to international construction projects. As mentioned above, most international standard forms do not contain multi-party arbitration agreements. Umbrella agreements are also rarely seen. Furthermore, it is not realistic to expect that contracting parties with divergent interests will agree on multi-party arbitration after the emergence of disputes. Hence, the parties' choice to refer to a certain set of arbitration rules addressing multi-party arbitration will not be sufficient *per se* for the conduct of such arbitration.

Theoretically, it may be argued that workable solutions can be found in arbitration rules that do not explicitly require the parties' consent to multi-party arbitration. However, the flexibility of these rules has divided scholars and practitioners. Whereas some are of the opinion that the provisions in these rules can be operated without parties' consent and that they create a jurisdictional basis for multi-party arbitration, others hold that these provisions only prescribe the procedure that should be followed and that they may not create parties' consent if such consent is not expressed in other ways. This has caused some uncertainty as to how these provisions should be applied. Statistical information reveals that requests for multi-party arbitration based on these flexible clauses are granted sparingly. A notable exception in that regard seems to be the consolidation provision under the HKIAC Rules. It remains to be seen whether the consolidation provision under the new SIAC Rules will follow the same path.

Only a few states have introduced multi-party arbitration provisions in their laws governing international commercial arbitration. When approaching the problem, most states have acknowledged the consensual nature of arbitration and adopted the view that multi-party arbitration may not be imposed in the absence of agreement between the parties. There are some exceptions to this general trend that allow for court-ordered consolidation even in the absence of parties' consent. The Netherlands has introduced an *opt-out* consolidation clause that applies by default, unless the parties exclude its application. Besides the Netherlands, court-ordered consolidation without the parties' consent is also possible in the United States but predominantly in domestic arbitrations.

It will be an illusion to believe that workable solutions to multi-party arbitration can be found in states' arbitration laws. Mandatory provisions dictating multi-party arbitration regardless of parties' agreement are inconsistent with the consensual nature of arbitration. Therefore, their application may result in the setting aside of the award or its non-recognition and non-enforcement. Statutory provisions in the form of 'opt-in' or similar clauses can be reconciled with the consensual premises of arbitration. However, these provisions are of little avail and have only had a marginal impact so far. The main purpose of these provisions is to underline the necessity of parties' agreement on multi-party arbitration. Contracting parties may well reach an agreement on the conduct of such arbitration regardless of a legislation that tells them that they may do so.

Thus, none of the discussed legal sources where regulation of multi-party disputes is to be found provides for workable solutions which contracting parties in the construction industry may readily utilize. The book contained some suggestions as to how this gap can be overcome. These suggestions found expression in two proposed approaches.

The first approach addressed the contractual regulation of multi-party disputes. For that purpose, the author has considered in detail the process of drafting multi-party arbitration clauses. In this way, the book has attempted to bridge the gap between the theoretical proposals regarding multi-party arbitration and their practical application. The author has endeavoured to provide some guidelines on the parties' regulation of multi-party arbitration in their contracts. The guidelines have tried to identify certain good practices that are likely to cause least problems in legal practice. In order to illustrate how a workable multi-party arbitration clause can be created on the basis of the matters discussed in these guidelines, the author has introduced an exemplary multi-party clause, which can be suitable for use with the FIDIC Red book.

The second proposal called for amendments in the regulation of multi-party arbitrations at the level of the arbitration rules. Under this proposal, arbitral institutions should introduce provisions that create an unequivocal jurisdictional basis for the conduct of multi-party arbitrations without necessarily requiring the parties' explicit consent to such type of arbitration. For that purpose, arbitral tribunals and institutions should be granted wider powers to order multi-party arbitration in cases where this may be needed.

Finally, drafters of international standard form agreements are in the best position to propose workable solutions to contracting parties in need of multi-party arbitration. Multi-party arbitration solutions should always be tailored to the specifics of the particular contract in use and the dispute resolution provisions contained therein of which these drafters are undoubtedly cognizant. Therefore, the drafters of standard forms should engage more actively in proposing multi-party arbitration clauses, which the parties using these forms may employ. It is the author's hope that the present book will give an impetus to this process.

Table 1 Summary of Multi-Party Arbitration Provisions under the Reviewed Arbitration Rules

Arbitration rules	**Form of multi-party arbitration**			
	Single request for arbitration against multiple parties	*Joinder*	*Intervention*	*Consolidation*
ICC Rules	*Article 9 subject to Articles 6(3)–6(7)* (requires, among other things, a prima facie arbitration agreement binding all parties and prima facie evidence that all parties may have agreed that the multi-contract claims can be reviewed in a single arbitration)	*Article 7 subject to Articles 6(3)–6(7)* (requires, among other things, a prima facie arbitration agreement binding all parties and prima facie evidence that all parties may have agreed that the multi-contract claims can be reviewed in a single arbitration)	No regulation	*Article 10* (if all parties have agreed or if they are bound by the same arbitration agreement)
UNCITRAL Rules	No regulation	*Article 17(5)* (requires a single arbitration agreement binding all parties)	No regulation	No regulation
CIArb Rules	No regulation	*Article 17(5)* (requires a single arbitration agreement binding all parties)	No regulation	No regulation

	Single request for arbitration against multiple parties	*Joinder*	*Intervention*	*Consolidation*
CEPANI Rules	*Article 10* (if all parties have agreed to have their multi-contract claims reviewed in a single arbitration and if the arbitration agreements are compatible (*see the presumptions in the article*))	*Article 11* (requires an arbitration agreement binding all parties)	*Article 11* (requires an arbitration agreement binding all parties)	*Article 13* (there is no requirement that the arbitrations should be between the same parties)
LCIA Rules	No regulation	*Article 22(1)(viii)* (requires the consent of the party requesting the joinder and the third party)	No regulation.	*Article 22(1)(ix)–(x)* (requires all parties' agreement to consolidation or a single arbitration agreement binding all parties)
Swiss Rules	No regulation	*Article 4(2)* (parties' consent is not explicitly required)	*Article 4(2)* (parties' consent is not explicitly required)	*Article 4(1)* (there is no requirement that the arbitrations should be between the same parties)
CIAR	No regulation	*R-7* (parties' consent is not explicitly required)	No regulation	*R-7* (parties' consent is not explicitly required)

(*Continued*)

Table 1 (*Continued*)

	Single request for arbitration against multiple parties	*Joinder*	*Intervention*	*Consolidation*
ICDR Rules	No regulation	*Article 7* (parties' consent is not explicitly required)	No regulation	*Article 8* (if all parties have agreed or if they are bound by the same arbitration agreement)
Vienna Rules	No regulation	*Article 14* (parties' consent is not explicitly required)	*Article 14* (parties' consent is not explicitly required)	*Article 15* (if all parties agree or if the same arbitrators are appointed in the separate proceedings)
DIS Rules	No regulation	No regulation	No regulation	No regulation
SCC Rules	No regulation	No regulation	No regulation	*Article 11* (only if arbitrations are between the same parties)
DIA Rules	No regulation	*Article 9(3)* (parties' consent is not explicitly required but there should be 'an arbitration agreement covering the third party')	*Article 9(3)* (parties' consent is not explicitly required but there should be 'an arbitration agreement covering the third party')	*Article 9(1)–9(2)* (there is no requirement that the arbitrations should be between the same parties)

	Single request for arbitration against multiple parties	*Joinder*	*Intervention*	*Consolidation*
CIETAC Rules	*Article 14* (if contracts consist of a principal contract and its ancillary contract, disputes arise out of the same series of transactions, and the arbitration agreements are compatible)	*Article 18* (if there is an arbitration agreement binding all parties)	No regulation	*Article 19* (if (a) claims are made under the same arbitration agreement, (b) claims are made under multiple compatible arbitration agreements, and the contracts consist of a principal contract and its ancillary contract, or (c) all parties have agreed to consolidation)
SIAC Rules	*Article 6* If (a) all parties have agreed, (b) claims are made under the same arbitration agreement; or (c) the arbitration agreements are compatible and the disputes arise out of: (i) the same legal relationship, (ii) contracts consisting of its principal contract and its ancillary contract, or (iii) the same transaction or series of transactions.	*Article 7* If (a) the additional party is *prima facie* bound by the arbitration agreement, or (b) if all parties, including the additional party, have consented.	*Article 7* If (a) the additional party is *prima facie* bound by the arbitration agreement, or (b) if all parties, including the additional party, have consented.	*Article 8* If (a) all parties have agreed to consolidation, (b) claims are made under the same arbitration agreement; or (c) the arbitration agreements are compatible and the disputes arise out of: (i) the same legal relationship, (ii) contracts consisting of its principal contract and its ancillary contract, or (iii) the same transaction or series of transactions.

(*Continued*)

Table 1 *(Continued)*

	Single request for arbitration against multiple parties	*Joinder*	*Intervention*	*Consolidation*
HKIAC Rules	*Article 29* (if, among others, all parties are bound by each arbitration agreement giving rise to the arbitration)	*Article 27* (upon the existence of an arbitration agreement binding all parties)	*Article 27* (upon the existence of an arbitration agreement binding all parties)	*Article 28* (if (a) parties agree to consolidate, (b) claims are made under the same arbitration agreement, or (c) claims are made under more than one arbitration agreements, there is a common question of law or fact in the proceedings, the rights to relief claimed arise out of the same transaction, and the arbitration agreements are compatible)
JCAA Rules	*Rule 15* (if all parties have agreed in writing or the claims arise under the same arbitration agreement)	*Rule 52* (if all parties agree in writing or there is a single arbitration agreement binding all parties)	*Rule 52* (if all parties agree in writing or there is a single arbitration agreement binding all parties)	*Rule 53* (if all parties have agreed in writing or the claims arise under the same arbitration agreement)

Notes:

[1] *The present table is drafted for ease of reference only. The table should always be read together with the full content of the specified article and the analysis in Chapter 4.*

[2] *The table reflects only the most up-to-date editions of the reviewed sets of arbitration rules as of 01 November 2016.*

[3] *The table describes the approaches in the reviewed arbitration rules to the type of construction disputes discussed here, i.e. multi-party disputes arising under two or more contracts binding non-identical parties. Approaches that are not relevant to these disputes (e.g. the possibility of consolidation of arbitrations pending between the same parties) are not included in the table because of their irrelevance.*

[4] *Wherever the table refers to 'No regulation' with regard to a specific form of multi-party arbitration, this does not necessarily mean that this form of multi-party arbitration cannot take place under the relevant set of arbitration rules. For example, if a third party's joinder is requested in pending arbitration, such a joinder may be possible if all the parties consent to it regardless of the lack of explicit regulation in the rules.*

Table 2 Summary of Multi-Party Arbitration Provisions under Arbitration Laws

Arbitration law	**Form of multi-party arbitration**			
	Single request for arbitration	*Joinder*	*Intervention*	*Consolidation*
UNCITRAL Model Law	No regulation	No regulation	No regulation	No regulation
English Arbitration Act 1996	No regulation	No regulation	No regulation	*Section 35* (consolidation is only possible if the parties agree to confer such power on the tribunal)
Arbitration (Scotland) Act 2010	No regulation	No regulation	No regulation	*Rule 40 of Schedule 1 (Scottish Arbitration Rules)* (consolidation is only possible if the parties agree to confer such power on the tribunal)
The Netherlands Code of Civil Procedure	No regulation	*Article 1045* (to be ordered by the arbitral tribunal; requires a single arbitration agreement binding all parties)	*Article 1045* (to be ordered by the arbitral tribunal; requires a single arbitration agreement binding all parties)	*Article 1046* (*opt-out* clause; consolidation can be ordered by a third person designated by the parties or by the provisional relief judge of the district court of Amsterdam)
Belgian Judicial Code	No regulation.	*Article 1709* (to be ordered by the arbitral tribunal; requires a single arbitration agreement binding all parties)	*Article 1709* (to be ordered by the arbitral tribunal; requires a single arbitration agreement binding all parties)	No regulation
New Zealand Arbitration Act 1996	No regulation	No regulation	No regulation	*Subsection 2 of Schedule 2* ('*opt-in*' clause; to be ordered by the arbitral tribunal or the High Court)

(*Continued*)

Table 2 (*Continued*)

	Single request for arbitration	*Joinder*	*Intervention*	*Consolidation*
2011 Hong Kong Arbitration Ordinance (Chapter 609)	No regulation	No regulation	No regulation	*Article 2 of Schedule 2* ('*opt-in*' clause when it comes to international arbitrations (applies by default in domestic arbitrations); to be ordered by the court) Does not explicitly require parties' consent
Canada *(no federal regulation)*	No regulation	No regulation	No regulation	*Article 8 of the Alberta International Commercial Arbitration Act, Article 27(2) of the British Columbia International Arbitration Act, Article 8 of the Manitoba International Commercial Arbitration Act, Article 9 of the Newfoundland and Labrador International Commercial Arbitration Act, Article 9 of the New Brunswick International Commercial Arbitration Act, Article 7 of the Ontario International Commercial Arbitration Act, Article 9 of the Nova Scotia International Commercial Arbitration Act, Article 8 of the Prince Edward Island International Commercial Arbitration Act, Article 7 of the Saskatchewan International Commercial Arbitration Act, Article 10 of the International Commercial Arbitration Act (Northwest Territories), Article 10 of the Nunavut International Commercial Arbitration Act, and Article 6 of the Yukon International Commercial Arbitration Act.* (consolidation is possible if all parties consent to it)
Australian International Arbitration Act 1974	No regulation	No regulation	No regulation	*Article 24* (*opt-in* clause; to be ordered by the arbitral tribunal(s))

	Single request for arbitration	*Joinder*	*Intervention*	*Consolidation*
Malaysian Arbitration Act 2005 (Act 646)	No regulation	No regulation	No regulation	*Article 40* (consolidation is only possible if the parties agree to confer such power on the tribunal)
Singapore Arbitration Act (No. 37 of 2001)	No regulation	No regulation	No regulation	*Article 26* (applicable to domestic arbitrations only; consolidation is only possible if the parties agree to confer such power on the tribunal)
Irish Arbitration Act 2010	No regulation	No regulation	No regulation	(consolidation is only possible if the parties agree to confer such power on the tribunal)
Italian Civil Procedure Code	No regulation	Article 816-*quinquies* (to be ordered by the arbitral tribunal; requires all parties' consent)	Article 816-*quinquies* (to be ordered by the arbitral tribunal; requires all parties' consent)	No regulation
US *(no federal regulation)*	*The Federal Arbitration Act is silent on multi-party arbitration. However, it pre-empts any state laws that contradict parties' arbitration agreements*			
California Code of Civil Procedure	No regulation	No regulation	No regulation	*Section 1297.272* (applicable to international arbitrations; to be ordered by the superior court; requires all parties' agreement) (applicable to domestic arbitrations; consolidation is possible even if the arbitration agreements are inconsistent)
Texas Civil Practice and Remedies Code	No regulation	No regulation	No regulation	*Section 172.173* (to be ordered by the district court; requires all parties' consent)

(*Continued*)

Table 2 *(Continued)*

	Single request for arbitration	*Joinder*	*Intervention*	*Consolidation*
Ohio Revised Code				*Section 2712.52* (to be ordered by the court of common pleas; requires all parties' consent)
Georgia International Commercial Arbitration Code (Senate Bill 383)	No regulation	No regulation	No regulation	*Section 9-9-46(d)* (consolidation is only possible if the parties agree to confer such power on the tribunal)
General Laws of Massachusetts	No regulation	No regulation	No regulation	*Chapter 251, Section 2A* (mandatory consolidation provision, which can prevail over any parties' agreement; to be ordered by the superior court)
New Jersey Alternative Procedure for Dispute Resolution Act	No regulation	No regulation	No regulation	*Section 2A: 23A-3* (does not require parties' consent)
Revised Uniform Arbitration Act (RUAA)	No regulation	No regulation	No regulation	*Section 10* (does not require parties' consent)

Notes:

[1] *This table is drafted for ease of reference only. The table should always be read together with the full content of the specified article and the analysis presented in Chapter 5.*

[2] *The table reflects the position in the reviewed arbitration laws as of 01 November 2016.*

[3] *The section concerning the United States should always be read in conjunction with the case law discussed in Section 5.10.2.*

Appendix 1

Second Alternative Clause of Clause 20 of the FIDIC Subcontract[1]

EXAMPLE PROVISIONS WHERE A DECISION AND/OR ARBITRAL AWARD UNDER THE MAIN CONTRACT CONCERNING A SUBCONTRACTOR'S CLAIM OR AN EMPLOYER'S CLAIM SHALL BE BINDING UNDER THE SUBCONTRACT: Delete Clause 20 [*Notices, Subcontractor's Claims and Disputes*] of the General Conditions of Subcontract and substitute:

20 Notices, Claims and Disputes

20.1 Notices

Without prejudice to the generality of Clause 4 [*The Subcontractor*], whenever the Contractor is required by the Main Contract to give any notice or other information to the Engineer or to the Employer, or to keep contemporary records (whether in relation to a claim or otherwise), to the extent that these terms apply to the Subcontract Works, the Subcontractor shall give a similar notice or other information in writing to the Contractor and keep contemporary records that will enable the Contractor to comply with these terms of the Main Contract. The Subcontractor shall do so in good time to enable the Contractor to comply with these terms. Provided always that the Subcontractor shall be excused from any non-compliance with this requirement for so long as he could not have reasonably known of the Contractor's need of the notice or information from him or the contemporary records.

Notwithstanding this Sub-Clause and Sub-Clause 3.3 [*Contractor's Claims in connection with the Subcontract*], each Party shall immediately give notice to the other Party of any delay event which has occurred, or specific probable future events or circumstances, which may adversely affect the other Party's activities or delay the execution of the Subcontract Works and/or the Main Works. The Subcontractor shall immediately give notice to the Contractor of any event which has occurred, or specific probable future events or circumstances, which may increase the Subcontract Price and/or the Contract Price.

[1] The clause has been reproduced with permission of FIDIC. It is contained in the Guidance for the Preparation of Particular Conditions of Subcontract to the FIDIC Subcontract, pp. 23–35.

Multi-Party and Multi-Contract Arbitration in the Construction Industry, First Edition.
Dimitar Kondev.

If the Subcontractor considers himself to be entitled to any extension of the Subcontract Time for Completion and/or any additional payment, under or in connection with the Subcontract, the Subcontractor shall give notice to the Contractor describing the event or circumstance giving rise to the claim, and setting out the contractual basis for the claim. Notice shall be given as soon as practicable but in any case not later than 21 days after the Subcontractor became aware (or should have become aware) of the event or circumstance. If the Subcontractor fails to give notice of a claim within the period of 21 days referred to above, the Subcontract Time for Completion shall not be extended, the Subcontractor shall not be entitled to additional payment, and the Contractor shall be discharged from all liability in connection with the claim.

20.2 Subcontractor's Claims

Within 7 days of receipt of the Subcontractor's notice of claim in accordance with Sub-Clause 20.1 [*Notices*], the Contractor may notify the Subcontractor, with reasons, that the Subcontractor's claim:

(a) arises from an event or events that may also give rise to additional payment and/or an extension of time as may be claimable in accordance with the Main Contract;
(b) concerns issue(s) which is/are the subject of a Contractor's claim in accordance with Main Contract Clause 20.1 [*Contractor's Claims*]; or
(c) involves issue(s) which is/are also involved in a dispute between the Contractor and the Employer under the Main Contract;

(a 'Related Claim').
Unless the Contractor so notifies the Subcontractor, the claim shall thereafter be considered an Unrelated Claim for the purposes of Sub-Clause 20.3 [*Unrelated Claims*]. If the Contractor does so notify the Subcontractor the claim shall thereafter be considered a Related Claim for the purposes of Sub-Clause 20.4 [*Related Claims*] and the Subcontractor shall have no right to pursue this claim under Sub-Clause 20.3 [*Unrelated Claims*] save:

(a) where it is decided by the pre-Arbitral Referee in accordance with this Sub-Clause that this claim is an Unrelated Claim, or
(b) to the extent expressly provided for under Sub-Clause 20.4 [*Related Claims*].

Upon receipt of the Contractor's notice, unless the Subcontractor raises a written objection to the Contractor's opinion that the claim is a Related Claim within 7 days, this opinion shall be deemed to be accepted by the Subcontractor. If the Subcontractor raises an objection the Contractor shall give all due consideration to this objection and shall give his written response, with reasons, within 7 days of its receipt.
If the Subcontractor is dissatisfied with this response then, by notice in writing, he may refer the question of whether the Subcontractor's claim is a Related Claim or an Unrelated Claim to a pre-arbitral referee for an order. Save where the provisions of this Sub-Clause require, the ICC Rules for a Pre-Arbitral Referee Procedure shall apply.

With reference to Article 2.1.1 of the ICC Rules for a Pre-Arbitral Referee Procedure, the Referee's sole power shall be to decide the question of whether the Subcontractor's claim is a Related Claim or an Unrelated Claim. The Referee shall issue his Order within 21 days from the date on which he receives the file from the Secretariat (as defined in the ICC Rules for a Pre-Arbitral Referee Procedure) and

(i) the costs arising out of the Pre-Arbitral Referee Procedure shall be borne in equal shares by the Parties;
(ii) the Order of the Referee (who shall not be considered to be an arbitrator and whose decision shall not be considered as an arbitral award) shall be binding on both Parties, and Articles 6.3 and 6.4 of the ICC Rules for a Pre-Arbitral Referee Procedure shall not apply.

Whether the Subcontractor's claim is a Related Claim or an Unrelated Claim, the Subcontractor shall keep contemporary records that may be necessary to substantiate the claim, shall comply with any Contractor's Instruction to keep further contemporary records, shall permit the Contractor to inspect all these records, and shall (if instructed) submit copies to the Contractor. Unless the Subcontract has already been abandoned, repudiated or terminated, the Subcontractor shall continue to proceed with the Subcontract Works in accordance with the Subcontract.

20.3 Unrelated Claims

If a Subcontractor's claim is an Unrelated Claim in accordance with Sub-Clause 20.2 [*Subcontractor's Claims*]:

1. Within 42 days after the Subcontractor became aware (or should have become aware) of the event or circumstance giving rise to the Unrelated Claim, or within such other period as may be proposed by the Subcontractor or and approved by the Contractor, the Subcontractor shall send to the Contractor a fully detailed claim which includes full supporting particulars of the basis of the claim and of the additional payment and/or extension of time claimed;
2. If the event or circumstance giving rise to the Unrelated Claim has a continuing effect:
   (a) this fully detailed claim shall be considered as interim;
   (b) the Subcontractor shall send further interim claims at monthly intervals, giving the accumulated delay and/or amount claimed, and the further particulars that the Contractor may reasonably require, and
   (c) the Subcontractor shall send a final claim within 28 days after the end of the effects resulting from the event or circumstance, or within the other period that may be proposed by the Subcontractor and approved by the Contractor;
3. Within 42 days after receiving a claim or any further particulars supporting a previous claim, or within the other period that may be proposed by the Contractor and approved by the Subcontractor, the Contractor shall respond with approval or disapproval and

detailed comments. He may also request any necessary further particulars, but shall nevertheless give his response on the issue of the Subcontractor's entitlement to the Unrelated Claim within this time;

4. The Contractor shall consult with the Subcontractor in an endeavour to reach agreement on the additional payment and/or extension of the Subcontract Time for Completion to which the Subcontractor may be entitled for this Unrelated Claim. If agreement is not reached, the Contractor shall make a fair decision as to the appropriate and applicable additional payment (if any) and/or extension of the Subcontract Time for Completion (if any), taking due account of the Subcontractor's submissions, the extent to which his claim for additional payment and/or extension of time has been substantiated, and all other relevant circumstances; and
5. The Contractor shall make the additional payment (if any) and/or grant the extension of the Subcontract Time for Completion (if any) to the Subcontractor that he has decided is appropriate and practicable. Unless and until the particulars supplied for the Unrelated Claim are sufficient to substantiate the whole of this claim, the Subcontractor shall be entitled to additional payment and/or extension of time only for the part that has been substantiated.

20.4 Related Claims

If a Subcontractor's claim is a Related Claim in accordance with Sub-Clause 20.2 [*Subcontractor's Claims*]:

1. The Contractor shall submit a notice of claim, including the subject of the claim which the Contractor considers to be a Related Claim, to the Engineer in accordance with Main Contract Clause 20.1 [*Contractor's Claims*] and in good time to ensure compliance with such provision, regardless of any objection or referral by the Subcontractor under Sub-Clause 20.2 [*Subcontractor's Claims*];
2. The Contractor shall use all reasonable endeavours to secure from the Employer and the Engineer, for both the Contractor's and the Subcontractor's benefit, any additional payment and/or extension of time as may be claimable in accordance with the Main Contract in respect of the Subcontract Works and shall regularly keep the Subcontractor informed of the progress of these endeavours;
3. The Subcontractor shall have no right to pursue this claim under Sub-Clause 20.3 [*Unrelated Claims*] save as expressly provided under this Sub-Clause 20.4. The Subcontractor shall comply with any Contractor's instruction regarding the keeping of contemporary records relevant to the event or circumstance giving rise to the Related Claim. The Subcontractor shall permit the Contractor and the Engineer to inspect all these records;
4. The Subcontractor shall submit the Related Claim to the Contractor, which shall include full supporting particulars of:
   (a) the contractual or other basis of claim; and
   (b) additional payment claimed, and/or
   (c) the extension of time

and any interim claims in accordance with Main Contract Clause 20.1 [*Contractor's Claims*] and in good time to enable the Contractor to comply with such provision;

5. The Contractor shall submit a claim to the Engineer, which includes the supporting particulars and any interim claims of the Related Claim provided by the Subcontractor, in accordance with Main Contract Clause 20.1 [*Contractor's Claims*] and in good time to ensure compliance with such provision, regardless of any objection or referral by the Subcontractor under Sub-Clause 20.2 [*Subcontractor's Claims*];
6. The Contractor shall give the Subcontractor all reasonable opportunity to be involved in any consultation with, and to attend any meeting convened by, the Engineer which concerns the Related Claim. Unless the Subcontractor is permitted by the Engineer to be involved in consultation and/or to attend a meeting but the Subcontractor refuses or fails to do so, the Contractor shall not reach any agreement with the Engineer concerning the Related Claim without prior consultation with the Subcontractor. Where an agreement is reached under the Main Contract or the Engineer makes a determination concerning the Related Claim, the Contractor shall as soon as practicable but not later than 7 days of its receipt, notify the Subcontractor of this agreement or determination. If the agreement or determination insofar as it concerns the Related Claim is such that the Contractor has no entitlement to additional payment and/or extension of time, unless the Subcontractor notifies the Contractor of dissatisfaction with the agreement or determination within 7 days of his receipt of the Contractor's notice, this agreement or determination shall be deemed to be accepted by the Subcontractor and, as between them, shall be binding on the Parties. If the Subcontractor notifies his dissatisfaction with the agreement or determination within 7 days of receipt of Contractor's notice, the Subcontractor's notice shall be deemed to be a Notice of Dispute and Sub-Clause 20.6 [*Subcontract Disputes*] shall apply.
7. If it is agreed under the Main Contract or the Engineer determines under the Main Contract that the Contractor is entitled to additional payment and/or extension of time, within 28 days of receiving this contractual benefit from the Employer, the Contractor shall pass on to the Subcontractor a share of the benefit as may be appropriate and applicable to the Related Claim. In the case of a Related Claim concerning additional payment, the receipt of payment by the Contractor from the Employer that includes a sum in respect of the claimed amount shall be a condition precedent to the Contractor's liability to the Subcontractor in respect of this share. The Contractor shall consult with the Subcontractor in an endeavour to reach agreement as to this share. If agreement is not reached, the Contractor shall promptly and with due diligence make a fair decision as to the appropriate and applicable share, taking due account of the Subcontractor's views and all other relevant circumstances. The Contractor shall, making reference to this sub-paragraph, give notice to the Subcontractor of his decision with reasons and supporting particulars. Unless the Subcontractor notifies the Contractor of his dissatisfaction with this decision within 28 days of receipt of the Contractor's notice, the share decided by the Contractor shall be taken as accepted by the Subcontractor in full and final settlement of the Related Claim; and
8. If the Subcontractor notifies the Contractor of his dissatisfaction with this decided share within 28 days of receipt of the Contractor's notice, the Contractor shall give all

due consideration to this dissatisfaction and shall give his written response within 7 days of its receipt. If the Contractor fails to so respond to the Subcontractor's notice of dissatisfaction, the Subcontractor shall be entitled to treat this non-response as if the Contractor maintains that the decided share is appropriate and applicable. Any dispute concerning this share shall thereafter be considered an Unrelated Dispute which shall be finally settled as between the Parties under the Rules of Arbitration of the International Chamber of Commerce, and Main Contract Clause 20.6 [*Arbitration*] shall apply to the Unrelated Dispute except that the dispute may be settled by one arbitrator appointed in accordance with the Rules.

20.5 Failure to Comply

If, by reason of any failure by the Subcontractor to comply with the first and the third paragraphs of Sub-Clause 20.1 [*Notices*] and/or the provisions of Sub-Clause 20.2 [*Subcontractor's Claims*], the Contractor is prevented from recovering any sum other than in respect of Subcontractor's claims from the Employer under the Main Contract in respect of the Subcontract Works, then without prejudice to any other remedy of the Contractor for this failure the Contractor shall, subject to Sub-Clause 3.3 [*Contractor's Claims in connection with the Subcontract*], be entitled to deduct this sum from the Subcontract Price.

20.6 Subcontract Disputes

If a dispute (of any kind whatsoever) arises between the Parties in connection with, or arising out of, the Subcontract or the execution of the Subcontract Works, then either Party may give a notice of the dispute to the other Party (the 'Notice of Dispute').

If the Subcontract dispute arises from an Unrelated Claim (as referred to in Sub-Clause 20.2 [*Subcontractor's Claims*]), then it shall be considered to be an 'Unrelated Dispute' and Sub-Clause 20.7 [*Unrelated Disputes*] shall apply.

If the Subcontract Dispute arises from a Related Claim (as referred to in Sub-Clause 20.2 [*Subcontractor's Claims*]), then it shall be considered to be a 'Related Dispute' and Sub-Clause 20.8 [*Related Disputes*] shall apply.

If the Subcontract dispute does not arise out of an Unrelated Claim or a Related Claim:

(a) within 14 days of receiving or giving a Notice of Dispute, the Contractor may notify the Subcontractor, with reasons, of his opinion that the Subcontract dispute involves issue(s) which are also involved in a dispute between the Contractor and the Employer under the Main Contract. If the Contractor so notifies the Subcontractor within such period of 14 days then, subject to sub-paragraphs (b) and (c) of this Sub-Clause, the Subcontract dispute shall be considered to be a 'Related Dispute' and Sub-Clause 20.8 [*Related Disputes*] shall apply. If the Contractor does not so notify the Subcontractor within such period of 14 days, then the Subcontract dispute shall be considered to be an 'Unrelated Dispute' and Sub-Clause 20.7 [*Unrelated Disputes*] shall apply;

(b) upon receipt of the Contractor's notice, unless the Subcontractor raises a written objection, to the Contractor's opinion that the Subcontract dispute is a Related Dispute within 7 days, this opinion shall be deemed to be accepted by the Subcontractor. If the Subcontractor raises an objection the Contractor shall give all due consideration to this objection and shall give his written response, with reasons, within 7 days of its receipt; and

(c) If the Subcontractor is dissatisfied with this response then, by notice in writing, he may refer the question of whether the Subcontract dispute is a Related Dispute or an Unrelated Dispute to a pre-arbitral referee for an order. Save where the provisions of this sub-paragraph require, the ICC Rules for a Pre-Arbitral Referee Procedure shall apply. With reference to Article 2.1.1 of the ICC Rules for a Pre-Arbitral Referee Procedure, the Referee's sole power shall be to decide the question of whether the Subcontract dispute is a Related Dispute or an Unrelated Dispute. The Referee shall issue his Order within 21 days from the date on which he receives the file from the Secretariat (as defined in the ICC Rules for a Pre-Arbitral Referee Procedure) and:

    (i) the costs arising out of the Pre-Arbitral Referee Procedure shall be borne in equal shares by the Parties; and

    (ii) the Order of the Referee (who shall not be considered to be an arbitrator and whose decision shall not be considered as an arbitral award) shall be final and binding on both Parties, and Articles 6.3 and 6.4 of the ICC Rules for a Pre-Arbitral Referee Procedure shall not apply.

Whether the Subcontract dispute is an Unrelated Dispute or a Related Dispute, unless the Subcontract has already been abandoned, repudiated or terminated, the Subcontractor shall continue to proceed with the Subcontract Works in accordance with the Subcontract.

20.7 Unrelated Disputes

If a Subcontract dispute is an Unrelated Dispute:

1. It shall be decided by a Subcontract DAB, which shall be jointly appointed by the Parties within 42 days after the date of the Notice of Dispute or any other time as may be agreed in writing. Unless it is stated in the Appendix to the Subcontractor's Offer that it shall comprise three members, the Subcontract DAB shall comprise one suitably qualified person. In all respects other than as stated in this Sub-Clause, Main Contract Clause 20.2 [*Appointment of the Dispute Adjudication Board*] shall apply to the appointment of the Subcontract DAB, save that Rule 1 to 4 of the Procedural Rules annexed to the General Conditions of Dispute Adjudication Agreement shall not apply;
2. If the Parties fail to agree upon the appointment of the Subcontract DAB within 42 days after the date of the Notice of Dispute, or upon the appointment of a

replacement person within 42 days after the appointed person declines or is unable to act, then the President of FIDIC or a person appointed by the President shall, upon the request of either or both Parties and after due consultation with both Parties, appoint the Subcontract DAB. This appointment shall be final and conclusive. Each Party shall be responsible for paying one-half of the remuneration of the appointing official;

3. Either Party may refer the Unrelated Dispute in writing to the Subcontract DAB for its decision, with a copy to the other Party. The referral shall state that it is given under this Sub-Clause. In all respects other than as stated in this Sub-Clause, Main Contract Clause 20.4 [*Obtaining Dispute Adjudication Board's Decision*] shall apply to the resolution of the Unrelated Dispute, save that Main Contract Clause 20.8 [*Expiry of Dispute Adjudication Board's Appointment*] shall not apply;
4. The Subcontract DAB's decision shall be binding on both Parties unless and until it shall be revised in an amicable settlement or an arbitral award, as described in this Sub-Clause below;
5. If either Party serves a notice of dissatisfaction with the Subcontract DAB's decision within 28 days after receiving the Subcontract DAB's decision, both Parties shall attempt to settle the Unrelated Disputes amicably before the commencement of arbitration. However, unless both Parties agree otherwise, arbitration may be commenced on the twenty-eighth day after notice of dissatisfaction was given, even if no attempt at amicable settlement has been made;
6. Unless settled amicably, any Unrelated Dispute in respect of which the Subcontract DAB's decision has not become final and binding in accordance with Main Contract Clause 20.4 [*Obtaining Dispute Adjudication Board's Decision*] shall be finally settled under the Rules of Arbitration of the International Chamber of Commerce and Main Contract Clause 20.6 [*Arbitration*] shall apply to the Unrelated Dispute except that the dispute may be settled by one arbitrator appointed in accordance with the Rules;
7. In the event that a Party fails to comply with any decision of the Subcontract DAB whether binding, or final and binding in accordance with Main Contract Clause 20.4 [*Obtaining Dispute Adjudication Board's Decision*], then the other Party may, without prejudice to any other rights it may have, refer the failure itself to arbitration under the Rules of Arbitration of the International Chamber of Commerce for the purpose of obtaining an award (whether interim or other) to enforce that Decision, and in all other respects Main Contract Clause 20.6 [Arbitration] shall apply to the obtaining of such an award except that the award may be rendered by one arbitrator appointed in accordance with the Rules. There shall be no requirement to obtain a Subcontract DAB's decision or to attempt to reach amicable settlement in respect of this reference.

20.8 Related Disputes

If a Subcontract dispute is a Related Dispute:

1. The subject of the Related Dispute shall be referred by the Contractor to the Main Contract DAB in accordance with Main Contract Clause 20.4 [*Obtaining Dispute*

Adjudication Board's Decision], with a copy to the Subcontractor, within 28 days of the Notice of Dispute. If, on the date of the Notice of Dispute, there is no Main Contract DAB in place, the Contractor shall refer the subject of the Related Dispute to the Main Contract DAB in accordance with Main Contract Clause 20.4 [*Obtaining Dispute Adjudication Board's Decision*], with a copy to the Subcontractor, within 56 days of the Notice of Dispute. If the Contractor fails to refer the subject of the Related Dispute to the Main Contract DAB within the period of 28 days or 56 days, whichever is applicable, the Subcontract dispute shall thereafter be considered an Unrelated Dispute and Sub-Clause 20.7 [*Unrelated Disputes*] shall apply;

2. Where the subject of the Related Dispute is referred to the Main Contract DAB, the Contractor shall use all reasonable endeavours to pursue the dispute on the Contractor's and the Subcontractor's behalf and for both the Contractor's and the Subcontractor's benefit, and shall regularly keep the Subcontractor informed of the progress of these endeavours;
3. The Subcontractor shall, in good time, afford the Contractor all information and assistance that may be required to enable the Contractor to diligently pursue his dispute which includes the subject of the Related Dispute on the Contractor's and the Subcontractor's behalf;
4. If the Main Contract DAB proposes a period other than 84 days for giving its decision in respect of the subject of the Related Dispute, in accordance with Main Contract Clause 20.4 [*Obtaining Dispute Adjudication Board's Decision*], then the Contractor shall not give its approval to another period without prior consultation with the Subcontractor;
5. In any adjudication under the Main Contract which concerns the subject of the Related Dispute, unless the Employer or the Main Contract DAB objects, the Contractor shall give the Subcontractor all reasonable opportunity to:
   (a) be involved in the preparation of any written submission to the Main Contract DAB,
   (b) attend any site visit or hearing convened by the Main Contract DAB,
   (c) make any oral submission to the Main Contract DAB,
   (d) receive copies of all submissions and other documents submitted in the adjudication which concern or relate to the Related Dispute, and
   (e) be involved in any discussions about the general strategy to be adopted in the adjudication which concern or relate to the Related Dispute including, but not limited to, choice of legal representation (if any), experts (if any) and witnesses.

   If the Subcontractor is given such opportunity by the Employer or the Main Contract DAB, the Contractor shall not reach any settlement with the Employer concerning the Related Dispute without prior consultation with the Subcontractor[2];
6. Where the Main Contract DAB gives a decision which concerns the Related Dispute, the Contractor shall as soon as practicable but not later than 7 days of its receipt from the Main Contract DAB, notify the Subcontractor of this decision;

[2] In the author's opinion, there is a mistake in this paragraph. The latter should start with 'If the Subcontractor is **not** given such opportunity' instead of 'If the Subcontractor is given such opportunity'.

7. Unless the Subcontractor notifies the Contractor of his dissatisfaction with the Main Contract DAB's decision within 7 days of his receipt of the Contractor's notice, this decision shall be deemed to be accepted by the Subcontractor insofar as it concerns the Related Dispute. Whether or not a notice of dissatisfaction has been given, this decision shall be binding on both Parties unless and until it shall be revised in an amicable settlement or an arbitral award as described below;
8. If the Subcontractor so notifies the Contractor of his dissatisfaction and the Contractor responds by concurring with this dissatisfaction, the Contractor shall serve a notice of dissatisfaction with the Main Contract DAB's decision to the Employer in good time to prevent the Main Contract DAB's decision from becoming final and binding under the Main Contract Clause 20.4 [*Obtaining Dispute Adjudication Board's Decision*];
9. If the Subcontractor so notifies the Contractor of his dissatisfaction but the Contractor responds by not concurring with this dissatisfaction, or fails to respond to this notice of dissatisfaction within 7 days of its receipt or fails to serve a notice of dissatisfaction with the Main Contract DAB's decision to the Employer in good time to prevent the Main Contract DAB's decision from becoming final and binding under the Main Contract Clause 20.4 [*Obtaining Dispute Adjudication Board's Decision*], the Subcontract dispute shall thereafter be considered an Unrelated Dispute and Sub-Clause 20.7 [*Unrelated Disputes*] shall apply;
10. If the Main Contract DAB's decision entitles the Contractor to any contractual benefit, the Contractor shall use all reasonable endeavours on the Contractor's and the Subcontractor's behalf to obtain this contractual benefit, and shall regularly keep the Subcontractor informed of the progress of these endeavours. Within 14 days of receiving this contractual benefit from the Employer the Contractor shall pass on to the Subcontractor a share of the benefit as may be appropriate and applicable to the Related Dispute. In the case of a Related Dispute concerning additional payment, the Contractor's receipt of payment from the Employer which includes a sum in respect of the disputed amount shall be a condition precedent to the Contractor's liability to the Subcontractor in respect of this share. The Contractor shall consult with the Subcontractor in an endeavour to reach agreement as to this share. If agreement is not reached, the Contractor shall promptly and with due diligence make a fair decision as to the appropriate and applicable share, taking due account of the Subcontractor's submissions concerning the Related Dispute and all other relevant circumstances. The Contractor shall, making reference to this sub-paragraph, give notice to the Subcontractor of his decision with reasons and supporting particulars. Unless the Subcontractor notifies the Contractor of his dissatisfaction with this decision within 28 days of receipt of the Contractor's notice, the share decided by the Contractor shall be taken as accepted by the Subcontractor in full and final settlement of the Related Dispute;
11. If the Subcontractor notifies the Contractor of his dissatisfaction with this decided share within 28 days of receipt of the Contractor's notice, the Contractor shall give all due consideration to this dissatisfaction and shall give his written response within 7 days of its receipt. If the Contractor fails to so respond to the Subcontractor's notice of dissatisfaction within 7 days of its receipt, the Subcontractor shall be entitled to treat this non-response as if the Contractor maintains that the decided share

is appropriate and applicable. Any dispute concerning this share shall thereafter be considered an Unrelated Dispute which shall be finally settled as between the Contractor and the Subcontractor under the Rules of Arbitration of the International Chamber of Commerce, and Main Contract Clause 20.6 [*Arbitration*] shall apply to the Unrelated Dispute except that the dispute may be settled by one arbitrator appointed in accordance with the Rules;

12. If the Main Contract DAB's decision has not become final and binding under the Main Contract, unless the Employer objects, the Contractor shall give the Subcontractor all reasonable opportunity to be involved in the attempts, if any, to settle the Related Dispute amicably under the Main Contract before the commencement of arbitration. If the Contractor is not given such opportunity by the Employer, the Contractor shall not reach any amicable settlement with the Employer concerning the Related Dispute without prior consultation with the Subcontractor;
13. If the Contractor shall reach such an amicable settlement with the Employer, he shall immediately notify the Subcontractor. Within 28 days of the day of this settlement, the Contractor shall consult with the Subcontractor in an endeavour to reach agreement as to the Subcontractor's entitlement to contractual benefit in connection with the Related Dispute. If no agreement is reached within 56 days of the date of the settlement, the Parties' disagreement shall thereafter be considered an Unrelated Dispute which shall be finally settled as between the Contractor and the Subcontractor under the Rules of Arbitration of the International Chamber of Commerce, and Main Contract Clause 20.6 [*Arbitration*] shall apply to the Unrelated Dispute except that the dispute may be settled by one arbitrator appointed in accordance with the Rules;
14. If no amicable settlement is reached between the Contractor and the Employer under the Main Contract concerning the subject of the Related Dispute, the Contractor shall refer the Related Dispute to arbitration under Main Contract Clause 20.6 [*Arbitration*]. If the Contractor or the Employer does not refer the subject of the Related Dispute to arbitration within 63 days, or any other time as may be agreed, after the day on which either the Contractor or the Employer has served a notice of dissatisfaction with the Main Contract DAB's decision, the dispute shall thereafter be considered an Unrelated Dispute which shall be finally settled as between the Contractor and the Subcontractor under the Rules of Arbitration of the International Chamber of Commerce, and Main Contract Clause 20.6 [*Arbitration*] shall apply to this dispute except that the dispute may be settled by one arbitrator appointed in accordance with the Rules;
15. In any arbitration under the Main Contract which concerns the Related Dispute, the Contractor shall use all reasonable endeavours to pursue his dispute which includes the subject of the Related Dispute on the Contractor's and the Subcontractor's behalf and for both the Contractor's and the Subcontractor's benefit, and shall regularly keep the Subcontractor informed of the progress of these endeavours. Unless the Employer or the Arbitral Tribunal objects, the Contractor shall give the Subcontractor all reasonable opportunity to:
    (a) be involved in the preparation of any written submission to the Arbitral Tribunal,
    (b) attend any site visit or hearing convened by the Arbitral Tribunal,

(c) make any oral submission to the Arbitral Tribunal,
(d) receive copies of all submissions and other documents submitted in the arbitration which concern or relate to the Related Dispute, and
(e) be involved in any discussions about the general strategy to be adopted in the arbitration which concern or relate to the Related Dispute including, but not limited to, choice of legal representation, experts and witnesses.

If the Subcontractor is not given such opportunity by the Employer or the Arbitral Tribunal, the Contractor shall not reach any settlement with the Employer concerning the Related Dispute without prior consultation with the Subcontractor;

16. Where the Arbitral Tribunal makes an award which concerns the Related Dispute, the Contractor shall as soon as practicable but not later than 7 days of its receipt, notify the Subcontractor of this award. Insofar as it concerns the Related Dispute, this award shall be deemed to be binding on the Subcontractor to the same extent as it is binding on the Contractor;
17. If the Arbitral Tribunal's award entitles the Contractor to any contractual benefit, the Contractor shall use all reasonable endeavours on the Contractor's and the Subcontractor's behalf to obtain this contractual benefit, and shall regularly keep the Subcontractor informed of the progress of these endeavours. Within 14 days of receiving this contractual benefit from the Employer the Contractor shall pass on to the Subcontractor a share of the benefit as may be appropriate and applicable to the Related Dispute. In the case of a Related Dispute concerning additional payment, the Contractor's receipt of payment from the Employer which includes a sum in respect of the disputed amount shall be a condition precedent to the Contractor's liability to the Subcontractor in respect of this share. The Contractor shall consult with the Subcontractor in an endeavour to reach agreement as to this share. If agreement is not reached, the Contractor shall promptly and with due diligence make a fair decision as to the appropriate and applicable share, taking due account of the Subcontractor's submissions concerning the Related Dispute and all other relevant circumstances. The Contractor shall give notice to the Subcontractor of his decision with reasons and supporting particulars. Unless the Subcontractor notifies the Contractor of his dissatisfaction with this decision within 28 days of receipt of the Contractor's notice, the share decided by the Contractor shall be taken as accepted by the Subcontractor in full and final settlement of the Related Dispute;
18. If the Subcontractor notifies the Contractor of his dissatisfaction with this decided share within 28 days of receipt of the Contractor's notice, the Contractor shall give all due consideration to this dissatisfaction and shall give his written response within 7 days of its receipt. If the Contractor fails to so respond to the Subcontractor's notice of dissatisfaction within 7 days of its receipt, the Subcontractor shall be entitled to treat this non-response as if the Contractor maintains that the decided share is appropriate and applicable. The dispute concerning this share shall thereafter be considered an Unrelated Dispute which shall be finally settled as between the Contractor and the Subcontractor under the Rules of Arbitration of the International Chamber of Commerce, and Main Contract Clause 20.6 [*Arbitration*] shall apply to this dispute except that the dispute may be settled by one arbitrator appointed in accordance with the Rules;

20.9 Employer's Claims under the Subcontract

If the Contractor notifies the Subcontractor that the Employer or the Engineer has given notice of claim under Main Contract Clause 2.5 [*Employer's Claims*] and that the subject of such a claim concerns the Subcontractor's performance of the Subcontract:

1. The Contractor shall provide a copy of this notice, and of all particulars given by the Employer or the Engineer in connection with the Employer's claim, to the Subcontractor;
2. The Subcontractor shall comply with any Contractor's Instruction regarding the keeping of contemporary records relevant to the event or circumstance giving rise to the Employer's claim. The Subcontractor shall permit the Contractor and the Engineer to inspect these records;
3. The Contractor shall use all reasonable endeavours to defend against the Employer's claim on the Contractor's and the Subcontractor's behalf, and shall regularly keep the Subcontractor informed of the progress of these endeavours;
4. The Subcontractor shall, in good time, afford the Contractor all information and assistance that may be required to enable the Contractor to diligently defend the Employer's claim on the Contractor's and the Subcontractor's behalf;
5. The Contractor shall give the Subcontractor all reasonable opportunity to be involved in any consultation with, and to attend any meeting convened by, the Engineer which concerns the Employer's claim. Unless the Subcontractor is permitted by the Engineer to be involved in consultation and/or to attend a meeting but the Subcontractor refuses or fails to do so, the Contractor shall not reach any agreement with the Engineer and/or the Employer concerning the Employer's claim without prior consultation with the Subcontractor;
6. If it is agreed under the Main Contract, or the Engineer determines under the Main Contract, that the Employer is entitled to be paid an amount by the Contractor, the Contractor shall consult with the Subcontractor in an endeavour to reach agreement as to the share of such amount that shall be paid by the Subcontractor to the Contractor. Receipt by the Subcontractor of evidence of the amount paid by the Contractor to the Employer in respect of the Employer's claim shall be a condition precedent to the Subcontractor's liability to the Contractor in respect of this share;
7. If agreement is not reached as to the share referred to in sub-paragraph (6) above, the Contractor shall promptly and with due diligence make a fair decision as to the appropriate and applicable share, taking due account of the Subcontractor's views and all relevant circumstances. The Contractor shall, making reference to this sub-paragraph, give notice to the Subcontractor of his decision with reasons and supporting particulars. Unless the Subcontractor notifies the Contractor of his dissatisfaction with the decision within 28 days of receipt of the Contractor's notice, the share decided by the Contractor shall be taken as accepted by the Subcontractor;
8. If the Subcontractor notifies the Contractor of his dissatisfaction with this decided share within 28 days of the Contractor's notice, the Contractor shall give all due consideration to this dissatisfaction and shall give his written response within 7 days of its receipt. If the Contractor fails to so respond to the Subcontractor's notice of dissatisfaction, the Subcontractor shall be entitled to treat this non-response as if the Contractor maintains that the decided share is appropriate and applicable;

9. If a dispute between the Employer and the Contractor arises from the Employer's claim and is referred to the Main Contract DAB under Main Contract Clause 20.4 [*Obtaining Dispute Adjudication Board's Decision*], the Contractor shall provide to the Subcontractor a copy of the reference to the Main Contract DAB, and of all additional information provided to the Main Contract DAB;
10. Sub-paragraphs (2) to (17) of Sub-Clause 20.8 [*Related Disputes*] shall apply to the dispute and:
    (i) any reference to "the Related Dispute" shall be read as a reference to this dispute;
    (ii) sub-paragraph (10) of Sub-Clause 20.8 [*Related Disputes*] shall be amended to read: "If the Main Contract DAB's decision required the Contractor to make payment to the Employer, and the Contractor makes such payment, the Contractor shall consult with the Subcontractor in an endeavour to reach agreement as to the share of such payment to be paid by the Subcontractor to the Contractor. Receipt by the Subcontractor of evidence of such payment by the Contractor to the Employer shall be a condition precedent to the Subcontractor's liability to the Contractor in respect of this share. If agreement is not reached, the Contractor shall promptly and with due diligence make a fair decision as to the appropriate and applicable share, taking due account of the Subcontractor's submissions concerning this dispute and all relevant circumstances. The Contractor shall, making reference to this sub-paragraph, give notice to the Subcontractor of his decision with reasons and supporting particulars. Unless the Subcontractor notifies the Contractor of his dissatisfaction with this decision within 28 days of receipt of the Contractor's notice, the share decided by the Contractor shall be taken as accepted by the Subcontractor and the Subcontractor shall immediately make payment of such share to the Contractor.";
    (iii) sub-paragraph (13) of Sub-Clause 20.8 [*Related Disputes*] shall be deleted; and
    (iv) sub-paragraph (17) of Sub-Clause 20.8 [*Related Disputes*] shall be amended to read: "If the Arbitral Tribunal's award requires the Contractor to make a payment to the Employer, and the Contractor makes such payment, the Contractor shall consult with the Subcontractor in an endeavour to reach agreement as to the share of such payment to be paid by the Subcontractor to the Contractor. Receipt by the Subcontractor of evidence of such payment by the Contractor to the Employer shall be a condition precedent to the Subcontractor's liability to the Contractor in respect of this share. If agreement is not reached, the Contractor shall promptly and with due diligence make a fair decision as to the appropriate and applicable share, taking due account of the Subcontractor's submissions concerning this dispute and all relevant circumstances. The Contractor shall, making reference to this sub-paragraph, give notice to the Subcontractor of his decision with reasons and supporting particulars. Unless the Subcontractor notifies the Contractor of his dissatisfaction with this decision within 28 days of receipt of the Contractor's notice, the share decided by the Contractor shall be taken as accepted by the Subcontractor and the Subcontractor shall immediately make payment of such share to the Contractor."

Appendix 2
Multi-Party Arbitration Provisions under the Blue Form[1]

I. *FCEC Form of Sub-Contract (Revised September 1984), for use in conjunction with the ICE Contract, 5th Edition*

Clause 18

1. *If any dispute arises between the Contractor and the Sub-Contractor in connection with or arising out of this Sub-Contract or the carrying out of the Sub-Contract Works including any dispute as to any decision, opinion, instruction or direction of the Contractor and/or Engineer or any dispute as to payment under Clause 15 it shall, subject to the provisions of this clause be referred to the arbitration and final decision of a person agreed between the parties, or failing such agreement, appointed upon the application of either of the parties by the President for the time being of the Institution of Civil Engineers and any such reference to arbitration may be conducted in accordance with the Institution of Civil Engineers' Arbitration Procedure 1983 or any amendment or modification thereof in force at the time of the appointment of the arbitrator.*
2. *If any dispute arises in connection with the Main Contract and the Contractor is of the opinion that such dispute touches or concerns the Sub-Contract Works, then provided that an arbitrator has not already been agreed or appointed in pursuance of the preceding sub-clause, the Contractor may by notice in writing to the Sub-Contractor require that any such dispute under this Sub-Contract shall be dealt with jointly with the dispute under the Main Contract in accordance with the provisions of Clause 66 thereof. In connection with such joint dispute the Sub-Contractor shall be bound in like manner as the Contractor by any decision of the Engineer or any award by an arbitrator.*
3. *If at any time before an arbitrator has been agreed or appointed in pursuance of sub-clause (1) of this clause any dispute arising in connection with the Main Contract is made the subject of proceedings in any court between the Employer and the Contractor and the Contractor is of the opinion that such dispute touches or concerns the Sub-Contract Works, he may by notice in writing to the Sub-Contractor abrogate the provisions of sub-clause (1) of this clause and thereafter no dispute under this Sub-Contract shall be referable to arbitration without further submissions by the Contractor and Sub-Contractor...*

[1] The clauses have been reproduced with permission of CECA.

Multi-Party and Multi-Contract Arbitration in the Construction Industry, First Edition.
Dimitar Kondev.

II. FCEC Form of Sub-Contract (September 1991, prior to the 1998 amendments), for use in conjunction with the ICE Contract, 6th Edition

Clause 18(8)

If any dispute arises in connection with the Main Contract and the Contractor is of the opinion that such dispute touches or concerns the Sub-Contract Works and the dispute is referred to a conciliator or an arbitrator under the Main Contract the Contractor may by notice in writing require that the Sub-Contractor provide such information and attend such meetings in connection therewith as the Contractor may request. The Contractor may also by notice in writing require that any such dispute under this Sub-Contract be dealt with jointly with the dispute under the Main Contract and in like manner. In connection with any such joint dispute the Sub-Contractor shall be bound in like manner as the Contractor by any recommendation of the conciliator or any award by an arbitrator.

III. FCEC Form of Sub-Contract (September 1991, as amended in 1998), for use in conjunction with the ICE Contract, 6th Edition

Clause 18(10)

(a) *If, when a dispute in connection with the Main Contract (hereinafter called a Main Contract Dispute) is referred to a conciliator or an adjudicator under the Main Contract, and the Contractor is of the opinion that the Main Contract Dispute has any connection with the Sub-Contract Works then the Contractor may by notice in writing require that the Sub-Contractor shall as soon as is practicable provide such information and attend such meetings in connection with the Main Contract Dispute as the Contractor may request.*

(b) *If a Main Contract Dispute has been referred to conciliation or adjudication under the Main Contract and the Contractor is of the opinion that the Main Contract Dispute has any connection with a dispute which is to be (but has not yet been) referred to conciliation or adjudication under this Sub-Contract (hereinafter called a Connected Dispute), the Contractor may by notice in writing require that the Connected Dispute be referred to the conciliator or adjudicator to whom the Main Contract Dispute has been referred.*

(c) *If the Contractor is of the opinion that a Main Contract Dispute has any connection with a dispute in connection with the Sub-Contract (hereinafter called a Related Sub-Contract Dispute) and the Main Contract Dispute is referred to an arbitrator under the Main Contract, the Contractor may by notice in writing require that the Sub-Contractor provide such information and attend such meetings in connection with the Main Contract Dispute as the Contractor may request. The Contractor may also by notice in writing require that any Related Sub-Contract Dispute be dealt with jointly with the Main Contract Dispute and in like manner. In connection with any Related Sub-Contract Dispute the Sub-Contractor shall be bound in like manner as the Contractor by any award by an arbitrator in relation to the Main Contract Dispute.*

(d) *If a dispute arises under or in connection with the Sub-Contract (hereinafter called a Sub-Contract Dispute) and the Contractor is of the opinion that the Sub-Contract Dispute raises a matter or has any connection with a matter which the Contractor wishes to refer to arbitration under the Main Contract, the Contractor may by notice in writing require that the Sub-Contract Dispute be finally determined jointly with any arbitration to be commenced in accordance with the Main Contract. In connection with the Sub-Contract Dispute, the Sub-Contractor shall be bound in like manner as the Contractor by any award by an arbitrator concerning the matter referred to arbitration under the Main Contract.*

IV. CECA Form of Sub-Contract (November 1998, as amended in June 2008), for use with the ICE Contract[2]

Clause 18C(4) '*Related Main and Sub-Contract Disputes*':

(a) *If, when a dispute in connection with the Main Contract (hereinafter called a Main Contract Dispute) is referred to a conciliator or an adjudicator under the Main Contract, and the Contractor is of the opinion that the Main Contract Dispute has any connection with the Sub-Contract Works then the Contractor may by notice in writing require that the Sub-Contractor shall as soon as is practicable provide such information and attend such meetings in connection with the Main Contract Dispute as the Contractor may request.*

(b) *If a Main Contract Dispute has been referred to conciliation or adjudication under the Main Contract and the Contractor is of the opinion that the Main Contract Dispute has any connection with a dispute which is to be (but has not yet been) referred to conciliation or adjudication under this Sub-Contract (hereinafter called a Connected Dispute), the Contractor may by notice in writing require that the Connected Dispute be referred to the conciliator or adjudicator to whom the Main Contract Dispute has been referred.*

(c) *If the Contractor is of the opinion that a Main Contract Dispute has any connection with a dispute in connection with the Sub-Contract (hereinafter called a Related Sub-Contract Dispute) and the Main Contract Dispute is referred to an arbitrator under the Main Contract, the Contractor may by notice in writing require that the Sub-Contractor provide such information and attend such meetings in connection with the Main Contract Dispute as the Contractor may request. The Contractor may also by notice in writing require that any Related Sub-Contract Dispute be determined by the arbitrator appointed to determine the Main Contract Dispute consistently with the determination of the Main Contract Dispute. In the event of such a notice, the arbitrator appointed to determine the Main Contract Dispute shall conduct a tripartite arbitration between the Employer, Contractor and Sub-Contractor if the Employer agrees. If the Employer does*

---

[2] The wording of the cited clause is the same as the wording which appears in the later CECA Form of Sub-Contract, November 2011, which was drafted for use in conjunction with the Infrastructure Conditions of Contract 2011, which replaced the ICE Contract.

not agree, the arbitrator appointed to determine the Main Contract Dispute shall conduct the arbitration of the Related Sub-Contract Dispute concurrently with but separately from the arbitration of the Main Contract Dispute.

(d) *If a dispute arises under or in connection with the Sub-Contract (hereinafter called a Sub-Contract Dispute) and the Contractor is of the opinion that the Sub-Contract Dispute raises a matter or has any connection with a matter which the Contractor wishes to resolve under the Main Contract (hereinafter called a Related Main Contract Issue), the Contractor may by notice in writing require that the Sub-Contractor provide such information and attend such meetings in connection with the Related Main Contract Issue as the Contractor may request. In the event that the Related Main Contract Issue develops, or in the opinion of the Contractor may develop, into a Main Contract Dispute, the Contractor may also by notice in writing require that the Sub-Contract Dispute be determined by the arbitrator appointed or to be appointed to determine the Main Contract Dispute consistently with the determination of the Main Contract Dispute. In the event of such a notice, the arbitrator appointed to determine the Main Contract Dispute shall conduct a tripartite arbitration between the Employer, Contractor and Sub-Contractor if the Employer agrees. If the Employer does not agree, the arbitrator appointed to determine the Main Contract Dispute shall conduct the arbitration of the Related Sub-Contract Dispute concurrently with but separately from the arbitration of the Main Contract Dispute.*

Appendix 3

Multi-Party Arbitration Clauses under the ENAA Model Form – International Contract for Process Plant Construction, 2010 and Related Subcontracts[1]

I. *Multi-Party Arbitration Clause to be inserted in the Special Conditions to the ENAA Model Form – International Contract for Process Plant Construction, 2010*

Where the Contractor procures that a sub-contract, including a contract for the supply of goods or services, provides for arbitration of disputes and differences and incorporates the clause (with any necessary changes in points of detail) set out in Appendix 10, then the following provisions shall apply:

If any dispute or difference to be referred to arbitration pursuant to the Contract,

raises issues which are substantially the same as, or connected with, or touch upon, or concern issues raised in any dispute between the Contractor and any Sub-contractor or any supplier of goods or services; or
arises out of, or touches upon, or concerns substantially the same facts as are the subject of any dispute between the Contractor and any Sub-contractor or any supplier of goods or services; or
is such that the Owner and the Contractor declare that a dispute or difference between the Contractor and any Sub-contractor or any supplier of goods or services is one of interest to them in connection with the resolution of any dispute or difference under or in connection with the Contract;
the Owner and the Contractor hereby agree that the Contractor may refer any related dispute as is mentioned in (a) or (b) above and that the Contractor shall refer any related dispute as is mentioned in (c) above, to the arbitral tribunal appointed or to be appointed

[1]The clauses have been reproduced with permission of the Engineering Advancement Association of Japan (ENAA). The draft clauses are contained in the Attachment '*Draft Joinder Clauses for Multi-Party Arbitration*' to the Guide Notes, pp. 73–75, to the ENAA Model Form-International Contract for Process Plant Construction, 3rd edn, 2010.

Multi-Party and Multi-Contract Arbitration in the Construction Industry, First Edition.
Dimitar Kondev.

pursuant to the Contract. The arbitral tribunal shall have the power to make all necessary directions as to the joinder of the parties as the arbitral tribunal considers appropriate to achieve such purpose and any award made by such arbitral tribunal shall be final and binding.

II. Multi-Party Arbitration Clause to be inserted in sub-contracts with Sub-contractors and suppliers

The clause is contained in Appendix 10 which is referred to in the multi-party arbitration clause under item I above.

1. ***Settlement of Dispute***

   1.1 If any dispute or difference of any kind whatsoever shall arise between the Contractor and the [Sub-contractor] in connection with or arising out of the [Sub-contract], including, without prejudice to the generality of the foregoing, any question regarding its existence, validity or termination or execution of the [Sub-contract] works, whether during the progress of the same or after their completion and whether before or after the termination, abandonment or breach of the [Sub-contract], shall be settled by arbitration under [the Rules of Arbitration of the International Chamber of Commerce (ICC)] which rules are deemed to be incorporated by reference into this clause. The award of the arbitral tribunal shall be final and binding on the parties.

2. ***Joint Arbitration***

   If any dispute or difference capable of being referred, to be referred or referred to arbitration under this [Sub-contract]:

   raises issues which are substantially the same as, or connected with, or touch upon, or concern issues raised in any dispute or difference arising out of or in connection with the Contract between the Owner and the Contractor ("the Main Contract"); or

   arises out of, or touches upon, or concerns substantially the same facts as are the subject of any dispute between the Owner and the Contractor pursuant to the Main Contract; or

   is one that the Owner and the Contractor declare to be of interest to them in connection with the resolution of any dispute or difference to be referred or referred to arbitration pursuant to the Main Contract;

   (a dispute or difference under the Main Contract which falls within any of (i) to (iii) above shall be referred to as a "related dispute under the Main Contract"),

   then notwithstanding that an arbitrator(s) may have been agreed or appointed under this [Sub-contract], the Contractor may, by written notice to the [Sub-contractor] and the arbitrator(s) who has (or have) already been agreed or appointed hereunder, require that any such dispute under this [Sub-contract] be referred to and finally settled by the arbitral tribunal appointed or to be appointed under the Main Contract in respect of any such related dispute under the Main Contract ("Joint Tribunal").

   The Joint Tribunal shall become the arbitral tribunal in respect of any dispute or difference between the Contractor and the [Sub-contractor] thus referred hereunder. The

Contractor and the [Sub-contractor] shall be bound by any directions or orders made by the Joint Tribunal as to their joinder in any arbitration proceedings under the Main Contract, and shall also be bound by any procedural directions and any subsequent award made by the Joint Tribunal.

The language of the arbitration and the place of arbitration shall be as fixed under the Main Contract.

The provision of sub-clause 2.1 above shall not apply in respect of any dispute or difference under this [Sub-contract] after a hearing on the merits has commenced in any arbitration under Clause 1 hereof.

In the event of the revocation of the authority of an arbitrator(s) who has already been agreed or appointed under this [Sub-contract] by reason of the notice given by the Contractor under sub-clause 2.1 above, the cost of the cancelled arbitration (including the arbitrator's fees) shall be dealt with by the Joint Tribunal as costs in that arbitration. Pending a determination as to liability for such costs, the fees of the arbitrator(s) whose authority has been revoked shall be paid by the Contractor.

It is not intended that the machinery in this Clause shall operate so as to deprive any party of anything which, apart from this Clause, would be a valid claim or defense. Accordingly, all claims and defenses which were originally made in any cancelled arbitration shall be deemed for all purposes to have been brought when made and not to be affected in any way by the revocation of the authority of the arbitrator or the cancellation of the arbitration pursuant to sub-clauses 2.1 and 2.3 so that the position of either party to the dispute shall not thereby be prejudiced with respect to any rule of law, statute, regulation or contractual provision which imposes a time limit on the commencement of the proceedings or the right to any remedy.

The Joint Tribunal in determining any dispute or difference shall consider all evidence which it may think pertinent to that dispute which is filled or called by a party to the arbitration proceedings.

Bibliography

I. Books

Adriaanse, J. (2010) *Construction Contract Law. The Essentials*, 3rd edn, Palgrave Macmillan, Basingstoke.

Anderson, R. (2001) *Adjudication under the NEC*, Thomas Telford Publishing, London.

Bastianelli, A. and Sink, C. (eds) (2014) *ADR Construction*, American Bar Association, Forum on the Construction Industry, Chicago.

Bellet, P., Bernardino, P., Bernini, G. *et al.* (eds) (1991) *Multi-party Arbitration: View from International Arbitration Specialists*, Publication No. 480/1, ICC Publishing SA, Paris.

Berger, K. P. (1993) *International Economic Arbitration*, Kluwer Law and Taxation Publishers, The Hague.

Binder, P. (2013) *Analytical Commentary to the UNCITRAL Arbitration Rules*, Sweet & Maxwell, London.

Blackaby, N. and Partasides, C. with Redfern, A. and Hunter, M. (2015) *Redfern and Hunter on International Arbitration*, 6th edn, Oxford University Press, Oxford.

Böckstiegel, K., Kröll, S. and Nacimiento, P. (eds) (2015) *Arbitration in Germany: The Model Law in Practice*, 2nd edn, Kluwer Law International, Alphen aan den Rijn.

Born, G. (2009) *International Commercial Arbitration*, Kluwer Law International, Alphen aan den Rijn.

Born, G. (2012) *International Arbitration: Law and Practice*, Kluwer Law International, Alphen aan den Rijn.

Born, G. (2013) *International Arbitration and Forum Selection Agreements: Drafting and Enforcing*, 4th edn, Kluwer Law International, Alphen aan den Rijn.

Born, G. (2014) *International Commercial Arbitration*, 2nd edn, Kluwer Law International, Alphen aan den Rijn.

Brekoulakis, S. (2010) *Third Parties in International Commercial Arbitration*, Oxford University Press, Oxford.

Carbonneau, T. (2007) *Cases and Materials on Arbitration Law and Practice*, 6th edn, American Casebook Series, Thomson West, St Paul.

Caron, D. and Caplan, L. (2013) *The UNCITRAL Arbitration Rules, A Commentary*, 2nd edn, Oxford University Press, Oxford.

Conrad, N., Munch, P. and Black-Branch, J. (eds) (2013) *International Commercial Arbitration, Standard Clauses and Forms Commentary*, Helbing Lichtenhahn C. H. Beck Hart Nomos, Basel.

Croft, C., Kee, C. and Waincymer, J. (2013) *A Guide to the UNCITRAL Arbitration Rules*, Cambridge University Press, Cambridge.

Multi-Party and Multi-Contract Arbitration in the Construction Industry, First Edition.
Dimitar Kondev.

Derains, Y. and Schwartz, E. (2005) *A Guide to the ICC Rules of Arbitration*, 2nd edn, Kluwer Law International, The Hague.

Dore, I. (1990) *Theory and Practice of Multiparty Commercial Arbitration with Special Reference to the UNCITRAL Framework*, Graham & Trotman, London.

Eggleston, B. (2015) *The NEC3 Engineering and Construction Contract, A Commentary*, 2nd edn, Wiley Blackwell, Chichester.

Eksi, N., Martinez-Fraga, P. and Sheehy, W. (eds) (2007) *International Commercial Arbitration: A Comparative Survey*, ICOC Publication, No. 2007/45, Istanbul Chamber of Commerce, Istanbul.

Evald, J. and Schaumburg-Müller, S. (2004) *Retsfilosofi, Retsvidenskab og Retskildelære*, Jurist- og Økonomforbundets Forlag, Copenhagen.

Friedland, P. (2007) *Arbitration Clauses for International Contracts*, 2nd edn, New York: JurisNet.

Fry, J., Greenberg, S. and Mazza, F. (2012) *The Secretariat's Guide to ICC Arbitration*, ICC Publication No. 729, ICC Publishing SA, Paris.

Gaillard, E. and Di Pietro, D. (eds) (2008) *Enforcement of Arbitration Agreements and International Arbitral Awards: The New York Convention in Practice*, Cameron May, London.

Garnett, R., Gabriel, H. and Waincymer, J, (2002) *A Practical Guide to International Commercial Arbitration*, Oceana Publications, New York, NY.

Glover, J. and Hughes, S. (2006) *Understanding the FIDIC Red Book: A Clause-by-Clause Commentary*, 2nd edn, Sweet & Maxwell, London.

Godwin, W. (2013) *International Construction Contracts. A Handbook*, Wiley Blackwell, Chichester.

Hanessian, G. and Newman, L. (eds) (2009) *International Arbitration Checklists, Baker & McKenzie*, 2nd edn, JurisNet, LLC, New York, NY.

Hanotiau, B. (2005) *Complex Arbitrations: Multiparty, Multicontract, Multi-issue and Class Actions*, Kluwer Law International, The Hague.

Hansen, M., Schmidt, J. E., Sørensen, N. *et al.* (1993) *AB 92 for Praktikere, En Kommentar til AB 92*, Byggecentrum.

Hinchey, J. and Harris, T. (2008) *International Construction Arbitration Handbook*, Thomson West, Eagan, MN.

Huleatt-James, M. and Gould, N. (1999) *International Commercial Arbitration. A Handbook*, 2nd edn, LLP Reference Publishing, London.

Jaeger, A. and Hök, G. (2009) *FIDIC: A Guide for Practitioners*, Springer, New York, NY.

Jenkins, J. (2013) *International Construction Arbitration Law*, 2nd revised edn, Kluwer Law International, Alphen aan den Rijn.

Jenkins, J. and Stebbing, J. (2006) *International Construction Arbitration Law*, Kluwer Law International, Alphen aan den Rijn.

Kelley, G. (2012) *Construction Law: An Introduction for Engineers, Architects and Contractors*, John Wiley & Sons, Inc., Hoboken, NJ.

Klausegger, C., Klein, P., Kremslehner, F. *et al.* (eds) (2015) *Austrian Yearbook on International Arbitration, Volume 2015*, Manz'sche Verlags- und Universitätsbuchhandlung, Vienna.

Klee, L. (2015) *International Construction Contract Law*, Wiley Blackwell, Chichester.

Lew, J., Bor, H., Fullelove, G. and Greenaway, J. (eds) (2013) *Arbitration in England with Chapters on Scotland and Ireland*, Kluwer Law International, Alphen aan den Rijn.

Lew, J., Mistelis, L. and Kröll, S. (2003) *Comparative International Commercial Arbitration*, Kluwer Law International, The Hague.

Ma, G. and Kaplan, N. (eds) (2003) *Arbitration in Hong Kong: A Practical Guide*, Sweet & Maxwell Asia, Hong Kong.

McIlwrath, M. and Savage, J. (2010) *International Arbitration and Mediation, A Practical Guide*, Kluwer Law International, Alphen aan den Rijn.

Meier, A. (2007) *Einbezug Dritter vor internationalen Schiedsgerichten*, Schulthess, Zurich.

Merkin, R. (2004) *Arbitration Law*, Informa, London.

Mistelis, L. (ed.) (2010) *Concise International Arbitration*, Kluwer Law International, Alphen aan den Rijn.

Mistelis, L. (ed.) (2015) *Concise International Arbitration*, 2nd edn, Kluwer Law International, Alphen aan den Rijn.

Moses, M. (2012) *The Principles and Practice of International Commercial Arbitration*, 2nd edn, Cambridge University Press, New York, NY.

Nairn, K. and Heneghan, P. (eds) *Arbitration World, Jurisdictional Comparisons*, 4th edn, Thomson Reuters, London, 2012

Nielsen, R. and Tvarnø, C. (2011) *Retskilder og Retsteorier*, 3rd edn., Jurist- og Økonomforbundets Forlag, Copenhagen.

Pair, L. (2012) *Consolidation in International Commercial Arbitration, The ICC and Swiss Rules*, International Commerce and Arbitration Volume 10, Eleven International Publishing, The Hague.

Paulsson, J., Rawding, N. and Reed, L. (2011) *The Freshfields Guide to Arbitration Clauses in International Contracts*, 3rd edn, Kluwer Law International, Alphen aan den Rijn.

Permanent Court of Arbitration (ed.) (2009) *Multiple Party Actions in International Arbitration*, Oxford University Press, New York, NY.

Pihlblad, S., Lundblad, C. and Søgaard-Christensen, C. (2014) *Arbitration in Denmark*, Djøf Publishing, Copenhagen.

Polish Chamber of Foreign Trade (1982) *International Arbitration in Multi-Party Disputes, Materials of an International Symposium Warsaw June 29th – July 2nd 1980*, Wydawnictwo Prawnicze, Warsaw.

Poudret, J.-F. and Besson, S. (2007) *Comparative Law of International Arbitration*, 2nd edn, Sweet & Maxwell Schulthess, London.

Reisman, W. M., Laurence Craig, W., Park, W. W. and Paulsson, J. (1997) *International Commercial Arbitration. Cases, Materials and Notes on the Resolution of International Business Disputes*, The Foundation Press, New York, NY.

Reisman, W. M., Laurence Craig, W., Park, W. W. and Paulsson, J. (2015) *International Commercial Arbitration. Cases, Materials and Notes on the Resolution of International Business Disputes*, 2nd edn, The Foundation Press, St Paul, MN.

Sanders, P. (1999) *Quo Vadis Arbitration? Sixty Years of Arbitration Practice, A Comparative Study*, Kluwer Law International, The Hague.

Schütze, R. (ed.) (2013) *Institutional Arbitration, Article-by-Article Commentary*, C. H. Beck Hart Nomos, Munich.

Sheridan, P. (1999) *Construction and Engineering Arbitration*, Sweet & Maxwell, London.

Siems, M. (2014) *Comparative Law*, Cambridge University Press, Cambridge.

Steingruber, A. M. (2012) *Consent in International Arbitration*, Oxford University Press, Oxford.

Strong, S. (2009) *Research and Practice in International Commercial Arbitration, Sources and Strategies*, Oxford University Press, New York, NY.

Thornton, A. and Godwin, W. (ed.) (1998) *Construction Law: Themes and Practice, Essays in Honour of I.N. Duncan Wallace Q.C.*, Sweet & Maxwell, London.

Turner, P. and Mohtashami, R. (2012) *A Guide to the LCIA Arbitration Rules*, Oxford University Press, Oxford.

Tweeddale, A. and Tweeddale, K. (2007) *Arbitration of Commercial Disputes, International and English Law and Practice*, Oxford University Press, Oxford.

Uff, J. (2013) *Construction Law*, 11th edn, Sweet & Maxwell, London.

Vienna International Arbitration Centre of the Austrian Federal Economic Chamber (ed.) (2014) *Handbook Vienna Rules, A Practitioner's Guide*, WKÖ-Service Gmbh, Bad Vöslau.

Voser, N. (ed.) (2014) *Ten Years of the Swiss Rules of International Arbitration*, ASA Special Series No. 44, JurisNet LLC, New York, NY.

Voskuil, C. and Wade, J. (eds) (1985) *Hague-Zagreb Essays 5 on the Law of International Trade, Reservation of Title, Multiparty Arbitration*, Martinus Nijhoff, The Hague.

Waincymer, J. (2012) *Procedure and Evidence in International Arbitration*, Kluwer Law International, Alphen aan den Rijn.

Webster, T. and Bühler, M. (2014) *Handbook of ICC Arbitration. Commentary, Precedents, Materials*, 3rd edn, Sweet & Maxwell, London.

Weigand, F. B. (ed.) (2009) *Practitioner's Handbook on International Commercial Arbitration*, 2nd edn, Oxford University Press, Oxford.

Williams, L. (ed.) (2015) *The Baker & McKenzie International Arbitration Yearbook 2014–2015*, JurisNet, LLC, New York, NY.

Wood, D., Chynoweth, P., Adshead, J. and Mason, J. (2010) *Law and the Built Environment*, Wiley Blackwell, Chichester.

Youssef, K. (2009) *Consent in Context: Fulfilling the Promise of International Arbitration. Multi-Party, Multi-Contract and Non-Contract Arbitration*, Thomson West, Eagan, MN.

Zuberbühler, T., Müller, C. and Habegger, P. (eds) (2005) *Swiss Rules of International Arbitration: Commentary*, Kluwer Law International, Alphen aan den Rijn.

Zuberbühler, T., Müller, C. and Habegger, P. (eds) (2013) *Swiss Rules of International Arbitration: Commentary*, 2nd edn, Schulthess/Juris, Zurich.

Zweigert, K. and Kötz, H. (1998) *Introduction to Comparative Law*, 3rd edn, Oxford University Press, Oxford.

II. Articles and other contributions in books

Athanasakis, D. (2007) 'Has Multi-Party Arbitration Failed in Construction Disputes? Legal and Practical Issues in Drafting Joinder Provisions', in D. Boyd (ed.) *Procs 23rd Annual ARCOM Conference, 3–5 September, Belfast, UK, Association of Researchers in Construction Management*, pp. 107–116, http://www.arcom.ac.uk/-docs/proceedings/ar2007-0107-0116_Athanasakis.pdf (accessed 24 July 2016).

Bärtsch, P. and Petti, A. (2013) 'Consolidation and Joinder (Article 4)' in Tobias Zuberbühler, Christoph Müller, and Philipp Habegger (eds) *Swiss Rules of International Arbitration: Commentary*, 2nd edn, Schulthess Juris, Zurich, pp. 52–67.

Benedict, C. (2015) 'Part IV – Selected Areas and Issues of Arbitration in Germany, Construction Arbitration in Germany', in K. Böckstiegel, S. Kröll and P. Nacimiento (eds) *Arbitration in Germany: The Model Law in Practice*, 2nd edn, Kluwer Law International, Alphen aan den Rijn, pp. 829–845.

Bernardini, P. (1991) 'Examination of the Issues Involved in Drafting Arbitral Clauses', in P. Bellet, P. Bernardini, G. Bernini *et al.* (eds) *Multi-Party Arbitration: Views from International Arbitration Specialists*, Publication No. 480/1, ICC Publishing SA, Paris, pp. 97–101.

Bernini, G. (1991) 'Organization of the Arbitral Proceedings. Overview of the Issues', in P. Bellet, P. Bernardini, G. Bernini *et al.* (eds) *Multi-Party Arbitration: Views from International Arbitration Specialists*, Publication No. 480/1, ICC Publishing SA, Paris, pp. 161–169.

Bitter, J. W. (2009) 'Consolidation of Arbitral Proceedings in the Netherlands: The Practice and Perspective of the Netherlands Arbitration Institute', in the Permanent Court of Arbitration (ed.) *Multiple Party Actions in International Arbitration*, Oxford University Press, New York, NY, pp. 221–235.

Bloomquist, M. (2004) 'Chapter 26, Consolidation and Joinder' in D. Brennan, R. Lowe, J. Nielsen and J. Spangler (eds) *The Construction Contracts Book, How to Find Common Ground in Negotiating Design and Construction Contract Clauses*, American Bar Association, Forum of the Construction Industry, Chicago, IL.

Bond, S., Paralika, M. and Secomb, M. (2015) 'ICC Rules of Arbitration, 2012', in Loukas Mistelis (ed.) *Concise International Arbitration*, 2nd edn, Kluwer Law International, Alphen aan den Rijn, pp. 347–568.

Bredow, J. (2013) 'Arbitration Rules and Country Reports: Germany', in N. Conrad, P. Munch and J. Black-Branch (eds) *International Commercial Arbitration, Standard Clauses and Forms Commentary*, Helbing Lichtenhahn C. H. Beck Hart Nomos, Basel, pp. 455–498.

Bredow, J. and Mulder, I. (2015) 'Part III – Commentary on the Arbitration Rules of the German Institution of Arbitration (DIS Rules), Section 13 – Multiple Parties on Claimant or Respondent Side', in K. Böckstiegel, S. Kröll and P. Nacimiento (eds) *Arbitration in Germany: The Model Law in Practice*, 2nd edn, Kluwer Law International, Alphen aan den Rijn, pp. 629–631.

Casey, B. and Doria, C. (2012) 'Canada', in K. Nairn and P. Heneghan (eds) *Arbitration World, Jurisdictional Comparisons*, 4th edn, Thomson Reuters, London, pp. 309–326.

Castello, J. and Digon, R. (2012) 'Maximizing Possibilities for Joinder in International Arbitration' in Arthur Rovine (ed.) *Contemporary Issues in International Arbitration and Mediation. The Fordham Papers 2011*, Martinus Nijhoff Publishers, Leiden, pp. 104–120.

Conejero Roos, C. (2009) 'Multi-party Arbitration and Rule Making: Same Issues, Contrasting Approaches', in Albert Jan van den Berg (ed.) *50 Years of the New York Convention, ICCA International Arbitration Conference, ICCA Congress Series No. 14*, Kluwer Law International, Alphen aan den Rijn, pp. 411–433.

Conrad, N., Baumann, B. and Cilingir, Ö (2013) 'Sample Clauses for International Arbitration Agreements', in N. Conrad, P. Munch and J. Black-Branch (eds) *International Commercial Arbitration, Standard Clauses and Forms Commentary*, Helbing Lichtenhahn C.H.Beck Hart Nomos, Basel, pp. 11–34.

Craig, W. (1991) 'Means of Recourse and Enforcement of Awards', in P. Bellet, P. Bernardini, G. Bernini *et al.* (eds) *Multi-Party Arbitration: Views from International Arbitration Specialists*, Publication No. 480/1, ICC Publishing SA, Paris, pp. 217–233.

Dannemann, G. (2006) 'Comparative Law: Study of Similarities or Differences', in Mathias Reimann and Reinhard Zimmermann (eds) *The Oxford Handbook of Comparative Law*, Oxford University Press, Oxford, pp. 388–419.

de Boisseson, M. (1991) 'Constituting an Arbitral Tribunal', in P. Bellet, P. Bernardini, G. Bernini *et al.* (eds) *Multi-Party Arbitration: Views from International Arbitration Specialists*, Publication No. 480/1, ICC Publishing SA, Paris, pp. 147–157.

De Winter, K. and De Vroey, M. (2015) 'Belgium', in L. Williams (ed.) *The Baker & McKenzie International Arbitration Yearbook 2014–2015*, JurisNet, LLC, New York, NY, pp. 43–50.

Dika, M. (1985) 'The Problem of Multi-Party Arbitration from the Standpoint of Yugoslav Law', in Cornelis Voskuil and John Wade (eds) *Hague-Zagreb Essays 5 on the Law of International Trade, Reservation of Title, Multiparty Arbitration*, Martinus Nijhoff, The Hague, pp. 125–138.

Drahozal, C. (2007) 'International Arbitration Law in the United States', in N. Eksi, P. Martinez-Fraga and W. Sheehy (eds) *International Commercial Arbitration: A Comparative Survey*, ICOC Publication, No. 2007/45, Istanbul Chamber of Commerce, Istanbul, pp. 63–83.

Gilliéron, P. and Pittet, L. (2005) 'Part 1: Introductory Rules', in Tobias Zuberbühler, Christoph Müller, and Philipp Habegger (eds) *Swiss Rules of International Arbitration: Commentary*, Kluwer Law International, Alphen aan den Rijn, pp. 36–44.

Godwin, W. (1998) 'Arbitration or Litigation? Multi-Party Disputes and Arbitration Clauses', in Anthony Thornton and William Godwin (ed.) *Construction Law: Themes and Practice, Essays in Honour of I.N. Duncan Wallace Q.C.*, Sweet & Maxwell, London, pp. 245–272.

Goedel, J. (1991) 'Examination of the Issues Involved in Drafting Arbitral Clauses', in P. Bellet, P. Bernardini, G. Bernini *et al.* (eds) *Multi-Party Arbitration: Views from International Arbitration Specialists*, Publication No. 480/1, ICC Publishing SA, Paris, pp. 103–113.

Greenberg, S., Feris, J. R. and Albanesi, C. (2010) 'Consolidation, Joinder, Cross-Claims, Multiparty and Multicontract Arbitrations: Recent ICC Experience', in Bernard Hanotiau and Eric Schwartz (eds) *ICC Dossiers VII, Multiparty Arbitration*, ICC Publication No. 701E, ICC Publishing SA, Paris, pp. 161–182.

Guterstam, K., Ragnwaldh, J. and Andersson, F. (2015) 'SCC Arbitration Rules 2010', in L. Mistelis (ed.) *Concise International Arbitration*, 2nd edn, Kluwer Law International, Alphen aan den Rijn, pp. 709–761.

Hanotiau, B. (2009) 'Multiple Parties and Multiple Contracts in International Arbitration', in the Permanent Court of Arbitration (ed.) *Multiple Party Actions in International Arbitration*, Oxford University Press, New York, NY, pp. 35–67.

Hanotiau, B. (2010) 'Introduction', in B. Hanotiau and E. A. Schwartz (eds) *Multiparty Arbitration*, Dossiers VII, ICC Publication No. 701E, ICC Institute of World Business Law, Paris, pp. 7–8.

Herrlin, H. (1991) 'Issues to be Discussed', in P. Bellet, P. Bernardini, G. Bernini *et al.* (eds) *Multi-Party Arbitration: Views from International Arbitration Specialists*, Publication No. 480/1, ICC Publishing SA, Paris, pp. 131–136.

Jansen, N. (2006) 'Comparative Law and Comparative Knowledge', in Mathias Reimann and Reinhard Zimmermann (ed.) *The Oxford Handbook of Comparative Law*, Oxford University Press, Oxford, pp. 305–338.

Jarvin, S. (1991) 'Issues Related to Consolidation', in P. Bellet, P. Bernardini, G. Bernini *et al.* (eds) *Multi-Party Arbitration: Views from International Arbitration Specialists*, Publication No. 480/1, ICC Publishing SA, Paris, pp. 199–205.

Karrer, P. (2013) 'Chapter V, Swiss Rules', in Rolf Schütze (ed.) *Institutional Arbitration, Article-by-Article Commentary*, C. H. Beck Hart Nomos, Munich, pp. 361–412.

Karrer, P. and Straub, P. (2009) 'Switzerland', in Frank Bernd Weigand (ed.) *Practitioner's Handbook on International Commercial Arbitration*, 2nd edn, Oxford University Press, Oxford, pp. 815–876.

Kondev, D. (2015) 'Can Arbitral Rules Resolve Multi-Party Multi-Contract Construction Disputes?' in Giovanni Iudica (ed.) *Construction Contract, Arbitration and ADR, Papers from the Annual Conference of the European Society of Construction Law (Milan, 10 October 2014)*, Editoriale Scientifica, Naples, pp. 69–81.

Lloyd, H. (1991) 'A National Experience', in P. Bellet, P. Bernardini, G. Bernini *et al.* (eds) *Multi-Party Arbitration: Views from International Arbitration Specialists*, Publication No. 480/1, ICC Publishing SA, Paris, pp. 61–79.

Mantilla-Serrano, F. (2010) 'Multiple Parties and Multiple Contracts: Divergent or Compatible Issues?', in B. Hanotiau and E. A. Schwartz (eds) *Multiparty Arbitration*, Dossiers VII, ICC Publication No. 701E, ICC Institute of World Business Law, Paris, pp. 11–33.

Marrin, J. (2009) 'Multiparty Arbitration in the Construction Industry', in the Permanent Court of Arbitration (ed.) *Multiple Party Actions in International Arbitration*, Oxford University Press, New York, NY, pp. 395–425.

Marzolini, P. (2012) 'Is the Parties' Consent Still an Overriding Principle for Joinder and Intervention of Third Parties in International Commercial Arbitration?', in D. Favalli, X. Favre-Bulle, A. Furrer *et al.* (eds) *Selected Papers on International Arbitration: Volume 2 Series on International Arbitration SAA*, Stämpfli Verlag, Bern, pp. 105–137.

Mayer, P. (2009) 'Extension of the Arbitration Clause to Non-signatories under French Law', in the Permanent Court of Arbitration (ed.) *Multiple Party Actions in International Arbitration*, Oxford University Press, New York, NY, pp. 189–199.

Megens, P., Bonnell, M., Darian-Smith, M. and Cubitt, B. (2012) 'Australia', in K. Nairn and P. Heneghan (eds) *Arbitration World, Jurisdictional Comparisons*, 4th edn, Thomson Reuters, London, pp. 249–269.

Michaels, R. (2006) 'The Functional Method of Comparative Law', in Mathias Reimann and Reinhard Zimmermann (eds) *The Oxford Handbook of Comparative Law*, Oxford University Press, Oxford, pp. 339–382.

Muir Watt, H. (2006) 'Globalization and Comparative Law', in M. Reimann and R. Zimmermann (eds) *The Oxford Handbook of Comparative Law*, Oxford University Press, Oxford, pp. 579–607.

Nesbitt, S. (2010) 'LCIA Arbitration Rules', in Loukas Mistelis (ed.) *Concise International Arbitration*, Kluwer Law International, Alphen aan den Rijn, pp. 401–466.

Oberhammer, P. and Koller, C. (2014) 'Article 14, Joinder of Third Parties and Consolidation' in Vienna International Arbitration Centre of the Austrian Federal Economic Chamber (ed.) *Handbook Vienna Rules, A Practitioner's Guide*, WKÖ-Service Gmbh, Bad Vöslau, pp. 69–88.

Öhrström, M. (2013) 'Chapter XII, SCC Rules', in Rolf Schütze (ed.) *Institutional Arbitration, Article-by-Article Commentary*, C. H. Beck Hart Nomos, Munich, pp. 815–862.

Park, W. (2009) 'Non-signatories and International Contracts: An Arbitrator's Dilemma', in the Permanent Court of Arbitration (ed.) *Multiple Party Actions in International Arbitration*, Oxford University Press, New York, NY, pp. 3–31.

Pitkowitz, N. (2015) 'Chapter II: The Arbitrator and the Arbitration Procedure, Multi-Party Arbitrations – Joinder and Consolidation under the Vienna Rules 2013', in C. Klausegger, P. Klein, F. Kremsiehner *et al.* (eds) *Austrian Yearbook on International Arbitration*, Volume 2015, Manz'sche Verlags- und Universitätsbuchhandlung, Vienna, pp. 301–319.

Platte, M. (2008) 'Multi-Party Arbitration: Legal Issues Arising Out of Joinder and Consolidation', in E. Gaillard and D. di Pietro (eds) *Enforcement of Arbitration Agreements and International Arbitral Awards: The New York Convention in Practice*, Cameron May, London, pp. 481–499.

Reiner, A. and Aschauer, C. (2013) 'Chapter II, ICC Rules', in R. Schütze (ed.) *Institutional Arbitration, Article-by-Article Commentary*, C. H.Beck Hart Nomos, Munich, pp. 25–201.

Rubino-Sammartano, M. (2009) 'Italy', in Frank Bernd Weigand (ed.) *Practitioner's Handbook on International Commercial Arbitration*, 2nd edn, Oxford University Press, Oxford, pp. 543–616.

Savage, J. and Dunbar, S. (2015) 'SIAC Arbitration Rules 2013', in Mistelis, L. (ed.) *Concise International Arbitration*, 2nd edn, Kluwer Law International, Alphen aan den Rijn, pp. 763–834.

Schramm, D. (2013) 'Chapter 3, Part II: Commentary on the Swiss Rules, Article 4 [Consolidation and Joinder]' in M. Arroyo (ed.) *Arbitration in Switzerland: The Practitioner's Guide*, Kluwer Law International, Alphen aan den Rijn, pp. 360–369.

Sedrati-Müller, M. (2013) 'Arbitration Rules and Country Reports: Austria', in N. Conrad, P. Munch and J. Black-Branch (eds) *International Commercial Arbitration, Standard Clauses and Forms Commentary*, Helbing Lichtenhahn C. H. Beck Hart Nomos, Basel, pp. 231–306.

Sheppard, A. (2010) 'English Arbitration Act 1996 (Chapter 23), 1996 – Arbitration Law in England, Wales and Northern Ireland', in Loukas Mistelis (ed.) *Concise International Arbitration*, Kluwer Law International, Alphen aan den Rijn, pp. 719–872.

Siig, K. M. (2006) 'Multi-Party Arbitration in International Trade: Problems and Solutions', in Sylvia Mercado Kierkegaard (ed.) *Business, Law and Technology: Present and Emerging Trends*, Volume **2**, International Association of IT Lawyers, Hellerup, pp. 21–33.

Smits, J. (2006) 'Comparative Law and its Influence on National Legal Systems', in Mathias Reimann and Reinhard Zimmermann (eds) *The Oxford Handbook of Comparative Law*, Oxford University Press, Oxford, pp. 513–538.

Stackpool-Moore, R. (2014) 'Joinder and Consolidation – Examining Best Practice in the Swiss, HKIAC and ICC Rules', in Nathalie Voser (ed.) *10 Years of the Swiss Rules of International Arbitration*, ASA Special Series No. 44, JurisNet LLC, New York, NY, pp. 15–34.

Tao, J. (2010) 'CIETAC Arbitration Rules, 2005', in Loukas Mistelis (ed.) *Concise International Arbitration*, Kluwer Law International, Alphen aan den Rijn, pp. 513–580.

Tao, J. (2015) 'CIETAC Arbitration Rules 2015' in Loukas Mistelis (ed.) *Concise International Arbitration*, 2nd edn, Kluwer Law International, Alphen aan den Rijn, pp. 617–707.

Van Houtte, H. (1991) 'Due Process in Multi-Party Arbitration', in P. Bellet, P. Bernardini, G. Bernini *et al.* (eds) *Multi-Party Arbitration: Views from International Arbitration Specialists*, Publication No. 480/1, ICC Publishing SA, Paris, pp. 189–195.

Voser, N. (2009) 'Multi-party Disputes and Joinder of Third Parties', in Albert Jan van den Berg (ed.) *50 Years of the New York Convention, ICCA International Arbitration Conference, ICCA Congress Series No. 14*, Kluwer Law International, Alphen aan den Rijn, pp. 343–410.

Whitesell, A. M. (2009) 'Multiparty Arbitration: The ICC International Court of Arbitration Perspective', in the Permanent Court of Arbitration (ed.) *Multiple Party Actions in International Arbitration*, Oxford University Press, New York, NY, pp. 203–212.

Winstanley, A. (2009) 'Multiple Parties, Multiple Problems: A View from The London Court of International Arbitration', in the Permanent Court of Arbitration (ed.) *Multiple Party Actions in International Arbitration*, Oxford University Press, New York, NY, pp. 213–220.

III. *Journal articles*

Athanasakis, D. and Morgan, R. 'Joinder of Arbitrations: an Overview of English and Hong Kong Construction Industry Practice', in *Asian Dispute Review* no. **1** (2008), pp. 17–23.

Austmann, A. 'Commercial Multi-Party Arbitration: A Case-By-Case Approach', in *1 The American Review of International Arbitration*, no. **3** (1990), pp. 341–363.

Bamforth, R. and Maidment, K. '"All join in or not"? How well does international arbitration cater for disputes involving multiple parties or related claims?', in *27 ASA Bulletin*, no. **1** (2009), pp. 3–25.

Bartels, M. 'Multiparty Arbitration Clauses', in *2 Journal of International Arbitration*, no. **2** (1985), pp. 60–66.

Bevilacqua, T. 'Voluntary Intervention and Other Participation of Third Parties in Ongoing International Arbitrations: A Survey of the Current State of Play', in *1 World Arbitration & Mediation Review*, no. **4** (2007), pp. 507–538.

Brekoulakis, S. 'The Relevance of the Interests of Third Parties in Arbitration: Taking a Closer Look at the Elephant in the Room', in *113 Penn State Law Review*, no. **4** (2009), pp. 1165–1188.

Bruner, P. 'Dual Track Proceedings in Arbitration and Litigation: Reducing the Peril of "Double Jeopardy" by Consolidation, Joinder and Appellate Arbitration', in *31 International Construction Law Review*, part **4** (2014), pp. 537–557.

Brunner, C. 'The Swiss Rules of International Arbitration: An Overview for Prospective Users', in *8 Zeitschrift für Schiedsverfahren*, no. **5** (2010), pp. 243–251.

Butler, J. 'AAA Construction Rules', in *65 Dispute Resolution Journal*, no. **2/3** (2010), pp. 96–103.

Caprasse, O. 'The Setting up of the Arbitral Tribunal in Multi-Party Arbitration', in *International Business Law Journal*, no. **2** (2006), pp. 197–216.

Cohen, M. M. 'A Missed Opportunity to Revise the 1996 Arbitration Act', in *23 Arbitration International*, no. **3** (2007), pp. 461–465.

Dasser, F. 'International Arbitration and Setting Aside Proceedings in Switzerland: A Statistical Analysis', in *25 ASA Bulletin*, no. **3** (2007), pp. 442–472.

Fai, E. T. C. and Dewan, N. 'Drafting Arbitration Agreements with Consolidation in Mind', in *5 Asian International Arbitration Journal*, no. **1** (2009), pp. 70–94.

Fan, K. 'The New Arbitration Ordinance in Hong Kong', in *29 Journal of International Arbitration*, no. **6** (2012), pp. 715–722.

Figueres, D. J. 'Multi-Tiered Dispute Resolution Clauses in ICC Arbitration: Introduction and Commentary', in *14 ICC International Court of Arbitration Bulletin*, no. **1** (2003), pp. 71–74.

Gaillard, E. 'The Consolidation of Arbitral Proceedings and Court Proceedings', in *14 ICC International Court of Arbitration Bulletin, Complex Arbitrations – Special Supplement* (2003), pp. 35–42.

Gaillard, E. and Pinsolle, P. 'The ICC Pre-Arbitral Referee: First Practical Experiences', in *20 Arbitration International*, no. **1** (2004), pp. 13–37.

Galloway, P., Martinez, L. and Marra, M. 'Dispute Resolution under FIDIC – The Parties' Options', in *9 Transnational Dispute Management (TDM)*, no. **7** (December 2012), pp. 1–15, https://www.adr.org/aaa/ShowPDF?doc=ADRSTAGE2009402 (accessed 24 July 2016).

Gravel, S. 'Multiparty Arbitration and Multiple Arbitrations', in *7 ICC International Court of Arbitration Bulletin*, no. **2** (1996), pp. 45–53.

Habegger, P. 'The Revised Swiss Rules on International Arbitration – An Overview of the Major Changes', in *30 ASA Bulletin*, no. **2** (2012), pp. 269–311.

Hanotiau, B. 'Arbitration and Bank Guarantees. An Illustration of the Issue of Consent to Arbitration in Multicontract-Multiparty Disputes', in *16 Journal of International Arbitration*, no. **2** (1999), pp. 15–23.

Hanotiau, B. 'Multiparty – Multicontract Arbitration: A General Presentation with Special Emphasis on Energy Disputes', in *The Lebanese Review of Arbitration*, no. **27** (2003), pp. 6–10.

Hanotiau, B. 'Non-signatories, Group of Companies and Group of Contracts in Selected Asian Countries: A Case Law Analysis', in *32 Journal of International Arbitration*, no. **6** (2015), pp. 571–619.

Hanotiau, B. 'Problems Raised by Complex Arbitrations Involving Multiple Contracts-Parties-Issues, An Analysis', in *18 Journal of International Arbitration*, no. **3** (2001), pp. 251–360.

Hanotiau, B. 'The Res Judicata Effect of Arbitral Awards', in *14 ICC International Court of Arbitration Bulletin, Complex Arbitrations – Special Supplement* (2003), pp. 43–51.

Hardy, C. 'Multi-Party Arbitration: Exceptional Problems Need Exceptional Solutions', in *66 Arbitration: The Journal of the Chartered Institute of Arbitrators*, no. **1** (2000), pp. 15–20.

Hascher, D. 'Consolidation of Arbitration by American Courts: Fostering or Hampering International Commercial Arbitration, in *1 Journal of International Arbitration*, no. **2** (1984), pp. 127–144.

Hök, G.-S. 'Dispute Adjudication in Civil Law Countries – Phantom or Effective Dispute Resolution Method?' in *28 International Construction Law Review*, part **4** (2011), pp. 413–438.

Jarvin, S. 'Consolidated Arbitrations, the New York Arbitration Convention and the Dutch Arbitration Act 1986 – a Critique of Dr. van den Berg', in *3 Arbitration International*, no. **3** (1987), pp. 254–257.

Kazutake, O. 'Party Autonomy in International Commercial Arbitration: Consolidation of Multiparty and Classwide Arbitration', in *9 Annual Survey of International & Comparative Law*, no. **1** (2003), pp. 188–226, http://digitalcommons.law.ggu.edu/cgi/viewcontent.cgi?article=1077&context=annlsurvey (accessed 26 July 2016).

Kim, K. and Mitchenson, J. 'Voluntary Third-Party Intervention in International Arbitration for Construction Disputes: A Contextual Approach to Jurisdictional Issues', in *30 Journal of International Arbitration*, no. **4** (2013), pp. 407–430.

Koch, C. 'Judicial Activism and the Limits of Institutional Arbitration in Multiparty Disputes', in *28 ASA Bulletin*, no. **2** (2010), pp. 380–391.

Kondev, D. H. 'Do Recent Overhauls of Arbitration Rules Respond to the Need for Multi-Party Arbitration in the Construction Industry?', in *32 International Construction Law Review*, no. **1** (2015), pp. 63–94.

Kondev, D. H. 'Is Dispute Adjudication under FIDIC Contracts for Major Works Indeed a Precondition to Arbitration?', in *31 International Construction Law Review*, part **3** (2014), pp. 256–268.

Kondev, D. H. 'Joint Adjudication of Related Disputes under NEC3', in *10 Construction Law International*, no. **4** (2015), pp. 13–18.

Kondev, D. H. 'Statutory Approaches to Multi-Party / Multi-Contract Construction Arbitration', in *19 The Vindobona Journal of International Commercial Law and Arbitration*, no. **1** (2015), pp. 31–54.

Kratochvilova, E. and Mendelblat, M., 'Testing the Water – A New FIDIC Subcontract', in *28 International Construction Law Review*, part **1** (2011), pp. 47–66.

Leboulanger, P. 'Multi-Contract Arbitration', in *13 Journal of International Arbitration*, no. **4** (1996), pp. 43–99.

Lécuyer-Thieffry, C. 'First Court Ruling on the ICC Pre-Arbitral Referee Procedure', in *20 Journal of International Arbitration*, issue **6** (2003), pp. 599–607.

Lewis, D. 'The Hong Kong Arbitration Ordinance – Proposed Changes', in *5 Asian International Arbitration Journal*, no. **2** (2009), pp. 109–141.

Lloyd, H. 'Some Thoughts on NEC3', in *25 International Construction Law Review*, no. **4** (2008), pp. 468–483.

Lu, S. 'The New CIETAC Arbitration Rules of 2012', in *29 Journal of International Arbitration* Volume, no. **3** (2012), pp. 299–322.

Meredith, I. and Birch, M. 'The ICC's pre-arbitral referee procedure. How valuable is it?', in *Cross-border Quarterly, January–March* 2008, pp. 49–53, http://www.klgates.com/files/Publication/ab0be67f-01ef-4206-9c12-6e91f5b4837e/Presentation/PublicationAttachment/bae41c65-1f1b-43c3-b963-7de5c496b5bc/article_meredith_icc_0108.pdf (accessed 24 July 2016).

Miller, H. 'Consolidation in Hong Kong: the Shui On Case', in *3 Arbitration International*, no. **1** (1987), pp. 87–90.

Naegeli, G. and Schmitz, C. 'Switzerland: Strict Test for the Extension of Arbitration Agreements to Non-Signatories' in *7 Zeitschrift für Schiedsverfahren*, no. **4** (2009), pp. 185–188.

Ness, A. and Peden, D. '*Arbitration Developments: Defects and Solutions*', in *22 The Construction Lawyer*, no. **10** (2001), pp. 10–17, 44–47.

Nicklisch, F. 'Multi-party Arbitration and Dispute Resolution in Major Industrial Projects', in *11 Journal of International Arbitration*, no. **4** (1994), pp. 57–72.

Nottage, L. and Garnett, R. 'Top 20 Things to Change in or around International Arbitration Act', in *6 Asian International Arbitration Journal*, no. **1** (2010), pp. 1–43.

Piers, M. and De Meulemeester, D. 'The Adoption of the UNCITRAL Model Law Encourages Arbitration in Belgium', in *b-Arbitra (Belgian Review of Arbitration)*, no. **2** (2013), pp. 367–404.

Platte, M. 'When Should an Arbitrator Join Cases?', in *18 International Arbitration*, no. **1** (2002), pp. 67–81.

Rethman, C. M. and Lim, W. T. 'Some Contractual Approaches to the Problem of Inconsistent Awards in Multi-Party, Multi-Contract Arbitration Proceedings', in *1 Asian International Arbitration Journal*, no. **2** (2005), pp. 161–168.

Saunders, K. and Mosey, D. 'PPC2000: Association of Consultant Architects Standard Form of Project Partnering Contract', in *2 Lean Construction Journal*, no. **2** (2005), pp. 62–66, http://www.leanconstruction.org/media/docs/lcj/LCJ_05_004.pdf (accessed 24 July 2016).

Schöer, H. '"*Something is rotten in the state of Denmark" – was Shakespeare right?*' in *4 Construction Law International*, no. **2** (2009), pp. 6–8.

Schwartz, E. 'Multi-Party Arbitration and the ICC: in the Wake of Dutco', in *10 Journal of International Arbitration*, no. **3** (1993), pp. 5–19.

Schwartz, F. and Konrad, C. 'The New Vienna Rules' in *23 Arbitration International*, no. **4** (2007), pp. 601–643.

Schwarz, F. and Konrad, C. 'The Revised Vienna Rules. An Overview of Some Significant Changes (and a Preview of the New Austrian Arbitration Law 2014)', in *31 ASA Bulletin*, no. **4** (2013), pp. 797–811.

Seppälä, C. 'International Construction Contract Disputes: Commentary on ICC Awards Dealing with the FIDIC International Conditions of Contract', in *9 ICC International Court of Arbitration Bulletin*, no. **2** (1998), pp. 32–45.

Seppälä, C. 'International Construction Contract Disputes: Commentary on ICC Awards Dealing with the FIDIC International Conditions of Contract', in *International Construction Law Review*, no. **3** (1999), pp. 347–353.

Seppälä, C. 'International Construction Contract Disputes: Third Commentary on ICC Awards', in *23 ICC International Court of Arbitration Bulletin*, no. **2** (2012), pp. 23–45.

Seppälä, C. 'Multi-party arbitrations at risk in France', in *12 International Financial Law Review* (1993), pp. 33–35.

Seppälä, C. 'The Arbitration Clause in FIDIC Contracts for Major Works', in *22 International Construction Law Review*, part **1** (2005), pp. 4–15.

Seppälä, C. 'The New FIDIC International Civil Engineering Sub-Contract', in *12 International Construction Law Review*, part **1** (1995), pp. 5–22.

Seppälä, C. and Gogek, D. 'Multi-Party Arbitration under the ICC Rules', in *8 International Financial Law Review* (1989), pp. 32–34.

Siig, K. M. 'Multi-party Arbitration in International Trade: Problems and Solutions', in *1 International Journal of Liability and Scientific Enquiry*, no. **1**/2 (2007), pp. 72–84.

Stackpool-Moore, R. 'Asian Arbitration: Positive Developments in Hong Kong, in *11 Zeitschrift für Schiedsverfahren*, no. **5** (2013), pp. 279–280.

Stippl, C. 'International Multi-party Arbitration: The Role of Party Autonomy', in *7 The American Review of International Arbitration*, no. **1** (1996), pp. 47–69.

Strong, S. 'Research and Practice in International Commercial Arbitration: Special Skills, Special Sources', in *20 The American Review of International Arbitration*, no. **2** (2009), pp. 119–158.

Tao, J. and Zhong, M. 'A Quick Read of the CIETAC Arbitration Rules 2015', in *31 Arbitration International*, no. **3** (2015), pp. 455–463.

Ten Cate, I. 'Multi-party and Multi-contract Arbitrations: Procedural Mechanisms and Interpretation of Arbitration Agreements under U.S. Law', in *15 The American Review of International Arbitration*, no. **1** (2004), pp. 133–159.

Thomson, C. and Finn, A. 'International Commercial Arbitration: A Canadian Perspective', in *18 Arbitration International*, no. **2** (2002), pp. 205–218.

Ugarte, R. and Bevilacqua, T. 'Ensuring Party Equality in the Process of Designating Arbitrators in Multi-Party Arbitration: An Update on the Governing Provisions', in *27 Journal of International Arbitration*, no. **1** (2010), pp. 9–49.

Van den Berg, A. J. 'Consolidation Arbitrations, the New York Arbitration Convention and the Dutch Arbitration Act 1986 – A Replique to Mr Jarvin', in *3 Arbitration International*, no. **3** (1987), pp. 257–262.

Van den Berg, J. 'Consolidated Arbitrations and the 1958 New York Arbitration Convention', in *2 Arbitration International*, no. **4** (1986), pp. 367–369.

Van Haersolte-Van Hof, J. 'Consolidation under the English Arbitration Act 1996: A View from the Netherlands', in *13 Arbitration International*, no. **4** (1997), pp. 427–430.

Veeder, V. V. 'More News from the Front-Line – The Second Shui On Case', in *3 Arbitration International*, no. **3** (1987), pp. 262–266.

Veeder, V. V. 'Multi-Party Disputes: Consolidation under English Law *The Vimeira* – a Sad Forensic Fable, in *2 Arbitration International*, no. **4** (1986), pp. 310–322.

Verbist, H. 'Multiparty and Multicontract Arbitration under the 2013 CEPANI Arbitration Rules', in *17 Vindobona Journal of International Commercial Law and Arbitration*, no. **1** (2014), pp. 1–24.

Verbist, H. 'New Belgian Arbitration Law of 24 June 2013 and New CEPANI Arbitration Rules of 1 January 2013', in *30 Journal of International Arbitration*, no. **5** (2013), pp. 597–618.

Voser, N. 'Overview of the Most Important Changes in the Revised ICC Arbitration Rules', in *29 ASA Bulletin*, no. **4** (2011), pp. 783–820.

Wallace, R. 'Consolidated Arbitration in the United States, Recent Authority Requires Consent of the Parties', in *10 Journal of International Arbitration*, no. **4** (1993), pp. 5–17.

Wöss, H. 'The ICC Model Turnkey Contract for Major Projects', in *3 Construction Law International*, no. **2** (2008), pp. 6–11.

IV. International conventions and arbitration laws

International conventions and related sources

Convention for the Protection of Human Rights and Fundamental Freedoms of 4 November 1950, http://www.coe.int/fr/web/conventions/full-list/-/conventions/rms/0900001680063765 (accessed 24 July 2016).

Convention on the Recognition and Enforcement of Foreign Arbitral Awards, 10 June 1958, http://www.uncitral.org/pdf/english/texts/arbitration/NY-conv/XXII_1_e.pdf (accessed 24 July 2016).

Recommendation Regarding the Interpretation of Article II, Paragraph 2, and Article VII, Paragraph 1, of the Convention on the Recognition and Enforcement of Foreign Arbitral Awards, adopted on 7 July 2006, http://www.uncitral.org/pdf/english/texts/arbitration/NY-conv/A2E.pdf (accessed 24 July 2016).

Arbitration Laws and Related Sources

1982 Hong Kong Arbitration Ordinance, Chapter 341, Section 6B, http://oelawhk.lib.hku.hk/items/show/3286 (accessed 1 August 2016).

2011 Hong Kong Arbitration Ordinance (Cap. 609), http://www.legislation.gov.hk/blis_pdf.nsf/6799165D2FEE3FA94825755E0033E532/C05151C760F783AD482577D900541075/$FILE/CAP_609_e_b5.pdf (accessed 24 July 2016).

Arbitration (Scotland) Act 2010, http://www.legislation.gov.uk/asp/2010/1/contents (accessed 24 July 2016).

Australian International Arbitration Act 1974 (Act no. 136 of 1974), https://www.comlaw.gov.au/Details/C2011C00342 (accessed 24 July 2016).

Belgian Judicial Code, Chapter 6: Arbitration, English translation http://www.cepani.be/en/arbitration/belgian-judicial-code-provisions (accessed 24 July 2016).

English Arbitration Act 1996, http://www.legislation.gov.uk/ukpga/1996/23/contents (accessed 24 July 2016).

Explanatory Note by the UNCITRAL Secretariat on the 1985 Model Law on International Commercial Arbitration as amended in 2006, http://www.uncitral.org/pdf/english/texts/arbitration/ml-arb/MLARB-explanatoryNote20-9-07.pdf (accessed 24 July 2016).

French Code of Civil Procedure, Book IV Arbitration, Title II – International Commercial Arbitration, English translation http://www.iaiparis.com/pdf/FRENCH_LAW_ON_ARBITRATION.pdf (accessed 24 July 2016).

French Law on Subcontracting (n 75-1334), English translation www.legifrance.gouv.fr/content/download/1952/13689/version/4/file/Code_23.pdf&prev=search (accessed 24 July 2016).

German Arbitration Act, English translation http://arbitrationlaw.com/files/free_pdfs/German%20Arbitration%20Act.pdf (accessed 24 July 2016).

Housing Grants, Construction and Regeneration Act 1996, http://www.legislation.gov.uk/ukpga/1996/53/contents (accessed 24 July 2016).

Irish Arbitration Act 2010, http://www.irishstatutebook.ie/eli/2010/act/1/enacted/en/pdf (accessed 24 July 2016).

Italian Civil Procedure Code, Book IV, Section VIII, an English summary of its provisions is available at http://www.arbitration-icca.org/media/4/67832367324249/media012571315850070bernini_arbitration_italy.pdf (accessed 24 July 2016).

Malaysian Arbitration Act 2005 (Act 646), http://www.newyorkconvention.org/11165/web/files/document/1/6/16298.pdf (accessed 24 July 2016).

New Zealand Arbitration Act 1996, http://www.legislation.govt.nz/act/public/1996/0099/latest/DLM403277.html (accessed 24 July 2016).

Polish Code of Civil Procedure, English translation http://sakig.pl/uploads/upfiles/pdf/kpc-ang.pdf (accessed 24 July 2016).

Singapore Arbitration Act 2001 (No. 37 of 2001), http://statutes.agc.gov.sg/aol/search/display/view.w3p;page=0;query=DocId%3A%22e8687d02-1aae-42ff-9afa-92c086e168c0%22%20Status%3Apublished%20Depth%3A0%20TransactionTime%3A20151010000000;rec=0;whole=yes (accessed 24 July 2016).

Spanish Arbitration Act 2003 (Act 60/2003 on Arbitration), English translation http://www.voldgiftsforeningen.dk/Admin/Public/Download.aspx?file=Files%2FFiler%2F2011%2FNationale_love%2FSpanien.pdf (accessed 24 July 2016).

The Netherlands Code of Civil Procedure, English translation of its part concerning arbitration is available at http://www.nai-nl.org/downloads/Text%20Dutch%20Code%20Civil%20Procedure.pdf (accessed 24 July 2016).

UNCITRAL Model Law on International Commercial Arbitration, 1985, as amended in 2006, http://www.uncitral.org/pdf/english/texts/arbitration/ml-arb/07-86998_Ebook.pdf (accessed 24 July 2016).

Canadian International Arbitration Acts

Alberta International Commercial Arbitration Act, http://www.qp.alberta.ca/documents/Acts/I05.pdf (accessed 24 July 2016).

British Columbia International Arbitration Act, http://www.bclaws.ca/civix/document/id/complete/statreg/96233_01 (accessed 24 July 2016).

International Commercial Arbitration Act (Northwest Territories), https://www.canlii.org/en/nu/laws/stat/rsnwt-nu-1988-c-i-6/latest/part-1/rsnwt-nu-1988-c-i-6-part-1.pdf, (accessed 24 July 2016).

Manitoba International Commercial Arbitration Act, https://web2.gov.mb.ca/laws/statutes/ccsm/c151e.php (accessed 24 July 2016).

New Brunswick International Commercial Arbitration Act, http://laws.gnb.ca/en/showfulldoc/cs/2011-c.176//20120307 (accessed 24 July 2016).

Newfoundland and Labrador International Commercial Arbitration Act, https://www.canlii.org/en/nl/laws/stat/rsnl-1990-c-i-15/latest/rsnl-1990-c-i-15.html (accessed 24 July 2016).

Nunavut International Commercial Arbitration Act, https://www.canlii.org/en/nu/laws/stat/rsnwt-nu-1988-c-i-6/latest/rsnwt-nu-1988-c-i-6.html (accessed 24 July 2016).

Ontario International Commercial Arbitration Act, https://www.ontario.ca/laws/statute/90i09 (accessed 24 July 2016).

Nova Scotia International Commercial Arbitration Act, http://nslegislature.ca/legc/statutes/internlc.htm (accessed 24 July 2016).

Prince Edward Island International Commercial Arbitration Act, http://www.gov.pe.ca/law/statutes/pdf/i-05.pdf (accessed 24 July 2016).

Saskatchewan International Commercial Arbitration Act, http://www.qp.gov.sk.ca/documents/English/Statutes/Statutes/I10-2.pdf (accessed 24 July 2016).

Yukon International Commercial Arbitration Act, http://www.gov.yk.ca/legislation/acts/incoar.pdf (accessed 24 July 2016).

United States Legislation

California Code of Civil Procedure, http://www.leginfo.ca.gov/.html/ccp_table_of_contents.html (accessed 24 July 2016).

Federal Arbitration Act (USA), http://sccinstitute.com/media/37104/the-federal-arbitration-act-usa.pdf (accessed 24 July 2016).

General Laws of Massachusetts, https://malegislature.gov/Laws/GeneralLaws (accessed 24 July 2016).

Georgia International Commercial Arbitration Code (Senate Bill 383), http://www.legis.ga.gov/Legislation/20112012/127687.pdf (accessed 24 July 2016).

New Jersey Alternative Procedure for Dispute Resolution Act, http://www.mediationandarbitrationadr.com/the-new-jersey-alternative-procedure-for-dispute-resolution-act/ (accessed 24 July 2016).

Ohio Revised Code, http://codes.ohio.gov/ (accessed 24 July 2016).

Texas Civil Practice and Remedies Code, http://www.statutes.legis.state.tx.us/?link=CP (accessed 24 July 2016).

Uniform Arbitration Act (USA) drafted by the National Conference of Commissioners on Uniform State Laws with Preparatory Note and Comments, http://www.uniformlaws.org/shared/docs/arbitration/arbitration_final_00.pdf (accessed 24 July 2016).

V. Arbitration Rules

2000 CIArb Arbitration Rules, http://www.ciarb.org/docs/default-source/das/arbitration/ciarb-arbitration-rules-2000.pdf?sfvrsn=6 (accessed 24 July 2016) (*replaced by the 2015 CIArb Arbitration Rules*).

2015 CIArb Arbitration Rules, in force as from 1 December 2015, https://www.ciarb.org/docs/default-source/das/ciarb-arbitration-rules.pdf?sfvrsn=2 (accessed 24 July 2016).

Arbitration Rules of the Arbitration Institute of the Stockholm Chamber of Commerce or SCC Rules, in force as from 1 January 2010, http://sccinstitute.com/media/40120/arbitrationrules_eng_webbversion.pdf (accessed 24 July 2016).

Arbitration Rules of the Arbitration Institute of the Stockholm Chamber of Commerce, Draft for Public Consultation, 26 April 2016, http://www.sccinstitute.com/media/93603/16-draft-14-26042016-arbitration-rules-2017_for-consultation.pdf (accessed 22 October 2016).

Arbitration Rules of the Belgian Centre for Arbitration and Mediation, in force as from 1 January 2013, http://www.cepani.be/sites/default/files/images/hayez_reglement_arbitrage_cepani_en_dec2014_1.1.pdf (accessed 24 July 2016).

Arbitration Rules of the German Institution of Arbitration of 1998 (DIS Rules), in force as from 1 July 1998, http://www.dis-arb.de/en/16/rules/dis-arbitration-rules-98-id10 (accessed 24 July 2016).

Arbitration Rules of the Singapore International Arbitration Centre (5th edn), in force as from 1 April 2013, http://www.siac.org.sg/our-rules/rules (accessed 24 July 2016).

Arbitration Rules of the Singapore International Arbitration Centre (6th edn), in force as from 1 August 2016, http://www.siac.org.sg/our-rules/rules/siac-rules-2016 (accessed 22 October 2016).

China International Economic and Trade Arbitration Commission CIETAC Arbitration Rules, in force as from 1 January 2015, http://cn.cietac.org/rules/rules.pdf (accessed 1 August 2016).

China International Economic and Trade Arbitration Commission CIETAC Arbitration Rules, in force as from 1 May 2012 (*replaced by the 2015 CIETAC Rules*), http://cn.cietac.org/rules/rule_E.pdf (accessed 1 August 2016).

Construction Industry Arbitration Rules and Mediation Procedures, Including Procedures for Large, Complex Construction Disputes, in force as from 1 July 2015, https://www.adr.org/aaa/ShowProperty?nodeId=/UCM/ADRSTG_004219&revision=latestreleased (accessed 1 August 2016).

Construction Industry Model Arbitration Rules, CIMAR 1998, 1st edn 1998, http://www.constructionarbitrators.org/sites/default/files/local/browser/documents/cimar_final.pdf (accessed 24 July 2016).

FOSFA Rules for Small Claims Single Tier, in force as from 1 September 2008, http://www.fosfa.org/arbitration/guide-and-rules/ (accessed 24 July 2016).

FOSFA Rules of Arbitration and Appeal, in force as from 1 January 2012, http://www.fosfa.org/arbitration/guide-and-rules/ (accessed 24 July 2016).

GAFTA Arbitration Rules No. 125, in force as from 1 June 2014, http://www.gafta.com/write/MediaUploads/Contracts/2014/125_2014.pdf (accessed 24 July 2016).

Hong Kong International Arbitration Centre Administered Arbitration Rules, in force as from 1 November 2013, http://hkiac.org/arbitration/rules-practice-notes/administered-arbitration-rules (accessed 24 July 2016).

ICC Rules for a Pre-arbitral Referee Procedure, in force as from 1 January 1990, http://www.iccwbo.org/products-and-services/arbitration-and-adr/pre-arbitral-referee/rules-for-a-pre-arbitral-referee-procedure/ (accessed 24 July 2016).

ICDR Rules, in force as from 1 June 2014, https://www.icdr.org/icdr/ShowProperty?nodeId=/UCM/ADRSTAGE2020868&revision=latestreleased (accessed 24 July 2016).

ICE Arbitration Procedure (2010), published by the Institution of Civil Engineers, https://www.ice.org.uk/ICEDevelopmentWebPortal/media/Documents/Disciplines%20and%20Resources/09-2-ICE-Arbitration-procedure-2012-04-30.pdf (accessed 24 July 2016).
IChemE Arbitration Rules, The Pink Book, 4th edn 2005, published by the Institution of Chemical Engineers.
JAMS Engineering and Construction Arbitration Rules and Procedures, in force as from 15 November 2014, http://www.jamsadr.com/rules-construction-arbitration/ (accessed 24 July 2016).
JAMS International Arbitration Rules, in force as from 1 August 2011, http://www.jamsinternational.com/arbitration-rules (accessed 1 August 2016).
Japan Commercial Arbitration Association Commercial Arbitration Rules, in force as from 1 February 2014, http://www.jcaa.or.jp/e/arbitration/docs/Arbitration_Rules_2014e.pdf (accessed 24 July 2016).
JCT/CIMAR 2011 Construction Industry Arbitration Rules 2011, http://www.jctltd.co.uk/docs/JCT_CIMAR_2011.pdf (accessed 24 July 2016).
LCIA Arbitration Rules, in force as from 1 October 2014, http://www.lcia.org/Dispute_Resolution_Services/lcia-arbitration-rules-2014.aspx (accessed 24 July 2016).
Practice Note on Consolidation supplementing the Hong Kong International Arbitration Centre Administered Arbitration Rules, in force as from 1 January 2016, http://220.241.190.1/en/arbitration/arbitration-rules-guidelines/practice-note-on-consolidation-of-arbitrations (accessed 1 August 2016).
Procedural Regulations of Arbitration of the Abu Dhabi Commercial Conciliation and Arbitration Centre, in force as from 1 September 2013, available http://globalarbitrationreview.com/cdn/files/gar/articles/New_ADCCAC_Rules.pdf (accessed 24 July 2016).
Rules of Arbitration by the International Chamber of Commerce, in force as from 1 January 2012, http://www.iccwbo.org/uploadedFiles/Court/Arbitration/other/rules_arb_english.pdf (accessed 24 July 2016).
Rules of Arbitration Procedure adopted by the Board of the Danish Institute of Arbitration, in force as from 1 May 2013, http://voldgiftsinstituttet.dk/wp-content/uploads/2015/01/rules_1_may_2013_-_pdf-uden-logo.pdf (accessed 24 July 2016).
Rules of Arbitration Procedure for Disputes Relating to Building and Construction (VBA Arbitration Rules), in force as from 1 January 2011, an English version of the rules is available at http://voldgift.dk/wordpress/wp-content/uploads/2014/09/C-Voldgiftbehandling-2010-Engelsk.pdf (accessed 24 July 2016).
Swiss Rules of International Arbitration (Swiss Rules) of the Swiss Chambers of Commerce Association for Arbitration and Mediation, in force as from 1 June 2012, https://www.swissarbitration.org/sa/download/SRIA_english_2012.pdf (accessed 24 July 2016).
UNCITRAL Arbitration Rules (as revised in 2010), http://www.uncitral.org/pdf/english/texts/arbitration/arb-rules-revised/arb-rules-revised-2010-e.pdf (accessed 24 July 2016).
VIAC Rules of Arbitration and Mediation, in force as from 1 July 2013, http://www.viac.eu/en/arbitration/arbitration-rules-vienna (accessed 24 July 2016).

VI. Court Decisions

Canada

Javor v. Francoeur 2003 BCSC 350, http://www.newyorkconvention1958.org/index.php?lvl=notice_display&id=957# (accessed 24 July 2016).

Western Oil Sands Inc. Allianz Insurance Co. of Canada [2004] A.J. No. 85, 2004 ABQB 79, https://wcart.files.wordpress.com/2012/03/western_oil_sands_inc_v_allianz_insurance_co_of_canada.pdf (accessed 24 Julyl 2016).

England

Abu Dhabi Gas Liquefaction Co Ltd .v. Eastern Bechtel Corp., in *21 Building Law Reports* (1983), pp. 117–126.

Bay Hotel & Resort Ltd. v. Cavalier Construction Co. Ltd. [2001] APP.L.R., http://www.nadr.co.uk/articles/published/ArbLR/Bay%20Hotel%20v%20Cavalier%202001.pdf (accessed 24 July 2016).

Channel Tunnel Group Ltd. v. Balfour Beatty Construction Ltd. And others, in *56 Building Law Reports* (1991), pp. 19–42.

City & General (Holborn) Ltd. v. AYH Plc., in *56 Building Law Reports* (2006), pp. 55–65, http://www.nadr.co.uk/articles/published/AdjudLawR/City%20&%20General%20v%20AYH%202005.pdf (accessed 24 July 2016).

Dredging & Construction Co Ltd & Delta Civil Engineering Co Ltd., in *68 Construction Law Review*, pp. 87–95, http://www.nadr.co.uk/articles/published/ArbitrationLawReports/Dredging%20v%20Delta%201999.pdf (accessed 24 July 2016).

Dredging & Construction Co Ltd & Delta Civil Engineering Co Ltd. (No. 2), in *72 Construction Law Review*, pp. 99–117.

Enco Civil Engineering Ltd. v. Zeus International Development Ltd., in *56 Building Law Reports* (1991), p. 43.

Erith Contractors Ltd. v. Costain Civil Engineering Ltd., in the *Arbitration and Dispute Resolution Law Journal (ADRLJ)* (1994), pp. 123–128.

Great Ormond Street Hospital NHS Trust v. Secretary of State for Health and others, in *56 Construction Law Reports* (1997), pp. 1–30.

Higgs & Hill Building Ltd v. Campbell Denis Ltd, in *28 Building Law Reports* (1982), pp. 47–75.

Hyundai Engineering and Construction Co Ltd. v. Active Building and Civil Construction Pte Ltd, in *45 Building Law Reports* (1989), pp. 62–71.

Lafarge Redlands Aggregates Ltd (Formerly Redland Aggregates Ltd) v. Shephard Hill Civil Engineering Ltd, Judgment by the House of Lords, http://www.publications.parliament.uk/pa/ld199900/ldjudgmt/jd000727/lafarg-1.htm (accessed 24 July 2016).

M J Gleeson Group Plc v. Wyatt of Snetterton Ltd., in *72 Building Law Reports* (1995), pp. 15–25.

M J Gleeson Plc v. Wyatt of Snetterton Ltd., An Editorial Case Note, in *12 International Construction Law Review*, part **2** (1995), pp. 341–346.

Multi-Construction (Southern) Ltd v. Stent Foundations Ltd and Others, in *41 Building Law Reports* (1988), pp. 98–109.

Oxford Shipping Co Ltd. v. Nippon Yusen Kaisha (The Eastern Saga), in *2 Lloyd's Law Reports* (1984), ref. p. 373, digested in *2 Journal of International Arbitration*, no.**1** (1985), pp. 79–81.

Property Investments (Developments) Ltd. v. Byfield Building Services Ltd, in *31 Building Law Reports* (1986), pp. 47–56.

Taunton-Collins v. Cromie and Others, in *1 The Weekly Law Reports* (1964), pp. 633–638.

Trafalgar House Construction (Regions) Ltd. v. Railtrack plc, in *76 Building Law Reports* (1995), pp. 55–90.

France

Siemens AG and BKMI Industrienlagen Gmbh v. Dutco Construction Company, Cour de Cassation, 7 January 1992 (*XVIII Yearbook Commercial Arbitration*, 1993, pp. 140–142).

Hong Kong

Chun Wo Building Construction Ltd. v. China Merchants Tower Co Ltd & Others [2000] 2 HKC 255.
Dickson Construction Co. Ltd. v. Schindler Lifts (HK) Ltd. & Another (unreported, MP No. 545 of 1992).
Karaha Bodas Co. v. Perusahaan Pertambangan Minyak Dan Gas Bumi Negara, in *21 ASA Bulletin* no. 3 (2003), pp. 667–684.
Linfield Ltd. v. Brooke Hillier Parker [2003] 2 HKC 624.
Re Shui On Construction C. Ltd. And Schindler Lifts (HK) Ltd. [1986] Hong Kong Law Reports 1177.
Shui On Construction Co. Ltd. v. Dah Chong Hong Ltd. (Unreported, MP No. 1275 of 1987).

Singapore

PT First Media TBK v. Astro Nusantara International BV & Others [2013] SGCA 57 in *1 Singapore Law Reports* (2014), pp. 372–452, https://leeshih.files.wordpress.com/2013/11/judgment-ca150151.pdf (accessed 1 August 2016).

United States

American Centennial Ins. Co. v. National Casualty Co., 951 F.2d 107 (6th Cir. 1991), http://law.justia.com/cases/federal/appellate-courts/F2/951/107/258151/ (accessed 25 July 2016).
Atlas Plastering, Inc. v. Superior Court of Alameda County, 72 Cal. App. 3d 63, 68, 140 Cal. Rptr. 59, 63-64 (1977), http://law.justia.com/cases/california/court-of-appeal/3d/72/63.html (accessed 25 July 2016).
Baesler v. Continental Grain Co., 900 F. 2d 1193 (8th Cir. 1990), http://www.leagle.com/decision/1F2d1193_11904/BAESLER%20v.%20CONTINENTAL%20GRAIN%20CO (accessed 25 July 2016).
Balfour, Guthrie and Company, Limited v. Commercial Metals Co., 93 Wn.2d 199 (1980), 607 P.2d 856, http://law.justia.com/cases/washington/supreme-court/1980/46338-1.html (accessed 25 July 2016).
Bateman Construction, Inc., v. Haitsuka Brothers, Limited, 889 P.2d 58 (1995), 77 Haw. 481, http://law.justia.com/cases/hawaii/supreme-court/1995/17745-2.html (accessed 25 July 2016).
Bay County Building Authority & Spence Brothers, 140 Mich. App. 182 (1984), 326 N.W.2d 739, http://www.leagle.com/decision/MichApp182_1299/BAY%20COUNTY%20BUILDING%20AUTH.%20v.%20SPENCE%20BROS (accessed 25 July 2016).
Biber Partnership v. Diamond Hill Joint Venture LLC, 404 N.J. Super. 96, 960 A.2d 774 (App. Div. 2008), http://law.justia.com/cases/new-jersey/appellate-division-published/2008/a1766-07-opn.html (accessed 25 July 2016).
Blimpie International Inc. v. Blimpie of the Keys, 371 F.Supp.2d 469 (S.D.N.Y. 2005), http://www.leagle.com/decision/FSupp2d469_1784/BLIMPIE%20INTERN.,%20INC.%20v.%20BLIMPIE%20OF%20THE%20KEYS (accessed 25 July 2016).
Certain Underwriters at Lloyd's London v. Westchester Fire Ins. Co., 489 F.3d 580 (3rd Cir. 2007), http://law.justia.com/cases/federal/appellate-courts/F3/489/580/574065/ (accessed 25 July 2016).
Children's Hospital of Philadelphia v. American Arbitration Association, 231 Pa. Super. 230, 331 A.2d 848 (1974), http://www.leagle.com/decision/PaSuper230_1426/CHILDREN'S%20HOSP.%20of%20PHILA.%20v.%20AM.%20ARB.%20ASSN (accessed 25 July 2016).
Compania Espanola de Petroleos, S.A., v. Nereus Shipping, S.A., 527 F.2d 966 (2nd Cir. 1975), 1 (accessed 25 July 2016).

Conejo Valley Unified School District v. William Blurock & Partners, Inc., 169 Cal. Rptr. 102, Civ. 57894 (1980), http://law.justia.com/cases/california/court-of-appeal/3d/111/983.html (accessed 25 July 2016).

Connecticut General Life Insurance Co. v. Sun Life Assurance Co. of Canada, 210 F.3d 771, 775 (7th Cir. 2000), http://caselaw.findlaw.com/us-7th-circuit/1281923.html (accessed 25 July 2016).

Consolidated Pacific Engineering, Inc. v. Greater Anchorage Area Borough, 563 P.2d 252 (Alaska 1977), http://www.leagle.com/decision/P2d252_1813/CONSOLIDATED%20PAC.%20ENG'G%20v.%20GREATER%20ANCHORAGE%20AREA%20BOROUGH (accessed 25 July 2016).

County of Sullivan et al., v. Edward L. Nezelek, Inc., and Edward Durell Stone and Associates, 42 N.Y.2d 123, 366 N.E.2d 72, 397 N.Y.S.2d 371 (1977), http://law.justia.com/cases/new-york/court-of-appeals/1977/42-n-y-2d-123-0.html (accessed 25 July 2016).

Dean Witter Reynolds, Inc. v. Byrd, 470 U.S. 213, 221 (1985), https://supreme.justia.com/cases/federal/us/470/213/case.html (accessed 25 July 2016).

Del E. Webb Construction v. Richardson Hospital Authority, 823 F.2d 145 (5th Cir. 1987), http://law.justia.com/cases/federal/appellate-courts/F2/823/145/221658/ (accessed 25 July 2016).

Dockser v. Schwartzberg, 433 F.3d 421 (4th Cir. 2006), http://caselaw.findlaw.com/us-4th-circuit/1252061.html (accessed 25 July 2016).

Employers Insurance Co. of Wausau v. Century Indemnity Co., 443 F 3d 573 (2006), http://openjurist.org/443/f3d/573/employers-insurance-company-of-wausau-v-century-indemnity-company (accessed 25 July 2016).

Exber, Inc. v. Sletten Construction Company, 92 Nev. 721, 558 P.2d 517 (1976), http://law.justia.com/cases/nevada/supreme-court/1976/8236-1.html (accessed 25 July 2016).

Garden Grove Community Church v. Pittsburgh-Des Moines Steel Co. (1983) 140 Cal. App. 3d 251 [191 Cal. Rptr. 15], http://law.justia.com/cases/california/court-of-appeal/3d/140/251.html (accessed 25 July 2016).

Gavlik Construction Co. v. H.F. Campbell Co., 389 F.Supp. 551 (W.D. Pa. 1975), http://law.justia.com/cases/federal/district-courts/FSupp/389/551/1591873/ (accessed 25 July 2016).

Georgia Casualty & Surety Co. v. Excalibur Reinsurance Corp., Case No. 1:13-CV-00456-JEC (ND Ga, 12 March 2014), http://02ec4c5.netsolhost.com/blog/data/20/1/142/136/1957625/user/2137514/htdocs/blog/wp-content/uploads/2014/03/Georgia-Casualty-v.-Excalibur-3.13.2014-Order-and-Opinion.pdf (accessed 25 July 2016).

Glencore Limited v. Schnitzer Steel Products Co., 189 F.3d 264 (2nd Cir. 1999), http://caselaw.findlaw.com/us-2nd-circuit/1011784.html (accessed 25 July 2016).

Government of the United Kingdom of Great Britain v. *The Boeing Company*, 998 F.2d 68 (2nd Cir.1993), http://law.justia.com/cases/federal/appellate-courts/F2/998/68/48624/ (accessed 25 July 2016).

Green Tree Fin. Corp. v. Bazzle, 539 U.S. 444 (U.S. S.Ct. 2003), https://supreme.justia.com/cases/federal/us/539/444/case.pdf (accessed 25 July 2016).

Grover-Diamond Associates, Inc. v. AAA, 297 Minn. 324, 211, N.W.2d 787 (Minn. 1973).

Hoover Group, Inc. v. Probala & Associates, 710 F.Supp. 677,681 (N.D. Ohio 1989), http://law.justia.com/cases/federal/district-courts/FSupp/710/677/1462587/ (accessed 25 July 2016).

International Paper Co. v. Schwabedissen Maschinen & Anlagen Gmbh, 206 F.3d 411 (4th Cir. 2000), http://caselaw.findlaw.com/us-4th-circuit/1451869.html (accessed 25 July 2016).

James Steward Polshek & Associates v. Bergen County Iron Works, 142 N.J.Super. 516 (1976), 362 A.2d 63, http://law.justia.com/cases/new-jersey/appellate-division-published/1976/142-n-j-super-516-0.html (accessed 25 July 2016).

J. Brodie & Son, Inc. v. George A. Fuller Co., 16 Mich. App. 137, 167 N.W.2d 886 (1969), https://www.courtlistener.com/opinion/1932977/j-brodie-son-inc-v-george-a-fuller-co/ (accessed 25 July 2016).

Karaha Bodas Co. v. Perusahaan Pertambangan Minyak Dan Gas Bumi Negara, 364 F.3d 274 (5th Cir. 2004), in *23 ASA Bulletin* no. **2** (2005), pp. 360–378, http://caselaw.findlaw.com/us-5th-circuit/1207034.html (accessed 25 July 2016).

Litton Bionetics, Inc., v. Glen Construction Company, Inc., et. al, 292 Md. 34 (1981) 437 A.2d 208, http://www.leagle.com/decision/Md34_1321/LITTON%20BIONETICS%20v.%20GLEN%20CONSTR (accessed 25 July 2016).

Louisiana Stadium and Exposition District v. Huber, Hunt & Nichols, Inc., 349 So.2d 491 (La. App. 1977), http://www.leagle.com/decision/So2d491_1718/LA.%20STADIUM%20&%20EXPOSITION%20DIST.%20v.%20HUBER,%20HUNT%20&%20NICHOLS,%20INC (accessed 25 July 2016).

Matter of Chariot Textiles Corp., 21 A.D.2d 762 (N.Y. App. Div. 1964), https://casetext.com/case/matter-of-chariot-textiles-corp-1 (accessed 25 July 2016).

Matter of Kallas v. Milberg Weiss LLP, 61 A.D.3d 451 (2009), App. Div. N.Y.S.C., http://law.justia.com/cases/new-york/appellate-division-first-department/2009/2009-02683.html (accessed 25 July 2016).

Moses H. Cone Memorial Hospital v. Mercury Construction Corp., 460 U.S. 1 (1983), 103 S.Ct. 927, 74 L.Ed.2d 765, https://www.law.cornell.edu/supremecourt/text/460/1 (accessed 25 July 2016).

Nath v. Merrill Lynch, Pierce, Fenner & Smith Inc., WL 2438435, 4 (NY Sup, 21 May 2014), http://www.leagle.com/decision/In%20NYCO%2020140530361/NATH%20v.%20LYNCH (accessed 25 July 2016).

New England Energy Inc., v. Keystone Shipping Co., 855 F.2d 1 (1st Cir. 1988) cert. denied 489 U.S. 1077, 109 S.Ct.1527, 103 L.Ed.2d 832, http://openjurist.org/855/f2d/1/new-england-energy-inc-v-keystone-shipping-company-keystone-shipping-company (accessed 25 July 2016).

Pedcor Management Co., Inc. Welfare Benefit Plan v. Nations Personnel of Texas, Inc., 343 F.3d 355 (5th Cir. 2003), http://caselaw.findlaw.com/us-5th-circuit/1411299.html (accessed 25 July 2016).

Protective Life Insurance Corp. v. Lincoln National Life Insurance Corp., 873 F. 2d 281 (11th Cir. 1989), http://openjurist.org/873/f2d/281/protective-life-insurance-corporation-v-lincoln-national-life-insurance-corporation (accessed 25 July 2016).

Robinson v. Warner, 370 F. Supp. 828 (D.R.I. 1974), http://law.justia.com/cases/federal/district-courts/FSupp/370/828/1801675/ (accessed 25 July 2016).

Sarhank Group v. Oracle Corporation, 404 F.3d 657 (2nd Cir. 2005), http://www.newyorkconvention1958.org/index.php?lvl=notice_display&id=746 (accessed 25 July 2016).

Seretta Construction, Inc., v. Great American Insurance Co., 869 So. 2d 676 (Fla. Dist. Ct. App. 2004), https://www.courtlistener.com/opinion/1601984/seretta-const-inc-v-great-american-ins-co/ (accessed 25 July 2016).

Shaw's Supermarkets, Inc. v. United Food & Commercial Workers Union, 321 F.3d 251, 254 (1st Cir. 2003), http://openjurist.org/321/f3d/251/shaws-supermarkets-inc-v-united-food-and-commercial-workers-union-local (accessed 25 July 2016).

Sparwick Contracting, Inc., v. Tomasco Corporation, 335 N.J. Super. 73, 761 A.2d 90 (N.J. Super. App. Div. 2000), http://caselaw.findlaw.com/nj-superior-court-appellate-division/1372901.html (accessed 25 July 2016).

Stolt-Nielsen S.A. v. Animalfeeds Int'l Corp., 130 S.Ct. 1758, 1774 (U.S. S.Ct. 2010), http://www.supremecourt.gov/opinions/09pdf/08-1198.pdf (accessed 25 July 2016).

The North River Ins. Co. v. Philadelphia Reinsurance Corp., 63 F.3d 160 (2nd Cir. 1995), http://openjurist.org/63/f3d/160/north-river-insurance-company-v-philadelphia-reinsurance-corporation (accessed 25 July 2016).

The School District of Philadelphia v. Livingston Rosenwinkel, P.C., 690 A.2d 1321 (Pa. Commw. Ct. 1997), http://caselaw.findlaw.com/pa-commonwealth-court/1280458.html (accessed 25 July 2016).

The Stop & Shop Companies, Inc. vs. Gilbane Building Company, 364 Mass. 325, 304 N.E.2d 429 (1973), http://masscases.com/cases/sjc/364/364mass325.html (accessed 25 July 2016).
Travellers Casualty and Surety Company of America Inc. v. Long Bay Management Company, 58 Mass. App. Ct 786 (2003), http://masscases.com/cases/app/58/58massappct786.html (accessed 25 July 2016).
Vigo Steamship Corp. v. Marship Corp. of Monrovia, 26 N.Y.2d 157, 309 N.Y.S.2d 165, cert. denied, 400 U.S. 819 (1970), http://www.leagle.com/decision/197018326NY2d157_1161/MATTER%20OF%20VIGO%20CORP.%20(MARSHIP%20CORP.%20OF%20MONROVIA) (accessed 25 July 2016).
WM. C. Blanchard Co. v. Beach Concrete Co., 150 N.J. Super. 277, 375A.2d 675 (App. Div. 1977), http://www.leagle.com/decision/NJSuper277_1386/WM.%20BLANCHARD%20CO.%20v.%20BEACH%20CONCRETE%20CO.,%20INC (accessed 25 July 2016).
Weyerhauser Co. v. Western Shipping, 743 F.2d 635 (9th Cir. 1984), cert. denied 105 S.Ct. 544, 469 U.S. 1061, http://openjurist.org/743/f2d/635/weyerhaeuser-company-v-western-seas-shipping-co (accessed 25 July 2016).
Yuen v. The Superior Court of Los Angeles County, 121 Cal. App. 4th 1133 (2004), http://caselaw.findlaw.com/ca-court-of-appeal/1010328.html (accessed 25 July 2016).

VII. Arbitral Awards

Ad hoc award of 17 November 1994 in *Banque Arabe et Internationale d'Investissement* et. al. v. *Inter-Arab Investment Guarantee Corporation*, in XIII Yearbook Commercial Arbitration, 1998, pp. 644–654.
ICC Case No. 12171, Award on Third Party Person Notice, 7 April 2004, in *23 ASA Bulletin* no. **2** (2005), pp. 270–277.
Final Award in ICC Case 6535 of 1992 (Extract), in *9 ICC International Court of Arbitration Bulletin*, no. **2** (1998), ref. p. 60.
Interim Award in ICC Case No. 5898 of 1989, in *9 ICC International Court of Arbitration Bulletin*, no. **1** (1998), ref. p. 83.
Partial Award in Cases 6276 and 6277 (Extract), in *9 ICC International Court of Arbitration Bulletin*, no. **2** (1998), ref. p. 58.
Partial award in ICC Case No. 5333, in *4 International Construction Law Review* (1987), pp. 320–333.
Award of 28 November 1997 in ICC Case No. 7061 (unpublished).

VIII. Soft Law Instruments

AAA Guide to Drafting Alternative Dispute Resolution Clauses for Construction Contracts revised on 1 July 2015, American Arbitration Association, https://www.adr.org/aaa/ShowPDF?doc=ADRSTG_002542 (accessed 25 July 2016).
CIArb Guideline 15: Guidelines for Arbitrators on how to Approach Issues Relating to Multi-Party Arbitration, https://www.ciarb.org/docs/default-source/practice-guidelines-protocols-and-rules/international-arbitration-guidelines-2011/2011multipartyarbitrations.pdf?sfvrsn=6 (accessed 25 July 2016).
Drafting Dispute Resolution Clauses – A Practical Guide, last revised in 2013, American Arbitration Association, https://www.adr.org/aaa/ShowPDF?doc=ADRSTG_002540 (accessed 25 July 2016).

IBA Guidelines for Drafting International Arbitration Clauses of 7 October 2010, International Bar Association, http://www.ibanet.org/ENews_Archive/IBA_27October_2010_Arbitration_Clauses_Guidelines.aspx (accessed 25 July 2016).

IBA Guidelines on Conflict of Interest in International Arbitration of 23 October 2014, http://www.ibanet.org/Publications/publications_IBA_guides_and_free_materials.aspx (accessed 25 July 2016).

IX. Other Sources

Electronic Articles

Aiken, S. 2009 *Private Arbitration Update, Consolidation of Separate Arbitration Proceedings*, http://www.ashrlaw.com/dox/SKA-arb-consolidation.pdf (accessed 25 July 2016).

Alitz, J. and Dunlap, B. *The New AIA and ConsensusDOCS: Beware of the Differences – The Professional Services Agreements*, http://www.nspe.org/sites/default/files/resources/pdfs/Professional_Services_Docs.pdf (accessed 25 July 2016).

Gould, N. *NEC3: Construction Contract of the Future? A paper presented to the Society of Construction Law international conference in Singapore, February 2007*, Paper No. D84 (September 2007), published by the UK Society of Construction Law (this can be purchased from https://www.scl.org.uk/papers/nec3-construction-contract-future, accessed 25 July 2016).

Harness, S. 2007 *Revisions to AIA Contract Documents*, http://www.aia.org/groups/aia/documents/document/aiab078763.pdf (accessed 1 August 2016).

Harness, S. and Cobleigh, K. 2007 *AIA Contract Documents: Key Issues of Interest to Owners*, http://www.aia.org/groups/aia/documents/pdf/aiab078725.pdf (accessed 1 August 2016).

Jankowski, J., Harness, S. and Bomba, M. AIA 2007 *Update: How does it affect Architects?* http://www.aia.org/groups/aia/documents/pdf/aiab078767.pdf (accessed 1 August 2016).

Kesikli, O. *United States: International Arbitration and Arbitrability from the United States Perspective*, http://www.mondaq.com/unitedstates/x/309172/Arbitration+Dispute+Resolution/International+Arbitration+And (accessed 25 July 2016).

McCallum, M. *Getting Directly to the Point of the Contested Matter: Dispute Mitigation and Resolution in ConsensusDocs Construction Forms*, https://www.consensusdocs.org/News/Download/fbb7a767-bf76-4f3d-8447-9fb400e5f768?name=Dispute%20Mitigation%20and%20Resolution%20in%20ConsensusDOCS%20Construction%20Forms.pdf (accessed 25 July 2016).

Nielsen, M., Thomsen, K. C. *A Greener Pasture*, http://www.cdr-news.com/categories/expert-views/5245-a-greener-pasture (accessed 25 July 2016).

Ricketts, R. *Judicial Review of Arbitral Awards*, http://gablelaw.com/wp-content/uploads/2015/06/2013-08-02-Judicial-Review-of-Arbitration-Awards.pdf (accessed 25 July 2016).

Ruzicka, L. and Scavotto, A. *A Review of the New Family of Construction Agreements, ConsensusDocs*, https://www.consensusdocs.org/News/Download/0a100c49-8b27-4946-ae0f-9fb400de4d49?name=ConsensusDocs-042009.pdf (accessed 25 July 2016).

Seppälä, C. *The New FIDIC International Civil Engineering Subcontract*, http://fidic.org/sites/default/files/red_subcon_intro.pdf (accessed 25 July 2016).

Yuen, P. *The New HKIAC Arbitration Rules and How they Compare to Other Institutional Rules*, http://us.practicallaw.com/3-542-4605?q=&qp=&qo=&qe= (accessed 25 July 2016).

United Nations Documents

Working Group II, *3rd Session (16–26 February 1982, New York)*, UN Doc A/CN.9/216.
Working Group II, *45th Session (11–15 September 2006, Vienna)*, UN Doc A/CN.9/614.
Working Group II, *46th Session (5–9 February, New York)*, UN DOC A/CN.9/619.
Working Group II, *47th Session (10–14 September 2007, Vienna)*, UN Doc A/CN.9/WG.II/WP.147/Add.1.
Working Group II, *49th Session (15–19 September 2008, Vienna)*, UN Doc A/CN.9/665.
Commission Sessions, *32nd Session (17 May–4 June, 1999, Vienna)*, UN Doc A/54/17.
Commission Sessions, *32nd Session (17 May–4 June, 1999, Vienna)*, UN Doc A/CN.9/460.

Theses

Athanasakis, D. (2008) The Law and Practice of Multiparty Construction Arbitration. Unpublished PhD thesis, Queen Mary University of London.
Jafari, D. M. (2012) Resolution of Multiparty Construction Disputes under the Singapore International Arbitration Legal Framework. Unpublished PhD thesis, National University of Singapore.

Other Sources

'2012 Statistical Report', in *24 ICC International Court of Arbitration Bulletin*, no. 1 (2013), pp. 5–18.
'2014 ICC Dispute Resolution Statistics', in *1 ICC Dispute Resolution Bulletin*, no. 1 (2015), pp. 7–19.
'*Arbitration Bill gazetted in June 2009, Automatic Opt-in for Subcontractors*', prepared by the Administration for the Bills Committee on the Hong Kong Arbitration Bill, http://www.legco.gov.hk/yr08-09/english/bc/bc59/papers/bc590512cb2-1477-3-e.pdf (accessed 25 July 2016).
'The Key Points of the 2014 Amendment to the Commercial Arbitration Rules', in *31 JCAA Newsletter* (2014), pp. 1–12, http://www.jcaa.or.jp/e/arbitration/docs/news31.pdf (accessed 25 July 2016).
2015 International Arbitration Survey: Improvements and Innovations in International Arbitration, conducted by Queen Mary University of London and White & Case LLP, http://www.arbitration.qmul.ac.uk/docs/164761.pdf (accessed 25 July 2016).
AAA Construction Rules Updated: An Interview with Catherine E. Shanks, Vice President, Construction Division, American Arbitration Association, in *64 Dispute Resolution Journal*, no. 4 (November 2009–January 2010), ref. p. 44
Bartlett, A., Hitching, I., Alleyne, E., *et al.* (2011) *Emden's Construction Law by Crown Office Chambers*, LexisNexis, London.
Cairns, D. and Ortiz, A. L., *Spain's New Arbitration Act*, http://www.voldgiftsforeningen.dk/Admin/Public/Download.aspx?file=Files%2FFiler%2F2011%2FNationale_love%2FSpanien.pdf (accessed 25 July 2016).
Comair-Obeid, N., *Arbitration Guide, IBA Arbitration Committee, Lebanon, February* 2012, http://www.ibanet.org/Document/Default.aspx?DocumentUid=9D05A58F-F3E7-4585-A3F9-C69B8309D42D (accessed 5 August 2016).
Commentary on AIA Document A201-1997, http://www.umich.edu/~cee431/AIA/A201-1997Commentary.pdf (accessed 25 July 2016).

Commentary on AIA Document B141-1997, http://www.umich.edu/~cee431/AIA/B141-1997Commentary.pdf (accessed 25 July 2016).

De Meulemeester, D., *Multicontract Arbitration under the CEPANI Arbitration Rules (Article 10)*, Kluwer Arbitration Blog, http://kluwerarbitrationblog.com/blog/2013/10/23/multicontractarbitration-under-the-cepani-arbitration-rules-article-10/ (accessed 25 July 2016).

Departmental Advisory Committee on Arbitration, 'The 1996 DAC Report on the English Arbitration Bill' in *13 Arbitration International*, no. **3** (1997), pp. 275–316, http://uk.practicallaw.com/6-205-5120 (accessed 25 July 2016).

Diamond, A. *The New (1998) LCIA Rules, Multi-Party Arbitrations – Formation of and Vacancies in the Tribunal – The Removal of Arbitrators – Truncated Tribunals*, London Court of International Arbitration, New Arbitration Rules 1998, Centre of Construction Law and Management Conference at King's College London (5 June 1998).

Gearing, M. and Hodgson, M., *CIETAC's New Arbitration Rules*, http://www.allenovery.com/publications/en-gb/Pages/CIETAC's-New-Arbitration-Rules-2015-.aspx (accessed 25 July 2016).

ICC Commission on International Arbitration, 'Final Report on Multi-party Arbitrations', in *6 ICC International Court Arbitration Bulletin*, no. **1** (1995), pp. 26–50.

ICDR International Arbitration Reporter, September 2013/Volume 4, https://www.adr.org/cs/groups/international/documents/document/z2uy/mde1/~edisp/adrstage2015007.pdf (accessed 25 July 2016).

Kreindler, R., Kopp, T. and Rother, N., *Arbitration Guide, IBA Arbitration Committee, Germany, November 2013*, http://www.ibanet.org/Document/Default.aspx?DocumentUid=72111D60-6585-412C-B239-189ABF22108F (accessed 25 July 2016).

Kruzewski, B. and Diehl, M., *Arbitration Guide, IBA Arbitration Committee, Poland, September 2013*, http://www.ibanet.org/Document/Default.aspx?DocumentUid=DE8F3274-8525-432D-9118-88300110F445 (accessed 1 August 2016).

Lloyd, H. (2004) *Multi-Party Clauses and Agreements*. A paper for use by the University of London LLM students, pp. 1–19.

Statistical information on the number of cases filed with CIETAC, http://cietac.org/index.php?m=Page&a=index&id=40&l=en (accessed 25 July 2016).

Statistical information on the number of cases filed with SIAC, http://www.siac.org.sg/2014-11-03-13-33-43/facts-figures/statistics (accessed 25 July 2016).

Tan, K., *New Year, New Practice Note: HKIAC Issues Practice Note on Consolidation of Arbitrations*, http://www.ciarb.org.sg/new-year-new-practice-note-hkiac-issues-practice-note-on-consolidation-of-arbitrations/ (accessed 1 August 2016).

van den Berg, A. J. (1989) 'Shui On Construction Co. Ltd. V. Moon Yik Co. Ltd., Xipho Development Co. Ltd., High Court of Hong Kong, Not Indicated, 12 September 1986', in Albert Jan van den Berg (ed.), *Yearbook Commercial Arbitration 1989–Volume XIV*, Kluwer Law International, Alphen aan den Rijn, pp. 215–223.

Index

Multi-Party and Multi-Contract Arbitration in the Construction Industry, First Edition.
Dimitar Kondev.

Printed and bound by CPI Group (UK) Ltd, Croydon, CR0 4YY
16/09/2026
14963478-0002